A History of Women

IN THE WEST

Georges Duby and Michelle Perrot, General Editors

I. From Ancient Goddesses to Christian Saints

A HISTORY
OF WOMEN
I N   T H E   W E S T

I. From Ancient Goddesses
to Christian Saints

Pauline Schmitt Pantel, Editor

Arthur Goldhammer, Translator

The Belknap Press of
Harvard University Press
Cambridge, Massachusetts
London, England

Originally published as *Storia delle Donne in Occidente,* vol. I,
L'Antichità, © Gius. Laterza & Figli Spa, Roma-Bari, 1990.

This book is printed on acid-free paper, and its binding materials
have been chosen for strength and durability.

Text design by Lisa Diercks

Library of Congress Cataloging-in-Publication Data

Storia delle donne in Occidente. English
   A history of women in the West / Georges Duby and
Michelle Perrot, general editors.
      p. cm.
   Translation of: Storia delle donne in Occidente.
   Includes bibliographical references and index.
   Contents: 1. From ancient goddesses to Christian saints /
Pauline Schmitt Pantel, editor.
   ISBN 0-674-40370-3 (alk. paper)
   1. Women—History. 2. Women—Europe—History. I. Title.
HQ1121.S79513   1992
305.4'094—dc20

91-34134
   CIP

Contents

A New Kind of History

Natalie Zemon Davis and Joan Wallach Scott

THIS FIVE-VOLUME HISTORY of women is of Italian origin. The publishers Giuseppe and Vico Laterza broached the idea to a group of French historians. As a result, the two general editors are French, and most of the volume editors are from the country that has given us in the past decades some of the best of the new social history. Long before they came to the general editorship of *The History of Women,* Georges Duby had redefined the nature and dynamic of French feudalism and medieval social thought and Michelle Perrot had given her readers a fresh understanding of workers' resistance and prison systems in nineteenth-century France. But curiously enough, the study of women and gender was long ignored by vanguard social historians in France and had little role in curriculum reform. Georges Duby's course on medieval marriage was a rarity a decade ago; Michelle Perrot's seminar was celebrated for years as one of the few places in Paris one could discuss the history of women in the nineteenth century.

But if in France one could not count on lecture halls filled with students of the history of women, one could count on the long-standing appetite of the French reading public—in and out of academe—for books of high quality on history. The same is true in Italy, where there are few university courses in women's history, but many readers willing to learn about the subject. From this situation the plan for a multivolume history of women emerged, one written by an international team. These volumes, edited and written by historians recognized for their work on the history of women, demonstrate what the study of gender can include, how fascinating it can be, and where it can lead.

Inspired by a European encyclopedic tradition, the *History of Women* is not a conventional textbook, nor does it simply trace a set of themes as they change over time. Its approach is more eclectic and open-ended than might be the case if an Anglo-American team had been organizing the project today. The questions that preoccupy so many American historians of women—questions about equality and difference; about the complementarity of male and female roles; about the interconnections of race, class, and gender; about the construction of gender and of sexuality (heterosexuality and homosexuality)—do not systematically organize either the individual essays, the single volumes, or the entire series. To be sure, there is much material in these volumes that bears on these questions, and some essays deal with them directly. But they do not provide a single analytical axis around which all five volumes are arranged.

Instead *The History of Women* is a work in process. Rather than giving exhaustive coverage, it focuses mainly on the western European experience, with some attention to North America. Rather than providing a final synthesis, the volumes present a history that consists of many aspects. They explore the range of meanings that "women" have had in different contexts and epochs; they look at the ways gender has been constituted by, and has in turn constituted, the organization of social, political, and economic life; they demonstrate the varied methodological and theoretical approaches that can be used to study women's lives. Throughout, the situations of women are analyzed in terms of experience and in terms of representation. Women are seen as both the objects of discourse and as active subjects. The distance between what women say about themselves and what men say about them is one of the most intense landscapes mapped in the five volumes.

The essays draw on original research and existing bodies of literature. As such they reflect something of the state of the field, especially as it has developed in western European scholarship. Women's work and domesticity, heterosexual families and religion, and internal state policies are more fully treated than, say, sexual practice and homosexuality, ethnicity and colonialism. The relative weight given some areas of women's experience rather than others is not intended to suggest an absolute scale of values about what is important and what is not. Instead the volumes provide a sampler for those interested in exploring the extent and variety of the field of women's history and a stimulus for future work and exploration. Their most important contribution is to establish that women's history is as open to investigation and interpretation, as rich and unlimited in scope and substance, as history itself.

Writing the History of Women

Georges Duby and Michelle Perrot

AT ONE TIME a history of women would have seemed an inconceivable or futile undertaking. The roles for which women were destined were silent ones: motherhood and homemaking, tasks relegated to the obscurity of a domesticity that did not count and was not considered worth recounting. Did women so much as have a history? In the minds of the ancients, they were associated with cold: they were inert constituents of an immobile world, while men, burning with heat, were active. Remote from the stage of history, upon which the men who controlled their destinies clashed, women were poorly placed to serve as witnesses. At times they might play minor roles, but they rarely took the leading parts, and when they did their weaknesses were all too apparent. Generally they were subjects, ready to hail conquerors and to weep when heroes went down to defeat. No tragedy was complete without a chorus of women in tears.

What, moreover, do we know about women? The tenuous traces they have left did not originate with themselves—"nothing knowing, nor ever letters reading"—but were filtered through the gaze of the men who held the reins of power, defined official memory, and controlled public archives. The selection criteria of official scribes shaped the primary record of what women did and said. Indifferent to private life, these men focused exclusively on the public, in which women played no part. And when women did burst upon the public scene, men inevitably saw disorder: from Herodotus to Taine, from Livy to today's police, women on the public stage have been cast in familiar stereotypes. Even the census neglected women. In Rome only heiresses were counted. Not until the third century after Christ did Diocletian order that women be included in the count, and then only for fiscal reasons. In the nineteenth century the labor of female farm workers and peasants was consistently underestimated because only the head of family's occupation was recorded. Thus the state of relations between the sexes is inscribed in the sources themselves: information about women is less abundant than information about men.

From antiquity to the present the absence of concrete, detailed information about women stands in sharp contrast to the profusion of discourse and imagery. Women are more likely to be "represented" than to be described or to have their stories told—much less be allowed to tell their own stories. It may be that the more women are absent from the public arena, the more abundant the representations. Olympus is filled with goddesses, but Greek city-states had no female citizens. The Virgin reigns above altars at which (male) priests officiate. Marianne is the incarnation of the French Republic, that most virile of regimes. Woman—imagined, imaginary, even fantasized—epitomizes everything else.

How did images and fantasies of women evolve? Because the question is so important, we have given a great deal of space in the volumes of this series to "picture archives," which we think of not as mere illustrations but as data to be deciphered. Fifth- and sixth-century B.C. Attic vases do not simply transcribe everyday life, any more than does the Bayeux tapestry or contemporary billboard advertising. Only by analyzing the way in which such images change over time can we begin to understand the representation of gender. Marriage rites commonly stress the physical transfer of the bride from one place to another; the newly married woman is spirited away from her own surroundings and ensnared in a series of acts that symbolize separation and integration. Thus marriage has a structure. When the virtuous woman is portrayed as a spinner of yarn in a society indifferent to the value of labor, or when feminine beauty is associated more with adornment than with the body itself, all but shapeless and hidden from view, then we can begin to glimpse the way in which the feminine has been perceived. From such manifestations we can determine not how the sexes actually stood in relation to each other but how men construed their relation to, and thus their representation of, the opposite sex.

Literary images possess greater depth. The suppleness of language allows for greater freedom than is possible with visual imagery, which is subject to fairly strict rules. Literature is perhaps freer and more inclusive than the plastic arts, yet here too the desire of the Master predominates. The "Lady" of "refined love" of whom Guillaume de Poitiers sang in the twelfth century may appear to be sovereign over men's hearts, but one must always bear in mind that "these poems show not woman" but "man's image of woman," or at any rate an image that some men, having chosen a new sexual strategy, chose to promote. The game had changed, but men remained in control. Much the same thing can be said of the sophistications of romantic love. Balzac said: "Woman is a slave that one must learn to place upon a throne" by showering her with flowers and fragrances. Men celebrate the Muse and exalt the inaccessible Madonna and Angel. In singing societies lusty males sang ribald songs about "Mademoiselle Flora" stripped bare and considered her qualifications "for the degree of whore."[1] Meanwhile, woman's real visage remained masked, shrouded by a thick veil of images.

What are we to make of the diversity of ways in which thinkers, social theorists, and other spokesmen for the thought of the ages discussed women? Philosophers, theologians, jurists, doctors, moralists, and educators have been tireless in their efforts to define women and prescribe their proper behavior. Women were defined first and foremost by their social position and duties. When Rousseau, in book five of *Emile,* came to write of Sophie, the woman he imagined for his eponymous hero, he had this to say: "To please [men], to be useful to them, to raise them when they are young, to take care of them when they are grown, to advise them, to console them, to make life pleasant and agreeable for them—these are the duties of women in all ages, duties which they should be taught from childhood." In the Middle Ages, Bishop Gilbert of Limerick observed that "women marry, and serve, those who pray, work, and fight." The views of Aristotle, and indeed of men in general, were much the same; this view of women's duties changed little over the centuries. In the nineteenth and twentieth centuries women were invited, in the name of social utility, to leave the home and extend the benefits of maternity to society at large. The demands of religion and morality reinforced one another. Pagan or Christian, Rome insisted that young women remain virginal and celebrated female modesty and chastity. Women wore veils: in a respectable woman "one sees only the figure," said Horace, whose sentiments were approximately echoed by Saint Paul and, nineteen centuries later, by Barbey d'Aurevilly. Decent women remained shut up in their gynaeceums or Victorian homes. All but timeless, this practice of confining women reflects certain assumptions about their nature: that they are fragile and unhealthy as well as wild and undisciplined, a menace if not restrained. To be sure, physical barriers crumbled, only to be replaced by more sophisticated systems of education aimed at the internalization of social norms. These systems gave rise first to the "young woman" and later to that even more mysterious figure, the "little girl." Slowly—very slowly—women became individuals, people whose consent mattered. The history of these changes, reflected in discourse about women, is central to our study.

So is the evolution of thinking about the difference between the sexes, a question that has preoccupied Western consciousness since the time of the Greeks. Thinking on the subject has wavered between two extremes. Athenian and baroque thinkers allowed for the possibility of a combination of male and female elements in a single individual, as exemplified by the androgyne, the hermaphrodite, the transvestite. By contrast, classical thought emphasized the radical difference between the sexes: male and female were two species, each with its own distinct character, to be apprehended not so much by scientific knowledge as by intuition.[2] Primitive notions impeded study of the female body. From Galen to Raymond Roussel (and, more controversially, Freud), ideas about women's physical nature reinforced and reflected ideas about their moral nature. It took a long time for physicians to realize the consequences of discoveries concerning female physiology and sexuality (such as the seventeenth-century discovery of ovulation).

Discourse about women took many forms: mythical, mystical, scientific, normative, scholarly, and popular. Sometimes it is hard to perceive the modulations and shifts beneath the repetitious formulations. Thinking about the subject stemmed from a common *episteme* or conceptual matrix defined by men who referred to themselves as "us" and to women as "them." Listen to Rousseau: "Let us begin, then, by examining the similarities and differences between her sex and ours." Often the men who spoke were those—clergymen, for instance—whose status, function, and predilections ensured that they would have least to do with women and who imagined them from a distance and with a certain dread, at once drawn to and frightened by this indispensable yet unruly Other. What exactly is a woman? they asked.

And what did women say? In one sense the history of women is the history of their finding a voice. At first they spoke through others, that is, through men, who portrayed them on stage and later in the novel. In modern as well as ancient theater women were often merely mouthpieces for their male authors, whose obsessions they expressed. Aristophanes' Lysistrata and Ibsen's Nora symbolize not so much the emancipation of women as male fear of the female (although in very different ways, the difference being precisely that which makes comparison possible yet precludes any suggestion of equivalence). Writers were nevertheless compelled by the demands of realism to learn more about their characters. The works of Shakespeare and Racine, of Balzac and Henry James, abound with highly individualized female characters. Actresses, meanwhile, imbued the roles they played with their own personalities. Despite the many taboos surrounding a career on the stage, it was through this profession that women first achieved an individual identity and public recognition.

The voice of women also manifested itself in demonstrations, riots, and popular unrest, where it was transcribed and recorded with ever-increasing care by the guardians of law and order. From court and police records we learn of the importance ascribed to confession, an importance that was associated with a new conception of public order. Through the records of such confessions we can hear the quavering, chattering voices of insignificant people, of that *peuple* among whom women moved.

If we are to hear women's voices directly, they must first have access to the means of expression: gesture, speech, writing. Literacy is essential, and in general men acquired literacy before women, although in some areas it was the reverse. Even more important than literacy per se was the ability of women to enter the realm of expression, a realm that was considered sacred and thus hedged about with ever-changing prohibitions. Some genres were permissible to women: writing for private consumption, for instance, as in letters. The earliest texts we have by women are letters, those of the Pythagoreans. The letters of Madame de Sévigné are among early literary works by women. Later, maintaining correspondence became one of a woman's regular duties, and letters became an invaluable source of family and personal information. Religious writing was another form of expression open to women. We can hear the voices of renowned saints, mystics, and abbesses: Hildegard of Bingen, Herrard of Lansberg (author of the *Hortus deliciarum*), Protestant women caught up in the ardor of "revivalism," and charitable women engaged in preaching to the poor.

Women were all but excluded from certain other forms of expression: science; to an increasing extent, history; and, above all, philosophy. By the seventeenth century the Précieuses, aware of the stakes involved in the mastery of language, were already blazing new trails in the realms of poetry and the novel. Now the goal was not merely to write but to publish, and under one's own name. Anonymous authorship and the use of pseudonyms only confuse the issue, as do the mediocre quality and tediously uniform morality of the countless works whose similarity raises the question of the constraints imposed on expression by the requirements of virtue. Writing itself was no doubt sufficiently subversive that to go still further in the direction of protest or formal experimentation was out of the question.

Halting at first, the voice of women has gradually gained strength, particularly over the last two centuries thanks to the feminist impetus. The change cannot be understood in a linear fashion. Every statement must be examined in its proper context, every mode of expression compared with masculine forms. Speaking, reading, writing, and publishing raise the question of the relation between sex and creation, sex and the surrounding culture.

Preservation of women's memories is another difficult issue. In the theater of memory, women are mere phantoms. They take up little space on the shelves of public archives and have suffered from the widespread destruction of private archives. How many private diaries and letters have been burned by apathetic or vindictive heirs, indeed by women themselves who, after long years of suffering, poke the ashes of memories they would rather see destroyed than divulged? The memory of women has often been preserved in the form of objects: a charm, a ring, a missal, a parasol, an item of linen, a dress, or any of a hundred other treasures hidden away in an attic or closet. Women are remembered too through images seen in museums of fashion and dress:

memories of appearances. A rudimentary feminine archaeology of daily life can be found in museums of folk art and traditions, whose collections do not disdain the domestic. Since the nineteenth century feminists have sought to assemble collections, whose problematic survival is indicative of their marginal character. Various libraries feature collections pertinent to women's history: the Bibliothèque Marguerite Durand, the Bouglé collection at the Bibliothèque Historique de la Ville de Paris, the Feminist Library in Amsterdam, and Schlesinger Library in Cambridge, Massachusetts, to name a few. In Seneca Falls, New York, home of Elizabeth Cady Stanton, a Women's Rights National Historical Park was recently established in honor of the first Women's Rights Convention (held on July 19 and 20, 1848). Collections of documents have been published in the United States and France. Biographical dictionaries of "notable women" and feminists are in preparation. Such projects reflect the heightened awareness of women's history that has developed over the past twenty years.

What was missing before was the will to know. There can be no history of women unless women are taken seriously and gender relations are believed to influence events and social changes. In notes for her *Memoirs of Hadrian* Marguerite Yourcenar writes: "It is also impossible to take a female character as central figure, to organize the narrative, for instance, around Plotina rather than Hadrian. Women's lives are too constricted or too private. If a woman tells her own story, the first criticism people will make is that she is no longer a woman. It is difficult enough to place some modicum of truth in the mouth of a man."[3] For a long time historians shared the novelist's doubts. Greek historians had little to say about women, who were generally seen as victims of wars and thus classed together with children, the elderly, and slaves. Occasionally actresses were mentioned, for example when their secession *(stasis)* threatened the political order.[4] Medieval chroniclers liked to speak of queens and ladies, indispensable for arranging marriages and embellishing feasts. Commynes had great respect for Marguerite of Burgundy. By his day princesses could exercise power and make themselves "illustrious"—a sign of changing times and laws. The court of Louis XIV was a gendered world, and Saint-Simon was constantly attentive to the great family intrigues of the court, in which women, careful of what they said and with whom they slept, played a part that the great memorialist depicts in his own manner.

Romantic history paid vastly greater attention to women. Michelet, in his *History of France* and even more in his *History of the Revolution,* saw relations between the sexes as a motor of history. Social equilibrium depended on gender equilibrium. Yet in subsuming women under the head of Nature—a dualistic nature that wavered between two extremes, one maternal, the other savage—while placing men under the head of Culture, Michelet was echoing the prevailing view of his day, a view further developed by anthropologists such as Bachofen. In the late nineteenth century, when positivist history took shape as an academic discipline with an emphasis on rigor, women were excluded in two senses: from the subject matter, which was concerned exclusively with the public and political, and from the profession, a profession of men engaged in writing the history of men, which they presented as universal history, while murals of women covered the walls of the Sorbonne. Women, because they were not worthy of serious consideration, were left to the authors of books about everyday life, to biographers of edifying or scandalous lives, and to historians who thrived on anecdotes (Georges Lenôtre was the foremost French example). Alongside "scientific history" there grew up a "women's history" that still exists today, a genre that is variously edifying or stultifying, seductive or tear-jerking, and that finds its place primarily in women's magazines where it is tailored to the tastes of the mass reader.

The women's history to which the volumes of *A History of Women* are intended to contribute and which has shaped their conception is something quite different, a product of the last twenty years. Its development has been influenced by a number of factors, some proximate, others more remote. More than a century ago historians began once again to see the family as the basic cell of social structure and development. Today the family has become the central focus of one sort of anthropological history, which emphasizes kinship structures and sexuality and consequently the feminine. In France, moreover, the *Annales* school has steadily expanded the scope of history to include everyday practices, common behavior, and shared "mentalities." To be sure, relations between the sexes have not been the primary focus of *Annales* historians, generally more concerned with economic conjunctures and social categories. Nevertheless, the *Annales* school has been receptive to the new women's history. Another important factor, brought to the fore by decolonization and intensified by the events of May '68, has been a political concern with exiles, minorities, and members of cultures oppressed or reduced to silence by dominant powers, a concern that has led many historians to consider peripheral or marginal groups and their relations with the centers of power.

Nevertheless, women did not immediately become the focus of historical inquiry. It took the women's movement and the many issues it raised to place the question of women on the historical agenda. "Who are we? Where do we come from? Where are we going?" These were the questions women asked themselves in consciousness-raising groups. In the universities these questions had a decisive impact on teaching and research. English and American women opened new avenues of inquiry: in England *History Workshop* played a pioneering role, while in the United States the burgeoning field of "women's studies" gave rise to journals such as *Signs* and *Feminist Studies*. Most European countries followed suit—most countries in the West, that is, with Poland virtually alone in the Eastern bloc. France, Germany, and Italy led the way between 1970 and 1975; the ferment took longer to reach other countries. A great deal of good work has been done, although it is unevenly distributed. If some early work was fairly "primitive," that has long ceased to be the case. Women's history already has a history of its own, for its subject matter, methods, and views have changed over time. At first the primary aim was simply to give women visibility.[5] New problems have since come to the fore, as many scholars have turned from a purely descriptive to a more relational approach. A central concern in recent years has been the question of "gender," of relations between the sexes viewed not as an eternal fact given in some undefinable nature but as a social construct that it is the historian's task to deconstruct.

This series is thus a product of its times. Its timing is no accident. It is the result of fruitful interaction between women's history and the need for historians to reexamine the nature of their discipline. It has benefited from a vast range of historical inquiries too numerous even to summarize here. But our aim is not merely to report the results of recent research. We also hope to indicate new problems and to ask stimulating questions.

The *History of Women* is a history of the *longue durée*, of time conceived on a vast scale. It covers history from antiquity to the present. The history of women is often seen as static, and indeed it has resisted change to such a degree that it can sometimes seem virtually changeless. Yet change has occurred, and the question is first to identify it and then to determine what aspects of life it affected. How did religion, law, and education influence the inheritance of family and cultural legacies? What new departures and ruptures proved crucial? What were the major evolutionary factors in each period? What part was played by the economy, by politics, and by culture?

Comparison of different periods is useful. Admittedly we made a potentially controversial choice: we chose to use the customary periodization of European history, thereby implicitly assuming that this periodization is valid for studying the historical evolution of relations between men and women. Each volume in the series corresponds to one of the usual periods. The volumes are to some extent independent. Each has its own internal organization, its own guiding concepts, its own style. This was a convenient choice for us, and the only practical choice, but does it yield a useful conceptual framework? What do the birth of Christianity, the Renaissance, the Reformation, the Enlightenment, the French Revolution, and the two World Wars have to do with the history of women? Or put another way, what are the fundamental continuities in the history of women, and what are the major discontinuities and crucial events?

Our second key choice was to limit the geographical scope of our inquiry to western Europe and North America. We look first at Greco-Latin Europe, then at Judeo-Christian Europe, but scarcely at all at Islamic Europe. We touch on European expansion and colonization primarily in North America. Work is only just beginning on Latin America, where the importation of Iberian models of female behavior as early as the sixteenth century raised numerous issues for Indian society. Given the preliminary stage of current research, we have not been able to explore those issues. Similarly, we have not paid enough attention to the impact of colonization on sex and race relations, a matter with particular implications for the United States, where the earliest feminist groups were resolutely abolitionist. The issue is more peripheral but just as crucial for Europe. What we have written is essentially a history of white women, but that choice implies no deliberate exclusion or value judgment; it simply reflects our limitations as scholars and our need for help from others. We would like to see a history of Oriental and African women written by Oriental and

African women and men. Such a history would surely be very different from ours, because it would have to be written with one eye on the Orient and Africa and another eye on Europe and America. Neither feminism nor the representation of the feminine are universal values.

Although centered in Europe, our history is concerned not with women within the borders of particular countries (borders that in any case are of relatively recent date) but with the contribution of women to the common history of Europe. Its structure is thematic: we consider a variety of themes in comparative perspective. Authors have of course made use of their specialized knowledge of particular countries, but they have tried to situate their "cases" in a broader context. A general history like this one leaves plenty of room for less sweeping, more narrowly focused monographs. Our coverage may at times seem spotty. Deficiencies in the literature and in the editors' acquaintance with experts in various areas explain this shortcoming even if they do not excuse it.

This series is the product of a revolution—an ongoing, far-reaching revolution in the relations between men and women in Western societies. It is therefore legitimate that it should focus primarily on the particular region of the world in which it was born.

Another characteristic of the series is pluralism. Its volumes reflect many different, even contradictory, points of view, and we do not always seek to reconcile disagreement. The authors share certain common beliefs, most notably that the history of women is worth taking seriously; but they do not share any party line or stultifying jargon. The volumes are pluralist in another sense: they are concerned not with the history of *Woman* but with the history of *women*, some women, certain women. The women we study differ in social condition, religious belief, ethnic origins, and life experience. Wherever pertinent we have attempted to consider sex in conjunction with such other factors as class and race, factors that may at times cut across the sexual divide. Can sex be considered a form of class in the Marxist sense? Is there a real or potential "women's community"? Is the "second sex" unified in any sense other than conceptual, and, if so, what is the basis of that unity?

Finally, this series is intended to be not so much a history of women as a history of the relation between the sexes. Therein lies the crux of the problem, the source of woman's identity and otherness. It is our guiding concept, the thread that runs through and, we hope, unifies all five volumes. What is the nature of this relation? Considered in terms of representation, knowledge, power, and everyday practice, how does it function and how does it evolve over time? How does it operate in public life? In work life? In the family? The distinction between public and private does not necessarily coincide with the distinction between male and female, but it often figures as part of a recurrent, ever-changing strategy for defining sex roles and limiting men and women to their own respective spheres. Throughout history, so far as we can see, men have dominated women. This judgment is ratified today by the social sciences, including anthropology. Matriarchy appears to have been a concept invented by nineteenth-century anthropologists such as Bachofen and Morgan and taken up as a nostalgic wish by early American feminists. In societies accessible to historical inquiry we find no trace of it. Nevertheless, the modes of male domination vary widely, and it is this variation in which we are interested. Male domination does not mean that women are powerless, but it does mean that we must inquire about the nature of women's powers and how they relate to the powers of men. Can women's powers be described as forms of resistance, compensation, assent, or counter-power (in the guise of deception and ruse)? Thought must be given to the dialectical relation of influence to decisionmaking: the power ascribed to women is occult and diffuse; that attributed to men is clear and distinct.

How do men govern women? The question is existential as well as political, and it becomes increasingly complex as we approach modern times and the possibility of democratic politics. There are controversial issues here, as we shall see when we come to the role of women in Nazism. Women were relegated to the private sphere, but there they were honored and esteemed. Were they simply victims, or were they agents of a system to whose operation they contributed? To what extent are women political actors? From the time of the Greeks to the French Revolution and beyond, three major masculine preserves have been closed to women: religion, the military, and politics. The one that remains most refractory to this day is certainly politics. On such issues we seek not to draw conclusions but to raise questions.

The impulse for this *History of Women* came from Vito and Giuseppe Laterza, who in the spring of 1987 approached Georges Duby and Michelle Perrot, both of whom had participated in another series on the *History of Private Life* (which Laterza published in Italy and Harvard University Press in the United States). In due course the proposal was accepted and the two general editors set about putting together a team of historians. First to be chosen were the volume editors: Pauline Schmitt Pantel (volume I), Christiane Klapisch-Zuber (volume II), Natalie Zemon Davis and Arlette Farge (volume III), Geneviève Fraisse (volume IV), and Françoise Thébaud (volume V). The volume editors collectively worked out the principles of the series and took charge of the details of production. Together they assembled a group of nearly seventy historians, mostly academics with distinguished records of publication. Though the majority are women, that merely reflects the number of women engaged in this area of historical research. The contributors come from many different countries (if some countries are underrepresented, it is only because the editors happened to have few contacts there). In June 1988 all the contributors gathered at the Centre Culturel Italien in Paris to discuss the overall project, plan the contents of each volume, and compare views. Subsequently, work on each volume proceeded independently, while coordination was maintained through the editorial committee. Individual contributors were free to write what they pleased and were allowed the final say on their contributions, but all were asked to make an effort to ensure that the work would be conceptually coherent and stylistically consistent. We wish to thank one and all for venturing the impossible.

Sum up? Flaubert himself refused to try. Since we prefer to leave the questions open and the last word to women themselves, we will end this introduction with a quotation from Jane Austen's *Northanger Abbey:*

> "But history, real solemn history, I cannot be interested in. Can you?"
> "Yes, I am fond of history."
> "I wish I were too. I read it a little as a duty, but it tells me nothing that does not either vex or weary me. The quarrels of popes and kings, with wars or pestilences, in every page; the men all so good for nothing, and hardly any women at all—it is very tiresome."[6]

Perhaps Jane Austen would find a history from which women are not excluded somewhat less tiresome.

A History of Women

IN THE WEST

From Ancient Goddesses
to Christian Saints

Representations of Women

Pauline Schmitt Pantel

Regarding the virtues of women, Clea, I do not hold the same opinion as Thucydides. For he declares that the best woman is she about whom there is the least talk among persons outside regarding either censure or commendation, feeling that the name of the good woman, like her person, ought to be shut up indoors and never go out. But to my mind Gorgias appears to display better taste in advising that not the form but the fame of a woman should be known to many. Best of all seems the Roman custom, which publicly renders to women, as to men, a fitting commemoration after the end of their life . . . I have also written out for you the remainder of what I would have said on the topic that man's virtues and woman's virtues are one and the same . . . Yet, if in a convincing argument delectation is to be found also by reason of the very nature of the illustration, then the discussion is not devoid of an agreeableness which helps in the exposition, nor does it hesitate

> To join
> The Graces with the Muses,
> A consorting most fair,

as Euripides says, and to pin its faith mostly to the love of beauty inherent to the soul.

If, conceivably, we asserted that painting on the part of men and women is the same, and exhibited paintings, done by women, of the sort that Apelles, or Zeuxis, or Nicomachus has left to us, would anybody reprehend us on the ground that we were aiming at giving gratification and allurement rather than at persuasion? I do not think so.

Or again, if we should declare that the poetic or the prophetic art is not one art when practised by men and another
when practised by women, but the same, and if we should put
the poems of Sappho side by side with those of Anacreon, or
the oracles of the Sibyl with those of Bacis, will anybody have
the power justly to impugn the demonstration because these
lead on the hearer, joyous and delighted, to have belief in it?
No, you could not say that either?

And actually it is not possible to learn better the similarity
and the difference between the virtues of men and of women
from any other source than by putting lives beside lives and
actions beside actions, like great works of art, and considering
whether the magnificence of Semiramis has the same character
and pattern as that of Sesostris, or the intelligence of Tanaquil
the same as that of Servius the king, or the high spirit of Porcia
the same as that of Brutus, or that of Pelopidas the same as
Timocleia's, when compared with due regard to the most
important points of identity and influence.[1]

So reads Plutarch's introduction to his brief essay on "The
Virtues of Women" *(Gynaikon Aretai),* written in the early part
of the second century A.D. His proposal—to treat men and women
on an equal footing—was a worthy one, and we might do well to
take it to heart. It was a rather astonishing view for Plutarch to
hold, given that the opinion Thucydides imputes to Pericles reflects
the ancient world's prevailing view of women: the less said about
them the better. Unfortunately Plutarch does not keep his promise.
In the essay he does not explore the masculine virtues in parallel
with the feminine. Nor does he write a *Lives of Illustrious Women;*
to have done so would have been to acknowledge that women
have a right to a biography. He merely rescues one act from
oblivion, one exploit, which he takes to be a striking illustration
of feminine *arete* (the Greek means something closer to "valor"
than to "virtue"). Pointing out that certain actions and attitudes
regularly attributed to women are mere commonplaces of ancient
rhetoric, Plutarch denies that there is anything particularly distinctive about the female of the species. In his texts Pericles and
Fabius Maximus are born, gain glory, obtain power, and die, but
Aretaphila of Cyrene, after ridding the city of two tyrants, returns
to the gynaeceum and spends the rest of her days doing needle-
work. The women of Troy end the Trojans' wandering by burning
their vessels in the mouth of the Tiber; having done so, they lavish

kisses upon their husbands, begging their pardon for such a reckless act. We who would write of the ancient world thus face a
dilemma: either say nothing about women or submit to the tyranny
of familiar images. Is there no other choice?

Our ambition is grandiose: to cover more than twenty centuries
of Greek and Roman history, encompassing a territory ranging
from the North Sea to the Mediterranean, from the Pillars of
Hercules to the banks of the Indus; to explore sources ranging
from gravestones to floor plans, from stele inscriptions to papyrus
rolls, from vase paintings to Greek and Latin literary works that
talked profusely of women, though women were excluded from
their making. Although this world was essentially rural, we know
far more about the cities than we do about the countryside. It was
a world of inequalities, most of whose residents were nonfree or
foreigners while the minority of citizens occupied the center stage.
It was a world of linguistic and cultural diversity, whose cities,
states, monarchies, and empires emerged in brief interludes of
superficial and often precarious unity. Obviously a work of this
kind cannot take account of regional differences; we will have
nothing to say about important periods of history, and we cannot
do justice to the whole range of ancient documents and authors.
To learn about the role of female landowners in Hellenistic Boeotia, say, or about the place of women in the work of Diodorus of
Sicily and Ovid, the interested reader will have to turn to the
monographic literature.

The purpose of this book is not to replace the substantial literature that exists on subjects of this kind, nor is it to achieve some
sort of synthesis. We take up only a few of the questions that we
consider important for understanding the place of women in the
ancient world. Since this volume is part of a series dealing with
the history of women over the ages, it was important to consider
the formation of certain intellectual habits, legal forms, and social
institutions that endured through centuries of European history.
The content of this volume thus reflects a deliberate choice, partly
determined by the current state of research. Given the outpouring
of work on women in recent years, we asked ourselves which areas
we would like to see summarized. Many topics such as the economic role of women in the Greek city-states, the status of women
in Hellenistic and Roman Egypt, and the place of women in the
Roman family had been covered in other recent surveys, and it
seemed pointless to rehearse their findings here. But significant

3

subjects had been omitted entirely from other works, and interested readers had no choice but to embark on an arduous search for articles in specialist journals—one sign of the much-denounced fragmentation of women's studies. We therefore chose to focus attention on important areas, such as iconography, in which recent advances were more or less inaccessible to general readers. We also tried to highlight differences and similarities between Greece and Rome. It will emerge, for example, that the ecological and social conditions of reproduction were similar in both places. Two related articles on the role of women in Greek and Roman ritual point up areas of convergence and divergence. The structure of the book was in part dictated by our determination to deal with issues fundamental to both Greece and Rome.

We are deeply indebted to the scores of researchers whose archival research, methodological reflections, and historiographical debates have infused the subject with new life and rescued it from that insipid backwater known as "the history of everyday life." This is a work of history; we do not repudiate other approaches to the subject, but our method is strictly historical. All the contributors to this volume have worked on gender issues, even if gender was not the exclusive focus of their research. Many have contributed to "women's studies," yet they work in fields as varied as the history of law, religious history, political history, and the history of Christian thought. We do not follow any party line. What unites us is our determination to show how and why the history of male-female relations was an integral part of the history of the ancient world. Our approach is both internal and external. In a field that can all too easily degenerate into polemic, we have tried to exercise the critical function of historians.

The issues raised by Georges Duby and Michelle Perrot in the series introduction are pertinent to this volume on the Greco-Roman world. Some of the problems—sources, for example—are more serious here perhaps than elsewhere. The ancient world left very little writing by women, although the name of Sappho is frequently cited. In general the sources provide a man's view of women and of the world, and thus this book of necessity relies heavily on masculine discourse, even in its iconography. The only alternative, it seems to us, is to refrain from writing on the subject altogether. Because we are looking through men's eyes, there is little concrete information about women's lives; what we have instead is representations. Given the nature of the sources, we felt it best to confront the issue directly. We therefore look first at what the ancient documents give us, namely, masculine discourse about women, and more generally about *gender,* the difference between the sexes. We shall look at the sources chronologically in order to gain a better idea of how thinking on the subject evolved from the archaic Greeks imagining their goddesses to the Church Fathers inventing the figure of the martyred female saint and the Virgin Mary. But even after we have dealt with these texts and images, we still cannot describe how women actually lived. This deficiency may well exasperate or even outrage certain feminists— with good reason. We cannot even give a general description of women's culture. What we can do is describe certain social practices that influenced, shaped, or otherwise left their mark on women's lives: marriage, procreation, and religion. In so doing we touch on the place women occupied in the economic and social life, and more generally in the history, of the Greco-Roman world. Unfortunately, the women of the ancient world did not confide in diaries or anthropologists, so that it was impossible for us to follow Yvonne Verdier's advice "to take women at their word."

Even if we could not listen directly to the women of the past, we have tried to be attentive to the concerns of the women of today. The two brief historiographical essays included in the volume are intended merely to point out that the history of ancient women and of the relation between the sexes in the ancient world is also a living history, an ongoing saga, in which the contributors to this volume are modest participants.

More perhaps than subsequent volumes in the series, this first volume deals with representations, with the imagination. The first task ahead of us is to describe these representations. It is important to know exactly what Aristotle thought about gender and how the entirety of Roman law is based on the division between the sexes. We must learn about the female divinities and how they differed from other gods. We must explore the ways in which the Greeks, Romans, and early Christians used women in their religious rituals. Later of course these representations may be "deconstructed," but even then only with great care and with scrupulous attention to the type of discourse involved. We are wary of any all-encompassing system that would obscure the underlying diversity, a diversity not lessened by the passage of time, to which several of the essays in this volume are particularly sensitive. Only the reader can judge whether the attention devoted here to the discourse of men can help us understand our own relation to gender.

This volume was shaped by precise questions and by a determination to highlight certain ancient models that long obsessed—and perhaps still do obsess—the Western imagination. The first section is devoted to the ancient world's female models. It begins with the question, "What is a goddess?" Nicole Loraux goes on to examine not only the functions and significance of the goddesses in the Greek pantheon but, more generally, the place of the feminine in Greek representations. Giulia Sissa continues this line of investigation in the more specialized domain of philosophical thought. By examining the way in which Plato and Aristotle define gender, she explores ancient thinking about the respective position of men and women. Equally fundamental is the attitude of Roman law toward the division of the sexes. Yan Thomas shows that the key to the whole system is the fact that legitimacy could not be conveyed through women and that all of women's disabilities stemmed from the definition of the order of inheritance. Visual representations define a different model. The male perception of the female becomes the basis of a symbolic code that permeates the entire culture. François Lissarrague examines Greek perceptions as recorded in painting on ceramics. The method he employs, previously tested elsewhere, deserves to be tried on other periods (the Roman, for example) and other forms of artistic expression, such as sculpture.

The fact that we study female models in order to understand ancient discourse does not mean that we believe representation can be separated from reality, discourse from practice. It is generally accepted that any such division is artificial and that every social institution has its own representation, just as every discourse has its effect on real life. The division of the first two parts of the book is not based on any methodological preconception, and analysis of discourse is as prevalent in Part II as in Part I. The only difference is that in Part II the discourses under scrutiny are associated with practices that determine how women actually live.

Perhaps the most important of these practices is marriage, whose Greek manifestations Claudine Leduc explores. Her anthropological approach examines "the free gift of the woman" over a considerable expanse of time, from Homer until the fourth century, and in a variety of cities. With this novel approach it becomes possible to reformulate the question of the relation between marriage and citizenship in a new and fruitful way. In Rome the destiny of the married woman was to produce legitimate offspring. Aline Rousselle explores not only the biological but also the social and ethical consequences of this fact for women's lives. Among the topics considered are age at marriage, the number of pregnancies, the status of midwives, the sexual division of labor for women of various classes, and the slow emergence of new attitudes toward bodily self-control.

When we think of ancient women, we inevitably think of maenads and vestals, those frenetic and virtuous virgins about whom we began reading as children. Louise Bruit Zaidman traces the lives of Greek women from infancy to maturity and examines their participation in public rituals. She notes certain key stages and certain disabilities that John Scheid also finds in Rome: exclusion from sacrifice, the role of the female assistant in aiding certain kinds of priests, and, more generally, the subtle dialectic of presence and absence that is the religious counterpart of the ambiguous attitude toward the female element in the sphere of citizenship, where the presence of women is unavoidable and yet unrecognized. Yet in a further parallel between Greece and Rome, both societies give prominence to other forms of female participation in ritual: neither midwives nor vestals are Greek. Monique Alexandre shows how the modest, anonymous Christian women of the early church, as well as the emblematic martyrs, incorporated both aspects of the ancient image of the married woman: the procreative and the adoring. They also constitute a bridge between the ancient and the medieval worlds.

All history—and the "history of women" as much as any other—must bridge the gap between yesterday and today. Because so many people have some familiarity with the ancient world, we are often asked about Amazons and the whole question of women's power in antiquity, or whether Penelope and Clytemnestra are symbols of matriarchy. Stella Georgoudi reviews the content of Bachofen's *Mutterrecht* (Maternal Law) and shows how recent research has cast grave doubt on beliefs that once lent some semblance of reality to this nineteenth-century myth. Finally, since most ancient historians have little taste for the history of women, despite the rapid development of the field in recent years, I contribute a final chapter on the place of women's history in ancient history today.

The reader who makes his or her way to the end of the book

will find that the words of Perpetua, a young woman condemned because she was Christian to die in Carthage at the beginning of the third century, sound a hopeful note. This book will have achieved its goal if it helps the reader to understand "why Omphala did not manage to acquire lasting power."

one

Feminine Models
of the Ancient World

1

What Is a Goddess?

Nicole Loraux

A SCENE AT THE END of Euripides' tragedy *Hippolytus* features a goddess and a mortal. Young Hippolytus, his body broken as a result of his father's curse, is dying. Preceding the sad procession carrying home the shattered body of Theseus' son, Artemis has already arrived and begun to proclaim her outrage at thus being forced to watch the death of her protégé, "the man who, of all mortals, was dearest to me." Hippolytus is then laid upon the ground. A divine fragrance, the ineffable fragrance of the gods, has revived his senses. Within his body—a body he wished to ignore but that cruelly reminded him of its presence—the pain suddenly subsides. A dialogue begins between the mortal and the goddess:

— The Goddess Artemis [*Artemis thea*] is near this place?
— She is the dearest of the gods to you.

Soi philtate theon: for you, the dearest of the gods. Or should it read "the dearest of the *goddesses*"? In the Homeric language, which possesses the genitive feminine plural *theaon,* the question would not arise, but in classical Greek the form *theon* makes it impossible to say for sure whether

Artemis is here being classed with the group of gods in general or, more particularly, with the goddesses. And although Artemis openly expressed her affection for Hippolytus in his absence, she refrains from repeating her sentiments now that he is present. Hippolytus is simply confronted with his own feelings: to *you* Artemis is the dearest of the gods. For that reason perhaps he makes yet another attempt to penetrate the deity's reticence: "You see my suffering, mistress?" To which Artemis responds: "I see it. But the eyes are forbidden to shed a tear." The impersonality of this reply—the goddess avoids even the possessive, *my* eyes, *my* tears—is appropriate to the enunciation of a law: it is the gods in general, and not just Artemis, who are forbidden *(ou themis)* to weep for a mortal. [Compare Grene's translation: "Heavenly law forbids my tears."] For abject Hippolytus, however, the universality of the law is small consolation. It is the goddess—this particular goddess—of whom he asks tenderness and solace, but Artemis replies that what is *divine* in her, and therefore shuns human suffering, takes precedence over what is *feminine,* and with which, in the world of men, tears are closely associated.

Does this mean that a female divinity has nothing in common with the femininity of mortal women? Or should we rather attribute this reticence (or distance) to chaste Artemis' ferocious virginity? Hippolytus then resumes, as if trying one more time to tighten the bond between himself and the goddess:

— Gone is your huntsman, gone your servant now.
— Yes, truly: but you die beloved by me.
— Gone is your groom, gone your shrine's guardian.

But Artemis has not come for such effusions. She reveals the name of the goddess responsible for this disaster: Aphrodite, whom Hippolytus had disdained, and who took her vengeance. Artemis then turns to a more urgent task; to reconcile the son with the father. Then, as self-possessed as ever, she takes her leave, leaving the humans to themselves:

— Farewell, I must not [*ou themis*] look upon the dead.[1]
  My eye must not be polluted by the last
  gaspings for breath. I see you are near this.

The goddess has already gone before Hippolytus has finished his reply, a response not unalloyed with bitterness (lines 1440–1441):

> — Farewell to you, too holy maiden! Go in peace.[2]
> You can lightly leave a long companionship.

Has the mortal Hippolytus grasped the fact that it was precisely this long companionship *(homilia)*, of which he was as proud as if it were a privilege reserved for him alone (lines 84–86), that cost him his life? For Aphrodite's jealousy is not simply that of a woman when, in the play's prologue (line 19), she characterizes the companionship *(homilia)* between man and goddess as too lofty for a mortal. In any case she has no trouble adopting the language of offended divinity. Greek piety was based on distance between man and god; it was Hippolytus' error to have allowed his pleasure in proximity to the divine Huntress to overshadow this basic tenet.[3] Companionship with a god, even on the ephebic trails of the forest, was at best inappropriate, at worst impudent.

It may be, however—I propose this simply as a hypothesis—that Hippolytus had also committed another error, one more difficult to formulate in words. In following in the footsteps of a virgin goddess, he was no doubt combining repudiation of woman as mother with attraction for the feminine. Such an interpretation is suggested by the highly ambiguous words that he addresses early in the play to Artemis, words that, while apparently praising chastity, reveal a highly eroticized relationship.[4] Here, again, the interpreter is faced with a choice. Does the youth's error lie in his failure to recognize that the nature of femininity is not the same for mortal women as for goddesses? Or does it lie in his belief that he is protected from the race of women by a divine friendship, as if a goddess were nothing more than a god in the feminine? Who can say whether other goddesses will accept the law of which Artemis, sweetly distant, reminds Hippolytus in the hour of his death?

We will never know, and nothing can compel a text to reveal more than its words state. Nevertheless, we cannot decline to interpret. In this case the interpreter must admit that she finds herself embarrassed. We therefore end up with two hypotheses. Either "goddess" is nothing other than the grammatical feminine of the word "god," and in a goddess the feminine is an essential characteristic. Or a goddess is something other than a god, in which case there are two further possibilities: her femininity is essential, but it may be either a femininity of the same kind found in mortal women or of a different, more intense kind. In all our interpretations thus far we have wavered back and forth among these possibilities.

Theos, Thea: A Goddess

How Can a Feminine Be Ascribed to "God"?

Although feminists have attempted to find a feminine name for God (He/She-God), the divine sex appears to have been clearly masculine in all monotheisms. In polytheism—in those polytheisms that we denote, in our language, with a Greek word—"goddesses" would appear to be yet another way of expressing the underlying multiplicity *(poly-)* of the system.

Once the temptation arises to unify the divine under a single principle, however, a suspicion appears. The Stoics, for example, acted as if the question of the gods' sex were badly framed. If Zeus is all, as he was for Chrysippus, then there are no male and female gods but only *names,* each bearing a grammatical gender. Or gender may be a mere metaphor for aspects of the divine: "The Stoics maintain that there is but one god, whose names vary according to its acts and functions. One can even say, therefore, that the powers have two sexes, male when they are in action and female when they are by nature passive." Thus the sex of the gods stems from a mental operation that links the powers and elements to the masculine and feminine. By associating air with Juno (or Hera), men were said to have "feminized" *(effeminarunt)* her, because nothing is more tenuous than air. If, moreover, the gods are merely a fiction *(fictos deos)* that measures everything against the standard of human weakness, and if the attributes of the divine are set forth in two columns, one headed male, the other female, the difference between the sexes becomes merely one of the categories that make it possible to establish long chains of synonyms: "The Stoics say that there is only one god and only one power, which, according to its functions, is assigned different names by men. Thus, Sun, Apollo, and Liber are different names for the same thing. The same is true of Moon, Diana, Ceres, Juno, Proserpina."[5] But these are Latin quotations, and it might be objected that they reflect some unique feature of the Roman *religio*, even though Chrysippus, who initiated the controversy, was a Greek. Let us go back, therefore, to archaic and classical Greece, the periods with which this chapter is concerned. Gods and goddesses are in their places, yet anyone who considers the general nature of the divine will find that, considered as divinity, or "divine thing," the term is neuter *(to theion)*, while considered as god, the word is masculine *(theos)*.[6] Goddesses exist, but the divine cannot be expressed in the feminine.

Historians of religion frequently seem unsure what to do about this gendered dimension, to which they generally allude without analysis. Walter Burkert, for example, notes that the opposition of male and female is one of the "primary differentiations among the gods," but thereafter he interests himself only in family relations and pairs of gods (where gender differences may be irrelevant) and in relations between older and younger gods.[7]

Yet gender difference is an important element in Greek thinking about the gods, even though the difference between the sexes does not play the same role on Olympus as in the world of mortals. In the *Theogony,* the great narrative of the replacement of one generation of gods by another, Hesiod indicates that "all the gods . . . male and female" are involved in a great contest, the decisive battle between the children of Kronos and the Titans.[8] Given the immensity of the stakes, no Immortal, god or goddess, could fail to respond to the call. This suggests that in the world of the gods war is not, as it is among humans, the exclusive province of males. In combat Athena is the equal of Ares, and on the Trojan plain goddesses throw themselves wholeheartedly into the battle on both sides.

We must therefore yield to the evidence. In any investigation of the Greek gods, gender difference is an important heuristic category, and we must ask ourselves how a goddess differs from a god in attributes and modes of action. Before we can do that, however, we must analyze the multiple displacements to which the category "feminine" was subjected in being projected from the world of men onto that of the Immortals. At the same time we may ask how divine status might alter, or even deform, the definition of femininity.

Another point must be kept in mind. If we are talking about the very beginnings of the *kosmos,* we cannot formulate these questions in the same way as when we are speaking of the reigning generation of gods. What was there in the beginning: "*One* or a *Couple* or many? Male and/or female? A single *Mother* for all things, or one mother for the good and another for the bad?"⁹

A Problem of Gender

Grammar is as good a place as any to begin. While the Greek word for "god" is *theos,* there are two different and equally legitimate ways of designating a goddess: by using the word *thea,* the feminine form of *theos,* or by using the morphologically masculine word *theos* but preceded by a feminine article or rendered feminine by the context. Thus in official Athenian inscriptions Athena is *he theos,* a fact that led Aristophanes to make jests about a city "in which a *god born woman* [*theos gune geonuia*] appears armed from head to toe."¹⁰

Ho theos, he theos: the god, the goddess. There can be no doubt that, to use the terminology of the Prague school of linguistics, the phrase *he theos* is the "marked" form of the word "god." *He theos* denotes a divine being who happens to be marked by a feminine sign.

Consider the problematic amorous encounter between Aphrodite and the mortal Anchises. The goddess of desire is overcome by a violent desire for the young herdsman, and, "so that he might not take fright at the sight of her," she assumes what she believes to be the human shape and size of a young maiden. But Anchises is not deceived; he hails the apparition as Sovereign and wonders about her divine identity (is she perhaps Artemis, Leto, Aphrodite, Themis, or Athena, or possibly a nymph?). Aphrodite denies everything: "No, I am not *theos.* Why do you compare me to the Immortals? Mortal I am, and the mother who gave me birth was a woman" (*Homeric Hymn to Aphrodite,* 109–110). If I had to translate *theos,* I would not use the word "goddess" but rather "god," whose generality conveys the meaning that Aphrodite intends: that in her there is nothing divine.

Reassured, Anchises does not bother to inquire further and gives the goddess the pleasure she had hoped for. Now Aphrodite can admit to being what she had never ceased to be while in the young man's bed. The "divine among goddesses" *(dia theaon)* therefore allows herself an epiphany. Her poor human lover can only stammer: "The moment I saw you with my eyes, goddess [*thea*], I understood that you were *theos*" (*HHA,* 185–186). You are a goddess; I clearly recognized the divine in you. What better proof could there be than these lines of the *Homeric Hymn* that in a goddess there is both *thea* and *theos? Theos:* generic divinity beyond the difference in sex; *thea:* a female divinity.

The Goddesses: A System of the Feminine?

Theai: goddesses. If we were to forget for a moment that *thea* can always be replaced by *theos,* it might be tempting to look at each goddess as the incarnation of a feminine "type" in the hope of ultimately demonstrating that the *theai* as a group constituted a symbolic system of femininity. But this group scarcely exists apart from a few very general formulas associating the goddesses with the gods. More than that, there is no proof that each goddess is, as certain historians of religion claim, an archetype or idea (Hera the stilted wife, Aphrodite the seductress, Athena the sexless careerist, and so on). One historian who took pleasure in this sort of game, Paul Friedrich, saw Aphrodite as nothing more than a pure female symbol of love.[11] As a result, he was obliged to neglect or underestimate any aspect of the goddess' action that could not be easily accommodated under this head: her intimacy, for example, with the somber cohort of children of the Night, who constitute her train in the *Theogony;*[12] her association, which is not simply erotic, with Ares the killer, along with the epithet *Areia* which is attached to her name in certain cities; and her title *Pandemos,* which does not, as Plato perfidiously insisted, transform her into a Venus of the crossroads but rather describes her activity as proctress of the political, her role in maintaining the unity of all *(pan)* the people *(demos)* and protecting the city's magistrates.

This is not to say that the goddess cannot, in her most immediately perceptible aspect, "embody one face of feminine reality to the exclusion of others." But as Jean-Pierre Vernant observes, she then stands at an even greater distance from the "feminine condition" as mortal women must endure it, fraught with tension and conflict, because the feminine trait thus embodied is in its divine state almost chemically "pure."[13] To complicate matters still further, this remark needs to be qualified, for such purity can rarely be isolated wherever there is any depth at all to the divine personality. The attributes of a divinity are manifold, and its field of action is infinitely broad, so that upon examination even the virgin Hestia with her impoverished mythology turns out to be a murkier figure than she at first appeared.[14]

Consider the interpretive framework provided by the "ages" of woman, or, more precisely, by the biological and social *cursus* that constitutes a woman as such. In Nauplia every year Hera recovers her virginity by bathing in the Kanathos spring.[15] Does this mean that she "incarnates" not only the maturity of the married woman but also the virginity of the young maiden? At Stymphalos she is honored by three sanctuaries, in which she is revered, respectively, as "very young girl" *(Pais),* as "accomplished" woman *(Teleia),* and as "widow" *(Khera).*[16] Does this mean that the goddess is the very incarnation of the ages of woman? To make such a claim would be to mistake the unique nature of Hera's life, for at no time is she honored as a mother, the only figure of "accomplishment" for a mortal woman. On rereading Pausanias' text, it is clear that the three temples, far from having any purely symbolic intention, honor three phases in Hera's "personal" *story,* including the final phase, in which, according to this version, she separated from Zeus after a more than usually violent quarrel and went to live in Stymphalos.

The virgin goddesses give rise to similar reflections. If Athena, Artemis, and Hestia have chosen to remain *parthenoi* (virgins) forever, and if virginity is therefore one of their essential characteristics, the three offer very different interpretations of that state. One is a warrior virgin, much given to the use of ruse and magic. Another is a wild huntress, chaste yet also the goddess of childbirth. And the third is the guardian of the hearth in the city as well as in the home.

Yet another unpromising approach is to interpret relations between goddesses as analogous to kinship relations. Athena and Artemis might be interpreted symbolically as "sisters," for example.[17] In fact, only Demeter and Persephone, institutionalized as *Meter* and *Kore* in their cult, can be taken as symbols of mother and daughter. If attention is confined to myth, as in the *Homeric Hymn to Demeter,* one must still distinguish carefully between the "human" register of the story, in which the relation between mother and daughter is crucial to the central plot, and the quite independent divine register, in which mortals and their concerns play a largely marginal role.[18]

The word *thea* is a feminine form, and in sculpture the *thea* was always represented as a female; yet there is no evidence that in a goddess the feminine attributes had greater importance than the divine.

A Goddess, A Woman

Does the divine take precedence over the feminine in a goddess? This question, although not explicitly raised, was recently answered in the negative in a study of the Homeric poems, in which it was alleged that the dazzled desire of male gods and mortals always takes as its object "women," "whether divine or mortal."[19]

That may indeed be true as regards the *eros* and pleasure that males, heroic or divine, take in sexual union. While the preliminaries are eloquently recounted and the sequels fondly narrated, so little is said about the pleasure of the gods that we cannot be sure that in this specific realm Homer's imagination of distance did not fail him. But everything else is complicated and worthy of further attention.

There are of course maidens so similar to goddesses that no mortal eye can distinguish Nausicaa, say, from Artemis. In the *Homeric Hymn to Demeter,* for example, the daughters of King Keleos are "four in number, like goddesses, and of a ripe age." Aphrodite, moreover, wished to appear before Anchises as a "woman resembling a goddess," but as we saw the human semblance proved incapable of concealing the real goddess.

To say that a mortal woman *resembles* a goddess is to ascribe to the mortal some of the radiance inherent in the bodies of the gods (all the gods, male as well as female) as well as some of the magnitude of the goddess in epiphany.[20] For then, repudiating the various forms she has borrowed to present herself to humans, she touches the peaks of tall houses and gives off a divine fragrance.[21] But who can say whether epiphany is not a form—the theomorphic form—of metamorphosis?[22] One might easily think so at the sight of Demeter, in the *Homeric Hymn* devoted to her, exchanging *(ameipse)* one form, that of an elderly wet nurse, for another, that of a tall and beautiful woman.[23] Or again, when, after making love, Aphrodite appears to Anchises in all her glory: "A brilliant beauty gleamed in her immortal cheeks, like that of Kythaerea with the handsome crown" (HHA, 174–175). Kythaerea is one of Aphrodite's names. Did the goddess perhaps resemble the figure by which humans knew her in her sanctuaries?

Appearances may lead mortals astray. Let us content ourselves with an approximation, since, after all, the stories about the gods are fiction—in the present case, poetry. To compare maidens to goddesses is simply to characterize them as quintessentially beautiful. Divine beauty is in essence "pure," and it is also superlative in that it expresses the god-being. Thus Demeter was beautiful in her epiphany, as is Hera in the fourteenth canto of the *Iliad*, when she fixes herself up in preparation for the seduction of Zeus. The case of Hera is particularly interesting because it reveals how much beauty is essentially a manifestation of power. Not only is Hera beautiful, but she is described as "by far the most beautiful of the immortal goddesses, the glorious daughter of subtle Kronos and of Rhea the Mother, the venerated divinity whom Zeus with his immortal designs made his accomplished and respected wife."[24]

Accordingly, Hera the sovereign should have won the beauty contest judged by Paris, had that contest been, as Dumézil argues it was, simply a competition among the three Indo-European virtues, because sovereignty should have taken precedence. But no one, man or god, could resist the goddess of desire. Hence Aphrodite won, and, for humans as well as gods, the Trojan War was the result.

If beauty is the property of goddesses, women, being mortal, are in possession of voice. When Zeus orders Hephaestus to make a being of earth and water, he indicates that he wants it to have "the human voice" *(anthropou auden)*.[25] Ultimately it is cunning Hermes, who before giving the name Pandora to the female decoy created by Hephaestus, bestows upon her the ultimate gift: voice *(phone)*.[26] Here I shall concentrate my attention on the word *aude*, which lexicographers, based on abundant textual evidence, take to be the very name of human speech.[27] Upon contacting Ino, the daughter of Kadmos elevated by her death to divine honors but who, during her lifetime, was mortal and therefore normally equipped with a voice *(brotos audeessa)*, Circe (three times) and Calypso (once) are characterized as *deine theos audeessa:* "terrible goddess with the human voice."[28] This has embarrassed the commentators, who, ever since antiquity, have tried to replace *audeessa* with another adjective. It is clear, however, that *oudeessa* (terrestrial) and *auleessa* (accompanied by the sound of a flute) are derisory substitutes. We must therefore make do with the text, particularly since the expression juxtaposes the god-being, the human voice, and the feminine in a superb oxymoron. In two minor goddesses the divine and the female thus face each other in intimate confrontation, and the discordance of genders (the female ending of *deine,* the masculine form of *theos,* and the feminine *audeessa*) suggests that this intimacy dissimulates the irreconcilable.

Return for a moment to Pandora. In a chapter on "the divine and woman," a longer look is warranted at this woman who possesses not only "the human voice and capabilities" but also "the shape of a beautiful and desirable virgin, modeled on the immortal goddesses."[29] Traditionally Pandora was called the "first woman," which in itself would suggest that imitation of goddesses was not incompatible with the maintenance of a certain distance between the divine and the mortal. But Jean Rudhardt has shown that the designation "first woman" implied not only that Pandora was *mortal* but also that she was the first female member of *civilized* humanity.[30] Such a claim requires a systematic, and perhaps artificial, reordering of Hesiod's narrative to form a linear chronology. Still, while one may hesitate to agree with Rudhardt that "Pandora was not exactly the first female in the human race," he is clearly right that she "prefigures a certain distribution of male and female roles . . . very different from the distribution that obtains among the gods."[31] And there is a great deal in the idea that femininity, as Hesiod sees it, largely transcends the figure of Pandora, so that attention must be given to "all the female beings he mentions, from monsters to goddesses."

A goddess, then, is not a woman. The truth of this assertion is clear, but it was worth taking the time to establish the grounds on which it rests. How is the fact that a goddess is not a woman translated into action? For one thing, it is dangerous for a mortal man to have intercourse with a goddess, particularly if she is named Aphrodite.[32] Recall Aeneas' entreaty to the goddess who was for one night his lover: "Have pity on me, for a man who sleeps with immortal goddesses does not prosper."[33] However, a passage in Euripides' *Ion*[34] points out the danger inherent in any unequal union between humans and gods, a danger attested by the unfortunate fate of certain of Zeus's lovers, from Danae inundated by a golden rain to Semele thunderstruck at the sight of her omnipotent seducer in full glory.[35] In these examples, however, it is only too clear that the distance between gods and mortals is more important than the sexual identity of the partners. Since our interest here is in goddesses, I shall dwell at somewhat greater length on two cases that have so far been mentioned only briefly:

the virgin goddesses, for whom chastity is an eminently divine luxury that no mortal, male or female, can choose without being severely punished, as the examples of Hippolytus and Atalanta show;[36] and Hera, the protectress of marriage but herself a shrewish wife and dubious mother, the wife but also the sister of Zeus, whose paradigmatic union would have been regarded as incest under Athenian law, which authorized marriage between (half) brother and sister with a common father but prohibited it with a common mother.[37]

The Divine Wife and the Virgin Goddesses

Consider first Hera. Clémence Ramnoux observes that of all the divinities mentioned in the *Iliad,* she is the goddess most remote from humans.[38] It might therefore seem logical to say that this distance reflects her status as the wife of a powerful god, a statement with which Pindar, who begins one triumphal ode with an invocation of "Zeus most high and Hera who shares his throne," no doubt would have agreed.[39] From a cult standpoint, however, matters may be rather different. In cities where Hera was the protectress of marriage, honored with the title *Teleia,* meaning "perfect" or "accomplished," Marcel Detienne tells us that she owed this honor to "her exclusive competence in that which the word *telos* designates for women." Detienne calls attention to the Theogamies, a festival celebrated in Attica during the month of marriage *(Gamelion)* in honor of the marriage of Zeus and Hera, but in which Zeus is said to be attached to Hera *(Heraios),* while among men the inviting power is the wife and not the husband.[40]

Admittedly such a reversal can be found in the texts. Sometimes Hera's power is said to derive from the fact that she "sleeps in the arms of the great Zeus."[41] But other times her power is said to be her own, and the texts go so far as to refer to Zeus, not without rather labored condescension, as Hera's "bed companion."[42] Her statues, moreover, generally bear the imposing coif of the Great Goddesses. It should therefore come as no surprise that some historians of religion consider Hera to be a mother goddess.[43]

Yet as Mother (and even simply as mother), Hera leaves much to be desired, just as she is quite baffling in her role of *Teleia.* Recall the Hera of Stymphalos, whose image in her married state is flanked by two others celebrating her innocent youth and her separation from Zeus without so much as a mention of Hera *meter,* as if the married Hera were always fleeing toward a before and an after marriage. Walter Burkert, who notices this point, also remarks that the figure of the goddess is strangely lacking any maternal dimension.[44] In the *Iliad* Zeus avows his hatred for his legitimate son by Hera, Ares, a god steeped in conflict and so like his mother; but there is no indication that Hera cherishes this son who so resembles her. Think too of the mistreatment she previously had meted out to Hephaestus, and of her strange propensity to forgo the services of Zeus in order to conceive children who would owe nothing to anyone but herself, among whom Ares was sometimes included.[45]

In short, Hera was the protectress of marriage, but what a marriage she herself had! How problematic was the accomplishment of the goddess honored as *Teleia!* Clearly the "feminine condition" exists only among humans.

The divine virgins, or *Parthenoi,* whose existence and resolute chastity are sometimes taken as characteristic features of Greek religion, also avoided the feminine condition.[46] On Olympus the goddesses impervious to desire numbered three, and their names occur early on in the *Homeric Hymn to Aphrodite* as if to reinforce by contradiction the power of the smiling goddess:

> First is the daughter of Zeus who holds the aegis, bright-eyed Athene; for she has no pleasure in the deeds of golden Aphrodite, but delights in wars and in the work of Ares, in strifes and battles and in preparing famous crafts. She first taught earthly craftsmen to make chariots of war and cars variously wrought with bronze, and she also teaches tender maidens in the house and puts knowledge of the homely arts in each one's mind. Nor does laughter-loving Aphrodite ever tame in love Artemis, the huntress with shafts of gold; for she loves archery and the slaying of wild beasts in the mountains, as well as the lyre and dancing and thrilling cries and shady woods and the cities of upright men. Nor does the pure maiden Hestia love Aphrodite's works. She was the first-born child of wily Kronos and youngest too, by will of Zeus who holds the aegis—a queenly maid whom both Poseidon and Apollo sought to wed. But she was wholly unwilling and stubbornly refused; and touching the head of father Zeus who holds the aegis, she, that fair goddess, swore a great oath which has in truth been fulfilled, that she would be a maiden all her days. So Zeus the Father gave her a high honor instead of marriage,

and she has her place in the midst of the house and has the richest portion. In all the temples of the gods she has a share of honor, and among all mortal men she is chief of the goddesses. Of these three Aphrodite cannot bend or ensnare the hearts. But of all others there is nothing among the blessed gods or among mortal men that has escaped Aphrodite.[47]

Artemis, paradoxically clad in the garb of the huntress, is the most eroticized of the three and perhaps also the most terrifying for those under her protection: women in childbed die suddenly from her shafts, and hunters keen on living must forbear to gaze on the beautiful body of the naked goddess in her bath—as Actaeon learned to his peril. Euripides has her avow the hatred that the immortal *Parthenoi* bear toward Aphrodite: "of all the gods the most odious for us, who take our pleasure from virginity."[48]

Athena is supposed to be the least sexualized of the three, or so historians of religion like to tell us in order to avoid the riddle of her sexualization. It has even been claimed that "the Greek idea of god appears to have freed itself from all sexual features only in the virginity of Athena."[49] Perhaps these historians find the femininity of goddesses disturbing. They would do better to look at things as they are. Just because mortal women cannot settle on virginity as a permanent state, it does not follow that the goddesses' choice of virginity constitutes some sort of degree zero of femininity. Athena herself provides the proof. She is desirable enough to be pursued by lame Hephaestus, and the results are well known: the god's sperm fertilizes the earth, the child Erichthonius is born, and Athena, still a virgin, raises the miraculous offspring.[50]

Hestia, for her part, was said to be misogynist, and no woman was allowed into those highly political edifices, the prytaneums, which, though consecrated to her, symbolized the male city. Female in body, she "resides in the home in the twin guise of virgin and old woman."[51] Thus she, more than Athena, satisfied the quest for a deity "free" if not of all aspects of (female) sexuality then at least of any of the characteristic accomplishments of mature womanhood. Hestia had no, or at any rate very little, history, however. All that is known about her comes from the *Homeric Hymn to Aphrodite.*

The qualities of a goddess were confirmed but also complicated by divine virginity. Taken individually, the three *Parthenoi* of Olympus make it clear that to be *thea* was not to be a woman.

But, taken together, they are essential to an understanding of the divine configuration of the feminine. Because their femininity is arrested, hovering, as it were, on the threshold, it offers abundant food for thought concerning the essence of that "pleasure in virginity" of which Euripides' Artemis speaks. Perhaps "goddess" was the feminine form of "god," but we must henceforth focus our attention on both notions, feminine as well as god, as matter for speculation and material for reverie in the city of men.

Feminine Forms of the Divine

The term goddess generally refers to one of the females among the twelve divinities of the Olympian pantheon.[52] Despite certain ambiguities or overlappings of identity within this pantheon, these goddesses, like their male counterparts, are individuals.[53] Of course it makes little sense to speak of divine "personalities," because, as Jean-Pierre Vernant notes, "the Hellenic gods are powers, not persons," from which it follows that "a divine power exists only through its relation to the divine system as a whole."[54] It is clear, however, that there are goddesses and there are divinities, or, rather, there are individual goddesses and there is the divine in the feminine, of which number and name are the principal characteristics.

The Plural Feminine

We find in Greek literature not only individualized personalities but also collective identities. In the *Theogony,* for example, the "traditional divinities of the third generation" are followed by "civic choruses" of Horae and Charites.[55] Other examples include the Moirae, Keres, Nereides, and Oceanides. And do not forget the redoubtable Erinyes, or the unique Erinye who is at once one and three. But even when they are three, as in the choir in Aeschylus' *Eumenides,* they still have but one name for all: Erinye(s).[56] In considering these "multiple" divinities, one scholar has spoken of "the Greeks' taste for plural personages"[57] and suggested that they are "the *illustration* in the divine sphere of the problems involved in gaining mastery over numbers."[58] Another has proposed the bold hypothesis that "the Greeks, before learning from Pythagoras how to count groups represented by points, knew how to count groups representable as divinities."[59] No one, however, has paid sufficient attention to the obvious: these collective personages are frequently feminine, as if it were somehow no accident that the feminine and the plural should coincide.[60]

Naturally I would like to say more about this plural feminine, if only to account for these groups of divinities whose identity emerges only in the guise of multiplicity. I would then need to explore further the deeper link between the fondness for number and the common tendency to generalize—or at any rate to *de-individualize*—when talking about the divine in the feminine: one speaks of "goddesses" or even of the race of "goddesses," just as people refer to the "race," or better still, the "tribe" of women.[61] This would lead to a consideration of why female choruses tend to take the form of triads; this may well be the primary formulation of the plural, if plurality (as opposed to duality and singularity) is indeed the meaning of the number three.[62] But lacking specifically Greek conceptual tools, I shall say nothing more for the time being, except to suggest that the issue is crucial.[63] The important point to remember is that, because of this sharp contrast between strong Olympian personalities and relatively ephemeral choruses, femininity in the gods is less homogeneous than it is generally assumed to be in mortal women.

Female divinities also resist individuation in other ways. Certain names, for example, suggest a rather uncertain identity. An epiclesis, or qualifying epithet, may refer to a specific goddess, but it may also refer to a specific function shared by several different goddesses. Thus *Eileithyia* (she who has arrived) denotes the divinity whose arrival during labor brings about the birth of the child. But *Eileithyia* is a goddess about whom Pindar waxes enthusiastic in the Seventh Nemean Ode: "Eileithyia, seated beside the grave, wise Muses, child of almighty Hera, bringer of children to birth, Listen: without you we look not on daylight nor on black evening." Associated with the chorus of Moirae, daughters of Hera, the goddess belongs to a strictly feminine universe. Is it because of this that she is an unstable figure, plural as well as singular, whose being can equally well be summed up in a simple epiclesis? Thus Artemis, quite naturally, and Hera, when, as in Argos, she presides over childbirth, are both characterized as *Eileithyia*. Other epicleses are similarly shared, such as *Soteira*, the savior, who, though never embodied in any divine figure, wanders from city to city, attaching herself to Persephone or Artemis in Arcadia and to Athena in Piraeus or Delos.

We come next to such "divinized abstractions" as Renown. Hesiod says that "she too is a goddess," and Pindar calls her *Aggelia*, the Messenger.[64] In Pindar's poetry and on late-fifth-century vases by the painter Midias we find many such discreet goddesses, whose nature is generally summed up by a name denoting some human virtue. In Pindar, for example, we find *Eunomia* (good government), *Dike* (justice), her daughter *Hesukhia* (tranquillity), *Eirene* (peace), and *Nike* (victory) set against *Hubris* (harmful excess). Like *Aidos* and *Nemesis* (chastity and retributive justice) in Hesiod, or the host of Maladies to whom Zeus denies the power of speech,[65] they haunt the world of mortals, who at best endow the benevolent ones with generic "beautiful bodies" that remain unseen while avoiding any hint of biographical detail. Yet all these categories of the feminine divine communicate with one another. In this respect these various abstractions, naming qualities prevalent among humans, have more than one point in common with a goddess who, though an Olympian, is "scarcely developed as a person."[66] I refer to Hestia, "an almost geometrical figure," who, historians of religion generally agree, stands "aloof from the intrigues of mythology."[67]

Is it correct to say that "from the standpoint of the powers, the opposition between singular and universal, concrete and abstract, is irrelevant"?[68] I would modify this assertion by adding that it pertains primarily to the "female" powers.

Were it not necessary, finally, to end this digression between the concrete and the abstract, the singular and the plural, I would dwell at some length on another familiar but ill-defined group, the nymphs, or *Numphai*, that dwell in trees[69] and watch over the childhood of mortals.[70] Benevolent as goddesses, they eat ambrosia like the gods, but their lives, though long, are destined one day to end, and in this respect they resemble humans. They are not goddesses,[71] nor are they truly humanized; like mortals they can suffer from familiarity with the gods. I am thinking of the cry of pain uttered by the nymph Khariklo when Athena blinds her son.[72] Yet at the dangerous noon hour nymphs are known to take possession of mortals who go astray in the woods. According to the *Homeric Hymn to Aphrodite*, nymphs are neither mortals nor immortals; they are to be classed with other indeterminate beings such as the Gorgons (two of which are immortal and another, the one that kills Perseus, mortal), female monsters such as Ekhidna whose lair is "far from gods and men," and the Erinyes, about whose uncertain nature Athena and the Pythia agree in Aeschylus' *Eumenides*.[73]

Ge: Limitless or Circumscribed?

The time has now come to speak of the Great Indeterminate: *Ge*, or *Gaia pelore* (the monstrous Earth), in all her immensity.[74] *Io, gaia maia:* Ah! Earth, good mother![75] With this exclamation a tragic chorus regains its voice. We note the word *maia*: little mother, good mother, sometimes grandmother, or, when the word refers to a function in the world of men, midwife.

Ge is all that and much more. Yet this does not mean that, when her name occurs in a speech in a formulaic expression *(o ge kai theoi)* that links her to but at the same time distinguishes her from the gods of the earth, she is meant to rule over all the rest.[76] As for her relation with human beings, what are we to make of the adage that in reproduction "woman imitates the earth"? Plato is the author of this formula, which quickly became a topos that has since been repeated ad nauseam.[77] But the phrase really should be read in context before being interpreted, because it occurs in a pastiche of a funeral oration.[78] In the presence of Mother Earth, however, many scholars have a tendency to lose their bearings and throw caution to the winds in their haste to go straight to the essential—to the Feminine with a capital F. Historians of religion turn into worshipers of Ge.

The "Great Goddess" is presented as the "Earth Mother personified." Earth Mothers proliferate, with examples said to be "ubiquitous" from Anatolia to Greece and from Greece to Japan, to say nothing of darkest Africa.[79] Of course it is sometimes admitted that Ge "symbolizes" the feminine or is "a metaphor for the human mother." But at the first opportunity the mimesis theory is reinstated: the human female, reduced to little more than a womb, is said to be the "mortal image of the earth mother."[80]

Having gone this far, why not identify Demeter (decomposed into De-meter, with the syllable *De-* said to be a doublet of *Ge*) with Mother Earth? Despite the passage in Euripides in which Ge is associated with but also differentiated from Demeter,[81] and despite the fact that in the *Homeric Hymn to Demeter* Ge offers help to the abductor of a woman in tears,[82] it has also been suggested that the Earth is Persephone's mother. Dissenting voices have nevertheless been raised, sometimes from unexpected quarters: the Jungian Kerényi for one.[83] When attention is focused on differences rather than similarities, it becomes apparent that in the Greece of the city-states—as opposed to prehistoric Hellas with its profusion of Earth Mothers—the cult of Ge was as political as it was "agrarian,"[84] and that in Athens' autochthonous myth Ge is not only mother (and nurse) but also *patris,* the land of the *fathers,* and as such clearly defined by Attica's borders.[85]

Interpretation is then a matter of choice. One can opt for an interpretation in terms of "survivals," but one must then be prepared to allow for possible "resemanticizations." Or one can choose to emphasize the structural unity of a system analyzed in depth at a given point in time, but then one must confront the question of "mother goddesses," which has been generally neglected by anthropologists studying classical Greece, despite the fact that for some historians of religion it is the key to everything.

The Goddess: A Question of Maternity

Meter

The Mother did exist, and the Greeks did worship her. Belated evidence of this is provided by the antiquarian Pausanias in the second century A.D., a late date to be sure but still of greater relevance than Neolithic survivals.

The "Mother" was spelled with a capital letter or, as in Sparta and Lykosoura, coupled with the adjective "Great." Sometimes, as at Corinth or Delphi, she was called simply *Meter.* Other times she was characterized as *Dindumene* in reference to her Asiatic origins. This was the case in Thebes, where Pindar himself allegedly honored the goddess with a cult and statue.[86] More commonly she was honored, as in Athens, Corinth, and throughout the Peloponnesus (in Laconia and Messenia, at Olympia and Megalopolis, and in Arcadia) as the Mother of the gods.[87] In Dodona she was identified with the earth,[88] but even earlier, in the fifth century B.C., the Athenian Solon celebrated "the Great Mother of the gods, Earth the Black."[89] Pindar venerated her as "Great Mother, venerable Goddess," "venerable Mother," and "Cybele, Mother of the gods." Thus we see that the Mother was already clearly Asiatic in the classical period. Was she always so? And if so, what are we to make of the "divine Mother" mentioned in the Pylos tablets and therefore of Mycenian origin?[90] Let us hope that the Greeks had a clearer notion of all this than we do.

The fact that we are faced with many variations of a single name does not guarantee that we are dealing with a single goddess, but neither is there any evidence to the contrary. In short, nothing is certain.[91] But there our difficulties only begin, for among historians of Greek religion it is common to multiply the names of the Mother without making it clear whether all these names refer to exactly the same thing or indicate various ways of being a great maternal goddess. Modern scholars have only confused an issue about which the Greeks themselves were already in something of a muddle.

Great Is the Mother and Vast Is Her Domain

We have the Mother and Mothers, the Great Goddess and the Great Mother Goddess, to say nothing of the Goddess. How are we to find our way through this forest of names? I am not sure that I know the answer, and for now I wish to propose a simpler task, namely, to note some of the points repeatedly raised by the Mother's champions:

The Mother points the way back to our origins. In order to find her in her full glory, we must go back as far as the Neolithic or even Paleolithic era.[92] But to do this, scholars must give voice to mute "female idols."

The Mother reigns over territory that extends well beyond the borders of Greece, a territory without frontiers, so that the search for the Goddess has no limits.[93] It allegedly follows from this that her reign is universal: such is the standard of proof in a field where argument proceeds more often by association than by the rules of logic.

The womb stands as a metonymy for the Mother, a part fully expressive of the whole.[94] By extending the limits of time and space as broadly as possible, the Goddess is all the more effectively confined within her *metra*, the locus of motherhood in the female body. The logic appears inescapable. The Goddess' fervent devotees believe that her offspring have no need of a jealous Uranos but remain forever trapped in the depths of their mother's body.[95] Hence she is all. Her womb is a great receptacle that contains everything that exists.[96] So much for logic, because in this system of Russian dolls the innermost doll is as large as the outermost. (I had already hit upon this metaphor before learning that in Russian such dolls are referred to as *matriochka*.)

The Mother's strength comes from this faculty of her body to expand without limit. For Bachofen her reign was characterized by the "law of the corporeal-material." Believing that "matriarchal culture"[97] was unified by "the homogeneity of a dominant idea . . . all of whose manifestations come from the same mold,"[98] he sought to expound the notion of a culture of the sensible.

Assume for the sake of argument that the Great Mother was a reality. Does it follow that she was a material reality? Not at all. If maternity was singularly dramatized in those goddesses who were characterized as mothers, Jung and his followers argue that this was above all because the Great Mother was a *cosa mentale*, or, in Bachofen's terminology, a "dominant idea." According to Pierre Lévêque, moreover, the unity of the indivisible mother figure is never more clearly demonstrated than when she exhibits her two antagonistic faces: benevolent and terrifying.[99] For Lévêque, the terrifying Mother is a "concept."[100]

The Mother is thus everything (the All). For other scholars, she is the controlling Idea. She is therefore proof of the origin of the world, because she *is* the origin. It was as such, we are told, that the Greeks saw her, as the source of two carefully delineated families, one of gods, the other of men. And some modern historians of Greek religion agree, or at any rate they seem to take comfort in placing the indeterminacy of religion's beginnings under the protection of the great and limitless Goddess, the one and the many, whose traces are to be found not only in Greece but the world over.

Those scholars who look back to the beginning of time do not confine their remarks to prehistory, however. They shape their view of later ages to fit their view of the unrecorded past. The goddesses of Olympus thus do not emerge unscathed from the quest for *the* Goddess. Sometimes they are interpreted as mere clues for the understanding of the Mother. Other times they are read as "survivals" whose testimony can rescue what preceded them from oblivion. Thus Hera, ever so little maternal, is seen by some as Mother. But the urge to interpret has fastened above all on the virgin goddesses, the purpose being to extract from them a confession that they were not always *Parthenoi*. Take Artemis the huntress. Cast her as the heiress of an archaic Mistress of Wild Animals, and the Anatolian Great Goddess begins to loom in the background. Or take Athena, so firm in her refusal to marry. The chorus in one tragedy refers to her as *"mother,* mistress, and guardian" *(mater, despoina, phulax)* of the Attic soil, and for one scholar that is enough to restore her triumphally to her "primitive state."[101] Additional evidence for this view is said to lie in the fact that in Elis she bore the official epiclesis *Meter* because she brought fertility to married couples in times of population shortage.[102]

These arguments were not airtight, and objections were soon raised by other scholars among the Mother's admirers. Kerényi, for instance, insists that the qualification *Meter* cannot contradict Athena's "nature."[103] Hubert Petersmann can do research on pre-Hellenic Mother Goddesses and yet acknowledge that few goddesses in classical Greece bore the title *Meter* and that the mere attestation of an epiclesis, always connected with a specific cult, in no way implies the existence of a "cult of the Mother."[104] Eventually someone will conclude that, in Greece at any rate, there was no specific mythology of the *Meter*.[105] What, then, are these devotees of the Mother looking for? The Eternal Feminine, perhaps.

Variations on the Eternal Feminine

The Great Mother, prized though she is by students of ancient Greek religion, is actually an archetype, and Jung is her prophet—or so Erich Neumann argues in his monograph on the Mother.[106] An archetype is an internalized image, which is perpetuated in the *psukhe* as a focal point and unifying principle of psychic organization. It is immutable, or, as one writer puts it, "the name of that which reigns beyond all names."[107] Thus it hardly matters that the word "Mother" does not necessarily refer to actual motherhood or that the word "Great" means only "superiority of the symbol over all reality."[108] If we were to accept these assumptions, everything would be simple—alarmingly so. Yet still further simplifications are required. Thus Neumann contends that Bachofen's book is not really about the "law" of the mother; so much for the work's title and content. Rather, he says, Bachofen is concerned with the female "nature."[109]

There is no point multiplying examples of this sort, but one other statement of Neumann's deserves attention. The Egyptians, he says, referred to one of their goddesses as "The Great Goddess." This generic description allegedly is meant to symbolize the *impersonal anonymity* of the archetype in the same way as Goethe's use of the plural "mothers" in part two of *Faust*.[110] In other words, the feminine singular is generic, while the feminine plural is collective. The parallel with my earlier remarks is clear. Indeed, whether singular or plural, generic or collective, the archetype of the feminine—or, rather, the feminine, in essence archetypal—can be apprehended only in an impersonal or even "transpersonal" mode.[111] Perhaps this is so. But Bachofen long ago spoke, in more evocative language, of the "character of archaic sublimity" oblivious to "individual coloration" that he saw as intrinsic to cultures of the Mother.[112]

Is the Mother therefore a symbol of female impersonality? So we are told. Some writers add that because this impersonality touches on something primordial, it tends to promote unity. One speaks of the "myth of femininity in action as the mystery that brings about reconciliation in the world."[113] Yet none of these authors notices that what is all too apt to disappear in such neuter discourse is precisely the feminine, to say nothing of women, who have already been forgotten.

Nothing supposedly is more edifying than the Mother (or Mothers), however terrifying she (or they) may be. Thus she is cast as a figure of reconciliation, which some people find reassuring. But one may also feel, as I do, that such a view of both the category of the feminine and the structure of the psyche give short shrift to the conflict and unpleasantness that are also an essential part of life.

Mother and Daughter

When it comes to the Mother and her Daughter, that is, to Demeter and Kore, the edifying gives way to the sentimental. Prose turns lyrical to celebrate, with a profusion of capital letters, the "archetypal poles of the Eternal Feminine"—in other words, archetypes of an archetype—"the mature woman and the virgin," who together embody "the mystery of the feminine . . . capable of nev-erending renewal."[114]

Here is a good opportunity to test the validity of the impersonal generalities of archetypal thinking. In cults of the two goddesses in which Two is a variant of One, the archetype comes close to the mark. As was pointed out earlier, Demeter and Kore are the most apt of all the goddesses to symbolize the ages of woman. But there is also the myth, as well as the dynamic structure of the Olympian pantheon in which Demeter and Kore both have specific roles. And there is the whole structure of Greek religion: Demeter and Kore can hardly be said to provide a common denominator for the variety of Greek goddesses.

With the Daughter added to the picture the Mother is not alone, but it would be misleading to think she had found her opposite; for that she would probably need a son.[115] If the plural *Demeteres* (Demeters), which is attested in cults found in many cities, did in fact refer to the couple Demeter-Kore, there is reason to think that Demeter's powerful presence simply overwhelmed her daughter. (The opposite occurs in Arcadia, where the appellation *Despoinai* argues for a splitting of the daughter figure, there called *Despoina,* or Mistress.) The use, common in Athens, of the dual form *to theo* (the two divinities)[116] may correct this impression with its suggestion of a perfect equilibrium, a unified pair—One in Two, as some would have it.[117] In Eleusinian myth, however, Demeter and Kore also have a history in which their respective positions are neither interchangeable nor simply symbolic (the Maiden Persephone is a highly deviant paradigm of the maiden[118]). The distinction between myth and cult must be respected. Mother and daughter belong to the pantheon of twelve gods as two associated yet distinct and dissimilar divine persons. They participate in the community of gods in the form of a triad that includes a Zeus from a lower world that looks a lot like Hades. Between their common cult, in which the difference between them is effaced, and their participation in the pantheon the temporality of a narrative has intervened, along with the possibility of forming other associations.

Generalizing on the cultic form of the couple, it is sometimes asserted that *all* Greek mother goddesses are pairs consisting of fertile mothers and virginal daughters, the latter invariably described as drawn toward virile youths.[119] In light of the foregoing remarks, however, it would be better to refrain from such generalizations. It is quite plausible to argue instead that the close association of Demeter and Kore is a phenomenon peculiar to Greek religion. Hence there is no point looking for parallels in other places or in the obscure profusion of prehistory.[120] I am aware, however, that these historian's arguments are unlikely to be heard in a field where capital letters abound and the guiding impulse is to efface differences wherever they are found.

Series

Consider for a moment those cascades of equations (A = x = y = Mother) that allow champions of the Goddess to overlook the individuality of particular goddesses by reducing every goddess to some other goddess and that other goddess to the Mother, as if female divinities were interchangeable in some way that male divinities are not. Scholars thus speak of equivalences or avatars.[121] They claim that Artemis is the Great Goddess of Asia Minor, that the Gorgon is Artemis-Hecate, or that the wrathful Goddess is Demeter or Ishtar or Hathor or Hecate (thus proceeding full circle from Greece by way of Mesopotamia and an Egyptian hypostasis back to Greece again). Aphrodite is dissolved into Usa (the Indo-European Aurora), Kybele, and Ishtar, not to mention the "panoply of Aphroditoids," including Helen, Thetis, Penelope, Calypso, Circe, Ino, and Nausicaa, among others. As for Pandora, of whom Hesiod said that "she received a gift from all the gods," we are told that her name is a corruption of a very ancient word for a universal gift giver; thus Pandora too is linked to "Mother Earth, which she is as well."[122]

At this point I would like to recall Marie Delcourt's useful warning about the pitfalls of a practice that unfortunately she herself has not always avoided. Greek mythology, she reminds us, is "a language in which there are no synonyms."[123] Not that the Greeks themselves did not play this game: they were the first to propose the various interpretations disputed by modern scholars. Emperor Julian, for example, identified *Ge* or *Meter* with Rhea. Devotees of the Orphic cult transformed Demeter into the Earth Mother.[124] But such identifications were the work of later ages or mystical sects; Greek religion in its classical orthodox period generally avoided them. Raising the question of "series" touches once again on the many ways in which thinkers from Greek theologians to historians of religion have attempted to link the feminine with the plural.[125] But I must move on, and I will not consider this issue any further.

God the Mother?

The crucial question is whether the Great Mother actually reigned. The dream of those scholars who believe in her importance is to establish the Great Goddess as the supreme deity of what would have to have been a relatively informal pantheon, since her power was so great that it would have left little room for others. Thus a feminine deity would have reigned "in the place and stead of a god."[126] The She-God, we are told, preceded the He-God, or, as Marie Moscovici puts it, "God the Mother" took precedence over God the Father.[127]

Historians object to this formulation. Walter Burkert, for example, notes that even "Minoan religion [though supposedly pre-Hellenic and therefore impervious to Indo-European adulation of the father] also embraced a polytheism and not a quasi-monotheism of the Great Goddess."[128] Nevertheless, the scholars who raise such objections are aware that belief in the Great Mother is so strong among her devotees as to resist all argument; every challenge only confirms them in their undiminished fervor. In this realm, Burkert says, everything is a matter of interpretation; to himself he no doubt says speculation.[129]

Let me be perfectly clear about my own position: the maternal Great Goddess is a *fantasy,* a powerful fantasy with an astonishing capacity to resist criticism. It unites militant proponents of matriarchy with worshipers of a prehistoric goddess with great powers of consolation. The common ground that certain feminists have managed to stake out on this issue with certain distinguished academics is to say the least surprising. Consider the latter, since it is their work that has occupied us here.

What does one gain by unifying prehistory under the authority of a single maternal figure? The answer is that one satisfies, perhaps unconsciously, a longing for an undifferentiated stage of existence. It may also be that one wants to clear the paternal culture's name, as Freud, who may have believed in the existence of a primitive matriarchy but who was always suspicious of the Great Goddess, suggested when he said that the triumphant patriarchy invented mother goddesses "by way of compensation."[130] I admire Freud's audacity in rejecting obscure notions and comforting generalizations and in characterizing the Great Mother as a by-product of other purposes. Such a notion is a far cry from Jung's archetypes and from Rank's postulate of a "primitive mother of whose existence all subsequent representations . . . are tantamount to a denial."[131] On the contrary, Freud suggests that granting supreme power to a primitive mother is a way of compensating mothers for the dismissal of many or all of their claims to power in the present. The past and the present are two different things, and the past is the foundation of the present.[132]

Devi

Let us now take a brief excursion outside Greece to Hindu India, where a goddess of uncontested power reigns, one who is called simply the Goddess: Devi. At once terrifying and benevolent, she is everywhere, so much so that in certain sects she is ranked above the male aspect of divinity. Some scholars argue that her origins predate Brahmanism and even the Veda. Are we at last dealing with an unambiguous instance of the Great Goddess?

Madeleine Biardeau has put an end to a great deal of speculation. Earlier goddesses may well have existed, she writes, but "it is certainly more fruitful to see how carefully the place of the Goddess is carved out within the Hindu system . . . The foreign origins [of this element of the system] tell us nothing about what [its] nature might have been outside the structure from which [it] currently derives its meaning."[133] The Goddess is referred to as "Mother of the world," but she has no children. Furthermore, in Hindu thinking a mortal woman is first a wife and second a mother, "an indication that the ubiquitous mother-goddess concept is not as important in India as modern scholarship has tended to make it."[134] As an avatar of the great god Siva, in fact, the Goddess is bisexual. In some versions she is virginal only when she retires to her temple. If, moreover, she is a warrior given to the "sacrifice of battle," it is because she is an emanation of the male and therefore endowed with his qualities. Ready to bear any defilement, including that of spilling blood, she relieves the god of the inevitable risk to his purity involved in the fight against demons.[135]

Bearing this in mind, let us turn our attention back to the Greeks. Once again we see that if a pantheon is viewed as a structured system, there are no grounds for believing that a prehistoric Great Goddess somehow survives as a preeminent if occult presence. But we also see that the impetus to believe in the Mother is impervious to criticism: the Great Mother, whether she belongs to the Paleolithic era or to the culture of a remote land, is a constant figure in this kind of speculation. The Great Goddess is the name that has been given to a widely shared fantasy. Her reality is that which a fantasy takes on when reality testing cannot make it disappear.

The Feminine in the History of the Gods

Although there is nothing specifically Greek about goddesses, let me conclude by speaking Greek. Not that the Greeks necessarily have the last word on the subject. If we were to make that our methodological principle, how would we ever know what it never occurred to the Greeks to say? As it happens, however, the Greeks had a great deal to say about goddesses in the "histories" of the gods that were repeated, in much the same terms, in city after city.[136] The time has come to let the Greeks speak for themselves, or at any rate to take a look at Hesiod, whose work served as something like the theology of ancient Greece. As a guide to reading Hesiod I shall rely on Clémence Ramnoux's faithful yet independent interpretation of the Theogony.[137]

The Splitting of the Mother

The beginning of the story is not what we might expect, for at the outset there were *two* mothers. There is of course Gaia, the Earth, but there is also the redoubtable Night, who, in the *Iliad,* gives pause even to Zeus, who, wrathful though he is, is reluctant to displease her.[138] Night, in the theologian's conception, is thus an honored mother.[139] This splitting of the mother figure is not to everyone's liking, however, and various attempts have been made to diminish the role of Night. Since we have Hesiod's text, it is worth examining more closely.

Gaia preceded Night. Earth has existed from the very beginning, since right after Abyss—the very beginning, the crack or slit, the word for which, it should be noted, is neuter. Earth gave birth to Sky (Ouranos), less as a son (though he is one) than as a "her equal"; Abyss gave birth to Night. But it is almost as if the only point of this first period, barely a generation, was to end Earth's solitude. The rest of the story is played out between Earth and Night. No sooner does Earth give birth to a son capable of blanketing her in her entirety than she couples with him in love. From this union come dreadful offspring, who, having provoked their father's hatred, are driven by him into the depths of their mother, who, choking and moaning, set Kronos, her youngest, to wait in ambush, armed with a scythe. Ouranos is castrated. The second generation can be born at last.

Meanwhile, Night, born of the primordial cleft and aware of nothing but division, gave birth—without love, by fission only[140]— to progeny encompassing everything negative in the Greek imagination. Rhea, daughter of Earth and mother of the Olympians, corresponds precisely to Discord (Eris), daughter of Night and mother of many children, including Disaster (Ate) and that "scourge of mortals," Oath. The symmetry, to judge by the two sets of offspring, was purely formal: on one side, gods—*the* gods; on the other, groups of women (the Hesperides, Fates, Keres) and "abstractions" (as they are called, but since they constitute the actual experience of mortals, these abstractions might equally well be called presences). It may be that whatever asymmetry there is has to do with the clear opposition between the two modes of procreation: one by union, the other by fission; one that the gods share with men, the other exclusively divine (or at any rate inconceivable in the human world, even if Aristotle at times believes he has discovered it in the animal kingdom).[141] This nocturnal parthenogenesis is wholly divine and therefore miraculous (or monstrous): Night conceives and gives birth alone, out of contact with any masculine principle, whereas Earth, before rebelling against Heaven's insatiable lust, couples with him countless times. Clémence Ramnoux has frequently, and rightly, called attention to the importance of procreation by fission, a phenomenon which, we now can see, the Greeks traced back to the beginning of time. This *adynaton* in fact gives rise to the idea of a divine femininity closed upon itself and separate from the outset—a threatening idea if ever there was one.

The children of Night, in contrast to the gods, who seem to exist only for themselves, were brought into the world expressly to visit pain on the city of men. Can the perpetual threat of the "race of women" to subsist in self-enclosed isolation be an imitation of Night? At once a different kind of imitation emerges. Contrary to the usual topos, it goes not from woman to earth, but from *women,* the shunned race, to Night, the primal paradigm. This hypothesis was never formulated in Greek, as far as I know, but it is worth considering.

Hera Again

Consider once again the gods. Eros has presided over the divine births, so everything is in order, except that Night's child Oblivion (Lethe, hence a daughter) seems to be at work trying to undo the temporality of the divine generations. There are three generations of females—Gaia, Rhea, and Hera—or four, if we say that Earth is the mother of both Sky and the children of Sky. And there are three generations of males: Ouranos, Kronos, and Zeus. "Through the women" the Olympians belong to the fourth generation.[142] Now, "it is a law that the earlier the generation to which a god belongs, the more remote that god is" from human memory.[143] Aeschylus, for example, observes that a day will come when Ouranos' very existence will have been forgotten, since Kronos himself "has gone away."[144] But Zeus halts this process to his own advantage by cleverly preventing a more powerful successor from coming into the world.[145]

A father unwilling to be reduced to a mere patronymic, Zeus puts an end to any significant reproduction within the Olympian family. One could say a great deal about this action, beginning with Zeus's way of "gathering virgin daughters around his paternity."[146] But what interests me is what happens to the mothers. Things are not simple.

The mothers of the first two generations, Gaia and Rhea, are all-powerful. They protect their last-born sons against their fathers' judgment. With Hera, however, this power comes to an end. The archaic mothers, moreover, give their support to Zeus, who openly proclaims himself "Father of gods and men" because he is the successor of two generations of fallen fathers. In the *Theogony,* for example, the gods recognize Zeus as their king on the sage advice of old Gaia after the defeat of her sons the Titans.[147] Gaia profits from this result in that she is henceforth celebrated along with the gods, from whom she is set apart although not as the prophets of the Great Mother proclaim in a position of preeminence. In the *Choephore,* for example, Electra invokes "the gods, Earth, and victory-bearing Justice."[148] Here the various generations of divinities are confounded. Earth, the eldest ancestor, is named second, after the gods but before Justice, who is one of the Horae, or daughters of Zeus and Themis. Gaia's complicitous good will may be an effect of narrative, a narrative that accords omnipotence to women initially the better to deprive them of power later. Note that their consent is said to have been given immediately after the accession of Zeus. Gaia and to a lesser extent Rhea also gain from their consent in that, unlike the prehistoric fathers, they are not plunged into oblivion. Earth continues to be an object of prayer, but who would pray to Ouranos?

Only Hera protests, and for good reason. She knows that Zeus has put an end to the complicity between mothers and their younger sons and that no son of hers has been born more royal than his father, no son to whom she might lend a helping hand.[149] She is her husband's equal, but the ancient preeminence of the goddesses is finished. She therefore seeks vengeance, and with the shrewish, quarrelsome character that has so frequently been attributed to her since the time of Homer. But to blame Hera's bitterness on her character is a psychological and therefore superficial interpretation. The goddess' true vengeance is to give birth alone, without love and without a partner. She does so more than once: Hephaestus, Hebe (Youth), and even Ares (though in the *Iliad* he is portrayed as an ill-loved but nevertheless legitimate son of Zeus) are the fruit of parthogenetic pregnancies.

Can one say, however, that "she wants to prove that she can be both mother and father" or that "she incorporates the father"?[150] "Incorporation" is a term more properly applied to Zeus, who "really" swallows Metis so that he may remain Athena's sole progenitor. Detienne's later formulation is more satisfactory: that Hera's desire to produce children on her own "harks back to the deeds of the most autonomous powers," not only Night but also Earth. And Ramnoux remarks that the birth of Hephaestus is like "a return to the archaic world and the birth of Ouranos by scissiparity."[151]

Champions of the Great Goddess view Hera's gesture toward all-powerful maternity as evidence that they are right to regard her as a mother goddess and that their interpretation accords with authentic Greek tradition as recorded in the *Theogony*. But for a Greek such as Hesiod, living in historical times, the only real time was the eternal present, the static time of the reign of Zeus. To be sure, the history of the gods is not uniformly linear; there are trials and errors, advances and retreats. Hera's childbearing, prodigious as it may be, repeats the past but repeats it imperfectly. Because she does not produce a Son who is beyond challenge, her efforts may be seen as a series of failures. Ramnoux observes: "The specter of the solitary mother truly haunted Greece, no less than the specter of the mother without love. At the very beginning she was tolerated, because it was necessary for a woman to give birth to the first male in order to form with him the first amorous couple. But all of her subsequent fruit was bad."[152] Burdened by reminiscences of her powerful archaic forebears, Hera "the awkward" must adjust, like it or not, to her position as wife of Zeus. Her "prestige"[153] stems neither from her talents as a mother goddess nor even from the terror she inspires in Zeus. She always gives in to him, and when she wishes to deceive him, she has no choice but to arouse his desire *(eros),* of which Aphrodite is the sole mistress. Seducing her husband is the only way to circumvent the vigilance of the Father.

Then and Now

Myths tell us that once upon a time there were goddesses. Proponents of the Great Mother should not be too quick to read this as evidence for something that actually existed in prehistoric times; it may be simply a necessary component of a narrative. Now follows then, and historians of religion who prefer the father are perfectly comfortable with the "history" recounted in the *Theogony* (and portrayed in the *Oresteia*).

If space had allowed, I would have liked to set forth their reasoning. Instead I shall content myself with a few excerpts from the work of Walter Otto, who in 1929 published a book on the gods of Greece, or, more precisely, "the figure of the divine in the mirror of the Greek spirit." There he states that while "the feminine essence predominates in prehistoric religion," the reign of the ancient gods was characterized in other ways by an "excess of the feminine."[154] We must await the "explosion of the divine," which proves liberating when, like Athena and like Apollo in the *Oresteia,* it takes the part of the father.[155] Consider Athena. As the Father's daughter, she is tailor-made to please scholars like Otto. "She is a woman," he says, "and it is as if she were a man." A divine surprise if ever there was one. As "symbol of the ideal of ennobled masculinity," it is in Athena that "the masculine sense of harsh combat and joy in action appears divinized."[156]

These passages are enough to convey the overall tone of Otto's work. The exchanges between the adepts of the Mother and the adepts of the Father are, I hope I have shown, "half speeches," to borrow a phrase from Athena's description of the Erinyes' plea in Aeschylus.[157] Each camp presents one side of the argument, severed halves of a coherent case. Consider Poseidon. Plutarch observes that Poseidon lost out in every city where he was in competition with another deity for the prestigious title of god of the polis. For scholars on both sides of the argument the explanation is the same: "His name indicates that he is the husband of the Great Goddess."[158] Having said that, one side goes on to argue that it was therefore only natural for "mothers" (such as Athena or Hera) to win out over him, while the other side holds that there is nothing surprising about this since even in his time of glory Poseidon was "subordinated to the feminine" and that it was therefore inevitable that he should be vanquished by the Father's wife or daughter.

Thus we are faced with two symmetrical discourses, both committed and therefore impassioned. Fortunately, structuralism ultimately came along, not so much to show how the two sides complemented each other (Aeschylus' Athena had already done that) as to shift the focus of the analysis from the quest for origins (which is a perennial source of conflict because what is forever lost can never be regained) to the way in which structures of thought determine the possible configurations of a theological system. A new question then arises: If gender difference is one important element of such a system, what is a goddess? I am not sure that I have given any clear or consistent answer, but I have tried to indicate various ways in which Greek and modern thinkers have gone about trying to formulate one.

We have seen that there are points of contact between ancient and modern approaches. For the Greeks, divinity when it was feminine tended also to be plural, and the same is true of the moderns. Greek speculations about the Great Mother were revived with unparalleled vigor in nineteenth- and twentieth-century theories. The Greeks had all the answers. They were the first to note the implicit or explicit distinction between *theos* and *thea*, between "god" in the broadest sense of the term and "goddess" in a gendered sense. The challenge for modern theorists is to understand the subtleties of the issue: a goddess is not the incarnation of the feminine, yet she often represents a purified, and even more often a displaced, form of femininity.

The Greeks were quick to construct their gods in the genealogical mode; therefore it was necessary to pinpoint what they had to say about female contributions to the engenderment of the divine. I am still not sure, however, that the notion of a "history of women" is pertinent here, and I do not believe that such a history is possible in all periods. There can be no doubt, however, that in the Greek construction of the divine, the history of the gods was set in motion by goddesses and brought to a halt by a god.

Perhaps this circumstance explains why those who would write of goddesses quickly succumb to the lure of prehistory, while those who would write about the Olympian religion after it was constituted in the form of a pantheon are concerned primarily with structure. Are there perhaps two ways of approaching sexual difference: one defined, however theoretically (and perhaps spontaneously), by origins, the other by structures? I have proceeded as if this hypothesis were true, convinced that it makes a difference whether one begins by looking at *theos* and the "totality" of *theoi* or by asking, in order to define *thea,* what the word "goddess" might mean within a polytheistic system.

Constructing Gender

Nicole Loraux's discussion of how the Greeks created and imagined their goddesses raises a basic question that runs throughout the remainder of this volume: Did ancient thinking about gender difference simply reflect male dominance, or was it also an attempt by males to lay claim to a small part of what females possessed? To examine this question, authors situate discourse about the feminine in relation to other areas of knowledge in the ancient world: to study normative propositions about women in the works of philosophers and in ancient law, for example, and to examine the way in which women became the objects of supposedly realistic and positive disciplines such as medicine from Hippocrates to Galen.

In this volume we are concerned only with one aspect of a complex process: the concept of woman as constructed by Plato and Aristotle and as embodied in Roman law.[1] Giulia Sissa analyzes the way Plato and Aristotle construct the category of gender. She enables us to grasp the characteristic way in which philosophy sought to relate sexual difference to other kinds of difference. This shows how philosophers tended to minimize the opposition between the sexes—not in order to bestow equality on women but to call attention to their incapacities. Also implicit in this chapter is another possible approach to the question of women and philosophy: to treat women not as objects but as subjects of knowledge, to focus on the connection between women and cognition, between the feminine and language.

P.S.P

2

The Sexual Philosophies
of Plato and Aristotle

Giulia Sissa

IN HER DUAL RELATION to knowledge the
Greek woman is a curious figure. She is a fascinating object of thought and a very discreet but
theoretically exemplary subject. As an object,
woman appears first as that living thing whose
advent in the world the mythographer must imagine. Later she becomes a body for physicians to
explore in detail and a social figure whose place
in society philosophers must reason about. As a
subject, she appears only sporadically and on the
margins of philosophical, medical, and literary activity; the thinking woman is the exception who
confirms the rule of exclusive male dominance in
the intellectual arena. Yet as a subject of knowledge her role is exemplary whenever knowledge is
conceived in terms of receptiveness and groping
rather than as triumphant acquisition of an established competence. When Philo of Alexandria distinguishes between the intellect, which he calls
masculine, and sensation, which he calls feminine,
he sums up an important aspect of the Greek concept of sexual difference, an aspect that can also
be seen in Plutarch's ideas about oracular truth
and Plato's notion of the maieutic.[1] Unable to acquire a real education, women were thought of as
embodying an almost resistanceless availability or

permeability with respect to truth, a permeability compatible with their sexual vocation, which was to receive, to take into themselves.[2]

Few activities requiring skill and competence were attributed to women: as in most traditional societies these included weaving, management of the household, and child care. It took Plato to express astonishment and outrage at what he considered a paradoxical state of affairs, that the education of future citizens should be entrusted to women who were themselves so poorly educated.[3]

If, however, Metis, Eumetis, and the notion that the philosopher's soul must be impregnated in order to give birth to philosophical thought tell us something about how the Greeks conceived of knowledge, then imaginatively and metaphorically receptive intelligence and intellectual sensibility were feminine. The analogies linking conception in the intellectual sense, enunciation, and childbearing come primarily from Plato. In the *Symposium* the theory of love to which Socrates gives his assent is one formulated by a woman, a priestess, Diotima. According to this theory, the question of love is displaced from the immediate level of erotic desire and pleasure to the "higher" level of desire for knowledge. The link between the two levels is beauty, a quality that belongs to the body as well as the soul. The most common and spontaneous experience of love stems in fact from aesthetic attraction, from the effects produced by a beautiful body.

The sight of beauty, here envisioned as an individualizing attribute of a body, awakens the soul. The desire thus aroused only begins to manifest itself in this form, however. Rather than remain attached to the body, or to a large number of individual and concrete bodies, it may rise to a higher level and attach itself to an object that reduces multiplicity to a higher-order synthesis: beauty in itself. Turning aside from a virtually infinite collection of bodies, the amorous gaze may succeed in fixing on the very idea of beauty, an idea of which individual beautiful objects merely partake. From there it may rise still higher, to an even more perfect idea: that of beauty abstracted not merely from the multiplicity of its incarnations but also purged of all physical connotations. Once capable of appreciating the beauty of souls, desire finds its ideal object: beauty in and for itself, independent not just of sensible aesthetic figuration but even of spiritual realization in a particular person. This ultimate object of love is the original principle of the beautiful, that which is the cause of beauty in things or thoughts.

Although this love is as immaterial as it is intense, Plato continues to describe it in terms drawn from the language of eroticism and sexual procreation.

While heterosexual love allows the human race to reproduce itself physically, this other kind of love, which begins with love for handsome boys and ends with passion for the Beautiful and which requires an initiation, aims at a different sort of generation: of speeches, ideas, and above all proposals for achieving justice in the city. The subject who turns toward this kind of love aspires to immortality of an intellectual order. To that end he employs the fecundity not of his genitals but of his soul, or *psyche*. "Those whose procreancy is of the spirit rather than of the flesh—and they are not unknown, Socrates—conceive and bear the things of the spirit. And what are they? you ask. Wisdom and all her sister virtues . . . And if any man is so closely allied to the divine as to be teeming with these virtues even in his youth, and if, when he comes to manhood, his first ambition is to be begetting, he too, you may be sure, will go about in search of the loveliness—and never of the ugliness—on which he may beget . . . By constant association with so much beauty, and by thinking of his friend when he is present and when he is away, he will be delivered of the burden he has labored under all these years. And what is more, he and his friend will help each other rear the issue of their friendship."[4]

The soul gives birth to what it has conceived in eager dialogue with the object of its love, and it then cares for its fruit. The metaphor continues to speak of the most abstract degree of love, that of the Beautiful in itself. Beauty becomes an object of contemplation, with which the soul communes, and of this union is born the soul's fruit: not just thought but *truth* itself. The soul then continues to care for this fruit without interruption.[5]

Intellectual activity can thus be represented in all its aspects in terms of conception, birth, and nourishment. In homosexual love between males, the desiring subject identifies with a feminine notion. The displacement of the generative function from *soma* to *psyche* thus signals a feminization of the desire for knowledge and its consequences.

One could propose a purely linguistic explanation: the word *psyche* being feminine, other aspects of the metaphor follow. But to do so would be to overlook a pertinent, indeed crucial, feature of the underlying analogy. The comparison of childbirth with the enunciation of thought is dynamic. In both cases effort is needed to *bring out something that resists.* The important thing is not that reflection requires two partners, for Diotima clearly states that the philosophically inclined soul is pregnant from birth. Rather, it is that thinking and childbearing are both long and painful experiences that end in *delivery.*

"And so, when procreancy draws near the beautiful it grows genial and blithe, and birth follows swiftly on conception. But when it meets with ugliness it is overcome with heaviness and gloom, and turning away it shrinks into itself and is not brought to bed, but still labors under its painful burden."[6] As long as it does not encounter beauty, the procreant soul cannot bring anything forth, hence it must labor with the burden of a fruit that is already ripe. If beauty is absent, the soul clenches, curls up, turns in upon itself, thus precisely imitating the body of a woman if the divine powers that preside over childbirth do not unbind her womb. "And so," Socrates continues, "when the procreant is big with child, he is strangely stirred by the beautiful, because he knows that beauty's tenant will bring his travail to an end."[7]

Thinking becomes delivery in that rare, unpredictable moment when the soul, swollen and heavy with the fruit of thought and suffering in its travail, at last finds relief. The point bears emphasizing. Plato does not merely draw a parallel between delivery and thought. If he did, it would be possible to read him as primarily or exclusively concerned with effecting a displacement from the masculine to the feminine.[8] The point of the comparison is to bring out the idea of *adynaton,* impossibility, and *chalepos,* difficulty. The soul tries to hold on to what it has produced, to close itself off; in the absence of an outside agent, such as beauty, the obstinacy of desire, or a midwife, it clings to suffering. We see the same thing in the *Republic,* where the soul is engaged in a quest or struggle until at last it transcends appearances and attains the real.[9] Here unsatisfied love is the dynamic principle.

At a given moment thinking becomes childbirth: that moment arrives when resistance is finally overcome, when the tension between the infant *logos* and the soul, which, like the female body, resists delivery, at last comes to an end. We see this in the *Phaedrus,* where the metaphor of pregnancy is combined with that of wings of love, wings that grow despite the obstruction of the pores in which they originate.[10] We see it even more clearly in the *Theaetetus,* where Plato shows us a young mathematician whose psyche, having reached the term of its pregnancy, he assists in giving birth. The maieutic is like a purification that relieves the soul of the weight of false opinions, ignorance of its own ignorance, and ideas, doubts, and paradoxes picked up from various sources.

In the *Theaetetus* Socrates compares the articulation of thought to childbirth and questioning to the technique of a midwife; at the same time he calls attention to a radical difference between the maieutic of bodies and that of souls. The maieutic of the philosophers consists in the examination, judgment, and diagnosis of the product of delivery: the newborn *logos*. Thus the masculine form of childbirth is a delivery that liberates; it lightens the soul by freeing a thought that, though nothing but wind, still weighs heavily. Socrates goes to work on Theaetetus in order to relieve him of his burden and to judge it after delivery, having previously assured himself that his interlocutor is capable of withstanding, if necessary, separation from his offspring. For the young man giving birth means undertaking the difficult *(molis)* search for a proper expression of the idea that moves within him.[11] He knows, meanwhile, that the midwife who is assisting him is also mercilessly scrutinizing his *logoi* for whatever truth they may contain in order to judge whether or not they deserve to survive. This power of life and death over *logoi* has no parallel in the tasks of the midwife who assists in actual childbirth. Her role, fortunately, is precisely the opposite.[12]

In other words, the paradigm of childbirth in Plato is meant to bring the knowing subject into correspondence with his own soul, a soul that has no immediate or certain access to truth. The analogy enables the philosopher to dramatize what he considers the essence of intellectual experience: the difficult, contentious labor of unconscious discovery. Owing to ignorance, error, and of course ignorance of error, my soul may unbeknownst to me contain ideas, opinions, and words whose significance escapes me. The psyche is pregnant with all this—with the unspoken. To give birth is to speak, to discover that which is being thought within me. Why is this painful? Because it does not happen by itself or at my behest. It requires an external force, beauty, or the assistance of a midwife to compel or help the soul to deliver its contents. Those contents weigh heavily upon the soul, which must endure the burden; but unless the proper contacts are made, the soul tends to cling to its fruit. Delivery is paradoxical because it is urgent yet difficult; one feels an insistent need to speak, yet the words remain elusive.

For Plato feminizing the subject of knowledge is a way of indicating all that prevents the soul from appropriating truth, from penetrating directly to where it lies hidden. Later, Plutarch would base his theory of oracles on the idea that the soul of the Pythia transmits the divine wisdom of Apollo as the moon reflects the sun's rays, that is, with a diminution of their brilliance.

Woman as Object of Knowledge

Poets, philosophers, and physicians from Homer (sixth century B.C.) to Galen (first century A.D.) speak with remarkable consistency of women as object. Merely listing the obsessions of this learned discourse about women will not get us very far: women are passive, and even the best of them are inferior to men—the unquestioned standard of comparison—in anatomy, physiology, and psychology. Much has been written about Plato's supposed feminism in the *Republic,* but the case is undermined by the fact that, even if Plato conceived of a city in which women ought to be educated *like* men, and even if he would allow women to do whatever they wish, they would nevertheless perform the same tasks *less well* than men. The Hippocratic physicians, though prepared to concede that all individuals, male and female, produce identical, androgynous seeds, nevertheless maintained that the female portion of the seminal substance is intrinsically *less strong* than the male portion. Aristotle, for his part, held that women are systematically inferior to men in every respect—anatomically, physiologically, and ethically—and that this inferiority is a consequence of their metaphysical passivity. For us, this certainty, this unanimous belief in the inferiority and inadequacy of women, in their shortcomings, deformities, and incompleteness, makes the thinking of the Greeks distinctly unpalatable. Their bitter contempt and, even worse, condescension have encouraged rather unbecoming attitudes in some recent students of these ancient texts. How can one avoid feeling rage or bitterness, helplessness or superiority? How can one retain one's objectivity in the face of the obtuseness and injustice that crop up so frequently in what is supposedly the best that has been thought and said about the human condition in our Western tradition?

Still, one must try. Great men said terrible things about women. Great philosophies and respected sciences established false and contemptuous ideas about the feminine. At times it is tempting to reduce it all to anecdotes and personalities. Biographers and dox-ographers, chroniclers of lives and opinions, have told us about the social attitudes and behavior of famous men. From this liter-ature we learn that withdrawal from the world of women has almost always been considered a prerequisite of "professional" philosophy. This distance from women has generally been ratio-nalized in terms of smug superiority. Thales avoided taking a wife because for a learned man marriage always comes too soon or too late. Playing on words, Antisthenes said that a beautiful wife gives herself to everyone *(koine)*, while an ugly one is a punishment *(poine)*. The *bioi,* or lives of philosophers, that Diogenes Laertius so carefully reconstructed abound with factual detail, but no at-tention is paid to relations with women. Is it absolutely necessary to adopt the clinical approach of pseudo-Aristotle, the author of a celebrated work on melancholy, who held that one of the symp-toms of the disease, namely, repudiation of the world (and there-fore of sexuality), was a condition essential to philosophical re-flection?

It would be all too easy to respond by denouncing foolishness and error. In the first place, a feminist critique of science must make use of cumulative knowledge that is, in point of fact, not the work of women. We are able to laugh at Aristotle's biology only because we know for sure that his repetitious remarks on the inferiority of women are incorrect. We know that he is wrong not only about the relation between gender and behavior but, more important, about the very facts that he claims to be the results of observation. No matter what epistemological choices we make in our work as feminist historians, and regardless of what we may owe to Kuhn or Feyerabend, Popper or Foucault, the force of our arguments depends on the difference between positive truth and error (although the answers to every question are provisional and open to refutation or correction). I would go even further: our firm conviction that we are right and that ancient science is wrong is the *raison d'être* for our research as militants. We know that our position is defensible. This knowledge is indispensable, and it does not come from a noninstitutionalized feminine biological traditional, however true or rational. In the age-old competition between doctors and midwives, the midwives were not always right. Take one narrow but essential point, the anatomical corre-late of virginity, that is, the hymen, considered as a *sign* of sexual integrity susceptible to examination and protection. Some doctors showed themselves to be far more enlightened, critical, and solicitous of a woman's dignity on this score than did midwives who claimed to be experts on the subject of virginity.

The great debates out of which European biology evolved were debates among men. Would female scientists have made progress sooner? Much as we would like to think so, our critique of a tradition from which women were excluded is nonetheless indebted to the positive accomplishments of that very tradition. An aggressive attitude, a sweeping denunciation of science as a manifestation of male chauvinism, would prevent us from making use of those facts that enable us to do history in the conviction that truth is on our side, facts that were first glimpsed at times in spite of, but at other times by way of, the male gaze.

Furthermore, despite the use of subtle and rigorous methods, physicians and biologists often made erroneous observations or reached absurd conclusions. Historians of science are well aware that hypotheses and theories demonstrate their superiority in conflict and polemic. Winners and losers fight with the same weapons: the same intelligence, the same norms, the same determination to establish the truth. Hippocrates, Aristotle, and Galen have lost decisively. There is no equivalent in, say, gynecology of the durable contributions that such Greek mathematicians as Thales, Euclid, and Pythagoras made to geometry. Nevertheless, the ideas and, even more, the arguments, assumptions, and standards of evidence and logic of these surpassed thinkers deserve the closest scrutiny. This is so not only because we have the means to deconstruct those arguments or because it is only fair to take seriously reasoning since proved to have been erroneous. More than that, certain key ideas of ancient science can be seen in a new light thanks to recent discoveries. The more flagrant and tenacious the errors of the past, the more we must explore the reasons for their success and longevity. And let me suggest, by way of hypothesis, that fantasy played a part.

The Problem of Gender

In his commentary on *Genesis*, Philo of Alexandria, discussing the sixth day, writes that God "having given the genus *(genos)* the name *(anthropos),* distinguished its species *(eide)*": male and female. Even before the formation of the two individual prototypes, "man" was created as male and female, "since the closely related species are contained in the genus and appear as in a mirror to those capable of a penetrating vision."[13]

Philo displays a remarkable confidence in his ability to classify and construct taxonomies. Yet despite the confidence of this Old Testament exegete so thoroughly steeped in Greek culture, is a perceptive eye all that it takes to see sexual difference as constitutive of two distinct species within the human genus? For Philo things were simple. Male and female were created as virtual forms of the genus implicit in the original notion of *anthropos*. When the first male *(aner)* and the first female *(gyne)* were fashioned as distinct and singular material individuals, man witnessed the appearance before his very eyes of a sister-species, another member of the same genus as himself: woman. But woman saw no other animal species like herself. Kinship, fraternity, resemblance: Adam and Eve recognized one another as similar, as related beings. Out of this familiarity was born desire: "Love came, and, after inspiring in each the desire for union with the other, joined as it were the two distinct segments of a single animal into one for the purpose of procreation."[14] Enamored of their homogeneity, the two species discovered that they were parts of a single whole and came together in order to reproduce.

A biologist who, out of curiosity, looked into *De opificio mundi* would probably see the text as a mythological commentary on mythology. He might notice that masculine and feminine are symmetrical and appear simultaneously. The notion that Adam came first and that Eve was later created from one of his ribs is not Philo's; for him male and female are both essential aspects of the concept of human being. A geneticist might be struck by the naive way in which Philo conceptualizes procreation in terms of reproduction and treats the two sexes as different species. The modern notion of species depends on the capacity to reproduce similar individuals of either sex. A man cannot "reproduce" by himself, nor can a woman; but together they can procreate individuals whose genetic makeup partakes of both parents and is therefore unique.[15] The sex of the offspring is decided by chance. The notion of species is combinatorial rather than morphological. Sexual reproduction involving two parents is at its very core: "Species are natural population groups whose individual members are actually (or potentially) capable of interbreeding. From the standpoint of reproduction, each species is isolated from every other."[16]

Now that the classification of species is based not on distinctive features and typologies but on this "endogamic" principle, it no longer makes sense to ask about the specific nature of sexual difference, where "specific" is understood in the etymological sense. Philo's text may strike us as odd or insignificant, as totally alien to scientific tradition and unrelated to the language of classification. Is there any relation between the words "genus" and "species" as used by a first-century biblical scholar and the same words as defined in ever-changing ways by biological science? The two contexts are far apart. Nevertheless, the persistence of the word *species,* Latin for the Greek *eidos,* suggests a surprising possibility: that what separates Philo from, say, the ornithologist Ernst Mayr is a hierarchical inversion of a similar set of concepts. To put it another way, if sexual identity does not determine a species, it is because the identity of each species is based on the sexual dichotomy it subsumes.[17] The reciprocal independence of speciation and sexuation is obtained by the logical subordination of the latter to the former.

There would be no point to the foregoing remarks were it not for the fact that the relation of sex to species was one of the questions of greatest interest to the man whom biologists still celebrate as a precursor: Aristotle. When Aristotle's biological works are examined with the tools of philology, it becomes clear that the widespread notion that he was the inventor of taxonomy is mistaken. The author of the "History of Animals," "Parts of Animals," and "Generation of Animals," to say nothing of the fragments of *Parva Naturalia,* his brief monographs on sleep, locomotion, respiration, and the like, was both a logician and an anatomist, but he never conceived a system of classification with anything like the complexity or subtlety of the one in use today. For Aristotle the animal kingdom was not divided into phyla, classes, orders, families, genera, and species. Although he knew of some four hundred animal species, he used only two categories in attempting to describe and compare them: genus and species, *genos* and *eidos.* Hence it is misleading to say that Aristotle constructed a taxonomy or even that he possessed the requisite concepts to do so.[18] Yet there is no denying that, as a philosophical naturalist, his approach to science was characterized by his impulse to classify, to order, to establish typologies. What is extraordinary is that, even without an adequate nomenclature and a suitably complex hierarchy of categories, Aristotle nevertheless managed to develop a form of systematic zoology.

For Aristotle the language of logic was sufficient. Once *genos* and *eidos* were defined in terms of inclusion of the species in the genus, an operational if selective and relative criterion for discrimination became available. In other words, all birds taken together constitute a genus *relative* to the variety of their forms (in modern terms, a *class*). But when considered in comparison, say, to fish, birds constitute a species, one of the several forms of blood-bearing animals. In Linnaean taxonomy, birds form a class; the observer's choice of an object of comparison has no bearing on the classification. The class occupies a place in an abstract system, a place indicated by a name that uniquely defines the class's place in the animal kingdom. In the Aristotelian system, by contrast, it is the zoologist's point of view that determines whether birds constitute a genus or a species. If the naturalist considers "birds" in relation to their polymorphic varieties, they are a genus; but if he considers "birds" as belonging to a broader category, they are a species. The Aristotelian animal is not captured in a cage of fixed denominations; it is the object of a discourse whose vocabulary, restricted though it is, is conceived expressly for the purpose of classification.

The Platonic Heritage

Aristotle was a great synthesizer. He inherited the words *eidos* and *genos* from Plato, who had already invested them with meaning. The primary meaning of *eidos* is "form." In archaic Greek it meant "visible form," but in the language of the philosophers it had come to mean "intelligible form." Plato's "ideas" are *eide* that can be perceived by the inner eye, the eye of intelligence, with the aid of the dialectic. *Genos* is a comprehensive term signifying birth, family, lineage, race, or, more generally, any group that reproduces itself. Though distinct, the two terms were sometimes conflated. Plato offers a striking example of the interchangeability of *eidos* and *genos* that is pertinent to the question of sexual difference. When he recounts the creation myth in the *Timaeus,* he alludes to a race *(genos)* of women that supposedly joined another race *(genos)* of men. But in the *Statesman* he describes the *genos anthropinon,* or human race, as divided into males and females. This is the best way to dichotomize the race, he says, because it yields two *eide,* or species. The model is the same as the one Philo uses in his commentary on *Genesis.* But for Plato, who antedates Aristotle's prodigious efforts to fix the language of philosophy, *eidos* and *genos* are truly interchangeable terms of classification. Consider the following passage from the *Statesman:* "What kind of mistake do you say that we made in our division just now?—The kind of mistake a man would make who, seeking to divide the *genos anthropinon* into two, divided them into Greeks and barbarians. This is a division most people in this part of the world make. They separate the Greeks [literally, the *genos* of Greeks] from all other nations making them a class apart. Thus they group all other nations *(gene)* together as a class, ignoring the fact that it is an indeterminate class made up of peoples who have no intercourse with each other and speak different languages. Lumping all this non-Greek residue together, they think it must constitute one real class *(genos)* because they have a common name 'barbarian' to attach to it. Take another example. A man might think that he was dividing number into its true classes if he cut off the number ten thousand from all others and set it apart as one class *(eidos)*. He might go on to invent a single name for the whole of the rest of number, and then claim that because it possessed the invented common name it was in fact the other true class *(genos)* of number—'number other than ten thousand.' Surely it would be better and closer to the real structure of the forms to make a central division of number into odd and even or of humankind into male and female."[19] Thus, cutting a *genos* in two is an operation that may yield two *eide,* but it may equally well yield two *gene.*

The logical hierarchy is not clear. Indeed, owing to the system of division, it cannot be clear. There is no way of knowing how autonomous each part is in relation to the whole that is divided in two. Each part is defined by the *genos* and the manner of division. Thus woman = human being + female, where female is the opposite of male. Women are at once a part of the human race and a form opposed to the male form, part of the whole but the contrary of the other part.

In the *Republic* Plato attempts to make sense of a contradiction that threatens to undermine his model of the perfect city: the homogeneity of male and female guardians. Having indicated in the *Statesman* that the only correct way of dividing the human race in two is to divide it into the two species (or genera) male and female, he now shows that this general division cannot be applied to the concrete society that constitutes the city. Women are a part of the human race, just as bitches are a part of the canine breed; therefore they must perform the same tasks as men. Hence there is nothing specific about them.[20] On the other hand, the participants in the dialogue agree that different natures require different occupations and that woman's nature is different from man's.[21] Are men and women the same or different, parts of a whole or specific natures? Faced with this undecidable question, Socrates proposes an analytical argument.

Male and female must be differentiated "according to species." First, however, the pertinent division must be found. The difference is not, as in the *Statesman,* a general one, attaching to all aspects of the genus indiscriminately, but a specific one, depending on the question of the moment. Here the question is the organization of the city. In this connection nothing falls to women because they are women, nor is anything the exclusive province of men because they are men. As far as the city is concerned, the "natures" of male and female have been equally distributed. Socrates draws a radical distinction between the city and biological reality: the political is an autonomous realm, governed by its own laws. The only area in which man and woman are opposed is that of repro- duction: the female gives birth, the male engenders. From the standpoint of political theory, however, neither this distinction nor any other is relevant.[22]

Socrates imagines an adversary who argues that some function ought to be specially reserved for women. The embodiment of traditional common sense, this opponent is enlisted in an argument whose purpose is to show that gender discrimination is illegitimate in the administration of the state. What does it mean to have an aptitude or talent for something? To possess the ability to do that thing easily; to outstrip one's teachers quickly; to have a body that obey's one's will. Does gender determine whether or not one has an aptitude for specific tasks? No. All men and women possess various talents. But there is an important proviso: the gifted male always outstrips the gifted female in any particular type of per- formance.

In short, what Socrates has shown is that gender is not a pertinent criterion for dividing the human race except in the realm of biology, where childbirth and engendering are distinct functions. In social life, where personal aptitudes are all that matters, sex cannot be the determining characteristic. Was Plato therefore an advocate of equal rights for women, a male who acknowledged the aptitudes and talents of females? Shall we allow ourselves to fall under the spell of his thinking? If we do, we incur the penalty of Plato's overestimation of the identity of all human beings, his denial of difference. For within this identity emerges the worst of all differences: quantitative inequality, inadequacy, inferiority. The human race is homogeneous insofar as the organization of society is concerned, yet the male-female dichotomy subsists: men are better than women at performing those tasks for which both sexes have an aptitude. From a conceptual point of view, woman's image is exalted only to be systematically denigrated. How does Socrates deal with those activities traditionally reserved to women and in which, as a result, only women excel? He dismisses them derisively.

"Do you know any human activity in which the male sex does not surpass the female in all of these ways? Let's not waste our time talking about weaving and making pancakes or boiling stews, things at which women appear to have some talent and about which people would laugh if a woman were bested by a man."[23] What does this statement mean? Socrates is bluntly dismissive: "Let's not waste our time." He thus denies the specific nature of the work women actually do. He refuses to discuss it, not because women enjoy an unjustified reputation for excellence in these fields, but because women are in fact very good cooks and excellent seamstresses and weavers. One might almost say that it is because women are good at these things that the work is devalued. There is nothing to say about weaving and cooking because women are good at them, and therefore it would be ridiculous for men to possess these skills. Thus a level of performance that would confirm the quality of a man's work is automatically discounted when it might demonstrate the quality of a woman's work. There is no other word for it but pure sexist discrimination. And Glaucon responds in kind: "You are right that the one sex is far surpassed by the other in everything, one may say. Many women, it is true, are better than many men in many things, but broadly speaking, it is as you say."[24]

The upshot of this argument is a logical redistribution of powers. For Plato the human race is not, so far as its political organization is concerned, divided into two distinct groups whose faculties and functions stand in sharp contrast. Such division is to be avoided. Instead humans are seen as individuals, endowed with certain personal aptitudes that have nothing to do with gender.[25] The city is neither a collection of families nor a class composed of two biologically defined subclasses; it is nothing other than a group of individuals, of citizens.[26] Sexual difference must be redefined in terms of individual variation: different individuals will display greater or lesser skill in certain activities.

Gender: Classification or Generation

We have seen how Plato confused *genos* and *eidos*. In the classificatory sense, a *genos* is a group that can be divided into *eide*, or specific forms. Thus the genus *anthropos* subsumes two opposed forms, male and female, products of a logical dichotomy according to Plato's rules. In another sense, however, both Plato and Aristotle use *genos* to mean a group of living beings capable of reproducing itself through generation, or, more precisely, a group of living beings whose form is preserved by generation.[27] The *genos* is literally defined by *genesis*. Now, because there are two ways of defining *genos* (as classificatory group and as the locus wherein forms are transmitted), confusion can easily arise: it is all too easy to imagine that any group designated a *genos* can reproduce itself. Plato exploits this double meaning in the *Symposium*, where he has Aristophanes say that homosexual men are members of, and descend from, a doubly male *genos* and that this accounts for their attraction to other men. Thus the traditional reproductive connotation of *genos* prevails despite the absurdity of what would have to be a monosexual *genesis*.[28]

The anthropogony of the *Timaeus* is set forth in terms of the successive emergence of different *gene*. At first there were supposedly only *anthropoi* who were all *andres*, or males. In the beginning the human race, *genos anthropinon*, exhibited no sexual division. Later a degenerative mutation brought the *genos* of women into the world. The souls of men who had behaved in a cowardly manner were reincarnated in the bodies of women. Similarly, the other principal families of animals—quadrupeds, birds, and reptiles—are said to be the consequence of metasomatosis, changing bodies. Obese men with little curiosity received the bodies of cows. Light-spirited fools became birds, and the brutish became reptiles, forced to scrape the earth. Aristotle reasons in a similar way when he explains the birth of a girl rather than a boy as a deviation from the masculine model. Plato thus situates the origin of sexual difference at a moment in human history when an original state of perfection was destroyed.[29] Each new defect was embodied in a new *genos*.

The most mythical of all versions of the origin of women, Hesiod's *Theogony,* is based on the exact same reasoning.[30] In the beginning mortals, *anthropoi,* lived with the Immortals, the gods born of Heaven and Earth, of whom there were several families, sometimes in conflict. The children of Kronos, including Zeus, who replaced his father, the descendants of Ouranos, known as Titans, and men marked by death all lived side by side, visiting the same places and taking their meals together. The various genera of living beings, some of them mortal, others immortal, lived together in a society that was homogeneous in at least one respect: boundless happiness prevailed. But one day an accident occurred. One of the gods, Prometheus, son of a Titan, played a trick on Zeus while butchering an ox for a banquet. Instead of butchering the animal properly, Prometheus picked out the good meat from the gristle and bone, hid the inferior cuts and waste under a cover of fat, and presented the package of bone to Zeus. The great god, already sovereign over the Olympian tribe, thought little of his cousin's joke and avenged himself by taking fire away from Prometheus. Though this reprisal was intended to punish the miscreant god, it actually injured unfortunate mortals who bore no responsibility for Prometheus' act. Human beings paid the price for the frivolous behavior of Zeus's cousin. Prometheus then took back what had been taken away—the fire without which cooking was impossible—angering Zeus once more with this brazen theft. This time Zeus decided to punish man by afflicting him with an evil gift: woman. The gods fashioned an artificial creature from which the *genos* of women derived.[31] Woman aroused in man the appetite of desire, thus spelling an end to contentment and self-sufficiency. In another version of the story the first woman is called Pandora, and she foolishly opens a box full of afflictions, loosing them upon the world.[32]

In all these stories, regardless of genre or content, we find a similar narrative pattern: women are portrayed as a superfluous element, an unnecessary addition to a society that prior to their arrival was perfectly harmonious.[33] They form a *genos*, a distinct group, as if they reproduced themselves. They do not introduce sexual difference as such: in Hesiod female divinities, goddesses, already exist.[34] Reproduction also antedates the arrival of women. What women do initiate is misbehavior and human distress. The feminine is privation. This can be proved by contradiction. In an anthropogonic myth that begins in a state not of plenitude destined to decay but of utter destitution, woman is present from the beginning. After a flood destroys mankind and everything must begin anew, one couple remains, a man and a woman; they engender the human race anew by tossing stones over their shoulders. From the stones tossed by the man arise new men, from those tossed by the woman, new women. Survivors of a world where sexual difference already existed, Deucalion and Pyrrha reproduce the human race with its two genders.

The feature common to most stories of the advent of women is gender autonomy. If a group of living things is designated a *genos,* it can reproduce. Finer discriminations are sometimes involved. In a poem by Semonides of Amorgos, the female sex is divided into several genera, each said to descend from an animal and each exhibiting a characteristic flaw: gluttony, sensuality, untruthfulness, and so on. The clearest discussion of the *genos* as a group with the capacity to reproduce is given by Aristotle in the *Metaphysics*[35] (1024a, 29–30). But in considering reproduction Aristotle does not rely simply on the etymology of *genos.* He raises a theoretical issue: what is the significance of sexual difference with respect to the notions of form and generation? In other words, the fact that a *genos* is defined as a group with the capacity to reproduce tells us nothing about the possibility of a monosexual *genos.* A way must be found to include sexual difference in the concept of *genos* (in order to preserve *genesis*) but (in order to preserve specificity) without dividing the *genos* into two distinct forms. This is a stringent demand, whose consequences are worth pursuing.

Is Sexual Difference Specific?

In Aristotle's terminology the question is this: Is there a difference of species *(kat'eide)* between males and females? The question arises in Book Ten of the *Metaphysics* in the course of a reflection on the various types of relations among things.[36] For Aristotle there are two types of differences between entities: essential and accidental. Essential differences are differences of form, while accidental differences pertain to similar substances. A man and a horse differ in form, but the difference between a white man and a black man is accidental. Color, matter, and size are accidental predicates, a change in which does not alter an object's identity, its essential being *(ousia)*. Thus the question of the masculine and the feminine arises at a crucial point in a lengthy discussion of the relation between substance, form, and accident, a discussion that lies at the heart of Aristotle's theoretical concerns. It is in fact a true aporia.

Rather than make light of the question as Plato had done and as Philo would do after him, Aristotle asks whether or not it is correct to consider sexual difference a difference of form. His answer will be negative, but his reasons are very different from those one might propose today. Given the contemporary definition of species in terms of sexual reproduction, it is easy to see that sexual difference cannot be species difference. Had Aristotle been able to give such an answer, he might not have considered it worthwhile to pose the question. But he does raise the issue, because the notion of *eidos* implies nothing about reproduction: it refers to *identity* as such, independent of its transmission. Identity is perpetuated within the *genos*, the genus-line.

The philosopher's uncertainty is therefore significant. There is nothing in the concept of *eidos* that says stallion and mare, bull and cow, man and woman are not animals of different species. Where form is the only basis for comparison, the question is whether one is dealing with essential difference or accidental diversity.

With a predicate like color, it is not difficult to explain why the differences to which it gives rise are of secondary importance. But sexual difference affects all animals other than the few that reproduce by spontaneous generation. Can such dissimilarity be explained away as a mere coincidence? Nor is sexual difference like variation in size: half of all the individuals in each species differ from the other half in this fundamental way. How is the difference between dog and bitch related to the difference between dog and man? Does the morphological difference between the sexes justify the belief that a difference of species, an essential difference, exists between male and female? Aristotle is embarrassed by his own alternative. The male-female antinomy is too important to be accidental but not important enough to be counted as substantial. The choice is so difficult that Aristotle actually contrives to evade it.

The difference between male and female, he says, concerns

both "matter and bodies." So much is obvious. No one would deny that men and women are physically different. But to view this as an empirical statement is to misunderstand Aristotle's idea and the significance of his solution to the riddle of sex. The author of the *Metaphysics* is not observing an obvious fact. Rather, he is seeking to ascertain the status of a *diaphora,* or difference within the context of a constraining abstract scheme: that difference is either specific or accidental. If matter *(hyle)* were said to be the sole determining factor, then sexual difference would be like the difference between a bronze and an iron ring, a question of size and histology. In that case sexual dimorphism would be impossible to explain. So when Aristotle says that the difference between males and females is a question of both matter *and* bodies, he is adding a formal, anatomical and physiological, connotation to matter. Dimorphism is preserved, but at the cost of having surreptitiously smuggled in a criterion from the realm of *eidos*. For what is form for Aristotle if not the form of a living body? What is a body, if not an organism defined by its anatomical and physiological structure, which is to say, by its form? Birds and fish are different species, as is shown by the structural difference of their bodies. Thus the difference between masculine and feminine is neither accidental nor essential but some ambiguous combination of the two.

Is Sexual Difference Generic?

The concept of *eidos* assumes nothing about reproduction and is subject to a morphological criterion. Hence there is apparently nothing to prevent Aristotle from seeing males and females of a given type as two autonomous forms. Why does he refuse to do so? Because the two sexes exist for the purpose of *genesis,* and therefore for the *genos,* which is defined as "continual reproduction of beings possessing the same form." Every genos must therefore include both sexes as a necessary condition of reproduction. But in each genos there can be only one form, transmitted from individual to individual. A genos has only one identity. For Aristotle this is a theoretical constraint. If one begins with the "genetic" as distinct from the classificatory definition of genos, it is impossible to divide a genos into two *eide*. In hindsight we may ask why Aristotle did not hit upon the modern definition of genos in terms of endogamy. The answer is that he persisted in defining a genos in terms of form.

A genos consists of two sexes but possesses only one form. The two sexes permit the transmission of the one form, the unique *eidos*. Two sexes for one form: clearly things would be simpler if there were only one sex. Generation would then truly be the linear transmission of identity from one individual to another, and there would be no need to clarify the concept of sexual difference. Hesiod, Semonides, and Plato all wished that things might indeed be this simple, that a genos might be a family of males *or* females somehow miraculously capable of perpetuating itself. Aristotle gives this wish a theoretical basis. Despite the empirical existence of two sexes, he argues, only one form is transmitted in any genos: that of the father. In order to hold on to the formal unity of the genos without dispensing with reproduction, Aristotle takes a reductionist view of sexual difference. He develops this view in two ways: by reducing sexual difference to quantitative inequality and by defining it negatively, in terms of a lack relative to the masculine norm.

More and Less

Aristotle devotes a great deal of space to female bodies in his studies of animals. Females exist in all species not born by spontaneous generation, that is, from the moist earth or from decomposing matter. Female characteristics are described in two ways: by analogy with the male and by comparison of inferiority with the male body. To begin with, the dissimilarity between male and female is a matter of correspondence: where males have a penis, females have a uterus, "which is always double, just as in the male there are always two testicles."[37] A male is an animal capable of engendering in another animal; a female is an animal capable of engendering in herself. "Thus, since each sex is defined by a certain potential and a certain action, and since each activity requires appropriate instruments, namely, for the functions of the body, the organs, there must necessarily be distinct organs for childbirth and copulation, whence the difference between male and female."[38] Aristotle thus explains genital dimorphism as an anatomical consequence of the two modes of engendering: in oneself or in another.

Yet the female body also exhibits signs of deficiency, weakness, and incompleteness.[39] "The female is less muscular, and the body's articulations are less pronounced. In hairy species the hair of the female is finer, as is that which takes the place of the hair in species that have none. Females also have softer flesh than males; their knees are closer together, and their legs are thinner. In animals with feet the female's feet are smaller than the males. The female voice is always weaker and higher in all animals that have voice, except the bovine breed, where the female voice is deeper than that of the male. The parts that naturally lend themselves to defensive purposes—the horns, claws, and other parts of this sort—are found in the male of certain species but not the female. In other species these parts exist in both sexes, but they are stronger and more fully developed in the male."[40]

If the female is naturally unarmed and incapable of defending herself, the female brain is also small: "Among the animals, man has the largest brain in proportion to his size, and in man the male brain is larger in volume than the female . . . Man has more sutures than other animals, and men more than women, for the same reason: so that this region, and especially the larger brain, may breathe more easily."[41] The body of the female, like that of the child, is incomplete, and, like that of a sterile male, it produces no semen.[42] Sickly by nature, the female body remains longer in gestation because of its low heat, but it ages more rapidly because "anything small, whether a man-made work or a natural organism, comes to an end more quickly."[43] All of this follows from one premise: "Females are by nature weaker and colder [than males], and their nature must be considered naturally deficient."

Thus we come to the ultimate ground of the female's defects: feminine nature itself. The female is deficient. All of her characteristics signify some shortcoming. Since Aristotle regularly compares animals by size, one might think that the female would be credited at least with having larger breasts than the male. But no, he suddenly chooses a different criterion: consistency and firmness of tissue. Compared with the male pectorals, female breasts are spongy protuberances; always soft, they can fill with milk but are quickly emptied.[44] The flesh of the male is solid; that of the female is porous and moist. Thus even the breasts are a sign of female inadequacy. Woman, born female because of some impotence in her male parent, exhibits her own form of impotence, "that of cooking the sperm in a specially treated nutrient [the blood in creatures with blood or some analogue in those without] owing to the coldness of her nature."[45]

Comparison with the male brings out two aspects of the female body: not only equivalence in diversity but also deficiency, failure to conform to a superior model. Aristotle would say that the female body differs from that of the male as less differs from more. The importance of this quantitative measure of sexual inequality should not be underestimated. For Aristotle the difference between lesser and greater is something precise, the difference separating two birds or two fish, between a sparrow and an eagle, say, or a minnow and a bass. In other words, it is a difference between animals of the same *genos*. There is another, distinct kind of difference in biology: that of analogy. An analogy exists between birds and fish to the extent that natural functions such as respiration, alimentation, locomotion, and the like give rise to distinct but comparable organs. The fish's mouth corresponds to the bird's beak; the fish's fins correspond to the bird's wings. Each genus has its own anatomy, but that anatomy is "specifically" determined by functions common to all animals. Quantitative difference exists within each genus, but analogy distinguishes one genus from another with respect to form.[46]

Sexual difference is as problematic in this context as it is in the *Metaphysics*. If reproduction is a natural function common to all living things, one would expect the number of genders to be in one-to-one correspondence with the number of distinct but analogous anatomies. Are not penis and testicles the analogues of cervix and womb—disparate but equivalent embodiments of an identical function? When Aristotle discusses the genital apparatus, he is almost forced to conclude that male and female differ in form and must therefore be considered two autonomous genera. But since genus is defined in terms of the reproduction of a form, such a conclusion is unacceptable. Aristotle, though he never explicitly states the aporia, nevertheless managed to resolve it by insisting that sexual dimorphism is a matter of quantitative rather than formal difference, a matter of greater and lesser. He portrays male and female bodies as quantitative variants of a single form, the *eidos* that reproduces itself in the genos.

The Weakness of the Cold Body

Reducing sexual dimorphism to quantitative difference conforms with the logic of the Aristotelian system. The unity of the *genos* as reproductive entity is preserved. There are two sexes but only one indivisible *(atomos)* form. This *reductio ad unum* is not accomplished simply by stringing together a series of descriptive statements: the female is small, weak, and fragile, she has fewer teeth and cranial sutures, her voice is weaker, and so on. These distinctive traits, attentively observed by the naturalist, are mere epiphenomena of a mutilated *physis,* or nature. Why are women's bodies small and frail? Because they lack vital heat, which weakens their metabolism, or "cooking," as Aristotle calls it. The same lack explains the flow of menstrual blood. "In a weaker organism, there will inevitably be a greater residue of less fully cooked blood."[47] It is this residue that flows out of the female body once a month.

Menstrual blood is another sign of the coldness of the female body. Because it is the female's contribution to conception and thus to reproduction, however, it is probably the most important sign of all. Menstrual blood is analogous to sperm, but it is imperfect sperm because it is uncooked. Semen is produced by cooking the blood of the male, the blood being the ultimate form of nutriment for the organism's tissues. Owing to his vital heat, the male is capable of transforming blood into sperm. By contrast, the female is characterized by lack of sufficient energy, *adynamia,* to effect this transformation.

The opposition of sperm and menstrual blood demonstrates the irreducible difference between male and female. Yet the two are analogous: sperm is to the male what menstrual blood is to the female. Both are the result of the cooking of the blood, but the male is capable of carrying this cooking through to completion while the female is not. The two substances differ only as the products of two distinct phases in a single process. Evidence for this can be seen in the traces of blood present in incompletely cooked sperm. This theory of sperm production is not Aristotle's. He borrowed it from Diogenes of Apollonia without mentioning the source. Its usefulness is clear: it allows Aristotle to present a qualitative difference as a quantitative one. But it also takes on another function in the theory to become a central element in the Aristotelian system: in the metamorphosis of blood into sperm a metaphysical transformation occurs. The rapid cooking effected by coital motion just prior to ejaculation creates an absolute discontinuity between the hematic residue and its derivative. Henceforth the sperm possesses soul, form, and a principle of movement.

"As principles of generation one might reasonably propose the male and the female, the male as possessing the generative and motor principle, the female as possessing the material principle."[48] All of Aristotle's work on genetics is an elaboration on this division, which is set forth at the beginning of *On the Generation of Animals*. The interest of this "primitive genetics"[49] has to do less with the axioms on which it rests than with the form the argument takes. Let us take a careful look at the sentence just quoted. Generation, *genesis,* is said to rest on two principles. The male possesses the "generative and motor" principle, the female the "material" principle. The trick has already been played: in generation there is only one progenitor, *arche geneseos,* the father. Though Aristotle states that there are two principles, he is really interested in only one: the female is there only to provide the material, the menstrual blood. Maternity provides alimentary and physical support for a process that depends essentially on the male.

The father is the progenitor because his sperm possesses a threefold potency *(dynamis):* a principle of soul *(tes psuches arche),* a principle of movement *(arche kineseos),* and a principle of form *(arche tes eidous).* The sensitive soul, that is, the fundamental sensibility of the animal, is contained in the sperm, the "very essence of the male." Generation is accomplished by the male, because he is the one "who introduces the sensitive soul, either directly or by way of the semen." The sperm, because it is thoroughly cooked, is by nature hot and pneumatic; therefore it is capable of carrying the psychic principle. The father thus transmits soul to the embryo. The sperm also possesses "movement," movement that is not simply physical but biological. "The semen possesses the movement impressed upon it by the progenitor," simply because it is the residue of the blood and the blood naturally nourishes the body. The sperm inherits the power of blood to make the body grow and extends that effect to the embryo: "Since the sperm is a residue, and since it is animated by a movement identical to that by which the body grows as bits of elaborated nutriment [blood] are distributed throughout its extent, when it penetrates the uterus it coagulates and sets in motion the residue of the female by imparting to that residue its own animating motion." The development of the embryo is thus linked to the development of the father. The sperm is not simply a means of transmitting life or a vector of physiological force; it possesses the principle of form. That is why children resemble their parents.

Form, or the invariance of the *eidos,* is essential to generation.

The movement of the sperm is not merely a blind impetus applied to matter. It perpetuates itself in the embryo by reproducing a form: "The movement of nature resides in the product itself [the embryo] and comes from another nature, which contains the active form within itself." The growth force emanates from the father, who is already what the affected matter will come to be: out of this matter will grow something that resembles its progenitor. How does conception work? "When the seminal residue of menstruation has been suitably cooked, the movement that comes from the male will cause it to take on the proper form." In the manufacture of man-made objects, the craftsman is an intermediary who, by imparting a motion to matter, creates a certain shape or form (*morphe, eidos*). Similarly, in procreation, the male supplies the form and principle of movement. "The semen plays the role of the artist, because it is in possession of a prospective form." Transmission, continuity, homonymy: man engenders man. "Callias and Socrates are different from their progenitors with respect to matter, which is not the same, but identical with respect to form, because form is indivisible." Progenitor and progeny have different physical forms but the same "specific" form.

The father embodies and transmits the model of the species, the unique form whose destiny is to be transmitted within a *genos*. An active demiurge, he makes the child in his own image. He works on the body of the mother, which is a physical place, a kind of workshop. It is also inert matter: "The only thing it lacks is the principle of the soul." It is incapable of locomotion and absolutely passive: "The female, qua female, is a passive element." Her condition is that of taking, of receiving the male form. Her menstrual blood contains no *psyche*, no *kinesis*, no *eidos*. It is a product of *adunamia*, of an insufficiency of heat for cooking, and therefore lacks *pneuma*, the hot air that gives life. It is raw material, the primordial stuff, *prote hule*, of the generational process: "The female, qua female, is a passive element, and the male, qua male, is an active element. It is from him that the principle of motion emanates. Therefore, if we take each term in its extreme sense, the one as agent and motor, the other as object and thing moved, the sole product thereof is made as a bed is made by a carpenter and out of wood, or as molded wax is created out of molten wax and a mold."[50] These artisanal analogies demonstrate clearly what role Aristotle ascribes to the woman's blood in reproduction.

Matter and the Body

"The male provides the form and the principle of motion, the female the body and matter." This proposition from the very beginning of *On the Generation of Animals* links body and matter in the same way as the *Metaphysics*. Precisely what is the significance of the body's virtual presence in the hematic residue of females, a presence that Aristotle mentions several times? He asserts that "the parts of the embryo are potentially present in the matter." Furthermore, "the female component is also a residue, which contains all the parts potentially but not actually. Among the parts that it contains potentially are those that distinguish the female from the male." Here we encounter the difficulty of understanding the Aristotelian notion of body, or *soma*. It would appear to be impossible to conceptualize the body apart from its form, apart from a perception of anatomical distinctiveness. Aristotle contrasts body-and-matter with *eidos*. The parts of the embryo's future body, including the sexual parts, are already potentially present in the residue of the mother's body, so that continuous development is possible. Since development occurs, development must be possible. An animal grows not by adding new parts to those already present, but by developing possibilities already inherent in the female blood. "What is potentially possible cannot achieve existence without the action of a sufficiently energetic motor force. Nor can the motor possessing this necessary force operate on just any substance, any more than a carpenter can make a chest out of anything other than wood, or than a chest can be made of wood without a carpenter." The assertion that the female residue contains the parts of the future adult tells us nothing about their nature; it tells us only that this residue has the potential to develop into a living creature.

"The residue of the female is in potential what the animal will be by nature, and because all the organs are present in potential but not actual form, each of the parts is formed, and also because when an actor acts upon an object . . . one is active and the other passive. Thus the female provides the matter, and the male the principle of movement."[51] This passage is particularly clear: the menstrual blood contains the parts of the embryo's body, yet it is mere matter.

The Significance of Symmetry

Aristotle posits soul, form, and movement against body, matter, and passivity. The problem of gender—how to explain sexual difference as quantitative variation given a definition of *genos* in terms of reproduction and formal identity—leads to a series of dichotomies in which the feminine is always characterized as negativity, deformation, or lack.

In Hesiod, Semonides, and Plato we found a mythical concept of *genos* as an autonomous, monosexual lineage, and in Aristotle we noted a metaphysical reduction of the concept. But there is yet another body of ancient thought about women that deserves attention: that of the physicians, who attempted to reconcile certain positive knowledge with the need for a *double* principle of generation. No longer are the sexes self-sufficient, nor is the feminine reduced to the masculine. Rather, male and female are symmetrical categories.

According to the Cnidian physicians, women produce a seminal fluid analogous to the male sperm. This fluid is a sort of concentrated extract of all the bodily humors. It is secreted by the cervix of the uterus under exactly the same conditions that lead to ejaculation in the male: "In women, when the genitals are rubbed in coitus and the womb is set in motion, the latter is gripped by a sort of itch that brings pleasure and heat to the rest of the body. The woman also ejaculates from her whole body, sometimes in the womb (which becomes moist), sometimes outside it (if the opening of the womb is larger than it should be)."[52] Thus the female body actively contributes to procreation; conception is the result of a mechanical mixing process. The sex of the embryo is determined by the relative strength of the two contributions: "Sometimes the female secretion is stronger, sometimes the male. The man possesses both the male and female seed, as does the woman. The embryo must come from the stronger seed." Male and female differ in strength, and this difference is quantitative or, in Aristotelian terms, "a matter of greater and lesser." Both sexes possess a "hermaphroditic" seminal substance with stronger and weaker components. The ratio of strong-masculine to weak-feminine varies with each emission, and the sex of the child is determined by this combinatorial variation. "This is how it works: if the stronger seed comes from both partners, [the embryo] is male; if it is the weaker seed, [the embryo] is female." The decisive factor apparently is not the strength inherent in the masculine seed as such but rather the mass *(plethos).* "If the weak seed is more abundant than the strong, the latter, dominated by and mixed with the weak, turns into female seed; but if the strong seed is more abundant than the weak, the weak is dominated and turns into male seed."

This model is distinguished by symmetry of male and female. Both parents are progenitors, and it is quantitative predominance, the greater mass of one kind of seed as opposed to the other, that determines the sex of the child. In other words, the model strikes a compromise between acknowledgment of male superiority (in the strength of the sperm) and acceptance of a substantial equality of the two sexes in the determination of gender. Ultimately the deciding factor is chance. Which type of seed happens to be more abundant? The weaker sperm may win out, provided that it is present in greater mass than the stronger sperm—provided it is in the majority. The use of political language is scarcely stretching the point, since in the terminology of democratic politics *plethos* literally means majority.

The Probability of Gender

The most interesting word in this text, however, is the verb that expresses dominance: *kratein.* The word means "to prevail" in the sense that one opinion prevails over another in political debate. *Kratos* is power acquired through conflict and is often a synonym for victory. In contexts more closely related to the matter of sexual determination, and in particular in Aeschylus' *The Suppliant Maidens, kratos* refers to the triumph that Danaus' fifty daughters hope to win over the army of fifty male cousins who are pursuing the women for the purpose of compelling them to marry: "Lord Zeus, may he deprive us of an ill marriage and a bad husband, as Io was released from ill, protected by a healing hand, kind might did cure her. And strength may he assign us women [*kratos nemoi gynaixin*]."

In *The Suppliant Maidens,* where a family is divided along gender lines, the word used to express the hoped-for victory is the same word used in the medical literature to express the predominance of one sex over the other. It also turns out to be the word used to express the authority of the law: "If the deceased has not made disposition of his estate, and if he is survived by daughters, his legacy will change hands as they do. If he has no surviving children, the next of kin shall become masters *(kurioi)* of his property: the next of kin are brothers of the same blood if any, and if these brothers have children, the children inherit their father's share. In the absence of brothers or children of brothers [gap in the text], their children shall inherit shares according to the same rules. The males and children of males in a given line shall have priority *(kratein)*, even if they are more remote by birth. If there are no relatives on the father's side down to the children of cousins, the parents on the mother's side will inherit according to the same rules. If there are no relatives of this degree on either side, the nearest relative on the father's side shall inherit *(kurios einai)*."[53]

This text concerns inheritance *ab intestato*. The law prescribes what is to become of property and daughters belonging to the estate in the absence of direct male heirs. Priorities are established down to the fifth canonical degree in both the patrilineage and matrilineage of the deceased. The criterion is in all cases the same: the male takes precedence over the female. Maleness counts for more than proximity: a brother of the deceased is no closer than a sister, but the brother has priority. Furthermore, matrilineal descendants are always preceded by patrilineal ones: the daughter of a male cousin of the deceased takes precedence over a uterine half-brother or a maternal uncle. If there is no potential heir within the circle of relations thus defined, possible candidates are to be sought only on the father's side. Beyond the children of cousins, the mother's family cannot supply an heir.

The verb *kratein* refers in this context to the dominance of one sex over the other. That is not its only meaning in the language of the law. It can also refer, for example, to the assertion of possession of an inheritance by a potential heir. Nevertheless, it is remarkable that the use of this word in relation to gender is so similar in three quite heterogeneous vocabularies: those of medicine, tragedy, and law.

In each of the situations described—the dispute between the Danaids and the Egyptiades, the priority of inheritance, and the biological determination of sex—what is involved is not simply difference but also conflict between male and female. There is a prize at stake, a battle to be won, an advantage to be gained.

Kratein presupposes an agonistic or competitive situation dividing the two sexes. The word signifies an end to the conflict, but an end requiring a drastic choice. No conciliation is possible: one sex wins, the other loses. One dominates *(kratein)*, the other is dominated *(krateisthai)*. The antagonism, however, depends on the presence of two adversaries of comparable status and equal chance of winning. For victory to be possible or necessary, for one of the two to be declared, as in the law of inheritance, the victor, the dignity of the other must be acknowledged.

Accidents of Reason

Returning to Aristotle's theory, we may reasonably conjecture that he should have been obliged to avoid the verb *kratein*. In Aristotle there is no contest between the sexes at the moment of conception because the outcome is determined in advance. Form and soul come from the father through the movement imparted to the sperm; the male is the sole principle of generation, the *arche tes geneseos*. The mother is not a progenitor; she merely provides the inanimate material of which the embryo is made: the thickened, inert blood of menstruation. Hence she cannot transmit any form of her own that might compete with the patrilinear *eidos*. How, then, does Aristotle explain the birth of females? The answer is simple: a female is the product of a union in which there is an insufficiency of male *dynamis*, "owing to youth, old age, or some similar cause." Lacking demiurgic, creative energy, the father produces an imperfect, defective form, a form that is not so much a living portrait of the father as a sign of his aesthenia, of a falling off of his powers. A daughter's misshapen body *(anaperia)* is small and weak because her father flagged during coitus. In this unilinear model the female is merely a modification of the male. Aristotle draws the ultimate consequence: "The progeny that does not resemble its parents is already, in certain respects, a monster *(teras)*, because nature has to some extent departed from the generic type *(genos)*. The very first deviation from type is the birth of a female instead of a male." Femininity is a defective version of the *eidos* that reproduces itself within a *genos*. Taxonomy and genetics mesh perfectly.

Surprisingly, the verb *kratein* does occur in Aristotle's explanation of sexual determination. The idea of a test of strength, a contest in which one must either dominate or be dominated, is a central feature of his genetics. It appears at a very delicate point, when the philosopher considers the matter of resemblance. How can it be that a child may resemble its mother or mother's ancestors? The linear model of degeneration is no longer adequate. It is conceivable that the birth of a female results from a failure in the transmission of the father's form. But why should a daughter's face resemble her mother's?—something seen quite frequently, according to Aristotle. Such a phenomenon suggests that women possess a form of their own. If there is morphological similarity between a mother and her children, then there can be transmission on the mother's side, and indeed maternal heredity may sometimes outweigh paternal heredity: "When the seminal residue of menstruation has been suitably cooked, the movement imparted to it by the male will cause it to take on his form . . . If, therefore, the movement prevails *(kratein)*, a male rather than a female will result, and the offspring will resemble the progenitor and not the mother; but if it does not prevail, any potency that it lacks will also be absent in the offspring."[54]

Random dominance, the result of a contest between two progenitors either of whom may win out over the other, is necessary to account for individual characteristics, a subject Aristotle takes up in Book Four of the *Generation of Animals*. As long as the question of reproduction involves a continuity of form, of an *eidos* understood in the sense of a species, what counts is duplication of identity: man engenders man. The homonymy is perfect except when man engenders woman *(gyne)*, but that is a mere accident. But when Aristotle considers the problem of atavism and of features common to mother and child, he is thinking of particular individuals, probably human beings. Thus he is led to declare that "where generation is concerned, what is always most important is the particular, individual character."[55] This is to say the least an unexpected statement from a philosopher who thinks of *genesis* as the only chance of immortality for a form, an *eidos,* beyond the death of singular individual members of the *genos*. The explanation of "family resemblances" is nevertheless a crucial test for any genetic theory. Aristotle approaches it by adapting a theory that, given the absence of any notion of maternal form, appears to allow no place for any kind of affinity between mother and child. Suddenly his language becomes quite similar to that of the physicians.

"By individual I mean Coriscos or Socrates. Now, since things change by turning not into just anything but into their opposites, the same holds true in generation, and what has not been dominated *(kratoumenon)* must change and turn into its opposite, according as potency was lacking in the generative and motor agent in order that it might dominate. If it is the power whereby this agent is a male, a female is born; if it is that whereby it is Coriscos or Socrates, the child resembles not the father but the mother. For just as the general term mother is the opposite of father, a particular mother is opposed to a particular father."[56] The possibility that a mother may be a progenitor *(gennosa)* is here recognized. But the resemblance between mother and child is merely a distortion of the resemblance between father and child. Aristotle is actually combining his unilinear conception of engenderment with an inevitable concession to symmetry. But the concession is of considerable magnitude and threatens to undermine the whole system, because this intrusion of female otherness, this demonstration of material resistance, occurs in one birth out of two.

Aristotle grants that the mother may be a progenitor when he makes woman the subject of the verb *gennan,* to engender, a usage that is seriously at variance with his ordinary use of the word. Normally *gennan* refers to the masculine role in reproduction, to the transmission of form and life, soul and movement, as opposed to the material function assigned to the female body. *Gennan* is literally the exclusive province of the father. Therefore the decision to extend the meaning of the word to allow the mother to engender as well is not insignificant. Aristotle is yielding to the need to conceive of the feminine in positive terms. The female can win out in the contest over sexual determination because she too can engender, just like the male. The chance to *kratein* depends on the ability to *gennan.* Thus there are two progenitors, two sexes. One wonders why it was necessary to refute the Hippocratic theories with such ferocity only to arrive at a similar position.

Aristotle's genetic theory was thus shaped by two contradictory demands: to represent generation as a unilinear transmission of identity and to explain the incontrovertible phenomenon of resemblance.

An Indefensible Identification

Ancient physicians attributed active spermatic and phallic powers to the female body and thus parted company with the mythical and philosophical tradition. They argued that the semen secreted by the female intensifies the effects of the male sperm, that the uterus is the equivalent of the penis, and that the ovaries correspond to the testicles. This bipolar symmetry is tantamount to an identification of female with male. Is it really any less blind, any less serious in its consequences for the understanding of women, than the philosophical theory it countered? Does it warrant a judgment any less severe than Plato's political philosophy?

The answer to both questions, I believe, is yes, because the holistic reductive theory that Plato sets forth in the *Republic* is a vision for a totalitarian society. The nonspecific aptitudes of women serve to define their subordinate function in the ideal city. Out of disdain for such traditional female talents as weaving and cooking Plato praises the warlike virtues of the female guardians, whose behavioral characteristics are not unlike those of female dogs. Women owe their very presence on earth to the cowardice of certain primitive men, according to the anthropogony of the *Timaeus*. As the embodiment of pusillanimity, women have no claim on bellicosity and courage, by definition virile virtues, except by analogy with the animals, that is, with the bottom of the taxonomic scale. By nature lacking in boldness, women chosen to be guardians must be raised from early childhood, trained as animals are trained, to compensate for their innate defect. With this training they are capable of great things, yet always less distinguished, less glorious, than the deeds of *andres*.

Whenever knowledge and power are at issue, whenever the discussion turns to the philosophers whose role is to govern the city, women are not mentioned. Their utopia requires that children be taken from their mothers and nurses, who are held responsible for the miseducation of the city's future citizens. Thus Plato teaches the city the proper use of its female citizens by invoking what is unfortunately a transcultural suspicion of and disrespect for what women traditionally know how to do, beginning with maternity and motherhood.

Everything Plato says shows that for him women are never an end in themselves. The rules he sets forth with respect to women are never for their benefit or in their interest. Whenever he recommends maximum integration, as he does in the *Laws*, or worries about how women should live (common meals, residences, marital relations), the presumed needs and desires of society's female members are not considered. Plato's concern is always civic and collective, and women always figure as obstacles. They are a structural roadblock that must be circumvented, a dead weight that must somehow be turned to advantage. With their taste for gossip and secrecy they are by nature a troublesome presence, a threat to social homogeneity.

Social homogeneity is a utilitarian value and must therefore be fostered in spite of the nature of women and the biological difference between engendering and delivering. When Plato avoids the language of myth and politics, his argument anticipates Aristotle in every detail. Generation is a technical act. The father is the "principle of resemblance," the model or form, that governs all birth. The mother provides the material out of which the body is shaped. And the child is the finished product, the "metaphysical" offspring (*Timaeus* 50b).

Plutarch: From Identity to Inequality

The strategy, then, is to deny woman's otherness in order to emphasize her inequality. Plutarch, writing in the second century A.D., used similar reasoning to arrive at a conception of marriage based on a conflation of the notion of *koinonia,* or indivision, with that of the woman's submission to her spouse. In the symbiosis of marriage husband and wife ought, Plutarch tells us, to share the same friends, the same acquaintances, the same gods, the same property. Nature combines elements of both bodies so completely that no one can tell which parts of the child come from one parent and which from the other. Similarly, husband and wife must mingle whatever property each brings to the marriage. They must learn that nothing belongs to either of them as individuals but only to both as a couple. The couple is so intimate, so homogeneous, that nothing distinguishes the husband from the wife, and yet upon this intimacy is built a relationship in which the husband is invariably the more powerful of the two. Plutarch compares him to the sun, to a king, to a master, to a knight, all active and sovereign individuals, while the wife is compared to the moon (or to a mirror), a subject, a pupil, a horse. If a woman is active, if she takes the initiative, she is immediately accused of seduction, witchcraft, or shameful excess. A wife must remain consenting and passive; she must adapt in every way to her husband's style. Far from being a synthesis, marital symbiosis comes down to renunciation by the wife of anything she might call her own: gods, friends, occupations, and property. This is most striking in the case of property, where the quantitative effects of "mingling" two estates are most apparent. The two estates are joined into a single, indivisible estate, but it belongs to the husband, even if the wife is the larger contributor. Here, "mixing" is understood in the sense of *krasis,* or mixing of water and wine: the resulting liquid is still called wine, even if the quantity of water in the mix exceeds the quantity of wine. The wife always occupies the inferior position, just as water is less valuable than wine.

Plutarch's *coniugalia praecepta* constitute one of the more interesting interpretations of Plato's and Aristotle's theories of sexual difference.

Only in the medical literature do we find a theory coupled with empirical observations from which it is possible to extract a less reductive model of the female body and behavior. To be sure, the feminine is still marked by weakness: the female portion of the seed is less potent in both men and women. And female tissues exhibit greater softness, looseness, and porosity than male tissues, characteristics that make them particularly permeable to liquids and vapors. These are defects, because lack of firmness implied lack of muscular strength. The idea that the female sperm is lacking in energy is merely one more indicator of feminine inferiority. But to say that a sperm has less energy is nevertheless to recognize it as a sperm, hence as an active, effective substance capable of transmitting life, and thus this lack of energy is not so radical a defect as the absolute impotence that Aristotle ascribed to menstrual blood, the mother's only contribution to reproduction.

A few key ideas and preoccupations characterize the philosophical approach to the feminine: a concern to *classify* sexual difference in relation to other types of difference; a tendency to *reduce* the contrast between male and female by a variety of means, whether by transforming the antinomy of two autonomous and equivalent terms into a mere *alteration* of one of them, or by neutralizing all distinctive features (except that between childbearing and engendering) through the allegation of a *common nature*. This point cannot be stressed too strongly. When the feminine was included in the same sphere as the masculine, when females were allowed the same social functions, the same attitudes, and the same talents as males, the result was not liberal acknowledgment of equality but dismissal of the female as "obviously" inferior to the male, her defects being all the more apparent when set against a background of qualitative identity. Historically, conceptual homogenization of the sexes has served only to justify condescension toward one of them and systematic blindness as to its value. That brand of feminism which insists on woman's specificity and seeks to put it into practice through separation, to the point of treating women and children as a veritable *genos gunaikon*, is not mistaken in its wariness of assimilation. It errs, however, by shutting itself off, by rejecting any possibility of *transcending* the moment of pure affirmation of a fundamental otherness. Yet such transcendence is the only prospect truly worthy of women: equality of rights, recognition of *value*, respect for differences.

As long as scholars accept the prejudice of female inferiority as an article of faith, and as long as identification with the male model is used only to bring out the inferiority of the female, there will be no escaping comparison between the greater and the lesser.

Women and the Law

Another form of discourse concerning women is the law, where many of the necessary elements are already in hand, including municipal codes, inscriptions, and the speeches of Attic orators.[1] Roman law claims the lion's share of attention, which is only fitting given its importance in defining the legal status of women in many Western countries to the present day. Most writing about women and Roman law concerns the "incapacities" of women under Roman codes and the legal "inequalities" to which they were subjected. The traditional interpretation has been social and political: women were excluded from public life.

A lawyer by training, Yan Thomas shows that the exclusion of women from political life, and more particularly from those public offices that required deliberating in the name and on behalf of others, stems from a far more radical incapacity, namely, the inability to claim citizenship for one's offspring, or, put another way, the inability to transmit legitimacy. The order of inheritance is the key to understanding the logic of Roman law. Accordingly, the political order is not the primary consideration in expounding the logic of the legal system. Exclusion from political life can be explained in terms of sexual difference and its effects on the system of kinship.

P.S.P.

3

The Division of the Sexes in Roman Law

Yan Thomas

A Compulsory Norm

UNDER ROMAN LAW women did not form a distinct juridical species. The law was called upon to resolve countless conflicts involving women, but it never proposed the slightest definition of woman as such, even though for many jurists the common belief in woman's weakness of mind *(imbecillitas mentis)*, flightiness, and general infirmity *(infirmitas sexus)* served as a handy explanation for her statutory incapacities. On the other hand, the division of the sexes was a fundamental tenet of the legal system. To some this might appear perfectly natural: sexual reproduction is a fact of nature of which all legal systems tacitly take account. This is certainly true of the French Civil Code and other modern Western legal systems, where sexual division is so thoroughly taken for granted that it often goes unstated: it might be argued that, according to the letter of French law, applicants for a marriage license need not be of different sexes. By contrast, in the Roman legal tradition, as well as in canon law, obvious points were stated explicitly and even underscored. For the Romans sexual division was not simply a fact but a norm. Roman citizens belonged to one of two groups, *mares* or *feminae,* and marriage explicitly united a member of one group with a member of the other. The best way to understand this norm, however, is to look not at run-of-the-mill cases but at borderline ones. Indeed, it was in keeping with the casuistic style of Roman law that the principle was clarified by drawing artificial boundaries where natural distinctions failed: in cases involving hermaphrodites.

The Casuistry of Hermaphroditism

For Roman casuists, who as a matter of method collected rare species not readily classifiable according to the standard categories—cases in which, precisely because they were unclassifiable, judgment had to be based overtly on arbitrary, radical choices—hermaphroditism offered ideal ground on which to test the imperative of sexual division. Jurists found that there was no alternative to a system based on gender distinctions. In this they were merely conforming to standard institutional logic: regulate the social machine by drawing distinctions. I take this idea from Legendre's work on the dual tradition of Western dogmatics, which is based on both Roman and canon law. Structural anthropologists, fascinated by the combinatorial possibilities inherent in series of paired oppositions, have attempted to reduce all social distinctions to elementary structures of exchange and reciprocity. But social distinctions are always based on prior fundamental principles. Without such principles the oppositions that figure in anthropological analysis would not exist. Here, the fundamental principle is the legal rule that there must be two sexes. Because of this principle, the dichotomizations accomplished by law were guaranteed to be not just rational but also sound.[1]

Thus when the casuists of the Roman Empire, no doubt availing themselves of earlier republican (and even pontifical) jurisprudence, laid it down as a norm that humanity is divided into two categories, male and female, they were using the law as a laboratory in which to demonstrate an inescapable fact: the way to resolve nature's sexual ambiguities was to insist that every individual belong to one or the other of the two legally established genders. After careful examination, every androgyne had to be adjudged either male or female.

The questions the casuists raised were by no means absurd. They disclosed the true nature of sexual distinction as it emerged through legal controversy. Take one example. Could a hermaphrodite marry as a man and institute as his heir a child born to his legitimate spouse within ten months of the father's death (and thus legally considered his)? Ulpian, probably following earlier opinions of Proculus and Julian, answered affirmatively, but only "on condition that his virile organs predominate."[2] Implicit in this argument was the possible existence of "female" hermaphrodites who would not be allowed to institute posthumous heirs because under Roman law a woman by herself could not establish the legitimacy of her offspring. If such a "female hermaphrodite" died intestate, the law would not automatically define "her" heirs. Another question: Could a hermaphrodite witness the opening of a will, which in Rome was considered a "virile office"? Yes, the texts tell us, but depending on "the appearance of his genital organs when in an excited state."[3] Ambiguity was thus deliberately excluded from the law's response. The hermaphrodite was not a third gender. "One must decide that he belongs to the sex that dominates in him"—male or female.[4]

Because sexual division was so fundamental, jurists also felt obliged to consider the case in which both sexes were present in equal measure. Even then the hermaphrodite had to be classified as either male or female. This was a purely legal question; nature offered no grounds for decision. But Roman law considered the issue, as did canon law when it took up the question of what physical "abnormalities" might prevent a man from taking Holy Orders, given that masculinity was a crucial requirement.[5] By contrast, because ancient physicians did not feel obliged to classify human beings as either male or female, they were able to conceive of the *uterque sexus,* a veritable mixture of genders whose sexual nature was ultimately undecidable.[6] In religious tradition the phenomenon of hermaphroditism was treated as a freak of nature. The annals often mention the expulsion of hermaphrodites, many of whom were drowned in the Tiber.[7] Thus there was no difficulty at all in imagining the absurd case of a creature equally endowed with male and female traits; only the law could insist on the need for a definite either/or decision.

The Conjunction of the Sexes

Roman law thus treated sexual division as a juridical matter. It was not a natural fact but an obligatory norm. Until this crucial fact is recognized, it is impossible to understand the peculiarities of the legal status of women in Rome. That status cannot be explained solely by the structure of Roman society, nor can it be linked, as so many historians have tried to do, exclusively to the social and economic evolution of the Roman state. It was, rather, intimately associated with sexual difference and complementarity as an organizational norm. The question then is not so much the legal condition of women as the legal function ascribed to both sexes. The structure with which we are dealing could be reproduced indefinitely, because its perpetuation was ensured by the law of kinship responsible for the reproduction of society itself. It was this law that instituted men and women as fathers and mothers (in accordance with procedures about which I shall have more to say later on). With each new generation what was repeated was not life itself but the legal organization of life.

Society's foundational act could be represented only in terms of the model by which society legally perpetuated itself. Everything began, and would continue, through "the union of man and woman," *coniunctio* (or *coniugum* or *congressio*) *maris et feminae*.[8] Sexual division was inherent in the original foundation of society, as was legitimate union between the sexes. Therein lies the crux of the misunderstanding that divides jurists from historians and sociologists. The latter relegate the notion of social foundations to the sphere of ideology or mythology, where its importance is purely symbolic. But if one looks at the actual operation of the judicial apparatus, it is clear that invoking the founding norms of the society has a purpose: to renew, in a formal sense, the moment of inception as part of an ongoing process of reproduction.

The conjunction of the sexes fits into this context at two complementary levels: that of origins and that of the natural progress of institutions. Much as their ancestors had done with myths, Romans of the classical period frequently alluded to the inception of the social bond, but for the purpose of making solemn declarations, formulating laws, and establishing "the union of man and woman" as a fundamental human institution. Cicero traced all social development back to the primordial conjunction of the sexes. Out of this union came generations of offspring. Subsequently the first divisions appeared in the lineages descended from the original couple. The range of social bonds was then expanded in ever-widening circles through marriage, citizenship, and nationality. Similarly, the agronomist Columella, drawing on a Latin adaptation of Xenophon's *Economics*, linked the first sexual encounter to the destiny of the human race. For jurists of the Empire, a whole series of institutions stemmed from the existence of sexual relations between men and women. In that first union civil law joined natural law. Ulpian's *Institutes* (third century), later echoed by Justinian's *Institutes,* pointed out that "the union of male and female that we jurists call marriage" was a consequence of the existence of living species. When, also in the third century, the jurist Modestin attempted to define marriage, he began by subordinating all particular marriages to the general notion of *"coninunctio maris et feminae"* and based the legality of marriage on the legitimacy of the original encounter between the sexes, which each new marriage reproduced in the present.[9]

Although sexual relations were at the root of the first marriage, once a marriage was constituted, sex ceased to be essential. Physical consummation had no bearing on the legal status of a couple. This abstraction, this assumption of consummation, had various consequences for both men and women, as we shall see later on. For now it is enough to note that marriage had the same effect as physical relations because the legal system immediately transformed sexuality into statutory norms. Male and female roles were abstractly defined in a system that allowed no room for biological anomaly. Facts and actions of a physical nature were simply assumed without need for proof as the law substituted its own version of what nature required.

The Status of Men and Women

The juridical nature of the married man and woman was fully realized in the titles father and mother, or, more precisely, in the appellations *paterfamilias* for the man and *materfamilias* or *matrona* for the woman—appellations that pointed to a whole series of statutory requirements. These legal terms were largely independent of the actual condition of fatherhood or motherhood. Childless men and women were in some circumstances referred to as *pater* or *mater*. Conversely, not all legitimate fathers enjoyed the legal status of paterfamilias. But a woman could not be a materfamilias unless she was in a position to bear her husband legitimate offspring. Thus there were certain parallels as well as certain asymmetries between the two sexes. One parallel was the possibility of fictitious parenthood: citizens designated paterfamilias or materfamilias were not necessarily parents. But while not all men with legitimate progeny were legally invested with the paternal office, all women who bore their husbands sons or daughters were legally recognized as "mothers." The title carried with it honor, dignity, and even majesty appropriate to the civic, if not political, virtue of the function.[10]

Now if, as I am assuming throughout, the legal status of women cannot be understood without reference to relations between the sexes, it is important to pay close attention to similarities and differences between the paternal and maternal states. And, to begin with, it is important to analyze the institution of marriage. A wife without children was still a mother—a social fiction. Conversely, any mother of legitimate children was entitled to be called materfamilias—a social fact (to be contrasted with the fact that a man with children by his wife was not automatically considered a paterfamilias). Why did the notion of maternity (legally limited to motherhood within marriage) mix fact and fiction in this way? A woman derived her title from her physical nature, while a man possessed a right that had nothing to do with his being a progenitor: what was the legal significance of this difference? What does this disparity tell us about the functional division that Roman law established between the sexes? Finally, was the juridical status of Roman women—and perhaps of women in countries dominated by the traditions of Roman and canon law—shaped largely by the role attributed to women in the law of kinship?

The legal status of women was defined by a series of complex and changing rules, and we must be careful not to assume that this body of rules was internally consistent. The most distinctive subset of these rules, or at any rate the one to which legal historians have paid the most attention, pertained to the incapacities of women and appears to have been quite incoherent. Later we will discover a unifying principle: women were legally incapacitated not in their own right but only when it came to representing others. The sphere of a woman's legal action scarcely extended beyond her own person. In order to make sense of this analysis, I must show how it relates to the primordial division of the sexes with which we began. It is a truism to say that as social practice changed and as the law evolved, the modalities of sexual division were reshaped and adapted to the needs of a changing society. But from a jurist's point of view, a history that concentrates exclusively on change misses what is essential: the underlying structures. These remain the same, while the surface changes that have interested historians are merely ways of accommodating unchanging structures to changing times. What remains is the institution that establishes similarities and differences between men and women. The regime of incapacities, itself in evolution, is merely a symptom.

Inequality, legal and political inferiorities, and emancipation are all common themes in the historical study of Roman women.[11] The disparity between men and women is taken as a distinctive feature of Roman society. Looked at in this way, the incapacities of Roman women are merely an institutional reflection of the inferior position of women in a male-dominated society. P. Gide, whose work is still widely considered authoritative, argued that the subordinate position of women resulted from a social division by which women were confined to domestic activities while male citizens enjoyed a monopoly of public and political life. Indeed, the association of citizenship with maleness was considered tautological.[12] In the Greek as well as the Roman world, cities were "men's clubs," as Pierre Vidal-Naquet once put it.[13] Yet it is worth asking exactly what citizenship did mean in Rome. Citizenship could be transmitted through the male line to legitimate offspring, but it could also be transmitted outside marriage through mistresses and concubines. Bastards could become citizens. In this case, the law of motherhood was perfectly autonomous, while the law of fatherhood was not autonomous at all. Thus the old adage that "marriage is to women what war is to men" could be true in the realm of social representations yet false in the realm of institutional realities. Strictly speaking, marriage was indispensable only to men, and it was exclusively for them that the city instituted it. But let us leave that question aside for the moment. The point is that making inequality and exclusion the criteria for understanding male-female relations in the ancient world not only excludes women from public life but at the same time excludes sexual division from the realm of politics and law. But Nicole Loraux's work on the autochthonous religion of Athens shows how deeply the Greeks thought about the origins of sexual differentiation and how hard they tried to overcome it in their myths.[14]

Sexual division in Rome was a legal construct, not a fact of nature. It is therefore difficult to explain woman's legal inferiority without examining how sexual division affected Rome's central legal institution: the law of kinship and inheritance. Generally speaking, the legal status of males and females cannot be explained simply by saying that certain polities and societies were more favorable to sexual equality, others less favorable. It is misleading to treat equality as a measurable parameter and to write the history of women as a series of advances and retreats on this front. Equality itself needs to be historicized.[15] Statutes define a legal architecture within which differences are constructed, and it is with this construction of differences that history needs to be concerned. This narrowing of the question alters the object of investigation. No longer is the aim to understand the exclusion of women from an alien world. Nor is it even to explain their slow and partial integration into a man's world (one is reminded of those occasions when Latin translators remark that a certain "word of the masculine gender can be used in speaking of both sexes").[16] The problem is to explain how the law shaped relations between men and women and to show how statutes concerning women illustrate their complementary role in a system defined by the rights of men.

Women, the Family, and the Power of Transmission

Paternal Power and Continuous Succession

Let us begin with men, since the status of women can only be defined relative to that of men. Immediately we come upon a strange and paradoxical fact: the paterfamilias, or father of a family, did not owe this appellation to the fact of his having fathered legitimate offspring. It was possible to have children without being a "father." Conversely, it was possible to be awarded the title paterfamilias without either engendering or adopting a child. Not only in legal terminology but also in common forms of address the term paterfamilias was reserved solely for male citizens no longer subject to the paternal authority of any ancestor in the male line. The person so called occupied the summit of a line of ascendance. His father might have died, or he might have been emancipated by his father or grandfather, thereby severing all legal bonds of paternal authority. In turn the man found himself in a position to exercise paternal authority over his descendants, if any. Under Roman law the event that made a man a pater was not the birth of a child but the death of his own pater. At that moment the son ceased to be a son and came into possession not only of his inheritance but, at the same time, of authority over his offspring. The system was seamless: no hiatus was allowed. For the baton to be passed, the legal bond must not have been broken by emancipation, for example, or adoption or enslavement of the father or son—in short, by a removal of the successor from the deceased father's legally defined sphere of authority prior to and indeed up to the very moment of death.[17]

Women were strictly excluded from this order of succession. Of course daughters were subject to their father's authority just as sons were, so they were entitled to participate in probate. The principle of successoral equality was set forth in the Law of the Twelve Tables (450 B.C.), and there is no evidence from imperial legal practice to suggest that it was ever questioned. By contrast, children were generally excluded from their mother's succession (except in special circumstances which I shall discuss later). This was because the only bond between mother and children was natural, not legal. Maternal ties were recognized in Rome. The debate on this issue is pointless, because only an ill-informed historian would deny that this was the case. Nor is there any ground for comparison with agnatic kinship (kinship through the male line), which supposedly was predominant only in archaic times (although there is no irrefutable proof of this). The problem is that sociological history pays too little attention to the regulation of society by law. The question here is not one of kinship or even filiation but rather of an artifice of the law of inheritance that concealed these facts. Without paternal authority there could be no inheritance. The institution of paternal law supplanted kinship and filiation to such a degree that it either subsumed them entirely or allowed them to persist outside the law and devoid of juridical content (as, for example, after an adoption, which created a bond of authority that supplanted the prior bond of "natural" filiation and negated any associated patrimonial claim). In Roman civil law the succession from fathers to sons and daughters was not strictly subject to either an agnatic principle or a principle of filiation. Succession also required the legal cloak of paternal authority, which took the place of a blood tie between ascendants and descendants.

The case of children born after their father's death, which for theoretical reasons aroused passionate interest in legal scholars, was settled in the same spirit by a series of artifices that extended the power of the deceased into his pregnant wife's very womb. I have commented elsewhere on the highly original argument according to which, of all the food that a pregnant woman consumed for herself and her "womb," that which was destined exclusively for the still unborn child was deemed to come exclusively from the patrimony of the deceased father.[18] This legal fiction is an extraordinary example of the rigor with which Roman law conceived of male succession: it was regulated by power, by the continuous legal presence of a father under whose legal authority a person had to be at the moment of inheritance, even if that authority had to be artificially prolonged in the extreme case of posthumous paternity. There is no more telling expression of the Roman concept of succession than the legal definition of what constitutes a posthumous heir as formulated by Gaius: "Children born posthumously *who, had they been born during their father's lifetime, would have found themselves under his authority,* are legitimate heirs."[19]

In order to perceive the role ascribed to women under Roman civil law, we must first understand the nature of maternal filiation, and to do that we must contrast it to its male counterpart. The paternal authority of which women were deprived was not merely "power" in the patriarchal sense. There is in any case no point denouncing an archaic institution about which historians and sociologists are skeptical. Paternal authority was not about the exercise of real power as much as it was a reflection of an artificial, ideal, abstract institution—male filiation—which was in many ways the opposite of the natural bond of female filiation. Male filiation had legal value because it involved a new form of interpersonal bond, which the law called "authority." If for some reason that bond was broken, sons and daughters were eliminated from succession. Under this system the legitimate heirs were not the deceased's descendants of the first degree but the descendants who, at the moment of death, remained subject to his authority. As shorthand for this situation, the Romans coined the phrase *heres suus* (proper heir), which dates from archaic times and was still in use in the Justinian Code: it referred to the heir "under the authority of the deceased."[20] Toward the end of the republican period, when the urban praetor expanded eligibility for inheritance to include emancipated children of the *liberi* class, it was necessary to accredit the fiction that these new heirs, now joined with the proper heirs *(sui),* "were also ostensibly under the power of their father at the time of his death."[21] In other words, when praetorian law expanded the traditional order of civil successions, it was felt that some sort of justification was necessary, so a fiction was invented, an imaginary *potestas* that was supposed to continue beyond emancipation, because the system could not function without it.

.This legal procedure had nothing to do with the social situation, although efforts were soon made to identify the two. The institutions just described make sense in relation to other institutions, and in particular to the institution of maternal succession, whose concept was antithetical. It would be a methodological error, however, to compare the two until we understand the legal structure of which both were a part. Consider the *patria potestas,* which is at the heart of the legal division of the sexes. There is absolutely no point in looking at, say, such demographic data as can be derived from funerary inscriptions in order to determine what proportion of male and female citizens remained under their father's authority as adults. Suppose this proportion were as low as one-fourth. It still does not follow, as R. P. Saller maintains, that the institution of *patria potestas* had virtually no importance in the classical imperial period and was merely a formal survival from the much earlier period in which it was conceived.[22] For one would then have to assume that men lived longer in the archaic period, an assumption that not even the most imaginative historians are willing to make. The argument is absurd, hence the real problem lies elsewhere. An institution is never the reflection of a social practice, and its importance cannot be gauged by the ease with which it confirms or disconfirms the facts. So long as one believes that "paternal authority" refers exclusively to a concrete form of power, one will misjudge its importance wherever it can be shown that such power was not exercised.[23] But once one becomes aware of the fictional mechanisms that regulate all social life and begins to look for the way in which certain legal distinctions worked, the effectiveness of paternal authority becomes clear. It manifests itself not where sociologists have looked for and sometimes found it, in the form of patriarchal authoritarianism,[24] but in the regulation of succession among legitimate descendants. Authority was a "legal bond" (as a celebrated jurisconsult once called it) that supplanted the natural bond of kinship, a natural bond that was enough to establish maternity but not paternity. This legal bond was established not upon the birth of a child but upon the occurrence of a legally defined event. Events other than death could rupture it. Finally, that legal bond was enough to establish a legitimate succession, which could perpetuate itself by way of the patrimony.

Why was the system so complex? Clearly, kinship alone was

not the whole story. The reader may find it odd that so much attention is devoted to men's rights in a chapter on the history of women. But there is no other way to arrive at a sure understanding of intransmissibility in the female line that goes beyond the usual assertion that women suffered from statutory inferiority under Roman law. Even worse are the misleading conclusions drawn from the assumption that agnatic kinship was the only legally recognized form.[25] It is essential to understand why transmission in the male branch required continuity of power at the moment of inheritance. The absence of this same power might then be the key to understanding woman's status.

Understanding the legal artifices that allowed descendants in the male line to inherit is essential to explain why Roman mothers were excluded from the line of succession. From archaic times to the end of Roman legal history, marked by the Justinian compilations, women had no "proper" heirs. The principal reason for this was that the mother-child relation did not form part of the institutional apparatus of any "power."

It is true that the Roman law of sucession recognized only agnatic descendants, and this might suggest that the exclusion of heirs in the maternal line was a correlate of the kinship system. According to the Law of the Twelve Tables (450 B.C.), on which the whole system of intestate inheritance rested, only descendants in the male line (sons and daughters of the father, grandsons and granddaughters of the father's sons, and so on) stood in the principal line of inheritance.[26] Furthermore, the secondary line of inheritance consisted of collateral kin on the paternal side, those whom the law designated "agnates."[27] Within the class of descendants, males and females enjoyed equal rights. In the class of collateral kin the situation changed over time (beginning perhaps with the adoption of a new law, possibly the Lex Voconia of 169 B.C.), and ultimately the "agnatic circle" of women eligible to inherit was limited to consanguine sisters: a brother's daughters, paternal aunts, and patrilateral cousins were excluded.[28] Although Roman successoral law treated women as equal to men (daughters equal to sons, sisters to brothers), it excluded all kin in the maternal line. Children did not succeed their mothers; nephews did not succeed their mother's brothers or sisters; cousins did not succeed their mother's brothers' or sisters' children.

Insofar as the law of inheritance was concerned, the kinship system apparently attached no importance to maternal filiation.

But considerations of kinship alone cannot account for the system. A legal superstructure had to be erected on the kinship system, to some degree hiding its true nature. The "proper" heirs *(sui)* were not the same as the agnatic kin. They were also, indeed primarily, descendants under paternal authority. Sons with whom this legal bond was broken lost their status as heirs. But was this because all kinship with them was abolished? Certainly not, because they continued to be "natural" kin of their father, as the phrase went. When the law failed, nature served. Natural kinship served as the permanent substrate of a filiation deprived of its juridical cloak. A father was called "natural" if he emancipated his children or had them adopted and thus placed under another man's authority. Relinquishing the authority on which the whole system of succession depended did not, however, end all kinship. In areas such as joint responsibility, the obligation to nurture, and religious obligation the continuing natural filiation continued to be recognized by law.[29]

Mothers Lack Patria Potestas

Thus the kinship system as such was distinct from the mechanism of succession. The lack of a legal superstructure on the maternal side comparable to that which existed on the paternal side helps to explain why the maternal line was excluded. Too little attention has been paid to the fact that legal texts that attempt to justify this exclusion do not confine themselves to comments on kinship. No text states that children are not legitimate heirs of their mother solely because she is cognatic rather than agnatic kin. By contrast, the jurists stress that a mother lacked *patria potestas*.[30] Innumerable consequences resulted from this fact. Women could not, for example, choose an heir by adoption: "Women cannot adopt in any sense, since not even their descendants are under their authority."[31] Most important of all, the mother, unlike the father, had no proper heirs, children under her authority at the time of death and called upon to carry on after her, as they might have been inclined to do had the law joined them to her and treated children and mother as a single legal unit before and after death. Paul tells us that when an heir took possession of his father's estate, there was such perfect continuity that it was possible to confound death with life. In contrast, Gaius tells us that when a son took possession of his mother's property because she had included him in her will, the result was rupture and discontinuity. The son was not a *suus* but, as if he were a rank outsider, an "external" legatee. Hence he had the right to accept or refuse the inheritance after due deliberation: "Such of our descendants as may be instituted heirs by our will are considered 'external' legatees if they are not under our authority. Thus children whom their mother institutes as heirs belong to the category of external legatees, since women do not have their children under their authority."[32]

The system of intestate inheritance depended on regulations that ran against the grain of kinship. At a time when women still married under the so-called *manus* system, which subjected them to their husband's authority, they entered their husband's household as daughters *(filiae loco)* and became heirs along with other proper heirs under the husband's authority. The law could then treat mothers as consanguine sisters of their own children on the grounds that all fell within the jurisdiction and under the *potestas* of the same family head. Through this legal artifice children were allowed to inherit from their mother, not because she was their mother but because she was regarded as their agnatic kin.[33] This example shows how agnatic kinship could be reduced to nothing more than a bond stemming from having lived under a common authority. On examination this turns out to be the case with virtually all agnatic kin eligible to inherit: brothers and sisters were subject to the father's authority; uncles, paternal aunts, and nephews were subject to the authority of the father's father. The grandfather may not have lived long enough to exercise actual authority over two generations, but the mere possibility was enough to unite the group. A similar argument can be made in the case of patrilateral cousins. Taken as a whole, the agnatic successoral order was a juridical construct based on unity and continuity of power.[34]

The importance I have ascribed to institutional structure is confirmed by the extensive consideration in the *Digest* of cases involving the *heres suus* and ruptures of continuity. No descendant conceived after the death of a forebear was entitled to inherit from that forebear's estate. So much was clear. But what if the generation intervening between descendant and forebear had vanished or moved from one juridical sphere to another, so that the descendant had never been subject to the *potestas* of the deceased even at the time of conception? Such a descendant was neither heir nor even kin. "According to ordinary usage," Julianus wrote in the time of Hadrian, "grandchildren are kin of their grandfather even if conceived after his death, but this is an improper use of the term, an abuse of language."[35] In this jurisconsult's view no kinship existed with a grandfather unless a legal relationship existed, either *potestas* or, in the case of posthumous children, the fiction that stood in its stead. Legal symbiosis took absolute precedence over blood ties. The principle of legal continuity, of an unbroken link between one *potestas* and another, was reformulated to resolve a difficult case.

This continuity of power was precisely what the mother lacked, which is why she was excluded from the successoral line. A mother had no abstract authority that could be perpetuated through her estate and progeny in an invariant legal form. Maternal filiation was not subsumed in the abstract notion of a legal prerogative endowed with a life of its own and establishing regulations governing every aspect of the mother-child relationship. When a father's death put an end to his authority, his daughters became legally autonomous along with their brothers. Unlike the brothers, however, the female offspring were not invested with the transmissible power that was conveyed to the males and passed on from generation to generation. This was the crucial difference between the sexes under Roman law. Ulpian summed it up in a forceful aphorism: "A woman is the beginning and the end of her own family." Deprived of authority over others, she had nothing to transmit.[36] Kinship and lineage had nothing to do with the question.

The system was not justified by any custom of unilateral kinship, as kinship nomenclature makes clear. Further evidence is provided by the rules of incest: prohibitions on marriage applied equally to both sides. The prohibition on parricide applied to both parents, although a popular etymology *(patricida)* tended to suggest that it focused on the father, and various sources indicate that there was resistance to "abusive" attempts to apply the law to the murder of a mother.[37] But other sources state the law applied to murder of a *parens,* a word that could mean either father or mother, and mother-killers were subjected to the same punishment as father-killers, a form of execution presumably intended to ward off supernatural retribution: they were sewn into a sack and thrown into the Tiber.[38] Similarly, both men and women were subject to the obligation to provide nourishment to their progenitors.[39] Furthermore, with regard to obligations sanctioned by law, the reverence that one was expected to show both parents excluded taking them to court[40] or, more generally, committing any impious act against them.[41] Legal solidarities, as set forth in rules concerning sworn testimony and obligations to bring charges or defend against an accusation, applied to all kin of a given degree without hierarchy between the male and female branches.[42] Social practices, at least insofar as we are aware of them through sources dating from the late republican period, tend in the same direction. Take, for example, genealogical customs. When a Roman aristocrat enumerated his ancestors, he did not as a general rule give precedence to either the paternal or maternal line. In fact, if the maternal line was more illustrious, he might even list those ancestors first. Masks of forebears of both sexes in both lines were hung on the atrium wall. At funerals deceased kin on both sides were amply represented in the cortege that followed the body of the newly defunct: grandmothers and grandfathers, aunts and uncles, maternal as well as paternal.[43]

Kin on the mother's side were at no practical disadvantage, nor were they neglected in social and legal norms. But in Rome the function of bequeathing, insofar as it abolished discontinuities and gave rise to permanence, was a source of power. In speaking of male succession, one jurisconsult, Paul, spoke of a "continuation of dominion," that is, of the imperious force that a man enjoyed over his dependents once he ceased to be himself dependent on someone else. In a sense the order of life was transcended, legally speaking, by the order of power. This static perpetuation originated in a state of affairs of which nothing remained but the name, but it became current again whenever a foreigner was made a citizen of Rome. The law, or the emperor, granted citizenship not only to the man but also to his wife and children. With the man's citizenship came the right to exercise power over the family. The continuity of masculine rights was thus assured from the beginning.[44] Accordingly, it is correct to say that women could not transmit in one sense and one sense only: they were "the beginning and end of their own family." Women were deprived of institutional extensions of their singular personhood.

Women's Wills

Outside the realm of lawful successions, the bipolarity of Roman kinship allowed individuals considerable latitude in the expression of emotion and assumption of obligations toward kin. Wills were concrete manifestations of the importance of the maternal bond and of ties to maternal kin. Philippe Moreau has published an enlightening series of papers on the notables of Larinum in Umbria in the years 70–60 B.C., and S. Dixon has studied maternal bonds in Cicero's family. The fortune of Cicero's wife, Terentia, was apparently to be used to secure her children's future rather than returned to her agnates.[45] Women had property to transmit, because they inherited their father's property, in principle equally with their male co-heirs. They could also be named beneficiaries in wills, although the Lex Voconia of 169 B.C. prohibited citizens belonging to the first tax classification from naming a woman heir. In Cicero's time, however, this law was virtually unenforced and could be circumvented simply by ordering a male heir to pay a fraction of his inheritance to a woman.[46] Daughters and widows thus received property, which then became available for their children. Another source of wealth for women was the dowry, which was constituted in their behalf by fathers, relatives, and family friends and which normally went to the wife upon dissolution of the marriage. The dowry consisted of protected property, inalienable property, cash, clothing, slaves, lands, and buildings; in the upper classes it could amount to a considerable fortune. Sixty talents in gold was not enough for the heirs of Paulus Emilius to restore his widow's dowry, for example, while Terentia brought her husband a dowry of 400,000 sesterces, an amount equivalent to the wealth criterion for the equestrian, or highest, class. Cicero found himself in insuperable financial difficulties when forced to pay his daughter's dowry in three annual installments (and we know that the sum of 60,000 sesterces amounted to only a fraction of each payment). The burden was so onerous that when Tullia, pregnant and her dowry fully paid, decided in 46 B.C. to divorce, Cicero regretted bitterly that she had not made up her mind a year earlier, when the third payment was due on her dowry.[47]

Successions, wills, legacies, dowries: women of the wealthier classes had valuable possessions to pass on when they died. This is not the place to consider how, through the use of their wealth, women often were able to thwart the mechanisms of masculine power, which had its counterpart in women's incapacities. Let us begin by asking whether legacies from mothers to children did in fact, as some have argued, represent a shift from an agnatic to an undifferentiated system of kinship (because such legacies came at the expense of agnatic kin, especially the paternal collaterals).

S. Dixon's work on Roman mothers and J. A. Crook's on the legacies of Roman women leave the reader with the impression that Roman views of kinship changed profoundly in the late republican period. Wills gave cognates (not only maternal kin but also paternal kin with whom the legal bond of *potestas* had been broken, such as emancipated brothers and sisters) a place equal to those who had been the sole legitimate heirs under archaic law: the *sui,* or proper heirs still under paternal authority, and the paternal collaterals. New legal relations between previously excluded kin allegedly grew out of the ruins of the ancient law.[48] The praetorian edict ultimately granted cognates possession of their nearest relative's property, so that children, for example, assumed possession of their mother's estate under a procedure that complemented the system of legitimate succession. A new right of intestate succession, based on the jurisdictional power of magistrates, developed out of rights derived from ancient law. Can these changes be interpreted as signs of a closer bond between mothers and children?

When this new praetorian successoral right was first instituted toward the end of the republican period, it did not end the uncontested primacy of civil successoral vocations. When the praetor introduced "assignment in possession," the technical term for the authorization of a mother's children and kin to take possession of her estate, his purpose was not to establish equality between the maternal and paternal lines: cognates could inherit only in the absence of *sui* and agnates, who still took precedence. The new order of succession remained a secondary procedure, a recourse to be taken in the absence of other possibilities. Under the old system, property for which there was no "near" heir (probably down to the seventh degree) fell to the *gens,* or clan. Under the new system, this property could be claimed by the nearest cognate. The *gens,* which can be seen still pressing its claims as late as the first century A.D., was supplanted by the closest maternal kin. The *gens* was shut out in favor of closer kin owing to the intimate bonds that had always existed between potential heirs, their mother, and their mother's kin. Traditionally ignored by the law because unsupported by any form of power, these bonds ultimately gained a subsidiary place, after all other possibilities had been exhausted, in the earlier system, which continued in force.[49] Indeed the praetorian right had so little effect on that system that, according to the edict, children succeeded their mother not as "legitimate children" *(liberi)* but only as ordinary kin *(cognati).*[50]

Under the new order, which complemented but did not replace the old, the *liberi* were children emancipated by their father and therefore eliminated from the class of *sui*. The praetor's edict reestablished their claim to the estate as if they had not been excluded from the sphere of paternal power into which they had entered at birth. This was done by adopting the fiction that these children had never ceased to be *in potestate*.[51] This solution could not be adopted with respect to the children of a woman, however. There was no way to describe them as former *sui* who, after leaving the domain of paternal power, had their right to inherit restored: "No women can possess proper heirs [*sui*], or cease to possess such heirs by reason of emancipation or otherwise."[52] In their case it was impossible to restore via a fiction a right that had never existed. That is why the mother's children were not legally considered her descendants and simply included along with other cognates in last place in the order of succession.

It is misleading to argue that agnate ties were loosened and cognate ones tightened, and it is even more misleading to suggest that the old successoral law, based on the exercise of *potestas,* was somehow superseded. Of course there is no denying that maternal filiation was ultimately recognized by the laws of inheritance. In itself, however, this means very little. The significance of the change cannot be understood without first grasping the way in which this recognition was shaped by the absence of feminine "power." Only then can the increased importance of the maternal bond be seen in its proper light despite sociological prejudices that have caused scholars to mistake the central issue: the durable contrast between the regimes governing men and women, the inevitability of juridical signs of their dissimilarity.

Did the practice of making wills overcome the formal differentiation between masculine and feminine? There is no doubt that the making of wills gave new substance to the maternal bond. In this respect will-making can be regarded as one of many practices implicit in the kinship system. But does greater generosity toward a woman's offspring justify the contention that the law had progressed toward more equal treatment of the sexes? The answer is a tentative yes. But it must not be forgotten that Roman kinship was bilateral long before the first century B.C., the date of the sources from which we learn of will-making practices. Furthermore, the elimination of maternal successors (which the praetorian edict remedied only in part) meant that women were deprived not of heirs, whom they were permitted to designate in their wills, but of successors who would continue in their place uninterruptedly and by the operation of law.

What characterized the male hereditary system was the instantaneous nature of succession in the male line, and this was possible because of the continuity of power. When a woman in her will designated a son or daughter as her heir, she could not completely make up for her legal incapacity to bequeath what she had received and produced. Her choice had to be approved by her guardian and accepted by her heirs. Between the time of her death and the time her heirs assumed possession of her estate, there was a necessary waiting period, about which nothing could be done. It was precisely this discontinuity that differentiated a woman's legacy (whether by will or praetorian right) from the instantaneous succession of the male.[53]

Parity of Maternal and Paternal Wills

That certain ways of honoring the emotional and social ties to the mother should have been deemed necessary, that the transfer of property from mother to son by the mother's will should have come to be seen as the child's due, is different from the problem just considered. From first-century B.C. sources we know that these things happened, but did they represent a change in attitudes? Profound transformations are always tempting to imagine. But we know almost nothing about how women used wills in earlier periods, from the time they were first granted the right to make wills, probably around the fourth century B.C. The question does not arise for daughters under paternal authority, who, along with their brothers, enjoyed no patrimonial rights, nor for women under the authority of a husband, her property being mingled with his. Unmarried heiresses remained wards of their closest agnate (a brother or paternal uncle). Obviously these guardians would never have authorized their wards to dispose of their share of the family fortune.

There were some women who had broken ties with their agnates and who no longer had husbands: widows, who left the agnatic circle when they went to live under the husband's authority (legally becoming the spouse's "daughter") and who, on his death, became mistresses of a patrimony and free to make a will with the assistance of the guardian whom the late husband had chosen for her or whom the woman had been allowed by a provision in his will to choose for herself. True freedom to make a will belonged to the widow, and therefore to the mother. Did they favor their children or their agnates? If we had adequate sources from a time prior to Cicero, it might be possible to speak of a significant evolution, but unfortunately no such sources exist. In Cicero, Pliny the Younger, certain inscriptions from the imperial era, and above all in the many cases recorded in the *Digest* we see women making wills in favor of their children and grandchildren and sometimes in favor of their husbands, which shows that these women were not married under the *manus* regime (the authority of the husband). In short, women were most likely to choose heirs in the conjugal family and its progeny.[54] Lacking documents for the second, third, and fourth centuries B.C., however, we cannot say anything about what occurred earlier. For us history begins in the first century.

These attitudes and practices depended on a strict accountability of *officia,* or social duties. The jurists we read, most of whom lived after the second century A.D., expressly emphasized the equality of rights and duties. Sons and daughters could bring suit to have a will declared "inoperative" if they were unjustly excluded. It was held that such a finding required a serious breach, in which case the sanction was deemed appropriate. Fathers' wills were of course the first to come under scrutiny in this regard, fathers having always enjoyed the right to disinherit their children. "But [the right to bring suit for unjust exclusion] is accorded similarly to men and women who are not descendants in the male line. People may also challenge their mother's will, often successfully."[55]

This parity is attested at least since the time of Augustus, who himself invalidated the will of a woman who, after giving birth to two children, remarried in her old age and designated her second husband as sole heir. Toward the end of Domitian's reign, Pliny the Younger, along with other senators and equestrians, was named co-legatee in the will of a noble matron who chose to leave nothing to her son. The son, believing himself the victim of an injustice, begged Pliny to give him his share as a sign of the iniquity of his mother's will. The upshot was this astonishing scene: Pliny, the principal heir, formed a council of friends to look into what good and bad reasons the mother might have had for disinheriting the woman's son in favor of himself. The council agreed to hear the arguments of the son, whose exclusion benefited his judge; the son agreed in advance to accept his rival's judgment: "It is our view, Curianus, that your mother had just motives for her wrath against you."[56] There can be no doubt that society considered the loss of a mother's legacy a serious punishment, one that had to be weighed carefully. Conversely, a son had to have particularly severe grievances to omit his mother from his will, as is clear from a case that arose around A.D. 70, when Cluentius, a prominent citizen of Larinum, halted the drafting of his will because he could neither bring himself to mention his mother, who detested him, nor insult her by not including her, an action that might have been misunderstood by public opinion. Most likely Cluentius had calculated the risk that his will might be ruled invalid if his mother survived him.[57] In such case the court probably would have sought to establish "whether the mother, by dishonest actions or improper maneuvers, had attempted to entrap her son, or whether she had not concealed hostile acts behind manifestations of friendship, or whether she had not behaved as an enemy rather than a mother." This language, taken from a law of Constantine (321), could have been applied verbatim to the case of Sassia, Cluentius' mother, three and a half centuries earlier.[58]

There is no need to multiply examples. Suits to invalidate maternal wills are attested in legal documents from the second, third, and fourth centuries.[59] When it came to transmitting property to one's children, the duties of motherhood were so close to those of fatherhood that in A.D. 197 Septimius Severus awarded a share of a mother's estate to a child whose mother had died giving birth to him. She had failed to include the child in her will before the delivery, so that the unforeseeable "maternal fate" had unjustly disadvantaged the last-born relative to his two brothers, who had previously been named heirs. This case was related to that of the posthumous child whose father had failed either to name it as heir or disinherit it prior to his death. To be sure, a mother had no "proper" heirs, and for her the birth of a child was not subject to compulsory operations of the law that took precedence over her will. Yet even if imperial justice did not go so far as to nullify her will altogether, it did see fit to repair her negligence by restoring the share of her last-born child, "as if all the sons had been named heirs."[60]

Dissymmetry and Disinheritance

Did the conditions of men and women become more equal, and did the legal regimes governing their behavior tend to converge? In appearance, yes. But the subject warrants a closer look. A mother did not have to disinherit her children explicitly, because they were not legal continuations of her person. She was not required to indicate that she was eliminating them from a succession to which they would have been legally entitled had she not expressed her will to the contrary. All she had to do was omit their names from her will. From the sources we learn that sons who attacked the validity of their mother's will complained of having been "neglected" or "forgotten."[61] By contrast, a father could exclude his sons from succession, to which they were called by law, only by explicitly stating in a "disinheritance clause" that he did not wish them to be his heirs. In other words, "proper" heirs, heirs under the father's authority, had to be expressly excluded by an explicit declaration in the future imperative: "Titius, my son, shall be disinherited." Absent explicit disinheritance, omission of a son was *ipso jure* grounds for nullifying a father's will and reestablishing the regime of intestate succession. The external heir lost everything, and if the excluded son was still under the father's authority at the time of his death he succeeded to the entire estate. In the case of a daughter, the will was not nullified, but the excluded heiress was allowed to share the estate with the named heirs: half and half with external heirs and according to her share with proper heirs, which is to say with her own brothers.[62] In practice, therefore, a mother's silence about a son or daughter was equivalent to a father's explicit exclusion. In a society where bonds to both parents were equally affirmed, the mother's negligence was deemed the equivalent of the father's denial. Magistrates were as apt to grant judgments to children neglected by their mothers as to children disinherited by their fathers when the exclusion was adjudged to have been unwarranted. The history of law, however, allows us to delve below the surface. If one is willing to attend to subtleties that differentiate apparently similar attitudes, divisions not evident from the observation of behavior alone begin to appear. Fundamental differences emerge between types of behavior that might appear similar except for the fact that their institutional significance was diametrically opposed. Institutionally the mother's act of omission signified precisely the opposite of the father's formal act of exclusion. A woman had only to allow the law to act to exclude her children, whereas a man who wished to disinherit a child had to arrest the operation of law deliberately. Masculine continuity was fundamental and could be halted only by an express legal act: either emancipation or disinheritance. On the female side, however, discontinuity was the fundamental fact. An explicit decision was required to bridge the gap. Thus all signs point to a fundamental dissymmetry in the status of males and females: it was in the legal nature of the male to bequeath to his children, but it was not in the legal nature of the female.

Legitimate Maternal Succession in the Second Century A.D.

The praetorian edict only slightly altered this dissimilarity between men and women by making cognates subsidiary successors. Can the same be said of the senatus-consults "Tertullian" and "Orphitian," the former issued at the behest of Hadrian and the latter under Marcus Aurelius in 178? In these decrees the last vestige of gender difference would seem to have been eliminated. A true equality would seem to have been established between paternal and maternal succession. But appearances, as we shall see, are deceiving. Do these changes in the law prove that motherhood was gaining in authority in the second century? Masiello, for example, has shown that between the Antonines and the Severi it became common for women to be recognized in wills as guardians of their sons and daughters, whereas traditionally guardianship had been considered to be a "virile office" to be discharged by a male relative, even a distant one, rather than by the mother. It was not until 390 that a law of Theodosius validated this custom.[63] Nevertheless, the new successoral law put in place in the second century seemed to recognize customs that had been formed much earlier, customs associated, as we have seen, with true bilateral kinship. If, as some scholars believe, the Roman family was conjugal and nuclear, it may be that wealth acquired in the space of one generation was to be concentrated and passed on to the offspring of husband and wife. It is better, however, to sidestep the question of the nuclear family, epigraphic evidence for which is to be treated with caution. It is reckless to assume, as some historians do, that funerary epigraphs offer an accurate image of the family. There is no necessary connection between the conventional sentiments represented on tombs and actual social units.[64] The fact that one paid respects to and mourned for one's spouse, children, and parents but almost never one's sisters or brothers is not a reliable indicator of the extent of family groups. Tombs in today's cemeteries often refer to extended families, although we know by experience that the family unit in today's society is strictly conjugal and nuclear. Funerary epigraphs tell us something about the social conventions surrounding death, but we must not ask them for what they cannot reveal. Nevertheless, the hypothesis that the Roman family was nuclear cannot be dismissed out of hand, nor can the possibility that the law consecrated the patrimonial ties that developed among close relatives, principally parents and children. Let us consider the two great reforms of the second century.

Senatus-Consult Tertullian

The senatus-consult Tertullian granted to mothers of three children (four in the case of a freed woman) a claim on the estate of children who predeceased them. Counterclaims were held by the proper heirs of a male child and by the father of a male or female child, because in successions by forebears the father always took precedence over the mother. Among collaterals, however, only the deceased's consanguine brothers and sisters shared in the division with their common mother: other agnatic collaterals—uncles, nephews, cousins—were definitely excluded. Thus for the first time mothers were favored over agnates (or at any rate over relatively remote agnates) as the result of a law.[65] If one were forced to cite one document in support of the restricted-family hypothesis, this would be the one.

Senatus-Consult Orphitian

The senatus-consult Orphitian of 178 established a legitimate succession not from sons to mothers (a measure clearly designed to provide an incentive for free and freed women to have children) but from mothers to sons. With this law the successoral order in a woman's offspring was recognized and accorded the same legal status as the successoral order in a man's offspring. Ulpian's Rules, a fourth-century compilation that borrowed the name of the great

Severian jurist, clearly summed up the scope of the change in the legal system: "The Law of the Twelve Tables did not permit children of a mother who died intestate to succeed her, because women have no proper heirs. But later, through a law of Emperors Antoninus and Commodius presented to the Senate, it was decided that children should receive legitimate successions from their mothers even if the mother was not married under the *manus* regime [that is, even if the mother was not under the same paternal authority as her children, whereas under the earliest Roman law, if the mother had been under such authority, her children would have succeeded her, and she them, as consanguine brothers and sisters]. The mother's consanguine brothers and sisters and all agnates are eliminated from succession in favor of the deceased's children."[66]

A Mother's Heir Is Not Necessarily a "Descendant"

What was thus instituted for the first time, as other texts confirm, was indeed a *successio legitima:* a succession initiated by law, which went *ipso jure* to a woman's offspring without requiring her, as under the previous praetorian system, to resort to the fiction of an assignment of possession.[67] But when, in order to facilitate the procedure, possession was nevertheless claimed by this new class of legitimate heirs, the praetor did not always grant it on the grounds of the clause in the edict that covered the father's *liberi*—his offspring, whether emancipated or not. The descendants of the mother received their property in the next class, that of the *legitimi*.[68] This was the class traditionally reserved for the paternal collaterals (and possibly those paternal offspring who, after allowing the deadline for claiming the inheritance as *unde liberi,* legitimate offspring, to pass, settled for the position of second-degree candidates for succession). In other words, the status of the mother's children was lower than that of the father's children, even though according to the law of 178 they were the mother's primary heirs. Why this asymmetry? Why did magistrates continue to treat the mother's children under a different clause of the edict from the father's children when both now took precedence over all other heirs in their parent's succession? The longevity of certain juridical structures is astonishing. Apparently not even the law had the power to abolish them, even when its language was changed to give official and compulsory force to long-established customs.

Behind even the most significant social transformations (and regardless of whether what was actually occurring here was the restriction of the family to husband, wife, and children with concentration of the patrimony in the children's hands or, as I am more inclined to believe, an extension of concubinage encouraged by legitimation of patrimonial and successoral bonds between mothers and their children), a solid construct, identifiable from its formal signs, remained untouched. This was no useless superstructure maintained by conservatism but a manifestation of the society's deepest and most vital strata.

The New Laws and the Lack of Maternal "Authority"

The crucial question is: What prevented the praetor, after promulgation of the new law, from treating the children of women and the progeny of men as belonging to the same class? It was certainly not because their respective claims on their father's or mother's estate continued to be unequal: the reform of 178 was radical. In the absence of any will the children now took precedence over the agnatic collaterals and mother's forebears, just as the *liberi* had from the very first enjoyed absolute priority in their father's succession. There is no obvious practical reason for their having been placed in the second order of *legitimi*, since in such a case the first order of *liberi* was necessarily empty. This downgrading—or rather this incomplete upgrading, from the third rank of cognates in which they had been included previously to the second rank of *legitimi* but not all the way to the first rank of *liberi*, or free descendants—changed nothing about the fact that for them the second order had become the first. This second order was second not in relation to other heirs of the mother, over whom they now took priority, but *in relation to themselves insofar as they were also their father's heirs*. On the father's side they still came first, as *liberi*, just as they had always done. On their mother's side they also came first, but in the second order of *legitimi*. The reason for this strange disparity is given in Ulpian's Rules: "Women have no proper heirs." This principle is by now familiar. But whereas before the senatus-consult Orphitian the rule explained the fact that children could succeed their mother only as testamentary heirs or cognates of the third rank, after 178 (and through the fourth century) the rule explains that the same heir, *suus* of the father and therefore inscribed, even if emancipated, in the praetorian class of descendants, could not always be classified relative to his mother even though he had become her primary heir in the same category of descendants.

In order to understand such dissimilarity, the analysis must look beyond the transfer of property that was the ultimate consequence of every succession. At this level the difference almost ceased to have meaning. Must we regard the congenital legal incapacity of women to extend their existence through proper heirs as the fossil remains of an archaic system with no function in the present? By that token the power of men over their descendants should also have been a vestige; yet we have seen that, in the successoral order at any rate, it was not. The real question is what place should be ascribed to an institution seemingly devoid of practical consequences. We saw this earlier in connection with paternal authority. In order to understand its long-term significance, we found that the right method was not to look for some archaic period in which some have argued, although it is hard to see on what grounds, that the significance of the institution was obvious, after which that significance was allegedly lost, even though it is clear that the institution continued to function better than ever. Instead we had to refocus our attention away from domestic and patriarchal organization to the less obvious realm of masculine transmission of rights. Similarly, the fact that in the senatus-consult Orphitian it proved difficult to treat a mother's sons on a footing of equality with a father's sons suggests that we should focus attention not on the recognition of bilateral equality but on another dimension entirely, one apparently far removed from the realm of realist interpretation: the intrinsic incapacity of women to subsume ties of descent in ties of power. Instead of seeing the transformation of successoral law as a sign of changes in patrimonial solidarities, we emphasize the continuity in the way in which Romans organized gender division. Behind the emergence of a new institution (legitimate succession from mothers to sons) we see continuity in the way the law accommodated sexual difference to social needs—a continuity achieved at the price of certain formal distortions.

Legitimate as maternal succession became, it did not operate spontaneously. Before as well as after the new law, sons and daughters remained external heirs of the mother and had to indicate their willingness to accept her bequest. This was a necessary legal consequence of the mother's lack of authority over her family and was clearly stated in the senatus-consult: "If they wish the legacy to go to them."[69] Like all nonproper heirs, the children had to indicate their formal acceptance of the bequest. They were allowed a certain period of time to make up their minds, and if they did not accept prior to the expiration of this period, the mother's agnatic collaterals regained all their previous claims on the inheritance. In one recorded case a son refused his mother's bequest and her property went to her brother's son.[70]

A Woman's Posthumous Child

Jurists meanwhile sought to draw all the logical corollaries of the new situation in which women found themselves vis-à-vis men, namely, that of having legitimate, legally designated heirs of their own in the person of their children. How close did this change in the law bring the status of women to the status of men? What new bond existed between mother and child that could explain the convergence in status despite the fundamental dissymmetry between the sexes? Without defining that bond, as in the male case, in terms of power, could a legal basis be found for the new status of women? This, in my view, was the purpose of jurists who reflected, in a purely academic and hypothetical manner, on the case of a child born posthumously to a woman.

Consider the following, reported by Ulpian: "Suppose that a pregnant woman dies and that after her death her womb is cut open and the child removed. This child is legally eligible to claim the mother's praetorian succession as her closest cognate [which would place him after his mother's agnates]. Since the senatus-consult Orphitian, however, he is also eligible to claim the inheritance as a member of the class of legitimate heirs. Indeed, he was in his mother's womb at the time of her death."[71] In other words, a child delivered from the body of a dead woman was henceforth to be considered a legitimate heir, just as a child engendered by a dead man had always been considered his posthumous heir. That this parallel was drawn is confirmed by another passage in Ulpian concerning inofficious wills. Just as a posthumous child could challenge the will of a father who disinherited him, "provided that [the child] was already in the womb at the time of [the father's] death," so "the child extracted by Caesarian section from its mother's womb after she had drawn up her will could challenge that will."[72] Earlier, in the imperial constitution of 197, we encountered a similar tendency for the law to draw a parallel between the case of the child born to a dead man and that of a child whose mother died in childbirth. But in this case the mother has died prior to her son's birth. This hypothetical case, just barely within the limits of possibility, was once again a device for jurists not so much to resolve concrete problems as to draw clear lines so that in legal terms even the most improbable of events would have no ambiguity.

Once the law had created a legitimate succession for mothers that was in a sense symmetrical with that for fathers, it was tempting for jurists to consider the possibility of a posthumous child's being born to a mother. But children born posthumously to fathers were relatively common, and consideration of this case led to the idea of a fictive paternal authority that persisted throughout the time the child was in the womb. Posthumous children of mothers were rare and could mean only one thing: that every child had a mother, even if that mother died before the child was born, since it was from a woman's body that the child was extracted. The corpse was the mother's corpse, and the child was therefore its mother's heir. Posthumous fatherhood was associated with the legal definition of the period of conception and with the continuity of paternal authority that was the very basis of succession. What could posthumous motherhood—a freak of nature—mean unless the genetic bond was complemented by an autonomous legal bond. The senatus-consult Orphitian treated all of a woman's first-degree descendants as her legitimate heirs.[73] However, it was not the son who was legitimate but rather what the law made the son—an heir. There is a surprising conjunction between the legality of the succession and the illegitimacy of the filiation: *hereditas legitima* was recognized in bastards born to unmarried women as well as in legitimate offspring.[74]

Bastards and Heirs

"Children born indiscriminately [*vulgo quaesiti,* meaning children born out of wedlock] are not prevented from claiming their mother's legitimate succession, because by the same law under which their mothers could succeed them [the senatus-consult Tertullian] they could succeed their mothers." The *Pauli Sententiae* (early fourth century) sums up what we already know from earlier cases.[75] Julian, a contemporary of Hadrian, already held that a mother could succeed her children whether born in or out of wedlock. To enjoy this right a freeborn woman had only to have given birth to three children, and a freed woman born a slave had to have given birth to four. The only requirement was that the children had to have been born to a free mother. A slave freed while pregnant gave birth to citizens, upon whose succession the senatus-consult legitimated her.[76] The dispositions of 178 were based on the same legal nondifferentiation of motherhood as the measures adopted under Hadrian: "Children *vulgo quaesiti* are eligible along with other children to claim their mother's legitimate succession," according to Ulpian.[77] Nor did it matter whether the mother was freeborn or emancipated. Conception might take place while the woman was still a slave, provided she was free when the child was delivered. And this remained true even if emancipation was delayed because the person who inherited a slave through a will that instructed that that slave be liberated enjoyed a certain grace period before the slave actually had to be freed.[78]

In the second century the law did not distinguish between legitimate maternity and natural maternity. The same rights were accorded to mother and child regardless of whether conception took place within wedlock or not. This remained the case in the fourth and fifth centuries. No change is attested before the constitution of Justinian (529), which declared that among children born to a woman of "illustrious" rank, legitimate offspring were to be preferred to those conceived outside marriage, "because respect for chastity is a duty that falls particularly on freeborn women of illustrious rank, and it is an insult to our reign to allow bastards to be designated."[79] When a woman had legitimate offspring, this text was used to justify depriving her illegitimate children of any claim on her estate. It could be invoked, however, only if a woman had produced both legitimate and illegitimate progeny. One type of filiation was preferred over another. Even if this distinction was limited to the superior orders, it marked a considerable innovation relative to traditional Roman law and helps us understand what was singular in that law.

Children born outside wedlock were associated with no one but the mother. Even more important, there was no legal bond between children and mother, because no distinction was made between children conceived with a legitimate husband and children conceived with anyone else: the mother was purely and simply the mother. Her son was not characterized as an *iustus filius,* "son according to law," because this characterization made sense only in relation to the father.[80] A son conceived by, or presumed to have been conceived by, a man with his legitimate spouse was called *iustus*. There was no reason to characterize the mother as *iusta* because her identity as mother was determined not by the legal event of her marriage but solely by the birth of a child. By contrast, she was necessarily *certa:* for this the fact of her having given birth sufficed. The only legal appellation that one could require of a mother was that she be *mater civilis,* "mother of a citizen."[81] This expression had a precise meaning in the context in which it has come down to us. It meant that the right to succeed to the estate of a Roman woman was accorded only to those of her children who were, like her, citizens of Rome. Any children who had lost their citizenship were excluded from inheritance.[82] In a similar spirit Julian wrote that a Roman woman could not inherit from her children if, in the interim, they had become slaves and then been emancipated, because a free woman and citizen was assumed not to have sons and daughters who were slaves. The degradation in the children's status meant that she "ceased to be their mother."[83] Thus *mater civilis* meant mother of a citizen (male or female). Women's "legitimate successions" were awarded within the framework of civic law. One had to be a citizen to enjoy the benefits of the law. Being a "civil" mother thus did not define the bond of motherhood, whereas being a *iustus filius* signified that the bond of paternity derived from a lawful marriage.

Was this a second-century innovation? Were the rights of mothers and of children without mothers not recognized before the successoral reforms of Hadrian and Marcus Aurelius? And was it unnecessary to indicate the legal circumstances of conception, as was required after Justinian? Certainly not. A law promulgated under Augustus already freed women who had given birth to three children from the stewardship of their agnates, regardless of whether or not they were married. It was simply stated that they had to have "given birth three times," without further elaboration.[84] Similarly, a senatus-consult granted Roman citizenship to women of Latin status who had "given birth three times." This measure probably complemented the Augustan-era law that granted citizenship to Latin men who produced at least one child in a marriage with a Roman woman, provided that child had reached the age of one year.[85] When it came to legal benefits awarded for paternity or maternity, there was a clear contrast between the insistence on a *iustus filius* for men versus mere childbearing for women. This contrast is further heightened by the manuscript of the Rules of Ulpian, which, in discussing this senatus-consult, clearly states that it was enough for a woman to have "given birth to three bastards," an interpretation that was emended, oddly and in my view incorrectly, by the editors of the text when for no reason they replaced *"vulgo quaesito[s] ter enixa"* by *"mulier quae sit ter enixa"* (that is, a woman who "has given birth three times to bastards" by a woman who "has given birth three times").[86]

These legal texts were probably the inspiration of a clause in one will that granted freedom to a female slave, "on condition that she give birth to three children."[87] Thus in both public and private law childbearing conferred freedom and citizenship; it freed women from stewardship; and it established lines of succession between the mother and her offspring and vice versa. As far back in time as one can look this was the only law of maternity. When succession between mothers and sons was still governed by the praetorian edict in terms of cognation, no distinction was made between the *vulgo quaesiti* and other children. Claims on the estate by "the children *vulgo quaesiti* of the mother, the mother of these children, as well as by brothers among themselves" were recognized "because of the blood tie" or "because of proximity."[88] The need for legitimacy or marriage to establish such rights is never mentioned. There was no such thing as a mother by adoption or by conception in legal marriage or by any other legal institution.[89] The only thing that made a mother a mother was the actual bearing of children.

Legitimate Conception and Indeterminate Birth

We know from numerous sources that at the moment of delivery the newborn took on its mother's status: slave, peregrine, or Roman.[90] But this acquisition of maternal status at birth clashed with another principle, according to which the child conceived in wedlock "follows its father" *(patrem sequitur)*. In other words, the child's legal status at birth was that of its father at the moment of conception.[91] These two principles—"follow the mother" and "follow the father"—were incompatible: a person could be born free or a citizen in keeping with the father's or the mother's status but not with both. So we are faced with two antithetical sets of bonds.

Marriage conferred paternal status, while illegitimate birth conferred maternal status. Status was acquired either from a progenitor designated by law (presumed to be the mother's husband) or from a womb impregnated by an unknown individual *(vulgo)*. Hence the phrase "illegitimate birth" must be rectified: illegitimacy was a term that could properly be applied only to the act of engendering, which was an act of the man alone. A woman received *(concipit)* semen either from her legitimate husband or from an unknown male whom the law refused to recognize *(pater incertus)*.[92] The law characterized as legitimate or illegitimate the moment when the woman was impregnated by the man *(legitime, illegitime concipi)*. It characterized as legal or illegal the conjunction of the sexes, *coniunctio maris et feminae,* that is, the carnal union from which, it bears repeating, marriage took its generic name: "legitimate coitus" *(iustus coitus, legitima coniunctio)*.[93] Birth itself was not subject to these legal determinations. All the texts say that a child was "born" or "emerged from" the body of a woman whether or not she was legitimately or illegitimately impregnated. The mother caused the child to emerge from her body, brought it into the world *(edere)*, "procured" it (such was the original meaning of *pario,* the word for giving birth). This moment was never characterized in law. The only event with which the law concerned itself was the one that took place seven or ten months earlier, depending on the method of calculating the "legal time" *(justum tempus, legitimum tempus)*—an event in which the man played the leading role.[94]

As Bachofen to his credit understood, one of these two facts was immediately ascertainable, while the other had to be reconstructed.[95] Roman law is unique, however, in that it erected on this fundamental difference a set of institutions in which the contrast between the legal nature of men and women—a contrast made manifest by the difference in the nature of the event that attached every citizen to either one or the other—was incorporated into a system of filiation and succession in which the paternal bond was construed abstractly, the maternal bond concretely.

The Transmission of Status

The Materfamilias, *Wife of the* Paterfamilias

In the Roman legal system motherhood was never instituted or determined by law. By contrast, the title *materfamilias,* correlative of *paterfamilias,* depended entirely on marriage. Ancient formularies tell us in no uncertain terms that materfamilias meant the wife of a fully capable Roman citizen. When a Roman adopted a son before an assembly of curiae presided over by the grand pontiff and under the adoption law ratified by the comitia, he uttered a formula that embodied the fiction according to which the new son was as legitimate "as if he had been born to this paterfamilias and his materfamilias."[96] Similarly, in archaic marriage by simulated purchase, the man asked the woman "if she wished to be his materfamilias," that is, his wife.[97] To be sure, a husband was also a "father" to his wife, but there was no symmetry between the two appellations, because it was in an entirely different sense that the woman asked her future spouse, "And do you wish to be my paterfamilias?" In doing so she meant that the man who, in this form of marriage assumed authority over her, would become, legally speaking, like a "father" to her: head of the family, master of the household, and the power to which she and her children would be subject. A gloss by Servius confirms that when a woman addressed a man in this way, she meant that she would enter his household as a daughter and that her husband would "stand in her father's place."[98] "Father" thus characterized the status of the man possessing full legal capacity, whereas "mother" was applied to the wife subject to his authority. Attested by grammarians, jurists, and antiquarians, this was the specialized sense of the word in the archaic period, when the woman took a formal oath of obedience to her spouse's authority, symbolized by his hand. Later, in the lexicon of the imperial jurists, materfamilias meant simply "wife," a married woman without reference to this particular marriage convention. Nevertheless, a woman's matronal status in theory always depended on marriage.[99]

This term for wife and mother is of more than mere sociological significance: it meant that in Rome men looked at women essentially as mothers. In this respect Rome was no different from other ancient societies, or, for that matter, from nearly all societies prior to the emancipation of women in the modern industrial world. What is worthy of attention, however, is a fact of an institutional order that was unique to Rome: that the event by virtue of which a woman acquired the socially recognized status of materfamilias was not childbirth but marriage. Benveniste was careful to note the singularity of the Latin word for marriage, *matrimonium,* unique in that it signifies the "legal condition of *mater*": marriage was the state of motherhood for which a young woman was destined when she was given away by her father, accepted by her husband, and engaged by her own pledge.[100] But this maternal destiny was more than a function that women in virtue of their state were required to perform. It is not enough to say that women married in order to become mothers, although it is true that, according to the legal formula, men took wives "in order to obtain children" and that, from the third century B.C. on, one of the leading causes of repudiation of marriage was the sterility or infertility of the wife. What needs to be emphasized is that the law, in forging the term *materfamilias* for the legitimate wife, was construing maternity as a status achieved solely through marriage to a *paterfamilias*. The institutional nomenclature denaturalized maternity and subsumed it, ideally and fictively, in the status of wife of an adult citizen. Rigorously examined, this definition assumes that it was through marriage that the civic function of pubescent women was to be discharged: to supply citizens with a posterity by giving children to their husbands. That is why, as certain texts point out, the term materfamilias was applied to wives who had not yet given birth. The same was true of the *matrona*, who was distinguished from the materfamilias only in that she was not subjected by marriage to her husband's authority but retained her prior legal status. She too bore a name derived from *mater* even though her status derived solely from the dignity conferred on her by marriage and "even if children were not yet born."[101]

True, a different tradition does link the titles *matrona* and *materfamilias* to childbirth. A woman who had given birth to one child had the right to be called matrona, while one who had given birth to several children had the right to be called materfamilias.[102] But apart from the fact that this tradition was reported only to be challenged, it has against it all the archaic formulas mentioned previously as well as the common usage of matrona to mean either legitimate wife or, in certain contexts, "respectable woman," that is, a woman who, being neither an actress nor a prostitute nor a servant in a tavern or an inn was entitled to protection of her *dignitas* and to the honor of being made a wife.[103]

Thus "father" and "mother" were related legal terms in that, according to the most ancient law, only the wife of a *pater* could be a mother. They were also disparate terms, because the event by which a woman became a mother was quite different from the event by which a man became a father. In both there was room for a certain fiction. A childless man was a "father" if he had no male forebears, while a childless woman was a "mother" if she had a husband. An ineradicable difference thus arises: fiction played a far smaller role in defining the *materfamilias* than in defining the *paterfamilias*. By bearing children a woman placed in the household of a citizen became the mother that the title *materfamilias* anticipated and formalized, whereas a *paterfamilias* existed only as the direct heir of his male forebear. Thus the paternal function was accomplished in a purely successoral order, a logic of transmission initiated by death.

Unconsummated Marriage and the Presumption of Paternity

This new dissymmetry in the degree of fiction involved in the titles "father" and "mother" reveals a singular feature of Roman marriage. Although the purpose of marriage was overtly procreative and the legal term for marriage was derived from copulation, a marriage existed legally in Rome even without consummation. Sexual congress was not an essential element of marriage, failing which it could be annulled, as would later be the case in canon law. As Ulpian stated and many other jurists confirmed, "it is not sleeping together but consent that makes the marriage."[104] Certain contemporary jurists interpreted this as a sign of the purely consensual nature of Roman marriage (an interpretation that amounts to a tautology), but this was far from true. Rather, the rule of consent reflected the different status of husband and wife. Although consummation had no bearing on the existence of the marriage, this was not because the bride's virginity was valued and protected by law and still less because the couple's chastity was recognized, as it would be by Christian preachers from the third century on, as a means of achieving perfection within marriage. Behind the indifference of Roman law to physical realization of the *"coniunctio maris et feminae"* was indifference of another sort, related to the legal structure of kinship. Under the Roman system it was of little importance whether or not a father was the actual progenitor of the children born to his legitimate wife. It made little difference even if he was physically incapable of procreation.

Let us return to the legal nature of the conjugal tie, which Roman jurists defined in an entirely abstract manner, without reference to the body. Jurisprudence (even very early pontifical jurisprudence, as Tafaro has shown) took great care to establish criteria of puberty to be met by the male *pubes* and the female *viripotens* (literally, a woman "capable of supporting a man").[105] For boys the age of puberty was set at fifteen. According to some schools, the boy's maturity had to be confirmed by physical examination. It had to be shown on the basis of the *habitus corporis* that the young man was capable of engendering. Girls, on the other hand, were considered nubile at age thirteen without physical examination. Their capacity was judged on the basis of "legal age" *(legitima aetas),* to use an expression of the republican jurisconsult Servius; no facts could refute it. Reliable juridical sources show that prenuptial examinations of young women were prohibited. (In 529 Justinian would extend this prohibition to young men.) Further evidence can be found in the medical texts studied by Aline Rousselle.[106] This requirement of sexual maturity is a sign that the purpose of Roman marriage, notwithstanding the absence of insistence on sexual consummation, was procreation. In one way or another men and women were certified able to perform this task. This was a requirement of the institution, but the Romans did not go so far as to insist on actual performance.

The casuistic literature illustrates the principle that a marriage was complete even without physical consummation. A woman was required to wear mourning for a man whom she had married in absentia and never seen. In another case, in which D. Dala rightly sees a parallel with the former, a woman was permitted to sue for restitution of her dowry even though she still had not lost her virginity when the marriage was dissolved. The marriage was perfectly valid, and useful title to the property constituting the dowry had been transferred to the husband. As late as 475, moreover, a constitution attributed to Zeno advanced the Roman principle that unconsummated marriage is legally complete. In the case at issue, the Byzantine emperor had rejected the Egyptian custom of levirate (the requirement that the brother of a man who died childless must marry his widow) on the grounds of a taboo against marriage between affines, despite the fact that the dead brother's widow was a virgin, because, as the text of the law explains: "It is an error to believe that marriage is not truly contracted when husband and wife have not encountered in the flesh."[107]

Some jurists even speculated about marriages that could not be consummated because the husband was impotent. Such marriages remained valid, and any children the wife might bring into the world were considered legitimate children of the husband. There was a good deal of discussion of the paternity of the *spado,* which meant both eunuch and impotent. A eunuch had the right to marry and adopt. Like the hermaphrodite in whom the virile organs predominated, he was allowed to institute a posthumous heir. Children born to his wife would be legally ascribed to him.[108] As one can verify by reading the texts, Roman law coldly envisaged the procedure whereby Lady Chatterley's husband procured himself the heir he was incapable of engendering himself. The presumption of paternity in favor of the husband ensured that any man who married a fertile woman could enjoy the fruits of fatherhood.

The Abstraction of the Paternal Bond

In principle, and despite testamentary practices and reforms instituted by the praetorian edict and the law, a woman's legal personhood did not survive her. A woman's descendants, unlike a man's, did not prolong her existence *post mortem.* In the system of masculine transmission each male was a link in a chain, and the continuous process, which I described earlier as a union of contiguous authorities, transcended the individuality of any particular male. Power moved along a conveyor-belt. Each man designated a "proper" heir, one still under his authority, to assume the same power and patrimony that he had assumed from his predecessor. Thus Roman law carried the abstraction of the paternal bond to considerable lengths. Already abstract in principle and by virtue of its origin, the paternal bond was even more abstract by virtue of its duration. Its essence was fully realized only in and through death, when the son acceded to the status of paternity while at the same time acquiring legal autonomy and control of the patrimony. The presumption of conception founded a relationship within which an artificial truth wholly supplanted a natural truth: the institutional truth of paternal authority transcended the presumed truth of engenderment.

Hence the extent of paternal authority was never determined once and for all. A legitimately conceived child of course took its father's status at birth, including citizenship, but relations between father and son were not determined solely by the origin of the bond between them. Paternal authority was free to pursue its risky and tenuous destiny, subject as it was to being ended by *capitis deminutio* in one of its many degrees. If either father or son became a slave, the bond was dissolved, as it was also by loss of citizenship or by transference of the son to the authority of another man by adoption or to his own authority by emancipation. In this way the abstraction of the paternal bond was confirmed by derivative institutions: an idealization (of the son's presumed genetic origin); a sublimation (of a natural bond into a form of power that originated in and was renewed by death); and an autonomous legal regime (during the course of which the paternal bond could be perpetuated or ended).

"Follow the Mother"

By contrast, when the texts say that the child "follows its mother" because illegitimate conception gave the child the status of the woman who brought it into the world, we must understand that childbirth was more than just an event with these as its consequences. The birth stood for a lifetime of legal identification. Although circumstances might change the status of the mother or the child, nothing could change the nature of a bond that, because it did not enjoy the backing of law, could not be artificially extended or ended. The mother's legal biography could affect the child's status only *in utero*. Thus a slave freed while pregnant gave birth to a free child and citizen (assuming that she was freed by a Roman citizen). Conversely, a free woman who became a slave while pregnant necessarily gave birth to a slave child.[109] This rule was so firmly established and so clearly formulated in its principle ("children conceived out of wedlock take their status on the day of their birth") that it took a special writ from Hadrian to grant free status to the children of a woman sentenced to death. Execution of pregnant women was delayed until after they had given birth, but a death sentence automatically resulted in degradation to slave status; hence the child in the condemned prisoner's womb should have been born a slave. The imperial order countermanding this legal requirement shows more eloquently than any other document the strictness of the rule to which it created an exception.[110]

The full consequences of this rule have not always been recognized, probably because of changes that were made in the fourth century and consecrated by Justinian. Children born to a woman who conceived while in free or freed status but who fell into slavery during the course of her pregnancy were henceforth to be free.[111]

This *favor libertatis* relaxed the strict rule that status was determined not by conception but by birth, until ultimately it was accepted that a child conceived in a free womb would be born free regardless of the circumstances. This new view of the matter surely developed after the period in which the rule was still vigorously formulated, as it was in the second and third centuries. In a similar spirit we find discussion of the case in which a slave woman is freed while pregnant but subsequently finds herself once again reduced to slavery: ultimately it was decided that the child should enjoy freedom as a result of the intermediate time *(medium tempus)* spent in a free womb.[112]

Throughout the classical period, however, the rule was that the status of a child without a legitimate father was tightly bound to the body of the mother. Thus jurists once again focused considerable attention on borderline cases, cases in which the moment of birth had to be scrupulously observed because the birth itself affected the mother's status which in turn determined the child's. Consider the case of Arescusa, who, according to her master's will, was to be freed if she brought three children into the world. What would happen if she gave birth to two sets of twins? Which of the second set of twins would be born to a freed mother and therefore be free? Or suppose she gave birth first to one child, then to triplets: Which of the triplets would be free? According to the jurists, the exact sequence of births would have to be examined to determine which was the third child, whose birth would have set the mother free, and which was the fourth, which would then be free by virtue of having been born to a free mother. "Nature does not allow two children to emerge from their mother's body at the same time. It is impossible for the order of birth to be so ambiguous as to preclude a clear designation of one child as the third, born in servitude, the other as the fourth, born in freedom. The moment the [penultimate] delivery begins, the condition of the will is satisfied, so that the last child emerges from the body of a free woman."[113] Thus the question of status is a question of fact: What was the mother's status at the time of delivery?

The only events that matter are those that occur *in utero*, during which time the child is identified with its mother—"part of her viscera," according to Ulpian. At birth the child became an autonomous subject and kept only his or her mother's legal status; mother and child ceased to be treated as one. Subsequently, however, there was no legal bond between them. In law the relation between them was only one of fact; it was not affected by subsequent changes in the status of either party. According to one text, since a woman had no proper heirs, that is, heirs under her authority, she was never in a position to lose them through *capitis deminutio*.[114] Not even the relations between a woman and the "legitimate heirs" she enjoyed as a result of the senatus-consult Orphitian were affected by changes in her or their status, except for loss of civic rights, which deprived them of the benefits of Roman law but without severing a bond that subsisted outside the law.[115] The mother or her children could individually gain or lose legal autonomy or pass from one sphere of authority to another. These changes took place relative to a *pater*, not between mother and children, whose bond was extralegal. A decision reported by Ulpian went so far as to acknowledge that persons subject to capital punishment, who lost all status, were nevertheless entitled to succeed their mother if their citizenship was restored by pardon. The temporary loss of citizenship was not even taken into account since the natural tie to the mother was independent of any institutional structure.[116]

The status of the mother was identified with the status of the child only at the moment of birth, the moment of contact between lives wherein the one proceeded from the other. In this way, in the final contact between two bodies at the moment of separation, freedom and citizenship were transmitted from mother to child. From that point mother and child were independent, and the status of one could vary without affecting the status of the other. No legal mortar (except perhaps that of the common head of household in ancient times) held them together artificially. No legal artifice transformed mother and child into an indissociable unit, one that, through yet another artifice, persisted beyond the grave.

Citizenship and Birth

Parental bonds and modes of succession were complementary. Bachofen correctly perceived the nature of the opposition that Roman law established between the maternal and paternal bond: the former was physical or, as Bachofen called it, natural (based on birth); the other immaterial and abstract (based on conception). But in keeping with the evolutionist mode that dominated the institutional history of his day, Bachofen interpreted the antithesis between these two principles as the result of a transition from one to the other, as the imprint left upon the law when the paternal principle supplanted the maternal one.[117] In reality, it was within the same legal system, and not by gradual development, that the paternal principle was superimposed on the maternal one: in marriage the mother determines the paternity of the husband. We are not dealing with two successive legal systems with a perfectly consistent code spelling out the relation between the sexes. The principles underlying this code can be seen not only in the origins of paternal and maternal bonds (respectively spiritual and material) but elsewhere as well, as in the laws governing the duration of parental bonds. In this respect, successoral law is the most fully elaborated monument to the sexual order that the Romans had worked to establish since the archaic period, or at any rate since the Law of the Twelve Tables, which tells us of the necessary relation the Romans saw between masculinity, power, and continuous succession. This order was also political, since it governed the transmission of citizenship.

In the imperial period Roman citizenship was conveyed via a form of municipal citizenship to which jurists attached the technical name *origo*, origin. This system was probably instituted in the first few decades of the first century B.C. when the Italic cities and communities were integrated. From then on anyone who was born a citizen of a city included in the "common fatherland" was born a Roman. Offspring of a legitimate marriage followed the *origo* of their father; those born out of wedlock followed the *origo* of their mother.[118] At first sight the system seems quite simple: citizenship was transmitted through either men or women. Its complexity begins to emerge only when one notices the different time scales associated with the two branches of civic filiation. The father's *origo* was not his birthplace but the city from which *his* father derived his *origo* and so on, continuing back in time indefinitely as far as one could go. There was no limit to this regression in time, or, if you will, to the immobilization of time by law. In the political order, therefore, successoral continuity was based in a place that was not necessarily the place of residence but the place of membership in the civic community. Citizenship was thus perpetuated in the posterity of the first citizens.[119]

How was the mother's *origo* defined? Neratius, a jurist at the time of Trajan (early second century A.D.), tells us that the mother determined the *prima origo*, or primary origin: "He who has no legal father derives his primary origin from his mother, and this origin is counted from the day he comes into the world." In practical terms this text could have meant only that the *origo* acquired by the mother took effect at delivery, and that the child acquired the citizenship its mother possessed at that moment. In characterizing this origin as "primary," the jurist wished to indicate that the child's local citizenship could not be traced back any further than its mother.[120] If we compare this with the previously cited text of Ulpian, according to which a "woman is the beginning and end of her own family," we begin to understand that feminine transmission was not truly transmission. What originates with woman is not inscribed in the flow of time; it represents an absolute beginning.

The Regime of Incapacities

Was there a connection between the curtailment of women to individual personhood and the various legal incapacities to which they were subjected? These incapacities were varied, and the evolution of each was so different that it is difficult to form a clear idea of the system as a whole. In the stereotyped language of the jurists all differences between the legal status of women and that of men were justified by the natural inferiority of women: their congenital weakness, limited intellectual faculties, and ignorance of law.[121] And it was not only jurists who spoke this way. In 195 B.C. Cato the Elder delivered a speech whose intent perhaps can be understood more clearly in the version preserved by the Byzantine compiler Zonaras than from the entirely reworked version found in Livy. In it Cato praises a uniquely feminine form of wisdom, a mixture of reserve and moderation.[122] The natural subordination of women, an Aristotelian theme that may have found its Latin translation in the Catonian argument for superiority (*majestas*) of husbands over wives, was cited by Cicero as a reason for subjecting women to legal guardianship. Tacitus and the rhetors allude to the inferiority of women in their discussions of marriage. So there was nothing very original about the misogynist ideology of Roman jurists. Nor was there anything very original in the contrary ideas of someone like Gaius, who, in the age of the Antonines, said that he was not convinced that women are frivolous by nature. In his treatise on household economy Columella granted that in memory and vigilance women are men's equals.[123] Such commonplaces are of little importance for the history of institutions.

It makes more sense to try to identify the features common to all the legal incapacities of women so that we might go a little beyond the simple observation that the legal status of women was inferior to that of men. A work by J. Beaucamp is particularly valuable because of the use it makes of little-known papyrological sources. Beaucamp attempts to bring order to a subject on which scholars have too often contented themselves with didactic lists. He contrasts the incapacities of women with what he calls "protections." But is there much difference between the traditional ban that prevented Roman women from acting as proxies or representatives (an incapacity) and the law, in force from 41 to 65 A.D., that prevented them from vouching for another person or guaranteeing the debts of a third party (according to Beaucamp a "protection")?[124] Was not the protection a corollary of the incapacity? Can we not argue that both share the common feature of prohibiting women from appearing for or arguing on behalf of others? Beaucamp distinguishes three types of incapacities: public, judicial, and familial. His scheme is clear and logical. In the actual functioning of institutions, however, things were not always so clear. Was the exclusion of women from certain political and civic activities, for example, clearly distinguished from the provision in family law according to which women were not allowed to adopt male citizens or even to participate as wives in adoptions by their husbands? Without pretending to cover the whole domain of female incapacities, can we not attempt to identify a logic that was common to both public and private law? And can we not relate certain aspects of the legal status of women to the various elements that, as we have seen, entered into the law's definition of the difference between the sexes?

Lack of Authority and the Inability to Adopt

Having focused thus far on gender division in relation to the system by which wealth, power, and citizenship were transmitted, I shall begin this brief review of women's incapacities with one particular incapacity that can be taken, I believe, as a token for all the rest: Roman women were denied the right to adopt. "Women," Gaius wrote, "cannot adopt in any way, because not even their natural children are under their authority." The full import of this passage is apparent only in the light of the paragraph that precedes it, from which we learn that impotent males and eunuchs did have the legal power to adopt despite their physical inability to engender.[125] Thus the legal act of adoption was rooted directly in "authority," an authority denied to women.

An error that scholars have not always avoided is the belief that women were somehow involved in adoptions made by their husbands. Legal sources explicitly deny this. Not only do they tell us that "even unmarried men can adopt sons," but they also state that when a married man adopted a son, his wife had nothing to do with the transaction and did not become the child's mother.[126] That is why the judicial rite of adoption involved only the father and the adoptee. No woman played the role of mother, the lack of a mother being part of the very theory of adoption. True, in the archaic mode of adoption, where the ritual was held before an assembly of the people, the "adrogation formula" proposed a legal fiction in which the adoptee became the son of the adopting father *and* his wife. Lucius Valerius, for example, was to become the son of Lucius Titius, and his status was to be as legitimate as if he had been born to the latter and his *materfamilias*.[127] But this formula should be taken for what it was: a legal fiction. The adoptee was henceforth to be treated as if he had been born the son of his adoptive father, hence by implication as if he had been born the son of the father's wife. In this sense adoption "imitated nature," and for that reason there was supposed to be a sufficient difference in age between the adopting father and the adoptee that the former might indeed have engendered the latter.[128] The wife, however, is mentioned only as a presupposition of the legal fiction involved in adoption. Adoption itself required neither the wife's presence nor even her existence.

Because wives did not participate in the act of adoption, it had no effect on them. In the adoption ritual, however, there was a pretense of verifying the existence of a wife. This sham is attested only in the most ancient form of the procedure, the *adrogatio* before the comitia. It was not a part of the later "triple mancipation" of the son before the urban magistrate. Nor did it figure in the practice of testamentary adoptions, which not only excluded women but did not even allow them to be associated with their husbands in the choice of a successor to bear the family name.[129] It was not until the time of Diocletian, and then again in the sixth century, that the emperor expressly authorized a woman to choose a close relative to be treated as her own child in consolation and as replacement for a lost child of her own. Through the entire classical period, however, no exception was recorded to the principle that women may not adopt. Like the incapacity to designate "proper" heirs, the incapacity to adopt was a direct consequence of women's lack of authority.[130]

Authority and Guardianship

For similar reasons mothers were not permitted to act as guardians for their minor children. This had been so since the Law of the Twelve Tables designated as guardian of surviving minors the nearest male relative of their deceased father. Not only prepubescent children but women of all ages were subjected to the authority of the closest agnate: a brother, uncle, or cousin. The most authoritative interpreters of Roman civil law from the republican era to the third century A.D. agreed that guardianship was a *munus virile,* a male office.[131] In addition, women were not allowed to designate a guardian for their children in their wills, because such designation could be made only for proper heirs, that is, heirs under one's authority at the time of death.[132] Guardianship was a responsibility transmitted by men to other men: by those who held authority to those who would exercise it temporarily in their place over minors until they reached the age of majority and over women until they married and fell under the authority of another man.

The republican jurisconsult Servius Sulpicius defined guardianship as a kind of power, a power exercised directly on persons *in capite libero.*[133] But the guardian also joined his authority to administrative acts of the ward, thereby guaranteeing an act that would otherwise have been deemed invalid.[134] Thus guardianship meant power over persons together with authority to validate the legal acts of others, to give force to another person's will by ratifying its otherwise ineffective expression. Roman law excluded women from this office of confirmation, this faculty of giving legal force to the actions of legally incapacitated individuals. The reason for the exclusion was not that women were incapable but that their sphere of action was limited to their own person.

This limitation was the norm, the reflection of an all but invariant structure. In practice, however, there sometimes were rapid changes, as the law was adapted to meet the needs of a changing society. I want to emphasize again, however, that it would be missing the point if the historian of law were to content himself with describing these surface changes while neglecting the forms—the formal accommodations—that these changes in practice had to take in order to leave the permanent but hidden structures intact.

The fact that mothers could not serve as guardians conflicted with a Roman custom that is well attested as far back as the republican era. It was common for widows to raise their children, to oversee their upbringing and education until they reached adulthood. It was also fairly common after divorce for a woman, whether remarried or not, to receive from her first husband permission to raise their children, who often lived under the same roof as the children of the second marriage.[135] To be sure, this practice was not universal, as is shown by the fact that the first husband was entitled to retain a part of his ex-wife's dowry in proportion to the number of children he continued to raise *(retentio propter liberos)*, but it was common. Antoninus the Pious even issued an imperial writ granting a divorced mother the right to keep her children against her husband's will.[136] There was no difficulty in allowing widows to care for their minor children. A typical testamentary formula, cited by Quintus Mucius Scaevola around 100 B.C., prescribed "that [my] sons and daughters shall be raised wherever their mother wishes to bring them up."[137] Many well-known Romans were raised by their mothers: the Gracchi, Sertorius, Cato of Utica, Octavian, Claudius, and Caligula, to name a few. In every case the *custodia matrum,* as Horace called it in an epistle, complemented the proper legal administration of the official guardian designated by will or by law. Seneca is clear on this point in discussing the case of young Melitius, who lived under his mother's roof until she died. Until he reached the age of fifteen he was subject to the "guardianship" of his mother (legally speaking the term was incorrectly used) and to the "*cura* of his guardians."[138] In reality a dual administration was established, with the mother as actual guardian and the official guardians as nominal figureheads. What is striking about the large number of cases that arose from this complex system of family management is the care that jurists—and emperors—took to preserve the principle of women's incapacity to serve as and assume the responsibilities of a true guardian.

Concerning mothers' administration of their children's property, we have abundant evidence, much of it gathered long ago by

Kübler and analyzed more recently by Humbert, Masiello, and Beaucamp.[139] A mother could sell her daughter's land, decide her marriage, buy an apartment for a son, or invest the children's inheritance. But the mother's administration of the property did not suspend the responsibility of the guardian, who might insist on a guarantee, that is, a statement in which the mother agreed to assume the risks of her management. When the children reached the age of majority, moreover, they could bring suit against the guardian, and neither the mother's intervention (in the opinion of Papinian) nor the father's wishes as expressed in his will could "infringe the office." Even if the mother actually administered the property in the guardian's stead, the male guardian's obligations were not thereby nullified, and he alone was the person who could be compelled to provide a reckoning.

Heads of family often resorted to circuitous means to entrust their widows with responsibility for the property of minor heirs. One of these means was to disinherit the child in favor of its mother, who was in turn required to restore the property to the child when it reached majority.[140] The husband might even attempt to designate his wife directly as guardian in his will, though such a clause was not recognized as valid except by special favor of the emperor. We know of only one case in which the emperor granted such a request, during the reign of Trajan.[141] In the traditional law of certain provinces (such as Egypt) maternal guardians were recognized, but Roman law supplanted these alien traditions, and governors were ordered not to enforce their provisions.[142] It was not until 390, when Theodosius promulgated a new law, that the imperial chancellery began to accept women's applications for guardianship on condition that they swear never to remarry.[143] Despite ingenious means to circumvent it, an invariant structure of incapacity, related to women's lack of authority over others and above all to the narrowness of their sphere of legal action, remained intact through centuries of Roman legal history, from the archaic period until the end of the fourth century A.D.

Guardianship of Women up to the Beginning of the Empire

Nevertheless, women were not considered incapable of administering their own affairs.[144] Such, at any rate, was the opinion of the jurisconsult Gaius (second century A.D.), who argued against the traditional view that women needed guardians because of their "lightness of spirit": "It appears that no serious grounds have been advanced for maintaining adult women under guardianship. What is commonly alleged, namely, that women are usually misled by their *levitas animi* and that it is therefore more equitable for them to be governed by the authority of their tutors, appears to be more specious than true, because adult women handle their own affairs, and in some cases the tutor interposes his authority only for the sake of form. Frequently he is even forced by the magistrate to offer his guarantee against his will." Gaius goes on to say that where legal guardianship continued to exist in his day, it was justified by nothing other than the guardian's self-interest.[145]

Since the fourth decade of the first century A.D., women had been subject to guardians only if emancipated by a father or freed by a master, in which case the father or master became the guardian. For them, the advantage in this role was that as guardians they could control their wards' wills and prevent a disposition that might exclude them or damage their interests. According to Gaius, this was the reason why a woman's dependency did not end at puberty but continued throughout her life, even after her father's death: to safeguard the interests of men who were their heirs as well as guardians. In Gaius' day this system existed only for the benefit of masters who continued to control their former female slaves. The ancient guardianship that civil law since the Twelve Tables had granted to the closest agnate of a free woman was first limited by Augustus to women who had not given birth to three children; later it was abolished by Claudius. Now, when a father died, his free daughters were not subject to the control of their brothers, uncles, or cousins. If a woman was widowed (even if she had been married under the *manus* regime, which gave her husband authority over her), she was no longer subject to ratification of her acts by the agnates she acquired by marriage in place of her former relatives. She no longer required the authorization of her son (acting legally as her "brother") to make a will or constitute a dowry (that is, to remarry). And, in the absence of sons, she no longer required the authorization of her husband's brothers or other kin in the male line.[146]

The elimination of agnatic guardianship resulted in an emancipation of women. But this liberation was not so much a recognition of a new capacity that women supposedly had been denied previously owing to the imperfections of their nature as it was a weakening of the claims of family interests, which society now saw as less legitimate than in the past. Owing to changes in matrimonial law, a woman's legal center of gravity had shifted from her husband and her husband's agnates to her father and her father's agnates. During the final decades of the first century B.C., marriages with *manus* (authority of the husband or his father over the wife) declined and ultimately disappeared. Their existence is still attested two or three times by Cicero and in two cases by the *Laudatio Turiae,* an inscription from the Augustan era. But by the time of Tiberius this form of marriage had disappeared; only one *paterfamilias* needed to agree that his daughter become the wife of Jupiter's flamen, which according to tradition meant that she was placed in his "hand."[147]

This change of regime created a paradoxical situation, which leaves us with a false impression of archaism. In the most ancient law mothers of families enjoyed considerable autonomy. Because of the transfer of power that occurred at the time of marriage, these women were generally emancipated from their paternal families. If widowed, procedures were available that allowed them to gain freedom from the control of their husband's agnates. If divorced, they had the right to force the man who had held *manus* over them to grant them liberty.[148] When marriage no longer took women outside the legal sphere of their father's family, however, they found themselves trapped for life; neither widowhood nor death offered an opportunity to gain freedom from the guardianship of their family of origin. Now we can better appreciate the impact of the reforms instituted by Augustus and Claudius and, through them, the legal and social context within which the incapacities of Roman women must be interpreted.

Capacity for Oneself

When Gaius wrote his *Institutes,* the degradation in the legal condition of women had long since been repaired. First Augustus had ended all agnatic control of women, married or not, who had given birth to three children. The jurisconsults adapted their interpretation of the law to the demographic realities of the time: they did not insist that the children actually survive beyond birth. Children who died in infancy (as well as monsters, a possibility allowed for by the casuists) benefited their mothers just as much as healthy, viable children. So it was not three children but three full-term pregnancies (four for freed slaves) that liberated a woman from legal guardianship in the early Empire.[149] Then Claudius unconditionally ended agnatic guardianship for freeborn women, leaving only the authority of the patron over freed slaves who had not given birth to four children.

Most women released from paternal authority administered their own patrimony, with the exception of the dowry, which was entrusted to the husband's administration. In particular, women could make wills to dispose of their wealth without the approval of a guardian. Until Hadrian they had to resort to the formality of the fiduciary *coemptio, testamenti faciendi causa*—a survival of the time when matrons who wished to make a will first had to free themselves from the guardianship of their husband's agnates. This final archaism was eliminated at the beginning of the second century A.D.[150] From that time on the legal influence of family entourages was limited, as for men, to the power of the *paterfamilias*. Upon the death of the father a woman possessed a patrimonial capacity more or less comparable to that of her brothers.

At a time when most women were still prevented from contracting debts or selling property without the formal approval *(auctoritas)* of a guarantor *(auctor)*, however, women liberated by life's vicissitudes, left alone and free to control their own actions, ran the risk that those actions might not be accepted as fully valid. This was the case, for example, with matrons divorced under the *manus* regime; they had no guardian designated by law or will to assist them. The same was true for female slaves freed by a female patron, since women could not exercise this "virile office." To deal with these and similar situations (such as the female child without agnates and no guardian named by will), a law was promulgated in 210 B.C. empowering the urban praetor to designate a guardian. Later, under the Empire, this "dative" guardianship was systematically administered in Rome, Italy, and the provinces.[151] If necessary, any woman could be assisted by a guardian provided by the municipal authorities in her city. In practice women took the initiative in securing their own guarantors. They submitted a *petitio* with the name of the person chosen to the appropriate organ of government. The guarantor made sure that a woman's legal acts would satisfy all the formal requirements of the law.[152] It was "for form's sake" *(dicis gratia)*, Gaius wrote, that guardians were obliged to approve certain kinds of dealings. Unlike children, grown women could not bring action against the guardian. They could not claim compensation for imprudent or dishonest management that they had chosen of their own free will, because they administered their own affairs, and the guardian's role was restricted to adding formal *auctoritas* to transactions that the women themselves had full power to conclude.[153]

We know the types of transactions for which such formal ratification was deemed necessary. One was to contract an obligation—that is, to make a solemn, unilateral promise for which no quid pro quo was explicitly furnished—under the old civil law procedures. Another was the sale of property whose transfer required a formal act of mancipation (that is, land, buildings, and slaves).[154] Formal approval was not required for contracting a marriage, constituting a dowry (except in the form of a stipulated promise), making a will, entering into a contract, selling property whose transfer did not require the rite of mancipation (that is, all forms of merchandise), collecting a debt, or accepting an inheritance.[155]

Gaius was right: women handled their own affairs, *ipsae sibi negotia tractant*. The sources show that the women of the Roman Empire were perfectly conscious of their power to administer their property and to enter into legal transactions, especially those who enjoyed the "right of three children," which exempted them from the need to ask a magistrate to designate a "dative" guardian for those few transactions that still required the *auctoritas* of a third party. Women officially declared their legal capacity to the governor's staff, sometimes adding that they knew how to write, and this declaration was duly registered on the public books.[156]

This widespread legal capacity explains how so many Roman women besides those who served in aristocratic households (and who have been studied by Treggiari[157]) were able to engage in artisanal and commercial activities. There were of course specifically feminine trades, as Kampen has shown for the city of Ostia: wet nurse, midwife, actress, masseuse, weaver, seamstress, washerwoman. Few actually owned businesses, however, except possibly for the tavernkeepers who were more or less implicated in the world of prostitution. There were women merchants and even women who owned ships and ran shipping companies.[158] In addition to commercial activities, women were involved in legal actions of many kinds, as is attested by the large number of writs addressed to them. Huchthausen estimates that a quarter of all writs issued by the imperial chancellery in the second and third centuries A.D. were addressed to women. Petitions pertaining to all aspects of property management emanated from every province and apparently every segment of society.[159]

The Inability to Represent Others

Roman women were nevertheless still subject to various prohibitions. They could not adopt sons or serve as guardians because they possessed no power over other people. More generally, they were excluded from civil offices still described as "virile." In both private and public law, citizenship and masculinity were one whenever an action exceeded the limits of a single person or patrimony and affected others. This was precisely the sphere of those *officia* that women were forbidden to hold: representation, guardianship, intercession, proxy, advocacy, prosecution.

Consider advocacy in court. No party to a trial could choose a woman to represent it in court (that is, to serve as *procurator*), because the law stated that to plead the cause of another was a civil, public, and virile office.[160] A constitution of Septimius Severus is direct and to the point: "The affairs of others cannot be entrusted to women unless, through the actions they are directed to bring, they are pursuing their own interest and profit." Such a case might arise, for instance, if a woman sought to recover a debt that had been assigned to her by another creditor.[161] A brief allusion in a narrowly technical document tells more about the incapacity of women and its relation to gender division than do many more literary texts, which more often have to do with representations than with the actual functioning of institutions. Unless we understand how things really worked, we are all too likely to succumb to endlessly spiraling fantasies. In a word, better the *Code* than Juvenal. Better a crisply formulated rule than a thousand portraits of women by poets, satirists, and annalists critical of the presumptuousness of females ready to cast aside their reserve and behave in public like men. Methodologically it is sounder to study an institution like the legal incapacity of women by seeking to understand the underlying principle: that a woman cannot represent the interests of anyone but herself.

The unity of the domain that Roman law reserved for men and prohibited to women is not accounted for by the commonplace of *infirmitas sexus* or by the rationalizations of scholars who have attempted to distinguish between incapacities and protections. A common structure underlies the various modes of intervention associated with the notion of a civil and virile office: action on behalf of others. Representation in court is only the simplest example. Prosecution conforms to the same principle. Women were therefore forbidden to make accusations except to avenge their nearest male relatives.[162] For a woman to bring suit in her own name on behalf of a third party was considered an unnatural (and immodest) infringement of a male *officium*.[163] And from A.D. 41 to 65 the senatus-consult Velleien prohibited women from "interceding" between a debtor and creditor to guarantee a debt, such intercession being interpreted by jurists as yet another civil and virile office.[164]

Women's incapacities in public law were not fundamentally different in nature from their incapacities in private law. To be sure, the Roman city was, as has often been claimed, a "men's club." Nevertheless, a Roman woman was a *civis romana* who gave birth to a *civis romanus*. What women were denied in political life as well as in interpersonal relations was the capacity to transcend the narrow sphere of private interest, a capacity that "desubjectivized" action and gave it the abstract character of a function. It is not surprising that a woman could appear in court as a witness; her word was no less credible than that of a man.[165] But the fact that women were not allowed to witness wills does not contradict the rule just stated, because the male citizen who served as a *testis* validated the will by conferring on it the character of a public function.

In the earliest period of Roman law women could not make wills, because to make a will one had to belong to a comitia, or political assembly. Nor could they testify in court. Under archaic procedure testifying was a virile office because the entire body of citizens had to vouch for a claim in order for it to stand up in court. To testify in those days was to authenticate and therefore to assume the role of a third party par excellence. Women were of course excluded from this public function. They ceased to be excluded when the meaning of testimony changed from vouching for the existence of a claim guaranteed by all citizens to simply providing evidence. Women could testify because their testimony no longer had the abstract force of a kind of mediation, the general import of an *officium*.[166]

Images and Social Position

What was the place of the female image in a civilization that, it has often been said, devoted such extraordinary importance to figurative representation? A man walking in Athens' cemetery in the classical period might have seen, marking a gravesite, the statue of a smiling *kore* (young woman) draped in a gown of vivid colors. A few minutes later he would have encountered a grimacing female figure, head enveloped by serpents, tongue protruding, eyes fixed in a stare: the Gorgon's gaze. Looking up at the frieze of the Parthenon our classical stroller would have glimpsed the Canephorae, young women also wearing robes and carrying baskets associated with the procession of the Panathenae, a festival. Visiting the temple he would have been all but overwhelmed by the majestic statue of Athena Parthenos, the work of Phidias, which stood nearly forty feet high. He might have preferred the helmeted goddess in a more familiar form: on the drachmas that changed hands every day in the marketplace.

On a visit to a rural temple our Athenian would have seen countless female figurines, crudely made yet good enough to serve as objects of devotion. And in a pottery shop on the agora or stretched out on a couch for a banquet in the home of a friend, he might have coolly contemplated painted images of women engaged in activities that we would call erotic, their superb, naked bodies openly displayed on the drinking cups that passed among the guests. Figures of women were everywhere in the city, in forms that changed with the times. The changing image of Aphrodite and the social position of women can be seen in the Hellenistic statues of Aphrodite. In the chapter that follows François Lissarrague attempts a deliberately cautious approach in this kind of analysis.

P.S.P.

4

Figures of Women

François Lissarrague

EVERY SOCIETY BEARS a unique relation to the world of art, and ancient society is no exception. Not only Greece but also ancient Egypt, the Near East, and Rome were immersed in images. Each of these societies had a specific world view, which it expressed by characteristic representative means and according to distinct plastic conventions. In Greece different types of figurative objects served different needs, from the celebrated Kore of the Acropolis, marble statues presented to the temple of Athena by the city's young women, to the terra-cotta plaques of Locri in southern Italy, which depicted women paying homage to Demeter. Complex rules governed the modes of figuration, which varied according to the object's nature, functions, uses, and intended users.

Among the sources available to ancient historians, products of the plastic arts constitute a special case. Artistic evidence is not always used to best advantage, however, and everyone has seen ancient objects, statues, bas-reliefs, coins, and painted images in museums or in photographic reproduction. Such images usually serve to supplement an analysis based on written sources. Texts, speeches, and inscriptions form the bedrock of the historian's knowledge; images only confirm results arrived at by other means.[1]

Greek vases, owing to their number and variety, form a singular class. This chapter deals with Athenian vases of the fifth and sixth centuries B.C. In this period vases were not used for a single, exclusive purpose, and the images found on them were not all "feminine." The repertoire of imagery was quite broad, and it is a challenge to identify what role feminine imagery played and how it was related to masculine imagery.

Decorative imagery must not be seen in isolation from the object it embellished. Photographs and drawings of ancient vases tend to create a false impression. The images in question were not flat graphics, but vase paintings, and for the user a vase was primarily a utilitarian object with a definite function and only secondarily an object to look at. The utilitarian function was not the same for all vases, and we cannot always say with certainty what it was. But we do know the functions of many decorated vases, and this often provides the key to interpreting the decorative image.

Broadly speaking, vases can be classified according to use. Specific types of vases served in various rituals: marriages, funerals, initiations, sacrifices. Others were used in the consumption of wine when men drank among themselves *(symposion)*. There were special vessels for mixing wine, pouring wine, and drinking wine; for the most part these were used by men. Still other sorts of containers were used mainly by women: perfume jars, boxes for holding makeup and jewels, and bottles used in one way or another for grooming, makeup, and cosmetics. Imagery on ritual vases was of course the most strictly determined by function.

The significance of a vase painting is not immediately apparent from looking at it. In order to understand its meaning, one must first understand its function and construction, the logic according to which it was made. Painters looked at the world around them and chose certain subjects to represent. In representing a given subject they chose which details to include and which to exclude. What was left out may be as significant as what was put in (assuming that we are able, given the fragmentary nature of the sources, to find out). Hence in our exploration of Attic female iconography we shall be looking not only for signs and patterns of signs but also for omissions. And we shall be paying particular attention to plastic values in the selection of images and the handling of space.

The vases to be examined were made in the Ceramic Quarter near the gates of Athens in the fifth and sixth centuries B.C. They were not discovered until quite late, however: first in cemeteries in southern Italy in the eighteenth century and then in Etruscan tombs in Tuscany in the early nineteenth century.[2] The Etruscans were passionate admirers of Greek, and especially Attic, vases, and what we know today of the work of Athenian potters owes a great deal to the Etruscan custom of burying their dead in tombs sumptuously equipped with arms, vases, and jewels. At first in fact it was thought that the vases discovered in these tombs were of Etruscan origin and designed for this express purpose. But later in the nineteenth century similar vases were found in Greece, most notably in Athens during excavation of the Acropolis and Agora.

These Athenian products of the archaic and classical periods were products of a masculine world, and the vision they embody is also primarily masculine. Although there is evidence that some vase paintings were done by women (see fig. 45), and although several types of vases are thought to have been used exclusively by women, Athenian society was shaped by its male citizens, and the dominant ideology, the ideology that guided painters in their choices and defined their view in a system that left little room for individual initiative or what we would call inspiration, was chiefly masculine. Thus the images we will examine bear a double imprint. They are not an objective transcription of reality but the product of a gaze that reconstructed the real—and that gaze was masculine.

My approach, of necessity selective, is partly determined by the nature of the objects themselves, by the link between the form of a vase and the image it bears. We begin with marriage, a ritual in which the woman occupied a central place and which provided the occasion for the production of many kinds of vases. Then we will take a briefer look at funerals and women's role in them. Finally, we shall consider the problem of the space assigned to women. In doing so we shall bring together images of various types ranging from the fountain to the gynaeceum, from the dressing table to the workplace, as these were shaped by the male gaze in the context of the *symposion*. The discussion will thus be defined by two questions: How was ritual represented in images? and How did vase painters construct a plastic space?

Marriage

Many vases are decorated with scenes of marriage ceremonies. The nature of the scenes varies widely. Although certain details recur often, there seems to have been no canonical iconography of marriage. One has the impression that painters were quite free to interpret the ritual as they wished. The written sources, though incomplete, subjective, and sometimes of dubious authority, suggest that the marriage ceremony consisted of several phases. Marriage required a formal agreement, or *engye*, between the groom and the father of the bride-to-be. This agreement was linked to the payment of a dowry by the bride's father. The bride's consent apparently was not an issue. The marriage was completed by the transfer of the bride, which realized the *gamos*, or union, of the couple. At that moment the bride changed *oikos,* household, as well as *kyrios,* master, going from her father's dominion to her husband's. This rite of passage can be analyzed as consisting of three phases: separation, transition, and integration. In Athenian imagery these phases were not of equal importance; more attention was paid to transition than to the other two. The transfer of the bride took the form of a nocturnal procession of relatives and friends from one home to the other, either on foot or in carts. Certain individuals played special roles. The bride's mother carried a torch. A *parochos,* or companion, walked or rode alongside the couple. The procession was led by a *proagetes,* a guide. And finally, a *pais amphitales,* a child whose parents were both still alive, accompanied the bride and groom.

Images of marriage did not always portray all these characters or show all the phases of the marriage ceremony. No known painting exists of the *engye,* the agreement between the father and the groom. And no painting of a banquet can be identified specifically as a wedding banquet with the exception of images of the meal laid on by Pirithous for his wedding, which degenerated into a pitched battle between the Centaurs, who tried to kidnap the bride, and the Lapithae, who defended her.

Painters were particularly interested in the bride's preparations (bathing and dressing) and in the wedding procession. The painted imagery did not directly correspond to the phases of the wedding, however. Each image was a construct involving various actors in the ritual, among whom relations were established by means of gestures and glances. These devices established a plastic space within which the phases of separation, transition, and integration were inscribed. Objects such as vases, wreaths, and ornaments also played an essential role.

1. Marriage of Thetis and Peleus, *dinos,* circa 580. London, British Museum.

A Procession of Gods

In the archaic period figures painted as silhouettes in black varnish and heightened by undercutting and color stood out against the red background of the vase. The dominant theme in this "black-figure style" was that of the wedding procession. The couple rode in a chariot, and often gods were present in the cortege, suggesting that in some cases the bride and groom are to be taken as mythological figures.

The iconography of marriage begins with the wedding of Thetis and Peleus, which for a long time served as a paradigm for processional images. This was no ordinary marriage, involving as it did the immortal daughter of the god Nereus. According to an oracle, Thetis was fated to bear a son mightier than his father; hence no god wished to marry her. Despite her metamorphosis, the mortal Peleus managed to possess her and make her his wife. Achilles would be their son. All the gods came to the wedding to pay their respects to the goddess and her mortal husband. On one *dinos,* a large jar for mixing water and wine (fig. 1),[3] we find Peleus seated in front of the closed door of the couple's new home, welcoming the procession of divine wedding guests. The procession is led by Iris, messenger of the gods, who is followed by various figures on foot, including Chiron, the good centaur who will raise Achilles, and the household

goddesses Hestia and Demeter. Next comes a line of five chariots bearing gods, some in couples (Zeus/Hera, Poseidon/Amphitriton), others in pairs (Apollo/Artemis, Aphrodite/Ares). The chariots are accompanied by minor female goddesses on foot: the Horae, the Muses, the Charites, the Moires. Thus a pantheon was displayed in all its hierarchical degrees before the banquet guests in front of whom this vessel would have been placed. The greater gods ride in chariots in couples or pairs; the lesser gods walk in groups, for the most part designated by collective nouns, usually feminine. They are here to witness a marriage between a Nereid, one of their own, and a mortal. They are also guests at the new home of Peleus, who welcomes them with a drinking cup in hand to celebrate the marriage. The bride, however, is nowhere to be seen. We must surmise that Thetis is inside the house which the procession of the gods approaches.

A somewhat later version of the same scene is the principal decoration on the celebrated François Vase, a krater now in the Archaeological Museum of Florence.[4] The composition is the same: the divine procession forms a long frieze that continues all the way around the vessel. Gods, some on

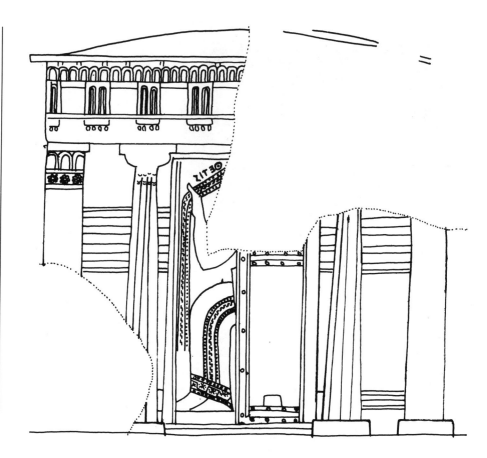

2. Thetis at home, krater, circa 570. Florence, Archaeological Museum.

foot followed by others in chariots, make their way toward the home of Thetis and Peleus. Peleus, standing at the door in front of an altar that calls attention to the ritual nature of the procession, receives the centaur Chiron, who has moved to the head of the cortege along with his wife Chariclo and Iris. The gods are arrayed much as they were in the earlier painting, but there is one important difference between the two: behind Peleus and to his right, the newlyweds' home is portrayed as having a portico and fronton, with the entryway located between two columns (fig. 2). Here, however, one of the doors is open, and we can see the legs of a woman who is lifting a portion of her garment, above which we read the name Thetis. Thus we catch a glimpse of the bride behind the open door. Her face was probably hidden by the other door, but the vessel is broken so we cannot be sure. The hand lifting a part of her garment reinforces the effect of the open door. The bride is present but partially hidden. She is unveiling herself in a gesture that has its counterpart in the marriage ritual, but one that we are not permitted to see. Her clothing, like her home, defines a private space that encloses her female body, a space removed from the public space in which the gods in procession show themselves to mortal men.

Door to Door

Painters often used the entryway in wedding iconography to mark a point of departure or arrival, as if the marriage itself were enacted between the doors of the two families' homes. For example, on one pyxis, or cylindrical terra-cotta container, the wedding procession emerges from a doorway in which one door is ajar (fig. 3).[5] A woman, perhaps the bride's mother, can be seen in the embrasure. She is turned toward the chariot, which is moving away from her. Her posture and gaze indicate that the doorway is the starting point of the procession rather than the destination. Again, though, it is a woman who remains inside. Following the archaic pattern, the wedding couple will ride in the chariot. The veiled bride has already taken her place, and the groom is about to join her. They are flanked by a young man and woman carrying

3. Newlywed couple in chariot, pyxis, circa 430. London, British Museum.

torches and followed by two women, one of whom carries a jewel box on her head and a large pot in her right hand, while the other raises a *lebes gamikos,* a large ritual vase that numbered among the bride's gifts. Several aspects of the marriage ritual are depicted here. The bride leaves her home, while members of her family stay behind. The marriage is represented as a linear transfer from one space to another, with the groom directing the process. The image emphasizes the gift-giving and transfer of property that are part of the marriage ceremony. And finally, the procession is led by a beardless youth with a caduceus, the god Hermes, who presides over transitions and changes of estate. The

4. Wedding procession, pyxis, circa 460. Paris, Louvre.

cover of this pyxis is decorated with celestial symbols—Sun, Moon, and Night—which revolve about the disk as they do about the vault of the heavens. These cylindrical containers were used exclusively by women, either as jewel boxes or for makeup. Its shape established a connection between two aspects of reality for which the Greek words stemmed from the same root: the *cosmos,* or celestial order, and *cosmetics,* or materials used in grooming. The iconography of the vase painting suggests a possible correspondence between marriage and the world order.

Another pyxis, this one in the Louvre (figs. 4 and 5), depicts a different kind of procession, in which there is no chariot.[6] This representation was more common in the classical period, from which some forty examples have survived. Once again the image wraps around the cylindrical terra-cotta container. We see an entryway with closed doors, but it is impossible to tell whether it is the starting point or the destination of the procession. The ambiguity seems deliberate: it turns the doorway into a special sort of icon, the center of the wedding ritual. At the leftmost extremity of the procession a woman reaches out to straighten the folds of the bride's gown. She may be either the bride's mother or the *nympheutria,* her governess. Situated next to the doorway, this woman symbolizes the space half-veiled and wears a wreath. With one hand she holds on to her gown, while with the other hand she reaches out to a young man who takes her by the wrist. The young woman's immobility contrasts with her husband's move-

5. Door to door, pyxis, circa 460. Paris, Louvre.

ment: he is already moving forward even as he turns back toward his wife, a sign that he is the leader of the procession that is taking her away. The *cheir' epi karpou,* or gesture of the hand on the wrist, is the ritual symbol of the husband's taking possession of his wife, the act by which he becomes her new kyrios, master. The bride is thus inserted in a symbolic web of gestures indicating separation and integration, two phases of the marital rite of passage. On the right side of the composition are four witnesses to the bride's departure. Apollo can be identified by the laurel he is holding and his sister Artemis by her bow and by the quiver that protrudes above her left shoulder. The two other figures are not easy to identify. The woman hands a bandelet to a man with a beard who leans on a scepter. Perhaps these are two other gods, in which case this scene would be reminiscent of the marriage of Thetis and Peleus, but the relatively undistinguished appearance of the two figures makes such an interpretation unlikely. It is not surprising to find gods among the wedding guests, particularly Artemis, who presided over the education of young women until the moment of marriage. One of the functions of images was to make the gods visible to human eyes. The painter could not represent the newly married couple by themselves, isolated from others. The door-to-door transfer had to be portrayed as a procession in which the couple was accompanied by friends and relatives. The presence of human and divine witnesses made the wedding a public act.

Processions of Chariots

Another transfer by chariot can be found on an archaic *dinos,* a variant of the krater used for mixing wine (fig. 6), which predates the pyxis just discussed by a half-century.[7] The body of this dinos is decorated with a frieze, which is continuous but composed of two distinct scenes. One features a

6. Top—wedding chariot;
bottom—warrior's chariot,
dinos, circa 530. Salerno,
Provincial Museum.

couple in a chariot, with the man in the foreground. The chariot is accompanied by two
women bearing gifts and a female torchbearer
along with Apollo and Dionysus. No starting point
or destination is indicated. The presence of the
gods is once again reminiscent of the wedding of
Thetis and Peleus, but no explicit sign or inscription indicates that such a mythological reading is
necessary. On the other side another chariot advances toward a seated old man. It is occupied by
two warriors and flanked by other warriors, both
hoplites and archers. At the time the painting was
made, however, chariots were not used for trans-
porting newlyweds or anyone else, nor were they
used in war, which was waged on foot by infan-
trymen in closely serried ranks. The only use of
the chariot was in games such as the Olympics. By
choosing to paint an old-fashioned vehicle associated with the great epic tradition, the painter
added a mythological dimension to his work. In
addition, by linking two different uses of the chariot, he established a parallel between marriage and
war: marriage represented the fulfillment of woman's destiny, just as war represented the fulfillment
of man's.

The departure of a wedding chariot can be seen
on a loutrophoros in the Berlin Museum (fig. 7).[8]
The loutrophoros was an elongated pitcher used
for carrying loutron, water for the bride's bath. A
marriage procession is portrayed on the tall, narrow body of this pitcher. On the left, under one
handle, a female torchbearer is preceded by a child
wearing a wreath, probably the pais amphitales,
or child with two living parents whose presence
was required at weddings but who was not represented in any of the other images looked at thus
far. The painter has chosen to give us a procession
with chariot. We see its wheels and chassis, on
which stands an auriga (charioteer) who has
turned to face the couple. The bridegroom,
crowned with laurel, has lifted his bride in his arms

7. Lifting the bride, loutrophoros, circa 430. Berlin, Antikenmuseum (in Furtwängler, Saburov Collection, pl. 58).

and is about to climb into the chariot. She, too, wears a wreath as well as a chiton, a portion of which she holds in her left hand. A small flying Eros holds a wreath (perhaps of myrtle) above the bride's head, and another wreath hovers over the groom. Underneath the right handle a column indicates the transition from one pictorial space to another. This graphic device is less explicit than the use of the doorway, which is more commonly found in this set of compositions. It does, however, create an area on the other side of the vase large enough to portray two figures: a female torch-bearer and a bearded male holding a scepter. Because they stand at the destination of the procession these figures may be the parents of the bridegroom, or perhaps the scepter indicates that they should be viewed as mythological figures.

The column that appears in this composition does not sever the pictorial space on one side of the pitcher from that on the other. The torch carried by the woman on the right appears on both sides. By contrast, the horses hitched to the chariot are not visible. This graphical ellipsis shows that, when necessary, painters included only those elements necessary to make their compositions intelligible. They did not seek to create a convincing illusion or to represent space as homogeneous and continuous. An image was a collage of elements intended to convey a meaning. Here the chariot wheel and the column are enough to convey the sense of a transition. Note the couple's movement: the groom lifts the bride. He takes the initiative in this quiet elopement. This was not, as we shall see, an abduction, but an assumption of possession analogous to the hand on the wrist. One additional innovation calls for comment: the presence of Eros. A slender, winged creature, the Attic Eros was an adolescent, not the pudgy putto made familiar by Roman art. I shall have more to say about him later on. For now, suffice to say that Eros is engaged in adding to the beauty of the bride, placing a leafy crown on her head. For the spectator he also calls attention to the convergence of gazes within the image. All eyes are on the bride, whose profile is half-hidden, half-accentuated by her veil. The image does not, however, respect the temporal sequence of procession, reception, and unveiling. The possession of the bride is here construed as a spectacle whose legitimacy is guaranteed by the gods themselves through their agent Eros.

Flowers, Eros, and Nike

As we have just seen, the form of a vase often had a strong influence on its iconography. In addition to the pyxis, used to hold perfumes and jewels, and the loutrophoros, used for carrying lustral water, the *lebes gamikos,* or nuptial cauldron, sat on a raised pedestal and appears to have been used exclusively as part of the wedding ritual. It was one of the gifts given to the bride, as can be seen

8. Wedding gift, lebes gamikos, circa 450. Copenhagen, National Museum.

on the London pyxis. One of these cauldrons, now in Copenhagen (fig. 8), is decorated with a painting that shows not a procession but a composition of which the bride is the central figure.[9] On her knees she holds a lebes gamikos, no doubt a recent gift. Above her hangs a *sakkos,* or bonnet. A woman is giving her other objects: one, oblong, is an alabaster perfume jar, while the other, mounted on a pedestal, resembles a pyxis. Behind the bride another woman holds a flower in her raised hand, but the drawing is obliterated. Between this woman and the bride a large, highly stylized floral decoration culminates in a budding palmetto. Usually such floral motifs were limited to less important areas of the vessel, such as the handles or neck. Here, however, the painting demonstrates the role of flowers and perfumes in the wedding ceremony. The floral decoration on this particular

vessel is disproportionately large and visually incongruous. The emphasis on the aesthetic function of the image suggests a possible link between women and flowers. The bud is not, as some scholars have suggested, simply a phallic symbol, but a symbol of growth in the plant kingdom, of plants ready to blossom and release their fragrance.

The back of the cauldron features a woman carrying a torch and another holding a scepter, again perhaps a divine witness of the wedding ceremony. Beneath the handles are floral motifs similar to the one on the principal face. Next to these are two winged females, also carrying torches, who fly horizontally toward the bride. These abstract figures are probably Nikes. The name Nike is often translated as Victory, but such figures occur frequently in the iconography of marriage, so Nike clearly cannot be interpreted simply as meaning victory in the military sense. Her presence seems rather to indicate divine approval, and, more precisely, approval of a favorable outcome. There is a possible parallel, as we have seen, between war and marriage. In both Nike represents

a positive conclusion, a successful outcome desired by the gods.

On one small lebes gamikos with a low pedestal and an alabaster perfume jar affixed to its cover (fig. 9) the painter has reduced the wedding iconography to a minimum.[10] His method is revealing. The picture contains only two winged figures in flight: a Nike and an Eros. As they fly toward each other, they frame an image that, though not present, is nevertheless implied by the form of the vessel: the bride. In their outstretched arms the winged figures hold barely visible branches festooned with huge buds. Finally, each figure is framed by two columns, reminiscent of the spatial structure of the compositions we looked at earlier. Thus here, ornamental elements and allegorical figures that were of secondary importance in other compositions have been promoted to the first rank as ideograms symbolizing the essential values of marriage: fecundity (marked by flowers and wreaths); transition (marked by the columns and by Nike representing success and fulfillment); and grace and beauty (symbolized by Eros).

9. Nike and Eros, lebes gamikos, circa 430. Copenhagen, National Museum.

157

10. Mythical marriages,
epinetron, circa 420.
Athens, National Museum.
Details on facing page.

The Marriage Paradigm

A more complex object (fig. 10) sheds additional light on the imagery of marriage.[11] The object in question is not a vessel but a terra-cotta implement used in weaving: the *epinetron,* as we know from a detail on a companion piece in Athens, was shaped to fit a woman's knee and thigh, and the upper, undecorated portion was used for winding yarn. It was a utilitarian object used by women in their domestic routine. The epinetron in question was found in an Eretrian tomb, and its quality suggests that it was a display object and possibly never used. Three decorative scenes portray mythical marriages. One end features a woman's bust surrounded by a circular frieze depicting the moment when Peleus grabbed hold of Thetis' waist just as she was changing into a hippocampus. Nereus, scepter in hand, stands on the right, while Thetis' sisters flee in terror toward their father. Two other scenes decorate the long edges of the epinetron; neither contains an image of an adult male. The first (fig. 10a) perhaps represents the preparations for the marriage of Harmonia, daughter of Ares and Aphrodite, to Cadmus, king of Thebes.[12] Inscriptions name Aphrodite, seated on the left, in front of her son Eros; and Harmonia, also seated and flanked by Peitho (Persuasion) and Kore (the Maiden). The bride has turned to her right to look at Hebe (Youth), who has turned toward Himeros (Desire). Seated, the latter holds a jewel box and offers Hebe a bottle of perfume. These figures are allegorical and mythical symbols

10a.

of the values of marriage: not only Persuasion, Youth, and Harmony but also Eros and his double, Desire. Aphrodite is both the mother of the bride and the goddess who has jurisdiction over these exact matters: seduction, beauty, amorous desire. Her province is not the domestic side of marriage, over which Hera presides, but everything that has to do with charm, grace, and beauty, all that is female and associated with grooming and fragrant perfumes.

The second lateral image (fig. 10b) is devoted to Alcestis, the exemplary wife of Admetus, king of Thessaly, who agrees to go to Hades in place of her husband. Nothing in this picture alludes to that episode, however. On the right side of the

10b.

159

composition Alcestis leans on the nuptial bed, which stands in front of a door that opens into the rest of the house. The limits of the room are indicated by a column. Alcestis faces five women, all named by inscriptions. Hippolyta, bird in hand, is seated in front of Asterope. On the left Theo and another woman are arranging branches in vases to be given to the bride: two *lebetes gamikoi* and a loutrophoros. Between them Charis, one of the three Graces, lifts a section of her gown. The composition also contains two wreaths and a mirror. Apparently the moment portrayed here is the *epaulia,* the giving of gifts on the day after the wedding. Now mistress of the house, Alcestis is shown in her new bedroom.

The image of the abduction of Thetis, the divine bride, contrasts with the two scenes featuring only women—one of preparation for the wedding, the other of the reception. In these two scenes there is no procession, only women among themselves. The cast of characters is not fortuitous: Alcestis was the model wife, faithful unto death, and Harmonia followed her husband, Cadmus, until both were transformed into serpents. What we have, then, is a yarn-spooling device decorated with images of women, mythical paradigms of marriage, and allegories of marital virtue. Male values were thus illustrated with female figures and used to decorate a household implement.

In Aphrodite's Garden

In the second half of the fifth century B.C. the variety of female personifications in Greek imagery increased. A series of representations of Aphrodite and her companions appeared, especially in the school of the Meidias painter. The values embodied in these works were similar to those already analyzed, although associated with the goddess and her powers rather than with marriage alone. On one compact lecythus, probably used as a perfume jar (fig. 11), the goddess is seated, her face turned toward Eros, who is perched on her shoulder.[13] She is flanked by five women distinguished by different hairstyles and identified by inscriptions: from left to right, we see Cleopatra (Noble Ancestry), who holds a flower and a necklace; Eunomia (Harmonious Order), who leans on Paidia (Games), also with a necklace; Peitho (Persuasion), decorating a sacrificial basket; and Eudaimonia (Happiness), picking fruits. The painting is filled with fruits and jewels, but the action is otherwise unspecified, even if Peitho seems to be engaged in preparing for some kind of ritual. All five women are turned toward Aphrodite, and their eyes are on Eros. The image seems to evoke a kind of paradise, a peaceful garden in which five women symbolize the various virtues of Aphrodite, patron of blissful love.

The aesthetic values that led the painter to present Aphrodite in this manner can be traced back to an earlier period, prior to the emergence

11. In Aphrodite's garden, lecythus, circa 410. London, British Museum (in Furtwängler Reichhold, pl. 78).

12. The beautiful bride, alabaster vase, circa 470. Paris, Bibliothèque Nationale.

of female allegories. Wreaths, flowers, ornaments, and Eros' participation in the wedding procession were all devices used to embellish portraits of brides. A central moment in the wedding ritual was the unveiling of the bride before her husband and his family. Wedding imagery underscored the aesthetics of marriage. A good example of this is an alabaster jar dating from about 470 B.C. (fig. 12).[14] It shows a seated young woman holding a floral wreath. A little girl holding another alabaster perfume jar identical to the one on which the painting appears approaches from behind. Flowers and perfume were of course the classical symbols of grooming. Facing the seated woman, a beardless man stands leaning on a staff, a symbol of citizenship. His right hand holds a sash, which he offers to the woman. The figures are identified: inscribed on the staff are the words *Timodemos kalos* (Timodemos is handsome). And the woman's work basket bears the words *he numphe kale* (the bride is beautiful). Note that he is called by name, while she is characterized by type. The asymmetry makes this image a sort of paradigm. The bride, busy grooming herself, receives a sash, which plays a crucial role in the wedding ritual. The standing male takes in the spectacle of the seated female: the painter has given us a narrative of what it is that makes a woman a beautiful bride.

Rituals

Other rituals, some private, others public, and still others exclusively feminine, were also recorded in paint.

Funerary Rituals

Paintings of funerary rituals share certain traits in common with paintings of weddings. The form of the vase on which the painting appeared strongly influenced the design, and careful attention was paid to the placement of figures in the composition. Women had a very definite place in funeral rituals, and male and female roles were clearly delineated.

Funerals. Certain phases of the funeral ritual were not represented. The dressing of the body was never shown, and there are few images of bodies being placed on biers or buried. From the earliest days of vase painting the painters seem to have settled on two aspects of the funeral: the *prothesis,* or laying out of the body, and the *ekphora,* or transportation of the body to the cemetery. These very ancient iconographic motifs can be traced back to the time when painters abandoned the geometric style and returned to the figurative.[15] Ceramic paintings from the middle of the eighth century B.C. depict animals, birds, horses, deer, and various kinds of human activities, mainly funerals. The painted objects were large vases—amphoras, kraters, and hydrias—that were used as steles to mark the location of a grave. Attic imagery thus began with the representation of the dead, or, more precisely, of the funeral ritual, on objects created expressly in their honor. What was celebrated was not so much the memory of the dead as the piety of the living.

These primitive forms of composition survived in the archaic and classical periods. One large loutrophoros with red figures that dates from circa 490 (fig. 13) features three complementary scenes on its neck, body, and base.[16] The same image is repeated on both sides of the neck. It shows two women, one of whom carries a loutrophoros similar to the one on which the painting appears. The water in it will be used to prepare the dead body for burial. (A similar vessel—but with different iconography—was associated with the bridal bath.) The other woman grieves by tearing her hair out. The base of the vase pictures a series of horsemen, perhaps a symbol of the social status of the deceased or of members of the funeral procession. Finally, the body of the vase depicts the deceased laid out on a bed (fig. 13a). Only his head, supported by a cushion, is visible. The jaw is held in place by a kind of chin strap. The rest of the body is wrapped in a winding sheet. Four women are arrayed around the bed. One holds the deceased's head, which appears to be the focal point of the scene, while the three others tear their hair out in

13. Salute to the dead, loutrophoros, and detail of neck, circa 490. Paris, Louvre.

Figure 13, and 13a, detail of the body.

grief. At the foot of the bed, on the other side of the body of the vase, five men gather (see page 165). The two on the right have their backs turned to the bed and have stretched out their right arms to greet the new arrivals, who are led by an adolescent.

The same arrangement can be seen in another painting from a slightly earlier period (fig. 14).[17] This is a *pinax,* or terra-cotta plaque in which holes were drilled so that it might be affixed to the tomb. Although the image on this particular example has been damaged, we can be confident of what it looked like by comparing it with other, better preserved, plaques. This plaque is interesting because of the inscriptions identifying the characters. The deceased is laid out on the bed, his head on a pillow. Around the bed are seven women, two of them adolescents. One is touching the dead man's head, and the inscription identifies her as *meter*, the mother. In front of her is *adelphe*, the sister. Facing the mother at the head of the bed is *thethe*, a grandmother, and on the far right, *thethis*, an aunt. Behind the mother on the left is *thethis prospater*, a paternal aunt. And on the left another aunt turns to look at the body. All but one of the women are looking at the deceased; grieving, they take hold of locks of their hair and, we know from inscriptions on other paintings, wail *oimoi* (alas!). As on the preceding vase (fig. 13), their attitude stands in sharp contrast to that of the men pictured on the left. The man with white hair who stands at the foot of the bed and turns to greet the others is identified as *pater*, the father. The entrance to the house or bedroom is indicated by a column, and it is there that the father stands to welcome the other men. One is the *adelphos*, brother of the deceased, and the other is a child.

14. Corpse with kinfolk, after a pinax, circa 500. Paris, Louvre.

Here, in its most generic form, is the kinship system. In this case the deceased is a young man whose parents' presence at the funeral heightens the drama of the scene and may account for the unusual inscriptions. Men and women not only play clearly distinct roles but adopt different gestures and occupy separate parts of the room. Within the death chamber itself the women, suffering in grief, bemoan the man's passing. From the entryway the men pay their last respects, betokening society's recognition of the deceased. In this domestic and familial phase of the funeral ceremony, the women occupy the private space closest to the corpse, whereas the men come from outside to honor the remains.

Other funerary plaques show similar aspects of the funeral ritual. Sometimes these were made in series to be affixed to the tomb side by side. One plaque (fig. 15) from the Berlin Museum dates from around 540 B.C.[18] Unfortunately it is part of a fragmentary series of at least fifteen. It depicts a group of eight women, five of whom are seated facing one another, while three others are standing. This is not a scene of prothesis. No bed or body is visible, and the women, rather than gesticulating wildly, are grave and seemingly contemplative. The woman standing in the center is passing an infant to the companion on her right; the one on the left holds out an item of linen. In the center foreground a woman with a veil stands out from the others. In her right hand she holds a lock of hair, symbol of her mourning, next to her cheek. Facing her is another woman, apparently younger than the rest and also distinguished by hairstyle. Given the funerary function of this painting, it seems likely that these women are mourning the death of the mother of the infant, now in their charge. There is little age differentiation; Attic vase painting indicated the age of males more carefully than that of females. Men were either beardless, bearded, white-haired, or bald, and these signs correlated with the

age classes that were of such great civic importance, particularly in war. Women, on the other hand, were portrayed as ageless. Only their status, married or unmarried, mattered. The Berlin plaque is a rare exception. Perhaps it portrays the death of a young mother whose child was entrusted to her kinswomen; if so, the two figures in the foreground might be the mother and sister of the deceased.

Burial Gifts. Many funerary paintings were devoted to another aspect of the funeral ritual: the practice of placing gifts in the tomb along with the body of the deceased. Apparently this was primarily a female function. Many vases show women laying wreaths, bandelets, or perfume jars before

15. Women in mourning, pinax, circa 540. Berlin, Pergamonmuseum (in *Antike Denkmäler*, pl. 9).

169

16. Grave offerings, based on lecythus, circa 450. Athens, National Museum.

funerary steles. These items were carried to the burial site in large, flat baskets. Some paintings show women preparing to visit the gravesite. It is not always easy, however, to tell their precise status: mistress or servant, mother or daughter? Such images usually appear on perfume jars that were themselves offered as burial gifts: form and decoration were closely related, and the ritual included a representation of its own protocol. One lecythus now in Athens (fig. 16) shows a woman carrying a basket approaching a stele encircled by a bandelet.[19] Pitchers and wreaths have been laid on steps at the foot of the stele. Facing the woman on the left and observing her actions is a young man wearing a tunic and carrying a lance. Comparison with other vases suggests that this figure represents not a male visitor but death itself. The tombstone marks the gravesite and preserves the memory of the deceased. This is where the living and the dead meet, where women come to offer gifts and attend to the memory of the departed. The stele on the vase not only symbolizes the deceased but links his image to that of the woman who has come to honor his memory.

The Return of the Warrior. Another important iconographic category consists of images of a slain warrior carried home by a comrade-in-arms. In some cases an inscription identifies the slain Achilles carried home by Ajax, but usually the figures are anonymous. Sometimes there are additional figures: other warriors, elderly men, women. Here I am particularly interested in images in which the soldiers are greeted by women, sometimes gesticulating like the mourning women around the deathbed in scenes of prothesis. These images are inconsistent with what we know of Athenian military practice. Normally, the dead were gathered up from the battlefield and burned on the spot; only their ashes were returned to the city. The iconography referred not to actual practice, however, but to epic literature. There the dead are generally carried off one by one. The slain were thus portrayed as heroes, and their deaths became occasions for private grief within the bosom of the family. One Tarquinian amphora (fig. 17) can be interpreted in this light.[20] In the center of the composition a soldier, leaning forward, carries on his back a lifeless comrade, his legs hanging limply.

17. Return of the dead, amphora, circa 520. Tarquinia, Archaeological Museum.

171

The soldier is also carrying two lances and a large notched shield decorated with images of a lion and a serpent. The pair is flanked by two women, one marching at a quick step, the other with her hand on her head in the characteristic gesture of lamentation and mourning. The iconography of the funeral ritual is here transposed into a martial context. The painters were of course also influenced by the ideology of warfare as set forth in epic poetry.

Women thus had an important place in funerary imagery. In scenes of prothesis they were shown occupying the place closest to the deceased. They appear more often than men in scenes depicting the bestowal of gifts upon the deceased. Even in the quintessentially male domain of warfare, women were shown welcoming home the slain hero's body. But mourning was not their only martial function.

Scenes of Departure

The series of paintings just described belongs to a larger series depicting women in relation to warriors, particularly in scenes showing the bestowal of arms on the warrior and his departure for battle. War was not simply a man's affair. It concerned the entire city, women as well as men.

Arming the Warriors. Warriors were often portrayed arming themselves before battle. Usually the soldier has already donned his breastplate and is shown strapping on an item of leg armor known as a greave. A helmet, round shield, sword, and lance completed the panoply of the hoplite, or foot soldier, who advanced in close ranks so that each man's shield partially covered that of his neighbor, thus forming a solid wall. Rather than portray this phalanx, however, painters preferred to depict single warriors as they prepared for battle. In these scenes women occupy a more important place than the written sources suggest. In many paintings a

woman stands facing the hoplite and holds his lance, shield, or helmet. On an amphora (fig. 18) in Munich, for example, a young warrior straps on his greave as a woman offers him a lance and shield.[21] The pair is flanked by two more hoplites ready to depart.

In some paintings other figures surround the hoplite as he straps on his arms: for example, archers, who were warriors of a less important category, or men too old to engage in combat. There was thus a contrast between those who went to war—hoplites and archers—and those who stayed home—women and old men. But who was this woman who assisted the hoplite in girding himself for war—his mother or his wife? In the

18. Arming the warrior, amphora, circa 520. Munich, Antikensammlung und Glyptothek.

173

19. Prayer at an altar, amphora, circa 530. Rome, Villa Giulia.

absence of iconographic signs marking the age of the female figure, we cannot be sure.

Like the return of the slain hero, these scenes of armament had a mythological source: the episode in which Thetis bestows arms on her son Achilles. This might be interpreted as a mother arming her son, in keeping with the idea that the role of women is to supply the city with warriors. But Achilles is a special case, because his mother is divine. The iconography of Hector, the Trojan hero, is more complex. In the oldest paintings he appears with his parents: Priam looks on as Hecuba gives him his helmet. Thus the mother is indeed arming the son. On a later vase, however, Hector, armed, turns toward Priam. A woman on the left hands him a phial, or flat cup, for the final libation. According to the inscription, her name is Andromache. So the figures in the two paintings are different.[22] Andromache has replaced Hecuba. But the action, too, changed: in the earlier painting a mother arms her son; in the later one a wife prepares a libation for her husband. The contrast between the images suggests the ambiguity of the woman's role, as well as the highly codified nature of these representations, which therefore took on almost ritual character, sometimes accentuated by the inclusion of a domestic altar.

On an amphora in the Villa Giulia (fig. 19), a bearded hoplite holding a lance and shield lays a plant offering on an altar while uttering the word *onaxs,* lord, to begin a prayer.[23] An inscription tells us that his name is Hippomedon, a companion of Adrastus and one of the Seven against Thebes. Facing him is a woman named Polycastes (a name unknown from any other context), who holds out a helmet and bandelet. The prayer and the offering give this scene, which alludes to the Theban epic, a strong religious cast. A painting (fig. 20) done several decades later exhibits a similar composition: a young warrior receives his helmet and shield from a woman, who passes them over an altar.[24]

20. Arming at the altar, krater, circa 450. Baltimore, Walters Art Gallery. Detail on facing page.

175

Always individual, these departure scenes contrast with the collective character of warfare. Women appear in a domestic setting as arms are bestowed on the warrior. These images promoted a martial ideology that emphasized heroic values and mythic paradigms but in association with the *oikos,* or household.

Libations. Later in the fifth century, as we saw in the case of Hector, image-makers turned from the bestowal of arms to the departure libation. A cup in Berlin (fig. 21) features a beardless young man with lance and shield.[25] On the right, an elderly man with a beard, probably the hoplite's father, looks on, leaning on a staff; he represents those who will not be going off to war. On the left a woman pours wine from a pitcher into the phial the young man is holding. In these libation scenes women often played the essential role of pouring the ritual wine. A libation was a brief but pregnant moment, an event that marked a turning point; it was presented sometimes in isolation, sometimes as part of a complex ritual sequence. In this respect it can be compared to the sign of

21. Departure and libation, cup, circa 430. Berlin, Antikenmuseum.

22. Woman carrying
breastplate, lecythus,
circa 460. Palermo,
Archaeological Museum.

177

the cross in Catholic ritual: both are spatiotemporal markers. A libation, however, was not an individual act but an exchange. At moments of departure or return the libation served to underscore the bonds that existed among the participants in the ceremony and between each participant and the gods. It is noteworthy that in this martial context women played this admittedly auxiliary but still essential role.

The association of women with the warrior's arms was so powerful that it could be merely suggested rather than spelled out explicitly. On a lecythus in Palermo (fig. 22), a woman appears alone, carrying a breastplate.[26] This isolated image ought to be part of a more elaborate composition. Perhaps the woman is one of the Nereids who accompany Thetis in the arming of Achilles, or perhaps she is some other woman bringing arms to a warrior. An amphora in Munich (fig. 23) offers a variant of this image in which an unarmed young man wearing a chiton leans on a staff.[27] His hat is pushed far back on his head, and he faces a woman who offers him a sword. Between them, on the ground, lie a helmet and shield, which contrast sharply with the youth's dress. This painting suggests not so much armament as a change of status from ephebe to hoplite, a change in which the woman's role was essential.

Consider, finally, one last variant (fig. 24).[28] This unique image links libation and armament in a composition involving Athena, the warrior goddess and protectress of the city. The woman on the left holds the libation pitcher and cup. A helmet lies on a shield on the ground between the woman and the goddess. Two interpretations are possible. The arms may belong to Athena, and the libation may be intended for her. Or it may be that the arms belong to an absent or slain warrior, and the libation is intended for him. In either case, warfare is here evoked solely by two female figures, one mortal, the other divine. Note that the

23. Arming of ephebe,
amphora, circa 440.
Munich, Antikensammlung
und Glyptothek.

24. Libation in the
presence of Athena,
oinochoe, circa 460.
Ferrara, Archaeological
Museum (in Aurigemma,
Spina, pl. 162).

25. Arming of warrior at a stele, based on lecythus, circa 450. Athens, National Museum.

vessel on which this painting appears is a pitcher similar to the one depicted.

The themes of armament and funerary ritual are combined on a lecythus now in Athens (fig. 25).[29] In the center of the painting stands a stepped stele festooned with bandelets. The woman on the left is holding a shield while handing a helmet to the young man in short tunic and armed with a lance. This is not a scene of armament in a cemetery but a collage of two different types of space: the household in which the warrior receives his arms before going to war, and the cemetery to which the living come to honor the dead. In both the woman's role is essential.

Bed and War

A lecythus in the Berlin Museum (fig. 26) draws a parallel between male and female.[30] This unique scene of departure can be interpreted in two ways. A standing woman holds a swaddled infant. Facing her is a man armed with a lance and holding a helmet in his right hand. This unusual portrayal of a family group—father, mother, and infant—is

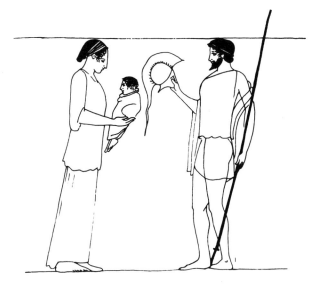

26. Departure of warrior, based on lecythus, circa 450. Berlin, Antikenmuseum.

of course reminiscent of the celebrated farewell scene between Hector and Andromache in the *Iliad*. But if that was indeed the model, many details that appear in the text have been omitted here. Furthermore, without any mythological reference, the scene can be interpreted as a comparison between male and female. Man's province is war, woman's is child-rearing. We encountered a similar parallelism earlier in paintings portraying both the wedding chariot and the chariot of war (fig. 6). On a funerary vase such an image would evoke the ever-present possibility of simultaneous death: the man in combat and the woman in childbirth.[31]

Achilles carried by Ajax, Thetis bringing arms to her son, Hector bidding farewell to Andromache—all these episodes can be transformed into images of anonymous soldiers departing for war, while the women remain at home ensuring the continuity of the oikos, home and family. Women are portrayed as mothers of children who will in turn become warriors, reflecting the masculine ideology according to which hoplites were defenders of the city.

Maternal scenes on Attic vases are rare. They

27. Mother and child: Alcmaeon and Eriphyle, based on hydria, circa 440. Berlin, Antikenmuseum.

are much more common on funerary steles sculpted in the late fifth and throughout the fourth century B.C. Because the steles commemorate the dead through the living who mourn their passing, they are relatively personal, and the inscriptions engraved on them identify the deceased and his or her kin. Certain steles refer to women who died in childbirth or to maidens who died before marrying. Nothing of the kind can be found on vases. The more generic images they contain were intended not to portray specific individuals but to evoke mythological models or paradigmatic moments.

There are a few vase paintings of mothers with children, usually set indoors. Children were most commonly depicted at play on small ritual vases used in the festival of the Anthesteriae.[32] Maternity was not an important subject for vase painters. Representations of childbirth are nonexistent, except for a series of images in which an ax blow delivered by Hephaestus, with assistance from the Eileithyiae, or midwife goddesses, splits the head of Zeus to allow his daughter Athena to spring forth fully armed—an impressive series of inversions compared with normal childbirth.[33] Child-

182

birth was women's business, not fit to be shown, or else of no interest to painters, who paid scant attention to biological functions. Even suckling was rarely portrayed, although there are a few scenes of Aphrodite feeding her son Eros. A hydria in Berlin (fig. 27) depicts what might at first sight be taken for an idyllic scene: the bearded man on the left leans on his staff and stares at a seated woman who is giving her breast to a child sitting in her lap.[34] Two cocks are fighting at her feet. A woman stands on the right next to a basket of wool, spinning yarn. This might appear to be a family portrait: parents, child, and servant together in tranquil harmony. But the inscriptions give the image a mythological resonance that transforms its meaning. The father is Amphiaraus, the mother Eriphyle, and the son Alcmaeon. Amphiaraus, king of Argos, betrayed by his wife, would die in the attempt to restore Polynices to the throne of Thebes. Alcmaeon will be killed by his mother to avenge his father. Thus the image is one of tragic irony, which, far from illustrating the charms of family life, implicitly alludes to a series of dramatic events. Now we can understand the presence of the fighting cocks, reminiscent of the fratricidal dispute between Eteocles and Polynices and a symbol, in the very heart of the oikos, of the discord and envy that divide families and cities. Not all images are simple transcriptions of everyday life. This genre painting makes sense only when its mythological dimension is restored. Once again we see how the mythological and the quotidian overlapped.

Rituals of Women

A smaller, more varied series of vase paintings depicts the performance of group rituals in the presence of an image of the divine: a statue, effigy, or sacrificial altar. In most cases it is difficult to associate these images with a particular festival among the large number included in the Attic calendar. Rather than rehearse the controversies that have divided historians of religion in this regard, it makes more sense to look at the role assigned to women, particularly in rituals in which only they participate.

Choruses.   Music and dance occupied a place of great importance in Greek religious life. Many festivals honored the gods with choral chants, of which there were many forms. Almost all Greek lyric poetry was associated with these chants. Today it is difficult to be sure about rhythm, music, or choreography, but some pictures of choral performances have survived. Most choruses were exclusively female: of some one hundred surviving paintings, nearly eighty depict choruses made up of women or girls.

A good example is the painting found on a *phiale* now in Boston's Museum of Fine Arts (fig. 28).[35] This type of vessel was generally used for libations, and the form adds a religious dimension to the scene painted on its inner surface: a female musician standing in front of an illuminated altar plays an *aulos,* or reed flute. The flames indicate that a sacrifice is in progress. On the ground to the right of an altar is a *calathos,* or basket, from which protrude bandelets. An offering to the gods, the basket symbolizes the woman's work of which it is an instrument. Above the basket hangs another bandelet, spread out for display: it is an ornament as well as an offering, a symbol of consecration that recurs in other contexts. The intended recipient of these offerings is not indicated. The painter was trying to represent not the divine figure but the ritual act. One used this image not to contemplate divinity but to admire a dance of women. A chorus of seven women, hand in hand, wraps around the vessel. Its rounded surface conveys a sense of the space around the altar. The composition reflects the triple etymology that the Greeks proposed for the word *choros.* Although

linguists may doubt the validity of this etymology, it was psychologically meaningful to the Greeks, who associated *choros* first with the verb *chairein*, to rejoice; second, with *chôros*, or circular space; and third, with *cheir*, or hand. And so we have a joyful festival of women holding hands as they dance in the round.

Sacrifice. The *bomos,* or altar, was often depicted as the focal point of ritual. In blood sacri-

28. Female chorus, phiale, circa 460. Boston, Museum of Fine Arts.

185

29. Woman carrying a sacrificial basket, lecythus, circa 480. Paris, Louvre.

fices women were represented as bearers of the *canoun,* the sacrificial basket, which contained seeds to be thrown into the fire, bandelets to be attached to the sacrificial animal, and the knife used to slit the animal's throat. The basket was made of wicker and had three projections. Many paintings portrayed women carrying such baskets.

A lecythus now in the Louvre (fig. 29) shows a woman approaching an altar, carrying a basket of the type just described.[36] Behind her a column suggests that the scene is taking place in a temple. There are no other details in this composition, which is like a minimalist pictogram pointing out the woman's role in the ritual.

30. The gardens of Adonis, lecythus, circa 390. Karlsruhe, Badisches Landsmuseum.

187

The Adonia. Other paintings are more explicit about the religious role of women. One interesting series is of rather late date, from the second half of the fifth century. The ritual portrayed in these images can be confidently identified as characteristic of the Adonia, a festival exclusively for women. A lecythus now in Karlsruhe (fig. 30) shows two women looking on while a third woman in the center stands perched on the first rung of a ladder.[37] On the right a winged Eros holds out, upside down, a broken amphora containing fresh green shoots. Another broken amphora lies inverted on the ground, while on the left we see a planter filled with plants. The moment depicted was the point in the festival when vessels containing ephemeral "gardens of Adonis" were to be carried up to the rooftops. This practice was part of an oriental ritual, supposedly inaugurated by Aphrodite to commemorate the premature death of handsome Adonis. In this particular composition the woman climbing the ladder may be an Athenian who is receiving help from Eros; or she may be Aphrodite herself, accompanied by her son. This is by no means an agrarian fertility ritual but rather an inversion of the festivals of Demeter. The tender green shoots will soon fry in the summer heat without bearing fruit. Familiar agricultural references are absent. These gardens of Adonis are planted not in the earth but in broken jars. They grow not in the ground but on rooftops. Adonis' premature death is celebrated with gardens that serve as a metaphor for the perishing of

31. Young she-bears, after kraters from the sanctuary of Artemis at Brauron.

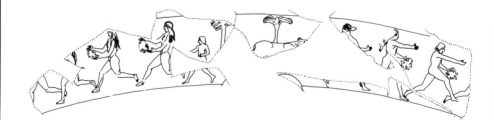

the hero. This ritual appears to have been strictly feminine. It was depicted on perfume jars in images that frequently stressed the link between Aphrodite and Eros. The painters' version of the festival was decidedly idyllic compared with the misogynist view of Aristophanes.

The She-Bears. Another series of paintings derived from Brauron's cult of Artemis.[38] The images (fig. 31) occur on small kraters given as offerings to the goddess in her temple; they portray young women performing, or preparing to perform, a bear-dance around the altar. Every picture is different. The series is difficult to analyze as a whole because there are so many gaps, but once again the iconography is closely related to the function of the object on which it appears: the paintings all relate to the ritual bear-dance performed in honor of Artemis at the annual Brauronia.

Dionysiac Rituals. Some seventy-odd paintings depict women dancing or serving wine in the presence of an effigy of Dionysus. Scholars are not sure whether the festival involved was the Lenaea or the Anthesteria. The details needed to settle the matter are missing, but certain features of the paintings attest to their ritual dimension. The compositions all center on an effigy consisting of a mask of Dionysus (sometimes carried to the site in a basket) and attached to a post decked with ivy and wrapped in a pleated covering. The mask is almost always shown head on, drawing the viewer's gaze to the center of the image. When the mask appears in profile, it is sometimes doubled. Often a table is placed in front of the effigy and set with *stamnoi,* vessels for mixing wine and water. The participants in the ritual are all women.

The most celebrated painting in this series occurs on a cup now in Berlin (fig. 32).[39] The mask of Dionysus is shown in profile, framed by branches, and the post is wrapped in richly embroidered cloth. In front of this statue and to the right is an altar, viewed from the side and stained with blood; it is decorated with a small, painted image of a seated individual. To the left of this group (the statue and the altar) is a woman playing the *aulos.* Dancing to the wild melody, a dozen women form a circle that winds all the way around the cup. Hair disheveled, each dancer is caught up

32. Dance around the pillar of Dionysus, cup, circa 490. Berlin, Antikenmuseum.

33. Under the gaze of
Dionysus, stamnos, circa
460. Rome, Villa Giulia.

in a whirl of her own rather than forming part of a continuous movement as on the Boston vase. Dancing around the mask of Dionysus, with which each dancer in turn comes face to face, seems to have been a crucial component of Dionysiac ritual.

A more common image depicted women pouring, mixing, or drinking wine. On a *stamnos* in the Villa Giulia (fig. 33) we also find an effigy of Dionysus.[40] This time the mask is seen from the front and occupies the center of the composition.

The post is covered by a tunic and ivy, and round cakes hang from the tunic's shoulders. In the foreground a table is set with round breads and two stamnoi similar to the one that bears the painting. On the left a woman pours wine from one of these vessels into a drinking cup, while on the right another woman holds a *skyphos,* a type of wine jug. The women are poised and solemn; their clothing is carefully arranged and their hair well groomed. There is no sign of a trance in this picture, in which everything suggests calm and control: proper mixing of the wine keeps these women in line.

The vision of Dionysianism presented here corresponds to the god at his most restrained and shows him most fully integrated into the Athenian order. It contrasts sharply with the image found in Theban tales, particularly the story of King Pentheus, whom Dionysus punishes for his incredulity by unleashing the murderous folly of his mother, Agave. Euripides' *Bacchantes* takes us a long way from this orderly, disciplined image of mastery over wine. Here, too, the vase on which the painting appears is represented. This reflexive type of representation offered a masculine version of a feminine ritual: the women of Athens are portrayed as maenads of a most unthreatening kind.

We will encounter more violent and threatening versions of maenadism a little later. Here I shall simply contrast the foregoing image with what seems to be a caricature (fig. 34).[41] The painting in question, which appears on a small skyphos, mocks the elements of the Dionysian ritual. The two faces of the vase must be considered simultaneously. One side shows a female dwarf with thick, misshapen features. Naked but for a leafy crown, she raises a skyphos to her lips. This is no dignified lady mixing wine before serving it but a wild barbarian who drinks alone without either mixing or sharing the wine. On the other side of the vase we see a post that is in fact a huge erect phallus with

192

34. Dionysiac parody,
skyphos, circa 440.
Munich, Antikensammlung
und Glyptothek.

an eye on the glans and wings at the base. It is
decked, like the pillar of Dionysus, with ivy. Here
the god is not a mask but an animate phallus.
What is evoked is not the fascination of the gaze
but the sexual energy over which the god Dionysus
rules. The *kanoun,* or three-pointed sacrificial basket, placed atop the phallic pillar symbolizes the

ritual dimension of the scene. Placed in front of the effigy is a table set with a skyphos, once again a vessel similar to that on which the image appears. In other words, a composition similar to those used in the series of *stamnoi* has here been adapted to show an obscene tippler. In a parody of the preceding image, the woman is portrayed as a drunk, as was often the case in Aristophanes' comedies as well.

The various images of ritual discussed thus far portray women as a group, acting collectively, whether around the body of a deceased individual or an effigy of a god. The convenient opposition between public and private does not always hold true in these images. Warriors are shown with members of their family, but the hoplite stands for the city in arms. Conversely, the pouring of a libation or the carrying of a sacrificial basket can be interpreted as elements of a public ritual, a blood offering to the gods by the city, or as private acts whose nature the artists did not fully specify.

Spaces

In explaining how the inhabitants of the Nile differed from the Greeks, Herodotus wrote: "In their manners and customs the Egyptians seem to have reversed the ordinary practices of mankind. For instance, women go to market and engage in trade, while men stay home and do the weaving" (II, 35). To the Greek historian this world seemed topsy-turvy. The very idea of women doing business on the public square and men doing the weaving at home was almost inconceivable. This passage attests, and other texts confirm, that for the Greeks the ideal was for women to stay at home, in the *oikia,* indeed in that part of it which, as the name suggests, was reserved for them: the gynaeceum. Few men had access to this part of the house, and to judge by the testimony in certain adultery cases, the women of the house—wife, daughters, servants, and sometimes other female relatives—did their work there and rarely went out. Women raised young children and worked among themselves, mainly spinning and weaving.

The image found in vase paintings differs somewhat. In scholarly debate over the status of women in Greece, and in Athens in particular, one of the most controversial issues has been the confinement of women. Was such confinement for women's protection, or was it, as we with our own preconceptions tend to see it, a limit on their autonomy? The question is badly framed, because it imposes our categories on the Greeks. Vase paintings can shed new light on it, although we must be careful to keep in mind that the painters construed space in conformity with Athenian male categories.

Two Models

Herodotus' contrast between inside and outside corresponds roughly to that between female and male. Except for banquets, most interior scenes in Attic vase painting involve women. There is an important series of images of women in the gynaeceum. Many of these occur on pyxides, and they often contain a door that is either open or ajar.

On one pyxis (fig. 35), which served as a jewel box and is now in London, we find portraits of six women in groups of two in an interior setting.[42] Nearly all have mythological names. On the left Helen sits winding yarn in front of a basket. Clytemnestra, facing her, holds out an alabaster perfume jar. A mirror stands between them, and a column separates them from the next pair: a woman holding out a basket to Cassandra, who is adjusting her robes. On the right, Danae takes a crown from a chest and advances toward an open door, through which we see Iphigenia wrapping a bandelet around her head. Note the inter-

195

35. In the gynaeceum, pyxis, circa 460. London, British Museum (in Furtwängler Reichhold, pl. 57).

play on this jewel box between images of the open and the closed. Removing the cover of the box exposes a necklace, and what we see through the door is a woman dressing. The mirror, alabaster jar, necklace, bandelet, and even Cassandra's gesture are all elements of the iconography of female beauty, dressing, and grooming. The mythological names attached to the figures do not correspond to any specific myth, but they do amplify the painter's aesthetic intent, which is not to illustrate everyday life but to give a poetic dimension to woman's space. The names attached to the figures are yet another kind of adornment.

Contrast this pyxis with another (fig. 36), which, though stylistically very similar, depicts an outdoor scene.[43] On the left we see a fountain in profile. Hippolyte looks on as her hydria is filled, while a companion awaits her turn. On the right Maspaura, arms askew, hastens toward a tree guarded by a coiled snake, while Thetis gathers fruit. The tree guarded by a snake is reminiscent of the famous garden of the Hesperides where Heracles is supposed to find the golden apples. In

196

36. At the fountain, pyxis, circa 460. London, British Museum (in Furtwängler Reichhold, pl. 57).

this painting, however, the hero does not appear; the scene is set outdoors, and only women and their activities (gathering fruits and fetching water) are shown. The painter uses the mythological allusion not to recount a heroic exploit but to add a mythical dimension to a scene combining two themes that can be traced back to the black-figure period: the orchard and the fountain.

These two vessels establish a parallel between women's work indoors and women's work outdoors, between the private space of the oikos and the public space of the orchard and fountain. Hence the distinction between male and female does not coincide precisely with that between exterior and interior.

Fountains

The feminine world as seen by vase painters was not limited to the gynaeceum. Numerous paintings depict women at fountains, but their interpretation is highly controversial. What was the status of the women shown fetching water? From the hypoth-

197

esis that free women never left home it follows that these women must be slaves. But there is little internal evidence in the paintings to support this conclusion. There are no graphic signs to distinguish the mistress from her servants or the free woman from the slave. Social status was not represented in painting any more than age. One of the rare exceptions to this rule is a hydria now in the Louvre (fig. 37), which shows three women carrying similar hydrias (again note the image of the vessel on the vessel itself).[44] Their hair is short

37. Tattooed slave women at the fountain, hydria, circa 470. Paris, Louvre.

and stiff, and they have tattoos on their arms and legs—signs that these women are Thracian slaves. But there is no other comparable image. Most of the paintings in this series emphasize the collective nature of what went on around the fountain, which frequently appears as a place for meeting and exchange generally involving only women. On one hydria (fig. 38) in Würzburg, for example, five

38. Women at the fountain, hydria, circa 530. Würzburg, Martin von Wagner Museum.

199

39. The space of a louterion, skyphos, circa 470. Brussels, Royal Museum of Art and History.

women have gathered.[45] One supervises the filling of the hydrias, while the others are either arriving or leaving. (The vessels carried upright are probably full.) From their gestures we gather that they exchange words as they pass. Vertical inscriptions give the women's names, which suggest the names of various flowers: Anthyle, Rhodon, Hegesila, Myrta, and Anthyla. The adjective *kale* means beautiful.

Here, then, the fountain is portrayed as the female equivalent of what the public square represents for men. It was a public place where one saw mainly women (or so the painters would have us believe). In certain paintings we see men who have come to look at the women. The image thus incorporates into the composition the male gaze of the spectator looking at the vase. In a more mythological vein fountains also served as settings for ambushes and violent encounters. We see, for example, Amymone taken unawares by Poseidon, or the young Trojan prince Troilus accompanying

his sister Polyxena to the fountain, where he is attacked by Achilles.[46]

Grooming and the Louterion

The *louterion,* a stone basin used for ablutions and grooming, appears frequently in paintings as a center of social activity. A skyphos now in Brussels (fig. 39) is a good example.[47] The same basin is depicted on both sides of the vessel. On one side (page 200) two pairs of women meet. The group on the left gathers around a louterion. One woman holds a flower in her raised hand, while the other lifts a mirror. On the other side (above) we see two pairs of men. A tree behind the louterion indicates that the scene is outdoors. Hanging in the branches is a grooming kit containing a sponge, a scraper, and a cylindrical jar of oil. These instruments were used by young athletes when they exercised in the palaestra. The man's grooming kit is the analogue of the woman's mirror. The athlete takes care of his body, while the woman takes care of her looks. In Attic imagery mirrors were an exclusively female accoutrement.

The central medallion of a cup now in the Louvre (fig. 40) depicts a woman with toilet accessories: a mirror and an oblong alabaster perfume jar.[48] Her body can be seen through her sheer chiton. We see her head on, looking at herself in the mirror but at the same time turned toward us. This is unusual in Attic vases, on which figures normally appear in profile, but it is no accident. The confrontation with self offered by the mirror is here amplified by the confrontation with the gaze of the person drinking from the cup. The woman looks in the mirror to reassure herself of her beauty. Two objects suggest what is going on in the scene: the basin for ablutions on the left, and the *calathos,* or basket of yarn, that sits on the chair. Good grooming and skill with wool are to men's eyes the essential ingredients of female beauty.

40. Woman with mirror, after cup, circa 490. Paris, Louvre.

41. Women grooming, krater, circa 440. Bologna, Civic Archaeological Museum.

Other paintings combine these same ingredients in different ways. In one (fig. 41), three women gather around a louterion bearing the inscription *kale* in large letters.[49] The one on the left is naked and holds a mirror. The woman in the center offers her an alabaster jar, and the one on the right is dressed and holds a small ankle-boot. Grooming provides an occasion to contrast the nude body with various accoutrements. The painter has tried to convey the beauty of the naked body rather than let it be glimpsed through a sheer garment. Similarly, on a small hydria now in the Louvre (fig. 42), a nude woman is grooming herself next to a basin as a hovering Eros arrives with her clothing.[50] Desire is thus embodied in the form of a winged youth dressing a naked female. In Athens, unlike Sparta, nude women were rarely portrayed, so these images of naked women doing their toilette are unusual. The female body as portrayed here is almost masculine, barely altered by the addition of breasts. Greek art in general, and Attic vase painting in particular, was fundamentally anthropomorphic, even in the representation of the gods. Images are invariably based on bodies, not volumes, objects, or landscapes. A great deal of attention was paid to anatomy, and it was the masculine form that shaped the painters' vision. Men and women did not groom themselves in the same way, however. Youths were perceived primarily as athletes. Almost always shown naked, they rivaled one another in strength as well as beauty. The painters emphasized this virile beauty whether painting games in the palaestrum or grooming around the louterion. Women were never shown engaged in gymnastic exercises. They appeared naked only in scenes of grooming. The ephebe's beauty was entirely in his body, but the woman's was just as much in her clothing and accoutrements.

Music

Painters were also interested in activities other than grooming. Music was important in Greek culture. It was featured in rituals and in festive choruses, chants, and dances. There are numerous paintings of female musicians; we have already encountered images of female choruses and flutists. Groups of musicians also appear in a series of red-figure paintings from the second half of the fifth

42. Eros at the bath, hydria, circa 430. Paris, Louvre.

43. Musicians, krater, circa 440. Würzburg, Martin von Wagner Museum.

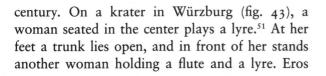

century. On a krater in Würzburg (fig. 43), a woman seated in the center plays a lyre.[51] At her feet a trunk lies open, and in front of her stands another woman holding a flute and a lyre. Eros

44. Dance lesson, krater, circa 460. Lecce, Provincial Museum.

flies overhead, holding a wreath in his outstretched hands. This image, like some of the pictures of women grooming, bears the mark of Aphrodite. Some paintings in this series can be interpreted as gatherings of the Muses, who were certainly the models for the women we see portrayed playing instruments or reading from open scrolls. In some cases explicit reference is made to the poet Sappho. The presence of Eros further conveys the ideas of grace and desire.

Music and dance played an important educational role in Greek culture, and school scenes appeared frequently from the late sixth century on. As far as the painters were concerned, it was mainly boys who read and recited in the classroom. Their tutors accompanied them to school. In musical performances men are often shown on stage in front of judges, sometimes receiving a wreath from a winged Nike, or Victory, while women usually appear indoors, among themselves, with Eros. Thus, according to the painters, the activities of the two sexes were parallel but different. The same is true of dance: apart from the *comos,* most dance scenes involve women. Even the Pyrrhic, a dance in arms generally associated with youthful males, was sometimes performed by girls. But it is hard to be specific about the context of paintings showing women studying music or dance. On a krater now in Lecce (fig. 44), a seated woman plays the flute for a girl wearing a short tunic who dances in front of her.[52] A kithara hangs in the background. Is this a picture of a home or a school? What is the relation between the woman and the girl: mother and daughter or mistress and servant? It has even been suggested that the girl is a young hetaera. But the painter was not painting for historians, and the image offers no answers to questions that undoubtedly did not arise for the ancients who contemplated this vase.

Woman's Work

Mirror, kithara, flute—the range of objects with which women were depicted was fairly limited. Each object defined not just an activity but the very status of women. The most common attributes involved spinning and weaving: distaffs (which sometimes look remarkably like mirrors), knitting baskets, portable looms. Above all, these symbols evoked the feminine virtue par excellence: *ergatis,* or industriousness, as exemplified by Penelope. These images do not exalt work for its own sake. The Greeks did not attach to work the same value as do modern cultures in which the ideology of effort has long held sway. In a slave society, such as that of fifth-century Athens, labor was even repudiated by the citizenry, whose chief occupation was politics. Industriousness was one of the virtues of women, and in this respect they differed from slaves, whose merits no one would have thought of celebrating, much less painting. There are precious few paintings of workshops or groups of artisans, and in the small number we know the presence of Hephaestus or Athena suggests that the image was intended to connote the favor of the gods. One hydria now in Milan (fig. 45) offers a remarkable example of this attitude.[53] Four artisans are sitting in what appears to be a potter's or bronzeworker's shop (it is hard to tell whether the vases are ceramic or metal). In the center Athena places a wreath on the head of a worker decorating a cantharus. Two companions also receive wreaths from winged Nikai in honor of their work. On a sort of podium on the right a woman is completing the decoration of a large krater. Her status does not appear to be inferior to that of her coworkers, but we cannot be sure. All we know is that of the four figures in this exceptional painting, she alone receives no wreath.

Few paintings actually depict women at work. One striking absence from the repertory is the kitchen. On one cup fragment (fig. 46), a woman, her cloak tied around her waist, is leaning over a stone basin and may be doing the wash.[54] Behind her a pestle evokes the pulverizing of grain. Such

45. Potter's workshop, hydria, circa 460. Milan, Torno Collection.

46. Washing or preparation of seed? cup, circa 480. Paris, Bibliothèque Nationale.

47. Preparing fabric, lecythus, circa 540. New York, Metropolitan Museum of Art.

209

48. Spinning, cup, circa 490. Berlin, Antikenmuseum.

activities appear in few paintings, however. The celebrated lecythus of Amasis (fig. 47) is in a class by itself.[55] Nine women, divided into four groups, are shown working with wool. Some are filling the basket with large balls of yarn, while others prepare a finer thread with the aid of a spindle. Three are weighing wool. Two others are operating a vertical loom. The fabric winds around the upper portion of this device. The remaining two women fold a piece of cloth. The documentary value of this image is undeniable, but it has nothing to do with the painter's intention. On the shoulder of the same vase we see a dancing chorus. The woman seated in the center is flanked by two standing men. Two half-choruses, each consisting of a young man followed by four women, converge toward the central group. Weaving and dance are thus complementary. The Greeks were struck by the similarity between the movement of the shuttle and that of dancers, and the two frequently occur together in imagery. This vase, moreover, was found with another featuring a painting of a wedding procession on the body and a chorus of women on the shoulder.[56] The juxtaposition of themes—weaving, wedding, dancing—shows what the Athenians considered to be the most important of women's activities.

Scenes of women spinning are common in the late archaic period. The usual symbols—distaff and basket—specify the nature of the activity. More than that, they characterize women as active; idleness was an exclusive province of the male. What interested the painters was not the techniques of weaving but the beauty of the women's gestures. Once again, the paintings aestheticize what they portray.

A cup in Berlin (fig. 48), for example, depicts two women.[57] The one on the left is sitting with her right leg bared and her heel resting on an *onos*, or low stool. From the basket in front of her she has taken a length of wool (highlighted in violet but partly effaced), which she is rolling around her shin in order to produce a finer thread. Her companion, standing, adjusts her robes, while her basket rests on a stool to the right. The elegant gesture of the standing woman, a gesture reminiscent of the bride's lifting of the veil, shows the aesthetic considerations at work here. The exterior of the cup features a cortege of eleven bearded males holding drinking flagons and dancing to the music of flutes. Thus this vessel, which would have been used by men at banquets, portrays on its inner surface the world of women and on its outer surface the world of men.

From the fountain to the louterion, from music to weaving, women moved in a diversified space that cannot be reduced to a simple contrast between inside and outside. The painters were in fact frequently interested in the relations that developed between different kinds of space and the encounters that took place as a result.

Encounters and Exchanges

Male-female relations were cast in images other than those intended for the *symposion,* or banquet. One series of paintings portrays encounters, conversations, and the exchange of gifts between men and women. In Attic imagery the exchange of gifts between lovers was first portrayed in the context of homosexual relationships. The black-figure painters of the late sixth century painted amorous encounters and embraces between adult males and youths. The *erastes,* adult lovers, offered various gifts to the *eromenes,* beloved youths: small animals such as cocks and hares, wreaths, and other objects.[58]

In the iconography of women we find similar items. On one *pelike* (fig. 49) a woman holds two flowers that set off her beauty.[59] On the reverse side of the vase a man holds the thigh of a sacrificial animal from which the bone has been removed. This offering is here given to the woman as a gift. If a man gave a woman a gift, it was expected that the woman give him a gift in return. In paintings men were always shown as gift-givers. Along with flowers, animals, and meats, some paintings show men giving small purses, and there has been a great deal of controversy about what these might contain. It is not clear that money is the answer. Such purses are almost never found in scenes of commerce. Perhaps they contained small bones or other tokens. Some commentators have interpreted these purses as signs of man's economic power over woman; by accepting money, she be-

49. Gifts of meat and flowers, pelike, circa 470. Present location unknown.

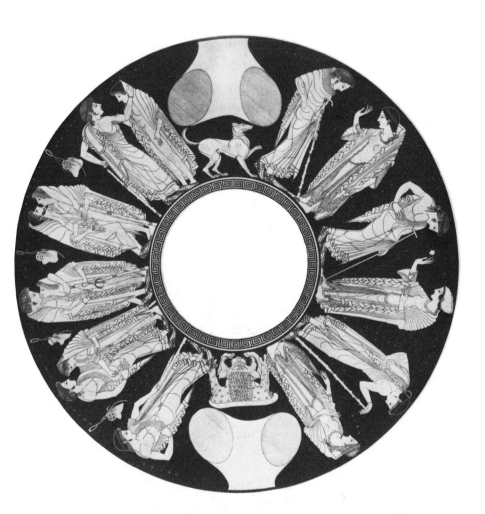

comes a prostitute. Thus the purse supposedly becomes an "economic phallus."[60] Although such an interpretation may sometimes be possible, it should not be generalized too broadly. Although men certainly dominated women, that domination was not necessarily mercantile. In scenes of courting and seduction the man seeks to attract not only with words but also with the gift of a desired object.

In translating this dialectic of desire into images, painters exploited different types of amorous exchange. Sometimes they drew parallels between

50. Two types of meeting, cup, circa 510. Berlin, Antikenmuseum (in Hartwig, Meisterschalen, pl. 25).

213

homosexual and heterosexual encounters. A cup in Berlin (fig. 50) exemplifies this in a particularly elaborate way.[61] On one side four young couples are more or less intimately entwined. A difference in size indicates that the erastes, the active partners, dominate the eromenes, whom they caress. The kit bags in the background indicate that the youths are athletes, as does the repeated inscription: *ho pais kalos,* the young man is handsome. On the reverse side we find only three couples, this time heterosexual; rather than embrace, the men and women are facing one another. The men lean on staffs, while the women are holding flowers, fruits, or their robes. The kit bags are gone, and the inscriptions alternate between the masculine and feminine gender: *ho pais kalos, ho pais kale.* The images thus bring together two different types of amorous intercourse. But desire and fulfillment are consistently shown from the point of view of the adult male. Obviously one cannot draw from this image any conclusions about the division of sexual roles. The themes of gift-giving, seduction, and copulation are common in archaic imagery. The particular juxtaposition of images on this cup reminds us that images of women cannot be studied as an autonomous unit within the whole range of Attic iconography. What is more, the central medallion of this same cup depicts another kind of relation between the sexes: abduction. The image shows Peleus grasping Thetis by the waist and struggling against her metamorphosis.

Pursuits

Many paintings depict amorous pursuits, often involving mythological figures. Abduction, along with its implicit violence, seems to have been favored as a means of expressing the relation of man to woman and of the gods to man, especially around the turn of the fifth century. Zeus, for example, was often shown in pursuit of mortal

women, for the most part anonymous. An example can be seen on a hydria now in the Cabinet des Médailles in Paris (fig. 51).[62] But Zeus was also shown frequently in pursuit of young Ganymede, suggesting an equivalence between homosexual and heterosexual desire. The violence of the god's desire and the fear it inspired in mortal women are also found in scenes of pursuit by heroic mortals such as Theseus. The iconography depicts the pursuing male as a hunter and the pursued female as his quarry.

The themes of gift and exchange stand in sharp contrast to the themes of abduction and pursuit. The latter involve chiefly mythological or metaphorical figures: the gods, Peleus, Theseus. Scenes involving satyrs and maenads also invoke these themes, as we shall see later.

51. Zeus pursuing a woman, hydria, circa 480. Paris, Bibliothèque Nationale.

52. Banquet, cup, circa 480. London, British Museum.

Wine, Banquets, and the Erotic

It was customary in Greece to drink in company after mixing wine and water in kraters. Drinking uncut wine was believed to be dangerous, but properly diluted wine, shared with male guests, was thought to have positive value. The *symposion* (literally, drinking together) that generally followed the meal was a time for conviviality among men. Friends and equals came together to talk and sing. Usually they lay stretched out on sofas. Woman had no place here: neither wives nor daughters took part in the symposion. The only women present were those who served in an auxiliary capacity, as it were. The ladies of pleasure who waited on the guests and played music were there not to enjoy themselves but to see that all went well. From various sources we know that these hetaerae, or companions, were hired for the occasion.[63]

The symposion theme is one of the most common in Attic imagery, particularly on drinking vessels, cups, and kraters. Such images were meant to serve as reflections of the banqueters' own activities; they were models (or warnings) to those who wished to perfect themselves in the art of drinking. One cup in London (fig. 52) features a circular

composition of four sofas without hierarchical dis-
tinction.⁶⁴ Two columns evoke the banquet hall;
next to each stands a servant, one holding a lyre,
the other a ladle and strainer for serving the wine.
Each sofa is occupied by a man, three of whom
are named by inscriptions: Demonikos, Aristo-
crates, Diphilos. Each is accompanied by a
woman. One of the women, seated, raises a cup
of wine at the foot of a sofa occupied by a young
man who is adjusting his bandelet. Another
woman, standing, plays the *aulos* in front of a
bearded man holding a *skyphos*. The woman sitting on the stool on the other side is blonde, perhaps Thracian. She too plays an *aulos,* next to a
bearded man who turns to hand a *skyphos* to a
neighbor. The latter, beardless, has allowed his
robe to slip from his shoulders, uncovering his
torso, and he is pulling toward him the young
woman seated at the foot of his sofa. From one
couch to the next we thus proceed from drinking
to music to amorous revelry.

In the period 520 to 470 B.C. these banquet
themes were taken up by a large number of vase
painters. Wine, women, song, and dance appear
in various combinations. Eros does not figure in
the paintings of this period notwithstanding the
proverb that "Aphrodite and Dionysus [love and

217

53. Erotic activity after a banquet, hydria, circa 510. Brussels, Royal Museum of Art and History.

wine] go together." Eros of course is part of Aphrodite's retinue and was the very symbol of sexual desire. But these symposion images represent not desire but its satisfaction: intoxication and physical pleasure. Aphrodite's place is elsewhere, in scenes of marriage and seduction. The symposion, at least as depicted in painting, was an occasion for gratifying men's appetites. Some forty paintings portray the act of copulation: although generally characterized as erotic and reproduced in most works on Greek erotic art, Eros does not appear in them. They are erotic in the modern sense, and most show women either stimulating or gratifying the desires of their male partners. To take just one example, a hydria now in Brussels (fig. 53) shows two couples.[65] On the left the youthful Polylaus is lying down and reaching out toward Egilla, who approaches on her knees; on the right young Kleocrates hugs Sekline, whom we see from the rear.

Although this theme disappears in the second half of the fifth century, the iconography of the banquet with its motifs of music and drinking continues. The figure of Eros becomes increasingly common, not only in Aphrodite's entourage but also in conjunction with Dionysus in the banquet setting. The change in repertoire marked the appearance of a new sensibility: desire, represented in allegorical form, took on greater importance.

In the archaic era women in banquets invariably played auxiliary roles, but it is hard to be precise about their status. Were they hetaerae? Were they freewomen or slaves? The iconography does not provide information to answer these questions, and no doubt the images were in large part projections. Consider the two women who lie, not side by side as at a banquet, but facing each other on a cup now in Madrid (fig. 54).[66] The woman on the left, like her counterparts on the London cup, is playing the aulos. The other woman, who is holding a skyphos, offers her companion a cup; an inscription records her words: *pine kai su,* you drink too. Both women are naked and isolated from the rest of the company. What are we to make of this scene? How are we to interpret one woman's invitation to another to drink in the absence of any male companion? This unusual image is certainly a manipulation of the

54. Female drinkers, cup, circa 510. Madrid, Archaeological Museum.

219

iconographic code, and perhaps it is best to refrain from imposing a meaning.

In some cases there is no doubt that we are dealing with a projection or fantasy. Consider the medallion of a cup in the Villa Giulia (fig. 55).[67] It shows a naked woman wearing only a *sakkos*, or bonnet, and earrings. She is astride an enormous bird whose neck is a long phallus with an eye on the glans. Recall that the Munich caricature (fig. 34) also portrayed a winged phallus in a Dionysiac context. Here the body and feet suggest a winged creature of some sort, and the female rider is definitely not of the maenad type but a hetaera. An

55. A strange bird, cup, circa 500. Rome, Villa Giulia.

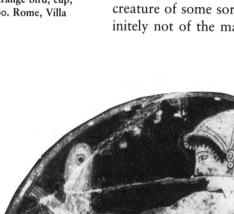

image like this at the bottom of a drinking cup is clearly the representation of an intoxicated male's fantasy.

Paintings of the *comos*—the chaotic procession of singing and dancing revelers—sometimes made use of Dionysiac symbolism. On occasion guests might dress as women. On the medallion of a cup now in the Louvre (fig. 56) a bearded male holding a parasol in his left hand walks with the aid of a walking stick.[68] He is wearing a long, pleated robe and a sakkos. Here, masculine attributes (the beard and walking stick) contrast with feminine ones (the long robe and sakkos): the comos was

56. Female disguise, cup, circa 480. Paris, Louvre.

221

one place where such temporary ambivalence was permissible. Examination of a series of paintings of such processions shows that such figures are actually men dressed as women. After drinking, men explored various forms of otherness: they behaved bestially, like satyrs, or barbarically, like the Scythians who drank undiluted wine. And they also explored the world of the feminine. The man who dressed as a woman temporarily became one, as a kind of joke. In such behavior we find further evidence for the proposition that Athenian men looked upon women as creatures of another species.

Mythical Models

Mythical models influenced the way the Greeks imagined the feminine. Two "tribes" of women occupied an important place in the repertoire: maenads and Amazons. These tribes transgressed the male order in various ways.

Maenads

One painting discussed earlier (fig. 33) portrayed women mixing wine beneath a mask of Dionysus. In certain ritual scenes these servants of the god are shown dancing in a frenzied manner as if in a trance, whence the name maenads (raving women). Vase painters usually depicted them in mythological scenes along with Dionysus himself and accompanied by satyrs.[69] The maenad was thus distinguished by her wild manner of dancing and her familiarity with wild animals. On one cup (fig. 57) a woman wearing a long, pleated robe has tied a panther skin around her neck and holds a live panther by a hind leg.[70] Her hair is disheveled, and she wears a snake for a headband. She is holding a *thyrsus,* or ivy-covered staff. Everything—clothing, plants, animals—contributes to

the transformation of this woman into a savage. But unlike the satyr, who is animalized in his very anatomy, the maenad's transformation is accomplished by the addition of these various attributes.

The relation between satyrs and maenads in Dionysus' entourage is not obvious. The oldest images, up to around 510 B.C., depict them as joyful companions, dancing together and on occasion copulating. With the inception of the red-figure period, this changes. Maenads usually are shown rejecting the advances of the satyrs who pursue them, in accordance with the pattern established by the amorous pursuits of gods and heroes. The satyrs' lubricity continues to be displayed in

57. Maenad in race, cup, circa 480. Munich, Antikensammlung und Glyptothek.

223

an obscene manner, however. They are in a constant state of erection, manifesting an insatiable sexual appetite.

The theme of abduction is most powerfully expressed in a series of images embodying fantasies of voyeurism and rape. A maenad on one hydria in Rouen (fig. 58), her eyes closed and her thyrsus in hand, sleeps quietly.[71] A satyr, having lifted her robe, places a hand on her, while on the left another satyr appears to be astonished by his virility. The nakedness of the sleeping maenad seems to arouse the lust of the satyrs, who are always game to satisfy their desires. But nothing happens: in this series of paintings the satyrs approach their quarry but never have their way.

Maenads appear to have entered their trance-like state more as a result of music and dancing than of drinking, and this, too, seems to please the satyrs. Sometimes, however, the maenads' trance erupts in violence: in image as in myth they then became capable of tearing animals to pieces with their bare hands after pursuing them into the mountains, far from the cities. Along with Dionysus the maenads practiced what was called *dias-*

58. Sleeping maenad, hydria, circa 500. Rouen, Départemental Museum.

59. Frenzied maenad, lecythus, circa 470. Syracuse, P. Orsi Museum.

paragmos, the tearing apart of raw flesh, as distinguished from civic sacrifice in all its forms, in which the animal was slaughtered, butchered, and roasted. The violence of *diasparagmos* is depicted on a lecythus in Syracuse (fig. 59), which shows a maenad, her hair undone and her thyrsus stuck in the ground on her left, tearing a young deer limb from limb.[72]

Thracians

Another myth provided painters with an opportunity to depict the murderous violence imputed to women. The story is set in Thrace, where the poet Orpheus charmed his male audience with his poems. Jealous, the women of the place put him to death. On a stamnos now in the Louvre (fig. 60), we see Orpheus lying on the ground, defending himself with his lyre.[73] The Thracian women, tattoos on their arms, assail him with stones and literally skewer him on the iron skewers that the Greeks used for roasting sacrificial meat.

Amazons

The twofold otherness of these Thracian murderesses—they are barbarians and they are women—is matched by the Amazons, a favorite subject of vase painters, more than a thousand of whose paintings of the tribe have survived. The Amazons were of course warrior women who lived apart and refused all contact with men. For an Athenian—citizen, hoplite, and defender of the city—they were the ultimate paradox, symbols of a world stood on its head. For Amazons were warriors without a city, a permanent menace to the

60. Thracian women killing Orpheus, stamnos, circa 460. Paris, Louvre.

civilized world. In paintings they were therefore repeatedly portrayed in combat with either the civilizing hero, Heracles, or the Athenian hero, Theseus.

On one epinetron (fig. 61), used by women for spinning wool, we see three Amazons taking up their shields.[74] Here they are equipped in the same way as hoplites, but in many paintings they are shown with barbarian weapons such as bows and hatchets and wearing striped clothing like the Scythians, which accentuated the strangeness of these troubling figures. An amphora in the Louvre (fig. 62) shows Theseus abducting Antiope, queen of the Amazons, who wears a Scythian bonnet and carries a bow and a quiver of arrows.[75] Here we have sexuality conceived as warfare and based on antagonism and violence but set in the mythical time of Athens' foundation, when women formed an autonomous tribe.

I shall conclude this survey of mythological themes with a unique but revealing image (fig. 63) found on an alabaster perfume jar.[76] It shows what I am tempted to call a logical combination of the maenad and Amazon themes. On the left a maenad wearing a panther skin and Thracian boots holds a serpent and a hare. Her name is Theraichme, the Huntress. Meanwhile the helmeted Amazon Pen-

62. Theseus abducts
an Amazon, amphora,
circa 510. Paris, Louvre.

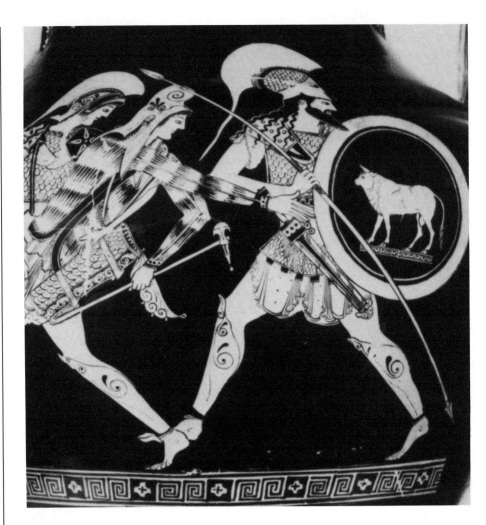

Detail of Figure 62.

thesilea arrives on the scene with bow and hatchet. This painting thus draws a parallel between the two mythical images of woman, one savage, the other barbaric. Since the perfume jar on which it appears would have been used by women, the image confronted Athenian women with two versions of their essential otherness as seen by men. This painting, though highly unusual, sheds new light on the function of Attic imagery. In painting, no radical distinction was made between the mythological and the everyday. Mythical paradigms were often used to dramatize certain moments in social life: Thetis bestowing arms on Achilles, Penelope at her loom. Conversely, the most commonplace images were mythologized by inscriptions identifying figures such as Alceste or Eriphyle. At the whim of a painter or his audience women could be lifted from anonymity to the mythical status of maenads or Amazons.

The use of a vase often determined its iconography. We find ritual themes on ritual vases and feminine themes on vases used by women. The context reinforced the power of the image. But Amazons and maenads most commonly appeared on objects used by men in banquets. These fanciful images of women were not destined for women's eyes. The images on Attic ceramics incorporated many different models. To the spectator they could serve as mirrors or admonitions. Women appeared in many guises, but whether portrayed as mother or wife, hetaera or musician, Amazon or maenad, they were always objects on display for the pleasure of the male viewer.

63. Maenad and Amazon, from alabaster perfume jar, circa 490. Athens, National Museum.

two

Traditional Rituals
Women Share

Marriage Strategies

In Part Two we take a different approach, though one still based on textual analysis. In contrast to Part One, here we focus on the everyday activities of Greek and Roman women, on practices associated with sexuality and reproduction; marriage, celibacy, and widowhood; property; and religious ritual and priesthood.[1] A common thread runs throughout these chapters, because a woman's biological nature became perceptible only as she grew up in a particular social context. A female child was not only a potential mother but also a commodity of interfamilial exchange, and there were specific religious functions for which she was suitable. As she grew older, these social functions changed.

"Marriage is to young women what war is to young men."[2] Jean-Pierre Vernant's celebrated dictum does not imply that marriage was unimportant for men in the city-states of the ancient world; matrimonial strategies are always an important aspect of social relations.[3] Claudine Leduc provides an uncompromisingly anthropological study of Greek marriage. Her basic assumption is that, from the time of Homer to the classical period, Greek marriage was organized as gift-giving: the gift included not only the bride but also certain items of property. The manner in which this gift was arranged can tell a great deal, Leduc argues, about the evolution of political structures in different city-states. As she examines marriage customs in Homer's texts and in the laws of Gortyn (in Crete) and Athens, we begin to understand the rationale behind the connection between legitimate marriage and real or movable property. Women and matrimonial strategies thus become central issues for understanding one of the most basic questions about ancient Greece: How did the *polis* (city-state) come to be?

P.S.P.

5

Marriage in Ancient Greece

Claudine Leduc

THE FIRST GREEK BRIDE, the bride in humanity's foundational myth, that of Prometheus, bears
a name—Pandora—belonging to the same lexical
group as the verb *didomi* (to give).[1] Pandora is
given in marriage by Zeus. Angry with Prometheus
for his duplicitous behavior at the time of the first
sacrifice, the Father of the Gods orders certain of
his children, those gifted with cunning intelligence,
to fabricate a trap in the form of a bride, which
the most powerful of the gods intends to spring
on mankind.[2] Pandora is taken by Hermes to the
home of a man simple enough to welcome her
with unreflective joy. Dressed for her wedding in
wreath, jewels, sash, veil, and embroidered gown,
she exudes a radiant charm.[3] The shimmering
bride brings with her a tightly sealed jar. When
she opens it, death and other evils are loosed on
the world, but hope will not emerge. The commentators have never been able to agree whether
the name Pandora signifies she who gave everything or she who was given by all the gods. For
our purposes the answer scarcely matters. The
etymological controversy brings to light a hitherto
hidden aspect of Greek marriage: the bride was a
free gift, and she came to her husband's home
polydoros (bearing gifts).

The free gift was, I believe, the organizing principle of the Hellenic system of legitimate reproduction. From the eighth to the fourth century B.C. a woman was always given *(didomi)* to her husband by another man, and this man always gave other riches *(epididomi)* along with her. Regardless of the social customs involved, the mother of a man's *legitimate children* (the sons who would succeed him and the daughters whom he would give away in marriage) was associated with (the Greek word means "settled on") certain possessions or expectations of wealth. This meant that in Greece a woman and her "patrimonial succession" were, in a fundamental sense, consubstantial.

Hellenic societies appear to have practiced what J. Goody and S. J. Tambiah have called "diverging devolution."[4] The term refers to a mode of inheritance "that includes women as well as men." But many questions remain. Did children of both sexes receive equivalent or identical legacies? Was devolution bilateral (in other words, did property "diverge" from both the father and the mother)? Was a distinction made between the owner, the recipient, and the usufructuary of the bride's portion? The concept of diverging devolution provides a useful tool for studying social relations in ancient Greece. It suggests a material basis for a fundamental social asymmetry.

Since brides, regardless of the composition of their phratry, had to be given with property, the number of possible combinations was limited. They are summarized in Table 1 and referred to in what follows by the letter T.

This way of posing the problem emphasizes the continuity of the system of legitimate reproduction. Our approach therefore differs fundamentally from that of the leading authorities in the field, who stress the system's discontinuities rather than its continuities. Thus Louis Gernet[5] and, following his lead, Jean-Pierre Vernant[6] and Joseph Modrzejewski[7] argue that Athenian marriage in the classical period (T/I1, II4, III2, IV2–3) was an "inversion," indeed a "total inversion," of Homeric marriage in its most common form (T/I2, II4, III1, IV1, 3). They see the dowry, or gift given by the bride's father, as a "sort of reversal" of the *hedna,* or gifts given by the groom's father, described in the *Iliad* and the *Odyssey.* Instead of "reversal," Claude Mossé prefers to speak of "rupture."[8] She sees two such "ruptures" in the evolution of the Athenian matrimonial system. The first is supposed to have occurred in the time of Solon, when the Homeric *hedna* were supplanted by the *pherne,* a gift by the bride's father that Mossé

Table 1. The Gift of the Bride in Greece (Ninth to Fourth Century B.C.)*

I. The gift of the bride: marriage within and without the social group
- I₁ True endogamy
- I₂ Virtual endogamy

II. The wealth of the bride's father
- II₁ House
- II₂ Land
- II₃ Livestock (movable chattel)
- II₄ Contents of household

III. The status of the bride and her retinue
- III₁ Placed in possession of groom (*ktesis*)
- III₂ Placed under authority of groom (*kyreia*)
- III₃ Neither *ktesis* nor *kyreia*

IV. The groom takes the bride and her retinue
- IV₁ Groom gives livestock to bride's father
- IV₂ Groom gives nothing to bride's father
- IV₃ Groom gives gifts to bride
- IV₄ Groom gives nothing to bride

*Marriages are classified in terms of four sets of parameters, here shown around the sides of the square. These parameters, indicated by Roman numerals, are: I. Social space to which the bride is sent, along with the wedding gifts; II. Forms of wealth placed in circulation by the bride's father as wedding gifts; III. Status of the bride and wedding gifts; IV. Gifts from the husband to his wife or to the father of the bride.

argues was roughly comparable to our trousseau. The second rupture came in 451 with the institution of the *proix,* or cash dowry. By contrast, my approach, based on continuity rather than reversal, inversion, or rupture, attempts to explain geographical and temporal variations in terms of a reorganization or restructuring of the matrimonial system.

To posit the free gift as the organizing principle of Hellenic marriage is to focus on two issues. The first is a question of origins. Why, from the time of Homer onward, was marriage in Greece located in the lexical domain of *didomi,* which according to Emile Benveniste[9] conveys the sense of free gift,[10] rather than in that of *oneomai/priamai* (purchase and bargaining)? Why is the mother of legitimate children in the *Iliad* and the *Odyssey* always given to her husband, and given with items of value? The second issue has to do with the manipulation of the institution of matrimony by Greek cities. It is true that in all ancient societies the bride was given to her husband along with a portion of her patrimony. But the conditions of the gift were such that the status of the wife and her property varied widely from city to city. Democratic Athens prided itself on having its female tribe firmly in hand. Sparta, the most restrictive, closed community in ancient Greece, reputedly allowed its women considerable freedom. What accounts for such differences if the organizing principle was the same?

To raise such questions is to ask about the interaction between the matrimonial and the social systems and to consider both as evolving systems. To approach this topic in a general way would be a daunting project. For now I shall focus my attention on three main sources: the Homeric corpus (ninth and eighth centuries B.C.); the law of Gortyn (ca. 460); and the speeches of the Attic orators (fourth century B.C.).

First Hypothesis. The gift of the bride and her portion was an integral element of Hellenic social structure at the end of the archaic period. Society was organized around what anthropological jargon calls segmented lineages, each located in a discrete household.[11] I claim that Hellenic societies gave away brides and practiced oblique marriage because they were discrete-household societies. Although this social structure was challenged as early as the archaic period, it nevertheless left indelible traces in the matrimonial practices of Greece in the era of the city-states.

Second Hypothesis. Between the eighth and the fourth century B.C., Hellenic societies continued to give away brides and their portions, but they abandoned unilineal households and moved from discrete to overlapping or interconnected households. Why was the status of women in Athens, the city of open citizenship and dynamic change, so different from what it was in Sparta, the city of restrictive citizenship and opposition to change? The answer is that the two cities defined the civic community in very different ways. In Claude Lévi-Strauss's well-known terminology, Athens was a "hot" city, Sparta a "cold" one.[12] Cold cities spurned history and sought to preserve their household structure and limit citizenship to landholders. Hot cities conceived of themselves as living in history. They moved away from a discrete-household structure and refused to limit citizenship. In cold cities the bride, tied to civic property, was mistress of her person and portion; in hot cities she was tied not to land but to a cash dowry and treated as a perpetual minor under the guardianship of her husband. To put it in a slightly different and perhaps more provocative form, women were the chief victims of the invention of democracy.[13]

The Gift of the Bride in Homeric Times

The Homeric Household

Discrete-household societies (Troy, Ithaca, and Phaeacia) are most clearly depicted in the *Iliad* (ninth century) and *Odyssey* (eighth century). Of course the validity of using Homeric sources to study Hellenic societies as they emerged from the dark centuries depends on three controversial assumptions. The first, due to Lévi-Strauss, is that mythical discourse "builds its ideological palaces with the debris of an earlier social discourse."[14] Second, it must be assumed, as M. I. Finley suggests, that this debris dates chiefly from the dark centuries.[15] And finally, one must accept Maurice Godelier's view that the societies depicted in the *Iliad* and the *Odyssey*, real and/or ideal, formed part of the social reality of Greece in the archaic and classical periods.[16]

If we grant these assumptions, how do we go about studying the use of the term *oikos*, household, in Homer? Historians and anthropologists give a static definition of the concept that has nothing specifically Homeric about it. According to Mossé, a household is "first of all a landed estate . . . It is also, and perhaps even more, a group of human beings with a fairly complex structure."[17] On this point specialists and generalists agree. Lévi-

Strauss, speaking with an eye to history in general and to Greek history in particular, defines a household as "a moral person in possession of an estate composed of both material and immaterial goods."[18] Thus scholars can be confident in stating what a household was, even though Homer, as R. Descat observes, never defined it.[19] In Homer we find an inventory of some of the things associated with the idea of a household: wife, children, and plot of land *(cleros)*.[20] Other passages refer to the household's raised roof and circular central hearth *(eschara)*, its livestock *(probata)* and reserves *(ktemata)*, the latter including both food supplies and items of value *(keimelia)*. The poet thus describes rather than defines. Perhaps Homer never attaches a referent to oikos because the term did not denote a concept. Household-structured society developed, I believe, out of a symbolic description of society in terms of "concrete signs." There appear to have been four such signs: the house, its contents, the plot of land, and livestock. Each is a concrete, material form of wealth, but it is also what G. Durand[21] calls "the epiphany of a mystery"—in this case the mystery of the individual's place in the larger society.[22]

The Homeric household is a symbolic object. It is first of all something extraordinarily concrete: a dwelling. A "well-built" household is composed of "well-built" elements. It can be recognized by its raised roof, supported by a central beam (the word oikos, it is said, referred originally to this beam). The roof covers the *eschara*, central hearth, which was not only circular but also womblike (the word *eschara* was used in fact for the female genitals). Every morning the hearth was opened to stir the fire smoldering beneath the ashes. Burning in the middle of the house "with a good odor of cedar and thuya,"[23] the fire shed its benevolent light on those who gathered round to eat. Thus we have a coherent assemblage of "well-built" components or, in Aristotelian terms, a "whole" enveloping its "parts."[24] For social thinkers this "mysterious epiphany" revealed a human group that was in no sense natural, a group whose reproduction was instituted by man. The house envelops, the hearth gives birth, the fire is born each day—symbols of the father recognized as progenitor, the mother married in conformity with the law, and the children brought legitimately into the world. There is a clear homology between people and things. The father, who bears the same name as the household, is, like the oikos, a "whole." He keeps the various components of the reproductive group together. The mother on her wedding day comes to sit beside the hearth. Children, if legitimate, were "born twice": five days after delivery the newborn was placed on the ashes of the hearth, and the father then lifted the child into an upright position—for man stands upright and flame, too, is vertical—and for the first time pronounced the name that gave the infant a place in family and phratry.[25] To have a name was thus to have been recognized by one's father and by his household; it was to join those blessed with a father, a name, and a house—the freeborn. In Homeric societies the *dmoes,* or nonfree, possessed neither name nor father nor household. They were referred to by their place of origin and given shelter by their master. Thus the household, the "epiphany" of recognized paternity and free birth, was the "concrete sign" that singled out a core group within the larger society.

If the house was the sign of belonging to this group, land determined a hierarchy within it. The status of a house depended on access to the land. Some houses were intimately associated with a certain plot. By eating the provisions *(bioton)* that came from a share in the land, invariably characterized as "fertile," each household became part of the *demos,* or territorial community, an amalgam of the nurturing land and the group that lived off its produce. Certain houses possessed land belonging to a different category (*temenos,* meaning royal land or perhaps land exempt from taxation) and enjoyed the privilege of collecting tribute from other households in the community. Thus the households of the king and certain important personages received "public" wine, flour, and cattle.[26] Still other households possessed no land at all; they received their provisions from households that did. *Thetes,* for example, were free men who worked the land of other men in exchange for a portion of what they produced. Men associated with households rooted in the nurturing earth participated in certain common meals and joined together in collective enterprises. At such times they constituted what was known as the *laos,* or community of warriors, which met on the agora to listen to the king and his counselors and answered the call to battle. Among those who talked and acted in concert there was a hierarchy that corresponded exactly to that established by access to the land. Possession of a plot of land ensured integration into the community or collectivity, and possession of special kinds of land conferred power.

Household and land were forms of wealth that determined

social status. These goods played a unique role in social classification, because they belonged to the category of the unchangeable and stood outside the realm of acquisition and possession. As generation succeeded generation in an unbroken line, these "concrete signs" of status were transmitted from one to the next. Household and land, being inalienable forms of wealth, could be possessed only by those with a rightful title. The wealth that "households set on foot" (that is, livestock) and the wealth "that they possessed" in the jars and casks that constituted their reserves belonged to a different category. These goods circulated and gave rise to relations of reciprocity. Such wealth could increase or be increased: within a given status group it determined rank. Transfers of livestock were involved in both sacrificial and matrimonial practices. Animals put to death according to prescribed ritual were shared by men and gods. The meat was then served at a banquet where each guest consumed his rightful share, thereby sealing the bonds of friendship. With each new marriage, cattle and sheep moved from household to household. Livestock served as an inducement to marriage. These archaic societies were also warlike, and the exchange of war booty was another token of friendship between households. Booty seized by force was the most precious and most tenaciously held of all forms of property.

What does this lengthy description of the Homeric household have to do with the gift of the bride? The answer is simple: knowledge of the household is essential if we are to approach the subject of marriage in the context of what Marcel Mauss called its "totality."

The Homeric household was always, to borrow Lévi-Strauss's apt formulation, "two in one."[27] It was founded on legitimate marriage, and it perpetuated itself by fashioning legitimate marriages. Regardless of the primacy of the whole over its parts, of the raised roof over the circular hearth, of the masculine over the feminine, no household could exist without a lawful wife, that is, a wife obtained according to the recognized rules of matrimony. As a duly recognized "part" of the household, this woman, the mother of the household's legitimate offspring, enjoyed a social existence denied to other women. It was only logical for a society that treated wealth as a concrete sign of status and position to treat a reproductive mother as a form of wealth. It was only logical, too, that a bride whose marriage was marked by a gift of land (that is, of wealth that could be used but not possessed) should occupy a position in the household different from that of a bride whose marriage was marked by a gift of valuable objects, tangible wealth of which a person could enjoy possession *(ktesis)*.

In Homeric societies the entire residential group was founded on, and perpetuated itself by enforcing, legitimate marriage. Insofar as wealth was a concrete sign of status and position, the social system made no distinction between heirs and successors: heirs inherited status along with property.[28] While recreational sexuality remained unfettered (large households were full of concubines and captives), society was intransigent on the subject of reproductive sexuality. Only legitimate offspring held a claim on the heritage/succession of a household. Illegitimate offspring were entitled only to a "bastard's portion" and had no status. These measures (whose residue can be detected in certain passages of the *Iliad*[29]) were clearly designed to preclude polygamy without forgoing its advantages (including perhaps demographic increase and unlimited expansion of the wealthiest households).

The question of marriage, I think, is best approached in terms of households rather than the usual welter of anthropological distinctions: endogamy versus exogamy, mobility of the wife versus mobility of the husband; patrilocal residence versus matrilocal residence; marriage with remote as opposed to near kin. Indeed, it would appear that, as Lévi-Strauss put it, Homeric societies made "an effort to transcend . . . theoretically irreconcilable principles."[30] What we must try to show is that this "effort" arose out of the difficulty of reconciling legitimate marriage with unilineal household units.

Before doing so, however, three points need to be made. First, households did not overlap. Descent was patrilinear, with the father of the household at the origin. Matrilateral kinship was at most a complementary system. Each household kept its sons as heirs/successors and sent its daughters to serve as mothers in other households. Second, households perpetuated themselves. A household with sons did so by taking in daughters-in-law. A household that had only daughters did so by taking in sons-in-law. The procedure was to incorporate the mobile partner into the household and treat him or her as consanguine kin. Surprising as it may seem, Homeric societies conceived of marriage in terms of consanguinity. Third, households divided (by "derivation," in the jargon of anthropology). When the father died, the sons divided the inheritance in equal parts and set up independent households. But a father also could divide his household while he was still alive by taking a son-in-law. In other words, Homeric households practiced two different types of marriage, which anthropologists call "daughter-in-law marriage" and "son-in-law marriage."

Daughter-in-Law Marriage: The Possessed Woman (Ktete Gyne)

Penelope was a bride given as a daughter-in-law. Before leaving for the Trojan War, Ulysses, king of Ithaca, marries Penelope, the daughter of King Ikarios of Acarnania (T/I2, II4, III1, IV1, 3). For several generations the husband's household has had only one son, so patrivirilocal marriage[31] and mobility of the bride are inevitable. Because Ulysses belongs to a royal household he cannot take a wife from his own kingdom; to do so would constitute hypogamy.[32] When no princess was available, the king married within his own household. Alcinous, king of the Phaeacians, reigned over an island that at intervals rose above the waves to permit passage between the Visible and the Invisible. Was it an accident that he married his sister?[33] To judge by Penelope's nostalgic recollection of lawful marriages in her youth, Ulysses and Ikarios scrupulously obeyed the rules.[34] Suitors who wished to marry the daughter of a good household were obliged to bring *hedna*, presents, always described as innumerable, and to woo their beauty with magnificent *dora*, gifts. (In what follows the *hedna/dora* distinction is preserved by a distinction, artificial in English, between "presents" and "gifts.") Arrayed before the gates of the household, the suitors vie with one another in largesse, and the most generous wins.[35] The father of the intended then gives his beautiful daughter to the winner and adds his own dora, also magnificent.[36] The lucky suitor thereupon takes his bride, and the gifts that accompany her, back to his own household.

The hedna, the "innumerable" presents, have hooves. As L. Di Lello Finuolli has shown, they consist of herds of cattle and flocks of the sheep brought by suitors to the household of the intended bride.[37] In Homeric societies livestock was a form of wealth that grew and multiplied; it was also exclusively masculine. Women and husbandry did not mix.[38] The significance of the great procession of herds is clear. A suitor offered a virile form of wealth, a herd that he had caused to reproduce, in exchange for a woman who would enable him to reproduce himself. In Homer's Greece as in the land of the Bantu, "livestock engenders children."[39] It did not, however, determine the status of either the offspring (legitimate or illegitimate) or the mother (wife or concubine). The purpose of the presents was to put the triumphant suitor in possession *(ktesis)* of a fertile womb. They did not make reproduction legitimate. This was the role of the magnificent gifts, which transformed the possessed woman, the *ktete gyne,* into the possessed wife mentioned in Hesiod: both mother of the household's legitimate offspring and guardian of its reserves.[40]

The magnificent gifts belong to the category of *keimelia,* precious possessions. The fact that they are described as "gleaming" suggests that a large number of metallic objects were included. Hidden in coffers in the recesses of the household, this repository of wealth was associated with the bride. In fact, it was the concrete sign of marriage.

The husband gave his wife "magnificent accoutrements" (including such items as an embroidered veil, necklace, and diadem), which she may have worn when she came for the first time to take up her place beside his hearth. These precious objects were removed from the storeroom briefly in order to indicate how highly the husband's family valued its new daughter-in-law and how much it wished to make her one of their own.[41]

Along with his daughter, the bride's father also gave the husband magnificent gifts. Taken from the father's own coffers, these precious objects indicated that the bride was not a reject, that she was not being repudiated by her own household, and that her family intended to establish with her children what anthropologists call "complementary filiation."[42] Removed from any concern with power or interest, relations between Homeric heroes and their maternal kin were always quite tender. Such relations were not merely emotional and ceremonial, however: legitimacy required matrilateral kinship. The gifts of the bride's family, stored in the coffers of the groom's family, signified that though the bride was a possession, she was a possession of an infinitely valuable kind, to be treated by the receiving family with the utmost care.

The bride, upon whom the groom heaped gifts in order to take her from her father and upon whom her father heaped gifts in order to give her to her husband, represented an alliance between two households. Son-in-law and father-in-law became *etai,* allies. Such bonds were very important in Homeric societies. Kin by marriage were represented at all rites of passage (birth, marriage, death). They frequently arbitrated disputes.[43] They took part in activities that required the participation of the household as a group, such as the trial of a murderer.[44] Kinship groups such as tribes and phratries played well-defined roles in Homeric societies, which appear to have been "parentela societies."[45]

The dora, the magnificent gifts, were thus a concrete sign of an alliance between two households, of the bride's integration into her husband's household, and of the legitimacy of the children she would bear him. The gifts established an unmistakable distinction between the freely given wife, the purchased concubine, and the captive seized in war. The story of Eurycleia, the faithful old servant in Ulysses' household, is an excellent example.[46] When she was in her prime, Laertes, the hero's father, had briefly entertained the thought of making her his concubine, but in the face of his wife's wrath he soon gave up this plan. His negotiations with Ops, the young girl's father and head of an old Ithacan family, were for the purpose of making a purchase *(priamai)*. The account is not very clear, but there is no doubt that Laertes offered twenty oxen, and it is clear that Ops sells his daughter since he gives her up without making any gifts. With his twenty oxen Laertes thus claimed possession of Eurycleia's genitals. Repudiated by her household, she had no social existence. She was a body, destined to serve the moment she ceased to give pleasure. Her children, deprived of maternal kin and therefore of a mother, would be bastards, excluded from their father's succession/inheritance. When their father died they would receive only a bastard's portion: one of the dwellings belonging to the household, but a dwelling without a plot of land.[47] This bequest signified that the bastard, someone with a name and a father, was a free man but not a member of the community or collectivity. The distinction in Homeric societies between the wife, or mother of heirs and successors, and the concubine (or captive), mother of free children, perhaps explains why brothers and sisters in Greek-speaking regions were called *adelphoi* (born of the same womb). Emile Benveniste suggests that this term was one residue of an early matrilinear kinship system.[48] I wonder if there is a simpler explanation. In patrilinear societies where monogamy coexists with concubinage, the legitimacy or illegitimacy of a phratry depends not on the father but on the mother. *Adelphos* is a residue of polygamy rather than matrilinearity.

The husband's household added the gifts that accompanied the bride to its reserves and the bride herself to its bloodline. In what sense did the bride become blood kin? The Homeric household, which expelled its daughters, was a polycephalous masculine "cell" consisting of the father and his sons, who always acted as a group. Kinship nomenclature was general and uninformative.[49] Homeric texts not being legal documents, it is difficult to characterize the position of the wife/mother in this system. Penelope's problems with her "proud suitors" suggest a possible answer.[50] The wife may have assumed the position of daughter to her husband and consanguine sister to her sons. In order for the drama that takes place in the palace of Ithaca to make any sense, Ulysses' wife must in one way or another be bound up with Ulysses' wealth.

Although the story is complicated, the essential points are easy enough to state. (1) Ulysses has disappeared into the Invisible, leaving behind a wife and a son who still has no "hair on his face" and is too young to claim his father's heritage/succession. (2) The suitors, the flower of Ithaca and her neighboring islands, are interested in Ulysses' widow but not in Ikarios' daughter. If for some reason Penelope returns to her father, none of these handsome youths will lead the "innumerable presents" back to Acarnania.[51] To win the hand of this woman, who is luring them toward death, the suitors jointly adopt two strategies. Their behavior is not so much indecent as ambiguous. (3) The first strategy of the suitors is aimed at effecting a "daughter-in-law marriage." They parade their herds in front of the palace gates and offer Penelope magnificent gifts, awaiting the moment when Telemachus, having attained "virility," will be in a position to give his mother, along with the usual magnificent gifts, to the highest bidder.[52] In this instance Penelope occupies the position of a legitimate daughter. With the father presumed dead, her "brother" is free to give her away in marriage along with precious items from the household reserves. (4) But the suitors simultaneously adopt another strategy. They take up residence inside the household itself, around the maternal hearth. They eat the fruits of the household's land and dream of killing Telemachus and of possessing Penelope on the conjugal bed that Ulysses hewed from the trunk of a solidly implanted olive tree.[53] In this case Penelope occupies the position of a legitimate daughter. If her brother is removed from the picture, she will be immobilized in her father's household and destined for a "son-in-law marriage."

A widow with son leaves her husband's household with a

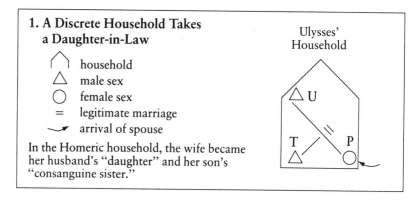

1. A Discrete Household Takes a Daughter-in-Law

Ulysses' Household

⌂ household
△ male sex
○ female sex
= legitimate marriage
↷ arrival of spouse

In the Homeric household, the wife became her husband's "daughter" and her son's "consanguine sister."

repository of wealth. A widow who has no son remains in her husband's household, occupying the house and land—forms of property associated with the bloodline and not subject to acquisition. Daughter-in-law marriage thus places the wife in the position of her husband's daughter. The widow's son gives his mother away in marriage along with magnificent gifts. This type of marriage therefore places the mother in the position of her son's consanguine sister. The structure of this matrimonial procedure is therefore oblique. The wife, as daughter of her husband and sister of her son, never attains "majority." She remains a girl, passed from one man to another: her father, backed by his brothers, gives her in marriage to her husband, backed by his sons. These are the two groups of men that a woman is obliged to love. If conflict develops between the givers and the takers, however, she sides with the givers.[54] If my analysis of the oblique structure of daughter-in-law marriage is correct, the status of the wife in Homeric societies might be characterized as follows: although the woman who was given by one household to serve as wife/mother in another household was a social being of great value (which is why gifts were heaped upon her), nevertheless she was always under the domination of one man, namely, the head of the household in which she resided.

If myths actually do "construct their ideological palaces with the residue of an earlier social discourse," it should be interesting to look for "residues" of daughter-in-law marriage in the great themes of mythology. I believe they can be found in two sets of myths. First, in Greek mythology certain widows, including Jocasta and Clytemnestra, are claimed by their second husband along with their first husband's inheritance/succession. Can this strange devolution be interpreted as a residue of daughter-in-law marriage? Second, in daughter-in-law marriage a woman ceases to be her father's daughter and becomes her husband's daughter. She thus passes from one state to another, and the only way this passage could be understood was as a symbolic death. Now, it so happens that the theme of the "infanticide father" is one of the best known in all Greek mythology, and it has been extensively studied by Pierre Brulé.[55] Whether he is called Agamemnon or Embaros, the father who snuffs out his young daughter's life (note that there is no case of a father who kills his son) offers her as a sacrifice, prior to marriage, to the Virgin Artemis, and the goddess is always willing to accept an animal in place of the young virgin. Could the theme of the "infanticide father" be the "ideological palace" constructed from the residue of a form of marriage in which the woman entered her husband's household as a possession?

Son-in-Law Marriage: The Married Woman (Gamete Gyne)

After my lengthy treatment of daughter-in-law marriage, what I have to say about son-in-law marriage may seem sketchy by comparison. The Homeric sources are to blame. Nevertheless, the texts do speak of the father-in-law's desire to "attract" a son-in-law and "keep him by his side."[56]

Whether or not the father-in-law has sons is an important factor. Alcinous, the father of Nausicaa, has many sons but still wishes to keep a son-in-law at his side. After wandering for a long time in the wondrous Invisible, Ulysses fetches up on the shores of Scheria, where the daughter of Alcinous discovers him, "his body naked and battered by the sea." The hero, "who has suffered so much," obviously has no splendid gifts or presents to offer, but he arouses the girl's interest and charms her father, who is delighted to discover "a man so handsome talking as he does."[57] Alcinous therefore proposes to "keep" Ulysses "with the name of son-in-law" and to give him his daughter, house, and possessions (T/I2, II1, 4, III3, IV2, 4). Ulysses declines the king's offer.

Iobates, king of Lycia, illustrates the other situation, in which the father-in-law has no sons. He manages to "attract" Bellerophon, son of Glaucus, to Ephyra.[58] There are four points to notice about this story (T/I2, II1–4, III3, IV2, 4). (1) Iobates has two daughters, Anteia, whom he gives away in daughter-in-law marriage, and Philonoe, whom he has kept by his side. (2) After Bellerophon triumphs over the Chimera, the Solymi, and the Amazons, Iobates finds reason to keep him by his side. He gives him Philonoe and half of his *time,* or royal honors, while the Lycians offer the hero a *temenos,* or royal land. (3) Hippolochus, the son of Bellerophon and Philonoe, is presented as the king of the Lycians. (4) Glaucus, the son of Hippolochus, on the battlefield of Troy evokes "the race of his fathers, who were always the best in Ephyra and in vast Lycia."

Analysis of these paradigmatic cases poses two problems: that of the marriage contract and that of the integration of the son-in-law into the father-in-law's kinship group. Consider first the question of the marriage contract, in regard to which son-in-law marriage differs from daughter-in-law marriage in two respects: the groom gives no presents; and the bride's father gives away not only his daughter but also property that confers status. In daughter-in-law marriage the acceptance of the livestock by the bride's father implies that she will take up residence in her husband's home and that she and her children will become his possessions. In son-in-law marriage, by contrast, the groom is *anaednos,* "without presents."[59] It might be objected that the exploits of Ulysses and Bellerophon take the place of presents, but I wonder if social ideas in Homer are not too concrete to permit such a parallel. Exploits, in my view, are not a substitute for presents but rather encourage the father-in-law to propose a marriage without presents to a man who has proved his valor—not the same thing at all. The father forgoes the usual parade of herds past his gates, in exchange for which he offers his prospective son-in-law a marriage contract that excludes patrivirilocal residence and possession of wife and children. Admittedly, Agamemnon proposes to Achilles a marriage without presents; he is to take with him to the house of Peleus one of his daughters, along with "gifts as sweet as honey" *(meilia),* and to accept seven of his "good cities."[60] But this contract is an exception designed to calm the hero's wrath by combining the advantages of both types of marriage.

In daughter-in-law marriage the father gives away his daughter along with certain possessions. In son-in-law marriage he gives real property that cannot be acquired or possessed, property that is bound up with his daughter and that confers status. Alcinous offers Ulysses a house and its contents, which would make him a member of the group of free residents. (An interesting question

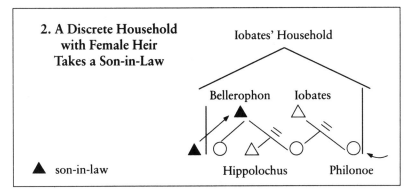

2. A Discrete Household with Female Heir Takes a Son-in-Law

Iobates' Household

Bellerophon   Iobates

▲ son-in-law

Hippolochus   Philonoe

for further research is why he does not offer Ulysses the plot of land that would make him a member of the community.) Iobates gives Bellerophon half of his royal honors. As Benveniste points out, these honors were "substantial advantages."[61] They probably included tribute of the sort that members of the community regularly paid to the king in the form of grain, wine, and cattle. Iobates thus shared his kingship with Bellerophon, and the community, by granting Bellerophon a royal plot, confirmed his kingly status. Alcinous and Iobates offered their prospective sons-in-law "continuous" wealth, wealth of the kind that could be transmitted from father to son or brother to brother. How was the kinship structure manipulated to permit the son-in-law to assume the place of consanguine kin?

The procedure depended, I believe, on whether or not the father-in-law had sons of his own. If not, the son-in-law was taken into the household as consanguine brother *(kasignetos)*. It was incumbent on Iobates to ensure the continuity of his household by availing himself of the nurturing, maternal qualities of his hearth and of his daughter's womb. Since the household could be inherited only by a male, Philonoe's sons had to occupy the same genealogical position as their mother in order to prevent any break in continuity. Oblique marriage of the brotherless daughter was a way of rearranging the order of filiation. Iobates proposed to divide the wealth that signified royal status equally with the daughter's husband, as if that husband were his own brother; thus he was in effect proposing that the husband become his brother. The carnal union of Bellerophon and Philonoe, symbolized by the circular hearth and raised roof, established a kinship between the hero and his father-in-law's entire household.

Son-in-law marriage established the following relations of consanguinity: the son-in-law became his father-in-law's brother; the husband was to his wife as paternal uncle to niece; the children belonged to their maternal grandfather's household; relations with their father's kin were of a secondary order. But they definitely had two fathers—one progenitor and one provider—who probably shared the job of choosing their names. The last representative of Iobates' household bore the name Glaucus, in use in the household that Bellerophon left when he entered that of Iobates.

If the father-in-law had sons of his own, he did not ask his son-in-law to enter his household, dividing his property instead. When Alcinous proposed giving Ulysses a house not within the sphere of acquisition, he was treating his prospective son-in-law as a blood relative. But Ulysses occupied a separate house of his own and did not join Alcinous' household. The king thus placed his son-in-law in the category of *anepsioi,* or nephews, which included consanguine kin who had ceased to belong to the royal household. The sons of Ulysses and Nausicaa were also to be classed as nephews. As members of a collateral line, they could claim their father and mother's heritage/succession only in the absence of a male heir in the direct line. Old Priam, who also kept his sons-in-law, did not put them in separate houses.[62] What place did he award them in his consanguinity?

The woman's position in son-in-law marriage was much stronger than in daughter-in-law marriage. She was not her husband's possession. No presents were given. The property on which she resided and which was consubstantial with her was situated outside the sphere of ownership. Her husband occupied the position of a paternal uncle and therefore did not possess the children of his "brother." Her marriage *(gamos)* did not give her husband total authority over her. Such a woman was presumably the *gamete gyne,* the married woman, whose husband's lack of authority Hesiod lamented.[63] Is it accidental that all the women who exhibit some measure of authority in Homeric society are involved in son-in-law marriages? Helen deplores the arrogance of Paris' sisters.[64] Priam "kept" his sons-in-law at his side. Alcinous' wife, Arete, enjoyed considerable prestige as her husband's niece or sister.[65]

Marriage in Homeric society implied the free gift of a bride along with certain property and the incorporation of the mobile spouse

252

into the consanguinity of the receiving household. Barring errors of interpretation, these two principles were intimately related to the establishment of monogamy in so-called discrete-household societies. The emergence of cities *(poleis)*, beginning in the eighth century, resulted in a restructuring of the household and the institution of marriage. Nevertheless, the matrimonial procedures of the earlier discrete-household societies left a certain residue. Certain seemingly irrational practices and taboos of the classical period regain a measure of rationality if they are interpreted in this way as survivals of an earlier form of social organization.

Hellenic marriage in the classical period is characterized by several features that are simply extensions or transformations of structural features of Homeric marriage. In the societies of the *Iliad* and the *Odyssey* the absence of conjugal bonds between spouses is a structural fact. Since the mobile spouse was integrated into the receiving household, marriage was conceived in terms of consanguinity rather than matrimoniality. Around 336 B.C. Aristotle observed in the *Politics* that in the Greek language "there is no specific term for the relation between husband and wife."[66] Historians have yet to explore the significance of this striking fact. Perhaps the reason why fourth-century Greeks found it so difficult to formalize marriage was that Greek culture had for a long time treated spouses as consanguine kin.

In the discrete-household societies of the *Iliad* and the *Odyssey* marriage within the parentela (or kinship group consisting of consanguine and affine kin) is also a structural fact. Whenever the household must act as a body, it calls upon both its consanguine and its affine kin. It was only logical for a household to seek to bolster its ties to this action group by marrying its daughters to group members. In the classical period marriage within the parentela was still a characteristic feature of matrimonial strategies.

Oblique marriage is another structural feature of discrete-household societies. Regardless of which marriage variant we consider, the groom belonged to the generation preceding that of the bride, occupying the position of father or paternal uncle. All studies of marriage in the classical period, and most notably that of Brulé, emphasize the age difference between husband and wife: a young girl, barely of marriageable age, was given to a man entering maturity.[67] Scholars frequently argue that there is a connection between oblique marriage and demographic concerns, the goal being to equalize the male and female populations in different age groups. Although I do not question the pertinence of such an argument, I believe that any functional purpose of oblique marriage was superimposed upon a structural feature inherited from discrete-household societies.

The inalterable residue of this earlier matrimonial structure may account for the contradictory regulations governing marriage with a half-sister in classical Greece. It was considered "impious" for a man to marry his sister (the word *incest* did not exist) but "pious" to marry, in Athens, his consanguine half-sister and, in Sparta, his uterine half-sister. Lévi-Strauss ascribes this difference to the relative power of "maternal" and "paternal" kin in the two cities.[68] But perhaps these restrictions should be viewed as the fossilized remains of daughter-in-law and son-in-law marriage. The following diagram offers a succinct expression of a complex hypothesis.

The diagram shows clearly that the taboo on the consanguine sister was associated with daughter-in-law marriage, while that on the uterine sister was associated with son-in-law marriage. With this hypothesis it may well be possible to account for the contradictory character of "impiety" in Athens and Sparta. It does not, however, explain why, at a given point in their history, both cities chose one taboo over the other. Nor does it explain why Athens organized its matrimonial system around daughter-in-law marriage and its regulation of incest around son-in-law marriage. In all probability this choice was based on a logic other than that of kinship.

The Age of City-States, Eighth to Fourth Century B.C.

The societies of Greece were organized into city-states *(poleis)* between the eighth and the fourth century B.C. The bride was still given away, together with certain riches or expectations of riches, by men authorized to do so. Although a homology continued to exist between the bride and her "patrimonial succession," matrimonial rules varied widely from city to city. Because an exhaustive inventory cannot be attempted here, I will focus on two cities that I believe to be representative: Athens and Gortyn.[69] Gortyn was, in Lévi-Straussian terms, a "cold" city, one that chose to preserve, insofar as possible, an archaic (perhaps even "neo-archaic") social organization. As late as the fifth century it preserved its discrete-

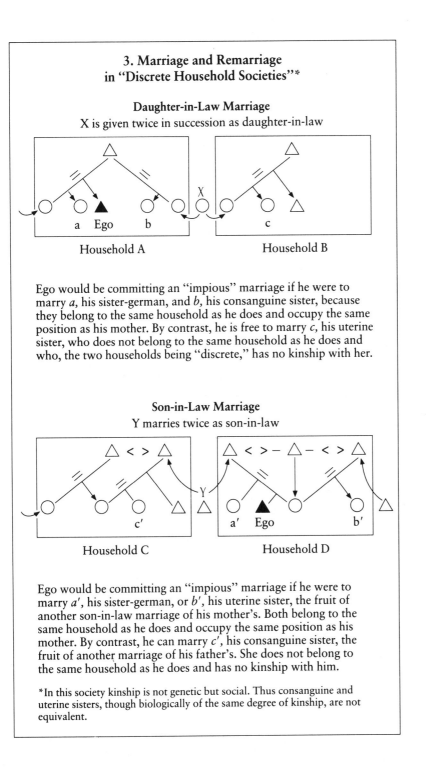

3. Marriage and Remarriage in "Discrete Household Societies"*

Daughter-in-Law Marriage
X is given twice in succession as daughter-in-law

a   Ego   b   c

Household A   Household B

Ego would be committing an "impious" marriage if he were to marry *a*, his sister-german, and *b*, his consanguine sister, because they belong to the same household as he does and occupy the same position as his mother. By contrast, he is free to marry *c*, his uterine sister, who does not belong to the same household as he does and who, the two households being "discrete," has no kinship with her.

Son-in-Law Marriage
Y marries twice as son-in-law

c′   a′   Ego   b′

Household C   Household D

Ego would be committing an "impious" marriage if he were to marry *a′*, his sister-german, or *b′*, his uterine sister, the fruit of another son-in-law marriage of his mother's. Both belong to the same household as he does and occupy the same position as his mother. By contrast, he can marry *c′*, his consanguine sister, the fruit of another marriage of his father's. She does not belong to the same household as he does and has no kinship with him.

*In this society kinship is not genetic but social. Thus consanguine and uterine sisters, though biologically of the same degree of kinship, are not equivalent.

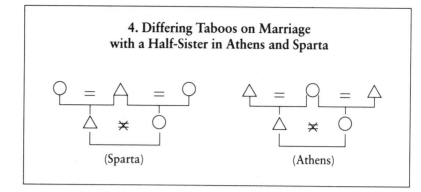

**4. Differing Taboos on Marriage
with a Half-Sister in Athens and Sparta**

(Sparta)   (Athens)

household structure; its politics, it has been said, were "immersed" in collective practices or in what Pauline Schmitt-Pantel calls "civic institutions."[70] Athens, on the other hand, was the "hot" city that permitted change and saw itself as part of history. The challenge posed to the discrete-household structure by the reforms of Solon (594–593) and Clisthenes (508–507) led to the invention of a new community organization and to "the emergence of the political."

Consideration of the matrimonial systems of Athens and Gortyn suggests two hypotheses. The first, based on the resemblances of the systems, proposes a correlation between the emergence of the city-state and the reorganization of the matrimonial system inherited from the dark centuries. The appearance of the city and the concomitant disappearance of kingship apparently went hand in hand with a reorganization of society. The system of discrete households that were divided up to provide for sons and sons-in-law was supplanted by a system of overlapping households. This manipulation of the kinship system was, I believe, the founding act of the Greek city-state. In Homeric societies each household was a unit, and society was held together by a concept of the royal household as a "whole" subsuming the households of the king's subjects. In the later system of overlapping households society was held together by the very overlap of lineages that gave the system its name. The city came into being with the establishment of a cognatic kinship system. The restructuring of the household stemmed from a reorganization of the system of legitimate reproduction.

The bride was given by her household in order to enable the groom's household to perpetuate itself.

The share of her father's patrimony that went with the bride was no longer given to the husband but was intended for the couple's children. This property, which stemmed from the mother's household, was in effect the "concrete sign" of the children's affiliation with their mother's family. This was no longer merely a supplementary affiliation but a parallel one. The wife retained legal title to the property provided by her household; the husband was only the usufructuary.

The interconnections among households obviated the procedures of daughter- and son-in-law marriage and the integration of the mobile spouse into the receiving household. Partners ceased to be treated as consanguine kin and came to be regarded as affine kin. In all city-states the crucial factor in determining marriage type became whether or not the bride had a brother.

This reorganization put an end to the practice of having the groom parade herds of livestock before the gates of the bride's home. Was it coincidental that the breeding of livestock began to decline at the same time, and that the descendants of the meat-eaters of Homer's time increasingly became vegetarians?

My second hypothesis, based on the differences between Athens and Gortyn, proposes a correlation between the choice of matrimonial system and the choice of political system. The conversion of discrete-household societies into societies of interconnected households did not necessarily undermine Homeric society's two organizing principles: that the residential group hierarchy was based on the possession wealth that conferred status, namely, the house (a concrete sign of freeborn status) and the plot of land (a concrete sign of integration into the community/collectivity, henceforth known as the city); and that both heritage and succession depended on legitimate reproduction.

Some cities, like Gortyn, chose to preserve these organizing principles. The "citizen" households, which did not include all residential units, established "interconnections" by transmitting their common possession, the civic lands, back and forth among their progeny without regard to sex. This was the simplest way to shut off access to the community of landowners and to limit its growth. By choosing to associate daughters with parcels of community land, these cities were led to develop matrimonial systems based on the son-in-law marriages found in discrete-household societies (Ulysses-Nausicaa) and to treat women as members of the community, mistresses of their person and property.

Other cities, like Athens, at some point in their history chose to reject the hierarchy of household societies. The "citizen" households, which in this case did include all residential units, established "interconnections" by transmitting the wealth they contained back and forth among their progeny without regard to sex. This was the easiest way to open up citizenship to those who did not own civic lands. By choosing to associate daughters with property, these cities were led to develop matrimonial systems based on the daughter-in-law marriages found in discrete-household societies and to treat women as perpetual minors, under their husbands' power and on the fringes of the community.

The Gift of the Bride in Gortyn

We know the law of Gortyn owing to "the great inscription of the laws," which dates from the first half of the fifth century B.C. (perhaps circa 460).[71] There it was stated that the legal code being written down was a new known, but the date and contents of prior legislation remain unknown.[72] We must analyze the Gortyn code to find out about its antecedents. In writing down its laws the city's purpose was simply, in Maffi's words, to "rationalize the public memory."[73] The code has nothing to say about the principles governing Gortyn's matrimonial system or the social system it was supposed to reproduce.

Gortyn's Matrimonial System

Organization. Marriage belonged to the lexical field of the verb *opuien/opuiethai:* men married (active form), women were married (passive form). It involved three of the four status groups mentioned in the text: the *hetaireioi* (citizens) and *apetairoi* (free men but not citizens) were of free status; the *foikees* (dependents) were not. *Douloi,* or slaves purchased on the market, were excluded from legitimate reproduction. Mixed marriages were not prohibited.

The code governing marriage was not formulated in terms of status. It was organized, as in all city-states at the time, around

Table 2. Residents of Gortyn (Crete) circa 460 B.C.*

Status of legitimate procreators			
Hetaireios	*Apetairos*	*Foikeus*	*Doulos*
belongs to hetairy (citizen who bears arms and sits in people's assembly)	does not belong to hetairy (free man, but not citizen)	dependent attached to civic land	slave could be bought or sold as commodity
Eleutheros		*Doulos*	
free		unfree	

*The table reflects the criteria by which inhabitants of Gortyn were distinguished: free/nonfree (free=*hetaireoi* and *apetairoi*; nonfree=*foikees* and *douloi*) and membership/exclusion (*douloi* were excluded from human society).

two cases: one where the prospective bride had a brother, the other where she did not.

The daughter who had a brother was given *(didomi)* in marriage by her father or brother.[74] This free gift had three effects: (1) It made the husband the master *(karteros)* of the couple's offspring, with full power to decide whether the newborn should be exposed or kept.[75] (2) It established the terms of the alliance between the contracting parties, who became "related by women" *(kadestai)*. (3) It raised the adult wife to the status of mistress *(karteros)* of her person and belongings. Giving a daughter away in marriage was a father's final act of authority over her, but it did not mean that he was placing her in the power of his son-in-law. If his daughter became widowed or divorced, she could remarry on her own, without any intervention on his part.[76]

When a brotherless daughter lost her father, she belonged by law to the rightful claimant *(epiballon)*, and it was her mother's brothers, her closest "relations on the female side," who supervised the operation. In Gortyn, regardless of the status of her husband, a wife was always linked to property. Any legitimately established domestic group possessed both *patroia,* paternal goods, and *metroia,* maternal goods. A bride who had no brother was said to be "settled" on her father's wealth. A bride who did have a brother was accompanied by a portion of that wealth, either at the time of marriage (dowry) or on the death of her parents (succession by reason of death).

The Classification of Wealth.   The code distinguished among four categories of *chremata,* or goods: the *stege,* or house; the contents of the house; livestock (large and small); and other property.[77] This classification is very similar to the Homeric one: wealth in Gortyn consisted of concrete signs indicating status (the house and other property) and rank (livestock and house contents).

The house was the residence (*stege* literally means roof). It was located in the *polis,* a term that was contrasted in the code with the *chora,* or countryside, and thus meant the city. Like the house in the *Iliad* and the *Odyssey,* the house in Gortyn was far more than a place to dwell. Homologous to the father, it gave its name to any child born within it, and this name signified that the child was recognized by its father and was a free man or woman. Recognition of paternity was a joint act of the father and household.[78] The code leaves no doubt on this score.[79] It considers, for instance, the case of a divorced wife who gives birth after her divorce. She was required to present the child to her ex-husband in his house and in the presence of three witnesses. If the former husband refused to admit the child to his household, the law stated that "it shall be the decision of the woman whether to nurse the child or to expose it."

Free status was also conferred, I believe, by the household. The code considered the status of children born to a free woman and a dependent.[80] If the woman went to live with the man, the children became dependents. If the man went to the woman's household, the children were free. The code did not treat the case of a child born to a free man and a dependent woman, and it is reasonable to assume that this case was omitted because such a child, being born in its father's household, was free by definition. In Gortyn to have a house was to have a name and a father, in other words, to belong to the group of those with house, name, and father—the group of free residents. The nonfree, whether dependents or market slaves, had no house of their own. The dependent could nevertheless enter into legitimate marriage because he lived in a dwelling belonging to his master and gave his children to his master's household. In fact, the code stipulated that a divorced female dependent must present a child born after her divorce to her ex-husband's master, who then chose whether or not to recognize the child as his dependent.[81] The master's household was clearly thought of as a "whole" that subsumed the dwellings of its dependents.

Other property was never explicitly defined in the code, but it was said to produce *karpos,* or fruit, of which there was much discussion in the regulation of devolution. Thus this "other" property consisted of the *claros,* or plot of land, which was located in the countryside and worked by dependents, who generally did not live in the city. This plot of land was, I believe, the concrete sign of citizenship. The citizen of Gortyn was called a *hetaireios,* which means "member of a hetairy." Much about these Cretan hetairies remains shrouded in mystery, but it has been established that they were groups of men who dined together from time to time.[82] The diners did not each bring a share, as in Sparta, and the food needed for the meal was supplied by the community's dependents. However this was done, members of the hetairy dined off the fruits of civic lands. In the fifth century their status probably depended on ownership of a plot of land. Just as the possession of a house was the concrete sign of free status, possession of land, and of the dependents attached to it, was the sign of citizenship.

In Gortyn house and land were forms of wealth that conferred status, just as in the Homeric societies. Thus they were forms of wealth that could be used and inherited but not acquired as property. The code hints, however, that under certain conditions these possessions could be alienated.[83] Thus Gortyn, "cold" society though it may have been, was not entirely unfamiliar with change. But status was associated with the possession of certain forms of wealth as late as the fifth century. In contrast to house and land, livestock and household contents were possessions that determined, as in Homeric society, not membership in a particular group but social rank. These possessions could be acquired as property. Since raising sheep has always been important in Crete, it is reasonable to assume that flocks were an important asset in evaluating a person's fortune.

The code's classification of wealth suggests that Gortyn in the mid-fifth century was still a household-structured society and that its component households formed a hierarchy. Some households were free but landless, while the households of citizens possessed both land and dependents. Like Homeric households, Gortyn's households were "two in one."

Daughters with Brothers (T/I1, II2 or 4, III3, IV2 and 4). A young woman with brothers received her share of her patrimony either when she married or when her parents died and maternal and paternal possessions were divided.

In Gortyn both father and mother exercised control over both their possessions and the time of their transmission, "which is not required as long as they are alive."[84] When the parents died, all their children, including any daughters who had not received dowries, shared in the division of their estate: "If a man dies, his houses in the city and all that is found in them . . . as well as the sheep and other large animals that do not belong to a dependent shall go to the sons. The rest of the property shall be divided in good faith. The sons, regardless of their number, shall receive two shares; the daughters, regardless of their number, one share." "If the mother dies, maternal property shall be divided in the same way as in the case of the father's death." "If there is no property other than the house, the daughters shall be entitled to a share of it in the proportion stated above."[85] Notwithstanding its extreme concision, the code thus established a distinction between the citizen's patrimony (the case where "other property" existed in addition to the house) and the free patrimony (where there was no "other property"). Both were subject to a bilateral diverging devolution, the technical term for the situation in which both mother's and father's property "diverged" by passing into the possession of children of both sexes.

Regardless of the status of her household, a daughter was always given status-conferring wealth. The daughter of a citizen household received land. Diverging devolution was organized in such a way as to ensure that the brothers would receive the bulk of the status-bearing wealth—the house and two-thirds of the land—and all of the rank-determining wealth, that is, household contents and livestock. Recall that livestock was exclusively a male possession. In Gortyn and the Homeric societies women were excluded from husbandry. What the daughter of a citizen received from her two parents was one-third of the civic land that signified citizenship. In the case of a daughter born to a free household, that is, a house without land, the house itself was divided and became the sign of the daughter's free status. To recapitulate, status-bearing wealth in Gortyn could be transmitted to both men and women, but wealth that constituted property in the full sense of the word could only be transmitted from man to man.

Not all daughters with brothers participated in the division of their parents' estate. Daughters who received dowries at the time of their marriage were excluded. The law permitted a father to give his daughter a gift when she married.[86] "He may give her her share as stipulated by law, but no more." This formulation is so concise that it can be read in two ways. The most common interpretation is that a dowry was an advance on the daughter's inheritance of both paternal and maternal possessions (land in the case of a citizen household). But it is also possible to read the text as implying that the dowry came out of the father's possessions, and that at the time of her marriage a daughter received those parcels of her father's land to which she would be entitled when he died. If the daughter who received a dowry from her father did not receive possessions belonging to her mother, either when she married or when her mother died, then the dowry significantly altered the form of devolution. In effect there would then be no diverging devolution from the mother. This second interpretation is fairly persuasive. Since a man could never dispose of his wife's property under the law of Gortyn, it seems unlikely that a father would have been permitted to give his daughter anything but what belonged to him. If the second interpretation is accepted, it follows that the law of Gortyn provided for two structurally different ways of determining the portion of daughters with brothers.

Daughters without Brothers. The *patrouchus,* the daughter "who no longer has a father or consanguine brother," was therefore her father's sole heir, and the law determined which male had the right to marry her.[87] Twelve articles of the law of Gortyn were devoted to the marriage of such a daughter (T/I1, II1–4, III3, IV2–4);[88] they have been analyzed in great detail by E. Karabélias.[89] The legal definition of the patrouchus was incomplete. The text did not point out, no doubt because the public needed no reminder, that she must be the daughter of a citizen household and established on a citizen's succession. Despite this omission, the code is quite clear. The issues are again the disposition of the house and the fruit of the earth. The law apparently took no account of brotherless daughters in free but noncitizen households. Two cases were considered: one in which the daughter who becomes a patrouchus is still unmarried; the other in which she is already married.

If the patrouchus had yet to be given in marriage, she was required to marry the closest relative having a claim on her. Priority went to her father's brothers, eldest first, or, if none was available, to her father's brothers' sons. The sons of the father's sisters were excluded. The mother's brothers, that is, the young

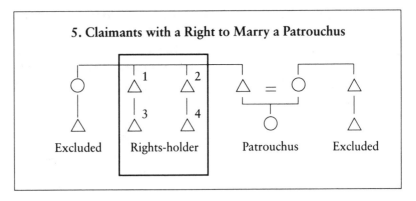

5. Claimants with a Right to Marry a Patrouchus

Excluded   Rights-holder   Patrouchus   Excluded

woman's closest maternal kin, had no right to marry her but were required to oversee her marriage. If no entitled candidate could be found, they were responsible for seeking a husband within the tribe. If no one offered himself, the patrouchus "shall marry another if she can." If the entitled candidate refused to marry the young woman, her maternal relatives took the matter to court. If the entitled candidate refused to comply with the decision of the judge, the patrouchus kept the property and married the next in line or a member of the tribe or, failing that, anyone who would have her. If the patrouchus refused to marry the entitled candidate, she kept the house and its contents and divided the rest of the property (livestock and land) with the entitled candidate.

Was the entitled candidate permitted to force a patrouchus to divorce in order to marry him? When the code takes up the question of the patrouchus who is already married, it considers only two cases: when she is a widow, and when she wishes to divorce the man she married before becoming a patrouchus without his consent. In either case, if the patrouchus was childless she had to marry the entitled candidate. If she had children and then divorced, she might marry "whomever she wished within the tribe," provided that she shared the property with the entitled candidate as specified earlier. If she was a widow with children, she could "marry whomever she wished within the tribe" and keep all the property.

Whatever compromise might be made with the entitled candidate, the patrouchus was an heiress with control over status-bearing wealth (house and land) and other rank-determining property (livestock and household contents). But these belongings were not destined to remain in female hands. To be sure, the code does not specifically state that the possessions of the patrouchus had to go to her sons, but the portion of the daughter with brothers being what it was, the maternal property that a patrouchus left to her daughters could consist only of land.

Whether she came from a citizen household or a free household or from a household with sons or one without sons, a married woman in Gortyn always possessed status-bearing wealth and controlled her own person, but she lacked power over her children. It remains to be seen what kind of household structure might have corresponded to a matrimonial system of this kind. Since the system of legitimate reproduction was conceived with an eye toward the reproduction of citizen households, as is shown by the number of articles of the code devoted to this question, study of the matrimonial system can tell us chiefly about how those households were organized.

Civic Organization and the Matrimonial System

With the house as the basis of free status, the plot of land as the foundation of citizenship, livestock and household contents as determinants of social rank, and legitimate husband and wife as guarantors of continuity, the citizen household in Gortyn would seem almost indistinguishable from the Homeric household. And yet households in this small Cretan city were in fact very different from those described in the *Iliad* and the *Odyssey*. Households in Ithaca and Scheria were also kinship groups, and wealth never passed between them. Daughter-in-law and son-in-law were incorporated into the household needing their reproductive services as consanguine kin, and children inherited wealth from only one household, that of the father in daughter-in-law marriage and that of the maternal grandfather in son-in-law marriage. The system of inheritance in Gortyn was far more complex. Although house, household contents, and livestock passed "discreetly" from father to son (as the son's "additional portion"), land was transmitted to children of both sexes. Consider the following diagram, which illustrates the reproduction of citizen households with sons.

This diagram of the transmission of wealth in Gortyn illustrates the city's social structure, one of interconnected, self-contained households. All citizen households possessed civic land. The original allocation of land remained present in both the vocabulary

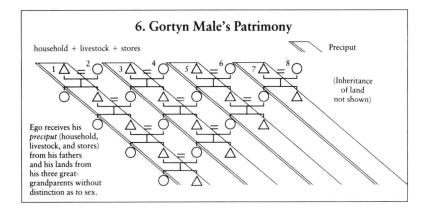

6. Gortyn Male's Patrimony

household + livestock + stores

Preciput

(Inheritance of land not shown)

Ego receives his *preciput* (household, livestock, and stores) from his fathers and his lands from his three great-grandparents without distinction as to sex.

and public memory of Gortyn, and the plot was the concrete sign of community membership. Unlike Homeric households, however, Gortyn's households partially redistributed the common land with each new generation. The decision that daughters should receive one-third of their parents' land altered the distribution of land parcels. This measure correlates with the closed nature of the civic community and the interconnectedness of households.

Gortyn needed no prescriptions to establish true endogamy, the obligation to marry within the group.[90] The decision to allow land to be passed on to both men and women was a way of saying that citizenship could be passed on by both men and women. Homeric households formed an open community. Both daughter- and son-in-law marriages allowed households to integrate foreigners and others excluded from the community (bastards). By contrast, Gortyn's households relied on a closed matrimonial system to reject all who were ineligible to inherit civic lands, including bastards and noncitizens. The city may nevertheless have anticipated the risks of overly restricting access to the civic community. The law stipulated, on the one hand, that a patrouchus unable to find a man of the tribe to marry her was permitted to marry whomever she wished. Furthermore, a child born to a nonfree father in the household of a free woman was considered to be free. Hence we may assume that if a citizen household was in danger of dying out for lack of a suitable reproductive partner drawn from the ranks of the community, the mistress of the household was authorized to maintain continuity by taking a husband from among the ranks of either free men or dependents. Such a provision allowed the citizens of Gortyn to avoid the danger of oliganthropy.

The decision to redistribute land in each generation gave rise to a structure of overlapping households. Land was not subject to purchase, sale, or exchange. It was considered a continuing entity to be transmitted from generation to generation. When a daughter received land at the time of her marriage or on the death of her parents, it was the parents' household that was being broken up for the benefit of the daughter and her children. Children who inherited parcels of land through both paternal and maternal forebears were considered kin of the families of both their father and their mother.

The Status of Women. The consubstantiality of "female citizen" and civic land in a city composed of interconnected households explains the woman's position in the community and household. Tied to the civic land as the concrete sign of her citizenship, the woman of Gortyn was considered a citizen even though her sex excluded her from those collective practices that subsumed the political sphere (communal meals, meetings on the agora, war). She owed her social status to her birth, not to her marriage or motherhood. For her social existence to be recognized it was not necessary that she be considered as reproductive agent. Given the nature of the document that is our only source, we cannot hope to discover anything more about the female citizen's place in the community of Gortyn. By contrast, however, the text is quite eloquent on a woman's position in the household.

In Gortyn the husband took his wife into his household. With this gift from his father-in-law he was able to reproduce legitimately and become the master of his children: paternal authority was based on the mobility of the bride. Yet this type of marriage was quite different from the daughter-in-law marriage of Homeric societies. The bride came either with a dowry or with expectations of a future inheritance; she was tied to a form of wealth that could not be acquired. The husband could no more integrate his bride into his household than he could take possession of his wife's parcels of land. The relation between husband and wife was conceived of in terms of kinship by marriage, not consanguinity. Dependency and subordination were excluded. The husband's property remained strictly separate from the wife's; both were destined to be inherited by the children. Because there was no consanguine kinship between the spouses, it was impossible for one to inherit

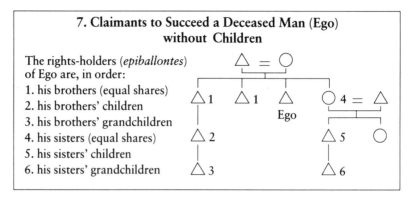

7. Claimants to Succeed a Deceased Man (Ego) without Children

The rights-holders (*epiballontes*) of Ego are, in order:
1. his brothers (equal shares)
2. his brothers' children
3. his brothers' grandchildren
4. his sisters (equal shares)
5. his sisters' children
6. his sisters' grandchildren

from the other. The husband had no power over his wife's belongings or person, and the wife had none over her husband's.

Thus the concept of the household in Gortyn was very different from the concept of the Homeric household. The household of the *Iliad* and the *Odyssey* was a male "whole" that subsumed its female component, whereas the Gortyn household was a kind of unequal partnership *(koinonia),* which pooled not the capital of husband and wife but the income on that capital. If the partnership ended by reason of divorce or death, persons and possessions regained their autonomy. A divorced woman could claim her maternal possessions, half the fruit they had produced, half of the woven goods, and, if the divorce was sought by her husband, a small indemnity.[91] A childless widow left her husband's household with her maternal possessions, half of the fruit they had produced, and half of the woven goods.[92] A widow with children could claim only her possessions and certain items such as clothing up to a specified value.[93]

The married woman was a guest in her husband's household, and her relation to her own consanguine kin is rather difficult to comprehend. The concept of devolution in the collateral line may help to clarify things.[94]

As the diagram indicates, a deceased man's sister and her children became successors when he had no brothers or brothers' children. Jurists referred to this situation as "the privilege of masculinity." On what kinship logic was such a privilege based? The relation of the married woman to her consanguine kin was based, I believe, on the relations that existed in a discrete-household society between a family with sons and the children of one of its

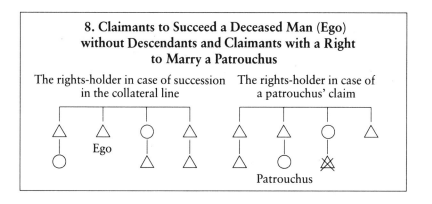

8. Claimants to Succeed a Deceased Man (Ego) without Descendants and Claimants with a Right to Marry a Patrouchus

The rights-holder in case of succession in the collateral line

The rights-holder in case of a patrouchus' claim

daughters in son-in-law marriage. These children were classified as consanguine kin, but in the category of "nephews," and the only way they could participate in their maternal grandfather's succession was if there were no "direct" descendants (that is, sons or sons of sons). In Gortyn a married daughter was a consanguine relative of the household from which she came, but one who resided elsewhere, a consanguine of another category. But the hypothesis that Gortyn's matrimonial system derived from Homeric son-in-law marriage has no chance of being accepted unless it can be shown that at some point in its history Gortyn was a discrete-household society. Evidence for this can be seen in the regulation of patrouchus marriage.

From Discrete to Interconnected Households. There was a clear disparity between the order of succession in the collateral line and the order of precedence of those entitled to marry a patrouchus. A brotherless daughter could not be claimed by the sons of her paternal aunt, whereas the sisters and sisters' children of a man who died childless could inherit from their brother. What was the logic behind the exclusion of the son of the patrouchus' father's sister?

R. F. Willetts, who has investigated this problem extensively, argues that the reason has to do with survivals of what he calls "a tribal organization" of the social group.[95] According to him, the regulation bears traces of a taboo on cross-cousin marriage and of tribal endogamy (when there is no eligible candidate, the kin on the female side call upon members of the tribe to marry the patrouchus). This may be correct. But is it not also possible to view these two regulations in the light of less distant survivals and to consider them as residues of a time when Gortyn's households were organized as discrete units? Four rules govern the attribution of the patrouchus: oblique marriage with the paternal uncle; priority to the father's eldest brother; exclusion of the father's sister's sons; and appeal to members of the tribe. While these rules are difficult to understand in a society of interconnected households, they retain their coherence in a discrete-household society.

When households are discrete units, the children of a sister given to another household as a daughter-in-law belong to their father's household and are only complementary kin to their mother's brothers. The brothers therefore cannot be asked to marry a woman linked to the succession of another household because they are not consanguine kin of that household. So much for the exclusion of the father's sister's sons.

At some point in time the tribe may have formed an endogamic unit. But the tribe is a lineage, a patrilinear group that includes all descendants of a common ancestor. When the code envisions two circles of entitled candidates, brothers of the patrouchus' father in the first circle, their sons and members of the tribe in the second, it implicitly refers to the two delimitations of collateral consanguinity in a discrete-household society.

The patrouchus is the daughter who is given to her *patros,* or paternal uncle. Such oblique marriage is characteristic of discrete-household societies, where a household without sons that takes in a son-in-law treats him as the father's brother. It is inherent in the logic of son-in-law marriage that when a man dies without having had the opportunity to "keep a son-in-law at his side," it is up to his brother to give him the son he never had. But why give preference to the eldest brother? This (noneugenic) provision of the law was intended, I believe, to preserve demographic and social equilibrium in discrete-household society. The eldest brother of the patrouchus' father would, by virtue of his age alone, already have seen to the reproduction of his own household. He could therefore leave his home in the hands of sons liable to succeed him and take up residence in the household of his brother in order to assure its continuity. Since households comprised discrete lineages, the marriage of the patrouchus to her uncle ensured demographic continuity without leading to a concentration of wealth. The switch to a society of overlapping households profoundly altered the effects of this provision: the patrouchus' uncle no longer left his household for his brother's, so the children of the patrouchus inherited from both their father and their maternal grandfather, thus concentrating in their hands the wealth of two households. Organized in such a way as not to disrupt the demographic and social equilibrium of a discrete-household society, patrouchus marriage became a factor of disequilibrium in a society of overlapping households.[96]

If I am correct in thinking that the regulation of patrouchus marriage allows us to glimpse the residue of a discrete-household society, then the social structure of Gortyn must have changed during the archaic period from a society in which citizen households were discrete to one in which they were interconnected. While it is relatively easy to identify the effects of this choice on the condition of the female citizen, it is much more difficult to understand the reasons for it. Anthropologists like to contrast the flexibility of undifferentiated filiation with the rigidity of systems of unifiliation, where, we are told, it is impossible to solve the problem of a shortage of sons or daughters. But the discrete-household societies of the *Iliad* and the *Odyssey,* with their son-in-law marriages that enabled a father-in-law to incorporate his daughter's husband into his household, appear to have found a rather ingenious solution to the problem of a shortage of sons in a patrilinear system. The general explanation therefore seems untenable. Instead, the social restructuring of Gortyn can be related to a historical phenomenon: the emergence of cities. What I am suggesting is that it was through a manipulation of its kinship system that Gortyn first organized itself as a city.

According to P. Lévêque, the emergence of the city coincided with the disappearance of kingship and the establishment of strictly closed communities (in the proper sense of the word).[97] Gortyn shows how a restructuring of households could lead to the "emergence" of a city. In a discrete-household society each household is an element. Social cohesion is ensured, materially and symbolically, by the royal household, which encompasses and binds together all the households in a given territory. Gortyn's overlapping households circulated daughters and parcels of land among themselves and thereby invented a new form of social cohesion based on marriage and redistribution of the common wealth. In a discrete-household society each household takes daughters- and sons-in-law wherever it pleases, and the group as a whole is quite open. But the circulation of daughters and land in a society of interconnected households meant that Gortyn was a closed community, one that excluded those, such as bastards and free noncitizens, who did not inherit civic land. Although the emergence of the city corresponded to a restructuring of the household, it did not undermine the social hierarchy, which was based on the homology between persons and things.

If the female citizen of Gortyn was mistress of her person and possessions and a member of the community, it may have been because citizenship status derived from the land and land could be transmitted to both males and females in a society of overlapping households. If my interpretation is correct, the "emergent" city chose this form of inheritance because it wished to define itself as a closed community of citizens possessing land. Athens may have been the most misogynistic of Greek cities because long before, in the archaic period, it had rejected the equation between possession of land and membership in the community and the interconnected-household structure that went with it.

The Case of Athens

The sources that enable us to study the gift of the bride in Greece's great democratic and seafaring city date for the most part from the fourth century. Athens' matrimonial system is well known from the speeches of the great Attic orators Isaeus and Demosthenes, which have been extensively studied—indeed, so extensively that the Athenian system is sometimes taken as a paradigm for Hellenic marriage in the classical period.[98] The Athenian system, like that of other Greek cities, was organized around two mutually exclusive possibilities: marriage of a daughter with brother(s) and marriage of a daughter without brothers. In both cases the Athenian bride was given to her husband by the man authorized to do so, and in conjunction with items of value. Given away by her father or, failing that, by her consanguine brother or paternal grandfather, the bride with brother was said to be *epiproikos,* or settled on *(epi)* her dowry *(proix).*[99] Awarded to the rightful claimant *(anchisteus)* by the archon eponymos, the brotherless bride was said to be *epikleros,* or settled on her father's *kleros,* a term that in the fourth century designated the whole of the father's estate.

In the time of the Attic orators Athens was no longer structured by households. To be sure, there is much discussion of the household and households (*oikos* and *oikia*) in their speeches, but in most cases I believe the term can be translated as "family," even though it included domestic slaves (in contrast to Lévi-Strauss's notion of "family").[100] The reforms of Solon (594–593) and Clisthenes (508–507) struck down the household system and the equivalence between persons and things on which it was based. With Solon the plot of land ceased to be the concrete sign of citizenship. With Clisthenes the name that indicated membership in the group of free men ceased to be that of the household and became that of the deme, the smallest subdivision of the city. Thus in fourth-century Athens there was no longer any form of wealth that conferred status, although possession of civic lands remained a privilege of citizens. The Athenians, moreover, classified their wealth according to two new categories very different from those used in the past. "Visible property" included houses, fields, and flocks, as well as directly and indirectly exploited slaves. "Hidden property" designated money saved or invested (as a mortgage, loan, or other remunerative investment).[101]

The Attic orators credited Solon with having established Athens' matrimonial system. Thus the same lawgiver both reorganized marriage and redefined the civic community by refusing to limit citizenship to those in possession of civic land. This coincidence raises the question whether there might have been a correlation between the regulation of the gift of the bride and the emergence of the new city.

The Athenian Matrimonial System in the Fourth Century

The clients of the Attic orators apparently accepted the dowry system fully, but they seem to have taken liberties, apparently with impunity, with the regulations governing marriages of brotherless daughters. Were these regulations obsolete?

The Dowry and the Marriage Contract (T/I1, II4, III2, IV2 and 3).   Before a dowried daughter could marry, her father (or his proxy) and the future husband (*eggue*) entered into an oral contract in the presence of witnesses. The term *eggue* meant "handful," signifying that the father placed the bride and her portion of the patrimony "in the hand" of his son-in-law.[102] Various formulas were repeated on these occasions; we know what they were because Menander cites them in several places.[103] Consider this dialogue from the *Perikeiromene* (The Woman with the Shaved Head):

> *Father-in-law:* I give you my daughter to sow for the purpose of producing legitimate children.
> *Son-in-law:* I take her.
> *Father-in-law:* I also give you a dowry of three talents.
> *Son-in-law:* I accept it, too, with pleasure.

The words are too commonplace to have been gratuitous. For children in fourth-century Athens to be legitimate, for sons to inherit and daughters to be given in marriage with an appropriate dowry, it was necessary for the father of the bride to give away his daughter and a portion of his capital and for the husband to accept both with pleasure. Give and take. The terms were the same as those used in Homeric daughter-in-law marriage, but the Athenian bride was not a *ktete gyne,* a possessed woman. What the father-in-law placed in his son-in-law's hand was not *ktesis,* or possession of the bride and her patrimonial succession, but *kureia,* power over her person and over the property that accompanied her. The marriage contract was not a contract of sale but one of guardianship. Its stipulations were those of daughter-in-law marriage but modified by the abandonment of unilineal kinship.

The father-in-law did not sell his daughter to the son-in-law, and the son-in-law did not take her on as a daughter. An Athenian woman did not become her husband's consanguine kin, even though, just as in Homer, on their wedding day the husband gave her presents from his household stores. Proof of this assertion lies in the fact that if a husband died without children, his property went to his collaterals. Although the kinship structure did not place the bride in the position of her husband's daughter, custom codified in law treated her as an eternal minor whose husband-guardian had to vouch for her every public act. When a woman was involved in a court case, her husband represented her, just as he represented his minor children and wards. A woman had to ask her husband for authorization, just as a minor child had to ask its father or guardian for permission, "to enter into a contract involving a value in excess of the price of one *medimna* (51.84 liters) of barley."[104] The marriage contract thus placed the wife in the position of her husband's ward.

Certain legal practices retained fossilized traces of an older kinship relation between spouses. Consider three examples. First, an attentive husband, like the father of Demosthenes, could, when he felt death to be near, engage his wife to marry a man of his choosing and go on to make what looks a lot like an augmentation of her dowry.[105] Giving his wife in marriage was the act of a guardian, but giving her a portion of his capital, and at the expense of his children, was the act of a father. Second, according to the Attic orators, although wives in this society were treated as minors, certain widows could occupy the paradoxical position of family head.[106] Although they were not considered to be consanguine kin of their husbands, they continued to live in their married residence, took care of their minor children, and administered the fortune left to the children by the deceased. These fourth-century Penelopes behaved as if they were eldest daughters when in fact they were only related by marriage. Third, an adult son in Athens had the right to give his widowed mother away in marriage. This power, which was properly that of the father's consanguine brother, was in all likelihood a survival of an authentic kinship between husband and wife.

The husband assumed guardianship over his wife, but she remained her father's daughter. Thus she automatically fell under his authority if for one reason or another (death of the husband, repudiation of the wife by the husband, abandonment of the husband by the wife) the marriage contract was broken. The bride therefore remained a member of her family, and she could inherit from her consanguine collaterals as long as the "privilege of masculinity" did not work against her. The bride's father granted his son-in-law guardianship not only over his daughter but also over her dowry. Joseph Modrzejewski has convincingly demonstrated that the dowry is best analyzed in functional terms and that one must distinguish between titulary, usufructuary, and the ultimate recipients.[107] The bride was beyond any doubt the titulary of the dowry. The marriage was indissoluble. In case of divorce, the husband was under an absolute obligation to return the dowry, even if the wife's conduct was not above reproach. Restitution was facilitated by the common practice of the dowry-mortgage: in making the marriage contract the husband acknowledged the dowry as a loan and put up his own land as security. Thus the husband was guardian of the dowry as well as of his wife. He administered the property and received any income that flowed from it as long as the marriage endured. The state fiscal authorities were in doubt about the nature of the arrangement, and their calculations always took account of the income from the wife's dowry.[108] The husband was thus the usufructuary of the dowry, but the ultimate recipients were his sons, who claimed possession upon the death of their mother. If they were minors, the father continued to act as guardian until they reached adulthood.

The contract, which places the bride and her dowry under the stewardship of her husband, is the act that constitutes marriage. The exchange makes the bride a legitimate wife and her sons eligible to become heirs: she becomes an *aste,* a woman of the civic community and future mother to sons who may become successors to their father (*polites,* the term for citizen, was rarely used in the feminine). This was a society where men took concubines, and what distinguished the wife from the concubine was the free gift given when the marriage contract was concluded. The acquisition of a concubine was also a matter of contract: a man received a woman from another man (or woman) authorized to enter into such a bargain.[109] But despite the relative scarcity of sources, it is clear that in contracts of this type it was the man acquiring the concubine who did the giving, who, as the texts put it without further elaboration, "gave to the concubine."[110] Whatever the personal status of the concubine may have been, her children were bastards, excluded from the heritage of the man who kept her and whose estate went either to his legitimate children or collateral kin. In any event, men did not take concubines in order to have children. One of Demosthenes' clients put it quite clearly: "[We have] concubines to take care of everyday needs; [we have] wives to bear legitimate offspring and to serve as faithful guardians of the hearth."[111] To judge by the speeches of Attic orators, it was mainly older gentlemen, already blessed with "legitimate offspring," who sought concubines to "take care of" their everyday needs.

The marriage contract made the wife a member of the civic community. In placing the bride under the guardianship of a citizen, her donor certified that both her father and her mother were members of the civic community. The marriage contract was to the young woman as inscription on the rolls of the deme was to a young man—an act signifying integration into the civic community. The conditions of introduction were quite similar. To be accepted by the deme the young man had to be the progeny of two citizens according to the so-called decree of Pericles (451 B.C.).[112] To figure in a marriage contract the young man had to be born a citizen. The law prohibited the donor of a bride, who was required to be a citizen, from contracting with a foreigner or passing off a foreign female as his "kinswoman."[113] The recipient was also required to be a citizen, and the law prohibited him from contracting to marry a foreigner. Violators of these laws were liable to prosecution for "usurpation of civic rights." The conditions of the gift were sufficiently strict that the marriage contract was accepted as proof of citizenship.[114] It was not, however, proof of legitimacy. The marriage contract had this in common with inscription on the rolls of the deme: both required citizenship, but the law posed no requirement of legitimacy.

The way in which the gift of the bride was regulated points up the clear distinction that Athenians drew between heritage and succession. The transmission of material and immaterial goods depended on legitimate filiation, while the transmission of status depended on "civic" procreation (that is, on the citizenship status of the parents). The family excluded bastards, but the city was willing to accept them, provided their parents were citizens and their illegitimacy was somehow acknowledged. One of Isaeus' speeches may help to shed some light on how a bastard female could become a wife of the civic community.[115] A man by the name of Pyrrhos died, leaving an adopted son, Endios, and a female bastard whose mother was Phyle, a citizen concubine. Endios inherited his adoptive father's estate, and, since Phyle was a bastard and he was therefore not obliged to marry her himself, he gave her, along with a small dowry, in marriage to a citizen. Because Phyle was a bastard, she was not entitled to a share of her father's estate, but that did not prevent her from contracting to marry and thus to enter the civic community. The dowry in some sense made her bastardy "official." A male bastard both of whose parents were citizens could also, it seems, join the group of citizens with the help of a portion of his father's patrimony. To be sure, there is much doubt about what Euktemon actually did when, at the age of ninety, he left his wife for another woman,[116] but it appears that he agreed to pass off the child of the woman who seduced him as his own bastard and that, in order to begin the process of making the boy a citizen, gave him some land.[117]

To recapitulate, the significance of the dowry in a city that had abandoned its household structure was complex and therefore difficult to interpret. At first it would appear that the dowry was the concrete sign of the wife's ancestry and of her affiliation with two distinct kinship groups. When the father of the bride gave his daughter away, along with a portion of his capital, he acknowledged that his daughter's children would inherit that capital as *thugatridous* and *thugatride,* his sons and daughters by his daughter. A more subtle analysis shows, however, that the dowry was a material element in a process for integrating into the city daughters excluded by birth from family membership.

The Dowry

Constitution. On the day the marriage contract was concluded, the daughter was "settled on the dowry" that the donor constituted, if not gladly then at least voluntarily, out of his capital. No law required a father or brother to marry off daughters over whom they exercised authority. But if they allowed daughters to grow into spinsters, they risked losing face in the eyes of the community and being judged stingy or impoverished. If a man had several daughters, he provided them with equal dowries. The patrimonial portion set aside for a daughter generally consisted of hidden property.

Table 3 indicates that daughters were given either with cash or with income-producing investments (such as mortgages or rental property). To be sure, custom dictated that on the wedding day the father-in-law was supposed to give his son-in-law robes and other precious objects and that the bride was supposed to take various household items with her to her new home. It was common, however, for the donor, whether from stinginess or prudence, to have an estimate made of the value of the gifts included in the dowry so that he might follow their fortune. Clearly, then, diverging devolution existed in Athens, but the devolution in the male branch was not the same as in the female branch. Daughters were placed in circulation along with sums of cash, while sons kept all the visible wealth, including the house and means of production, namely, land and slaves. Demosthenes' sister received a handsome dowry of 2 talents, but the young orator kept the cutlery and bed-making shops that were the source of the family fortune.

The two branches were not identical; neither were they equivalent. From the corpus of the Attic orators it is possible to extract

Table 3. The Dowries of Daughters

	Source	Dowry Established by	Number of Daughters	Composition of Dowry*
Lysias	XIX 15	father	2	1:40 mines 2:?
	XVI 10	brother	2	1:30 mines 2:30 mines
	XXXII 6	father	1	1 talent
Isaeus	II 3, 4	brothers	2	1:20 mines 2:20 mines
	III 28	brother	1	none?
	III 49	adoptive brother	1	1000 drach-mas
	V 26	?	1	rent estimated at 40 mines
	VIII 8	father	1	25 mines
	X 5	father	1	?
	X 25	brother	?	?
	XI 41	?	?	20 mines
		?	?	20 mines
Demosthenes	XXXVII 4	?	?	50 mines
	XXXVII 5	father	1	2 talents
	XXX 1	brother	1	1 talent or 80 mines
	XXXIX 7	father	?	1 talent
	XXXIX 20	father	?	100 mines(?)
	XLI 3–27	father	2	elder: 40 mines, includ-ing mort-gage on rented property younger: 40 mines, less value of trousseau bought back from first hus-band
	XLVII 57	?	?	"My wife for-bade them to touch property included in her dowry"

*One talent is worth 60 mines, and the mine is worth 100 drachmas.

Table 4. The Dowry of a Daughter and the Wealth of the Person Constituting It

	Source	Dowry established by	Dowry	Percentage
Lysias	XXXII 6	father: 12 talents	daughter: 1 talent	8.3
Isaeus	III 49	adoptive brother: 3 talents	sister: 1000 drachmas	5.5
	VIII 8	father: 90 mines	daughter: 1st time: 25 mines; 2nd time: 1000 drachmas	27.8 11.1
Demosthenes	XXVII 5	father: 14 talents	daughter: 2 talents	14.2
	XXXI	brother: 30 talents	sister: 1 talent	3.3

five cases in which the amount of the dowry can be related to the fortune of the man constituting it. The fourth of these is that of Demosthenes' father. In his will he provided for a dowry of 2 talents for his daughter, age five at the time, and left his son a fortune valued at 14 talents. In Athens the daughters' portions were but a small fraction of the sons'. A third aspect of diverging devolution in Athens has until now attracted little attention: it was not bilateral. The father's property was passed on to children of both sexes, but the mother's dowry apparently went only to her sons. In the whole corpus of the Attic orators there is not one example of a daughter receiving money from her mother. There is frequent discussion, by contrast, of sons inheriting their mother's dowry or expecting to inherit their mother's dowry in order to marry off their own daughters.[118] This arrangement was logical. Since a man did not have the right to dispose of his wife's dowry, he was obliged to constitute his daughter's dowry out of his own property. The dowry (and other property that she received from her collaterals) thus passed back and forth between the sexes.

Transmission of property defined two smaller groups within the larger kinship group: father, daughter, and daughter's son; and paternal grandmother, son, and son's daughter. Like Zeus's daughter in the *Eumenides,* an Athenian daughter stood entirely on her father's side.[119]

Circulation of Women and Money.   For the well-to-do clients of the Attic orators, to marry off a daughter was to set money in motion. How were these two forms of circulation related? Some scholars see the connection between the two as the reason for the devaluation of the condition of women. They have in mind Euripides' Medea's statements that "women are the most miserable of tribes," obliged to "lavish large sums to buy a spouse."[120] Other scholars wonder about the disequilibrium in phratries where there were fewer women than men. What was done with female children? Were they exposed because they cost too much to keep?[121] But no one has yet investigated the economic rationality or irrationality of the dowry.[122] Studies of dowry systems in Mediterranean societies have generally found the system to be irrational because the dowry represented immobilized, unproductive wealth. But these studies were concerned primarily with rural societies, which did little in the way of income-producing investments, and with Christian societies that condemned divorce. Their conclusions therefore are not applicable to fourth-century Athens, a seafaring city where dowry money easily found productive investment. It has been shown that the Athenians were past masters at the art of making their capital bear fruit.[123] The bride's dowry was not stored away in a coffer but immediately invested. Indeed, some marriages were nothing less than investment-bank mergers.[124] The dowry was not immobilized. Athenian women—or at any rate the wealthier ones—began their matrimonial careers early (age fifteen) and ended late (menopause). Owing to widowhood and divorce, many married more than once, the better to serve the interests of the men who acted as their guardians.

Whom was a father likely to choose as guardian of his daughter and of a (small) portion of his capital? The regulation of the marriage contract being what it was, fathers were obliged to choose their sons-in-law from the group of male citizens. The father's social position made it obligatory to find a husband whose fortune corresponded to the size of the daughter's dowry. Fourth-century Athenians behaved in much the same way that Greek and Cypriot peasants do today (according to L. Mair)[125] and that the peasants of Béarn did in the first two decades of the twentieth century (according to Pierre Bourdieu).[126] In the world of the Attic orators, princes never married shepherdesses and princesses never married chimney sweeps. It was often said that no man of means would ever marry a woman without a dowry and that no poor man could hope for much of a dowry when he married.[127] In democratic Athens "money always married money," even if such factors as the bride's beauty and her family's reputation were also taken into account. These conditions were so much taken for granted that in lawsuits involving disputed fortunes, a wife's small dowry was accepted as evidence that her husband's fortune had also been small.[128] Brides circulated, but not outside the social class of the family into which they had been born. In fact circulation was generally confined within even narrower limits. Men liked to marry their daughters to their own friends, thus to men of their own age. Fathers were particularly apt to give their daughters to relatives. If a young woman married a man from outside the family when a relative by blood or marriage was available, there was likely to be talk about her mother's virtue and the "purity" of her birth.[129] Much work has been done on intrafamilial marriages among the clients of the Attic orators as well as in other segments of Greek society.[130] The preferred marriage was one arranged between the children of two brothers or an oblique marriage between a paternal or maternal uncle and a niece. Thus late-classical marriage in Athens involved elements of both change and continuity. Functionally, the system was ideally suited to the needs of a "hot" society with no "inhibitions" (to borrow M. I. Finley's term) when it came to seeking profitable investments. But in form it remained similar to daughter-in-law marriage as practiced in the discrete-household societies of the *Iliad* and the *Odyssey*.

Adjudicated Marriage of the Brotherless Daughter

If a young woman had a brother or brothers, her guardian constituted a dowry and her marriage was settled by contract. She was said to be *epiproikos,* settled on her dowry. But when she had no father or brother, she was said to be *epikleros,* or settled on her father's succession, and the claim to her hand was settled by a decision of the court *(epidikasia)* rendered by the archon eponymous. The successful candidate became the guardian of both his wife and her succession, and its revenues were added to his own. If the marriage produced sons, the succession of their maternal grandfather was to be restored to them when they reached adulthood, and the sons were required to provide their mother with a pension (T/I1, II1–4, III2, IV1, 3).

The Designation of the Epikleros. Four requirements had to be met. First, the (deceased) father of the *epikleros* could have no legitimate sons eligible to inherit his property and succeed to his position. He might, however, have any number of daughters, all of whom were "settled on his succession" with equal shares. Second, the father of the *epikleros* could not be a member of the group of so-called *thetes,* citizens in the lowest wealth category. (Adjudication of a *thessa,* the daughter of a *thete,* was subject to a different set of regulations.[131]) The selected candidate was obliged either to marry the epikleros or to constitute a dowry for her based on his own fortune. The epikleros was an orphan, but not a poor one. Third, the epikleros' late father must not have stipulated, either during his lifetime or in his will, the manner in which he wished to dispose of his daughter or his property. Under Athenian law a father without sons could adopt a son and designate him as successor. The presence of a daughter was no impediment to adoption, but the adopted son was required to marry the daughter. This procedure seems to have been used quite frequently. If a man had more than one daughter, he married off the eldest ones and kept the youngest (?) at home to marry the kinsman he chose to be his adopted son (often a sister's son or brother-in-law). Fourth and last, the epikleros was required to be of legitimate birth. A daughter born to a concubine, regardless of the concubine's status, could not become an epikleros, at least to judge by the third speech of Isaeus: Pyrrhos, who had no son, adopted one of his sister's sons but did not have him marry his daughter Phyle, who was apparently a bastard.

The designation of the man destined to become the epikleros' husband was governed by a set of rules that E. Karabélias has pieced together from information contained in the speeches of the Attic orators.[132] The accompanying diagram gives a simplified version of these rules.

As in Gortyn the husband was selected from the consanguine kin of the epikleros' father, but the order of precedence was not the same as in the Cretan city. Priority in both places went to the father's eldest brother. In Athens, however, subsequent precedence

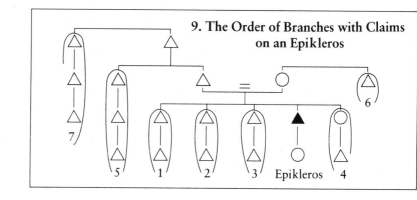

9. The Order of Branches with Claims on an Epikleros

was by branch rather than generation: the sons of the epikleros' eldest uncle took precedence over the next eldest uncle. Another difference compared with Gortyn was that the sons of the epikleros' father's sister were not excluded but came after the father's brothers and their sons. And a final difference was that when the father's phratry was exhausted, the selection turned next to his parents, and if need be to his paternal grandfather. In cases discussed by the Attic orators there is no instance where an epikleros went unclaimed. We may assume, however, that the judges had occasion to consider the fitness of a candidate to "visit the epikleros at least three times a month," as required by law.[133] The designee was not required to press his claim to the epikleros, but the income from a rich estate was hard to turn down. It was not unheard-of for a married designee to divorce in order to claim his due. "Protomachos was poor," one of Demosthenes' clients recounts. "A wealthy epikleros fell to him by inheritance. He hoped to find another husband for my mother, and he succeeded in gaining the assent of a friend of his, my father Thoucritos."[134]

If the epikleros was unmarried, the designee immediately became her guardian and the trustee of her estate. If she was married but childless, he could exercise his right of *apheresis,* abduction. Several passages in Isaeus leave no room for doubt on this score.[135] But if she had children, the law does not appear to have sanctioned the abduction of their mother. In that event the designee did not become the successor, and the epikleros' sons, on reaching adulthood, could claim the estate in exchange for providing their mother with a pension.

Was this always the system in Athens? It is possible that at some point in the history of epikleros marriage the designee was entitled to abduct her without regard to her matrimonial situation. In a discrete-household society the daughter had to return to her father's home if necessary to perpetuate the household. Regardless of how the right of *apheresis* might have evolved, the limitation of that right in the fourth century made it possible to overcome the effects of an age-old custom. A man who had no sons and who for one reason or another decided not to adopt one could choose sons-in-law for his daughters. Upon his death his estate would be divided among his daughters' sons, unless the sons-in-law decided to attribute one of their own sons to him in "posthumous adoption." Under this arrangement the adoptee was excluded from the paternal succession, but the adoption served as a way of avoiding both the sad fate of a household dying out without heirs and the fragmentation of inheritances in a society that strongly favored equal division among sons.[136] Was this a way for the adoptee's father to avoid inscription in the tax class obliged to pay for liturgies? The reflections of one of Isaeus' clients suggest that this was the case.[137]

Marriage and Politics

Whether *epikproikos* or *epikleros,* the Athenian woman never enjoyed power over her person, property, or children. She was a ward who served as a "silent link" in a chain of men: her father, her husband, and her sons. I take the phrase "silent link" from the title of E. Cantarella's book on women in the ancient world, *Tacita Muta*.[138] The situation of women was a consequence of a matrimonial system that combined the "rational" innovations of a profit-seeking society—the joint circulation of women and interest-free loans—and the "relics" of daughter-in-law marriage in the discrete-household societies of the *Iliad* and the *Odyssey.* The question then arises why Athens at a certain point in its history chose to transform the institution of daughter-in-law marriage, while at about the same time other cities were transforming the institution of son-in-law marriage. I propose this hypothesis: that the development of the matrimonial system was related to the abandonment of the household structure and the emergence of the political in the sixth century B.C.

The Origins of the Hypothesis. My hypothesis begins with the observation of a coincidence. According to a tradition that was well established by the fourth century, Solon was both the architect of the matrimonial system and the second founder of Athens, the man who gave new life to the city originally supposed to have been founded by the mythical King Theseus. This hypothesis, which is not easy to verify, rests on the idea that the emergence of the city was somehow connected with a restructuring of the kinship system. But the sources, most of which date from the fourth century, strictly distinguish between the laws governing political authority *(politeia)* and those governing private life.

It was the Attic orators who described Solon as the architect of Athenian marriage. He was credited with having forged the regulations governing adjudication of the epikleros and the thessa and with having set forth the conditions defining who was authorized to give a woman in marriage by contract.[139]

Solon's contribution to the matrimonial system is further described in a passage in Plutarch: "He prohibited dowries [*pherne*] and stipulated that a bride should take with her only three items of clothing, objects of relatively little value, and nothing else. He did not want marriage to become a lucrative affair."[140] What is the meaning of *pherne* in this context? Two interpretations are widely cited. According to Chantraine, who has the support of many other scholars, there were two words in Athens for dowry: *pherne,* the more poetic, and *proix,* the more technical legal term.[141] More recently, Mossé has proposed another interpretation: pherne refers to the bride's trousseau, *proix* to the cash dowry.[142] I am not convinced that pherne was the word for trousseau. Plutarch distinguishes too clearly between the dowry on the one hand and robes and household items on the other. Nor am I persuaded by Chantraine's view that pherne was a poetic word for dowry. To be sure, the tragic poets used the word in the classical period,[143] but Xenophon and Aeschines, who were not concerned with poetry, also use the word and give it a specific meaning: the pherne was land that used to accompany a bride at some time in the past.[144] Prohibiting the pherne may have been an attempt to halt fragmentation of landed estates.

In the *Constitution of Athens*[145] Aristotle called Solon the second founder (after Theseus) of the democratic city.[146] It would be presumptuous to attempt to summarize in a few lines pages that have been the subject of much authoritative commentary, so I shall limit myself to stating a few key points.

Early in the sixth century the community of Athens succumbed to civil war between the poor and a group that Aristotle characterizes as a rich and powerful minority of nobles. There were two reasons for this very violent conflict. First, "the land was in the hands of a small number of people . . . The poor were the slaves of the rich . . . They were called *hectemores,* because they were allowed to keep only a sixth of the harvest in exchange for the right to work on the estates of the rich . . . And if the peasants did not pay their rents, they could be reduced to servitude." Second, power, too, was concentrated in the hands of a few. The archons, or magistrates, and the Council of the Areopagus (consisting of archons no longer in office), were drawn from a minority of the population.

After a period of violence the two groups agreed to name Solon as archon and arbiter. He refused to redistribute the land once again. Instead he "made laws." First, "he abolished debts, both public and private, by a measure called *sisachthie,* or shedding of the burden." Second, "he divided the body of citizens in the following way. There were, as before, four classes based on taxable income: pnetacosiomedimnas; equestrians; zeugites; and thetes." Third, he decided that all magistrates would be drawn from the first three classes, each to be given responsibilities commensurate with his wealth. "The thetes were entitled only to take part in the assembly and courts."

Aristotle explains that after a time Solon's constitution ceased to be observed, so, toward the end of the sixth century, Clisthenes undertook to reorganize the polity in a more democratic fashion.[147] He not only increased the number of citizens but also changed their denomination. He made the inhabitants of each deme citizens of that deme, "in order to prevent them from calling one another by their father's names in order to discredit new citizens and to encourage them to use the name of the deme instead. For that reason Athenians are named after their deme."

Although the sources discuss the "constitutional" laws of the sixth century separately from the "matrimonial" laws, I shall try to show that there was in fact a close correspondence between the two because both were involved in the effort to transform a society of households into a political society.

Kinship and Politics in the Sixth Century

What I am proposing is not easy: I wish to use fourth-century sources to develop an interpretation of the crisis that Athens endured in the sixth century. Athenian society on the eve of Solon's archonate was one of households. When Solon, in one of his elegies, speaks of "the land murdered" by civil war, he describes it as "the most ancient Ionian land."[148] Thus it is hardly surprising to discover that "the most ancient land" was organized in a manner not unlike the societies described by the Ionian poets who created the *Iliad* and the *Odyssey*.

The existence of a household structure is attested by the most ancient of Athenian laws, that on "involuntary murder," promulgated by Dracon in 621. The law first specifies those who are authorized to negotiate "as a body" with the murderer. They include the father, brothers, and sons of the victim, in other words, the consanguine kin who constitute the victim's household. The law goes on to define three categories of kin who may join with the household in prosecuting the murder: the sons-in-law (husbands of daughters given in marriage), fathers-in-law (fathers of women acquired as wives), and nephews (consanguines separated from the household). Like the Homeric household, the Athenian household was a polycephalous cell whose members had no separate social existence.[149]

The portrait that Aristotle paints of pre-Solonian Athens sheds light on the society's dual organization: it was a community based on the possession of land and a collectivity engaged in joint actions. Since society itself depended on a system of obligations, Solon's abolition of "public and private debts" portended major changes. It is plausible to assume that the household hierarchy in "the most ancient Ionian land" was still related to the possession of different classes of land. At the top of the hierarchy stood those households whose land was not taxed, like that of the king and leading nobles in Ithaca and Scheria. These were the households of the "rich and powerful minority of nobles" mentioned in Aristotle. At the next level households with a plot of the communal land, or demos, were required to pay taxes, as well as a tribute to the minority that was probably very much like the tribute in "public flour, cattle, and wine" mentioned in Homer. At the lowest level were those households without land, whose inhabitants were considered hereditary "tenants" of those with a great deal of land. These tenants worked "the estates of the wealthy" and were required to pay "private dues" that amounted to perhaps as much as five-sixths of the harvest. If they failed to meet their obligations, they were sold as slaves. Men from households with communal lands participated in various kinds of collective action such as warfare and the punishment of crime.

There was a close parallel between the social hierarchy and the authority hierarchy. The minority mentioned by Aristotle was an order in the strict sense of the word, the order of the Eupatrides, in which the hereditary right to receive "public debts" was coupled with the hereditary right to command other men. The *hectemores,* meanwhile, were excluded from "political" institutions. Were they also excluded from military action? Much research remains to be done before we can answer this question, which is related to the question of the origins of the Athenian fleet.

Were the early-sixth-century Athenian households discrete, or had they already begun to overlap? The Athenian kinship system in the classical era still had such a pronounced patrilinear character that it is plausible to assume that the city was slow to give up lineage segmentation. Solon's marriage regulations imply, moreover, that Athenians were still engaging in practices quite similar to Homeric son- and daughter-in-law marriage as late as the beginning of the sixth century.

The Solonic Reorganization of Marriage and the Community (594–593)

By abolishing "public and private" obligations Solon destroyed the Athenian community's hierarchical organization. Henceforth all households in the residential group would have the same status. All were free and all were alike, but similarity did not imply equality. Now the classification of a household depended on the quantity rather than the quality of its wealth.

Once the "repudiation of burdens" had destroyed the cohesion of the community, the question became one of how best to weld individual households into a solid unit. In cities like Gortyn, the transmission of civic lands to both sexes fostered interconnection among households and encouraged the development of a close community of landholders. Such a solution was out of the question in Athens, where not all households held civic lands and where the lawgiver flatly refused to redistribute "the fertile soil of the fatherland." Instead, Solon attempted to restore the cohesion of the community by establishing a new matrimonial system.

Solon first named those men who were authorized to give a woman in marriage by contract, namely, the men of the household. He then prohibited the pherne, which was a way of tying a married woman to the land. What did the conjunction of these two measures signify? First, the marriage of a daughter with brothers was reduced to a single operation. In order for the city's households to constitute a homogeneous unit, the procedure for marrying daughters had to be the same for all. Second, among the various procedures inherited from discrete-household society, Solon chose one quite similar to daughter-in-law marriage: the bride was given together with wealth that lay hidden in the household. He rejected son-in-law marriage, in which the bride was given together with land. His decision was surely based in part on a desire for uniformity. If all households in the new city were supposed to marry their daughters in the same way, allowance had to be made for those households whose status did not allow access to civic land; a category of wealth that had never conferred status had to be selected for undifferentiated transmission. Once households ceased to take possession of their daughters-in-law and entered instead into marriage contracts that granted them guardianship over wives and their dowries, they ceased to be unilineal and began to perpetuate themselves through their sons' sons and daughters' sons. In Athens households were bound together and forged into a community by the circulation of women in conjunction with undifferentiated transmission of household contents.

How could a lawgiver forge a homogeneous community out of a group of wealthy households and poor households, particularly after several years of civil war? Solon attempted to solve the problem by instituting a generalized exchange of women. According to Plutarch, he limited the bride's portion to "three robes" and "a few items of relatively small value," and Plutarch provides a most edifying explanation of this measure. But Solon's objective may have been more political. By limiting the daughter's portion, Solon in a sense made all brides equal and eliminated social divisions based on wealth from the matrimonial domain. Wealthy and less wealthy households could exchange daughters, thereby forging bonds between them while at the same time ensuring their reproduction: bonds of kinship would lessen the risk of civil war. While Solon refused to redistribute civic lands or private wealth, he attempted to end the antagonism between rich and poor by staking out a matrimonial meeting ground where women could be exchanged on an egalitarian basis.

The limitation of the bride's portion may have responded to an even more concrete concern. Scholars have done a great deal of work on the origins of the Athenian crisis in the archaic period. G. Augustin, for example, notes that "in societies where the patrimony is divided equally, one generally finds two social strata: those who have land and those who do not."[150] In other words, the rich and the poor. In Athens, which strongly favored equal division of the patrimony among the sons, the exchange of women with unequal dowries resulted in an increase of social inequalities. The groom's inheritance and the bride's portion were always matched. By reducing the bride's portion Solon may have hoped to slow the development of a social crisis stemming from the equal division of the father's estate among the sons.

With his refusal to exclude landless households from the community, Solon became the second founder of Athens. This "political" decision resulted in the invention of democracy. But by building the new community on a generalized circulation of women and an undifferentiated transmission of household contents, Solon chose a matrimonial system that represented a defeat for Athenian women—and, owing to its perpetuation in law and literature, for women of the Western world generally. Estranged from the means of production and identified as items of private wealth to be placed, along with the bridal portion, under the guardianship of the husband, the brides of Solon's Athens had no more power, but far less value, than did women in Homeric society, whom their husbands treated as possessions.

Marriage and Citizenship

The abolition of the household hierarchy that had once determined who held office and wielded power in the community led Solon to revamp the forms of collective discussion and action. From now on all free men joined together to make war and govern the city, and each man had a share in the government proportional to his wealth, which was probably evaluated in *medimna,* a measure of grain equal to 51.84 liters.[151] Every man thus exercised the "profession of citizen."

The women of the new Athens were excluded from the practice of citizenship. Were they, like the women of Gortyn, members of the citizenship community? Or, to put it another way, did the right to be called "citizen" depend, owing to archaic legislation, on whether a person's father and mother had been citizens? Scholars agree that this provision was added to the law at a relatively late date.[152] In 594 and 593, the experts state flatly, Solon based citizenship on birth. Under Clisthenes' reforms (508–507) to be a citizen it was enough for one's father to have been a citizen. It was not until Pericles' decree of 451 that in order to be a citizen both of one's parents had to have been citizens.

The culmination of the process sheds light on its evolution. The decree of 451 signified both the closing of the civic community and the autonomy of the political. The father-mother rule established "true endogamy" and made it impossible for an Athenian man to marry a foreign woman. But by omitting any requirement that the progenitors had to have been legally married, the new rule violated one of the fundamental principles of household society: the equivalence of heritage and succession. A clear line was drawn once and for all between household and city, kinship and politics. It had taken nearly a century and a half for the Athenians to close the civic community and establish the autonomy of the political.

The slowness of this process can be correlated with the organization of the Solonian community, which perpetuated the household structure and gave women no specific place in the matrimonial system. Solon's abolition of public and private obligations did away with the hierarchy of households but not with households as such. By choosing a procedure based on daughter-in-law marriage, Solon allowed the households of the new community to retain their patrilinear character: they were masculine cells that engulfed their female elements. The bride became a ward of her husband, hence she had no social existence. She was a member of the community not as an individual but only as a part of a household belonging to the community. Thus it was lawful, provided the regulations governing the marriage contract were respected, for a man to take a wife outside the civic community, and great households did not forgo this opportunity to extend their matrimonial strategies. It is therefore plausible to argue that Solon based citizenship on legitimate birth within a household belonging to the community.

Perhaps we can find support for this hypothesis in an analysis of the Clisthenian reform. Aristotle does not exactly say that after Clisthenes citizenship required only a father who was a citizen. Rather, he says that the Athenian citizen after Clisthenes was supposed to add the name of his deme to that of his father. The significance of this double-naming is clear. The father's name indicated that the father had acknowledged paternity and the child was therefore legitimate. The name of the deme indicated that residents of the city's smallest subdivision had recognized the individual as one of their own and therefore as a citizen. After 507 B.C. the status of citizen was conferred by a person's lawfully married father and by his deme, that is, by men not of his own household. Prior to Clisthenes' reform Athenians were designated by their father's name and the name of their household. Citizenship was most likely conferred by a person's lawfully married father and by his household, that is, by continuous generations of fathers. The current state of my research does not permit me to say anything more, however.

Whatever the validity of the foregoing hypotheses, it is clear that in a society where the differentiation of the political sphere from the kinship system proceeded at a slow pace, marriage and the condition of the wife must be studied in the light of the emergence of a democratic polity.

I began with two questions. Why were women in Greece always given in marriage in conjunction with valuable goods of one kind or another? And why, in the Greece of the city-states, did the conditions under which such gifts were made differ so from city to city?

I end with two tentative conclusions. In Hellenic societies in the early part of the first millennium the free gift of the bride was associated with a social structure based on discrete, monogamous households. The reason why the Greek city-states ascribed such different status to women was that at some point in their history they made very different political choices.

This chapter is an interpretive, and therefore speculative, essay. It represents an approximation to truth, and any errors that may be lurking in my argument are subject to revision. In the *Metaphysics* Aristotle describes the philosopher's quest: "The investigation of the truth is in one way hard, in another easy. An indication of this is found in the fact that no one is able to attain the truth adequately, while, on the other hand, we do not collectively fail, but everyone says something true about the nature of things, and while individually we contribute little or nothing to the truth, by the union of all a considerable amount is amassed. Therefore, since the truth seems to be like the proverbial door, which no one can fail to hit, in this respect it must be easy, but the fact that we can have a whole truth and not the particular part we aim at shows the difficulty of it."[153] The door may be difficult to hit, but I am convinced that it leads straight to the heart of Hellenic societies.

The Hazards of Biological Destiny

Although Claudine Leduc's chapter has taken us to the heart of
the process of social reproduction in the Greek city-states,
women as such remain in the background. This shows the degree to which, even in marriage, the institution in which the existence of women was most fully recognized by society, the female's fate was determined by forces beyond her control. The
very structure of marriage is reminiscent of the vase paintings
examined in an earlier chapter, in which brides were shown in
the process of being transferred from one *oikos* or *kurios* to another.

But social reproduction depends first of all on biological reproduction, and Aline Rousselle exploits a wide range of sources
to shed new light on this crucial aspect of a woman's life. Birth
and death were intimately associated: death in childbirth, death
from abortion, death of the newborn. Biological destiny was cru-
cially modified, however, by social condition. Matrons—the legitimate wives of Roman citizens—were required to produce
three children; after that they were free to leave it to slaves and
concubines to produce the needed manpower and minister to
their husbands' sexual needs. This was how inequality, that fundamental feature of ancient society, manifested itself among
women. Eventually, however, the emphasis on female virtue gave
rise to a novel idea: men too could be virtuous spouses. But as
this noble idea of marriage took hold, wives once again became
the objects of their husbands' desires and were therefore forced
to confront the mortal risks that had previously been shunted
onto less fortunate women. Thus, as a group, women paid a
price for equality.

P.S.P.

6

Body Politics
in Ancient Rome

Aline Rousselle

IN GREEK MYTHOLOGY the world at first had
no women, indeed no humans. In the golden age
work did not exist, nor did woman.[1] Babylonian
mythology and the Bible also portray worlds without women, but these are worlds populated by a
single man. In the second century A.D. Lucian of
Samosata (125–195?), an Asian who wrote in
Greek, described a womanless society of Selenites
inhabiting the moon:

> They are born not of women, but of men.
> Marriages are between males, and the very
> word "woman" is totally unknown. A man
> can become a "bride" up to the age of
> twenty-five, after which he may marry an-
> other man as "husband." Selenite "mothers"
> carry children not in the belly but in the calf
> of the leg, which swells up after conception.
> When the time comes, they make an incision
> and extract the infant, who is lifeless until
> exposed open-mouthed to the lifegiving
> wind . . . Among the Selenites is a race of
> men called Dendrites. They are born in the
> following way. A man's right testicle is cut
> off and planted in the ground, and from it
> grows a large tree, which resembles a phallus.

It has branches and leaves and, for fruit, nuts a cubit long. When they are ripe, they are cut down and shelled to reveal a man inside. But the sexual parts are not genuine: some are made of ivory, and the poorer ones are made of wood. With these they impregnate the men they have married.[2]

In this exclusively male system of reproduction, the swelling of the calf substitutes for the swelling of the pregnant woman's belly and age difference substitutes for sexual difference, but the institution of marriage is maintained. Anthropologists working in Morocco recently discovered a similar story told there about the birth of angels. Iblis, leader of a band of rebel angels, is said to have fertilized his left calf with a penis protruding from his right calf. The resulting eggs hatch to produce other angels whose reproduction is bisexual.[3] Lucian's splendid text pretends that the very word "woman" was unknown to the Selenites, as if in the absence of a word the thing itself could not exist. Yet nature has thoughtfully provided "male" Selenites with all the equipment necessary for reproduction.

Already a century had passed since the apostle Paul predicted (in Galatians 3:28) that there would come a day when there would be neither men nor women in the world. But this new world without women would be a world without reproduction, for reproduction was woman's destiny.

In the Roman world, as elsewhere, biology was not the only determinant of women's lives. Society influenced reproduction as much as natural capacities. Each of the societies that made up the Roman Empire shaped reproductive life in its own way. Still, it makes sense to begin by reviewing the biological data. We shall then ask how the risks of procreation were distributed by society. Finally, we shall consider changes in social arrangements that profoundly changed the lives of women in late antiquity.

The Biological Destiny of Women

Mortality

Death in Childbirth. For the women to whom Saint Paul preached, those responsible for the reproduction of Roman society, maternity was destiny—as it was to all women prior to the advent of modern medicine. Consider these facts: in A.D. 117 the Roman Empire covered some 5.18 million square kilometers (subsequently reduced to 4.144 million square kilometers). Its population may have been as high as sixty million. Up to the age of marriage and motherhood, Roman females were as likely to survive as males. Life expectancy at birth was twenty to thirty years.[4] The infant mortality rate approached two hundred per thousand, comparable to that found in other preindustrial societies. In societies where the mortality rate is very high, differences between social classes are relatively insignificant; nevertheless, risks to women in childbirth depend on diet, which affects pelvic size and bone structure.

It is hard to gauge the age structure of the male population in Rome and harder still that of the female population. Children are underrepresented in the only available documentation, funerary inscriptions, which yield information almost exclusively about the urban upper and middle classes. In many cases a woman whose husband had died before her was buried without an inscription. In Roman Africa inscriptions honoring the memory of elderly women are very rare. In general women were discounted: the republican census included only those women who, as heiresses, were obliged to pay military taxes. In the late third century A.D. Diocletian ordered a census of the entire Empire for the purpose of assessing a head tax. Women were counted, but not as the equivalent of men: on rural estates in Thrace, for example, two women counted as one man. Before that, women had not been counted at all.

Childbirth was a mortal risk in all social classes. Perhaps 5 to 10 percent of pregnancies ended in the death of the mother either in delivery or afterward.[5] In the first century A.D. the grammarian Varro believed that Prorsa and Antvorta (Back and Front), the two faces of Carmentis, goddess of childbirth, owed their names to the two possible positions of the fetus. On January 11 and 15 matrons whose ancestors had dedicated the temple of Carmentis celebrated the goddess on the slopes of the Capitoline Hill. Five centuries later Augustine of Hippo, who had read Varro, wrote that the goddess Carmentis revealed the fate of the newborn.[6] The cult of the goddesses Antvorta and Prorsa was also related to the phases of the moon, which grows fat like a pregnant woman only to return to its prior thinness. Augustine warned Christian women not to turn to Roman goddesses and suggested Virtue and Felicity instead; but when danger loomed, his preaching was of no avail.[7] Felicity, a Christian martyr, had died with her mistress, Perpetua, in the amphitheater of Carthage shortly after giving birth. Lives of saints from late antiquity show women in the throes of puerperal fever invoking their names.[8] Midwives and physicians could never be certain that a delivery would go well. Perhaps to minimize their responsibility, it was often said that delivery after the eighth month represented a mortal danger to mother and child, whereas delivery of viable offspring at seven months was reputed to be easy.[9] "If the wife is that *rara avis,* a good and gentle woman, we wail with her in delivery and suffer if she is in danger," Seneca wrote in a book on marriage.[10]

It was well known that the size of the pelvis had a bearing on the ease of delivery. Doctors advised wealthy families to mold infants' bodies with bandages during the first two months of life. To reduce the circumference of a girl's shoulders and chest, her wet nurse or mother would bind them tightly, but the hips were left unbound to encourage a large pelvis. Boys' hips were bound.[11]

Prior to Christian accounts of miracles, we have little information about childbirth among the poor. Death in childbirth or from infections was common among aristocratic women, however. Following her divorce, Cicero's daughter Tullia gave birth to a boy and died a month after the delivery.[12] Her father, who loved her like a son, honored her with a eulogy replete with literary allusions usually reserved for the death of a male child. On one of his estates not far from Rome he built a small temple in her memory.

Despite the danger of childbirth, women worried more about sterility. Ancient physicians wrote treatises on amenorrhea, one of the signs of the uterine infections that can lead to sterility.[13] In pagan as well as Christian times Roman women prayed for divine assistance in having children. Ancient sources speak more often of the male impotence caused by malnutrition than of the related amenorrhea in women. When food was short, as it often was in the Roman Empire, particularly in the late fourth century, neither men nor women were in any condition to produce offspring.[14] When a child was slow in coming, families often turned to the gods (or to God), as we know from texts, inscriptions, and Christian tales of miracles.[15]

Infant Mortality. If women did not die in childbirth, there was a good chance they might have to watch their children die.

All social classes were accustomed to such losses. To console a woman friend who had lost a son, Seneca listed the great men who had suffered a similar misfortune.[16] Throughout the Empire women and their husbands prayed to the gods to protect their unborn, newborn, and growing children. Wood and stone carvings of swaddled babies were widely used as devotional objects in Etruria[17] and Gaul.[18] Prayers for the health of children were written on papyrus and other materials. One Egyptian amulet, in the form of a uterus sealed by a lock, shows a woman, her hair disheveled as in delivery, pressing on her belly; inscribed beneath the drawing are the words, "Womb, close thyself!"[19] Bowls from the vicinity of the Euphrates carry inscriptions warning against the Liliths, female demons believed to kill infants in their mothers' wombs. The prophet Elijah was believed to protect women against these attacks: "The Lilith encountered the prophet Elijah and said to him: Lord Elijah, I am going to the home of a woman on her childbed and in the throes of death . . . to bring her death's sleep and take the child she is carrying in order to suck its blood and the marrow of its bones and devour its flesh."[20]

There was no agreement as to the precise time at which the soul entered the infant's body, but everyone believed that it was difficult for the soul to attach itself to matter. As it came and went, unable to decide, the child momentarily came to life, then lapsed into death. The presence of holy men encouraged the soul to take root in the tiny body. Pagans shared these beliefs with Christians, and mothers waited for the moment when the child's soul would return. Christians believed that the soul briefly revisited the body of a stillborn child and that during this "respite" baptism was possible.[21] The bodies of deceased children were not wrapped in shrouds but buried directly in the earth, and not always in the cemeteries used for other burials. When ancient cemeteries are excavated, children's remains are sometimes found grouped together, often in numbers disproportionate to the total number of graves. Much of what we can say about infant mortality comes from our knowledge of other periods and from the anxious worries voiced by parents in the temples. Statistics could not possibly be more eloquent.

Edicts issued by Augustus concerning the marriage of senators and equestrians in 18 B.C. and inheritances in A.D. 9 made marriage and parenthood conditions of inheritance. Girls of twelve and boys of fourteen (the official ages of eligibility for marriage) were counted in the census. But child mortality was so high, even in the upper classes affected by the imperial edicts, that a person was considered a parent if he or she had produced two children who lived until the age of three or three infants who survived at least three days.[22] In his consolations to mothers Seneca noted examples of women who had seen their children die, most notably Cornelia, mother of the Gracchi, who had lost ten of her twelve children only to see the two survivors murdered.

Late-fourth-century Christians looked forward to lives of perfect continence after fulfilling the familial duty to procreate. When Melanie, a wealthy heiress whose parents had arranged her marriage at age fourteen, persuaded her husband of seventeen to embrace chastity along with her, she agreed to wait until they had produced two children. She lost a little girl not yet two years old and then an unborn son in a miscarriage, no doubt the result of long nights of prayer at holy gravesites. To illustrate the young woman's concern for others, Melanie's biographer chose an episode in which she called on a "woman in danger" because her dead fetus remained trapped in the uterus.[23] Melanie placed a sash that she had received from a holy man on the woman's belly, and the fetus immediately emerged. Two other late-fourth-century aristocrats—Paulinus of Nola and his wife Therasia—also decided to devote their lives to God but first sought to assure perpetuation of their line. When their child died, however, they saw it as a sign from God, had the body buried near a saint, and did not attempt to have any other children.[24] Not even the most attentive care in the wealthiest of homes was enough to prevent child mortality. During the high imperial period children of the aristocracy were not always nursed by their mothers, but wet nurses were chosen carefully on the advice of physicians and either resided in the parents' home or were kept under surveillance. The use of wet nurses did not kill children in Ancient Rome as it did in Enlightenment Europe.[25]

Women were concerned about their children's fate in the afterlife. They were touched by mythical tales of mothers who went down to the Underworld in search of their kidnapped progeny, as Demeter went in search of Persephone. Syrian coroplasts patterned their representations of mother-daughter reunions on Eros' embrace of Psyche.[26] They admired Demeter, who had offered to nurse the child of the king of Eleusis and had the ability to make the child immortal. Throughout the Empire women were moved by the story of Isis' search for Osiris, her dismembered son and husband, whose death they mourned every October 28. The name of Isis was invoked in funerary inscriptions commemorating the death of a son.[27] Even if at least half the inscriptions to Isis in Italy (up to 85 percent in the major port cities) were left by immigrants from the East, the remainder reflect the sentiments of Western adepts.[28] This identification with Isis was not a reflection of female masochism or lack of common sense, despite Seneca's crude remark: "They wail even though they have lost no one. It is all right to rave once a year."[29] It was rather a reflection of the experience of a mother's loss.

Society and Ecology

The "ecobiological" conditions of a woman's life were influenced largely by social organization. In the ancient Mediterranean world there was no room for choice: a woman did not choose celibacy, she did not choose marriage, and she did not choose remarriage after widowhood.

By now it should be clear that if there is such a thing as a pure demographic ecology for animals, there is no such thing for humans.[30] Social factors must be taken into account, since to a large extent society regulates the biological destiny and therefore the mortality of women. It no longer makes sense to speak of demographic ecology or ecological demography once human beings begin to act socially to regulate reproduction.[31] Women naturally become the focus of such efforts.

The Age of Marriage. The women of antiquity—not only Greeks and Romans but also Jews—were destined to marry and become mothers. Although daughters were sometimes exposed, the practice was not widespread, and before the age of Christianity very few women remained unmarried. Women did not choose when to marry. Marriage contracts were concluded between the bride's father and her future husband and originally did not require her consent.[32] When the Romans did begin to insist on the daughter's formal consent before her father could give her to another man, it was a major innovation.

Roman law fixed the age at which a daughter given to a spouse by her father officially became a matron, a recognized spouse with all the privileges set forth in marriage law. That age was twelve years. In other societies included in the Empire such early marriage did not exist, at least not until Roman influence made it a mark of distinction. In Greek areas girls married after puberty, between the ages of sixteen and eighteen.

Puberty. According to ancient physicians, girls reached puberty at about age fourteen.[33] They believed, however, that it was possible to influence the age of puberty in females. It was also observed that excessive exercise could stunt the growth of boys.[34] In the late first century a physician, Rufus, noted that puberty came early in girls who did not exercise, particularly those who did not work. He recommended early marriage but counseled caution, because the uterus was still too young to withstand a pregnancy.[35] Concerned about early onset of menstruation, he recommended physical exercise—games of skittles and choral singing—to prevent this condition.[36] Women observed that singing and dancing could delay puberty and disrupt the menstrual cycle. Many stopped menstruating during choral competitions, which required considerable effort.[37] Rufus' ideas on physical exercise were correct: recent studies have shown that regular participation in sports can delay puberty by up to three years.[38] Soranus recommended a diet intended to advance the onset of menstruation so that girls could marry early and still have reached puberty. His method was the opposite of Rufus': girls should not be overfed and should be allowed plenty of rest together with mild and generally passive forms of activity, such as carriage rides and massages.[39] Both sets of recommendations indicate that people were aware of the effects of athletic activity and physical labor on puberty in women. It would therefore be presumptuous to hazard a guess as to the average age of puberty; it is better to accept the ancient physicians' own estimate of fourteen.

Early Marriage. Marcel Durry, upon learning that Moroccan girls often marry before puberty and that these marriages are consummated immediately, turned to ancient Greek and Latin texts and found evidence of a similar practice. Much as scholars disapproved of this discovery, they were forced to yield to the evidence. The question now is how widespread the practice was. Evidence of very early marriage is relatively easy to come by: funerary inscriptions mention brides of ten or eleven. But were such marriages consummated? Written documents speak of mothers of thirteen, such as the wife of Quintilian, an illustrious rhetorician and a man jealous of his reputation for good teaching, irreproachable ethics, and general decency.[40] A papyrus source from Egypt during the imperial period also refers to a mother of thirteen.[41] Obviously if these young women were mothers at thirteen, they must have reached puberty by the age of twelve. And funerary inscriptions are hardly the place to look for evidence that girls who married at ten, before puberty, did or did not have sexual relations with their husbands.

The key to the problem lies in what ancient physicians had to say about marriage. Romans believed that there was a scientific reason for girls to marry before puberty, namely, that early sexual relations facilitated the onset of menstruation. Among those to whom the physician Soranus of Ephesus addressed his works it was firmly believed that virgins suffered from a blockage of the vagina.[42] Given the persistence of the notion that defloration ought to precede the onset of menstruation, prepubescent marriages must have been fairly widespread. Women—and above all those walking encyclopedias of gynecology, midwives—left the men of Italy in ignorance as to the nature of the female sexual parts, from the hymen (if any) to the cervix. But Roman women who had married early were by no means opposed to the practice. They were perfectly willing to oblige future husbands by examining prospective brides for suitability in childbearing. The judgment was based on such criteria as facial complexion, pelvic width, and general physical condition, it being taken for granted that a mother's body should not be too soft or feminine.[43]

Prepubescent marriage was widespread in the Roman Empire. Jewish girls married as early as age twelve.[44] Since Roman law did not recognize a marriage as permanent until the bride turned thirteen, husbands occasionally leveled charges of adultery at girls of twelve and under. The Severian emperors administered official punishment to such young adulteresses in the early third century.[45] But the Severians hailed from Syria and Africa, so it is difficult to say whether Roman law evolved under the influence of Jewish law or vice versa.

In Deuteronomy (22:13–21) there is discussion of how judges ought to deal with a husband's claim that his bride, contrary to her father's protestations, was not a virgin on the day of her marriage. The text recommends that the bride's parents be summoned to produce the stained linen from the marriage bed as proof of defloration. Otherwise the judges should find that the girl had been a prostitute while still living under her father's roof. Under the Roman Empire the rabbis considered the question in a new light. They used the text of Deuteronomy to determine the punishment for adultery by a fiancée.[46] But the issue was now the same as for the Romans: Had a girl too young to be officially married committed adultery?

The passage from Deuteronomy indicates that the linen of the marriage bed was the sole admissible proof of the bride's virginity. Thus any woman who married had to be capable of bleeding. The manual examination that so horrified Saint Ambrose in the late fourth century was probably a Roman invention. It was designed to determine, prior to the marriage ceremony, whether or not the bride had been defiled.[47] This Christian verification procedure was simply one of many tests administered by midwives to ensure the reproductive capacity of the bride-to-be, tests condemned by Soranus in the second century. For the Jews the bed linen, along with the fear of disclosure, was a sufficient deterrent. Yet women knew perfectly well that defloration was not always accompanied by bleeding. Carston Niebuhr's *Description of Arabia* (1773) discusses what proof of a bride's virginity Yemeni men demanded.[48] The prudent father of one young bride produced witnesses to testify that they had seen his daughter fall from a camel. Some families claimed that their women did not bleed and produced documentation going back many years to support their contention. In such cases prospective husbands were willing to settle for certification that the bride's vulva was tightly closed (Soranus having described the vulvas of virgins in these terms). Another test used in Yemen was chemical: lemon juice caused the blood of a virgin to turn green, that of a nonvirgin to turn black. Niebuhr reports that he was told by certain Muslim men that some young women whose bodies offered no proof of virginity often simulated proof or claimed that the necessary mark had been obliterated by an accident. In short, while a stained sheet was irrefutable proof of virginity, other tests could be substituted; and where a woman's anatomy did not provide the necessary evidence, an arrangement could always be found. In Palestine in the second century B.C. Jews had perfected a surgical procedure for restoring the foreskin to circumcised males so that they could participate in sports at Greek gymnasiums; it may be that a similar procedure for restoring the hymen existed. In any case such a procedure was actively sought, and Julius Africanus was reputed to have found one.[49] From the first to the eighteenth century is a long time indeed, but Niebuhr's detailed and subtle investigation shows that many other techniques could be substituted for the rigid anatomical test. The Jews of the Roman Empire believed that the first penetration, the one that produced a flow of blood indicating virginity, never resulted in pregnancy. To explain cases in which a woman became pregnant after her first experience of sexual intercourse, they therefore assumed that there must have been a prior defloration by hand.[50] In late antiquity virginity was such an important aspect of a bride's character that it figured as a key element in various pagan romances.[51]

Evidence of desire for a virgin wife can be found in the works of Christianity's great preachers. John Chrysostom in the late fourth century took a personal tone in attempting to dissuade young widows from remarrying: "As I said before, we men are made that way: out of jealousy, vanity, and who knows what other reasons we love most what no one else has used or taken advantage of before us, so that we are the first and only masters." He goes on to compare women to clothing and furniture.[52]

The story of Mary's virginity, which eventually became an accepted part of Christian doctrine, developed in a world where examinations of virginity were an accepted practice. Slave girls whose virginity could be proven sold for higher prices.[53] As the Roman custom of early marriage spread throughout the Empire, it became fashionable to marry girls of twelve or younger. Byzantine judicial records preserve traces of such marriages, as Evelyne Patlagean has shown. Women stated that they had married at age eleven, "before the appearance of pubic hair." Marriages were sometimes made on the condition that they not be consummated, but one document indicates that a husband, breaking his promise, mutilated a girl by forcing her to engage in sexual relations for which she was not yet ready. Despite the relative absence of documents, the commentaries of ancient jurists suggest that the practice was not uncommon.[54]

For the girl who married on reaching puberty or shortly thereafter, puberty was virtually coincident with childbearing. Roman women, who married early, were apt to become pregnant at any time between the ages of thirteen and fifty. A woman today who marries at twenty-four is capable of bearing seven or eight children if she nurses her offspring and ten or fifteen if she does not.[55] How many more children could a Roman woman bear, even allowing for her shorter life expectancy?

In premodern societies one pregnancy in five was likely to result in the death of the mother. In Rome, where early marriage increased the possible number of pregnancies, the risk to women would seem to have been correspondingly higher, unless some means of social control existed that allowed men to marry, as they clearly wished to do, very young girls without killing them.

Family Planning

When Tacitus reports that the Germans considered it shameful to limit family size, he makes it clear that this was an issue that concerned the Romans.[56] He also notes the condemnation of infanticide by the Jews, who he says are lustful because they force their wives to bear so many children.[57] Elsewhere surprise was voiced that the Egyptians kept so many of their children.[58] The Jews of the Empire, such as Flavius Josephus in the first century, differed with the Romans over the issue of keeping all children.[59] Even in Rome, Augustan laws encouraged parents to keep the first three children. Exposure of boys was as widely accepted as exposure of girls. We have no way of knowing for sure whether the number of girls actually exposed was higher than the number of boys, although there are strong indications that this was the case. Nevertheless, girls as well as boys counted toward the quota of three children required by Augustan edict. Roman fathers wanted insurance against another kind of risk: that of creating new claims on the family patrimony. The husband in a legal marriage had the power to decide the fate of each child at birth.

We do not know how many children were exposed or how the practice was distributed among the various classes of society. It was common enough, however, to require regulation by law and to be mentioned in inscriptions.[60] The law, for example, prohibited a man from taking in and then adopting an exposed child, a practice that was apparently common in Egypt. Nevertheless, one thing is clear: unwanted children were unwanted from the moment of conception, yet the pregnancies were allowed to continue to term. (Deformed babies were a special case: even before the father had an opportunity to accept or reject the infant, its fate was decided by the midwife, who simply ended the life of a child unfortunate enough to be born defective.)

At all times in the ancient world the poor abandoned or sold their children.[61] In 315 Emperor Constantine decided to provide the poor with food and clothing for their children in order to discourage infanticide, which was forbidden under new laws.[62] From the law we also learn that heirs sometimes attempted to do away with a still unborn child that might pose a rival claim to an estate.[63] Only a father could order that an infant be exposed at birth. Moreover, the father retained control of his progeny even after death, and he could indicate in his will that he wished for any posthumous child to be exposed. The will could also specify that, should a son be born after the father's death, the child should be disinherited, leaving it to the mother to decide whether to abandon it or not. If the child turned out to be a daughter and the father ordered that it be kept, the mother was entitled to receive an allowance of food for the child.[64] Hence abortion was not the principal means of limiting family size.

In all cases a father who was a freeborn Roman citizen had full power over his legitimate offspring. Under the Law of the Twelve Tables (fifth century B.C.) a wife could be repudiated for denying the father the *partum,* or product, of the marriage, of which he alone had the right to dispose.

Contraception. What could women do to avoid unwanted births and the consequent risks of exposure and infanticide? Coitus interruptus, which depended on the husband's cooperation, was ineffective and therefore little used. Physicians advised men not to withhold their sperm on the grounds that to do so was harmful to kidneys and bladder.[65] Surgical sterilization was not attempted, although the technique was used on animals, particularly sows.[66] Vasectomies were performed on athletes, according to Galen, who in the same text discusses the spaying of sows in Cappadocia.[67]

Roman women believed that it was possible to engage in intercourse and still prevent conception. Our knowledge of this belief of course comes from texts written by men, mainly physicians.[68] Conception was thought to be certain if the male's sperm was fully absorbed by the woman's womb. The way to prevent conception was to impede such absorption. If a woman rose quickly after intercourse and washed her genitals, she could prevent conception. Pessaries and vaginal injections were also used, but their efficacy was limited.

The principal means of preventing conception was the ingestion of various potions similar to those used to induce abortions. Violent purgatives and emetics were widely used in Mediterranean countries for such purposes, as if the womb, like the stomach, could be made to vomit up its contents. Hellebore was administered in difficult cases, although its potentially fatal side-effects were well known.[69] Even today, in the twentieth century, Berber women in the Atlas Mountains are known to use potions made with artemisia to protect their unmarried daughters against conception. The treatment is effective and does not cause sterility. Artemisia was also employed in ancient times.[70] It was not the only herb used, however, and we do not know whether effective concoctions were favored over ineffective ones.

Abortion and Its Dangers. It was known from spontaneous abortions that termination of pregnancy could be fatal, but that was not what kept physicians from intervening.[71] It was rather the fact that an abortion was potentially a means of concealing adultery, and a physician who participated in such a crime was liable to the same penalties as the adulterous lovers. Soranus would perform an abortion only in cases where the girl involved was so young that pregnancy threatened permanent damage to the uterus. Abortion, possibly by surgical means (probes), was then considered advisable.[72]

We know about Roman abortion from two types of sources: medical treatises and legal documents, the latter arising out of cases in which administration of a potion resulted in death. An abortion could result in murder charges if mechanical means were used (a metallic probe, for example).[73] If death followed the administration of a potion, the crime was classified as poisoning. The law thus punished not abortion or even the taking of the life of the child (which belonged to the father) but the death of the mother.

If a woman died in an abortion attempt, the person (male or female) who administered the potion could be accused of poisoning or evil magic. The Romans drew no clear distinction between poisons, love potions, and drugs.[74] A "venom" was all right as long as it did not kill. The effects of a potion being unpredictable, the patient herself bore no responsibility. Only the person administering it was subject to prosecution.[75] If poisoning was suspected, a confession of evil intent had to be obtained from the alleged poisoner. Abortion potions were a special case. The identity of the person administering the potion was known, and the trial could begin immediately. The same was true for aphrodisiacs.[76] It was up to the husband to decide whether his wife had been the victim of an *injuria* so that the case should go to court.[77] To judge from the texts of the laws, the person administering venoms, whether good or bad, was generally a woman.[78] A woman who killed a friend while helping her to end an unwanted pregnancy risked repudiation, loss of her dowry, and imprisonment.

The Division of Labor

In societies with high mortality rates—that is, in all societies prior to our own—the assignment of women's roles was a key determinant of demographic structure. In the ancient world certain women were designated for the purpose of reproducing select groups or classes: citizens, for example, or members of the Jewish community. Because women married very young, we may ask how, since nothing could be done about either the fertility of sexually active women or the rate of infant mortality, regulating this selection process was used to limit the total number of births.

In ancient Mediterranean societies the mortality rate was approximately forty per thousand. We have no information about the number of children conceived, the number of abortions and infanticides, or the deliberate exposure of girls. The ancients spoke easily about such practices until first the Jews, then the Christians, began to criticize them as "pagan." So we know that abortion, infanticide, and exposure of daughters took place, but we do not know how common these practices were.

The vast territory conquered by the Romans was inhabited by a variety of peoples, whose customary and written laws differed markedly in regard to family matters. Laws concerning incest, the transmission of civic or ethnic status, and the role of women in such transmission—laws once regarded as ethnic peculiarities—were compared, contrasted, and ultimately erected into a hierarchy of ethical norms. Rome's supremacy being acknowledged by all, those who wished to join the conquerors' community came to adopt the laws of Rome. The unification of the Mediterranean peoples under Roman law early in the third century and, later, under the rules established by the Christian church (rules that were not all integrated into the laws of the Western and Byzantine Empires) transformed the lives of women in the region that would become the cradle of Western civilization.

Reproduction and Status

Personal status was the basis for all social distinctions in Mediterranean societies. Women formed an integral part of the status
hierarchy. The fundamental status distinction was of course that
between free man or woman and slave. Reproduction of servile
labor, a task assigned to female slaves, was a vital concern of all
slave owners.

No Mediterranean society permitted members to enslave other
members. A Roman could not have a Roman slave, a Jew could
not have a Jewish slave, a Greek could not have a Greek slave. A
woman raped while in captivity retained her honor in Rome, just
as a citizen taken captive regained his full legal rights if freed and
returned home.[79]

The Reproduction of Slaves. Slave owners regulated childbirth among their slaves. This was true in the Greek world, including Roman Egypt, as well as in the western part of the Empire.[80] From Xenophon's *Economics,* a widely read Greek work
of which a digest had been prepared by a disciple of Aristotle and
which had been translated into Latin by Cicero, Roman readers
could have learned that wise management required keeping male
and female slaves apart; copulation was to be authorized only as
a reward. Slaves were prevented from having intercourse with the
slaves of other masters. After A.D. 52 a Roman woman who slept
with a slave without the consent of the slave's master herself
became a slave.[81] The sale of a sterile female slave gave rise to
heated legal controversy, the upshot of which was that the sale
was null and void if the sterility resulted from a disease but not if
it was congenital. The jurisconsults based their reasoning on an
analogy with the sale of a spayed sow, which the law required the
seller to take back if the buyer had not been duly informed prior
to the sale.[82] Another analogy was with the sale of a eunuch, who
could be returned to the seller if found to be suffering from a
disease not disclosed prior to the sale. (Handsome eunuchs brought
higher prices than other males.) The comparison of women with
sows is instructive. Sows not to be used for reproduction were
spayed to make their meat tastier and more tender. Thus some
sows were to be savored for pleasure, while others were to be used
for reproduction: a declaration had to be made prior to the sale.

It was the same with female slaves: some were for reproduction, others for their masters' pleasure. In the sixth century Bishop

Caesarius of Arles (470–543) asked if free women who took drugs to induce abortion would allow their domestic slaves or *coloni* to do the same.[83] But war had ceased to be a source of new slaves, and reproduction of slave labor was essential. Female slave owners acted in the exact same way as did males: they exploited the bodies of their inferiors. Status governed emotions. In late-second-century Alexandria, Christian women felt no compunctions about having themselves bathed by male slaves. They simply did not see slaves as men.[84]

The ancients believed that slaves were sexually uninhibited. A character in a fourth-century comedy written in Gaul holds forth on the joys of slavery: the slave can bathe at night with the serving women and hold naked in his arms bodies that the master can glimpse only fully clothed.[85] But the myth of total promiscuity is contradicted by slaves' funerary inscriptions, which mimicked the pious sentiments toward marriage favored by those of free birth.

Free Women and the Transmission of Civic and Ethnic Status. Until 212 there was, in theory at least, another important distinction in Mediterranean cities: between citizens and noncitizens. There were, however, ways in which foreigners could become citizens, and there were agreements about how status was to be transmitted when a man married a woman belonging to another nation or tribe. Jews, whose laws were unlike those of imperial municipalities, also made provision for marriages between Jews and non-Jews. The non-Jewish partner was integrated into the community: if a male through study and circumcision, and if a female through religious ritual. The Romans signed treaties with the Italian tribes they conquered, and in extending Latin rights to a city or people, they always allowed for legitimate marriage between the indigenous population and Romans. Greek cities were less generous in granting citizenship to "foreigners," including citizens of other Greek cities. The Greek cities of Egypt did not recognize marriages between Greek men and Egyptian women. Throughout much of the Greek-dominated Middle East—Syria, Palestine, Egypt, and so on—neither Greek nor Roman law held sway. When people from these places came to the West, they were treated as foreigners and not allowed to marry the locals. Questions of citizenship and ethnic status arose frequently.

In determining citizenship different societies ascribed different roles to women. If husband and wife shared the same status, no question arose. Everywhere the child of two slaves was a slave, the child of two citizens was a citizen, the child of two members of a tribe was a member of the tribe. There was a problem only when husband and wife were of different status or the child was illegitimate.

Under Roman law a woman who brought a child into the world fell into one of several categories: a lawful wife and *matrona* (mother and citizen); a concubine, either matrona or not; a victim of rape, but still a matrona; a woman accused of adultery or indecent sexual behavior, no longer a matrona. As long as the woman was classified as matrona, her child, legitimate or not, was a Roman citizen. Under Jewish law any child born to a Jewish mother, legitimate or not and regardless of rank, was a Jew. Funerary inscriptions sometimes emphasized this transmission of status in the maternal line: so-and-so, son of (mother's name).[86] In Greece illegitimate children of Greek mothers were not citizens.[87] In Miletus the child of a male citizen by a foreign woman was considered a bastard, and the child of a foreign man by a Miletan woman was considered a foreigner. To be a citizen both parents had to be citizens, as in Athens. But when, owing to a shortage of males, it was decided to grant citizenship to bastards, only children of male citizens by foreign mothers were counted. In other words, transmission of citizenship depended essentially on the father. The Greek custom thus contrasts sharply with both Roman law and Jewish law, under which children took their mother's status.

In all the societies in question the chief concern was to encourage lawfully married couples to produce offspring. With the Lex Iulia, Emperor Augustus granted rights to children of freeborn men and freed women, except in senatorial families.[88] By being thus brought under the jurisdiction of Roman law, these children enjoyed a wider range of permissible marriages. Similarly, Jews allowed non-Jews to join their community by converting to Judaism. They also accepted some freed pagan slaves and on occasion authorized marriages between men and women of different ranks.

Honorable Women

Augustus revamped Roman family law on three occasions: in 18 and 17 B.C. and again in A.D. 9. He compelled men and women in the upper reaches of Roman society to marry and reproduce by restricting the right of inheritance if they failed to do so. He encouraged legitimate marriage and made the state responsible for policing the fidelity of Roman women. Family and neighbors were compelled to turn in adulterers or face charges of proxenitism and consequent loss of honor.

The Fidelity of Wives. Fidelity was required of married women in all societies known to have been under Roman domination. Members of other ethnic groups and communities were sometimes permitted to marry Romans, and these marriages were protected to the same degree as marriages between Roman citizens. Communities that lived under their own laws took similar steps to prevent adultery.

Chariton's long romance *Chaereas and Callirhoe,* probably written in the first century after Christ, is the story of a man who marries for love but who, on receiving false word of his wife's infidelity, goes wild and kicks her in the stomach so violently that she loses consciousness and is taken for dead. She does not come to until after her burial.[89] After a series of adventures she is reunited with her husband, whom, despite his violent behavior, she still loves. A deceived husband, everyone agreed, was entitled to his rage.

Preventing Adultery. Men feared exposing themselves to the penalties for adultery. Satirists often portrayed the problems involved in relations with married women (for a man, such relations were the sine qua non of adultery): the couple's surprise and terror at the slightest sound, the servant in league with the master, spying on the couple's every move so that the master might catch them in the act. Although the satires were vague about the woman's social class, they were definite about how respectable women should dress—in clothes that allowed the face to be seen but nothing else. "If you wish to savor forbidden pleasures, pleasures defended as tenaciously as a fortress (which is what causes you to lose your head), a thousand obstacles stand before you: guards, litters, hairdressers, parasites, dresses extending down to the heels, and a great cloak that hides everything." Courtesans display their wares, Horace tells us, but when it comes to a respectable woman, "one sees only the face."[90] The end of the poet's life (he died in 8 B.C.) coincided with Rome's most licentious period, but it was at around this same time that Augustus issued his strict edicts against adultery. Among the risks of adultery mentioned by Horace were torture for slaves (their legs were broken) and loss of dowry for an unfaithful wife.[91]

The Augustan laws against adultery were in force when Horace wrote his second satire. In surveying the ways in which a man might cultivate the extremes with a clear conscience, the poet first discusses money, then sex (which ultimately was related to money). Some men liked the wives of citizens, fully clothed from head to toe, while others were interested only in prostitutes. Adulterers, according to Horace, lived in constant fear, which interfered with their pleasures. They were terrified of such things as being obliged to hide on a rooftop from which they might easily fall, of being flogged to death, even of being castrated.

For Horace, concerned with what lay beneath all that linen, respectable women who wore veils outside the house were dishonest about their wares.[92] The poet himself was interested mainly in buttocks and never mentions breasts. Respectable women did nothing to draw attention to themselves. They were not supposed to use cosmetics, perfume, or hairpieces to seduce their husbands. In Rome and the East, on the rare occasions when women left the home, they wore veils or hoods. Elderly women and young girls were sent out to buy clothing.[93] Under the Republic a man could divorce a wife who went out with her head uncovered.[94] Pliny was glad that his wife came to hear him read, "with an eager ear hidden behind a curtain."[95] In Rome the cult statues of the goddess Pudicitia were veiled.[96]

A veil or hood constituted a warning: it signified that the wearer was a respectable woman and that no man dare approach without risking grave penalties. A woman who went out in servant's dress, unveiled, forfeited the protection of Roman law against possible attackers, who were entitled to plead extenuating circumstances.[97] When Paul (I Cor. 11:10) urged all Christian women to wear veils, his purpose was to signify that, regardless of their status under other laws, they were untouchable for Christian men. Just as male slaves took the liberty of wearing the toga or pallium, symbols of free status, Christian women, regardless of status, wore veils and even dressed as matrons. Although the veil was a symbol of subjection, it was also a badge of honor, of sexual reserve, and hence of mastery of the self.

Marriage and Children. Roman law defined the purpose of marriage as procreation. Women who wished to be released from guardianship were required to produce three or four children (three for a freeborn woman, four for a freed slave). Under Augustus the law prohibited unmarried men between the ages of twenty and sixty and unmarried (even widowed and divorced) women between eighteen and fifty from receiving inheritances. Women were expected to marry and have at least one child by the time they were twenty, men by the time they were twenty-five. A widow was expected to remarry within a year, a divorcée within six months. Under Hadrian a woman could count her illegitimate children—children born while she was a concubine, probably of her master—along with those of her lawful husband, probably a freed slave whom she married with her master's permission.

Fear of Sterility. Not just society but the husband's family expected a woman to produce the three children required by law so that the husband might receive his inheritance. If she failed to do so, much of the husband's share might go instead to relatives with children or to the state. Since the law stated that women married "in order to make children," wives became anxious if children were slow in coming. Sterile couples like the parents of Pythagoras visited temples and prayed to the gods for help. Inscriptions in temples of Asclepius offer thanks for the birth of a child.[98] The drugs women took to counter sterility were as dangerous as those used to induce abortion. At a time when Christianity was already flourishing in the Empire, Eusebia, the wife of Emperor Constantius II, died of an antisterility medication.[99] Christian women turned to the saints and their relics for assistance. And there is a lengthy text praising a model woman, a childless wife who proposed that her husband divorce her and marry another woman capable of bearing children.[100]

Feminine Continence. Women feared miscarriages and turned to physicians for help in avoiding them. To protect the unborn the doctors recommended abstaining from sexual intercourse during pregnancy. To protect the nursing infant they recommended abstaining as long as the child remained at the breast.[101] Aristotle said a woman ceased to produce milk if she became pregnant again. When did sexual relations resume? Medical texts recommended that husbands carefully plan the date and circumstances of sexual intercourse in order to maximize the likelihood of conception. I read these texts as indicating that sexual relations in the wealthiest couples were no more frequent than necessary to produce the required number of children. Births came close together, particularly since Roman women ignored the physicians' recommendations that they nurse their children.

If a man of thirty married a girl of fifteen and the husband died at forty-five, the intervening fifteen years were sufficient to produce at least seven children (even assuming that the mother nursed her babies). It was highly likely, however, that the woman would die before giving birth to that many offspring. A woman who married at fourteen could fulfill the requirement of three children "for the census," as the Romans used to say, by the time she was twenty. What happened after that?

To answer the question we must resort to an indirect form of argument. The great families were dying out. Under Nerva, around A.D. 100, only half of the senatorial families listed in the census of 65 remained on the rolls. By 130 only one of forty-five patrician families restored by Julius Caesar in 45 B.C. was still in existence.[102] Why was this happening? It is hard to believe that children were being exposed after the third required birth. For this to be true, women would have had to make the decision to expose the infant. Among the poor in the sixth century, children under ten, especially females, were sold to proxenetes.[103] Divorce may have had some impact on the birthrate, but this would only have increased the number of children produced by the average men. And it was always more satisfactory to work out some kind of arrangement rather than divorce, which was in no one's best interest. Roman divorces were a matter of public notoriety, reported in the chronicles of the historians. Unlike Jewish women, Roman women could take the initiative in asking for a divorce, but they risked losing their dowry if they did so. Some Roman women who converted to Judaism challenged this loss. By contrast, Jewish women who became Roman citizens and who lived under both Jewish and Roman law could not leave their husbands.[104]

Some husbands wished to continue sexual relations with their wives even after producing the requisite three children. What was to be done? Contraceptive techniques were not effective. If a respectable woman sought out a physician to perform an abortion, she was suspected of wishing to get rid of a child conceived in adultery. After the prudish reign of the Flavians, under Domitian's tyranny and Nerva's earnest government, upper-class women took lovers and had abortions when necessary—at least according to the writers Juvenal and Martial (but they were reporting scandalous affairs that surely did not reflect the norm). The law concerned itself with abortion only when the woman had no relations with her husband, so that her pregnancy was proof of adultery. In cases of abortion-related poisoning it was the aggrieved husband who went to court. In short, unless we assume that abortions (and the deaths incident to them) were widespread, particularly among the upper classes, the only way to account for the low birthrate in aristocratic families is to assume that couples abstained from sexual intercourse.

In the Roman Empire the life expectancy of a woman at birth was twenty to thirty years. One-fifth to one-quarter (perhaps more) of all girls died before reaching the age of five. Those who survived usually married by age twelve and certainly before age eighteen. If they lived that long they might hope to go on living until forty or so, but they knew perfectly well that childbirth could easily prove fatal. Even if the first pregnancy went well, proving that the pelvic formation was suitable, there was no guarantee that subsequent pregnancies would be unproblematic, particularly if the fetus presented itself in a bad position.

Aristotle tells us that after three children, "women lose their taste for love."[105] "Owing to constitutional weakness the female attains adulthood and old age more quickly [than the male] . . . During all this time males are in better physical condition, whereas most women are ill from pregnancy." But the ancients did not think that the ravages of childbirth posed an obstacle to further intercourse, except in cases where the mother was extremely young.[106] In large cities, moreover, where people suffered from congenital malformations owing to lack of exposure to sunlight and short nursing periods, it may well be that many women had pelvises too narrow to permit easy childbirth.

The issue for the ancients may not have been one of limiting births as it was protecting upper-class women from the risks of pregnancy. The Romans never sought to fix the maximum number of births, only the minimum, and they sought to encourage legitimate marriage in order to maximize the number of citizens born of such unions. Why was no thought given to limiting births? Because the problem was easily solved: upper-class women simply abstained from intercourse. People approved of and admired married women who lived in continence, a fact that was not concealed.[107]

Rather than attempt to combine disparate sources to create a composite portrait of female mortality in the Roman Empire, let us begin by looking at the way in which society divided the known risks. How were risks shared (a question of ecology), and how were they distributed (a question of sociology)? In other words, how did women collectively contrive to meet the sexual needs of married male citizens?

The Concubine. There were respectable Roman men and women and there were those who were not respectable. The distinguishing criterion was basically sexual. The disreputable were those whose sexual habits were condemned as notoriously licentious, including those involved in theater, circus, and prostitution. Female citizens who prostituted themselves lost status and were not allowed to wear the robe of the matrona. The same was true of adulterous wives and concubines and freed female slaves who married their masters but separated without the master's approval. The disreputable were permanently deprived of the right to enter into legitimate marriage and transmit full citizenship. A similar category existed in Greek regions, but we know less about it.

Men were not brought up to believe that it was virtuous to refrain from sexual intercourse. Boys learned to lust after the household's female slaves, always available for their pleasure. For variety youths also visited prostitutes. Society so arranged things that citizens could draw upon the services of a whole population of men and women whose purpose was to satisfy their every desire—and physicians counseled that such desires ought not to be repressed. The population that met these sexual needs was composed of slaves and the disreputable.[108] Although brief sexual encounters were not uncommon, male citizens generally entered into more permanent relations with concubines.

Other societies within the Empire had their own means of limiting births. The Germans, who according to Tacitus kept all their children, were despised in Rome because they were reputed to practice sodomy.[109] In classical Athens citizenship was strictly regulated. It was denied to the sons of female citizens not married to male citizens. No freed slave was ever made a citizen of Athens. A male citizen of Athens therefore had to be careful not to have children with a foreign woman, a freed slave, or even an unmarried Athenian. Athenian men preferred amorous relations with younger males. This arrangement was peculiar to Greece at a certain point in its history. The Romans adopted it but never adhered strictly to Athenian practice.[110]

In contrast to pederasty, concubinage was authentically Roman. Romans protected female citizens from their husbands' desires by encouraging men to have sexual relations with slaves and freed women. In Epictetus and Philo we read of the frequent

319

inability of men to control their desires for slave girls.[111] Freed slaves, both male and female, acquired citizenship and could transmit it to their freeborn children. Foreign women purchased in the marketplace and girls born in their master's household eventually could become respectable Roman citizens and mothers of citizens. Rome elaborated a code of concubinage that imposed duties on concubines not unlike those required of wives. The minimum age for an official concubinage was the same as for an official marriage: twelve years. The concubine was required to be faithful to her master.[112] Only a freed woman concubine could initiate a separation; a slave obviously could not. Concubines dressed as wives did: by covering their heads and bodies they showed that they belonged to a citizen.

These women thus bore the risks of childbearing that official wives were protected against.[113] Yet men did not like to have large numbers of bastards by slaves and concubines. In Greek areas a bleak portrait was painted of the lives of these unwanted children in order to dissuade men from having them.[114] Freed slaves who served as concubines bore the burden of multiple pregnancies. As their bodies aged prematurely, they might be abandoned by the master and turned over to a freed man or slave. If the master did not wish to see them pregnant, they had to submit to abortion. Some chose abortion of their own accord. The physicians who wrote down various formulas for potions believed to prevent or abort pregnancy do not tell us much about the women to whom such potions were administered. They say only that the mixtures are not to be used to conceal adultery or to preserve a woman's looks. An ancient proverb gives us an idea of just how unpleasant some of these abortive potions were, particularly those involving the herb rue: "Your agony is nothing yet; you've still not come to parsley and rue."[115]

Conditions similar to these are known in other polygamous societies. Sometimes the first wife makes sure that if the husband takes a prepubescent concubine, he will not have sexual relations with the girl until after she reaches puberty. In Kenya poor rural families send young girls to serve as domestic servants in urban households. When a servant becomes pregnant, she is sent back home. Abortions, often carried out under horrible conditions, are common.[116]

Upper-class women in Rome had no problem with their husbands' having sexual relations with slaves and concubines. Some women even chose their husbands' partners. The wife of Scipio Africanus knew her husband's concubine. After his death she set the woman free and arranged a marriage with a freed slave.[117] Livia found virgins for her devoted husband Augustus to deflower.[118]

In Roman Africa, where some married women became devotees of a terrifying goddess, the African Ceres, they abstained from sexual relations and provided their husbands with concubines.[119] For pagan women chastity consisted in "not desiring to be desired."[120] The rules for admission to Christianity confirm that concubines aborted pregnancies and abandoned children: "If a concubine was once a man's slave, if she raised his children and was devoted to him alone, she shall hear [the Word]; if not, she shall be sent away. A man who keeps a concubine shall cease to do so and take a wife according to the law; if he refuses, he shall be sent away."[121]

Concubinage was so widespread that freed men commonly ordered funerary inscriptions for themselves and two or three women described indiscriminately as wives or companions. Some scholars believe that these inscriptions refer to a succession of wives, but in my view the women mentioned shared the man's life simultaneously, one as lawful wife, the other(s) as concubines.[122] From the Talmud we know that polygamous Jews had children by a first wife and ordered the second, the woman kept for pleasure, to "take the potion."[123]

The Difficulties of Continence

The practice of continence by upper-class women became a mark of distinction. A pregnancy as "late" as perhaps age twenty-five was taken as a sign that a woman had not mastered her desires. Listen to what Seneca says to his mother: "You were never ashamed of being pregnant past the age for such a thing . . . You never concealed your pregnancies as an indecent burden, and after conception you did not expunge from your innards the last vestige of hope that you might be permitted to have the child."[124] To be continent at twenty or twenty-five was no easy task, not even after having three or four children. If a husband abandoned his wife, the temptation of adultery was always there.

Sexual Love in Marriage. The well-bred Roman woman received her husband when the time came to produce a child. It was to her advantage to produce the requisite three offspring, so that when her father died she might enjoy her property without having to submit to the authority of a guardian. But not all women were lucky enough to have husbands who could amuse themselves with a slave or concubine. Some had to bear the burden—and it was a real burden—of multiple pregnancies. An amorous husband was a catastrophe.

A man who had more than the required three children by his wife was called "uxorious." The term was pejorative: it meant that the man was no better than his wife's property, that she held him as she did her possessions. It was applied to Tiber's attachment to Ilia, the mother of Romulus and Remus,[125] and to Aeneas' attachment to Dido.[126] The Jews of Rome, who may have renounced polygamy but who were not yet sufficiently acculturated to take concubines, were often seen with large families. Tacitus held their fondness for procreation in contempt.

Augustus, on the other hand, went so far as to put couples with large numbers of children on display. Rome was treated to the spectacle of a man from Fiesole being honored at the Capitol along with his eight children, twenty-seven grandchildren, and eighteen great-grandchildren.[127] Augustus' daughter Julia, widowed at eighteen, married Agrippa when she was twenty and produced five children in nine years of marriage. When Julia was widowed a second time, Augustus ordered Tiberius to divorce so that he could marry her. But Tiberius continued to love the wife he had abandoned. Julia, who had loved Agrippa, could not do without a husband's love and so deceived Tiberius. Her father was aware of her behavior. As an example of his clemency, Seneca cites the fact that Augustus granted Julia's lovers safe-conduct to exile rather than have them executed.[128] Vipsania Agrippina (Agrippina Major), daughter of Julia and Agrippa, was born in 14 B.C. and married Germanicus in A.D. 5. Her father died two years after she was born, and her mother had been condemned to exile. Agrippina had nine children by Germanicus[129] and followed him to Germania and the East.[130] Imprisoned in 29 by Tiberius, she died (perhaps by her own hand) in 33. Marcus Aurelius had thirteen children with a wife who, he wrote in his *Meditations,* was "perfectly obedient."[131]

Wives visited too often by their husbands developed a taste for sex that made them ripe to become adulteresses. If, after being widowed, they married less attentive husbands, they knew what they could expect of lovers. For that reason, Plutarch counseled, it was better not to teach wives about love. There was a contradiction between the wish to increase the number of legitimate children and enhance the value of marriage in procreation and the wish to punish manifestations of desire in wives. The only satisfactory solution was for husbands to have relations with their wives only for the purpose of procreation. Husbands, in other words, must not be uxorious.

Love between Women. One of Juvenal's satires portrays two women who repair to a temple of Pudicitia for an amorous encounter. The play is obscene, but if love between women supplanted heterosexual relations because of a wish to limit mortality in childbirth, the reality may have been quite different.[132]

The Inculcation of Reserve. Upper-class women were brought up to expect that one day they would abstain from sexual relations. They, and perhaps women of more modest station, were protected against multiple pregnancies by an inculcated reserve. Early defloration left many Roman women violent-tempered but frigid. Reserve—in speech, act, and gaze—had to be fostered by training. Women, who lived with their husbands from the time they were twelve or sometimes earlier, were required to observe a strict diet and forbidden to drink wine. Their education was severe. The constraints on their behavior were so fully internalized, so bound up with their sense of their own value, that in my view few women were attracted by pleasure, which could lead all too easily to social ostracism. If they were able to bring their daughters up oblivious of their bodies to the point of ignoring the possibility of pleasure, they did not turn to the physicians or the gods for deliverance from what we would consider an affliction: for them it was a blessing.

For the woman who thought of herself as philosophical, the ideal was to be a chaste wife who spent her time spinning yarn and carefully managing the household. Fragmentary texts (some perhaps apocryphal) attributed to women of the Pythagorean sect tell us that sexual desire for a man other than one's husband was considered the root of all evil and the cause of moral depravity in women.[133] We have two letters written by women advising wives to be patient about their husbands' attraction to other women. The letter writers are critical of women who turn men against their wives but are also certain that the wife who knows how to be patient can always get her man back. Plutarch offered the same advice to young wives: a woman must learn to put up with it if her husband slept with an *etaira,* concubine, or servant.[134] The other area where women could exercise their philosophical virtues was in the education of children. A letter from Pythagoras' wife Theano warns against permitting children to be indolent and self-indulgent; by "children," she means both boys and girls. Chastity was universally praised as woman's primary virtue. This was true for women freed from slavery as well as those born free.[135] Freed men praised their masters for the gift of a still chaste freed woman as a wife.

Average age at marriage is a fact of demographic importance if girls who marry young continue to have sexual relations throughout their fertile years. It loses that importance if women of certain classes cease to have sexual relations with their husbands after producing three or four children. What is important is the way in which society organizes reproductive practices and hence the lives of the women who bear much of the burden of reproduction. In addition, the Roman, Greek, and Jewish societies of the ancient world regulated not only sexual reproduction but also sexual pleasure so as to protect women of the upper classes.

The Changing Social Arrangement

How was the burden of sexuality divided? Consider the social arrangement that existed in pagan Rome during the first two centuries of the Empire. Many women—slaves and women freed to serve as concubines—had no hope of entering into legitimate, stable, durable marriages. Some concubines did of course marry freed men after their master had tired of them and with his permission. Some free women, citizens of Rome, married citizens of modest station or lived with noncitizens. Those who lived with soldiers were prohibited from contracting lawful marriages. Girls of modest station were presumably brought up strictly and prepared for lives as respectable matrons, mothers of Rome's future citizens. There is no evidence to suggest that women of the lower classes were any less strict in their ideals or practices than were aristocratic women. The scandals we read about in history and literature concern the aristocrats, not their inferiors.

Opposition to this social arrangement developed in the context of aristocratic resistance to imperial power. The courage that women showed in the first-century conflict between Roman nobles and emperors altered the way people thought about relations between men and women.

The Philosophy of Women: To Die with Philosophical Men. At first Augustus had tolerated freedom of expression.[136] But after the famine of A.D. 6–8 and in the wake of numerous incidents of arson, hostile pamphlets began to circulate and Augustus cracked down. "Action," Tacitus wrote, "had been taken against deeds, words went unpunished. The first who employed this law [the revived treason law] to investigate written libel was Augustus."[137] According to Suetonius, Tiberius often said that "in a free state, words and thoughts must be free."[138] But a century later Tacitus wrote that "natural death is rare among aristocrats."[139]

A professor of rhetoric was charged with an offense against the emperor for having discussed the marriage laws. Augustus ordered books to be burned and later condemned all the works of certain writers.[140] Under Tiberius (A.D. 14–37) the number of trials increased; repression continued under subsequent rulers. Some opponents of the regime moved beyond words to deeds and were found out. The emperors authorized some to commit suicide in lieu of execution.[141]

Women too were sometimes sentenced to suicide, either for crimes of their own or as punishment for their husbands' crimes. Other women chose to take their own lives rather than outlive a husband whose resistance to tyranny they had supported. Much earlier, in 42 B.C., Cato's daughter had taken her life following the defeat and suicide of her husband, Brutus. Both were following the example of Cato, who had chosen to die rather than owe his life to Caesar. Under Augustus no noble was sentenced to suicide by the emperor, but such sentences became common beginning with the reign of Tiberius. Sejanus' wife killed herself after the death of her children; Paxea, the wife of Pomponius Labeo, and Sextia, the wife of Scaurus, took their own lives even though they were not at risk.

The most famous of all these women was Arria Major, who, to encourage her husband, Caecina Paetus, condemned by Claudius, stabbed herself first, saying "Paete, non dolet" (Paetus, it does not hurt).[142] Her words evinced such concern for the feelings of another that they were repeated by Marc Bloch, the great French historian and founder of the *Annales* school, to a young man about to be shot with him for resisting the Nazis during World War II.

Although some women chose to accompany a husband or father in suicide, the ancients tell us that some husbands attempted to persuade their wives not to take their own lives. Seneca advised Paulina against suicide in 65; the Stoic Thrasea dissuaded Arria Minor in 66; and in 72, under Vespasian, Fannia survived Helvidius. Though they might have preferred to die, these women were induced to live for the sake of their children and their husband's memory. In perpetuating that memory in written form they took risks: it was a crime to own the works of these aristocratic philosophers, as it was to write, publish, or possess their biographies. Women shouldered this burden as an act of family piety and philosophical faith. The historian Cremutius Cordus, who during the reign of Tiberius was prosecuted for his outspoken admiration of Caesar's assassins, chose death by starvation over execution. His daughter, Marcia, who had two sons and two daughters of her own, defied an order to burn all copies of her father's works and later, under Caligula, was able to publish them. When her two sons died, Seneca wrote her a letter of consolation, a rather conventional example of the genre in which he noted that Marcia's courage had enabled her to escape "the infirmity of the feminine soul." Lives of Cato, Thrasea, and Helvidius Priscus thus enjoyed an underground existence even though their authors lived in mortal danger.

Models of Feminine Heroism. For Romans the two exemplary heroines were Lucretia, who stabbed herself rather than endure the shame of rape, and Clelia, who, beneath a hail of enemy arrows, swam the Tiber to rescue female hostages and then, to the admiration of both sides, plunged back into the river to continue her search for captured youths.[143] An equestrian statue of Clelia graced the Roman Forum. Obviously her qualities were virile.[144] "They have almost turned Clelia into a man," Seneca said.[145]

Both women set examples of political courage: there was as much civic virtue in protecting the purity of a citizen's progeny as there was in saving the city's youth. In the first century of the Roman Empire, however, the question was where a citizen's duty lay: with liberty or with obedience to the prince. Epicureans had taken part in the opposition to Caesar, but it was the Stoics who breathed life into the resistance against the new regime after Augustus.

Greek models attached greater importance to a wife's loyalty to her husband. Alcestis was remembered for having agreed to die in Admetus' stead.[146] The pagan Greeks of late antiquity honored women as heroines in marriage. Similarly, the romance *Joseph and Aseneth,* which originated in a Jewish community in Egypt in the second century, exalted a wife's sacrifice.[147]

The ancients also admired heroism in enemy women, such as Eponina, a Gaul who after a failed uprising lived with her husband in a cave and hid him for nine years.[148] Gallic women who had killed their husbands and children after a defeat were also admired.[149] The Trajan Column portrays Dacian women taking part in war against Rome and torturing Roman prisoners.[150] Stories were told of women's courage in defeat and readiness for suicide.[151] We do not know what the Romans thought of the mass suicide of Jewish women at Massada, but surely they must have admired them as they did the barbarians of the north. The Jews had their own exemplary female heroine: the mother of the Maccabees. The Fourth Book of Maccabee, which dates from the early second century A.D., portrays her exhorting her sons to die rather than violate the Law. After witnessing their execution, she marches off to her own. Through all these tales runs a common theme: philosophical conviction (or in the case of the Maccabees, the Law) outweighs all other considerations, including love of life and the love of a Jewish mother for her sons.[152] In the wake of Roman wives and Jewish mothers came the Christian martyrs, married women as well as virgins.[153]

Once women had demonstrated their philosophical capacities, their courage in a dangerous world, the whole social system began to totter. Women became heroes not by submitting to biology, to the risks of childbearing implicit in their maternal destiny, but by adhering to a philosophy. They obliged their husbands to give a new dimension to marriage. A new way of thinking about the nature of women and the faculty of courage precipitated a revolution.

The Theory of Female Courage. There was no intellectual obstacle to formulating a theory of female courage. "Feminine nature" was understood to be weak, but masculine and feminine natures were present in both sexes to varying degrees.

Consider what physiognomists had to say about feminine characteristics. Physiognomy, as developed first by the Greeks and later by the Romans, was the science of predicting character on the basis of physical signs. An anonymous treatise, written in Latin

327

but based on Greek sources, begins with a series of general comments on masculine and feminine types.[154] There are masculine traits in women and feminine traits in men, we learn, and all education must be directed at encouraging the pupil's virile characteristics. Most of the comments on the female type are connected with the observation of effeminate traits in women, traits that are taken as signs of an irresolute, contemptible character. More surprisingly, while effeminate men are scorned, overly virile men are also troubling: they are suspected of undue ardor for boys. Similarly, overly feminine women are suspected of making love with other women (sec. 85), whereas women of virile aspect desire men. Galen, in a misguided and little-noticed attempt to prove that women produce semen in coitus, used the example of sows spayed to improve the flavor of their meat. A woman could shed her feminine characteristics, just as a man could lose his male characteristics by castration.[155] The physical signs of a virile character must therefore be encouraged by the way girls are brought up. A virile woman was one who did not give in to the infirmities of female nature.

Musonius Rufus on Women. Musonius Rufus, a Stoic philosopher of the equestrian order, was exiled by Nero in 65; he returned to Rome in 68, only to be exiled again by Vespasian before returning a second time under Titus.[156] He was Epictetus' teacher when Epictetus—who also was later exiled—was the slave of an imperial freeman. Although Epictetus was much less assertive about the capacities of women than Musonius Rufus was, he too recommended that young men learn to control their sexuality.

Reading Musonius Rufus gives one the impression that he had a much higher opinion of the female gender than did the Pythagorean women whose letters are filled with what might seem like male propaganda but actually passed in the Greek world for conventional wisdom. Musonius wrote in a Latin culture, where the sexual inhibition of upper-class women left them time for serious study and philosophical reflection. He insisted that the gods granted women the same faculty of reason and the same natural predilection for virtue as men. The examples he gives are homely ones: women are shown in customary roles, yet these offer opportunities to employ philosophy, self-control, and even courage. The temperate woman, Musonius says, will be a good household administrator. She will find ample opportunity to stifle her anger and hide her sorrow. By dealing justly she will help her husband and children live in harmony. She will find ways to love her children more than life itself and, if ordered to perform a dishonorable act, will know how to face death without fear.

If women wish to study the intellectual side of philosophy—controversies, arguments, and syllogisms, techniques of thought rather than of practice—they are just as capable of doing so as men, whose study of intellectual things does not exempt them either from the need to employ philosophical arts in their daily occupations (fragment 3). Hence it is not only possible but also necessary to educate girls as well as boys, to teach them justice, temperance, and courage. "Some may say that courage is a subject fit only for males, but I do not share that view. Women too must act virilely, and if a woman is made of excellent stuff, she must be free of any trace of cowardice; neither fatigue nor fear should weaken her resolve. For otherwise how could she remain temperate if the first man to come along could, by terrorizing her or subjecting her to hard labor, force her to submit to something shameful? Women must be prepared to defend themselves if, by Zeus, they do not wish to appear inferior to hens and other female birds, which fight to protect their young from much larger animals. How can anyone say that women have no need of courage? They even participate in armed combat, as is shown by the race of Amazons, which defeated many nations by force of arms. If women fall short in this respect, it is because of want of exercise and not because they are not naturally gifted with courage." And, while Musonius concedes that women are weaker than men and should therefore be assigned less arduous tasks, he also argues that men might find it to their advantage if sometimes they spun the yarn while women did the heavy labor.

Challenges to the Social Order. Having recognized women's capacity for temperance, sexual self-control, and courage, Musonius went on to insist that men should demonstrate the same virtues. Men, he said, ought not to take advantage of the sexual opportunities offered by slavery. A man who slept with a slave, male or female, demonstrated a lack of self-control.

If women can learn to control themselves, so can men. If both husband and wife confine their sexual relations to marriage, as women had always done, then clearly lovemaking would be for the purpose of procreation, as the Roman definition of marriage insisted. But what about limiting the number of children? Abortion and infanticide, the traditional solutions, now had to be faced within the couple and inside the upper classes of society. For Musonius, there was no handsomer sight than that of a large family.

Thus things at first sight unrelated were in fact closely intertwined: the recognition of women's ability to think, men's renunciation of sexual relations with slaves and concubines, the rejection of abortion and infanticide. And circumstances conspired to give new importance to the married couple and the large family. The man who had many children with his wife demonstrated both his capacity for fidelity and his desire for her. And it all began with the observation that women could think.

The principal change in women's lives in the Roman Empire, a change that predated Christianity's expansion of the duties of both men and women, thus came about because of the idea that men could practice self-control as well as women, that men were capable of being faithful husbands to intelligent wives.

The idea that a married man could remain continent if he devoted himself to philosophical study gradually spread throughout the Empire. Among the Jews the Midrash reports that when Miriam saw that her sister-in-law Zipporah had ceased to wear jewels, she divined that Moses had ceased to have relations with her. When a young boy reported that two men were making prophecies, Zipporah is supposed to have cried out, "Pity their wives!" Thus the Jews of the Empire believed that a prophet's wife was likely to be neglected.[157] Was this a reflection of Christian influence, or did it reflect the view, current in pagan philosophical circles, that continence could be achieved through mastery of the passions? The male authors who recorded this tale portrayed the wives as upset by their husbands' neglect.

Changes in the Social System

Toward the end of the Roman Empire the philosophical challenge to the social system of reproduction was greatly amplified by Christianity. Early in the third century the emperor decided to make all free inhabitants of the Empire citizens of Rome. This required coordinating laws that applied to those who had previously lived in the Empire without being counted as citizens: Greeks, Egyptians, Jews, and others. The necessary coordination was never fully carried out, however, as people found ways to take

advantage of discrepancies between their own native laws and
Roman law. One such discrepancy concerned the legal definition
of nonincestuous marriage. Despite an edict from Emperor Claudius, it had not been easy to gain acceptance, even in Roman law,
for marriages between an uncle and a niece. In the late third
century, Diocletian, the last pagan emperor (not counting Julian
the Apostate in the fourth century), promulgated a series of laws
intended to establish uniform criteria for legitimate marriage
throughout the Empire. He also outlawed polygamy, and from the
text we learn that not even Roman citizenship had prevented the
Phoenicians, at whom this measure was aimed, from adhering to
their customary practices. The Jews too clung to their own ways.
Diocletian ordered that children born of unlawful marriages be
declared illegitimate[158] and that polygamous parents be branded
with dishonor, which meant, for example, that they could no
longer take or receive oaths.[159] Jews were forbidden to marry
according to their customs.[160] Fourth-century Christian emperors
strengthened the punishments for violation of the marriage laws,
and marriage between an uncle and his niece became punishable
by death.[161] Arcadius, in excluding the death penalty for men who
married their cousins or sisters-in-law, tells us that an edict ordering that penalty had actually been issued; in the Western Empire,
Theodosius took action against men who married their first cousins.[162] The marriage laws were not concerned solely with the taint
of incest, although this was the basis for first-century laws imposing on slave marriages the same restrictions imposed on marriages
between freeborn men and women. In the fourth century the
concern with status again appeared: a free woman who married a
slave could expect death by burning or bludgeoning.[163] The Christian who married a Jewish woman, the Jew who married a Christian woman, and anyone who married a barbarian could expect
the same fate.[164] In other words, differences that previously had
constituted only obstacles to lawful marriage but not concubinage
were now subject to criminal penalties.

Although the Christian church did not explicitly cause this
shift toward criminal penalties, it was concerned with defining the
criteria of a pure marriage. In the fifth century Bishop Caesarius
of Arles delivered a sermon: "Let no man take for his wife his
maternal aunt or his wife's cousin or sister. It is unholy that such
vile lust should cause us to lose our souls in return for a diabolical
pleasure."[165]

Christianity and Sexual Taboos. Christianity defined its own rules for admission to or exclusion from the City of God. Paradoxically, while prohibitions proliferated under Christianity, the church as early as the second century agreed to renunciations impermissible under Roman law. Persons whom Roman law classified as infamous for life and for all posterity could join the Christian community, provided that they ceased their dishonorable activities. Among these were careers in the theater and entertainment. The keeper of a brothel could become a Christian, but a prostitute (male or female) could not.[166] An adulterous woman could return to her husband, and an adulterous man (under the new definition) could return to his wife.[167] Christianity set great store by female purity and accepted Roman marriage law. Concubines were accepted as long as they had been the concubine of one man only and had kept all their children. Men were required to dismiss their concubines and marry according to law. Thus the social arrangement that had protected wives was undermined. Eventually the law of the Empire sanctioned the idea that concubinage was dishonorable and prejudicial to a wife's rights over her husband. Exclusive love scored a victory—but upper-class women, who lost their protection, suffered a defeat.

The End of Concubinage. In the Christian era the law permitted children born to a concubine to be legitimized, provided that the father was not married to another woman, because from the time of Constantine married men had been forbidden to keep concubines. Constantine prohibited bequests to a concubine's child without authorization, which previously had been granted by imperial writ. He also prohibited gifts to concubines and their children.[168] As a result, husbands either entered into brief relationships (not concubinage) with other women or had more frequent relations with their wives.

The means by which concubines disposed of unwanted children were strictly regulated. Both Christians and Jews prohibited infanticide and exposure of children. Infanticide had been illegal under Roman law since the first century, but undoubtedly it was still practiced. Constantine included it in the law against murder.[169] Most important of all, in the fourth century exposure was regarded as infanticide by indirect means; as such it was punishable by law. After 374 a father who ordered a child exposed risked capital punishment.[170]

Punishment, for poisoning, of women who helped other women abort their pregnancies was reaffirmed by the Christian emperors starting with Constantine (306–337). The list of valid reasons for repudiating a wife was reduced to the crimes of adultery, murder, poisoning, and casting spells.[171] A woman convicted of poisoning could be repudiated by her husband and lose her dowry. Poisoners were excluded from amnesties.[172]

Multiple Pregnancies. By encouraging sexual relations exclusively between married partners, Christianity placed upper-class women in a difficult position. Faced with multiple pregnancies, they had to deal with problems previously faced only by concubines and slaves. There was growing interest in contraceptive and abortive potions. Christian writers, aware of this development, condemned it in homilies and treatises. Concubines had already been admonished to keep their children, but now the problem spread to other classes of society.[173] Like Roman law and ancient physicians, the Church suspected that when a married woman sought an abortion it was to conceal adultery. Early in the fourth century, at the Council of Elvira, the first council held in the West even before Constantine granted the church official status, sexual issues were a top priority. A wife who "killed" (aborted) a child conceived in adultery during her husband's absence could never be reconciled with the Church (can. 63). An unbaptized woman who sought an abortion after adultery would never be baptized (can. 68). Even if the husband was aware of the adultery, the wife could not be reconciled with the church (can. 70). The council's final canon (number 81) prohibited women from receiving or sending mail directly. All letters had to be submitted to the scrutiny of their husbands. This measure was intended as a safeguard against adultery.

An Exalted Idea of Marriage. It is interesting to compare the Church's views on murder, adultery, and abortion. So exalted was the Christian idea of marriage that adultery, along with the abortion that was its sign, was considered a more serious crime than murder.

Society, even Christian society, was hierarchical. Upper-class women were bred to contribute to the reproduction of their class, not to the demographic maintenance of the city. They had no notion of the fact that other women were saving them from the risks of multiple pregnancies. At best they were aware of being women of quality, women whose continence entitled them to rights over their inferiors, including the right to use those inferiors to satisfy their husbands' needs. They could also alleviate tensions by scolding, shouting at, or striking their inferiors. Well-bred men of the upper class, who listened to the advice of philosophers, were told among other things to control their anger and check their violence. Women were believed incapable of exercising such self-restraint, at least insofar as they remained women; education of course turned them into men, and thus they acquired a capacity they otherwise lacked. Yet some women were ill-bred, among them the physician Galen's mother, who lived on an estate outside Pergamum and was in the habit of biting her male and female servants. Uncontrollable anger among women was so common throughout the Empire that the Council of Elvira determined a punishment to be meted out to any woman who in a fit of rage whipped her servant so severely that the servant died within three days. (In the case of a slow death, the benefit of the doubt went to the mistress.) The bishops declared that if the killing was intentional, the mistress should be denied communion for seven years; if it was unpremeditated, five years. Communion was allowed if the penitent fell ill (can. 5). Compare these punishments with those for abortion or for women who remarried after divorce (legal after 306). A woman who took the initiative in seeking a divorce and who later remarried was not allowed to receive communion, not even on her deathbed (can. 8). Nor was a woman abandoned by her husband (can. 9). If remarriage took place after baptism, the woman was treated as being on the same level as a prostitute (can. 12). Clearly murder was a less serious offense than adultery.

What was at stake was the exalted idea that the Christian church, like Roman law, held of legitimate marriage. The foundation on which society stood was more important than the protection of life. Marriage was kept in the divine light by the regularity and chastity of sexual relations. Intercourse, as Jean-Louis Flandrin has shown, was forbidden on many days of the year. This sanctity of legitimate marriage was far more important than the virginity of the unmarried servants to whom husbands might turn for compensatory gratification, much as they had turned to concubines in the past. The penitentials laid down harsher punishments for marital infractions than for the rape of a servant.[174]

What mattered was what had always mattered: from the time

when Augustus insisted that noble couples, and if possible all citizens, produce a minimum number of legitimate children, to the time when the Church chose to punish adultery more harshly than murder, the chief concern was with the ethical value of legitimate marriage. And women were to be limited, if possible, to taking just one husband in a lifetime.

Damnation and Equality. Musonius exerted a powerful influence on Christian writers. In the early third century Clement of Alexandria insisted that women were as capable as men of studying any subject.[175] Christians like Theodoret of Cyrrhus were certain that there was only one human nature, the same for male and female, and that both men and women were subject to the same laws, laws that God intended to apply to the whole human race. "Woman, like man, is endowed with reason, capable of understanding, and conscious of her duty. Like him, she knows what to shun and what to seek out. Sometimes she is a better judge than man of what may be useful and may be a good advisor."[176]

In the pagan underworld no women suffered the infinite tortures of the damned. The rare human who penetrated the depths of the underworld saw only men suffering.[177] Poets and historians being punished for their lies stood alongside adulterers who had made love to other men's wives. Jewish texts about the hereafter gave no descriptions of torture.

Peter's Apocalypse (part of the Christian canon in the second century but later excluded) described the tortures of hell in a way that would forever leave its mark on Western art and thought:

There were people hanging by their tongues: these were the blasphemers of the way of truth. A fire burning beneath caused them to suffer. There was also a great pool of burning pitch for those guilty of injustice; angels tormented them. Above the burning pitch adulterous women hung suspended by their hair. The men who had sinned with them hung by their feet, their heads immersed in the pitch . . . And I saw, in a pit full of worms, murderers and their accomplices . . . Nearby I saw another pit into which flowed, as into a lake, the blood and excrement of those being punished. Women waded in blood up to their necks. Facing them were children born prematurely, all wailing. Tongues of flame leapt from their bodies to lick the eyes of the women opposite, who had conceived out of wedlock or practiced abortion . . . Other men and women were thrown from a high wall . . . They had besmirched themselves by offering themselves as women. The women of this group had slept together as man and woman . . . Still others were burning. They were turned over the fire as on a spit and grilled. They had abandoned God's path.[178]

From Cult to Christianity

The ritualized relation between women and the gods is the subject of the next three chapters. Earlier, Nicole Loraux pointed out that divinity took precedence over femininity in the goddesses of ancient polytheistic religions. Nevertheless, the limitations imposed on women left an indelible mark on cult practice in Greece and Rome. Participation in religious cults was the quintessential form of symbolic expression in the ancient world. As such it was kept under close surveillance by men and permitted only insofar as it did not disrupt the business of cities and empires. Cult practice did not even allow women religious autonomy, let alone true liberty. Nevertheless, it is striking to note the degree to which oriental influences that came rather late in the day to the Greco-Roman world obliterated the notion that women can have no part in religious sacrifice, an idea that had excluded women from the heart of civic religion in the West.

Eventually Christianity evolved a new model of religious participation for women, based on suffering for Christ and bearing witness to his kingdom. Women converted men, and for a brief moment egalitarianism reigned in the Christian faith. Soon, however, women were excluded from the church hierarchy, leaving those who wished to embrace a life of religion only one choice: to renounce the world.

P.S.P

7

Pandora's Daughters and Rituals in Grecian Cities

Louise Bruit Zaidman

THE GREEK GODS WERE intimately associated
with urban life in ancient Greece. In order to understand woman's place in the rituals of this masculine society, one must first understand her place
in Greek civic culture and iconography. Excluded
on principle from political life and therefore from
sacrifice, women were nevertheless integrated in
various ways into the religious life of the city, so
much so that one scholar has characterized their
lot as "cult citizenship."[1] In the privacy of the
home, where women enjoyed a measure of autonomy, they bore responsibility for certain religious
rituals, particularly those having to do with birth
and death, as if men assigned to women that realm
of the sacred in which the least controllable forces
made their influence felt. Throughout this chapter
we have occasion to measure the ambivalence of
the male gaze, invariably fascinated by the "race
of women" but also placed on the defensive.[2]

Women were excluded from blood sacrifice
and the subsequent division of the meat of the
sacrificed animal. But blood sacrifice was central
to Greek religion; because it made visible the accord between gods and men and renewed the
bonds of human community, it was the foundation
on which political life was based. The fact that

women participated in this ritual only through their husbands was perfectly compatible with their exclusion from active civic and political life. There were no female citizens in ancient Greece, only mothers, wives, and daughters of citizens—except in Sparta, whose women were "the only females who give orders to men," as Plutarch put it in his *Life of Lycurgus* (14.8).

This picture is much too simple. It is correct to say that women were generally excluded from blood sacrifice and the handling of meat; they were left out of the group that Marcel Detienne has called "commensals," those who, by virtue of sharing the sacrificial meat, became civic equals.[3] Nevertheless, the women excluded from this group were included in the broader community of those on whom the community depended for its existence and invited to its great festivals. For women, excluded from the agora and from the assemblies in which the business of men and gods was conducted, and confined to the *oikos*, or household, great religious celebrations were opportunities to participate in social life outside the home. In the Panathenaea procession, the great festivals of Dionysus, the procession of the Eleusinian Mysteries, and other occasions that I shall describe later, women mingled with the men who came to witness the great public sacrifices.

Furthermore, while women were generally excluded from blood sacrifice, they played a central role in certain rituals, such as the Thesmophoria. The study of civic rituals raises the question of how the Greeks resolved the contradiction between the exclusion of women from political life and their inclusion in religious life. The tensions arising out of this contradiction were partially masked by male hegemony, particularly in Athens.

Athens of course was not all of Greece. As far as the place of women is concerned, the situation there was unusual, even extreme. Distrust of women, misogyny in rhetoric and law, were greater in Athens than anywhere else. Indeed, Athenian misogyny was so extreme that a myth was needed to explain why women there were not to be called Athenians and children were not to take their mother's name. Varro tells us that it was to quell Poseidon's ire, aroused when the women of Athens voted to name the city after Athena rather than himself (cited by Augustine, *City of God*, 18.9). According to the Periclean law of citizenship (451 B.C.), citizenship was granted to any man who could prove he was the son of both a citizen and "the daughter of a citizen." When a boy was registered in a phratry, the name of his mother's father was recorded but not that of his mother. If the father swore that the son was the product of a marriage with a "woman of the city," the mother's name was not mentioned. In the *gamelia*, the ceremony in which a citizen presented his wife to his phratry, he established the legitimacy of his marriage by affirming that his wife was the "daughter of a citizen" (Isaeus 3.76, 8.18). The legitimacy of a woman's status always depended on that of her father and husband.[4] This was true of all Greek cities, where families were based on patrilineal kinship.

If Athens was an extreme case, why focus on it? The answer is partly that we have more information about Athens than about other cities, but in this instance there is a better reason. The very fact that women were viewed with such suspicion in Athens and so resolutely excluded from political life makes their participation in religious ritual that much more significant.

Of the thirty festivals celebrated in Athens each year, many of which continued for two or three days, women participated actively in nearly half. Different celebrations involved different aspects of women's lives. Young girls carried baskets of offerings to Athena in the Arrephoria and Plynteria; married women took part in the Haloa and Thesmophoria of Demeter; women of a canonical age waited on the queen of the Anthesteria, over which Dionysus presided. The culmination was the Panathenaea (celebrated every year and with greater pomp every fourth year), in which women of all ages and conditions took part.

How did religious participation vary with social status? Up to age seven the upbringing of boys and girls was quite similar. From that point on, however, a girl's life was defined entirely by her future role as wife and mother. Adolescence was seen as a time of preparation for marriage, and in marriage the reproductive function was paramount. Thus the biological and the social were closely intertwined. Primarily defined as a wife and mother, the Greek woman changed status once again when, past the age of childbearing, she lost certain privileges but also ceased to be subject to certain prohibitions. Different religious practices were associated with each of these three stages of life.

Young Girls

Parthenoi, virgins, later to marry and become the mothers of future citizens, were socialized through a variety of rituals. What Pierre

Brûlé calls "the Athenian maiden's religion" comprised a distinct set of practices within the larger category of woman's religion. In order to understand it we must explore all aspects of Athenian religious practice and its constitutive myths.[5]

Myths endlessly repeated the notion that young girls are like untamed mares. At age seven they began the training that would turn them into accomplished and docile wives. Not all girls received this "feminine initiation," only selected daughters of the aristocracy.[6] Nevertheless, the cult of the *parthenoi* was of immense civic significance. Girls who did not participate directly felt as if they were participating indirectly, by proxy. This sense of participation no doubt accounts for a well-known passage in Aristophanes' *Lysistrata,* when the women's chorus says:

Bore at seven, the mystic casket;
Was, at ten, our Lady's miller;
then the yellow Brauron bear;
Next (a maiden tall and stately with a string of figs to wear)
Bore in pomp the holy Basket.

These lines are often interpreted as an idealization of the initiation process, a comical compression of various roles that a *eugenes,* young woman of good family, might be called on to perform.[7]

The Arrephorae

From a list of well-born girls *(eugeneis)* between the ages of seven and eleven the Assembly elected four arrephorae, or sacred casket bearers. The archon-king would then select two of these to take part in the weaving of the *peplos* that was given to Athena each year during the Panathenaea. The other two, "who live near the temple of the Polias . . . and spend time with the goddess in a certain way" (Pausanias 1.27.23), attend the festival of the Arrephoria, during which they take part in a peculiar nighttime ritual: in sealed caskets perched on their heads they carry objects they are forbidden to look at. Near the temple of Aphrodite, "in the gardens," they exchange these objects for other, equally mysterious, ones (biscuits in the form of snakes and *phalloi* according to some lexicographers). Scholars have long seen a connection between this ritual and the story of the Cecropides, the daughters of Cecrops, mythical first king of Athens. When Athena orders them to watch over Erichthonius, a son of the earth taken in by the goddess, the young princesses ignore the injunction not to look in the basket in which he is sleeping and are punished by death. The sources are vague, and numerous interpretations of the ritual have been proposed. It appears to have marked the end of an initiation period during which the young maidens left their homes to serve the goddess of the city. The ritual may have something to do with the city's founding myths, in which birth and sexual symbolism occupy a large place. Claude Calame sees it as a rite of entry into adolescence.[8] The whole question must be approached in relation to other forms of "service" involving young girls, about which we have even less information.

The festival of the Plynteria, devoted to cleaning cult statues, had equivalents in the many cities other than Athens that observed the month of Plynterion. Callimachus' *Hymn for Pallas' Bath* evokes a ritual performed by the girls of Argos. In Athens two girls *(korai)* known as plyntrides or lutrides were selected, probably on an annual basis, to cleanse Athena's *peplos* under the supervision of a priest.

The *aletrides* "grind the grain for sacrificial cakes," yet another way in which young women served the gods. The sources have even less to tell us about this ritual than about those previously discussed. Note, however, the similarities in the background and mode of recruitment of the girls who performed these various services. Pierre Brûlé sees a functional kinship as well: these girls "reproduce in the sphere of the sacred the labors that adult, unsanctified women perform in the gynecaeum."[9] But arrephorae, plyntrides, and aletrides were not simply being initiated into their future role as wives; they were also performing sacred functions on behalf of the city.

Little Bears

In the Temple of Artemis in Brauron, twenty-three miles from Athens, about a hundred girls, all "select virgins," the oldest of whom was ten, underwent an initiation of which our knowledge remains quite fragmentary. With the aid of written sources, archaeological data (not yet fully exploited), and some suggestive vase scenes, it is nevertheless possible to propose several hypotheses. The written sources (a few meager lines) and paintings on vases found in the temple suggest that the ritual involved having the girls "act like bears" *(arkteuein)* prior to marriage *(pro tou gamou).* What meaning should be attached to this phrase? Fragments of small ritual vessels, believed to date from the late fifth or early fourth century B.C., have been found in Brauron as well as in the temple of Artemis Brauronia in Athens.[10] (See Figure 31 in Chapter 4, "Figures of Women," by François Lissarrague.) Scenes painted on them portray running girls of various ages, some naked, others wearing short robes; some have hair down to their shoulders while others have their hair cut short. Two older women appear to be helping the girls prepare for some activity. Some of the fragments show animals (dogs, female deer) with the girls. In one of the scenes a she-bear occupies a central position, and the girls proceed away from her toward an altar. In another we see two adults, a male and a female, wearing animal masks that appear to represent bears.

There is no doubt that these scenes represent some sort of ritual, as the presence of the altar proves. The animals suggest a ritual hunt. Sourvinou-Inwood believes that these paintings celebrate the completion of an initiation period whose end coincided with the Brauronia festival.[11] During their initiation the young girls dressed in characteristic yellow robes *(crocotes)* and mimicked the behavior of she-bears. Shedding these robes symbolized abandonment of the "bear life" in order to enter a new stage of life, the phase of puberty, to be followed by marriage. Accordingly, Sourvinou-Inwood suggests that Aristophanes' text be read not as "having donned the *crocote*" but as "having removed the *crocote*."

Why the bear's life? What was the initiatory significance of this behavior? The she-bear belonged to the realm of Artemis, goddess of the hunt, and figured in any number of Artemisian myths. In Brauron a story was told about a nearly tame bear that often visited the Temple of Artemis. One day, while playing with a little girl, the bear clawed the girl's face, whereupon her brother killed the animal, triggering a series of disasters. An oracle suggested to the Brauronians that they might appease the goddess by having little girls pretend to be bears and wear *crocotes*. We know that these youthful cults of Artemis served a protective function, subjecting young boys and girls to a series of ordeals in order to tame the savage in them. It is tempting, therefore, to view the Brauron ceremonies, the culmination of long months of initiation, as a way of exorcising the "she-bear" (a symbol of the savagery of childhood) in every little girl. Initiation would thus prepare the girl for the next phase of her life, that of *canephora* (basket-carrier), which preceded marriage, the true goal of all social and religious education.

By way of the bear cult the city socialized the transition from prepubescent girl to nubile woman. The institution was obviously one of civic importance, as can be seen from the size of the temple and associated buildings, among which archaeologists have identified the "parthenons" where the young "bears" lived in segregation. Another sign of the importance of the cult was the organization of the Brauronia festival, which was overseen by the Hieropes, the ten magistrates responsible for overseeing the great annual festivals. What about boys? A role comparable to that of Brauron for girls may have been played by Munichia, another important Attic civic temple, also consecrated to Artemis and the site of another festival, during which ephebes took part in rituals related to their integration into the adult world.

The Canephorae

The canephora was a young woman who carried a *kanoun*, a basket containing sacred barley to be placed on the altar and on the head of the sacrificial animal just prior to immolation. The *makhaira*, or sacrificial knife to be wielded by the priest or his assistant, was hidden under the grains of barley. Every blood sacrifice required a basket of barley, though not necessarily carried by a *parthenos*. Carrying these baskets in the processions associated with the great civic festivals became an honorific sacred function reserved for well-born young ladies.[12] Attested for the festivals of Hera in Argos and Artemis in Syracuse, as well as in numerous festivities throughout Attica and in localities subservient to Athens, the carrying of baskets was an honor, particularly in the Great Panathenaea. The number of canephorae rose to a hundred in the third century, as is indicated by Stratocles' decree honoring Lycurgus, which states that Lycurgus had ordered "processional vases in gold and silver and accoutrements for a hundred canephorae." Ordinarily, no doubt, their numbers were smaller. But further evidence of the importance the city attached to their participation in the procession can be seen in their presence on the frieze of the Parthenon and, even more perhaps, in their presence on the list of beneficiaries of honorary shares in the great Panathenaean sacrifice, along with "generals and officers and Athenians who participated in the procession." Thus on a day when the city celebrated itself by honoring its civic deity, young girls chosen from among the city's elite and in the final stages of adolescence were treated as honorary citizens and granted a privilege rarely accorded to women: a share in the ritual sacrifice.

The water-carriers in the Bouphonia, another Athenian festival of sacrifice, also participated in the central act of the ritual: the slaying of the ox. A myth (Porphyry, *On Abstinence*, 2.29–30) explained the origin of this solemn sacrifice to Zeus Polieus. After the sacrilegious slaughter of an ox, Attica had been afflicted with a drought. On advice of the Delphic oracle, the Athenians decided to "share responsibility for the murder." To that end, "they chose young girls as water carriers. They carried water for use in honing the axe and the knife. When the implements were honed, one man lifted the axe, another took it and stunned the ox, and a third cut its throat . . . Then came the judgment of the murderer, and all who took part in the operation were called upon to justify themselves." Responsibility was traced back through the girls to the knife, which, being unable to defend itself, was condemned. The girls who carried water for use in honing the sacrificial axe thus performed a function parallel to that of the girls who carried a sacrificial knife hidden in baskets of barley. In the myth of the Bouphonia, water takes the place of barley, of which there is none because of the drought. In fact the purpose of the ritual is to bring back the vanished grain.[13] In both cases a key element of urban life, be it water or barley, is linked to an instrument of murder. The sacrifice of the plow-ox is the necessary mediator between men and the gods. The water-carriers intimately share responsibility for the murder, even though they, of all the participants, are farthest from the slaughter itself. In the Panathenaea too classical Athens sought to involve all of its inhabitants in the ritual sacrifice. The basket-carriers stand for all the future wives of citizens, guarantors of the city's permanence; it was as such that they were honored.

Canephoria and Marriage. In Aristophanes the canephora is called *pais kale*, beautiful child, meaning a young girl "in bloom," that is, past puberty, nubile. The adjective *kale* signifies physical maturity. It marks the age at which the young girl begins to exist in men's eyes. The function of the canephora coincides with her new status, as a young woman "in view." On vases she was shown wearing jewels and an embroidered chiton. The link between canephoria and marriage is clarified by a series of myths in which canephorae, or girls with the characteristics of canephorae, are abducted by gods or heroes. Corresponding to these myths are certain rituals. In Athens a daughter of the tyrant Pisistratus was said to have been kissed in public while serving as a canephora and later abducted. The story is reminiscent of the adventure of Oreithyia and Hersea, two daughters of Erichthonius who, while serving as canephorae, were noticed and abducted, one by Boreas (the North wind), the other by Hermes. The abduction of Oreithyia, a familiar theme of fifth-century ceramics, was recounted in several versions.[14] In some the locale shifts from the Acropolis to the banks of the Ilissos (as in Plato's *Phaedrus,* 229b–c) or elsewhere, and Oreithyia is shown playing or dancing with her companions.

Choral Activities

Young girls playing and dancing together were a regular feature of the iconography of adolescence. For Euripides choral dancing was a typical activity of young girls, "who bloom in chorus." The parallel versions of the abduction of Oreithyia make it clear that the age of canephorae was also the age of choruses, with their ritual, pedagogical, and social functions. That age ended in marriage, for which the mythical metaphor was abduction.

Groups of girls led by a choragus took part in cults and rituals. A good example of the nature and function of these choruses is the one led by Sappho on the island of Lesbos toward the end of the seventh century.[15] Under the aegis of Aphrodite, Sappho's group prepared adolescent girls for adulthood. This "pedagogical" function can be glimpsed in fragments of the poet's verse exalting grace and beauty, the qualities most cultivated by nubile adolescents. Many of these verses are from epithalamiums (wedding songs) or poems about marriage and invoke the goddess of sexuality and sensuality, protector of young brides. No doubt there were other circles of young women similar to Sappho's, but female choruses often figure in a broader civic context, in which young women participated along with other segments of the population.

Choruses and Festivals

Throughout the Greek world the entire population turned out to mark the end of adolescence and the renewal of the community.

Adolescent youths of both sexes were often summoned together to ceremonies honoring the civic deity or divine figures having a specific association with youth, such as Artemis and Apollo.

The festival of Artemis in Ephesus was typical of these adolescent rites of passage. First, all boys of sixteen and girls of fourteen marched out of the city in procession, each group led by the handsomest of its members. The marchers, carrying the usual torches, baskets, and perfumes, were followed by people who came from near and far to admire them. After the sacrifice boys and girls mingled, "so that the young men, having come of age, might find young women to marry." In Xenophon of Ephesus (1.2.2 ff.), from whom these words are borrowed, the ritual leads to the meeting of two exemplary youths, Habracomes and Antheia. The description of the occasion resembles that of the ritual of Artemis Daitis, in which a meal is prepared in a meadow outside the city as an offering to the goddess. The myth on which this ritual was based involved the youth of Ephesus, who, having transported a statue of Artemis to the coast, sing and dance in honor of the goddess and then prepare an offering of salt. As in so many other founding myths, an oversight—in this case the failure to repeat the offering the following year—brings disaster that can be halted only by establishing a ritual (*Etymologicum Magnum,* 252.11 ff.). Here, the scourge, initiated by Artemis, strikes the youth of the city, thus underscoring the meaning of the ritual: its purpose is to effect a normal transition from adolescence to adulthood, a transition that has been compromised by the youths' neglect of the very goddess who presides over their coming of age.

The Delia, an Athenian festival celebrated every four years in honor of Apollo, began in 525 B.C., when Pisistratus purified the island of Delos. Originally this was an Ionian festival in which the entire population, including women and children, took part. A chorus of so-called Deliades, servants of Apollo, played a central role, chanting a hymn in honor of Apollo, Leto, and Artemis. Callimachus (*Hymn to Delos,* 278 ff.) notes that every city in Greece sent a chorus to Delos annually, along with tribute and first fruit offerings for the cult of Apollo, in memory of the first sheaves of wheat brought to Delos long ago by the three daughters of Boreas and an escort of youths on behalf of a mythical people, the Hyperboreans, believed to be beloved of the gods. The youth of Delos made offerings in honor of Boreas, the girls giving locks of their hair, the boys shavings of their first whiskers. The Delia was thus a springtime festival of propitiation, essential to ensure the normal growth of the city's youth. Plato (*Phaedrus*, 58a–c) gives an interpretation of the festival according to which the *theoria*, or delegation dispatched annually from Athens to Delos, was intended to honor Apollo for having protected the seven young men and women who had gone with Theseus to Crete, which accords well with the interpretation given here.

In Amyclae, a town under Spartan domination, the whole population as well as foreign visitors and slaves turned out for the Hyacinthia, the most important festival in the religious calendar, to watch the town's young men and women march in procession and participate in military drill. A funerary ritual in honor of the hero Hyacinthus was followed by activities involving youths from all over the territory. The children played the lyre and sang Paeans in honor of Apollo; ephebes divided among numerous choruses sang and danced; girls rode in procession in ceremonial chariots made of plaited reeds sometimes designed to look like fantastic animals.

Thus in Athens, Sparta, and numerous other cities youths took part in the great civic festivals, marching in procession, singing, and participating in other ceremonies in honor of the gods. Nevertheless, just because boys and girls came together at the end of adolescence, it should not be assumed that their initiations were similar. For boys, initiation led to adulthood and citizenship, while for girls (assuming that it even makes sense to speak of initiation for girls), it led to marriage. This difference in the purpose of education was reflected in its content, timing, and extent.

For girls the period from late childhood to marriage can be broken down into several stages. The first ended at around age ten, for young Athenians the age of *arcteia* (the bear ritual). Next came menarche and thus puberty. In iconography girls of this age were distinguished from older women by their size and hint of budding breasts, symbol of the physical transformations accompanying puberty.[16] The iconography is all the more significant in that it was not motivated by any concern for realism (married women were not differentiated by age). It was rather a culturally determined representation of one stage in a woman's life. Early puberty ended at fourteen, the age at which a girl became marriageable. For the Greeks she was then fully mature.

Let us return to the case of Athens. It is striking that, while an entire age cohort (youths sixteen to eighteen) performed the various services required of ephebes, only a small number of girls rendered service to Athena and Artemis.[17] The select few were chosen democratically (arrephorae were elected by the Assembly and "she-bears" chosen by tribe), but those selected belonged to an elite. The texts all draw attention to the aristocratic birth of the *parthenoi* chosen to perform various services; the total number selected was small.

The integration rituals for girls were symbolic. The actual initiation of young women, their instruction in adult tasks, took place in the gynaeceum and in what Pierre Brûlé has called "women's workshops." In its religious dimension, however, the initiation of women required the active participation of only a very few, who acted as representatives for an entire age cohort. Young women participated, as we have seen, in certain great festivals, but only on those occasions when the civic religion involved the whole population.

In the end the city's treatment of its "young people" was just another manifestation of the inequality between men and women in the religious sphere. Despite a certain pretense of allowing all citizens equal participation in politics and religion, men and women were treated differently. Women and girls were integrated in ritual, but under the control and supervision of men. Paradoxically, the use of noble families *(gene)* and an aristocratic mode of recruitment allowed democratic Athens to reconcile the demands of the divinities, mostly goddesses, who presided over the city's prosperity with its male citizens' suspicion of the "demos of women." Girls were allowed their moment of participation in civic ritual, only to disappear into married life.

Wives

The Thesmophoria

"As is customary, I call on Pallas, friend of choruses, to appear among us . . . guardian of our city . . . Thou who detest tyrants, appear . . . The demos of women calls you." So says the chorus in Aristophanes' *Women of the Thesmophoria,* before invoking two other goddesses, Demeter Thesmophoros (from whom the festival took its name) and Kore. For three days every year the "demos of women" took possession of the political sphere abandoned by men, who ceased to meet in law courts or council. The women of the city assembled in the temple of the two goddesses on the Pnyx, the hill where the Assembly normally met. As portrayed by Aristophanes, the women of Athens, styling themselves demos, invoke Athena in her civic dimension, "guardian of our city." Thus the women "represent" the city in whose name they speak. They have adopted the vocabulary of men for the purpose of attacking Euripides, their declared enemy. Their prayers, formulas, and formalities mimic the traditional forms of the assembly meeting: "The Council of Women, Timochia presiding, Lysilla as clerk, Sostrata orator, decrees the following: An assembly shall be held the morning of the second day of the Thesmophoria, when our time is freest, primarily for the purpose of considering the punishment to be meted out to Euripides, given that we are all agreed as to the baseness of his behavior. Who wishes to speak?" It may be objected that this is a parody, as suggested by the subject of the meeting, the punishment of Euripides. But this play is different from *The Assembly of Women,* also by Aristophanes, in which women disguised as men take the floor to speak. Here the assembly of women is a regular institution. That the Thesmophoria had a political dimension is confirmed by epigraphs as well as by the speeches of various orators.

Within each deme women themselves chose which of them would "wield power" in the Thesmophoria *(arkhein eis ta thesmophoria).* Isaeus (8.19–20) tells us that the selected women would preside over the assembly on the days "fixed by tradition" *(kata ta patria)* and do whatever "was consecrated by custom" *(ta nomizomena).* This ritual, if temporary, reversal of the political order was not limited to Athens. Of all rituals in the Greek world devoted to Demeter, the Thesmophoria were the most important. Literary sources indicate that thesmophorions, or temples of Demeter Thesmophoros, existed in many cities, including Aegina, Phlius, Paros, and Ephesus. Archaeological excavation has turned up others in Corinth, Thasos, Knossos, and Cyrene. The festival was of ancient origin, as is shown by Herodotus' belief that it was brought to Greece from Egypt by the daughters of Danaus. The dating of the thesmophorions discovered so far suggests that they were built near the end of the eighth century B.C., when Greek cities were still new, as suburban temples at the place where city and countryside merged.[18] They were dedicated to the deity responsible for the fertility of women and the soil as well as for ensuring political cohesion through respect for the law. This twofold significance was reflected in the very name of the goddess: the words *thesmoi* and *thesmia* had both a concrete and an abstract meaning. They could refer either to what remained of the sacrificial piglets and seeds carried to the altar by the first day's celebrants or, more abstractly, in the institutional and legal vocabulary, to "laws."[19]

The stories associated with each of these temples emphasized their civic functions. In Aegina it was said that the most powerful men of the city had committed an impious act by killing a rebel who had taken refuge in the vestibule of the thesmophorion. The entire population paid for this sacrilege a few years later, when the Athenians expelled the people of Aegina from their city. When Miltiades laid siege to Paros, he tried to profane the thesmophorion and discover its secrets but was seized with panic on the threshold and forced to withdraw (Herodotus 6.88, 6.134).

The Thesmophoria, associated with the myth of Demeter and her daughter Kore, celebrated the fall sowing. On the first day of the festival, certain women were selected to gather the remains of piglets tossed into consecrated fissures in the temple during the preceding year. These remains were treated as an offering to Pluto, in commemoration of his abduction of Kore. They were mixed with the seeds for the coming year and consecrated on the temple's altars to ensure that the land would prove fertile in the year to come. The second day celebrated Demeter's mourning after the loss of her daughter. The women sat and fasted on cushions made from chaste trees *(agnus castus)*. On the third day there was a blood sacrifice. The sacred archives of Delos list sacrifices for the Thesmophoria and ingredients needed to prepare the sacrificial meal. Since women were temporarily in control of the political sphere, it was only logical that they should oversee the sacrificial ritual as well. But one major element of that ritual remained beyond their grasp: they were not allowed to deliver the fatal blow. Inscriptions mention the presence of a *mageiros* who actually performed the killing and was at once expelled from the temple. The regulations specified that the person who slit the throats of the victims was not to attend the banquet. This third day of the festival was consecrated to Kalligeneia, "she who gives birth to beautiful children," and celebrated the return of Kore and the promise of fertility (human as well as agricultural).

Only legitimate wives of citizens were admitted to this woman-supervised celebration of fertility and birth. Indeed, participation in the Thesmophoria was accepted as legal proof of legitimate marriage. The adjective *eugeneis*, well-born, that the women in Aristophanes' play apply to themselves expressed their pride as daughters and wives of citizens, as did the adjective *eleutherai*, applied to them elsewhere. Just as women adopted the political language of men, so too did they take on masculine pride and values in identifying themselves with the city. Unlike other festivals in which a small number of aristocratic girls represented the rest of their age cohort, it appears that in Athens and other cities all women married to citizens went to the tents on Pnyx Hill to participate in the Thesmophoria.

The Thesmophoria highlighted women's procreative role. To participate a woman had to be lawfully married, because the legitimacy of her children depended on the legitimacy of her marriage. The women sat on cushions made from the branches of the chaste tree, which symbolized both purity and fertility. Participants refrained from sexual relations for the duration of the festival. Far from being incompatible, chastity and fertility were actually complementary. Only chaste brides could expect to give birth to the beautiful children that women on the third day of the festival beseeched the goddess Kalligeneia to bring forth.

In the Thesmophoria women were isolated from men. As mothers, they enjoyed special, indeed exclusive, access to Demeter, whose maternal component was paramount in the myth on which the ritual was based. During the festival women were accepted as equals, but there were limits to that equality, because they were recognized as mothers of future citizens. Thus the festival honored not the women themselves but the "city of men" it was their function to reproduce. When the chorus in *Women of the Thesmophoria* insists that a woman should be honored if she gives birth to a man useful to the city, it is "conforming to the civic model" in making the woman's recognition depend on the value of her son. "The city asks nothing of them other than to do what is expected of them as women by bearing children who will perpetuate their father's name."[20] This interpretation is correct as far as it goes. But the Thesmophoria also recognized the unique contribution of women, even though Aeschylus puts these words in the mouth of Apollo: "The mother does not give birth to what is usually called her child . . . She simply plays nurse to a seed in her bosom . . . The one who truly gives birth is the man who impregnates. The mother merely protects the young plant" (*Eu-*

menides, 658–661). The ritual function confers dignity, and the praise of women echoes the chants and prayers they utter in the ceremony. The seriousness and dignity of the language stand out all the more in contrast to the usual mockery.

Weaving and Politics

Women seldom participated in sacrificial rituals and assemblies. The good wife traditionally was portrayed as a weaver. But weaving was also a symbolic activity, and studying it is another way of understanding the relation between women, ritual, and the city.

Innumerable vase paintings depicted the good wife in her home, working at the loom alongside servants and other women of the household. *Ergastis*, industrious, was a term of praise frequently applied to women. *Ergon gunaikon*, or women's work, meant primarily work with textiles, as exemplified by the figure of Penelope in Homer and confirmed by fifth-century epitaphs.

In Athens young virgins known as *ergastines* gathered on the Acropolis to weave a peplos for Athena. But this ritual was not the only connection between weaving and religion. The symbolic significance of weaving extended far beyond the work women actually did on their looms. Athena, the goddess who presided over this activity, was also the protector of other types of industry. Under Athena's patronage Pandrosos was "the first woman, along with her sisters, to make woolen garments for men" (*Photius*, under Pandrosos). In mythology weaving, like agriculture, symbolized culture, the basis of civil society. Arcas, who gave his name to Arcadia and was in a sense the founder of the country, is described by Pausanias as the man who showed the Arcadians how to grow wheat and bake bread and taught the women how to weave (*estheta huphainesthai*, Pausanias 8.4.1). The regular replacement of Athena's peplos was like the renewal of a contract between the goddess and her city, as if, in exchange for their offering, Athens' citizens expected a guarantee of permanence. Women played an essential role in the ritual. Although the peplos was woven by maidens, the process was directed by priestesses and *teleiai gunaikes*, mature women. The city's offering to its patron goddess was thus the work of women of all ages under the direction of priestesses and the supervision of the Assembly.

The culmination of these labors was the "peplophoria," a procession in which the peplos, symbol of Athens' unity, was

353

carried through the city. An image of this procession figured in the frieze on the Pantheon: men and women, young and old, mortals and gods, spectators and marchers all took part.

The peplophoria of the Panathenaea was not the only such procession in Greece. In the Laconian Hyacinthia a chiton was solemnly offered to Apollo, probably in the course of a procession in which youths, both male and female, participated. Pausanias (3.16.2) says that "every year the women wove a chiton for Apollo in Amyclae, and they called the room in which they did the weaving a chiton also." Here, the god's "technical" function was not at issue, but the civic function of the Hyacinthia and the consequent political importance attached to the weaving of the chiton are evident. The fact that so central a festival in the Spartan religious calendar was celebrated at a temple outside the city calls for explanation. The location of the temple appears to have been intended to commemorate the completion of Sparta's conquest of the Amyclae region around the middle of the eighth century. Aristotle corroborates this interpretation when he writes that the festival marked the presentation of the breastplate of Timomachus, the hero of this conquest.

The first day of the festival was devoted to mourning for Hyacinthus, son of Amyclas, for whom the city was named and who was given a Spartan genealogy after the conquest. The dual cult of Hyacinthus and Apollo was thus a response to the need to integrate the population of Amyclae into Sparta's empire. On the final day of the festival all the people of the city, and particularly the youth, were invited to join in the activities. The festival proclaimed Amyclae's unity with Sparta, and the tunic woven each year for Apollo was the contribution of the city's women to this civic celebration. This weaving was extended over a period of time, as if in counterpoint to adolescent rites of passage. The activity could be prolonged indefinitely or, what amounts to the same thing, restarted over and over again (just as Penelope undid at night the weaving she did during the day, thus giving her control over time: the suitors waited and grew old, while the mistress of the house gave her husband, Ulysses, time to return). In this respect weaving can be seen as a metaphor for the life of the mature woman, which is stable and enduring, in contrast to that of an adolescent, which is marked by successive changes. Weaving is an expression of duration and cohesion. The city hopes to endure under Apollo's protection, its various components as tightly bound as the strands of a woven fabric.

354

In Elis, near Olympia, a weaving project gave women a more direct role in maintaining political unity. When a conflict between Pisa and Elis threatened the survival of both cities, women quickly became the arbiters. Sixteen married women, chosen for their venerable age, wisdom, and reputation, represented the sixteen cities of the Elis region. The group continued to function even after the territory was restructured politically and divided into eight tribes, with each tribe now naming two women. This group was responsible for organizing the festival of Hera in Olympia. The selected women organized choruses of maidens and foot races, and every four years they arranged for a peplos to be woven for Hera. Choruses and races were among the initiation rites by which young women were prepared for marriage. The weaving of the peplos, on the other hand, honored a goddess, Hera, who reigned as the patron of marriage and childbirth. The peplos was offered not only in gratitude but also in propitiation.

Dionysian Women

In Greek mythology the bacchantes, frenzied followers of Dionysus, symbolized an inversion of the normal civic and familial order. They were women who, forgetting their wifely duties, in a paroxysm of sacrilege tore their own children limb from limb in wild mountaintop revels. Invariably these stories begin with a refusal to embrace the cult of Dionysus, whose adepts engaged in orgiastic rituals under the influence of that divine madness known in Greek as *mania*. The legend of the Minyades unfolds in the Boeotian city of Orchomenus. Minyas' daughters Leucippe, Aristippe, and Alkithoe refuse to accompany the other women of the town into the mountains to undergo the *teletai,* rites of initiation. "Absurdly industrious," according to Antoninus Liberalis, the Minyades remained at their looms; in retaliation, Dionysus destroyed them. In one version of the tale, ivy vines and serpents coil around the looms' uprights and render them unusable. In another, the looms drip with nectar and honey. Plucked from their familiar chores and stricken with madness, the three women tear a child limb from limb and head for the mountains. Other women, outraged by the crime, pursue them until they are transformed into birds of the night.

The Minyades were distinguished from other women by two "excesses": an excessive devotion to their looms causes them to spurn Dionysus; once transformed into bacchantes, their frenzy knows no bounds and they commit every kind of excess, including murder. They transgress the requirements of the two activities that defined the Greek woman: weaving and motherhood. Here these two activities are emblems for each other: the destruction of the loom precedes the dismemberment of the child. In the classical period several Greek cities celebrated the Agrionia, a festival that preserved some form of wild-animal hunt (Greek: *agrios,* wild). In Orchomenus a ritual whose existence is attested by Plutarch as late as the first century A.D. recalled the consequences of the Minyades' blinding. In a biennial festival there the priest of Dionysus set out in pursuit of women representing the Minyades, and "he was permitted to kill any that he caught."

Agave, Ino, and Antonoe, the daughters of Cadmus, founder of Thebes, at first refuse to recognize Dionysus, but later they lead a chorus of bacchantes into the mountains. Dionysus has this to say in the prologue to Euripides' *Bacchae* (here in William Arrowsmith's translation): "I have stung them with frenzy, hounded them from home up to the mountains where they wander, crazed of mind, and compelled them to wear my orgies' livery. Every woman in Thebes—but the women only—I drove from home, mad. There they sit, rich and poor alike, even the daughters of Cadmus, beneath the silver firs on the roofless rocks." As in the myth of the Minyades, the indoor work of women is opposed to the hunt in the wild: "I left my shuttle by my loom," Agave says, "in favor of a grander work, hunting wild animals with my bare hands!" Agave's quarry is her own son, whom she tears limb from limb in her frenzy. In contrast to the myth of the Minyades, however, the child here is a king, who, like his mother, has refused to recognize Dionysus. In Euripides' play the bacchantes are in fact the instrument by which Agave's son Pentheus is punished. The women serve as a manifestation of the god. Their dionysiac frenzy is accompanied by a reversal in the activities and appearance of the two sexes. Pentheus initially mocks Dionysus' feminine appearance; later, after being blinded by the god, he agrees to disguise himself as a bacchante in order to surprise his mother in the mountains. The bacchantes use the symbols of their dionysiac possession as weapons to defeat men: "They—these women—have only to lift their thyrsus to strike terror into men," says the ox driver who has come to recount their exploits. Pentheus takes arm against the bacchantes in part to defend his male status: "To allow women to treat us in this way is too much!"

In both myths women are the instrument for testing the interchangeability of male and female domains, the permeability of one to the other, the transgression of the cultivated by the wild and of the masculine by the feminine. Dionysian madness is a catalyst, not a final state.

The behavior of the Lydian women who accompany Dionysus to Thebes and who constitute the chorus in Euripides' tragedy differs markedly from that of the Theban bacchantes. The latter exhibit "murderous madness and demented rage," whereas the former never rave or succumb to *mania*. Jean-Pierre Vernant notes that the term "maenads," which is etymologically related to mania and often used as a synonym for bacchantes, was never applied to these particular dionysian women.[21] The difference is identical to that between the Minyades, driven from their home by madness, and the women who refuse to accept them after their crime. Note, however, that the Theban bacchantes themselves are peaceable as long as nothing gets in their way; they become wild only when threatened by men or taken by surprise in their secret retreats. Similarly, Dionysus is at once "the most redoubtable of the gods and the most gentle," as if the two states that Dionysus reveals were successive stages of a single experience: murderous frenzy and ecstatic purity. This ambivalence is captured in two effigies of the god, one in Sicyon, the other in Corinth: the frenzied Baccheios and the saving Lysios. In this opposition Marcel Detienne sees "Dionysus' dual power in an analytic staging of *mania,* which can be purification even in the throes of madness, but only because it is first knowledge of impurity in the violence of a frenzy that requires compensatory purification."[22]

The *oribasia*, or race through the mountains, and *diasparagmos,* the sacrificial dismemberment of the captured prey, reflect Dionysus' savage face. But that is only one of the god's aspects. While the experience ends tragically for those who refuse to see the god, those who accept him end in joy and peace. The god's revelation is given first to women, but it is directed to men and women alike.

In Athens we find Dionysus settled in the heart of the city. The queen (the wife of the archon-king) and *gerairai* (fourteen women) who officiate in the great festival of early spring, the Anthesteria, are not bacchantes. Respectable women, they are responsible for ushering in the new year and preside over the opening of jars of wine made from the previous autumn's grapes. The queen's ritual marriage with Dionysus in the Boukoleion, the ancient royal residence to which the marriage procession brings the couple, symbolizes the prospect of fertility and prosperity. The woman chosen to "celebrate the secret sacrifices on behalf of the city" had to be above reproach, hence a woman who had been a virgin at marriage. This requirement explains Demosthenes' indignation in *Against Neara*, a diatribe against the foreign courtesan who improperly accepted a role that put her in the position of receiving the oath of the fourteen servants of Dionysus. Like the secrets of Demeter, those of Dionysus Limnaeus (Dionysus of the swamp) were hidden from men's eyes. The queen and her attendants performed their rituals in private, whereas the opening of the wine jars and the concomitant drinking bouts took place in a public ceremony presided over by the archon-king.

The women who officiated in the Anthesteria were of high rank (the inheritors, according to Demosthenes, of an ancient royal tradition); their number was limited; and they played an important civic function. They resemble another group of women discussed earlier: those in Elis who wove a peplos for Hera. To be sure, the women of Elis were recruited differently and had no queen. But their duties included the organization of a chorus in honor of Dionysus: the chorus of Physcoa, named for Dionysus' lover, reputed to have been the founder of his cult in the Elis region. This chorus no doubt took part in the Thyia, the Elians' great dionysian festival. Plutarch recorded the invocation with which the chorus' chant began and ended: "Noble bull, come, Lord Dionysus, into the pure temple of the Elians, come with the Charites leaping on the hoof." The tone here is similar to that of the Lydian chorus at the beginning of the *Bacchae:* after recalling the birth of "the god with the horns of a bull," the singers evoke the ecstasy of the dancing maenads on the mountain after the fawn-skin race.

Meanwhile, 8 leagues from the city, at a place called Thyia (compare *thuein,* to leap), citizens and guests look on as wine spurts out when the priests open the vats in which it has been stored. Marcel Detienne remarks on the series of contrasts that distinguish the two rituals: "the officiants are female in one, male in the other; city versus periphery; temple versus house; citizens versus citizens *and* guests."[23]

In Delphi we also find traces of a Thyia that lent its name to the Thyiades, women shown attending Dionysus on the pediment of Apollo's temple. In the historical era the name Thyiades became synonymous with bacchantes; the women so called performed orgiastic rites connected with the cult of Dionysus. But Pausanias (10.4.3) also speaks of "women of Attica who went annually to Parnassus, where, together with women from Delphi, they performed *orgia* for Dionysus. It was customary for these Thyiades to stage dances along their route from Athens." Similarly, Plutarch (*De mulierum virtutibus,* 13.249c) reports an anecdote according to which Athenian Thyiades lose their bearings at night on the road to Delphi and wander into enemy territory. Tired and still out of their wits, they stumble into the marketplace at Amphissa and fall asleep wherever they happen to lie down. The women of the city, fearful that the Thyiades might be mistreated, hasten to the marketplace, silently surround the sleeping women, care for them as best they can, and bring them food to eat. Finally they persuade their husbands to allow them to show the visitors the way back to the frontier, with the women of the town forming an escort for greater security. According to Plutarch this incident occurred in 335 B.C., during the Sacred Wars.

The god who enticed women away from their looms and into the mountains was the same one who, at the end of his journey, coupled with the wife of the archon-king of Athens, the embodiment of the city's historical continuity and identity. He was the same as the god invoked, in the form of a bull, by that paragon of respectability, the Elian women's chorus. The thiasus that the women of Athens carried through the mountains was the link between the god's two manifestations, the sign of his underlying unity. The active complicity of the women of Amphissa represents a conjunction of both aspects.

Epiphanies of Dionysus are too numerous to consider here. In the two cities I have chosen to examine the god's arrival coincided with the opening of the wine jars and spurting of the fermented liquid. Dionysus was of course also the god who taught men the uses of wine, whose consequences sometimes included madness and death (as in the story of the Centaurs, intoxicated with uncut wine, or of Icarius, who, unversed in the art of mixing wine with water, persuaded his shepherd companions to drink too much) but also, for those who abided by the rules, the benefits of civilized life. In this respect the counterpart of Dionysus was Demeter and of wine, wheat. In *The Bacchae* Tiresias proclaims that "for men there are two fundamental principles: first, the goddess Demeter, or Earth, as she is also known. She is the source of nourishment, the power of solid food for mortals. Next, but equal in power, comes the son of Semele, who invented and introduced men to liquid nourishment, to the drink made from grapes. Poor humans alleviate their sufferings when they gorge themselves on the liquor of the vine; it gives them the gift of sleep, oblivion for their daily woes, and there is no other remedy for their pains. Wine, itself a god, is poured in libation to the other gods, and what good there is in man's lot he owes to it."

Women, owing to their role in the reproductive process, became the intermediaries between Demeter and the city. Wine, like the blood spilled in sacrifice and war, was masculine, yet women also played a mediating role with respect to it. Even after women married, they ostensibly retained something of their "natural savagery," which could always be reactivated. Wine too was "savage" and could be made beneficial only through a ritual that acknowledged the power of the god. Perhaps it was because of this secret affinity that docile women "in mild servitude" were designated to bring Dionysus from his "mountain bacchanals" in Phrygia "to the places where choruses dance in Greece" (ll. 86–87).

In the Oikos

Let us now turn our attention to ceremonies centered on the *oikos,* or household. In classical Greece there was no private sphere clearly differentiated from the public. The city, as we have seen, took an interest in the initiation of adolescents, especially girls. The marriage ritual completed the young woman's initiation into adult and civic life. Marriage marked a change in status from *parthenos* (maiden) to *gyne* (married woman). It also marked a change of oikos, as the bride left her father's household to take up residence with her husband. She left the family and friends among whom she had grown up to live in a strange household with a man who was also a stranger. The disorientation associated with this new life was often compounded by apprehension that sexual relations might bring not pleasure but violence. Signs of this ambivalence can be seen in various myths and images. Medea's lament is tinged with tragedy: "So thrown amid new laws, new places, why, 'tis magic she must have, or prophecy—home never taught her that—how best to guide toward peace this thing that sleepeth at her side. And she who, laboring long, shall find some way whereby her lord may bear with her, nor fray his yoke too fiercely, blessed is the breath that woman draws. Else, let her pray for death" (Euripides, *Medea*, trans. Gilbert Murray, ll. 238–243).

Marriage consisted not of a single religious ceremony but of a constellation of rites. These matrimonial rituals were both a private celebration and an occasion to reaffirm the bonds between family and community. They were also a service to propitiate the gods and ensure the couple's future prosperity. And finally they marked the most important transition in a woman's life. The most important of the matrimonial rituals revolved around the bride's change of household. The *gamos,* or marriage, comprised two phases: the bride's farewell to maidenhood and her integration into a new household.

As marriage approached the young maiden prepared to abandon the "savage" world of Artemis in which her initiation had taken place. Artemis, however, was the goddess of transitions and therefore one of the marriage deities, to whom both boys and girls offered locks of hair on the eve of a change in status. In Sparta, Plutarch tells us, brides shaved their heads before presenting themselves to their husbands. This sacrifice of hair was at once a propitiatory rite, a farewell to adolescence, and a redemption of virginity. Girls gave not only their hair but also their toys and other symbols of the childhood they were about to abandon forever. An anonymous epigraph in honor of the Laconian goddess Artemis Limnatis alludes to this symbolic offering: "Timareta, who is about to marry, dedicates to thee, O goddess of Limnes, her tambourines, a ball she loved, a hairnet that held her hair, and her dolls. She, a virgin, has dedicated these things, as is fitting, to the virgin goddess, along with the clothing of these small virgins. In return, O daughter of Leto, extend thy hand over the daughter of Timaretos and piously watch over this pious girl" (*Anthology,* 6.280). Young women went to a Sphairian temple dedicated to Athena Apaturia to consecrate their sashes prior to marriage. The offering of hair in one form or another is attested throughout Greece. In Delos the consecration took place in the Artemision, the temple of Artemis, on the tomb of the daughters of Boreas, the Hyperborean Virgins, who according to myth traveled from their remote homeland to make the first offering in honor of the birth of Apollo and Artemis. "The daughters of Delos, frightened by the hymeneal song, consecrated the hair of their childhood" to the daughters of Boreas. In local rituals elsewhere we find the same

Artemisian context and intercession of heroines whose adolescence was cut short by death. The two symbols apparently reinforced each other. Maidens gave a part of themselves, symbolically offering their lives, but at the same time this symbolic death freed them to be "born again" in their new lives as married women.

In Trezene the offering went to Hippolytus, the adolescent hero par excellence. His story illustrates nothing less than the refusal of marriage as submission to divine and human law, and the respect paid him by soon-to-be brides was a way of recognizing that law. A woman's refusal to marry is a feature of several myths. Atalanta, the female equivalent of Hippolytus, was a young Arcadian huntress, a subject of Artemis' domain. After being nursed by a bear, Atalanta lived in the mountains, where she liked to run. She refuses to marry until one day, thanks to a subterfuge, Melanion, the black hunter, beats her in a race. While running, he drops apples of another marriage goddess, Aphrodite.

In another Arcadian myth, the daughters of King Proetus refuse to marry. Stricken with madness by Hera, they flee into the mountains. Proetus implores Artemis to intervene, and the goddess restores his daughters' sanity, after which they marry. A sacrifice and women's chorus commemorated their reconciliation with the two marriage goddesses, Artemis and Hera. The conjunction of Artemis and Hera in the myth of the Proetides illustrates the specific function of each. Artemis accompanies the future bride to the threshold of marriage, where Hera welcomes her. Artemis presides over the critical transition period, whereas Hera, along with Zeus Teleius, is the divinity of Teleia (accomplishment) and of legal marriage. According to another tradition, Dionysus had a part in the story of the Proetides, and the soothsayer Melampus was called in to purify the daughters, whose madness had spread to all the women of the region. The point is that the refusal to marry was no mere private affair; it placed the whole city, the whole human order, in jeopardy—hence the many myths that dramatize the crisis in the form of individual refusal. Marriage was a central social institution. In the Hesiodic tradition it was marriage, along with sacrifice and agriculture, that defined the human condition as falling between that of god and beast. Whatever man may think of Pandora, that "lovely curse" the gods contrive for him, he cannot escape Zeus's will or the necessity embodied in "the accursed race of women."

The bride-to-be spent the final days of her adolescence in her father's house, where other women helped her to prepare for the wedding. The prenuptial bath, whose water was thought to bring purity and fertility, was an important ritual with many local variants. In some places the water was fetched from a consecrated river or fountain such as the Callirohë fountain in classical Athens in a special pitcher known as a loutrophoros.[24] In some cases it was carried by a young woman other than the bride, in other cases by the bride herself (who may have fetched her own water). Certain vase paintings depict interior scenes suggesting a gynaeceum in which we see a line of women each carrying one of these ritual wedding vases.

On the day of the *gamos,* or wedding, the bride began by bathing and dressing in the gynaeceum. All day long she went veiled from head to toe. Only at the end of the day did her husband remove the veil that symbolized virginity. The bride's mother, who together with the other women of the household constituted the *nympheuteria,* presided over the preparations for the wedding and accompanied the bride to the banquet hall. Representing the last link to the paternal household, the *nympheuteria* escorted the bride throughout the day and ultimately to the door of the husband's house. After a sacrifice to the gods of marriage, the guests sat down for the wedding meal, with men and women at separate tables. Artemis, Hera Teleia, Zeus Teleius, Aphrodite, and Peitho were always among the honored gods, though others were sometimes added to the list.

Before the assembled guests the bride left the comforting escort of women and went to stand at her husband's side. Only her veil remained to protect her and to single her out as a *parthenos.* Soon the moment would come to confront her adult life and join the "cultivated" world symbolized by the bread that was distributed to the guests by the *amphitales,* a child both of whose parents were alive, symbolizing prosperity and good luck. In distributing the bread this child uttered the words "I fled worse and found better," suggesting the existence of a close connection between cultivation and marriage. It wore a crown of thorns and nuts to symbolize the threatening proximity of untamed nature. Other symbolic objects recalled the specific role of the new bride in perpetuating this civilized life: a grill for toasting barley, a sieve carried by a child, a pestle that was hung in front of the wedding chamber. Grains and the implements for handling them were symbols of Demeter, the goddess who represented the link between agriculture, fertility, and social life.

All was now ready for the bride to leave her father's house.

Sometimes on foot but more often by chariot the young woman, accompanied by her husband and his young male escort, set out for her new home. A procession formed, with young men carrying torches, some people playing flutes, and others bearing gifts. Youthful voices sang the hymeneal. This was the final transition, and the bride was sent off to the musical accompaniment of those who only yesterday had been her companions, reminders of the past. They sang in honor of the bride and in anticipation of her impending transformation, which would see her shed "the bridle of Artemis" for "the new yoke of Eros," as Claude Calame has put it.

Among the many myths that evoke the implicit violence of the bride's rupture with her family and initiation into sexual life as a married woman, the abduction of Kore is perhaps the most familiar in the Athenian tradition. Hades plucks his chosen bride from games with her companions and carries her off to the underworld in his chariot. Maiden Kore dies but is reborn as Hades' wife and as the goddess, along with her mother Demeter, of wheat and the harvest. The nuptial chariot is a pale version of Hades' mythical vehicle. Many vase paintings depict the bride on her journey from one household to another. In one she rides in a chariot and is held tightly by her husband, who also holds the reins. In another she walks and is pulled along by the wrist, while another woman walking behind appears to be arranging the folds of her bridal veil.

The young bride, lifted from the chariot by her husband, is welcomed by his mother and father. Various rituals accompany the bride's integration into her new home. She is first taken to the hearth, the center of the household, to receive the *tragemata*, consisting of dried dates, nuts, and figs. This ritual, also used to receive a new slave, marked the final rupture with the wife's former home. Now firmly tied to her new home, the wife will never leave it. The time has come for her to pass to the protection of Aphrodite and her associate Peitho, persuasion. Aphrodite is the goddess no one, not even the gods, can resist; her arms are gentleness and seduction. She will bring to the marriage the harmony that depends on pleasure and without which there can be no fine children. Outside the *thalamos*, or wedding chamber, a chorus of maidens again sings the ritual hymeneal to reassure the bride and encourage the couple, whom the gods are beseeched to bless: "Be happy, young bride. Be happy, son-in-law of a noble father-in-law. May

Leto, nurse of infants, give you fine children. May Cypris make you equals in reciprocated love, and may Zeus, son of Kronos, bring you prosperity forever, passed from noble hands to noble hands" (Theocritus, *Helen's Epithalamion,* ll. 49–53).

Marriage from the Male Point of View

We have so far considered marriage strictly from the woman's point of view. A wedding was also an important milestone in a man's life. In the myth of Hippolytus marrying would have meant accepting a new status; his refusal endangered the young man's life. For girls the rituals of farewell to adolescence merged with the preparations for marriage. For boys they were connected with the access to ephebe status and thus citizenship, whence the now classic parallel between the two institutions: "Marriage is to girls what war is to boys." In the Apaturia, celebrated in Athens and many other Ionian cities, the *koureotis,* the third day, was devoted to the enrollment of the young men in the phratries. This was accompanied by a sacrifice, the *koureion,* and an offering of hair to Artemis. On the same day another sacrifice, the *gamelia,* was performed, this being the only occasion for recognizing the social aspect of a woman's existence. The offerings were provided by newly married men, and the ritual was followed by a banquet during which the new bride was presented to her husband's phratry.[25]

Another important difference between men and women was age at marriage. Men generally married after they were already embarked on adult life, so the significance of marriage for them was very different from what it was for women. Pierre Brûlé has shown that fifteen to twenty years' difference in age between husband and wife was deemed desirable. On this point Aristotle agreed with the view that Hesiod had expressed some five centuries earlier.[26]

Childbirth

Even after the young bride received the keys to her new home in a solemn ceremony and was initiated into "the labors of Aphrodite," she was still not a woman in the full sense of the word. No longer *parthenos* but not yet *gyne,* she was called *nymphe:* a young woman who had not yet given birth. Only after the birth of the first child, when the father recognized his firstborn son as being "in his father's likeness" or held up the daughter he would one day marry off to another man, did the wife become *gyne,* a fully mature woman.

Birth, like marriage, required female assistance. Except for recognition of the child, which was the father's province, childbirth was a women's affair. Marriage existed to produce offspring: Aristophanes' satirical portrait of the lengths to which some people would go to obtain a child corroborates this assertion. Pregnancy and delivery fell under the jurisdiction of a number of gods. Eileithyia guarded against problems in pregnancy and helped to alleviate the pain of delivery. She intervened to end Leto's suffering when Hera, to avenge herself against her rival, complicated the delivery of Apollo and Artemis. Goddess of legitimate marriage, Hera was also the guardian of young brides, helping them to fulfill their destiny as *gynaikes.* Her power thus extended to the realm of pregnancy. But it was Artemis, under the name Lochia (goddess of childbirth), who received the linen from the birthing bed as an offering. Surviving epigraphs tell us of the gratitude of mothers who successfully gave birth. Artemis' protection of mothers was an extension of the protection she offered to young brides: "Artemis, by thy will may the wedding day of Lysomedeides' daughter also be the day she becomes a mother." The goddess was also the protector of newborn infants and the deity responsible for the growth of animals and plants as well as humans. Birth fell within her purview because it was the first stage of growth. Another deity, a sort of negative image of Artemis, received the clothing of women who died in childbirth. According to Athenian tradition, Iphigenia was the priestess of Artemis at Brauron. At the end of *Iphigenia in Tauris* Euripides has Athena say: "And you, Iphigenia, near the sacred fields of Brauron, you shall carry the keys of [Artemis'] temple. You will be buried there after your death. The rich fabrics left by women who die in childbirth will be consecrated to you." Iphigenia, sacrificed by her father on the altar of Artemis, thus became Artemis' priestess in Brauron. Pierre Brûlé calls her "the paradigm of feminine suffering."[27] Inventories of offerings from the temple of Artemis speak of large numbers of textiles, mostly women's clothing, offered to the goddess by women, so that the temple was "like a vast gynaeceum." The temple of Artemis thus figured continuously in a woman's life, from the initiation of maidens to the culmination of childbirth.

After giving birth a woman was considered to be impure. She was expected to remain, together with her midwife, friends, and neighbors, away from her husband for several days until a ritual purification could be performed. At that time she was expected to make a sacrifice. This custom explains lines 1124–34 of Euripides' *Electra*, a dialogue between Clytemnestra and her daughter (cited here in Emily Townsend Vermeule's translation). Electra says: "I think you heard about my lying-in and son. Make me the proper sacrifice—I don't know how—as the law runs for children at the tenth night moon." Clytemnestra answers: "This is work for the woman who acted as your midwife." But Electra says she had no midwife, so Clytemnestra says: "Then I will go and make the gods full sacrifice for a child as the law prescribes."

The sources, fragmentary and imprecise, distinguish between two types of postpartum ritual. The roles of the various participants are not always clearly defined. It appears that a set of rituals known as the Amphidromia took place five days after the birth. As the name suggests, the ceremony was essentially one in which the father, having recognized his child, carried it in his arms around the hearth and then placed it on the floor. This ritual, which signified that the child was judged viable by the women and accepted by its father, marked the beginning of the child's social life.[28] To mark his acceptance the father placed the child next to the central hearth, in the "cultivated" area of the household presided over by Hestia. Contact with the floor of the oikos was itself a rite of integration by virtue of which the child was recognized as a human being. The baby's social as opposed to biological existence depended on its father's decision, which was tantamount to a second birth. If the child was to be abandoned, the decision was made earlier, either by the mother in case of rape or adultery or else at the behest of the father. In that case the child was cast out of the household and into the savage or unsocialized world, represented in myth by caves, mountains, and forests. After Creusa is violated by Apollo, she abandons Ion, her son born secretly, in the cave where Apollo took advantage of her. But Apollo arranges things so that Xuthus, Creusa's husband, finds Ion, who in the meantime has become a servant of the god, and, thinking that the boy is his own son, orders a banquet in his honor, accompanied by "the sacrifice that should have celebrated his birth" (Euripides, *Ion*, ll. 650 ff.).

According to ancient lexicons, those who attended at a birth, and perhaps the birth mother herself, were purified on the day of the Amphidromia. But according to the text of *Electra*, purification did not take place until the tenth day, when it would have coincided with another set of rituals connected with the naming of the infant. Thus women played a crucial role in the newborn child's first days. Religious solidarity united the women of the household in performing their womanly duties. The division of responsibilities between husband and wife would continue throughout the child's upbringing, which was left in the charge of women until the child reached the age when its sex and social needs determined what course further education would take.

Women and Death

Women were mistresses of birth and, consequently, in contact with the most occult forces, impure by virtue of that very familiarity. They also played a special role in rituals associated with death. Because their role in childbirth brought them face to face with aspects of the body governed not by the laws of culture but by the laws of untamed nature, in death it was their job to oversee the purification of the body prior to its display to family and friends. Socrates washed his own body before his death in order to spare women the need to perform this task. Significantly, the same women who assisted in childbirth aided in the preparation of the corpse. Once the cadaver was washed, anointed with perfumes, and dressed in white, it was set out to lie in state for a day or two. The woman of the house led the ritual wailing and sang the threnody. Only close relatives joined the procession to the cemetery, which took place at night. On the island of Cös the Lex Iulia listed those who were to avoid the defilement that came of attending funerals, but it also stipulated that the women closest to the deceased (mother, wife, sisters, daughters, and five close kinswomen) must take part in the ritual *(miainesthai)*, after which they had to undergo purification.[29]

Women prayed for the dead and poured consecrated libations on the tomb. The Choephores, or libation-bearers, named in the title of Aeschylus' play were servants who assisted Electra in performing a religious ceremony at Agamemnon's tomb. Just as "slaves [took] part in ablutions of the patrimonial altar," serving women participated in household rituals alongside their mistress. When Eurydice, mother of Hemon in Sophocles' *Antigone*, departs after learning of her son's death, a servant comments: "She is heading home, where, under her own roof, she will gather her serving women to wail over this death in the household."

The Pure and the Impure

Birth and death were often linked as sources of impurity. In Epidaurus it was forbidden under sacred law to die within the temple walls, and women were not allowed to give birth there. On Delos, an island sanctified by the birth of Apollo, a similar prohibition applied. Speaking of Artemis, Iphigenia says: "If a mortal has contact with a murderer or so much as touches a woman who has given birth or a dead body, she [Artemis] prolongs the defilement by driving that person from her altars." Birth and death were thus on a par with the ultimate defilement, murder.[30] Both were feared because they were unpredictable and uncontrollable and therefore invested with a menacing if sacred value that could be tamed and held in check only by means of strict ritual. Women, who were believed to have a "savage" side (another way of defining their difference), were the "natural" intermediaries between these sources of impurity and men, who were thereby protected. Men were sheltered from the impurity of childbirth: they did not touch the mother (and possibly the child) until after the purification ritual, which took place on recognition day. Contact with death was mediated by women; men were not asked to view the corpse until it had been washed, perfumed, and dressed.

Impurity was a confusion of categories, a coming into contact of things that ought to be kept apart. Women were "by nature," that is, by virtue of their biological function, liable to become impure. Hence in the eyes of Greek males women enjoyed a mysterious and awe-inspiring relation to the sacred, a category whose ambiguity in archaic and classical thought has been analyzed by Jean-Pierre Vernant.[31] "A 'defilement,'" Vernant tells us, "was a contact that contradicted a certain order of the world because it established communication between realities that were supposed to remain perfectly distinct." Hence "it was possible for certain supernatural realities to be seen as both defiling and sacred." Ultimately the opposite poles of pure and impure merged. Pushed to the limit, this logic meant that in order to be perfectly pure, something had to be totally taboo. It is easy to see how to men women became indispensable intermediaries with the impure as well as the sacred.

The Quotidian

The ritual community of women, which enjoyed institutional existence for only three days a year, during the Thesmophoria, existed on a smaller scale in all the major events affecting the oikos: marriage, birth, death. It also functioned in daily life, where the mistress of the household was assisted in her routine by daughters, female relatives, and serving women. The women's community extended beyond the limits of the oikos to link women of different houses and neighborhoods through an exchange of information and skills. The religious life of the oikos reflected the male monopoly of social and political power, but women played a specific role. The bond between oikos and community was maintained by the family head, who performed the crucial acts of integration and presided over the sacrifices conducted under his roof. But the whole household participated in the principal daily rites. Wife and children were often shown together in images of sacrificial offerings at the family altar. The mistress of the household exercised religious authority over the women in her charge. Although women could not make sacrifices themselves, they often participated with other women in prayers and libations. They could also visit temples. The fourth mime of Herodas (third century B.C.) describes a visit to the temple of Asclepius by two common women accompanied by a servant. Having come to ask the god to heal someone who is ill, they repeat the ritual invocation that precedes the sacrifice and set down a votive object, then hand the sacristan a cock. When he returns with the bird's remains, they give him his share, a thigh, then place an obol in the temple crypt and some cakes on the table of offerings. One of the women then announces that they will eat the rest of the bird quietly at home, but not before asking one last favor of the god: "May we return with still more valuable offerings to make an even greater sacrifice, with the aid of our husbands and children?" One of the two women, more familiar with the ritual than the other, initiates her younger, more timid companion. For the poet this was a convenient dramatic situation, but it is also a plausible portrait of female solidarity in religious practice.

Rituals helped to bind together the community of women inside and outside the oikos. Neighbors joined neighbors, as Clytem-nestra's remark about her daughter's delivery indicates. Midwives went from house to house, and their duties extended well beyond assisting with childbirth: they helped prepare the bodies of the dead; they served as matchmakers; and some became involved in the sale or elimination of unwanted children. Women were re-doubtable not only for their skills but for the knowledge they possessed, and many people classed them with the magicians and viewed them accordingly with suspicion.

Indeed, a variety of suspect practices flourished on the fringes of ritual, practices in which, as men imagined them, women lost all sense of proportion and abandoned themselves to their pas-sions, to sexual license and animal behavior. The male imagination saw women as more than ready to succumb to excess and savagery. Theocritus describes one such woman: Samaitha uses love potions and sacrificial rituals to regain the love of Delphis. "Who was that old woman," she asks, "that chanter of incantations whose house I left without visiting?" (*The Magicians,* l. 91). The bacchantes shared the same malevolent image. Pentheus compares them to stray drunks: "Our women, they say, have left their homes to seek adventure in the mountain shadows . . . In their camps they fill their cups, and then each one goes off to lie with a man on the pretext that they are under the maenads' spell, whereas in reality Cypris is more important to them than Bacchus."

The Adonia

Thus the city favored the image of woman as chaste and prolific wife, and women who rallied round the flag of Cypris-Aphrodite were excluded from women's cults. Yet it was permissible for women to engage in a private cult of Adonis, Aphrodite's ephem-eral lover, who was killed by a boar. In the Adonia women placed on their housetops planters containing seeds that would briefly sprout tender shoots before succumbing to the hot August sun.[32] These plants were the antithesis of the agriculture protected by Demeter. Instead they symbolized the sterility of seduction as em-bodied by Adonis and expressed as mourning for the wilted roof gardens. Simultaneously, in private, women and their lovers glee-fully collected fragrant herbs, symbols of sexual pleasure. These herbs were taken down from the rooftop by the same ladders that were used to carry up the planters. The city exploited the ambiguity of the festival, which was generally tolerated but occasionally denounced as a symbol of feminine debauch. In Aristophanes' *Lysistrata* (ll. 387–398) the speech of one official is like a coarser echo of Pentheus' denunciation of the bacchantes: "Ah! Women's debauch is out in the open again, revealed by the beating of drums, the repeated shouts of 'Long live Sabazios,' and the festival of Adonis that is celebrated on the rooftops, of which I heard one day when I was in the Assembly. That is the sort of misbehavior of which women are capable!"

Women and the Priesthood

There is a striking contrast between the limited but strategically important part that women were permitted to play in public cults and the role assigned to priestesses. In some cults priestesses, whether elected or chosen by lot, occupied positions of great importance and received a share of every sacrifice, just as priests did.

Priestesses

The priestess of Athena Polias in Athens was the city's most important religious dignitary. When the *hiera,* the sacred objects, were transported in great splendor from Eleusis to Athens for the Great Mysteries, it was the priestess of Athena who was formally notified of their arrival in the city. The same priestess was also in charge of the Arrephoria; it was she who confided to the arrephorae the secret objects they were to carry. She also presided over the Kallynteria and the Plynteria. This important priestess, who served for life, was chosen from the Eteoboutades family.

In Eleusis the priestess of Demeter and Kore was, along with the hierophant, one of the two principal officials of the temple. Either elected or chosen by lot from among the daughters of the Philleides *genos,* she lived in a "sacred house" inside the temple and was entrusted with major responsibilities: she handled funds, was the principal celebrant of the festival of the Haloa, and played a role in the Eleusinia and Thesmophoria. On occasion (according to a fourth-century inscription) she fought legal battles to defend her sacred rights against the encroachments of the hierophant.

In Perge, a city of Pamphylia in Asia Minor, the priestess of

Artemis, the civic goddess, received a choice portion, "a thigh and other parts," of every sacrificial offering (F. Sokolowski, *LSA*, no. 73). Every year, on the twelfth day of the month of Heraklion, the priestess celebrated the great official sacrifice over which the prytanes (chief magistrates) presided.

Whereas inequality between the sexes was the rule in the political sphere, it appears that honors and responsibilities in the religious sphere were divided according to some other principle. Priestesses seem to have had the same rights and duties as priests. Those who did not hold hereditary posts were elected annually or chosen by lot; when they left office they had to submit an account of their activities. Like priests, they sometimes enjoyed the privilege of *eponymia* (as in the case of the Eleusinian Demeter or Athena Polias, *IG* II[2] 4704, 2586, 3559), or of *proedria,* a place of honor in the theater or at the stadium. The priestess of Demeter Chamynea in Olympia sat facing the judges of the Olympic Games (Pausanias 6.20.9).

Nevertheless, this appearance of equality should not be allowed to conceal the fact that those who voted or drew lots to choose priestesses were male citizens. When the purchase of priestly offices became common in Asia Minor, men were allowed to buy offices for themselves or to give to women, while women were allowed only to buy for themselves (F. Sokolowski, *LSA*, nos. 25, 73). Finally, priestesses were forbidden to make blood sacrifices. Those few examples of myth or ritual in which women wielded the sacrificial knife were exceptions that confirmed the rule.

Biological considerations and their socially constructed meanings had an important influence on the status of the priestess. Purity, associated with chastity, was required of both priests and priestesses. But the distinction between *parthenoi* and *gynaikes* applied not only to women as members of society but also to women in their relation to the divine. Priestesses were not always virgins. Cult requirements determined the marital status of the priestess. Bear in mind that in ancient Greece priests did not form a clergy apart but were citizens like other citizens. Often they were like magistrates, who as long as they held their position served a specific god at a specific temple. Priestesses, chosen for their purity and respectability to perform a prescribed service, were in a similar situation. In Athens, for example, the Basilinna, or wife of the archon-king, who served in the Anthesteria and assisted in sacrifices believed to be essential to the city's prosperity, conformed to this description. Her role was akin to that of a priestess, as were the roles of the *gerairai* who assisted her. A similar situation existed with regard to the services rendered by groups of women in Elis and Delphi. Although the relative equality of priests and priestesses in their religious functions did not efface the fundamental inequality between women and men, religion offered the only sphere in which Greek women could be treated as citizens.

Certain gods required the services of young men or, more commonly, young women, set apart by their status as *parthenoi,* virgins. At Thespiae in Boeotia the priestess of Heracles was required to remain a virgin all her life. Usually, however, priestesses were required to remain virgins only for a limited time, at the end of which they married. This was true of the priestess of Poseidon on the island of Sphaeria, for example, and especially of priestesses of Artemis in Egira, Triclaria, and elsewhere. All these were cults connected with adolescence and the transition to adulthood. The arrephorae and plyntherides of the Acropolis, chosen by election, were in a similar position. It is as if these functions preserved some ancient rite of initiation transformed into an honorific service at the behest of the civic authorities.

Some priestly offices, like the priesthood of Sosipolis in the temple of Ilythia, required not *parthenoi* but *presbytides,* elderly women beyond menopause. This requirement was a religious version of the rule according to which the power to deliver other women's children should go to those who could no longer be delivered of their own. Artemis "assigned the privilege [of midwifery] to women who were past childbearing, out of respect to their likeness to herself" (Plato, *Theaetetus,* 149b).

Prophetesses

In her most prestigious role, that of prophetess, the priestess was the direct instrument of a god. Plato, when he speaks of *mania,* the delirium inspired by the gods (*Phaedrus,* 244b), links the words *prophetis* and *hiereia,* alluding to both the prophetess of Delphi and the priestesses of Dodona, and then mentions the Sibyl and "others who by the power of inspired prophecy have so often foretold the future." The passage suggests that the function of prophecy was thought of as primarily, if not exclusively, feminine. By studying the Pythia of Delphia, the most famous of the Apollonian priestesses, we can begin to understand why this was so.

Direct contact with the sacred was a frightening thing, and men were more than willing to assign the task to women. In Greek the word *enthousiasmos* means the presence of a *theos*, or god, in a person in the grip of delirium, of what Plato calls *mania*. Diodorus of Sicily (16.26) tells how, before the institution of the Pythia was established, those who wished to consult the oracle of Delphi simply went to a hole in the earth (accidentally discovered by a goat) from which the divine breath emanated. After breathing in its vapors, they became capable of delivering oracles to one another. But "since many people, owing to their state of possession, leapt into the hole and disappeared, the inhabitants of the region decided to eliminate the danger by naming one woman to act as prophetess for all, and from then on the consultation involved her as intermediary." Seated on a sacred tripod placed on the ground in the *adyton* (forbidden zone) of the temple, the unseen prophetess manifested her presence by her voice alone. Her words were transcribed by priests and delivered to those who came to consult the oracle. An "instrument" of the god, the Pythia had to be pure; she also had to give her consent in order that the *pneuma*, or divine breath, might pass through her. To ensure that these two conditions were met, the Pythia had first of all to be a woman "pure of any carnal union and completely isolated throughout her life from all contact and relations with strangers" (Plutarch, *On the Disappearance of Oracles*, 438c, 1–2). In another dialogue Plutarch described the Pythia who officiated in his day as a virgin "raised in a poor peasant household. To the prophetic place she takes with her not one iota of art, knowledge, or talent . . . It is truly with a virgin soul that she approaches the god" (*On the Oracles of the Pythia*, 405c, 3–11). Prior to the consultation a sacrifice was offered; if not acceptable, it meant that the priestess was not ready to receive the god. To ignore this sign was to endanger the Pythia's life, as an anecdote related by Plutarch indicates. The Pythia, he says, was as docile an instrument of the god as a young wife was a docile servant of her husband. Her virginity was a necessary condition for serving as Apollo's intermediary.[33] Mediation was necessary if the god's voice was to reach man's ears. The role of mantic procedures was analogous to that of sacrifice in the relation between men and gods. The Greek idea of woman was ambivalent: it allowed for the possibility of contact with the impure, and it was this possibility that enabled women to serve as intermediaries to the sacred.

The oikos was the domain of women. What went on there went on under their control. But because the oikos was governed by the rules of society, the law of men, masculine law, was ultimately sovereign. Conversely, civic activity in its religious aspect could not ignore women entirely. The sacred required the presence of women because they alone possessed certain keys to the renewal of life and therefore to the perpetuation of the city. The gods spoke to women and expected to be served by women. A door had to be kept ajar for them: women were permitted to perform certain rituals, but only under the close surveillance of men. The story of Battus, first king of Cyrene, who paid for his attempt to gain knowledge of the mysteries of Demeter Thesmophora with the loss of his virility, tells us a great deal about men's fascination with, and anxiety about, the power of women. To the male imagination female control of the instruments of sacrifice seemed dangerous. The ambivalent figure of Pandora, born at the dawn of the seventh century in a historical and economic context that goes some way toward accounting for the bitterness of the myth, is an essential element of the Greek tradition. The virgin dressed by the gods to resemble a young bride so as to seduce and deceive men is the very image of woman and of the destiny of man separated from the gods: a mixture of good and evil, like the "lovely curse" sent by Zeus to avenge himself for Prometheus' ruse:

> For the famous limping god molded from earth the image of a girl, a modest virgin, through the plans of Zeus. Gray-eyed Athene made her belt and dressed the girl in robes of silver; over her face she pulled a veil, embroidered cleverly, marvelous to behold, and on her head Pallas Athene set a lovely wreath of blossoms from spring grasses, and a crown of gold, made by the famous limping god, worked with his hands, to please his father Zeus . . . When he made the lovely curse, the price for the blessing of fire, he brought her to a place where gods and men were gathered, and the girl was thrilled by all her pretty trappings, given by mighty Zeus's daughter with gray eyes. Amazement seized the mortal men and gods, to see the hopeless trap, deadly to men. From her comes all the race of womankind, the deadly female race and tribe of wives who live with mortal men and bring them harm.[34]

8

The Religious Roles
of Roman Women

John Scheid

IN HIS MEMOIR of childhood Elias Canetti recalls that prayer in the synagogue meant little to
his mother because, being a woman, she was excluded from the religious ritual. Such an attitude,
frequently described by Jewish writers, might just
as well have been expressed by a Roman matron.
As a woman, she was, if not excluded from religious practice, at least relegated to a marginal role.
In fact women were so thoroughly excluded from
Roman religion that they frequented suburban
sanctuaries and the temples of foreign gods and,
if the censorious comments of the pious are to be
believed, threw themselves into all sorts of deviant
religious practice and thought. Were Roman
women religiously "incapacitated"? Yes and no.
They were, to be sure, excluded from the celebration of the most important rites, but Roman religion was a complex affair in which women,
though subordinate, remained a necessary complement to men.

Roman Religion: A Man's Affair

Roman religious life had three main aspects. A
public religion was practiced in the forum and

temples. A private or semipublic cult was observed in neighborhood squares and wherever Roman citizens gathered. Within the household each family organized religious life as it saw fit, with its own gods, rites, and holy days. These overlapping religious communities all shared a common religious culture, but within this shared tradition, women never filled the leading roles.

Sacerdotal Roles

Public sacerdotal responsibilities were always exercised by men. Important public liturgies were presided over by magistrates, sometimes assisted by priests chosen from among the people of Rome. Priests and magistrates shared the religious responsibilities of the res publica and formulated and interpreted sacred law. Only they were authorized to announce the will of the gods, determined by consulting auspices or the Sibylline Books. Together with the Senate, the magistrates examined any religious problems that arose and in consultation with the priests prescribed remedies. High priests were elected by the comitiae, that is, by the citizens of Rome. Since the public religion was limited to these prescribed activities, religious power was almost entirely in the hands of these men.

In one public liturgy for which we possess extensive epigraphic records—the sacrifice to Dea Dia—women played no role. Men—the *flamines* (flamens, or priests) of the Fratres Arvales (Arval Brethren)—even represented the powers and functions of the goddess. They officiated in ceremonies wearing crowns of grain, presumably symbols of the ripe harvest made possible by Dea Dia, goddess of fair skies.[1] Indeed, all the great Roman goddesses—Ceres, Flora, Pomona, and Furrina—were represented by *flamines*.

Domestic cults were no different. The paterfamilias was in charge. Observance of family cults was one of the established duties of the paterfamilias, and failure to discharge this duty could lead to trouble with the censor.[2] In his treatises on agronomy Cato insists that sacrifices are performed on behalf of the entire family by the *dominus*, or master of the household.[3] Minor private rituals, such as the daily libation to the Lares, the household gods, were also his responsibility. More important domestic rituals were also supervised by males. In rituals to honor the dead in February (the *Parentalia*) and May (the *Lemuralia*) the paterfamilias played the leading role. Funeral processions were always led by men, who delivered eulogies and celebrated the prescribed sacrifices.

Other examples can be found in colleges of artisans and other citizen groups. Bas-reliefs depicting religious subjects show men as the principal actors. The evidence is clear: in religion, which was always related to the expression of community power, men played the leading role in every situation.

Women's Unfitness for Sacrifice

Women (along with foreigners and prisoners) were forbidden to participate in sacrificial rituals. According to Paulus Diaconus, abridger of the dictionary of Festus, a second-century compilation based on an even earlier source, "custom dictated that in certain liturgies the lictor cry out, 'Away with [exesto] the foreigner, the prisoner in chains, the woman, the girl!' The injunction exesto indicated that these people were forbidden to attend the sacrifices in question."[4] We do not know what rituals these were, but no doubt they included more than just sacrifices to virile or "savage" deities such as Hercules, Mars, and Silvanus. In any case, the exclusion of women from ritual is attested by another, more general rule: they were excluded from sacrifice, or at any rate from key moments in the sacrificial ritual.[5]

Plutarch's Eighty-Fifth Roman Question (second century A.D.) asks "why in ancient times were women not permitted to grind or prepare meat?" His answer involves the rape of the Sabine women and a treaty that was signed after the ensuing war, under the terms of which no woman could grind (alein) or prepare (mageireuein) meat for her husband. What exactly is the significance of these taboos? They have to do with two key moments in the two major domains of food production: the grinding (alein) of grain and the slaughter, skinning, and butchering (mageireuein) of animals. This prohibition on butchering not only made life more agreeable for the first women to marry Romans (as one version of the legend of the Sabines suggests) but excluded them from the sacrificial scene. The slaughter of the victim was ordered by the celebrant of the ritual—the magistrate, priest, or paterfamilias; the actual slaughter and butchering was done by lanii (butchers).[6] The prohibition on grinding (actually pounding) grain complemented the prohibition on sacrificial butchering. It excluded women not from the sacrifice itself but from the preparation of an essential ingredient of the sacrifice, *far,* a kind of flour made by pounding kernels of spelt, which was itself an offering and which, under the name *mola* (ritual flour), was also used as a bed for carrying the offerings of mortals to the gods.[7] The connection between ritual flour, pounding, and the sacrificial ceremony is also established by the term *molucrum,* which means both "broom for sweeping flour mills" and "block of wood for immolation."[8]

According to Plutarch, this rule was enforced "in ancient times" *(to palaion).* Does this mean that it was no longer in force under the Roman Empire? We do not know. Plutarch's phrase might indicate that the prohibition was supposed to date back to the time of Romulus, or it might simply apply to a strict rule enforced at some time in the past, perhaps as recently as the time of Christ's birth. If spinning and weaving were the traditional virtues of the Roman matron,[9] then the Eighty-Fifth Roman Question defined what it was that women were not supposed to do.[10] Whether ancient or not, the rule seemed important enough for Plutarch to include in his *Roman Questions,* in which he attempted to explain surprising and picturesque Roman customs. Hence we may assume that, even if the rule was not strictly enforced under the Empire, it was still one of the defining characteristics of the Roman matron in the second century A.D. We may even speculate that in the historical era the rule had ceased to be enforced except in regard to sacrifice. Antiquarians may even have used this prohibition to read a more general taboo back into "ancient times."

A third prohibition excluded women from another aspect of the sacrificial ritual: the old rule that women were not allowed to drink undiluted wine *(temetum).* Cazanove is correct in thinking that this exclusion left women out of the sacrificial ritual, which was the way in which men entered into contact with the gods.[11] For undiluted wine was an essential offering in every sacrifice, and its consumption was limited to men and gods.

Vestals, *Flaminicae,* and Other Priestesses

It would seem that because of their sex women were deemed unfit to take part in the most important elements of religious ritual: the slaughter, butchering, and distribution of the meat of the sacrificial victim. These fundamental roles were reserved for men. In relations between communities and gods, men were in charge, and their distribution of the sacrificial victim's "profane" parts defined the social hierarchy.

The Extent of Woman's Sacrificial Incapacity

The exclusion of women was not absolute. According to the letter of Plutarch's text, for example, the prohibition on grinding and preparing meat was not all-encompassing.[12] It applied to one specific situation: wives (Sabines) were not allowed to grind or prepare meat "for their Roman husbands [*andri Romaioi*]." This detail can of course be interpreted as a concession required by the circumstances of the mythical war between the Romans and the Sabines. In the *Life of Romulus* (15.5) Plutarch wrote that the Sabines forced the Romans to exempt their wives from all physical labor other than weaving. Just as obviously, both texts I have cited reflect the status of the Roman wife. The proviso that Plutarch mentions in his answer to the Eighty-Fifth Question was thus a real limitation: the rule applied only to relations between women and their husbands, that is, in a domestic religious setting. It was not necessarily valid for public rituals. Plutarch was perfectly well aware that women were almost entirely excluded from active roles in the religious community. If he nonetheless refrained from stating that the taboo on grinding and preparing meat applied to women in all situations, it was because he knew of exceptions to the ancient rule. These exceptions all related to public religious life, where certain sacerdotal and sacrificial positions were held by women.

The Vestals

Consider the six Vestals of the historic period. Like wives of the *flamines* and the *rex sacrorum* (king of sacred rituals), the Vestals were public priestesses—a rarity in Roman religion. Under the authority of the *virgo Vestalis maxima* (the Great Vestal Virgin), their function was to tend the fire in the public hearth in the temple of Vesta at the southwest corner of the Roman Forum. Chosen before the age of puberty, in principle Vestals served for thirty years, ten as apprentices, ten in service, and ten as teachers. Housed in a large building adjoining the temple of Vesta, they were required to remain virgins as long as they served. Afterward they were free to marry, although few did: their vow was not one of total sexual abstinence but rather of chastity *(pudicitia)* similar to that required of the Roman matron, who was expected to remain faithful to one man and austere in conduct and dress.[13] Like other Roman priests, the Vestals represented the nature of the goddess they served: their chastity reflected the purity of Vesta and the flame of the hearth.

The Vestals were "taken" *(captae)* by the *pontifex maximus* (grand pontiff) in a ceremony that resembled the Roman marriage ritual. The girl's father delivered her into the hands of the high priest, who then said: "In celebration of the sacred rites prescribed for a Vestal on behalf of the Roman people and Quirites, I take thee, Beloved, as a candidate chosen in keeping with the purest of laws, as Vestal priestess."[14] Throughout the service the Vestal wore the *flammeum,* or red headdress, and the *sex crines,* or six braids, of the bride.[15] After this ceremony the pontifex maximus and pontifical college enjoyed the same power over the girl as a pater-familias and family council. If she allowed the fire of Vesta to go out, the pontifex maximus could order her to be subjected to severe corporal punishment. And if she appeared to violate her vow of chastity (a crime known as "incest"), she could be buried alive.[16]

Despite these feminine aspects of the Vestals' role, and despite certain rather domestic responsibilities (such as the cleaning of the temple of Vesta from March 7 to 15), the Vestals did encroach on men's territory. Servius, a commentator on Virgil, reports that "from May 7 to 14 the three great Vestal virgins place *far* in the harvest workers' baskets. The virgins themselves roast, pound, and grind the spelt and store the resulting flour, out of which, three times a year, they make the *mola,* for the Lupercalia [February 15], Vestalia [June 9], and Ides of September [September 13], by adding cooked and raw salt."[17] The resulting *mola salsa* was sprinkled on every animal destined for public sacrifice (and on all other offerings to the gods). It is from this preliminary rite that we get the word "immolate," which literally means to sprinkle with *mola.* This sprinkling with flour served as a reminder of the land from which all offerings to the gods ultimately sprang, as well as of the human labor and Roman knowledge needed to make the land bear fruit.[18]

Thus the Vestals had an indirect hand in every great public sacrifice. According to some sources, they may also have played a more direct role, even making blood sacrifices of their own.

Cazanove[19] notes that the Vestals were given a kind of sacrificial knife, the *sescepita*.[20] Thus they had the power to sacrifice, although there is no proof that this power was to be used on animal offerings. Some texts, however, seem to imply that Vestals did participate by word and deed in common sacrificial rites. In the Fordicidia (April 15), a festival during which a pregnant cow was sacrificed to Tellus (Earth), pregnancy being a symbol for the desired growth of grain,[21] the Vestals took part in the complex butchering ritual: "After the officiants removed the calves from [the cow's] entrails and placed the butchered pluck [*exta*] in smoking vessels, the eldest of the Vestal virgins burned the calves, the ashes from which were used to purify the people on the day of Pales [April 21]."[22] To be sure, the Vestal did not participate in the sacrifice proper, but she did take part in the subsequent butchery. A better example perhaps is the sacrifice offered to the god Consus by the Vestals and the flamen of Quirinus on August 21, the festival celebrating the storage of the harvest: "Sacrifices were made [in honor of Consus] . . . on the twelfth day before the calends of September by the flamen of Quirinus and the Vestals."[23] Finally, if Georges Dumézil is correct,[24] on August 25 the Vestals took part in the pontiffs' sacrifice in honor of Ops Consiua (Abundance) at the Regia (the pontiffs' official residence). Final confirmation comes from a text of Prudentius, who mentions that the Vestals "immolated lustral victims underground . . . allowing their blood to flow into the flame."[25]

These sources are of course open to question. In the Fordicidia, for example, the Vestals took part only in the final phase of the sacrifice, burning just that part of the victim that the sacrificer passed on to them. In the other two examples it is possible that the Vestals played only a passive role, while the flamen of Quirinus or the pontifex maximus took the active part. Finally, a passing mention in a polemical text by Prudentius probably does not carry much weight. Still, the Vestals' right to the sacrificial knife and their role in the festival of Bona Dea suggest that they did indeed possess the power to sacrifice, and we have seen that they were also permitted to pound grain. Vestals therefore were exempt from the traditional taboo.

On the other hand, Vestals were neither matrons nor maidens, as Beard (1980) has shown. They were not matrons because they had neither husbands nor children. And they were not maidens, because they wore the long robe *(stola)* and hairbands *(vittae)* of the married woman. Vestals participated in certain rites along with matrons. They enjoyed, at least until the inception of the Empire, some of the same legal privileges as men, privileges not extended to matrons or maidens: they had the benefit of a lictor, could testify in court, and were not wards of a father or a husband, which meant that they could freely dispose of their property and make wills.[26] In other words, the sexual status of the Vestal was ambiguous, in-between, just as the fire she tended was of indeterminate nature.[27] Because of this special status Vestals were allowed to wield some of the religious powers traditionally reserved for men.

The Flaminica *and the* Regina Sacrorum

The Vestals were not the only exception. Some priests had wives who made sacrifices, particularly to the deities of time.[28] The fragmentary sources give information only about the wives of the *flamen* of Jupiter and the *rex sacrorum,* but it is reasonable to assume that the wives of other priests had similar responsibilities. The priest of Jupiter was required to sacrifice only once a month, on the ides (the thirteenth or the fifteenth day, depending on the month), but his wife, the *flaminica Dialis,* sacrificed a ram on every market day *(nundinae).*[29] The *regina sacrorum* offered Juno a sow or female lamb on the first of every month.[30] Like the Vestals, the *flaminica Dialis* was permitted to keep a sacrificial knife.[31]

Were these cases really exceptions to the rule? As in the case of the Vestals, the "male" powers of these priestesses may have been a consequence of their special status. Unlike *pontifices, augures,* and other priests, the *flamines* of Jupiter and the *rex sacrorum* were priests in their capacity as masters of households with full family lives. They were required to be married; indeed, their offices were not for individuals but for couples. The flamen of Jupiter had to resign if his wife died. Plutarch points out that there were many ceremonies this priest could not perform without his wife's assistance. The priestly couple was a unit and invested as such with the sacerdotal function, and it may be that the sacrificial powers of the *flaminica* derived from that fact. Perhaps the *regina sacrorum* was in a similar position. Bear in mind that the master of a household could delegate powers to his wife.[32]

Other Sacerdotal Women

There were many other special cases, such as the Salian virgins (*saliae virgines*), female counterparts of the Salii, who officiated in processions marking the opening and closing of the military campaign season. We know virtually nothing about these women, other than that they wore the *apex* (pointed hat) and martial garb of the Salii and offered a sacrifice in the Regia.[33] Although this seems to have been an ancient institution, it cannot be shown that the virgins actually performed sacrifices. Owing to the absence of sources, it is almost impossible to reconstruct the initiatory rites to which Roman girls were subjected.[34] At a later date Empress Livia served in the capacity of flaminica of the divine Augustus, a role that, unless we assume that her priesthood was totally passive, would have required her to perform sacrifices. But the position of the empress was ambiguous, between male and female, between mortal widow and divinized human being. As Augusta she enjoyed public privileges, hence her case cannot be taken as representative. Priestesses of naturalized foreign deities were in a similar ambiguous position. The cult of Ceres, for example, with a temple on the Aventine, was entrusted to a priestess from Greater Greece. Later, priestesses were allowed or tolerated in other naturalized cults, such as those of Magna Mater (Cybele) and Isis.

In these cases, however, it was the "foreign" status of the priestess that gained her exemption from the rule. Furthermore, these foreign customs were often contrasted with ancient "local" customs. Women assumed responsibility for rites that local law prohibited men from celebrating (Dionysius of Halicarnassus 2.22.1).

Matronal Liturgies

The most common instances of women in autonomous sacerdotal and even sacrificial roles involve rites both old and new celebrated by matrons. During certain traditional festivals matrons offered "nonblood sacrifices." In the Nonae Caprotinae (July 7), which celebrated fertility in women, free women and servants made Juno an offering of the sap of a wild fig tree.[35] In the Matronalia (March 1) matrons offered flowers to Juno on the anniversary of the dedication of her temple on the Esquiline. On the same day men prayed for their wives' health and gave them gifts and pocket money, money used both for the celebration of the rites and to pay for a banquet that the matrons prepared with their own hands for the family's male slaves. Ancient explanations of this festival, for the most part obscure, refer to birth, especially that of Romulus, and to the fertility of women.[36] In any case, the fact that women themselves paid for all the costs of the liturgy, admittedly with coins received from the paterfamilias, suggests that they bore the entire responsibility. Yet these ancient rites did not explicitly contradict the rule prohibiting women from taking part in the butchering of sacrificial victims. Indeed, it appears that no animals were sacrificed, and the rites concerned the city as a whole, not just the family. Finally, it must be admitted that we know next to nothing about these liturgies. All we have is two or three lines from a few grammarians and antiquarians, so we cannot determine exactly what these matrons did or how they did it.

The Matralia

Another ancient liturgy, the Matralia (June 11), exemplifies the close association of matronal and feminine rites with Roman mythology. In the Matralia well-born matrons *(bonae matres)* in their first marriage *(univirae)* went to the temple of Mater Matuta on the Forum Boarium. Violating the usual rule, they brought a slave into the temple, then angrily drove that slave out. Next, the matrons took their sisters' children in their arms and called on the goddess to bless them. Using comparative methods, Georges Dumézil was able to show that this ritual sequence, which contemporaries of Augustus no longer understood, was the vestige of a myth of Aurora (called Mater Matuta in Rome) transcribed into ritual.[37] The matrons, representing Aurora, drive away the evil, formless shadows of the night, represented by the slave (the opposite of the well-born matron). They then bring the Sun, child of Dawn's (Aurora's) sister Night, into the world liberated from darkness. Dumézil's reconstruction of the meaning of this ritual does not take account of all of Mater Matuta's qualities, in particular her attributes as midwife and nurse, derivatives of her primary function.[38] Nor does it take account of the complex relation between the goddess of the Forum Boarium and similar goddesses in nearby cities, as well as Fortuna. For our purposes the interesting point, apart from the mythological character of the liturgy, is the absence of any allusion to a sacrifice, or at any rate to one celebrated by the matrons. Dumézil compared this ritual transcription of a mythological theme to the Nonae Caprotinae, which may represent a lost myth of Juno.[39] He also pointed out the connection between this ceremony and his interpretation of the statue of Angerona, about which virtually nothing else is known.[40]

Admittedly the evidence is skimpy. But perhaps it is worth entertaining the hypothesis that women could be allowed to celebrate important public rituals when they were directly involved as women and when, as mothers, they could symbolize the honored deity. In this instance their presence was apparently necessary because their fertility was central to the ritual. The sources do not indicate whether men attended, or were even allowed to attend, these liturgies.

Festivals of Venus Verticordia and Fortuna Virilis

There is another ritual over which much ink has been spilled: the festival of Venus Verticordia and Fortuna Virilis.[41] On April 1, according to the epigraphic calendar of Prenesta, "women [*mulieres*] in great numbers, including many of modest station, beseeched Fortuna Virilis in the (men's) baths, because it was there that men bared that part of their anatomy with which they desired the favors of women."[42] Ovid added the name of a second deity, Venus Verticordia, as well as a more detailed account of the sequence of rituals in which all women, courtesans as well as matrons, participated.[43] The first rite, and no doubt the principal one in the first century, was a *lavatio*, a bath the women administered to the cult statue of Venus Verticordia, the Venus who was supposed to turn hearts toward chastity and the faithful discharge of matrimonial duties. Later the statue was decked out with jewels and flowers. Then the women, wearing wreaths of myrtle, plunged into the hot baths. While they bathed, they burned incense to Fortuna Virilis and then drank *cocetum*, a beverage composed of milk, honey, and poppies and traditionally served to new brides as a sedative. Clearly this liturgy was organized around the rites that preceded the consummation of a marriage. The matrons first bathed the statue of Venus and then themselves, as if preparing for the act of love. The myrtle and *cocetum* were also symbols of preparation for lovemaking. Ovid points out that Venus also drank *cocetum* before going to join her husband.[44]

Venus Verticordia's magic made sexual unions possible, but guided them toward marriage. In this task she was assisted by Fortuna Virilis, who ensured that women, even those with imperfect bodies, would arouse their men.[45] So far as we can tell, the festival of the first day of the month of Venus (April) consisted of an invocation to Venus Verticordia and Fortuna Virilis by women of all ranks and conditions. Imitating certain prenuptial acts, they asked the two goddesses to crown their sexual unions with success. It is not surprising that these rites were probably celebrated in the valley of the Great Circus, which was traditionally associated with the rape of the Sabines and therefore to the *aition* (origin) of Roman marriage. It may be that the ritual bath took place earlier in a public bathhouse some distance from the temple of Venus Verticordia, a bathhouse first built in 114 B.C. on a site that had been marked by a statue since the end of the third century.[46] When this bathhouse was destroyed at around the time of the Empire's inception, the bathing ritual may have moved elsewhere. Scholars disagree about the age of this rite. Some say it was archaic, and originally honored Fortuna Virilis, but after being Hellenized came to include Venus Verticordia (Aphrodite Apostrophia). Others argue that the whole liturgy was of more recent origin.[47] Given the scanty sources available, it is difficult to resolve the controversy, but it seems plausible to assume that the core of the festival had existed for a long time and that complexity was added over time. Since we are interested in rituals of the historic period, the issue is relatively unimportant for our purposes. The crucial point is that women of all ranks bore responsibility for a public festival, but again one that concerned them directly and involved no blood sacrifice.

Fortuna Muliebris

In a number of other religious services, however, matrons did indeed perform sacrifices. The first of these services is obscure, and our knowledge of the rite comes exclusively from an etiological legend. On July 6 matrons went to the fourth milestone of the Via Latina, close to the archaic (and idealized) boundary of Roman territory, where they made a sacrifice to Fortuna Muliebris. According to legend, the priestess of this cult was a woman legitimately married to her first husband (*univira*), that is, neither a virgin nor a remarried woman nor even an unremarried widow.[48] We know nothing else about either the priestess or the rites that took place in the temple of Fortuna Muliebris. Legends concerning the cult's foundation allow us just a glimpse of how the ancients interpreted this festival.[49] As the antiquarians tell it, the foundation of the sanctuary took place during the war against Coriolanus. When their men became impotent, women, led by Coriolanus' mother and wife, marched in procession to his camp at the fourth milestone of the Via Latina and persuaded him to lift his siege. To commemorate this event—when the republic was saved not by men in arms but by women in robes—the Roman authorities agreed to grant women any privilege they wished. The women of the city asked that a temple to Fortuna Muliebris be built on the site and that they be allowed to perform an annual sacrifice there.[50] The matrons also decided to offer the temple a second statue in honor of Fortuna Muliebris, which they dedicated on the same day as the statue provided by the republic.

Accounts of this legendary event, though often quite rich in detail, have given rise to innumerable exegeses, many of which are not only dubious and unverifiable but miss the essential point.[51] There is no question that the cult of the goddess was a cult of matrons. If the legends are to be believed (and I, for one, refuse to confuse legend with historical fact), the central element of the cult of Fortuna Muliebris was the opposition between the women's robes (*stola*) and men's arms. On this occasion matrons acted like men at war, and so too they acted like men in the commemorative cult. This is the fundamental conclusion to be drawn from the various traditions, apart from other interpretations of the *aition* based chiefly on the study of relations that may exist between the two women who are the principal actors in the tale and the two statues in the temple.[52]

What struck the ancient mythographers more than anything else was the active role that matrons played in the temple of Fortuna Muliebris: they performed sacrifices, and the priestess of the temple was herself a matron. The etiological legend calls attention to what was unusual about the cult: matrons were actually the founders of the temple and dedicated one of the cult images, whereas normally only a superior magistrate or special representative of the Roman people could found a cult or make a dedication. The matrons were said to have encountered resistance, and

Fortuna intervened directly to establish the legitimacy of their initiative—further signs of how unusual it was for women to be granted such privileges.[53] The extraordinary nature of this cult therefore does not contradict the general rule stated above. If a legitimately married adult woman and mother was considered the equal of the adult male citizen of arms-bearing age and even of a magistrate, it was only by virtue of a privilege accorded by the Senate and duly justified by an unprecedented exploit. That privilege, moreover, lasted only one day and was limited to a place on the fringes of the old Roman territory. It was in no sense a general rule.

Pudicitia

Even less is known about the cult of Pudicitia (matronal chastity), so little in fact that some scholars doubt its existence. Here too matrons functioned as a group with the power to make decisions and award or deny rights. According to tradition, a patrician woman who had married a plebeian man (and therefore lost status) was expelled from the cult of Pudicitia. This took place early in the third century B.C., at a time when patricians and plebeians were fighting over public priesthoods. In protest, the expelled woman founded a new cult dedicated to Pudicitia Plebeia and limited to plebeian women. According to Livy (10.23.3–10), the rules of the cult allowed matrons who were chaste and *univirae* (faithful to their first husbands) to make sacrifices *(ius sacrificandi)*. Ostensibly, then, matrons, whether patrician or plebeian, were able to establish cults, determine their rules, and, so the sources state explicitly, perform sacrifices. True, the sources for this information are legends, and the rite may have been affected by Hellenistic influences. Nevertheless, this cult, which was located on the Forum Boarium (hence not in the center of Rome though presumably within the *pomerium*), permitted matrons to perform sacrifices. Yet these sacrifices (which were not explicitly said to be blood sacrifices, by the way) were celebrated behind closed doors on one day of the year only and with no males in attendance. Hence no general rule can be deduced from it. Nor can much be made of brief indications that matrons also sacrificed to Rumina[54] and Carmenta.[55]

Bona Dea

All the distinctive features of the matronal cults attested by tradition are present in the festival of Bona Dea, which is notorious for the political scandal that erupted around it in 62 B.C. The origin and history of the cult of Bona Dea are ambiguous. Some scholars argue that Bona Dea was a Damia of Greater Greece that was imported into Rome and honored with a Greek-type cult.[56] Others (such as Piccaluga, 1982) say that it was an archaic Roman cult and that only the etiological myths were of Greek derivation. In any case, by the beginning of the Christian era, Bona Dea, considered the goddess of women (*he theos gynaikeia*,[57] *feminarum dea*[58]) was honored with a fairly unusual cult. There were two services. On May 1 a sacrifice was offered to the goddess in her temple, built on rocky ground at the foot of the Aventine.[59] Virtually nothing is known about the temple or the service, except that neither myrtle nor men nor wine (under its own name) were allowed in. An etiological tale also seems to imply that an elderly woman presided while young women took part in certain games.[60] Other sources say that in the temple there were serpents "who neither felt nor inspired fear" (*nec terrentes nec timentes),* and elsewhere serpents are associated with representations of Bona Dea.[61] More is known about the second service, which was held on the night of December 3 behind closed doors in the residence of a magistrate *cum imperio,* that is, invested with superior powers of civilian and military command, such as consuls and praetors. Matrons of high rank, aided by their female slaves and together with the Vestals, officiated in this ceremony. In 62, when Clodius sparked a scandal, the service was held in the home of Caesar, at that time praetor. Aurelia, Caesar's mother, presided, assisted by Caesar's wife Pompeia (who would be compromised in the affair) and her sister Julia.[62]

According to Plutarch's account of the affair and its political and legal consequences, the cult was headed by the eldest matron in the house where the service was conducted. But in 62 the ceremony was disrupted by Clodius, disguised as a woman, and had to be recelebrated by the Vestals, which suggests that, if they did not actually control the rite, they nevertheless wielded a power in sacred matters analogous to that of the pontiffs. Later we shall see that when matrons celebrated a public cult, the Vestals appear to have served as guarantors and repositories of their sacred right much as male priests did for magistrates. In any case the matrons in the cult of Bona Dea wore purple headbands.[63] They roasted a sow on the sacrificial hearth, and the animal's stomach (*abdomen*—we would like to know further details) went to the goddess,[64] in whose honor a libation was poured.[65] Dancing and singing were part of the ceremony.[66] Men were not admitted to these nocturnal sacrifices (although there is no evidence that would permit us to call them "mysteries").[67] In fact, no male was even allowed in the house where the service was conducted. To Plutarch, this rule, as well as the exclusion of myrtle, the plant of Venus, symbolized sexual abstinence.[68]

At first sight it appears that this sacrifice and libation were celebrated by matrons and Vestals "for the people" *(pro populo)*.[69] Since men were forbidden to take part, the butchering of the sacrificial animal and the pouring of the libation had to have been done by women. We may assume that the sacrifice and libation were followed by a sacrificial banquet, during which the matrons partook of the meat and wine that fell to them as sacrificial celebrants. Juvenal's remark about the Vestal Saufeia's penchant for wine suggests that matrons were reputed to help themselves generously to a beverage they were normally forbidden to drink.[70]

All the ancient sources agree that this was an unusual service and stress the presence of wine, which was all the more striking in that the rules of the temple of Bona Dea prohibited bringing in wine. Like women themselves, Bona Dea's temple was not supposed to come into contact with undiluted wine. Wine could be used in the temple only if referred to as "milk" and placed in a vessel called a "honey pot."[71] The purpose of such subterfuges apparently was to make undiluted wine appear to be diluted or "domesticated" wine such as the *passum* made from dried grapes that were placed in a basket and beaten with tree limbs, then stored in a "pot like honey."[72] It is plausible to assume that the same rules applied to the December service.

According to the founding myth of the cult of Bona Dea, the goddess herself was ambiguous. Bona Dea was supposedly the divine name of Fauna, wife of the archaic Faunus. In one version of the story, Fauna is beaten with myrtle branches and tortured for drinking undiluted wine in secret.[73] In another version she refuses, even though drunk and battered, to give in to the incestuous advances of her father, Faunus, who has his way with her only after assuming the form of a serpent.[74] In short, all the sources portray the cult of Bona Dea as an upside-down world in which women assume masculine roles.[75]

But this world was not only upside-down. It was also, like the Roman view of feminine chastity, deeply ambiguous. The seemingly contradictory attitudes of Bona Dea and her matrons toward wine, sex, and men are in some ways reminiscent of the ambiguous status of the Vestals.[76] The matrons both accept and reject undiluted wine and sex, signifying an ambivalence of masculine and feminine, active and passive. Thus the cult of Bona Dea ritually enacted a theory of matronal status. The role of women in the cult was portrayed in both ritual and exegesis as an exception. Women did what they did in secret, at night, in a private residence, and in disguise. It would be interesting to know how they went about butchering the sacrificial animal. Their behavior was the exact opposite of the behavior of men in other sacrificial ceremonies, who performed their services in public, during the civic day, in the presence of all, and in the open, without disguises of any kind. Note that the mythographers placed the origin of Bona Dea and her cult among the Fauna, legendary inhabitants of the woods surrounding what would become the city of Rome.

Supplications

The temporal, spatial, and structural estrangement of the cult of Bona Dea from Rome, from the urban center and its measured, civilized conduct, reminds us that almost all the ceremonies in which matrons and nubile girls participated were of foreign origin. This was true, in particular, of the supplications (prayers of congratulation or request, possibly accompanied by offerings) that became so common around the end of the third century B.C. Supervised by the (quin)decemvirs, these belonged to what the Romans called the Greek Rite (ritus Graecus). The great processions of the Greek Rite, such as that of 207 B.C., during which nubile girls sang a carmen (cantata), also took place outside the pomerium, or urban center. One route went from the temple of Apollo, between the Tiber and the southwest corner of the Capitol, and the temple of Juno Regina on the Aventine.[77]

We possess unusually detailed and exceptionally interesting information about one of these supplications: the triple supplication associated with the great liturgy of the Secular Games, which is described in epigraphic chronicles for A.D. 204.[78] Since this is virtually the only document describing a cult celebrated by matrons, it is worth quoting in its entirety. (The lacunae in the text are due to chips in the marble plaque.)

IV,4: [June 2, night] [gap in text] their *sellisternes*.

IV,9-Va,30: [June 2, day, after a sacrifice to Jupiter and a sacrificial banquet on the Capitoline Hill] Septimius Severus and Antoninus Augustus [the emperor and his son Caracalla], along with Geta Caesar [the emperor's second son] and accompanied by the prefect of the praetorium [Plautian] and all the other quindecemvirs [priests in charge of ceremonies associated with the Games], went to the *cella* of Juno Regina [one of the three naves of the temple of Jupiter Capitoline]. There [Emperor Septimius] Severus Augustus, flanked by the Vestal Virgins Numisia Maximilla and Terentia Flavola, imparted to Julia Augusta, mother of the camps and wife of the emperor, and to the hundred and nine matrons who had been convoked, the following formula: Juno Regina, if something can be of still greater benefit to the Roman people of the Quirites, allow us to supplicate and implore you to [gap in text] the hundred and ten mothers of families of the Roman people of the Quirites, all married, and [permit us] to ask you urgently to increase the power and sovereignty of the Roman people of the Quirites both without and within, and may the Latin remain forever subject [gap in text] may you grant eternal integrity, victory, and vigor to the Roman people of the Quirites, may you support the Roman people of the Quirites and its legions, may you keep the republic of the Roman people of the Quirites safe and sound, may you increase it further, and may you show yourself propitious and benevolent toward the Roman people of the Quirites, the quindecemvirs, ourselves, our homes, and our families. For this we supplicate, invoke, and implore you, we, the mothers of the families of the Roman people of the Quirites, all married, on our knees [gap in text]. This supplication was made by the following matrons [the names of those participating were listed, all of senatorial or equestrian rank]. Afterward they celebrated a *sellisterne* [sacrificial banquet for the statue of a "seated" goddess] for Juno [gap in text]. Another *sellis-*

terne was celebrated following the same rite and by the same matrons for Juno.

Va,52: [June 3, night] Julia Augusta, mother of the camps, and a hundred and nine matrons celebrated the *sellisternes* for Juno and Diana.

Va,83–90: [June 3] On the same day Julia Augusta, mother of the camps, and a hundred and nine matrons celebrated their [*sua*] *sellisternes* as on the two previous days; they immolated young sows [and] consumed the sacrificial banquet [gap in text] and performed dances.

In three religious services matrons, led by the most eminent of their number, Julia Domna, the empress, celebrated rites that are called their own *(sua)*, for which they enjoyed full responsibility. They sacrificed sows, at least on the third day. If we assume that the description of the sacrifice on June 3 gives the full context of the *sellisterne,* we can even conclude that the matrons performed sacrifices on all three days. This time the sacrifice was performed publicly, in the heart of the city, near the Capitoline Hill. The rites the women celebrated, including even the prayer they uttered, were in some ways a counterpart to those celebrated by the emperor, his sons, and the quindecemvirs on the Capitoline Hill. But once again this was not an "autochthonous" ritual, because the Secular Games were part of the Greek Rite, which differed from the Roman Rite *(ritus Romanus)* in various subtle ways. Hence it can be argued that sacrifice by women was permissible in this context because the rituals in question were governed by non-Roman rules. But does this argument hold up? The rituals of the Secular Games were borrowed in part from the cities of Greater Greece. While it is true that women in those cities could perform priestly functions, it is not clear that they always had the right to perform sacrifices.

However that may be, matrons, even in this "foreign" context, had a particular role to play. Their supplications and *sellisternes* followed the principal rituals of the Games celebrated by men. The matronal services came second and closed the ritual sequence, which in Roman eyes made them secondary. Furthermore, the autonomy of the matrons was limited, as is clear from both text and images. A bronze coin commemorating the Secular Games of 88 shows matrons on their knees facing the nave of Juno Regina.[79]

They are raising their hands and reciting the prayer of supplication whose text is preserved in the chronicle of 204. But Emperor Domitian stands before them dictating the text, just as in the 204 inscription Septimius Severus recites the prayer first *(praeire verba)*. This was always the role of the person responsible for ensuring that the proper words were spoken in prayer (for example, the pontiffs assisting a magistrate). Thus supreme religious authority lay ultimately in the hands of Septimius Severus and Domitian, who were supreme pontiffs as well as emperors. The question then arises whether the sacrifice performed by the matrons was not also supervised by a man.

The account of the Secular Games of 204 raises other questions. The enumeration of the matrons' actions recalls other matronal rituals, not just the supplications so common in Roman religious life from the third century B.C. on, but the rituals associated with the temple of Fortuna Muliebris or the festival of Bona Dea. Note the composition of the group of matrons. The hundred and ten matrons of 204, wives of senators and equestrians, are the equivalent of the *bonae matres* of the Matralia[80] and the *matrones honestissimae* (most honorable matrons) of the festival of Bona Dea.[81] And just as the matrons allowed to take part in the cult of Pudicitia or the Matralia were required to be *univira,* the matrons of 204 twice indicate in their prayer that they are *nuptae,* that is, neither widowed nor divorced. (Though admittedly being a "married *materfamilias*" was not the same thing as being *univira,* the emphatic repetition makes the point.) Furthermore, the supplication ceremony, like the festival of Bona Dea, was presided over by the oldest matron in the most powerful household, and in 204 that was obviously the imperial household. As in the rites of Bona Dea, moreover, the matrons were assisted by Vestals, who played a special role. When Septimius Severus dictated the words of the supplication to Julia Domna and the hundred and nine matrons, he was flanked by two Vestals, who were thus closer to the magistrate than the matrons and assisted him in his duties, much as pontiffs, augurs, and quindecemvirs assisted him in other rituals. We are also told that the matrons "performed dances" (*[antr]uau[erunt]*: only three letters of the original word remain), which reminds us of the singing and dancing mentioned in connection with women's festivals in other sources. Finally, just as in the festival of Bona Dea, the matrons sacrifice sows, which are young, possibly in the image of the new century that is the object of the celebration.

On the Fringes of Religious Life

The customs examined thus far show that women were either excluded from public and private religious life or confined to its "alien" and fringe aspects. Women participated in the ceremonies of imported cults, those governed (in Roman eyes at any rate) by the Greek Rite. When they exercised religious responsibilities, they did so at night or behind closed doors or in suburban or frontier temples, in some cases by special dispensation. In some cults, such as that of Fortuna, they mingled with slaves and others from the fringes of Roman society.[82]

The more marginal a woman was, the less she was subject to the authority of a paterfamilias or husband, the more religious responsibility she exercised.[83] Under the so-called Numaic Code, for example, a widow who remarried prematurely was supposed to immolate a pregnant cow,[84] and a courtesan (or *paelex*, whose partner was not her husband) who touched the altar of Juno was supposed to sacrifice a she-lamb.[85] We do not know the status of the "elderly woman" *(anus)* who officiated at the annual festival of Liber, but she was probably a widow of the lower classes.

Women and Superstition

These cases were direct extensions of the kinds of rituals already described. Women also participated in various forms of deviant religious behavior. Woman's affinity for superstition is a commonplace of Roman literature. Worshipers of Isis and other such deities are a central element of Juvenal's famous satires,[86] and allusions to "old ladies' superstitions" *(anilis superstitio)* were proverbial.[87] The number of sorceresses and female magicians was legion.[88] The celebrated affair of the Bacchanalia is a good example of women's participation in religious deviance, and the only one about which we possess detailed information. It was a complex business, and J. M. Pailler's skillful reconstruction of the event from the extant sources was more complex still. Although the whole of Italy was involved, I shall concentrate on events in Rome and the interpretations formulated by the authorities and passed on through tradition.

The Bacchanalia

In 186 B.C., scandal erupted in a Rome already shaken by the consequences of the Punic Wars and Roman expansion. The affair, which drew considerable attention and led to severe repression, affected men most directly, but women played central roles, at least in Rome. The incriminatory rites of Bacchus involved a perversion of two female cults: the Campanian rites of Ceres and the old cult of Stimula. Along with other matronal cults (such as those of Bona Dea, Venus Verticordia, and Ceres), these cults flourished on the Aventine, a section of Rome with a rather dubious reputation; they were consequently the subject of many rumors.[89] They were concentrated on the northwest slope of the Aventine, at the foot of which lay the Tiber and the Forum Boarium. Annia Pacula, a woman born in Campania, had reformed the matronal cult, and, according to Livy (39.8 ff.), another matron, Duronia, was instrumental in causing the scandal. What was the nature of Annia Pacula's reform? Essentially it was to initiate men—very young men—into this woman's cult. She began by initiating her two sons, who later became high priests of the cult. Duronia tried to initiate her son Aebutius. What most concerned the Roman authorities about the Bacchanalia, however, was not the cult's secret, nocturnal, orgiastic character, nor was it the presence of both men and women. It was not even the political difficulties associated with the newfound prominence of women, youths, allies, and other formerly marginal actors on the Roman political scene. For the authorities, the most alarming aspect of this gathering of marginals, which immediately led to charges of conspiracy, was the fact that very young men were initiated by their mothers (whether natural or ritual). In short, women were taking the place of both the father and the city.[90]

According to Pailler, this Bacchic initiation threatened to supplant the civic initiation of young Roman citizens. The Bacchanalia allegedly substituted "largely homosexual orgies and counterfeits of warrior initiation rituals for the traditional rites marking the *juvenes'* accession to their two distinguishing capacities: that of engendering a posterity for family and city, and that of defending family and city by arms."[91] Combine this subversive intent with such common crimes as misappropriation of wills and it becomes clear how the Bacchanalia might have appeared to be an attack on traditional Roman values. Women were at the center of the "conspiracy." Significantly, particular attention was devoted to the punishment of women when the conspiracy was finally suppressed. Whereas the men involved were punished publicly, the women were turned over to their parents or other guardians. Only if no one met the necessary conditions for administering private punishment was the penalty inflicted on women publicly.[92] By thus reverting to the strictest possible tradition, emphasizing women's public incapacity in all areas, the authorities clearly meant to reaffirm the patriarchal order and restore women to their normal place.[93]

The (real or alleged) role of women in the scandal of 186 and the reaffirmation of the authority of fathers, husbands, and guardians point to a larger problem that Rome had had to face since the end of the third century: matrons. Because the Punic Wars had lasted so long and cost so many lives in all strata of society, matrons had continued to play a public role. They not only took part in the great rituals of propitiation but often seemed to encroach on areas reserved for men. One of the best-known incidents other than the Bacchanalia was a demonstration that took place in 195 B.C., when matrons marched on the center of Rome to demand that the magistrates abolish a law first promulgated in 216, the Oppia Law, which prohibited wearing certain expensive items.[94] Roman conservatives looked upon this and other women's demonstrations as an attack on the male monopoly of public life and proof of a challenge to their domestic authority. As they would do again later, in 186, in 195 the authorities recommended that these feminine excesses be dealt with, and if necessary punished, at home.[95]

Conflicts between men and women, the most notorious of which involved the most prominent families, were often associated with deviant religious behavior. Occasionally fear of women erupted in panic. Matrons were regularly accused of poisoning their husbands. Several allegations of widespread poisoning are mentioned in the sources, one in 331,[96] another between 184 and 180,[97] and still another in 153 B.C.[98] These charges usually stemmed from epidemics, but many Romans agreed with Cato the Elder that every adulterous wife was a potential murderess.[99]

Poisoning was subject to criminal prosecution, but the crime itself, like the crimes attributed to the bacchants, was blamed on deviant religious practices. The Romans looked upon matronal magic as the antithesis of lawful religion. Magic was not subject to anyone's control, least of all to men's. Its practice was opposed point by point to traditional rituals. Women had a natural affinity for this kind of mischief because of their association with Venus and her charms as well as with medicinal herbs.[100] Macrobius reports that the sanctuary of Bona Dea contained an *herbarius*, a plant collection, that the priestesses used to manufacture medications.[101] Some ancient exegetes cite this same plant collection as a reason for identifying Bona Dea with Medea the Magician.[102]

Clearly women were excluded from public religion and largely confined to certain specific rites as well as to various forms of heterodoxy. This religious marginalization of women was justified by the widely held opinion that women were incapable of practicing any religion in a rational and reasonable manner. Hence it is difficult to speak of female or matronal cults because in the end these cults were invariably said to be exceptional and strictly limited or else denounced as intolerable excesses. Religion—the one true religion—was essentially a man's affair.

Disqualified but Indispensable

Women were not summarily excluded from religious life. Their exclusion, their marginality, was justified by a certain representation shared by women themselves. Thanks to that representation, women did indeed participate in religion, but in a very specific way. They were no more excluded from religion than goddesses were excluded from the pantheon. Their role, though subordinate, was indispensable.

The Vestal Virgins and the Sibylline Books

The very destiny of Rome was intimately bound up with the Vestals and the sacred fire of Vesta. No public sacrifice could be celebrated without their indirect but indispensable assistance, because they made the necessary *mola salsa*. If for any reason the fire of Vesta went out, the public life of Rome ground to a halt; without a fire in the city's sacred hearth, Rome had no identity.

Now we can understand Horace's comforting belief that his glory, and Rome's, would endure "as long as the pontiff and the silent Vestal climb to the Capitol."[103]

Like the Vestals and their rites, the prophecies of the Sibyl were indispensable to the functioning of Rome, since they enabled the magistrates and the Senate to resolve crises and restore peace with the gods. A native of Cumae (and thus, as is only to be expected, a "foreigner"), the Sibyl was so important that her words became one of Rome's talismans. As late as the fifth century A.D. the poet Rutilius Namatianus complained of Stilicho's destruction of the Sibylline Books, which he called "prophetic tokens of an eternal empire" *(aeterni fatalia pignora regni).*[104]

These two examples (the Vestals and the Sibyl) suggest the paradoxical nature of woman's place in religion. Though subject to men and confined to marginal roles, women performed tasks essential to the survival of Rome. Their indispensable reproductive function was of course celebrated in a number of rituals and cults, but they were also honored as an essential component of society. Celebrating a sacrifice at the Capitol might seem more "religious" and more important than preparing *mola salsa* in the Vestals' residence, but without such preparation no sacrifice was possible, just as religious life could not proceed if the sacred fire went out. Thus the Vestals' humble activities established communication between men and the gods. Similarly, the wisdom of Apollo, so essential to the government of Rome, was dispensed through the mouth of a woman. One can object that the Vestals were not exactly women and that the Sibyl was not really Roman. But certain phenomena that the Romans themselves classed as native prove that these facts are irrelevant.

The "Completeness" of the Flamen of Jupiter

The flamen and flaminica of Jupiter were supposedly an ideal couple. Antiquarians tell us that for good luck brides wore a veil the color of fire. The flaminica, who was not allowed to divorce, wore her veil continuously.[105] No other man was permitted to sleep in the marriage bed of the flamen and flaminica, and the flamen was not allowed to sleep elsewhere more than three consecutive nights.[106] The flaminica was required to be *univira.*[107] She knitted the *laena,* the ritual garment worn by her husband and symbol of their marriage. Flamens were married in the most formal rite, the *confarreatio*. This marriage was probably part of the investiture of the flamen; a couple was chosen for the post, not an individual.[108] The flamen of Jupiter could not be separated from his wife and could not discharge his duties without her. If the flaminica died, the flamen was required to quit his post. Plutarch pondered the significance of these requirements: "Is it because a man who has married and then lost his wife is unhappier than one who has had none at all? The married man's household is complete. That of a man who, after marrying a woman, loses her, is not only incomplete, it is mutilated. Or is it because the wife participates in her husband's sacred ministry (since there are many ceremonies that he cannot perform without her assistance)? For him to marry a second wife immediately after losing the first is perhaps impossible and in any case inappropriate."[109] After discussing the sinister Domitian's willingness to authorize the divorce of a flamen of Jupiter, Plutarch concludes: "This procedure may seem less astonishing given the rule that if one of the two censors died, the other was required to resign his post."

This commentary makes several points. Rapid remarriage was incompatible with the image of the model couple. The flaminica performed numerous ritual functions with her husband. Far more interesting is the characterization of the married man's household as "complete" *(oikos teleios)* and of the widower's household as "not only incomplete, it is mutilated" *(ateles . . . kai peperomenos)*. Notice first of all that Plutarch speaks of the husband's household. It is the man who gives the orders, who is master of the household. The possibility of the husband's death is not even mentioned, because the consequences in that case were obvious. What required explanation was why the flamen's household should be considered incomplete without the flaminica. Without a wife the master of the household was incapable of discharging his important duties: it was the flamen and flaminica together who symbolized the powers of Jupiter and not either of them separately, not even the man.[110] Equally important is the parallel with the censors that Plutarch draws by way of conclusion, because it implies an analogy between the flaminal couple and the two censors with respect to unity and completeness. This comparison underscores better than anything else could the flaminica's indispensable public role, which, though discreet, can hardly be called marginal. Simply put, the flaminica enabled the flamen to play his part. It may also be illuminating to compare the "completeness" of the married priest with the status of children known as *patrimi matrimi* (having both father and mother), who assisted magistrates and priests in the celebration of public cults. Children chosen for this role had to belong to "complete" families, although the sources do not tell us whether the couples involved had to consist of natural parents.

We do not know whether these rules applied to other flamens. The silence of the sources may imply that this was not the case. If other sacerdotal couples were not subject to the same rules, it would not have affected the coherence of the religious system as a whole, which was not conspicuous for its consistency. Jupiter being not only the sovereign but also the best *(optimus)* of the gods, the sacerdotal couple that represented him may have been the only one that needed to project an image of perfection ("completeness"). Other flamens and priests may have been subject to different rules determined by the functions of "their" gods.

For other priests, as for any paterfamilias, "completeness" probably could be restored by remarriage. Plutarch's comments on the customs of the Arval Brethren confirm this indirectly. As we have seen, the two censors (the most venerable Roman magistrates) were required to exhibit a perfection similar to that required of the flamen and flaminica of Jupiter. Now, in order to celebrate the sacrifice to Dea Dia, the annually elected master *(magister)* of the Arval Brethren required the assistance of a flamen, who was not elected and whose role throughout the year and for the duration of the liturgy was passive and subordinate. The magister gave his name to the year, performed the sacrifice, and convoked and administered the Arval Brethren. He also publicly chose the flamen (as a man takes a wife). If the magister died, the flamen immediately resigned, and the new magister chose a new flamen in the days following his election. If, however, the flamen died, the magister simply chose another flamen.[111]

These rules show that the flamen's presence, though passive and subordinate, was indispensable. The magister, if I may add my own gloss to the rules, was not *complete* unless accompanied by a flamen. But in contrast to the case of the two censors or the flamen and flaminica of Jupiter, the magister of the Arval Brethren could remain in his post even if he lost his "other half," provided he found an immediate replacement. Clearly the rules governing the magister's behavior were not as strict as those governing the censors or the flamen of Jupiter; nevertheless, he could not act without a flamen at his side.

The Domestic Setting

In general, the religious customs of families that were Roman in the strict sense of the word largely conformed to the principles already set forth. The exclusion of women from sacrificial ceremonies applied to domestic as well as public cults. Texts and images amply confirm the husband's religious preeminence. Women nevertheless took part in most domestic rites, not just in weddings and funerals. On so-called marriage sarcophagi women are portrayed handing boxes of incense to their husbands, who accomplish the sacrificial rite. In other words, the paterfamilias is shown in a state of "completeness," a perfection afforded by the presence of his wife. Similarly, the censor Cato delegated his domestic religious responsibilities to his steward, but he did not forget the steward's wife.[112] The steward was made responsible for all affairs involving the gods (rem divinam facere).[113] The steward's wife is supposed to "supplicate" the Lar familiaris, or family god, and honor the deity by placing a wreath on the hearth on a certain day each month (the first, fifth, seventh, thirteenth, or fifteenth, depending on the month). In other words, the steward's wife, like her patroness, was not allowed to take the initiative in religious matters, and in particular she was not permitted to sacrifice live animals or pour libations of incense and wine. But like the matrons in the Matronalia of March 1, she was allowed to place a wreath of flowers on the hearth. Assuming that the gift of the wreath was part of a more complex liturgy that began with a sacrifice to the Lar familiaris, the placing of the wreath can be interpreted as part of the "second course" of the god's banquet. The ritual would then establish a further order of precedence between the steward and his wife, an order reminiscent of that obtaining among the priests, magistrates, and hundred and ten matrons who participated in the ceremonies marking the Secular Games of 204. It will come as no surprise to discover that the women of one great senatorial family, the Pompeii Macrini of the second century A.D., discharged sacerdotal and initiatory duties in a domestic cult of Bacchus of Greek origin. The role of women in private cults may also have depended on whether the rite was Greek or Roman.

The foregoing examples show that there was no significant difference between the role of women in domestic cults and the role assigned to them in public ceremonies. It was woman in her private as much as (if not more than) in her public role who was the butt of the satirists' sarcasm, the proverbial clichés, and the outrage that erupted in the poison scandals.

Were Roman women religiously incapacitated? Let me stress that it is purely for reasons of convenience that I separate religious behavior from other social practices. Such a separation facilitates the classification of different sources of community practice. Women's religious roles are a corollary of their social situation in general. The advantage of an approach focused relatively narrowly on religion is that it gives access to a global view of women's roles, because the ancients used the cult of the gods to formulate totalizing representations of the city and its component parts. These representations stemmed as much from liturgical gestures and attitudes as from the exegeses the Romans themselves provided. While not as precise or systematic as legal texts, the conceptualizations implicit in Roman ritual and explicitly expounded by Roman antiquarians offer a vital image of women in Roman society. These conceptualizations bridge the gap between theory and practice, between rule and custom.

What is at stake when one asks whether or not Roman women were religiously incapacitated is the general representation of the female sex. And that representation was the result of a ritually constructed and repeated paradox: women were both excluded from and included in public and private liturgies.

Which women? Except for certain rituals specifically designed to celebrate female sexuality or the stages of a woman's life, the matron was the religious woman par excellence. Often the rules insisted on a matron in her first marriage and the mother of children. The further a woman was from matronal status, the less likely she was to play an important religious role. A woman who was a widow, elderly, of low birth, or simply separated from her husband was presumed to be susceptible to superstitions of all sorts.

Although matrons had religious importance, they lacked religious capacity. They were not allowed to perform important rites in the Forum or the family atrium. Their role was secondary, and in normal times and regular places of worship they were not permitted to officiate at sacrifices. Sacrifice, a central element of Roman religious life, was a three-stage ritual, sometimes accompanied by optional secondary rituals. In the first stage, the *prae-*

fatio, or preface, the sacrificer invoked and welcomed the gods by pouring a libation of incense and wine. In the next stage, the immolation, the sacrificer transferred ownership of the sacrificial victim from human to divine hands. In the final stage, after the animal was slaughtered on the express orders of the officiant, it was butchered and its meat was divided up. Women were excluded from all three stages because they were not permitted to handle undiluted wine and not allowed to butcher animals.

Women's incapacity had even deeper roots. All the sacrificial acts mentioned required the issuance of commands and therefore the power to speak in the name of a community, whether public or private. No sacrifice, and no important ritual, was celebrated by and for the individual making the offering. A sacrifice was always for the benefit of, and performed in the name of, a community. The officiant was always a representative of that community. So the sacrificial incapacity of women was another manifestation of women's general incapacity to represent others.[114] In fact, the prohibition on the pulverization and milling of flour, in particular the *mola salsa* used in sacrifices, stemmed from the same incapacity. In the eyes of the ancients, pounding and milling, as operations that enabled humans to consume cereal grains, were therefore symbols of human nutrition. The *mola salsa* made on the public hearth of Rome conferred a Roman identity on every offering. Only Vestals or millers were allowed to pound the kernels of grain into flour. Women qua women were not allowed to serve as sources of identity; only men or individuals who, like the Vestals, partook of both sexes enjoyed that privilege. The myth of the Sabine women, which served as the legendary foundation of Roman marriage, exemplifies the same paradigm: it describes the first wives of the Romans as "foreigners."

Nevertheless, matrons were permitted to officiate at certain sacrifices. There was not necessarily any inconsistency in this, because the circumstances in which they could make sacrifices were special. In some festivals, such as those of Venus Verticordia, the Nonae Caprotinae, and the Matronalia, matrons appear to have officiated not so much for the people of Rome as for themselves, for the women of the city. As individuals women were free to participate as observers in any cult they wished, as long as their observance did not disturb the domestic or public peace. All these practices can be related to woman's juridical incapacity to represent anyone other than herself and therefore her capacity to act in her own name.[115]

To be sure, many matronal rituals, such as the festival of Bona Dea, were included in the official calendar and celebrated on behalf of the people of Rome. In naturalized cults, moreover, women exercised sacerdotal functions. In some cases, at least, women were capable of acting on behalf of others. The apparent paradox disappears upon closer examination. Recall that men could play their roles properly only if they were complete, that is, married. Plutarch's commentaries on the flamen and flaminica of Jupiter suggest that the same necessity existed at the level of the city. Male officiants in public cults could claim perfection or completion only if assisted by women, or, more precisely, matrons. Thus in the annual economy of public festivals, the function of matronal liturgies may have been to ensure the "completeness," hence perfection of cults in which men officiated. Like the flaminica, matrons were permitted to perform certain sacrificial acts in these cults; they thus enjoyed a kind of religious existence.

The matrons in question played these masculine roles as a reversal or displacement of "normality." One might even say that liturgies involving women dramatized the reasons for excluding them from other ceremonies: their incapacity to conduct themselves "normally," that is, as citizens strictly governed by public traditions. As I see it, the bizarre character of women's rituals sheds considerable light on the role of women in public religion. The Romans carefully distinguished between rites reputed to be Roman in their religious tradition and rites alleged to be of foreign—Greek or Etruscan—origin. Now, all these rites belonged to a single religion. The public priestesses of Ceres, for example, were natives of Naples or Velia, hence born outside Rome, but they were required to be daughters or wives of Roman citizens. The "foreign" rites often were supposed to represent more passionate and violent religious sentiments than did the calmer rituals sprung from Latin soil. These cults symbolized something other than the rationalism of Rome's civic religion, namely, the powerful and terrifying otherness of the gods. Thus the naturalized foreign cults were an essential counterpoint to the civic religion of Rome. The feminine complement to Roman religious life can be interpreted similarly.

In view of the excesses attributed to women's cults and the affinity of women for foreign cults, women's secret and unusual liturgies dispensed with the proprieties of male religion in favor of the mysteries and dangers of intimate relations with the gods. Orgiastic cults, a religious exaltation believed typical of women, and goddesses such as Fortuna, who flouted male criteria of action and judgment, suggested an unfathomable, infinite otherness of the gods that the orderly, dignified rituals of the male-dominated public liturgy could not embrace. The city repressed these dangerous aspects of religion, relegating them to its borders and to figures of relatively low rank in the social hierarchy, but it could not ignore them entirely. Roman women—of foreign origin, according to the myth of the Sabines—were placed in charge of those murky border realms where Rome's civilizing influence came to an end. Through ritual and at times through extravagant excess, their mission was to remind Romans of the dangers of a religion at odds with the rules and spirit laid down by the city.

The religious incapacity of Roman women thus masks a more complex structure. Although certain women were able to exploit the religious roles they were permitted to play, in general the religious role of women in Rome signified their religious incapacity. In other words, their inclusion came about through demonstration of their exclusion.[116] Women were obliged to play out their religious incapacity in order to construct, through ritual, an image of what threatened male citizens: superstitious deviance leading to catastrophe, impotence, and ridicule. Women portrayed the gamut of men's errors; in so doing they stood beside their men as if supervising their actions. In this way women's liturgies, interpreted in countless exegeses and proverbs, bestowed perfection on the city's religious actors.

This ritual and intellectual construct conveyed a warning to women. Women were no more capable than the masters of the city of wielding supreme responsibility by themselves. When the requirements of the system forced them to do so, as before the tent of Coriolanus or in the temple of Fortuna Muliebris, they unabashedly adopted male behavior. Even for women the religious paradigm was male.

9

Early Christian Women

Monique Alexandre

IN THE EARLY CENTURIES of Christianity women were sometimes condemned, sometimes exalted. In "The Grooming of Women" Tertullian berates his female readers and reminds them of the third chapter of Genesis: "You give birth, woman, in suffering and anguish. You are under your husband's spell, and he is your master. And do you not know that you are Eve? She still lives in this world, as God's judgment on your sex. Live then, for you must, as an accused. The devil is in you. You broke the seal of the Tree. You were the first to abandon God's law. You were the one who deceived man, whom the devil knew not how to vanquish. It was you who so easily overcame him who was made in the image of God. For your wages you have death, which brought death even to the Son of God. And yet you think of covering your tunics with ornaments."[1]

But the glory of Mary, the new Eve, reflected upon all women. Proclus of Constantinople praised her: "Through Mary all women are blessed. No longer is the female accursed, because her race now has what it needs to surpass even the angels in glory. Now Eve is cured, the Egyptian ignored, Delilah wrapped in a shroud, Jezebel forgotten, and even Herodias goes unmentioned. Now the whole range of women is admired. Sarah is praised as the fertile seedbed of nations, Rebeccah is honored as a clever purveyor of blessings, Leah too is admired as ancestral mother, Deborah is praised because she overcame nature to become a leader in combat, Elizabeth too is called blessed because she bore the precursor in her bosom and leapt with joy at the approach of grace, and Mary is adored as mother and servant, the Lord's arch."[2] Paul declared sexual difference irrelevant: "There is neither Jew nor Greek, there is neither bond nor free, there is neither male nor female: for ye are all one in Christ Jesus."[3] Yet a pastoral epistle declared: "Let the woman learn in silence with all subjection. But I suffer not a woman to teach, nor to usurp authority over the man, but to be in silence. For Adam was first formed, then Eve. And Adam was not deceived, but the woman being deceived was in the transgression. Notwithstanding she shall be saved in childbearing, if they continue in faith and charity and holiness with sobriety."[4] The contradictions in these seminal texts cannot be ignored. They justified a reinforcement of the traditional subordination of women, yet at the same time they opened up a realm of freedom.

The presence of women in this realm is remarkable. Women like Mary Magdalene followed Jesus to the cross and waited at his empty tomb.[5] Martha and Mary welcomed him.[6] The Good Samaritan listened to him.[7] In the first mission, described in Paul's Epistles and the Acts of the Apostles, women "labored in the Lord" from city to city: Lydia, "a seller of purple of the city of Thyatira," the first convert among the Philippians;[8] Priscilla,[9] wife of Aquila, tentmaker at Corinth and Ephesus; Phebe,[10] *diakonos* of the church of Cenchrea, chosen to carry an epistle from Paul to the Romans. The tenacious faith of women in the face of persecution was not forgotten in Christian circles: Thecla in Acts,[11] the slave Blandina martyred in Lyons in 177,[12] Perpetua the matron and Felicity, perhaps a slave, who died in Carthage in 203,[13] and virgin martyrs like Agnes in Rome.[14] "The most illustrious of Christ's flock, the virgins,"[15] lived ascetic lives at home or elsewhere. At first most were anonymous, but later they found advisers and biographers. Gregory of Nyssa, for example, wrote a *Life of Macrina,* his sister, while heading a monastery she founded near Annisa in the Hellespont, not far from a monastery for men founded by his brother Basil.[16] In his treatises on virginity Jerome offered abundant advice to the "brides of Christ." Eusthochium was a young Roman aristocrat.[17] After the barbarian invasions in

410 Demetrias took refuge on his African estates with his mother and grandmother.[18] A few maxims of Amma Theodora, Amma Sarra, and Amma Syncleticus have been preserved along with the works of the Desert Fathers.[19] For his sister Caesaria, abbess of Saint John of Arles, Caesarius in 534 drafted the first monastic rule explicitly intended for women.[20]

Some widows opted for the "holy word," including Melania the Elder, who traveled from Rome to Jerusalem to found a monastery in which she lived for twenty-seven years, not far from the monastery of Rufinus of Aquileia.[21] Marcella, who remained in Rome,[22] and Paula, Eusthochium's mother, who went with her daughter to live in cloistered exile in Bethlehem, were celebrated by their friend Jerome in a long *Epitaphium*.[23] In Constantinople the noble Olympias, for whom Gregory Nazianzen composed an epithalamium, clung to widowhood in the face of imperial pressure and founded a monastery adjoining the episcopal church. Having enjoyed the support of John Chrysostom, she later supported him in exile, as indicated by John's responses to her lost letters and as reported in an anonymous *Life*.[24]

Married couples sometimes agreed to renounce conjugal relations: Melania the Younger persuaded Pinianus to accede to her wishes in this regard. Scattering their vast fortune in various countries from Italy to Sicily, North Africa, and Egypt, they made their way to Jerusalem, where they finally settled. There Melania founded a convent for virgins and later a monastery for men on the Mount of Olives. Gerontius, the priest who wrote her *Life*, celebrated her ascetic heroism and spiritual power.[25] Legends grew up about women who repented of past sins, legends that were all the more effective because of the glaring contrast between sinfulness and repentance. Pelagia, a fallen woman who had been a mime in Antioch, repented and lived as a recluse on the Mount of Olives.[26] Mary the Egyptian lived as a wandering hermit in the Jordanian desert.[27] The early Christians were fond of reading about pilgrimages. The *Peregrinatio Silviae*, for example, is a lengthy account of the journey of a woman named Egeria (or Etheria), probably a native of southwestern Gaul, to Sinai, the Holy Land, Mesopotamia, and Asia Minor.[28] Wives and mothers were less prominent, although Gregory Nazianzen celebrated his mother, Nonna[29] and delivered a eulogy for his sister Gorgonia.[30] Basil of Caesarea and Gregory of Nyssa spoke of their grandmother Macrina and mother, Emmelia.[31] And Augustine, "son of many tears," wrote of the virtues of his mother, Monica.[32] Gregory of Nyssa's funeral sermons for Empress Flacilla, wife of Theodosius I, and her granddaughter Pulcheria can no doubt be read as offering an official image of women associated with the most Christian emperor.[33]

The presence of women is almost always perceived indirectly, however. Women's voices are rarely heard: there is Perpetua's account of her imprisonment in Carthage; a letter from Paula and Eusthochium urging Marcella to join them in the Holy Land;[34] Egeria's account of her travels and prayers; a few maxims of the Desert Mothers; and later a letter and some sayings of Caesaria the Younger.[35] The only vision of women to which we have access is the idealized, normative one put forward by clerics and monks. This vision exalts the "stars" and, by the end of the fourth century, aristocrats of both the east and the west who had become fascinated with the new forms of monastic asceticism and whose friends and relatives celebrated their spectacular renunciations. But what of the many others about whom we hear little or nothing: Anthony's sister, placed in the safekeeping of trustworthy virgins;[36] Pachomius' sister, who was called upon to establish a convent for virgins near her brother's *koinooion* (commune);[37] Augustine's sister, who, after being widowed, became the director of a woman's convent near Hippo, for which Augustine's own Rule, written for men, was adapted;[38] and the anonymous majority of ordinary women, both slave and free?

Men expressed themselves in voluminous theoretical writings. The apostolic Fathers led the way with their teachings; apologists defended the chastity of Christian women to the pagans; and, more systematically, Clement of Alexandria offered ethical counsel and rules for daily life in his *Paedagogus*.[39] In the third century women became a subject of theoretical texts, some of which were addressed to them specifically: Tertullian wrote "On the Grooming of Women" and "On the Wearing of Veils by Virgins,"[40] while Cyprian imitated him with his "On the Conduct of Virgins."[41] Two letters attributed to Clement were addressed from Rome to "eunuchs for the kingdom of the heavens and holy virgins."[42] Methodius of Olympus, inspired by Plato, wrote a *Symposium* in which ten virgins celebrate *parthenia* (virginity) and *para theou* (a life close to god).[43] Several of Athanasius' writings deal with these topics.[44] Basil of Ancyra wrote "On the True Integrity of Virginity."[45] Gregory of Nyssa wrote a treatise on the subject,[46] as did John Chrysostom.[47] In the west Ambrose of Milan published three books "On Virgins."[48] Augustine wrote "On Holy Virginity."[49] In counterpoint to these idealized writings we have, for example, Basil of Caesarea's still highly theoretical Forty-Sixth Letter to a fallen virgin and Niceta of Remesiana's treatise *On the Fall of a Consecrated Virgin*.[50] There are Christian texts on widowhood by Tertullian,[51] John Chrysostom,[52] Ambrose, and Augustine.[53] Rarer but crucial are treatises on marriage such as Augustine's *The Good of Marriage*.[54] Precepts on marriage were sometimes set forth in homilies, such as those of John Chrysostom.[55] Paul's epistles, as well as a series of exegeses of Genesis, situated woman in the order of Creation, the Fall, and Salvation. No doubt feminine metaphors in the discourse on God and the soul are also significant.[56] So are pagan judgments of Christian women, a subject as yet little explored.[57]

Conciliar decisions, episcopal letters from Rome and the Orient on disciplinary matters,[58] and collections such as the *Apostolic Constitution*[59] tell us a great deal about the slow elaboration of ecclesiastical law in this area and offer a glimpse of commonplace transgressions: adultery, abortion, divorce and remarriage, rape, abduction, concubinage, fornication, breaking of religious vows, anti-institutional asceticism, usurpation of powers. While juridical issues have attracted the attention of a number of investigators, on certain points the papyrological, epigraphic, and iconographic evidence has barely begun to be exploited.[60]

In the classification of discourse and imagery we must move beyond stereotypes to grasp variations and mutations. The first charismatic urban communities were supplanted by a hierarchical church. Organized as well as sporadic persecutions of Christian missions were ended by the Peace of the Church (which followed the Edict of Milan in 313). A minority that had seen itself as "the soul of the world,"[61] whether immersed in that world or repudiating it, became a majority, which for some time coexisted with the last unconverted pagans.

Little by little the fluid variety of individual experience gave way to institutionalization. Private and collective asceticism was supplanted by organized monastic communities governed by a rule, subject to an authority, and cloistered (more strictly for women than for men). The rhythms of the ascetic life imposed themselves on the laity as well. Geographic variations were important. The first communities of converts, "god-fearing Jews," began to accept Gentiles. But the status of women was not the same in Jewish, Greek, and Roman cultures.

No doubt the "proud saint,"[62] the liberty exhibited by patrician Roman women on the Aventine or in the Holy Land, contrasted sharply with the self-effacement of oriental women, who generally led retiring if not segregated lives. Rural northern Egypt, the still-pagan territory in which Pachomius and his sister were born, and the abandoned village of Tabennisi, where the pair established their monasteries, were quite different from Annisa, the family estate and retreat where Basil and his sister Macrina founded their monasteries. It was different too from the heart of Constantinople, where Olympias established a commune in the shadow of the episcopal church. Social differences are more easily sensed than analyzed.

The first urban communities in Philippi and Corinth, notable for their female artisans and merchants, gave way in the second century to mixed fraternities: in Lyons in 177, for example, the slave Blandina testified to her faith in Christ along with her mistress, a physician, a lawyer, and some Roman citizens and native Greeks.[63] In the third century, however, Clement addressed the advice in his *Paedagogus* to the master and mistress of a well-to-do household with numerous slaves. The couple were members of Alexandria's "leisure class." The converted aristocracy, whose contacts and alliances forged a spiritual as well as material bond between east and west, overshadowed other social groups in the fourth and fifth centuries. What are we to make of the serving women who entered convents with mistresses such as Macrina, Olympias, and others?[64] Or of those simple women in convents near Hippo or in Arles who came in contact with women of more refined upbringing and who, according to Augustine's Letter 211 and the Rule of Caesarius, were to be treated with tact?[65] Account must be taken of strains within the Church, particularly between rigorism and pastoral realism. When Jovinian denied that virginity was a higher state and praised the equal merit of Christian wives, Jerome mocked marriage in his response, *Against Jovinian* (393). But Siricius, the bishop of Rome, while acknowledging the honor accorded to virgins, showed that the Church through its participation in the wife's *vellatio* was receptive to the marriage vows.[66] Meanwhile, heretical versions of Christian doctrine took shape outside the Church: the Encratites, for example, emulated the Marcionites in advocating absolute continence, while the Montanists recognized women as prophets and educators.

Recent historiography has cast this whole subject in contrasting lights. In what respects were Christian women, Jewish women, Greek women, and Roman women similar, and in what respects were they different? The dividing line between Judeo-Christian and Greco-Roman is no longer as clear as it once seemed, thanks largely to the work of Michel Foucault,[67] Aline Rousselle,[68] Paul Veyne,[69] and Peter Brown.[70] Well before the advent of Christianity pagan philosophers and physicians had elaborated an ethical system, a set of techniques for the "care of the self," that placed considerable emphasis on monogamous marriage, continence, and virginity. Scholars still have to expound the religious origins of Christian ideals and practices in certain contemporary Jewish movements and in the eschatological expectations of the earliest Christian communities, which expressed a desire to live a life not divided between God and the world. Another area of active research is to understand, in psychological and social as well as ascetic and mystical terms, the powerful attraction that the new monastic life-style exerted on aristocratic women. The ascetic life promised liberation from the solitude and constraints of marital and family life; it promised autonomy as well as greater spiritual, intellectual, and even emotional intensity; it offered possibilities of male friendship and foreign travel; it could bring fame and contacts in the secular world; and it could serve as a means of birth control and estate management.

Judgments of early Christian women have been sweeping, crude, and often contradictory. To this day the Church maintains that it was, from the very beginning, a defender of the dignity and vocations of women.[71] Simone de Beauvoir, on the other hand, is peremptory in her condemnation: "Christian ideology contributed in no small measure to the opression of women."[72] A so-called feminist theology emerged in the 1960s, only to be attacked from various quarters. Thus present-day concerns often color the investigation of early Christianity: the controversy over the sex of God, the theology of sin and salvation, the status of women in the ecclesiastical hierarchy, access to the priesthood, woman's role in marriage and the family, the question of celibacy, a woman's right to control her own body and to seek an abortion, woman's place in work and politics. In exploring these issues contemporaries have returned to a period when modern attitudes were still in a formative stage and the masculine hierarchy was just establishing itself. Women in this same period took part in the "Jesus movement" and served as prophetesses, martyrs, deaconesses, virgins, ascetics, nuns, and Christian mothers. Among those who have taken a polemical as well as historical approach to the past are Karl Borresen,[73] Rosemary Ruetner,[74] Elizabeth Schlüsser-Fiorenza,[75] and Elizabeth Clark.[76] Their work, incomplete and biased though it is, has not been without success, although a consistent overall view has yet to emerge.

Jewish Women in the Christian Era

In Palestine during the time of Jesus women, excluded from public life, were expected to conform, as wives, mothers, and housekeepers, to the model of the "virtuous woman."[77] When they left home, they wore veils.[78] Men maintained a prudent silence, as Josi ben Johanan admonished them: "Do not speak much with a woman." This precept was glossed as follows: "Do not speak much with thy own wife, say the sages, much less with thy neighbor's wife." Whence this maxim: "He who speaks too much with women invites evil, neglects the study of the Law, and will end in Gehenna."[79] Only princesses and common women, particularly in the countryside, were exempt from this ideal of reclusiveness. In Alexandria, Greek custom reinforced Jewish moral teaching: "While outdoor life is suitable for men in time of peace as well as war," for females "domestic life and diligence in the home are best. Maidens, cloistered within the home, must not venture further than the door of the gynaeceum. Grown women may not venture further than the door of the house."[80]

At age twelve or even sooner girls passed from their father's authority to their husband's. If Jewish women could be divorced not only for "something shameful"[81] but, according to Hillel's interpretation, for nothing more than immodesty or a disagreeable appearance, they also enjoyed exceptional rights when it came to divorce. The *ketouba,* or marriage contract, carefully specified the amount of the dowry due the husband, but this same amount had to be repaid to the woman in case of divorce.[82] The wife retained ownership of certain property of her own, of which the husband became the usufructuary. The token to be paid in case of separation or death of a spouse was also specified. A woman's testimony was not admissible evidence in court, according to Flavius Josephus, "owing to the frivolity and temerity of the sex."[83] The Talmudic treatise *Nidda* specified how long women were to remain excluded from society because of contagious impurity following menstruation, other loss of blood, and childbirth (forty days after the birth of a boy, twice as long after a girl).[84]

Because of this destructive potential the participation of women in religion was also restricted. Women were exempt from pilgrimages to Jerusalem at Passover, Simchas Torah, and Succoth and excluded from the morning and evening Sh'ma (the prayer "Hear, O Israel! the Lord our God, the Lord is one").[85] These positive religious precepts thus did not apply to women, but many negative precepts did. Thrice daily the pious Jew repeated this prayer: "Blessed be God for not making me a Gentile . . . for not making me a peasant . . . for not making me a woman, because women are not required to observe the commandments."[86]

At home women were responsible for dietary and sexual purity but played little religious role in the strict sense. True, they enjoyed the privilege of lighting the sabbath candles and baking the sabbath bread, and it was their task to wash and dress the bodies of the dead and to mourn their passing. But blessings and prayers were reserved for men.

Polytheism had its goddesses and priestesses,[87] but monotheism boasted a hereditary priesthood, from which women were excluded more stringently than ever during the time of the Second Temple. Flavius Josephus described "the unbreachable barriers that protect purity . . . four concentric porticoes, each with its own particular guard according to the law . . . Anyone could enter the outer portico, even strangers. Only menstruating women were barred. The second portico was open to Jewish men and their wives, so long as they were free of all taint. The third was open to male Jews, spotless and purified. And the fourth was open to priests wearing their sacerdotal robes. As for the Holy of Holies, only the chief rabbis in their special robes could enter."[88] Gone were the days when women tended "the door of the tabernacle."[89]

Women were not required to attend synagogue for sabbath readings and sermons, which were already common at the dawn of the Christian era. Even if present, they did not count toward the *minyan,* the minimum number of men necessary for public prayer. "Out of respect for the congregation," they could not be called upon to read. They probably sat in a separate section of the synagogue, although the archaeological evidence is not very clear. Perhaps they were separated from the male congregation by a low wall, such as that described by Philo in his accounts of sabbath meetings of the Therapeutae in Alexandria.[90]

But there may be another side to the story. Bernadette Brooten has examined nineteen Greek and Latin inscriptions dating from the first century B.C. to the sixth century A.D. and from various sites in Asia Minor, Italy, Egypt, and Palestine.[91] In them women are designated as heads of synagogues *(archisynagogos/archisyn-agogissa),* leaders *(archegissa/arche),* elders *(presbytera/presbyter-issa),* mothers of the synagogue (one Latin inscription reads *pateressa!),* and even priestesses *(hiereia/hierissa).* These honorific titles are similar to those applied to men, and there is evidence as well of donations made by women. Clearly women were generous givers, and wealthy, prominent women did have influence, particularly in Asia Minor and Italy. But did they have religious duties in the synagogue?

Women were exempt, or excluded, from the study and teaching of the Torah, which, following the destruction of the Temple, became more than ever the central focus of Judaism. In the first century A.D. Rabbi Eliezer, who was married to the learned Ima Shalom, nevertheless said that "to teach Torah to one's daughter is to teach her obscenities." To be sure, the statement was controversial.[92] But legendary traditions pertaining to Ima Shalom and Beruriah, the daughter of Rabbi Hanania ben Teradyon, martyred under Hadrian, and wife of Rabbi Meir, and who was said to be "capable of reading three hundred traditions of three hundred masters in a winter's night," were apparently exceptions that confirm the rule.[93] And was not the fate of Beruriah an object lesson? For all her defiance of the rabbis' low opinion of women's intelligence, she was almost seduced by one of her husband's students and committed suicide out of shame.

To be sure, Jews honored the memory of the "Mothers" of *Genesis:* Sarah, Rachel, and Rebeccah.[94] They honored the seven prophetesses of old, especially Miriam, Deborah, judge of the people, and Huldah under King Josiah.[95] They exalted the women who had freed the people of Israel: Esther, the widow Judith, chaste wives like Susannah who triumphed over calumny, and martyrs like the mother of the Maccabees.[96] Yet not even the brilliance of these figures can blind us to so sweeping a condemnation as Flavius Josephus': "Woman, the Law says, is inferior to man in all things. Hence she must obey not force but authority, because God has given power to man."[97]

Women of the Gospel

With the gospel texts a marked change occurred. The genealogy of Joseph, "the husband of Mary," in Matthew[98] is unusual for a biblical text in that it names four atypical women: Thamar, the foreign woman who, with face veiled and by means of prostitution, deceived her father-in-law in order to perpetuate the lineage; Rachab, the Jericho prostitute, who ensured Israel's survival upon entering the Promised Land; Ruth the Moabite; and the woman "that had been the wife of Urias," the beloved of David, Bathsheba, whose sin was pardoned by the birth of Solomon.[99]

The gospels of Matthew and Luke[100] emphasize the virginity of Mary, who is made pregnant by the Holy Spirit as foretold by Isaiah 7:14: "Behold, a virgin shall conceive, and bear a son, and shall call his name Immanuel."[101] Joseph's dream, the adoration of the magi, the flight to Egypt in Matthew and even more prominently in Luke, the annunciation, the visitation, the nativity, the announcement to the shepherds, the presentation in the Temple, Jesus lost and found among the Doctors—all these are narrative fragments that were ripe for further development, which they received in the second-century Apocrypha, especially the Protoevangelium of James.[102] All the new episodes—Anne's encounter with Joachim, the childhood of Mary and her presentation at the Temple, her wedding with Joseph, the virgin birth and the incredulity of Salome, the midwife whose desiccated hand is healed—encouraged Marial piety and the ideal of virginity.[103] They also furnished future Christian iconography with a rich supply of images.[104] In Luke the figures of Elizabeth, the sterile woman who becomes the mother of John the Baptist, and Anne, the prophetic widow who heralds the deliverance of Israel, accompany the central figure of Mary, with her "fiat" of submission and "magnificat" of exultation in weakness. Subsequent allusions to Mary are rare, as religious bonds took precedence over ties of blood,[105] but such episodes as the marriage at Cana[106] and Mary standing at the foot of the cross with the beloved disciple of Jesus[107] left an indelible mark on Christian memory, as did Mary's presence among the apostles praying for Jesus after the Ascension.[108] The earliest allusion to Mary is in Paul: "God sent forth his Son, made of a woman."[109] The importance of this feminine role in the theology of the Incarnation is clear.

Jesus' relations with women seem to have been remarkably free, given the reserve that Jewish custom in his day required. He is received by Martha and Mary, neither of whom is married,[110] and demonstrates his friendship by resurrecting their brother Lazarus.[111] When his disciples find him talking to a Samaritan at Jacob's well in Sichem, they "marvelled that he talked with the woman. Yet no man said, What seekest thou? or, Why talkest thou with her?"[112] Barriers were broken down in the most surprising ways. Jesus preached to foreign women like the "schismatic" Samaritan[113] and healed even the daughter of a Canaanite.[114] The traditional hierarchy was overturned in favor of the despised: "The publicans and the harlots go into the kingdom of God before you," Jesus tells the high priests and elders of the Temple.[115] In a well-known passage he forgives the many sins of a woman who "loved much" because she, to the horror of the Pharisees, is willing to anoint his feet with ointment.[116] The pardon granted to the adulterous woman and the disarray of her male accusers can be seen in the same light.[117] So can the message to the Samaritan woman who has been married five times and is now living as a concubine.[118] Even female impurity is transcended: a bleeding woman touches the hem of Jesus' cloak and is cured.[119] He also takes pity on the poorest of women, the widows protected by the Law: he resurrects the only son of the widow of Nain,[120] as Elijah before him had resurrected the son of the widow of Sarepta.[121] The poor widow who casts in "two mites" is praised more than the rich men making their gifts to the temple treasury.[122]

The identity of the "saved" women who followed Jesus out of Galilee varies with the source. In Luke, after the passage about the anointment, we read: "And the twelve were with him. And certain women, which had been healed of evil spirits and infirmities, Mary called Magdalene, out of whom went seven devils, and Joanna the wife of Chuza, Herod's steward, and Susanna, and many others, which ministered unto him of their substance."[123] It is a diverse group of women that sets out with Jesus on the road in defiance of custom. In all the lists Mary Magdalene comes first.[124] Unlike the Twelve, these women have not received an explicit call, nor are they dispatched on clear missions. Yet in contrast to the abandonment of Jesus by the disciples, the presence of the women is emphasized—at a distance according to the Synoptics[125] but near the cross according to John.[126] As was customary in Judaism, the women are present when Jesus is wrapped in his shroud,[127] and it is they who prepare perfumes and fragrances for anointing the body.[128] Matthew names Mary Magdalene and the other Mary; Mark, Mary Magdalene, Mary, mother of James, and Salome; Luke, Mary Magdalene, Joanna, and Mary, mother of James; and John, only Mary Magdalene.

All four versions break with Jewish custom by making women, and particularly Mary Magdalene, witnesses to the resurrection and responsible for informing the disciples.[129] To be sure, masculine incredulity is apparent in Mark and Luke. But the special place of women, who are the first to see the resurrected Christ, is therefore all the more significant, especially in the celebrated *Noli me tangere* scene in John. Memory of that special role would be preserved in prayer and imagery.

The First Christian Mission: Conversion and Action

In Acts we read that the first group of Christian faithful included "women, and Mary the mother of Jesus."[130] The expression reminds us of the "women who followed Jesus." The text goes on to speak of conversions of men and women in Jerusalem and Damascus.[131] Certain names are mentioned, including the widow Tabitha-Dorcas, a disciple *(mathetria)* and a woman "full of good works and almsdeeds which she did."[132] When she dies, Peter, who is in Joppa, is sent for, and in a house still full of coats and garments the woman had made and in the presence of widows, he resurrects her. Another name is that of Mary, mother of John, surnamed Mark, to whose handsome house with porticoes Peter goes when released from bondage. A servant, Rhoda, opens the door, and "many were gathered together praying."[133] In the Greco-Roman world households played an important role in sustaining oriental cults.[134] And women were important to the functioning of these "household churches."[135]

Paul, in the course of travels through Syria, Cyprus, Asia Minor, Macedonia, and Greece, converts many women. He and his followers go to Philippi, for example, and on the sabbath day they preach to a group of women by the side of the river, where the

Jews pray. "And a certain woman named Lydia, a seller of purple, of the city of Thyatira, which worshipped God, heard us."[136] The Lord opens her heart so that she can attend to Paul's words. After being baptized along with her household, she welcomes the Apostles into her home. She was probably a freed woman, as her name ("the Lydian") indicates, and the text states that she was a dealer in luxury goods, hence familiar with the eastern trade routes. Lydia is portrayed as an independent woman with material and spiritual authority over her oikos. Emphasis is placed on her hospitality, which was essential in these early years of wandering Christian missions. Later, in Thessalonica, the crowd that comes to hear Paul preach in the synagogue includes "of the devout Greeks a great multitude and of the chief women not a few."[137] In Berea the congregation included Jews of the synagogue, many distinguished Greek women (euschemones), and not a few men.[138] In Athens the woman Damaris joins Dionysius the Areopagite in following Paul.[139] Many Jews were among those affected by Paul's preaching.

In Corinth, Paul encounters "a certain Jew named Aquila, born in Pontus, lately come from Italy, with his wife Priscilla, because Claudius had commanded all Jews to depart from Rome; and came unto them. And because he was of the same craft, he abode with them, and wrought: for by their occupation they were tent-makers."[140] This Jewish couple belonged to a group of artisans who clearly were well-to-do, familiar with the travel routes of both east and west, and even more apt to travel owing to their banishment from Rome. On their own they attempt a mission to Ephesus. They encounter another Jew named Apollos, born in Alexandria, who "taught diligently the things of the Lord" but knew "only the baptism of John." So Aquila and Priscilla "took him unto them and expounded unto him the way of God more perfectly."[141] Their house in Ephesus becomes the meeting place for a congregation (ekklesia), as later so does their house in Rome. In the final chapter of the Epistle to the Romans, Paul places husband and wife on a footing of equality: "Greet Priscilla and Aquila, my helpers (synergous) in Christ Jesus. Who have for my life laid down their own necks: unto whom not only I give thanks, but also all the churches of the Gentiles."[142]

The long list of recommendations and salutations that ends the Epistle to the Romans mentions some thirty names, of which a dozen are of women. Their roles were diverse, but not noticeably subordinate to those of men. First to be mentioned is "Phebe, our sister, which is a servant of the church which is at Cenchrea: That ye receive her in the Lord, as becometh saints, and that ye assist her in whatsoever business she hath need of you: for she hath been a succourer *(prostatis)* of many, and of myself also."[143] Phebe thus appears to have been an itinerant missionary who kept up contacts between various Christian churches, but no details of the nature of her service are given, and we must be careful not to assume that her duties were similar to those of the later deaconesses, whose hierarchical position was clearly subordinate. Her importance is evident from her place in the list, ahead of Priscilla and Aquila, and from Paul's praise of her services as *prostatis,* provider of material and spiritual assistance. Mary, Tryphena, Tryphosa, and Persis are mentioned among those who "labored much [*kopiao*]" for Christ and the Christians of Rome. Family ties appear: Rufus is saluted along with "his mother and mine."[144] Nereus and his sister are mentioned—ties of blood along with spiritual ties.[145] Above all we find the names of couples: "Andronicus and Junia, my kinsmen and my fellow prisoners, who are of note among the apostles, who also were in Christ before me."[146] Philologus and Julia are also mentioned.[147] Small groups of missionaries were sent forth, and couples—conjugal and/or spiritual, perhaps—were active in them. The Epistle to Philemon mentions "our beloved Apphia."[148] And in the Epistle to the Corinthians, Paul asks: "Am I not an apostle? Am I not free? . . . Have we not power to lead about a sister, a wife, as well as other apostles, as the brethren of the Lord, and Cephas?"[149]

The varied vocabulary that Paul uses in speaking of these women, whether singly or in groups, is similar to that which he uses in his own works. In the Epistle to the Philippians he calls for a reconciliation between Euodias and Syntyche and asks others to "help those women which laboured with me [*synethlesan*] in the gospel."[150] Here too there is no sign that women's tasks were in any way considered inferior to men's. In this fundamentally important missionary work women found space in which to act in equality with men.

An Institutional Place?

As the Church moved toward greater institutionalization, however, women did not hold well-defined ministries. Certain distinct groups of women did form, however. One such was the *cherai,* or widows, who, according to biblical tradition, enjoyed the special protection of the Law and of God.[151] From the widow of Sarepta[152] to Judith and Anne the prophetess,[153] an image took shape of the widow as a person closer than other people to God. Christian communities took it upon themselves to aid widows without other means of support.[154] Although remarriage was tolerated,[155] even encouraged for young widows,[156] and although the children of widows were reminded to care for them, widows past the age of sixty who had demonstrated maternal and charitable qualities in a single marriage were called upon to live lives of continence and prayer.[157] In setting forth the duties of elders *(presbytai),* young people, and slaves, the Epistle to Titus stated that elder women *(presbytides)* should occupy themselves with instructing other women: "The aged women likewise, that they be in behavior as becometh holiness, not false accusers, not given to much wine, teachers of good things; that they may teach the young women to be sober, to love their husbands, to love their children; to be discreet, chaste, keepers at home, good, obedient to their own husbands, that the word of God be not blasphemed."[158] Despite Paul's advocacy of virginity, there is no sign of any special group of virgins among unmarried women in these early Christian communities.[159]

Apart from these informal roles for women, there was probably also "a category of female ministers without specific titles."[160] In the First Epistle to Timothy, after the section on the *episcopes,* in the middle of the section on the *diakonoi,* "those who serve," we read: "Even so must their wives be grave, not slanderers, sober, faithful in all things."[161] Here "their wives" seems to suggest a category of women parallel to that of the male *diakonoi,* exhibiting similar traits and sharing similar duties.

The Charisma of Prophetesses

Although the institutional place of women was strictly limited and women, in keeping with Jewish custom, were excluded from positions of authority, they played a more important charismatic role. In Luke three women—Mary, Elizabeth, and Anne—are reminiscent of the prophetesses of the Old Testament. The early Christian community experienced the outpouring of the Holy Spirit at Pentecost: "And it shall come to pass in the last days, saith God,

I will pour out of my Spirit upon all flesh: and your sons *and your daughters* shall prophesy."[162] A passage in the Acts alludes to Paul's visit to the home of Philip the Evangelist, one of the Seven, who "had four daughters, virgins, which did prophesy."[163] In the congregation of Corinth men and women both prayed and prophesied. But while men were enjoined to bare their heads, women were required to keep theirs covered as a sign of power *(exousia)*, dignity, and decency, and out of respect "for the angels" present as mediators of human prayer. Thus the order of creation was respected, with man enjoying priority over woman and interdependence in the Lord. This complex passage is still a matter of debate among exegetes.[164]

Already true prophetesses were distinguished from false. In Revelations there is a denunciation of Jezebel, a woman of Thyatira "who claims to be a prophetess" and teacher.[165] The gift of revelation would continue to flourish for a long time to come. In the second century Justin spoke of "Christian men and women who receive gifts from the Spirit of God."[166] In 203 in Carthage the martyr Perpetua experienced visions.[167] But these gifts were difficult to control, and heretical sects could lay claim to them as readily as the orthodox. When the Montanists made such claims in the second century, the Church began to play down the importance of prophecy, particularly among women.

Prohibitions on Public Speaking and Instruction

The Church Fathers celebrated the memory of women who had labored in Christ. John Chrysostom, in a fourth-century homily on "Salute Priscilla and Aquila," contrasted the worldly vanity of the women of his day, which he deplored, with the zeal of Priscilla, Persis, Mary, and Tryphena, which he extolled.[168]

In later years women served in positions with titles similar to their predecessors but with different duties. One late-fourth-century epitaph draws an explicit parallel: "Here lies the servant and virgin of Christ, Sophia the deaconess, the second Phoebe, who rests in peace."[169]

Late Pauline texts were frequently cited, however, to justify, on biblical grounds, strict limits on the female role. Religious submission was linked to submission within the family. One passage frequently cited was 1 Corinthians 14:34–35, which scholars today generally agree is an interpolation at odds with the logic of the text: "Let your women keep silence in the churches: for it is not permitted unto them to speak. But they are commanded to be under obedience, as also saith the law. [cf. Genesis 3:16] And if they will learn any thing, let them ask their husbands at home, for it is a shame for women to speak in the church."[170] Another was 1 Timothy 2:11–14: "Let the woman learn in silence with all subjection. But I suffer not a woman to teach [*didaskein*], nor to usurp authority [*authentein*] over the man, but to be in silence. For Adam was first formed, then Eve [cf. Genesis 1:27; 2:7, 22]. And Adam was not deceived, but the woman being deceived was in the transgression [cf. Genesis 3:6, 13]." Thus women were forbidden to speak or teach in public. In his homily on Priscilla and Aquila, John Chrysostom went so far as to argue that Priscilla taught Apollos only in private and only because no qualified male teacher was available.

The Fear of Heretical Women

Prohibitions on women's activities were clarified and extended in polemical attacks on heterodox movements, in which women often played important roles. Over time orthodox authors evolved a standard litany of female heretics, to the point where the rhetorical *topos* obscured the reality. In 415, for example, Jerome attacked Pelagius and his female followers by reciting a satirical list of *mulierculae* (little women) who had followed heretics from Nicholas of Antioch to Priscillian and who, "both sexes aiding one another, [had] contributed to the 'mystery of iniquity.'"[171]

In Gnostic texts certain secret revelations were vouchsafed to the women who had followed Jesus, such as Salome and above all Mary Magdalene.[172] In the gospel attributed to her, Mary Magdalene affirms that "Jesus prepared us and made us men" and, despite Peter's hostility, becomes Jesus' companion of choice.[173]

Although Gnostic symbolism was highly complex, scholars, simplifying to some degree, have called attention to the importance the Gnostics attached to "God the Father and God the Mother" among the appellations attached to *Sige*, or Silence.[174] Other important topics included *Bythos*, or Abyss; the origins of the two Eons, constituents of the Pleroma (the plenitude of divine being);[175] the female Spirit;[176] the Hebrew word *ruah*; and Wisdom.[177] Attention has been called to the "romances of the soul," stories of women fallen and redeemed.[178] The importance of models of redemption has been noted, including models in which the male-female opposition is abolished;[179] women are made virile;[180] and primordial androgyny is restored.[181]

It is difficult to tell, however, whether there was indeed a relation between these Gnostic myths, which have become better known since the discovery and decipherment of the Nag Hammadi papyri, and the role of women as prophets, teachers, and functionaries in these religious movements. According to their opponents in the official Church, women used their resources and influence to herald the Gnostic truth.

There is a certain consistency to the heresiologists' findings, despite the diversity of the systems and cases studied. Simon Magus, for example, was supposedly accompanied by Helen—the same Helen held responsible for the Trojan War and since then fallen into prostitution in a final avatar of *Protennoia,* or Primary Thought, but destined to be received into the Pleroma.[182] Marcion was alleged to have sent a woman to Rome to prepare the souls of the women he deceived.[183] In the church he founded, women were allowed to perform sacerdotal functions, including baptism.[184] Marcellina brought Carpocrates' teachings to Rome.[185] Apelles was influenced by Philomena, a virgin prophetess whose teachings were collected in a Book of Revelations.[186] Irenaeus of Lyons provides many details of the activities of the Gnostic Mark Magus, a dissident follower of Valentinus: "He lavishes attention on women, and primarily the wealthiest and most elegant among them. When he wishes to make himself attractive to one of them, he resorts to flattering speech: 'I want to give you a share in my Grace, because the Father of all things sees your Angel constantly before his face . . . Make yourself ready, like a wife who awaits her husband, so that you may become what I am and I, what you are. Bring the seed of Light into your nuptial chamber. Receive from me the Husband, make room for him within yourself. Grace has descended upon you . . . Open your mouth and say anything, you will be making prophecy.'" Upon hearing these words, foolish—Irenaeus says impudent—women believe themselves to be prophetesses and give Mark their property and their bodies, "in order to descend in him into the One."[187] In demonstrations of magic, moreover, a woman assisting Mark was accused of "Eucharistizing" a cup.[188]

In Carthage at the beginning of the third century Tertullian attacked heretics for acting "without authority and without discipline, wholly in keeping with their faith." He denounced the women who joined these groups: "What impudence! Do they not dare to teach, argue, exorcise, promise cures, and perhaps even baptize?"[189] In another attack on a female leader of the Cainite sect, "one of the most venomous of vipers," he wrote: "This monster of a woman has found a way to cause these little fish to die, a way to entice them out of the water."[190] In his treatise on baptism he criticized women who used the apocryphal example of Thecla to justify their administration of the sacrament of baptism: "Is it likely that the apostle [Paul] would have granted women the right to teach and to baptize after restricting a wife's right to educate herself? 'And if they will learn anything, let them ask their husbands at home.'"[191] Although he cited Montanist prophetesses such as Priscilla even before his conversion, he limited the communication of prophecies to after the celebration.[192] During his Montanist period he reminded virgins, "who must remain veiled," of what they must not do: "Women are not permitted to speak in church, much less to teach, bathe, make offerings, or claim for themselves any of the functions that properly belong to men, most notably the sacerdotal ministry."[193]

Within the Church the most pointed attacks on the exorbitant power of women were triggered by Montanism. This wave of enthusiasm first arose in Phrygia in the middle of the second century and quickly spread throughout the east and west. Montanus was joined by Priscilla, Maximilla, and Quintilla in preaching the end of the world, the need for continence, and the coming of the millennium on earth. Seven of the nineteen extant Montanist oracles come from these women. "The Cataphrygians [a Montanist sect] say that in Pepuza, Priscilla was asleep when Christ came and lay with her. In the guise of a splendidly dressed woman Christ came to me. He gave me wisdom and declared that this place was holy and that the heavenly Jerusalem would descend from heaven here."[194] After the death of Montanus, Maximilla became the movement's leader. Under attack by the Church, she issued this oracle: "I am hunted far from the flock like a wolf. I am not a wolf. I am Word, Spirit, Power."[195] First described as virgins, Priscilla and Maximilla were characterized in later polemics as women who, when they became filled with the Spirit, abandoned their husbands.[196] In the third century it was rumored that a prophetess in Cappadocia was celebrating the Eucharist.[197] According to Epiphanus of Salamis, who in 374–377 composed a refutation of some eighty different heresies, Montanist women were ordained as priests and even bishops on the authority of Galatians 3:28: "There is neither male nor female, for ye are all one in Christ Jesus."[198]

The Montanist prophetesses claimed that their prophecies were in keeping with biblical tradition. But Origen replied that no woman in the Bible had ever issued a prophecy in a congregation. It was an absolute rule that women must remain silent in congregation, just as they must not teach in public or lay down the law for men. Origen offered this gloss: "If women wish to learn about some point, let them ask their husbands at home," or if they are virgins, let them ask a parent or brother, or if they are widows, let them ask a son.[199] Didymus of Alexandria also criticized the anthology of Montanist oracles, pointing out that no woman from Deborah to the Virgin Mary had ever written a holy text. Origen then repeated the Pauline prohibitions and recalled Eve's sin and the omnipresent danger.[200] Epiphanus argued that Christian women must wear veils and recalled the "curse" of Genesis 3:16: "And thy desire shall be to thy husband, and he shall rule over thee."[201] Ecclesiastical, domestic, and social hierarchies joined forces in this battle.

Widows and Deaconesses in the Church

In the Church hierarchy the bishop was the dispenser of the sacred word and sacraments. He was assisted by priests and deacons. As the distinction between clergy and laity grew increasingly rigid, women were allowed a place in the ecclesiastical institution, but a limited one.[202] In both east and west widows took on a spiritual and charitable role that gradually became confounded with the growing women's monastic movement in the last thirty years of the fourth century. At certain times and in certain places, mainly in the east, deaconesses who fulfilled a variety of functions were invested with ministries until roughly the tenth century. Here too feminine monasticism eventually subsumed these roles.

Widows. Along with orphans, the poor, the sick, prisoners, and strangers, widows had been portrayed as people in need of assistance in Christian texts from 1 Timothy 5:16 onward.[203] A portion of the Sunday collection was set aside for them.[204] In Rome in 251 Bishop Cornelius counted 1,500 widows and paupers receiving aid from the Church.[205] In return, the recipients of such aid were covered by certain special precepts in "apostolic" texts. Thus Polycarp wrote to the Philippians: "May they be wise [*sophronousas*] in the faith they owe the Lord, intercede constantly for all, avoid calumny, slander, false witness, love of money, and all evil, in the knowledge that they are the altar of God."[206]

But, as already in 1 Timothy 5:5, one group of widows stood out: those who pledged themselves to remain continent, to join an order *(tagma ton cheron, cherikon; ordo viduarum, viduatus)*. This ideal of chaste renunciation at first seemed to make these widows a model for virgins, with whom they were sometimes associated. Ignatius referred to "virgins called widows."[207] Other reports mention a similar confusion.[208] Soon, however, the luster of virginity would outshine that of widows, not only in merit but also in competition for precedence within the Church.[209]

Did widows have a place among the ecclesiastical orders? Tertullian in passing says that they did.[210] But Hippolytus of Rome, in his third-century *Apostolic Tradition*, noted that widows of long standing could, after a period of probation, "be instituted by speech [and] joined to others but not ordained." No hand was to be placed on such a widow, because she was not making an oblation and had no liturgical duties, whereas ordination *(cheirotonia)* was for clerics with liturgical services to perform. The widow was not ordained but instituted *(kathistatai)* for prayer, which was for everyone.[211] Most of the texts state that a widow, in order to be instituted, had to have been married only once (Greek: *monandros;* Latin: *univira*).[212] Her profession and vow of continence had to be irrevocable. For Basil of Caesarea breaking this vow meant excommunication.[213] The age of admission was set at fifty or sixty, though it was not always respected.[214]

Foremost among the obligations of the widow was prayer; 1 Timothy 5:5 had established this principle, and Hippolytus had followed it in *Apostolic Tradition*. We find it too in the *Didascalia Apostolorum*, a compilation that probably originated in Syria in the third century. When ordered to do so by a bishop, widows were supposed to pray at the bedside of the sick, lay on hands, and fast.[215] The asceticism of the widow's commitment was further emphasized in *Apostolic Constitutions*, a late-fourth-century compilation from Syria or Constantinople. Prayer was to be coupled with fasting and vigils on the model of Judith.[216]

In both the *Didascalia* and the *Constitutions*, however, the limits of widows' activities were carefully circumscribed. They were subject to the authority of bishops and deacons. Without express orders, no widow was permitted to visit any person's home for the purpose of eating, drinking, fasting, receiving gifts, laying on hands, or praying.[217] The inner life came first: widows were the "altar of God" and must prove themselves to be just as solid as an altar. They were *cherai* (widows), not *perai* (sacks used by mendicants). They were to pray at home and go out to help others.[218] They were at first advised,[219] then ordered,[220] not to perform baptisms. They were denied the right to teach, especially about Christ's passion and redemption. At most they were permitted to repeat elementary answers to basic questions: Christians must not worship idols, there is only one God.[221] Such warnings suggest that women, instead of devoting themselves to prayer, may have been encroaching on territory that male clerics considered their own private preserve.

Deaconesses. Second-century texts offer no clear evidence concerning women's service to the Church. In Hermas' *The Shepherd* the woman representing the Church proposes that one copy of her book be sent to Clement, who will circulate it to other cities, and another to Grapta, who will alert widows and orphans.[222] In a letter to Trajan, Pliny speaks of *ancillae . . . ministrae* whom he has subjected to torture in Bithynia.[223] The Latin word may correspond to the Greek *diakonos,* but we are told nothing about what services these women might have performed.[224] Pliny is contemptuous, seeing in their religion nothing more than "an absurd, extravagant superstition." His contempt may have been heightened by the humble status of these female slaves, who had been invested with official responsibilities by a community consisting of "many people of all ages and walks of life and of both sexes . . . in the cities, towns, and countrysides infected by this contagious superstition." Like Blandina in Lyons in 177 and Felicity in Carthage in 203, who were also slaves but without official religious functions, these victims of torture were notable for their courage. Note too the confidence of this *ekklesia* of mixed composition.

In the third century the *Didascalia Apostolorum* defined the status of the female deaconess *(he diakonos, gyne diakonos)* in the east. In the ecclesial typology the bishop was said to be in the image of God; the deacon, of Christ; the deaconess, of the Holy Spirit; and the priests, of the Apostles.[225] The bishop named deacons to perform certain necessary tasks and deaconesses to serve women. The number of deacons and deaconesses depended on the size of the congregation. The deacon's duties were extensive and included assisting the bishop, especially during the celebration of the Eucharist, and maintaining decorum in church.[226] By contrast, the deaconess' duties were limited to the service of other women: "Let a deaconess anoint the women" during baptism. "And when the woman being baptized emerges from the water, let the deaconess welcome her and teach her how the seal of baptism is to be preserved intact in purity and sanctity." Furthermore, "a deaconess is necessary to visit pagan homes in which there are female believers, and to visit women who are sick, and to wash those who are recovering from an illness." The *Didascalia* stressed the importance of this apparently new ministry by pointing out that Christ was served by deaconesses: Mary Magdalene; Mary, daughter of James and mother of Josiah; the mother of the sons of Zebadiah; and others.[227]

In the fourth century these prescriptions were revised and amplified by the *Apostolic Constitutions*. The bishop chose the deacons from the congregation at large, but deaconesses *(diakonissai)* were recruited among widows and virgins, a choice that gave a marked ascetic cast to the office.[228] The functions of the deaconess were still to visit sick and incapacitated women and to assist in the baptism of women.[229] But they could also be messengers.[230] Their presence was required when a woman came to see a deacon or bishop.[231] They welcomed women to religious services, and, along with their male counterparts, they maintained decorum.[232] The limits of their responsibilities were clearly delineated: "The deaconess does not make benedictions or perform any of the services for which elders and deacons are responsible. She simply guards the doors and, for reasons of decency, assists the elders in the administration of baptism."[233]

Deaconesses took precedence over other virgins and widows, for example in communion.[234] They belonged to the clergy. The bishop placed his hands on them and prayed for them in the presence of the *presbyterion,* deacons, and deaconesses: "God . . . creator of man and woman, who hast filled with Spirit Miriam, Deborah, Anne, and Hulda [prophetesses of the Old Testament], and who did not disdain for thy only Son to be born of woman, thou who hast designated in the Tent of Witness and in the Temple . . . the guardians of thy holy gates, deign now to look down upon this, thy servant, candidate for the deaconate. Bring unto her the Holy Spirit and purge her of every impurity of flesh and spirit so that she may worthily discharge her assigned task."[235] Along with the priests, the deaconesses were the sole recipients of the *eulogies,* breads distributed for the Eucharist.[236] The deaconesses' rank was not fixed, however. Their "ordination" came immediately after the deacons, and they communicated ahead of other widows and virgins but after priests and ascetics.[237]

Deaconesses were consecrated, and any transgression of their vows was considered a profanation. Ecclesiastical canons and legal texts were quite severe.[238] Basil of Caesarea wrote: "We will no longer permit the body of a deaconess, which has been consecrated, to be used for a carnal purpose." The minimum age for becoming a deaconess was increased to forty, fifty, or sixty, depending on the document. Exceptions were not uncommon, however: in Constantinople in 391 Bishop Nectarius ordained Olympias, widow of Nebridius (who had died four years earlier), despite her youth.[239]

To be sure, the duties of the deaconess had a spiritual dimension, as is evident from the beautiful prayer for the laying on of hands. But the institution of a feminine ministry for the purpose of administering baptism and visiting sick women suggests an impulse toward prudent segregation, an impulse that is evident in other respects as well. In the *Physiologus,* a fourth-century Christian bestiary, an article on flaming rocks illustrates the issue: "There are stones which, when brought together, catch fire and ignite anything that chances to fall upon them. By nature they are male and female and quite remote from one another. And therefore thou, noble ascetic, must shun women, lest you come near one and catch fire with pleasure and burn up all the virtue that is in you. For Samson, when a woman came near, saw his strength destroyed, and many others, it is written, have gone astray on account of the beauty of women."[240] The message here is addressed to an ascetic, but it applies to all men. Hippolytus, speaking of catechumens in the *Apostolic Tradition,* wrote: "Women, whether of the faithful or catechumens, shall pray in a separate part of the church. When they have finished praying, they shall not exchange the kiss of peace, for their kiss is not yet holy. The faithful shall salute one another, men with men and women with women. But the men shall not salute the women. The women shall cover their heads completely with a *pallium,* but not simply with linen cloth, for that is not a veil."[241] Within the church the *Didascalia* and *Apostolic Constitutions* recommended sorting "the flock by species, men, then women, with each age group in its proper place within these two groupings."[242] Deacons and deaconesses were responsible for maintaining this orderly arrangement.

An anecdote in John Moschus' *Pratum Spirituale* illustrates why it is dangerous for women to be too close to the church, particularly during baptism. A priest named Conon, responsible for administering baptisms at the monastery of Pentoucha, did not trust himself to anoint with oil the body of a beautiful young Persian girl, but no deaconess could be admitted into the monastery. The priest fled. John the Baptist appeared to him, and, after making the sign of the cross three times below his navel, sent him back to the monastery. "There, on the next day, he anointed and baptized the Persian without noticing that she was a woman, and he continued anointing and baptizing for twelve years without experiencing any movement of the flesh or noticing any woman."[243]

From the fourth century on we find more frequent mention of deaconesses in the east. Like deacons, they frequently figured in inscriptions, such as this one from Philippi in Macedonia: "Tomb belonging to Poseidonia, deaconess, and Pancharia, most humble *kanonike* [nun]."[244] Or this from Edessa: "Monument of Theodosia, woman deacon, and Aspilia and Agathocleia, virgins."[245] Or, from a sepulcher *ad sanctos:* "[Tomb] of Akakios, martyr, [tomb] of . . . deaconess."[246] And, on a devotional object from Stobi: "In virtue of her vow, Matrona, most pious deaconess, made the mosaic in the nave."[247]

Literary and legal texts abound with examples. In Constantinople, John Chrysostom ordained "deaconesses of the Holy Church, his three relatives Elisanthia, Martyria, and Palladia, so that the four services [*diakoniai*] may continue without interruption in the holy monastery established by" Olympias.[248] In the baptistry, about to depart for exile, he bids farewell to Olympias and two other deaconesses, Procla and Pentadia.[249] Deaconesses are mentioned in his correspondence from exile.[250] A deaconess, his aunt Sabinian, joins him in remote Cucusa.[251] In the sixth century Justinian enumerated the clerics attached to the Great Church (today Hagia Sophia): sixty priests, one hundred deacons, forty deaconesses, ninety subdeacons, one hundred lectors, twenty-five cantors, one hundred porters.[252] Clearly deaconesses were attached to secular and monastic churches. The documents suggest an evolution that was linked to the development of monasticism. In the monastery of Olympias in Constantinople deaconal duties were performed by nuns, as we have just seen. Superiors or adjuncts were often chosen. At the monastery of Arnisa in Pontus, Lampadion "directed the choir of virgins, with the rank of deaconess."[253] Sixth- and seventh-century Syriac texts from the Edessa region offer a possible glimpse of their duties: baptism of women and visits to sick women are still mentioned, but also, in the absence of a priest or deacon, the deaconesses "share the mysteries with the women under their authority." They could also read the gospels or other holy books in congregations of women. The ability to substitute for the deacon or even the sacristan was limited strictly to the monastery, and John bar Qursos' answers to the questions raised by the *Priest Sargis* suggest its limits: praying aloud was forbidden, for example, as was access to the sanctuary during menstruation.[254]

Deaconesses disappeared in the east around the turn of the twelfth century, as the institution was swallowed up by monasticism and baptism was extended to children. Yet traces of the deaconess' role persisted in liturgical and canonical texts.[255]

Exclusions

An elaborate argument was developed to justify limiting the role of widows and deaconesses. The *Apostolic Constitutions* attributed the following to the Apostles themselves: "We do not allow women to teach in the Church. We allow them only to pray and listen to the masters. Indeed, our Master himself, Jesus Christ, when he sent us Twelve to teach peoples and nations, did not send women to preach, although there was no lack of them, for with us were the mother of the Lord and her sisters, as well as Mary Magdalene and Mary, mother of James, and Martha and Mary, the sisters of Lazarus, and Salome, and others. If it were necessary for women to teach, he himself would have been the first to order them to instruct the people. If 'the head of the woman is the man' [1 Corinthians 11:3], it is not right for the rest of the body to command the head."[256]

A similar argument applied to the administration of baptism: "It would be hazardous, or worse still, contrary to the Law and impious. Indeed, if 'the head of the woman is the man,' and if man is chosen for the priesthood [*hierosyne*], it would not be just to abolish creation and abandon the head in favor of the body's extremity. For the woman is the body of the man, extracted from his flank and made subject to him from whom she was separated for the purpose of producing children [Genesis 2:21–23]. And it is written that he shall be her master [Genesis 3:16]. If, in view of the foregoing, we do not allow her to teach [1 Timothy 2:12], why would anyone go against nature by allowing her to exercise priesthood [*hierateusai*]? It was out of impious ignorance that the Greeks ordained priestesses for their female deities. In Christ's law no such thing is possible. If baptism by women were necessary, surely the Lord would have been baptized by his mother and not by John. And when he sent us to baptize, he would have sent women with us for that reason. He knew what conformed to nature because he was both the creator of nature and the author of its laws."[257]

This argument is based explicitly on the Bible. The order of the Old and New Testaments is opposed to the pagan disorder of priestesses and goddesses. The story of the creation and fall reveals the *nature* of woman. Created after man, she is his inferior, necessarily subordinate. Jewish law established a precedent by excluding her from the priesthood. Neither by deed nor instruction did Jesus include her in the mission of baptism of preaching, hence in the new priesthood. Paul's prohibitions, which established a connection between the social and religious hierarchy, fitted the pattern established by this historical and theological argument. It was no longer as common as it once had been to justify women's disabilities on the grounds of impurity. True, in the fourth century the Canon of Laodicea prohibited women from approaching the altar.[258] But in the fifth century, in Syria, the *Testament of Our Lord Jesus Christ* placed deaconess widows next to the bishop and inside the veil stretched in front of the altar during the eucharistic sacrifice.[259] The same document tells us that during menstruation deaconesses were allowed to remain in the church but not to approach the altar, not because they were impure but so that the altar could be honored.[260]

Women's defects were sometimes emphasized. In the fourth-century Egyptian *Ecclesiastical Canons of the Apostles*, for example, two widows are assigned to assist with prayers and another to help with sick women[261] but the Apostles are made to recall an event connected with the Last Supper to exclude women from the

436

oblation of body and blood: "John says: 'You have forgotten, brothers, that our Master, when he . . . blessed the bread and cut it, saying, "This is my body and my blood," did not allow the women to stand with us.' Martha says: 'It is because of Mary, because he saw her smile.' Mary says: 'It is not because I laughed. For he told us before that what is weak will be saved by what is strong.'"[262]

In the *Panarion* Epiphanius of Salamis attacked the heresy of the Collyridians, so called because they treated the Virgin as a deity by offering her a *collyre,* a small loaf of bread which they then used for communion. He rehearses the usual arguments to show that women may serve as deaconesses but not as priests. There are no Christian *presbyterides* or *hierissai* (priestesses). The race of women is weak, fickle, of mediocre intelligence, and an instrument of the devil—how can it aspire to a sacerdotal function?[263] In a dialogue *On the Priesthood* John Chrysostom declares: "When it comes to such high functions as the government of the Church and the direction of souls, women are excluded and only a small number of men are called."[264]

In the West

The institution of the deaconess was not widespread in the west, where some authorities associated it with heresy.[265] Sulpicius Severus says that the title "deaconess" was introduced in the west by Priscillianists, a heretical movement supported by noble women in southern Gaul and Spain.[266] In any case western councils from the fourth to the sixth century repeated the prohibition on allowing women access to the Levitical ministry or even to deaconal duties. In 441, for example, the Council of Orange stated: "No deaconesses should be ordained in any way, and if any still exist, let them bow their heads before the benediction given to the people."[267] Pope Gelasius wrote to the bishops of southern Italy: "Women are performing services at the holy altar, doing what has been ascribed to the ministry of men alone."[268] In the sixth century three bishops in northern Gaul issued a warning to certain itinerant Breton priests who traveled about preaching with female assistants *(conhospitae)* who raised the chalice containing the blood of Christ in the manner of the Pepudian *(sic)* sect.[269] Women in the west were exhorted to accept the consecrated status of virginity or widowhood. Occasional transgressions were of course not ruled out. The terms *diacona* and *diaconus* were occasionally applied to women as honorific titles. When Radegund decided to refuse to go on living with Clothaire I, she persuaded Medardus, bishop of Noyon, to consecrate her as deacon.[270]

Women's Powers

The major prohibitions (against entering the priesthood and teaching) did not prevent some women from exercising a kind of informal power, not least in ecclesiastical politics. In the third century the Neoplatonic philosopher Porphyry attacked this unwarranted intrusion in *Against Christians*. A century later Jerome referred to this work: "Let us take care lest, as the impious Porphyry maintains, matrons and women constitute our Senate."[271] After Constantine nearly all aristocratic women turned to Christianity, and social status and influence at times became major factors to be reckoned with inside the Church. John Chrysostom deplored this situation: "Divine law has excluded [women] from ecclesiastical office, yet they still try to push their way in, and since they can do nothing on their own, they rely on intermediaries for everything. They have acquired so much power that they can see to it that the priests they want are elected and others rejected. Everything is upside down . . . Those who are subject to authority command those who possess it, and may it please God that they are men and not women, who have not been trusted with teaching. And why do I say teaching? The blessed Paul did not even allow them to speak in the congregation. I heard someone say that they take such liberty [*parrhesia*] that they speak more harshly than masters to their slaves."[272] This diatribe, which John issued from Antioch, sheds light on his later conflicts in Constantinople with Empress Eudoxia and her cadre of powerful widows: Marsa, Castricia, and Eugraphia.[273] These conflicts continued until John was deposed and exiled to Isauria. Thereafter, as his correspondence shows, the exiled bishop received material, diplomatic, and spiritual support not only from Olympias and her companions but also from numerous other aristocratic correspondents in both the east and the west. Note especially, in his letters to Olympias, the requests for help from bishops who supported her and the intervention in an episcopal succession among the Goths.[274]

With ardent faith, culture both profane and religious, and

social influence, women also intervened in theological disputes such as the Origenist controversy. Under Pope Anastasius (399–402), Jerome tells us, Marcella was initially a supporter of the Origenists: "She produced witnesses instructed by them but since corrected of the heretical error. She introduced the impious volumes of [Origen's] *On First Principles* and showed that they had been expurgated ... The heretics, convoked by frequent letters to defend themselves, did not dare come, and the weight on their conscience was such that they preferred to be condemned absent rather than refuted present."[275] Melania the Elder defended Rufinus, Origen's translator, who came under attack.[276]

In the *Lausiac History* Palladius recalled how Melania, with her wealth and patrician assurance, had supported martyred bishops and priests in Palestine during the anti-Nicaean persecution of Valens.[277] He also praised her, along with Rufinus, for having restored unity in Jerusalem after the Pauline schism, which had involved some four hundred monks, "persuading all the heretics who fought against the Holy Spirit and bringing them back into the Church."[278]

Her granddaughter, Melania the Younger, was described by her biographer, Gerontius, during a stay in Constantinople while Nestorianism flourished there: she received "many senators' wives and some of the most eloquent of men, who came to discuss the orthodox faith with her. And this woman, in whom the Holy Spirit resided, talked theology from morning till night, bringing many stray sheep back to the orthodox fold, offering support to others in doubt, and in a word aiding all who came to seek out her teaching, inspired by God."[279]

In Christological debates women were involved on both sides of every issue. The empress Eudocia, exiled to Jerusalem, long remained faithful to her Monophysite convictions. She was brought back to the orthodox Church only through the influence of Euthymius and Simeon Stylites.[280] By contrast, Pulcheria played a major role in the anti-Monophysite victory at the Council of Chalcedon (451). She, along with Marcian, was declared one of the two "beacons of the orthodox faith."[281]

Yet even for such women propriety demanded a certain effacement. This, according to Jerome, was Marcella's supreme virtue: "All that we have been able to learn by dint of long study ... she has imbibed, she has learned it and possessed it, so that if, after my departure, a controversy arose on any text in Scripture, she was called upon to offer a judgment. And since she was very prudent and knew what the philosophers call *to prepon*, what is appropriate, when questioned she answered in such a way as not to offer her own sentiment as her own but as mine or someone else's, so that, even in her teaching, she appeared to be a pupil. Indeed, she knew the words of the Apostle: 'I do not allow a woman to teach,' and she did not wish to appear to do injury to the men, some of them priests, who questioned her on obscure and ambiguous issues."[282]

Women enjoyed power as donors and founders. They played a role in the transition from ancient euergetism to Christian charity, church assistance of the poor, and monasteries.[283] Some were obscure, like those who donated inscriptions in honor of their husbands. Others stood alone: "In virtue of her vow, Peristeria has made the mosaic in the nave" of the Stobi basilica; Matrona too was mentioned as the donor of a mosaic, as we saw earlier.[284] Aristocratic donors in the east and west were celebrated by their ecclesiastical biographers. After doing penance for a divorce followed by remarriage, Fabiola (died 399) founded the first hospital *(nosokomion)* in Rome, where she took care of the sick and the aged. She was generous to clerics, monks, and virgins throughout Italy. Upon her return from Jerusalem with Pammachius, who became a monk after the death of his wife Pauline, Fabiola founded a hostelry for travelers *(xenodochium)* at Porto Romano.[285]

The generosity of widows had long been an important source of wealth for the Church. Porphyry accused Christians of "persuading women [to distribute] their fortunes and their property among the poor," reducing them to beggary.[286] When Melania the Elder left Rome for a pilgrimage to Egypt, she brought with her a casket containing 300 pieces of silver and gave it to Pambo, a hermit.[287] She supported orthodox deportees in Jerusalem and later founded there a monastery, where, according to Palladius, she and Rufinus received "all who come to pray: bishops, monks, and virgins, edifying them and aiding them from their resources . . . They gave gifts and food to the clergy of the city."[288]

Olympias, the wife of the prefect Nebridius, became a widow in 386 after twenty months of marriage. Emperor Theodosius accused her of "wantonly wasting [her husband's] fortune" and pressed her to marry Elpidius, a kinsman. When she refused, the emperor named the prefect of Constantinople trustee of her property until she reached the age of thirty.[289] (She actually took control in 391.) She gave donations of money, land, houses, equipment, rents, and commodities to the church of Constantinople, initially during the episcopate of Nectarius: "She served him, and in the affairs of the Church he obeyed her completely."[290] John Chrysostom succeeded Nectarius as bishop. "For the benefit of the Holy Church she gave John 10,000 pieces of gold and 10,000 of silver along with her properties . . . in the provinces of Thrace, Galatia, Cappadocia, and Bithynia; the buildings she owned in the capital, including the one near the great church called 'Olympias's house' together with the court buildings and baths . . . and all the surrounding buildings, including the *Silignarion* [bakery?], and also, near the public baths of Constantius, the house that belonged to her and in which she lived, and finally another house of hers called the 'house of Evandrius,' as well as all her properties in the suburbs."[291] Later she added "all her other property in real estate, scattered throughout the province, and her share in the public product."[292] She used buildings and workshops adjoining the southern corner of the church to found a monastery that was later joined to the church narthex.[293] She was famous for receiving visiting bishops, giving gifts of money and property, and taking care of ascetics, virgins, widows, orphans, old people, and paupers.[294] She was also renowned for the sustenance she provided John, even in exile.[295] This impressive inventory gives some idea of her immense fortune, as well as her total commitment to the Church and the modicum of power she obtained in return.[296]

Early in the fifth century Melania the Younger and her husband, Pinianus, renounced the world and rid themselves of an even more stupendous fortune: an annual income of 12 myriads of gold, vast possessions, thousands of slaves set free or sold. They sent enormous sums to Egypt, Antioch, Palestine, and Constantinople "for the service of the poor," endowed monasteries of monks and virgins, and donated items of silk and silver to churches.[297] Once they had disposed of all their property in Rome and Italy, they went to Africa, where they also owned vast estates, the product of which went to feed the poor and redeem prisoners but also to provide money, offerings, jewels, and rich fabrics to the church of Thagaste. Meanwhile they founded and endowed two monasteries of eighty men and a hundred and thirty virgins.[298] After a pilgrimage through Egypt also marked by generous gifts, they settled in Jerusalem, where Melania, following her mother's death, built a convent for women on the Mount of Olives,[299] and, following Pinianus' death, a monastery for men in memory of the blessed.[300] She also built the chapel of the Apostoleion[301] and a martyrium to hold the relics of Zachariah, the Forty Martyrs of Sebaste, and Stephen.[302] She and Empress Eudocia fought over possession of the relics of Saint Stephen.[303]

The Theodosian empresses demonstrated their desire for religious action through generosity. When a male heir was born, Eudoxia fulfilled a pledge by building a basilica in Gaza on the ruins of the razed temple of Zeus Marnas.[304] Eudocia demonstrated her love of the holy land by transferring Saint Stephen's relics from Constantinople to Jerusalem, by building an episcopal palace and shelters for pilgrims, and by reconstructing the Church of Saint Stephen *extramuros*.[305] Pulcheria sent precious objects to Jerusalem, donated one of her robes to cover the altar of the Great Church of Constantinople during communion, and above all built next to her home martyria for Saint Lawrence, Isaiah, and the Forty Martyrs of Sebaste. She contributed to the worship of Mary by building three churches—Saint Mary's of Blachernes, the Hodegoi, and the Chalkoprateia—on the ruins of the synagogue, where relics of Mary (her shroud, icon, and sash) were venerated.[306]

Most important of all, women's power from the inception to the final victory of Christianity lay in the communicative character of their faith. It was easier for women than for men to free themselves from the social and political constraints of the ancient city, and often women seem to have been in advance of men from the same family. Their influence at home encouraged others to convert, so that women played a crucial role in the transmission of the faith. In 2 Timothy 1:5 we read: "I call to remembrance the unfeigned faith that is in thee, which dwelt first in thy grandmother Lois, and thy mother Eunice."[307]

To pagans this susceptibility was a sign of the weak-mindedness of women and of an odious subversion of their spirit. In 178 Celsus wrote: "Look . . . in the private homes of the yarn-makers and cobblers and fullers, the coarsest, most uneducated people. They dare not breathe a word before masters full of experience and judgment. But when they take their children aside, along with foolish common women *(gynaion tinon . . . anoeton)*, they speak in strange ways: without regard for father and teachers it is they alone who must be believed; the others are mere stupid dodderers, ignorant of the true good and incapable of bringing it about, preoccupied with vile twaddle . . . completely corrupt."[308]

Echoing the Pauline corpus is a letter from Basil of Caesarea to the residents of his grandmother's birthplace, Neocaesarea: "What clearer proof of our faith could there be than to have been raised by a grandmother who was a blessed woman from your midst? I refer to the illustrious Macrina, who taught us the words of the blessed Gregory [Thaumaturgus] as preserved by oral tradition, which she remembered and used to educate, to inculcate pious dogma, in the infants we then still were."[309] Thus Basil recalled his childhood in a family of "old Christians" of Cappadocia, where his "paternal grandmother was widely renowned: she had done battle, several times preaching Christ" while hiding in the mountainous forests of Pontus with her family when Christians were persecuted by Galerius and Maximinus Daia.[310] Basil's brother, Gregory of Nyssa, wrote a life of their sister, Macrina the Younger, whose *nomenomen* foretold that she, too, would live a life of ascetic martyrdom, another Thecla. Gregory describes how his mother Emmelia oversaw his little sister's biblical education.[311] Faith was a family affair, transmitted by women from generation to generation.

Women also played an important part in converting many families to Christianity. The history of the *gentes* of the Roman aristocracy in the fourth century, a period of "pagan reaction," illustrates this "law." André Chastagnol has studied the case of the Caeionii Alpini.[312] The first members of this family to convert, around midcentury, were women. One of them had two daughters who chose an ascetic life: Marcella after being widowed, and Asella, who chose to remain a virgin. Pammachius, the son of the other, chose asceticism after his wife died. All were friends of Jerome and corresponded with him after he moved to Bethlehem. By contrast, the older Volusianus Lampadius remained a leader of the pagan community. He married a priestess of Isis, and his children remained pagans. But two of his sons married Christians. In 403 Jerome portrayed Volusianus' younger brother Caecina Albinus, the pontiff of Vesta, as a man surrounded by Christian progeny (except for his eldest son, Caecina Decius Albinus, one of the guests at Macrobius' pagan *Saturnalia*): "Who would believe that the granddaughter of the pontiff Albinus was born in answer to her mother's prayer, and that in her grandfather's presence, to his great joy, the stammering child would sing the Hallelujah, and the old man would place a virgin of Christ on his knee? Our hopes have been rewarded. A holy religious family has sanctified an unbelieving elder. He is a candidate for the faith, this man surrounded by a flock of believing sons and grandsons."[313] But Volusianus, who headed the family's elder branch, remained a pagan. Despite pressure from family members and letters from Augustine and Marcellinus,[314] he resisted until 436, when, on his deathbed in Constantinople, he was converted *in extremis* by Melania the Younger who had hastened all the way from Jerusalem for the purpose.[315]

In the fourth and fifth centuries, when the Church still tolerated mixed marriages, we find abundant evidence of women's efforts to convert men and of the men's resistance. In his eulogy for his sister Gorgonia, Gregory Nazianzen recalls the favor she obtained on the eve of her death: "She wanted only one more thing: for her husband, too, to accede to perfection . . . He was her husband . . . She therefore wanted her entire body to be consecrated to God, rather than to depart having acquired only a half perfection, leaving something in herself unfinished. And in this request too she was not to be denied."[316] Augustine's mother, Monica, likewise tried to win her husband, Patricius, over to God, "preaching Thee unto him by her conversation."[317] And who can forget the impatient words of the bishop consulted by Monica during Augustine's Manichaean period: "It is not possible that the son of these tears shall perish."[318] The recently discovered correspondence of the bishop of Hippo contains two letters to Firmus, who, though an avid reader of the *City of God,* was in no hurry to take the next step of baptism. Augustine exhorts him to follow his wife's example and to enter the Church: "For if this be a difficult thing, consider that the weaker of the two sexes is already there; if this be an easy thing, there is no reason why the stronger should not be there also."[319]

Women also led the way to still greater religious commitment. After obtaining a cure for Evagrius and restoring him to his anchoritic life, Melania the Elder returned to Italy from Jerusalem.[320] There "she met the blessed Apronianus, a most worthy man, who was a pagan. She taught him the catechism and made him a Christian. And she persuaded him to remain continent with his wife, his niece Avita. With her counsel she fortified the resolve of her granddaughter Melania and her husband Pinianus and taught the catechism to her daughter-in-law Albina, the wife of her son. Then, having persuaded them all to sell what they possessed, she took them back to Rome and showed them how to live a noble and serene life."[321]

three

Yesterday
and Today

Matriarchy and Myth

Because women have been deprived of their history, it is tempting to recreate one for them in response to today's aspirations. Militant women of the liberation movement are demanding a history. Young feminists enthusiastically are discovering their heroines, their odes, their myths, and their ancient conflicts.

Such projections of modern concerns are often focused on the ancient world. In Crete, in Ephesus, in Sparta, we are told, there was once a time when women played leading roles. We may smile at this new mythology, but the assumptions on which it is based exert an influence that extends far beyond militant feminist circles, as Stella Georgoudi's study of Bachofen's *Mutterrecht* (Maternal Law) shows. The mythology of the matriarchy may even serve as an alibi for historians who sometimes feel that the nonsense that has been written about the Amazons is reason enough to pass quickly over questions of sexual difference. The history of women cannot be written until a proper autopsy has been performed on this myth.

P.S.P.

10

Creating a Myth
of Matriarchy

Stella Georgoudi

A VAST, PARCHED LAND, every year inundated
by the floodwaters of a great river; a vigorous,
impetuous tide penetrating the earth's dark and
mysterious entrails; an exuberant world of plants,
a rich profusion of swamp vegetation springing
from the union of water and soil, from the marriage of the Egyptian earth and the Nile. This was
the powerful, all but overwhelming image that inspired the Swiss jurist Jacob Bachofen (1815–
1887). Bachofen was an enthusiastic philologist
who set out to provide a theory of the origins of
natural life, an interpretation of myth, an insight
into the essence of the remote era that he saw as
governed by the *Mutterrecht,* maternal law, and
by the power *(kratos)* of women—in a word, "gynecocracy" (German: *Gynaikokratie,* from Greek
gyne, woman, + *kratos,* rule). Lost in the night of
time, this earliest age of humankind elicited all of
Bachofen's ardor and learning. He described, analyzed, and championed this lost era in a fundamental work published in Basel in 1861: *Das Mutterrecht,* whose subtitle was "Research into the
Religious and Juridical Nature of the Gynecocracy
of the Ancient World."

That the theoretical edifice Bachofen constructed rests primarily on Egypt is chiefly a con-

sequence of Plutarch's treatise *Isis and Osiris,* a work deeply influenced by Platonism and written around A.D. 120. Plutarch's discussion of the Egyptian myth, together with the image of Egyptian lands alternately flooded and drained by the Nile, furnished the essential ingredients of a scenario that Bachofen adapted and interpreted to fit his own ideological preconceptions.[1]

The General Scenario

Bachofen's theoretical edifice rested on two related but profoundly antagonistic principles: a feminine principle, in Egypt embodied in the goddess Isis, the supreme "Mother" and none other than the fertile Earth itself; and a masculine principle, crystallized in Osiris, brother and husband of Isis and identified with the Nile, the male and fecundating power of the waters.

Of these two vital entities, the "feminine" formed, according to Bachofen, the corporeal "receptacle," the "passive matter" of birth, the universal nurturer, the pure "telluric" element. The other, "fecundating virility," constituted active, "humidifying" energy, the seed that engenders, the immaterial, noncorporeal element, the expression of a pure spirituality. The whole of the *Mutterrecht* is Bachofen's absorbing, impassioned account of the conflict between these two great forces, which govern all human life. At the beginning of history Isis dominated Osiris; the Mother imposed her natural law and her cult; the maternal breast gripped, enclosed, and held the "generative fluid" in a subordinate position.[2] It was therefore natural to present Egypt as a prototype, a model of "gynecocracy" against which the mores of other nations could be measured.[3] This model status ascribed to Egypt would prove to be persistent: more than forty years after the publication of *Das Mutterrecht,* the "French Feminist Study Group" would characterize Egypt as "the unshakable source and last refuge of matriarchy."[4]

Although "matriarchy" (literally, mother power) is generally considered to have been Bachofen's great discovery (compared by some to Columbus' discovery of America[5]), the term does not appear in his work. Bachofen used the terms "maternal law" and "gynecocracy," often side by side, without establishing any firm distinction between them.[6] It is clear, however, that in his mind these two compound terms referred to a series of social and juridical facts exhibiting two inextricable characteristics: the superiority of women over men in the family as well as in society; and the exclusive recognition of maternal kinship, or, in the jargon of anthropology, matrilinear filiation, which meant that only daughters could legally inherit property. The term matriarchy, forged in the late nineteenth century by analogy with patriarchy, had the advantage of suggesting both of these characteristic concerns; no doubt that is why it caught on among Bachofen's admirers as well as his foes.

The Theory of the Matriarchy

What is Bachofen's theory of matriarchy? What are its principles and laws? To answer these questions is no easy task. Not only is the work long, but some specialists regard it as a "mystical" text, part poetry, part science, hard to read and "forbidding of approach."[7] It is indeed a book filled with contradictions, repetitions, and digressions.[8] Like Darwin's *Origin of Species* and Marx's *Capital*, *Das Mutterrecht* is more renowned than read.[9]

Out of Bachofen's "romantic prose" let us try to extract the main outline of an explanatory scheme whose purpose is not merely to establish historical facts but to explain "the origin, the development, and the end of all things."[10] Like individuals, peoples too are organisms. In order to "germinate" and reach maturity, they need a firm "guiding" hand that can only be that of the Mother. Humanity's origins are placed under the auspices of one supreme force: Woman, or rather the maternal body, which gives birth in imitation of the original Mother—Earth.[11] The era of triumphant maternity is an age entirely dominated by "matter" and the "physical laws" of existence. Ever since Plato and Aristotle, Bachofen says, woman has been identified with *hyle,* or brute matter, which is variously characterized as the "mother," "nurse," "seat," and "site" of generation.[12]

Aphrodite's Hetaerism

In keeping with his characteristically dualist method, Bachofen depicts this childhood of the human race as a period divided into two successive stages, each corresponding to a different type of maternity, a distinct form of materiality.[13] In the first, more primitive stage, "telluric life" knew no bounds or impediments. This was a period of profoundly "chthonian" materialism, during which pure natural law *(ius naturale)* attained its height. The most spectacular manifestations of the reign of natural law were, first, the exuberant but chaotic and undisciplined manner in which sexual relations were accomplished, leading to open "animal promiscuity"; and, second, the luxuriant flora, the vegetation that spontaneously arose out of the chaotic fertility of the swamps.[14] Bachofen called this the stage of *Hetärismus* (from the Greek *hetaera,* courtesan). Marriage, he said, was completely foreign to it. Children recognized no father but were "sowed at random" *(spartoi)* like the "marsh plants" that stemmed from maternal matter alone.[15] In this stage freedom was unlimited, and neither individual possessions nor private rights existed.[16] It was a time of nomadic life, when human beings were bound together only by "Aphroditean desire." In religion, moreover, Aphrodite took precedence over all other deities; and Aphrodite, Bachofen argues, vehemently opposed marriage.[17]

Demeter's Gynecocracy

In the second stage, the "sensualist materiality" of Aphroditean hetaerism was transformed into an "ordered materialism," symbolized by two important institutions over which the goddess Demeter presided: marriage and agriculture. This "cereal-conjugal" stage, as Bachofen called it, was nevertheless still governed by natural laws. The material-maternal framework of the previous period was maintained, but there was "a new impulse toward a higher morality," and a new law, "conjugal maternal law," was gradually extended to all spheres of life. Agriculture became the model for human marriage, and the seed and tassel of wheat became sacred symbols of maternity and its mysteries.[18]

Earth *(Gaia)* was no longer a mother in a universal, unlimited, absolute sense. She owed her motherhood to contact with man, who knew how to "plow, sow, plant, and work the earth" (all of these being masculine activities, according to Bachofen) and to whom she ultimately delivered up the fruit of her womb.[19] Woman, who merely imitated the Earth, was now elevated by her exclusive union with a man to the status of mother. Since marriage was a mystery of Demeter, women swore an oath of marital fidelity to the goddess and her daughter Kore.[20]

Although man's role was now active and indispensable, and although the institution of what might be called "Demetrian monogamy" in some ways presaged the restrictions of patriarchal monogamy, the priority of the fertile female over the fertilizing male remained unshaken.[21] The male procreative force bowed before the superior law of matter, the matter that conceived and bestowed life.[22] Woman, as a human replica of the grain-producing earth with its strong overtones of *sanctitas,* took on still greater importance in the "magico-religious" context in which agriculture flourished.[23] Throughout this phase of human existence religion played a primordial role. No creature is more profoundly religious than woman, Bachofen argued, and the female sex derived irresistible authority and power from its intimate insight into divinity. It was in fact during this Demetrian stage that true gynecocracy developed and the Mother came to dominate both family and state. Humankind entered an era of totally positive matriarchy.[24]

How and why did this transition from Aphroditean hetaerism to Demetrian gynecocracy take place? Bachofen identified the cause as the promiscuity of primitive times, when the male, restive under maternal constraint, used his physical superiority to abuse women sexually, "fatally exhausting them with his lubricity."[25] Woman, feeling an imperative need for a more disciplined life, a "purer civility," rebelled against the violation of her rights and became an Amazon, resisting the male by force of arms. Amazonism, in Bachofen's view, was a necessary transitional phase in the evolution of humanity. Despite its "savage depravity," it expressed "the revolt of maternity, which opposed its higher law to the sexual violence of males" and thus laid the groundwork for the Demetrian phase, during which the Amazon abandoned the bellicose and nomadic life and rediscovered her natural vocation: motherhood in a context of sedentary married life.[26]

Although the transition from hetaerism via Amazonism to the Demetrian phase was driven by "material laws," Bachofen considered both hetaerism and Amazonism to be "degenerate forms of the female sex."[27] There were, moreover, significant differences between the Aphroditean or Amazonian woman and the Demetrian woman. The first two types were governed, like the animal world, by the most unbridled *ius naturale,* whereas the Demetrian was restrained by the positive institution of *matrimonium.*[28] The difference was illustrated in the symbolic and religious sphere by the dual aspects of the moon. The Amazon saw the nocturnal star as having an austere, sinister nature, hostile to lasting union of any kind. The moon was a grimacing death's head, personified by the evil Gorgon. By contrast, the Demetrian woman saw the moon as having a mixed, androgynous nature (although the material-feminine component of course predominated). The cosmic union of Sun and Moon was for the Demetrian the prototype of human marriage.[29]

The Advent of Paternal Law

However much the various forms of "maternal predominance" may have differed from one another, taken together they constitute, for Bachofen, the most primitive stage of human history. The development of humankind inevitably led to what he considered the most important transformation of the relation between the sexes: the replacement of the maternal by the paternal principle, which he describes as a major step forward. When man liberated himself from the Mother and her gynecocratic mores, he ceased to be a child and became an adult. The peoples of the world shed their childhood and entered the age of maturity and responsibility. Thus began the reign of the father and of "paternal law." (Bachofen does not use the term "patriarchy" any more than he used "matriarchy.")[30]

Man's emancipation did not come about with a single stroke, however, but in three stages, symbolized by the sun's daily course. As the new age dawns, the "radiant son" is still dominated by the maternal principle. When the sun reaches its zenith, man attains to a triumphant and resplendent paternity. In the religious realm this corresponds to the age of Dionysus, to the realization of "Dionysiac paternity," in which the father searches constantly for a woman in whom he may kindle life. At first Dionysus is an ally of Demetrian woman and an enemy of the Amazonian women who refuse to bow before the superiority of his phallic-male nature. In a sudden reversal, however, these warrior women are vanquished by Dionysus' irresistible seductive powers and become "the hero's stalwart guard." This radical change demonstrates, Bachofen tells us, "the difficulty that female nature has in behaving with moderation and measure."[31] Dionysus, having become "the god of women," the god of carnal desire and mystical impulse, brings about a return of the old Aphroditean hetaerism. According to Bachofen, this transformation of "Demetrian gynecocracy" into "Dionysiac gynecocracy" demonstrates the fragility and precariousness of the father's victory.[32]

Before that victory could become solid, the paternal principle had to free itself from all association with woman; paternity had

454

to become purely spiritual. This goal was achieved in part by Apollo of Delphi but most of all by that male empire, Rome. Only the Roman system, staunchly supported by its juridical structure and political constitution, was capable of warding off all the attacks mounted by the maternal principle, which attempted to reconquer through religion what it had lost in political power. What this history shows, Bachofen concludes, is "how difficult it is for man in all times and under all religions to free himself from the weight of material nature and attain the supreme goal of his destiny, namely, the elevation of this earthly existence to the purity of divine paternity."[33] The danger, therefore, is not completely behind us, particularly since a step backward, a restoration of the "age of Mothers," will plunge humanity into bestiality.[34]

Praised by some, criticized by others, Bachofen's work on maternal law and gynecocracy remains the starting point for all histories of matriarchy. Apart from his influence on psychoanalysis, which deserves fuller evaluation,[35] he remains a reference for a certain type of Marxist or Marxist-influenced thought, all too appreciative of Engels' enthusiastic approval of *Das Mutterrecht*, whose publication he said led to "a total revolution" in his thinking: "The discovery of a primitive matriarchal stage prior to the patriarchal stage has for humanity the same significance that Darwin's theory of evolution has for biology, the same value that Marx's theory of surplus value has for political economy."[36] Nor should we underestimate the support that Bachofen's notion of gynecocracy has received from certain contemporary feminist quarters. But modern feminist writers who seek to prove the existence of a prehistoric matriarchy rely not so much on Bachofen's texts, which for the most part they have not read or have read badly, as on a simplified, often inaccurate, Bachofenian "vulgate."[37]

Ideas Derived from Bachofen

It is worth enumerating some of the ideas borrowed from *Das Mutterrecht* and sometimes reworked or elaborated in subsequent studies of women in antiquity.

> Ethnological evolutionism, in other words, the notion that human societies evolve in linear fashion from "savagery" or "barbarism" to civilization, from the lower to the

higher. In Bachofen this theory is coupled paradoxically with a cyclical model: certain societies devolve from the higher to the lower.[38]

The notion, apparently derived from Hegel, that the transition from one stage to another comes about through a violent confrontation between opposing principles, here the feminine and masculine. A series of other antitheses revolves around this fundamental clash of male and female: nature versus culture, matter versus spirit, earth (or moon) versus sun, darkness versus light, east versus west, Aphrodite versus Apollo, left versus right, death versus life, and so on.

The emphasis on the importance of religion, which the discoverer of matriarchy regarded as the primary cause of social development, the motor of all civilization. If woman dominated man at the dawn of humankind, it was because of her penchant for the divine, the supernatural, the marvelous, the irrational. Ultimately matriarchy rests on religion, whence the importance of the archetype of the Great Mother or Great Goddess or Mother Earth, symbol of the maternal reign, with whom nearly all the ancient goddesses have been identified.

The methodological axiom of Bachofen and his followers that myth can substitute for history, that the mythological tradition is a vast mirror that faithfully reflects the reality of the past, indeed that it is the most authentic evidence we have, the most direct and truthful manifestation, of primitive times.

The conviction that matrilinear systems are necessarily more primitive than patrilinear ones, a conviction that has led to confusing matriarchy with matrilinearity and matrilocality.

Keeping these ideas in mind, let us consider specific examples of the consequences of Bachofen's theories for the study of the ancient world.

The Reconstruction of Greek Prehistory

Convinced that gynecocratic forms predominate at the dawn of all civilization, Bachofen patiently painted a vast fresco of the ancient world comprising countries, peoples, and tribes from the

Iberian Peninsula to India, from Scythia to Africa. In this fresco real countries such as Lycia, Crete, and Egypt appeared alongside peoples such as the Pelasgians and the Minyans, whose historical reality has been contested, as well as frankly mythical tribes such as the Pheacians and Teleboans. Some of these gynecocratic societies flourished outside Greece; others lived on Greek soil, such as the Etolians, the Arcadians, and the Elians, the inhabitants of the western Peloponnesus, which, according to Bachofen, occupied "a preeminent place among the gynecocratic countries," as evidenced by "its religiosity, its festivals, and the conservative spirit of its people from both the civil and religious points of view."[39] Bachofen ranged widely in space and time. Less attention was paid to "well-known classical antiquity" than to those earlier periods in which contemplation of the Great Mother was still possible. Among the Greeks, for example, gynecocracy originated with the "barbarians" who were the "first pre-Hellenic inhabitants of Greece and Asia Minor, the migrant peoples who represent the dawn of ancient history," such as the Carians, the Leleges, the Caucones, and the Pelasgians.[40] These various tribes left "recognizable vestiges" of the "matriarchal" system, preserved mainly thanks to its religious foundations. From these "survivals" (within Greece as well as beyond its borders) one can, according to Bachofen, reconstruct the entire system.

A Lukewarm Reception

Bachofen's ambitious reconstruction did not meet with a uniformly favorable reception from specialists in Greek studies. Some great Hellenists deliberately ignored his work, while others barely mentioned it. That veritable encyclopedia of Greek religion, Arthur Bernard Cook, mentions *Das Mutterrecht* just once in his monumental work on Zeus, and then only to refer immediately to other scholars who disprove the existence of maternal law in archaic Greece.[41] Martin P. Nilsson, the acknowledged dean of Greek religious studies, dismisses *"mutterliche Spekulationen"* (matriarchal speculations) in a footnote and refers the reader to H. J. Rose's critiques of "alleged proofs" of the existence in "prehistoric" Greece of a so-called maternal law, which in any case is not to be confused with "gynecocracy."[42] Walter Burkert, in a treatise on Greek religion, warns of the dangers of a systematic dualism that opposes a so-called Indo-European element (associated with the masculine, the Olympian, Heaven, spirit, and patriarchy) to a non-Indo-European element (associated with the feminine, chthonian, earth, instinct, and matriarchy). The existence of "maternal law properly so called," he says, has not been demonstrated anywhere in the prehistoric Aegean or Near East. "It plays no role for the historian of Greek religion, despite the myth of Bachofen and the orthodoxy of Engels."[43] Similarly, W. K. Lacey, a student of the Greek family, refuses to take account of theories he believes to be based on "totally false premises, such as the matriarchal organization of society."[44]

The Use of Bachofen by Hellenists

Some Hellenists, however, have taken a more favorable position toward Bachofen's ideas, especially since notions such as matrilinear filiation, matriarchal system, maternal law, and gynecocracy have found a place in anthropological discussion. H. J. Rose even argues that at the beginning of this century a majority of scholars, inclined to look favorably on evolutionary theories, accepted the idea that a "maternal law stage . . . necessarily preceded the stage of paternal law."[45] For some specialists in Greek religion that priority was embodied above all in the "august" figure of the Great Goddess, also known as the Mother Goddess, Great Mother, or Mother Earth. Thus many scholars, whether or not they refer explicitly to Bachofen, have accepted the general, and often vague, notion that a feminine divinity, a mistress of nature, was the dominant religious figure in prehistoric or pre-Hellenic Mediterranean societies. Two cases in point are W. K. C. Guthrie and Jane Harrison.[46]

Jane Harrison was an eminent representative of what has been called the "Cambridge School," whose "anthropological Hellenism" has been deemed dangerous by some specialists in the study of ancient Greece.[47] She called *Das Mutterrecht* the most complete collection of ancient evidence for the survival of matriarchal conditions in Greek myth.[48] In two now classic works Harrison embraced the matriarchy-patriarchy dichotomy and explored the conflict between the old and the new social order as reflected in Greek mythology. Like Bachofen, she believed that myth was a projection of a real past. For Harrison, however, the primitive society was not matriarchal but matrilinear: woman was not the dominant force but, owing to her status as mother and "nurturer of sons," the social center.[49] Harrison saw the model of this type of society in the divine figure of the *kourotrophe* goddess, the nurturer of *kouroi,* young men.[50]

Similarly, Karl Kerenyi based his study of Hera and Zeus on the interplay between matriarchal and patriarchal. He set out to find archetypal images of the Father, the Mother, the Husband, and the Wife. This bipolar scheme enabled him to pinpoint the emergence of the "Olympian divine family" and to discern its correlations with a "matriarchal past."[51]

No Hellenist was a more fervent champion of the theory of matriarchy than George Thomson. A scholar steeped in Greek literature as well as an orthodox Marxist, he revised and elaborated on Bachofen's argument, which he complemented with a reading of Engels and with "principles of historical materialism." What he called his "reinterpretation of the Greek legacy in the light of Marxism" required an evolution of society in several stages.[52] Prehistoric Greece, whose matriarchal character Thomson took for granted, was a central element of this picture, in which the Mother Goddess assumed her proper place, crystallized in various "matriarchal" deities such as Demeter, Athena, Artemis, and Hera. Matriarchal society eventually disappeared, but it left traces everywhere, so Thomson set out to track down these "survivals" and to identify those places where "the maternal law reigned long enough to bask in the light of history."[53]

Other Hellenists followed Thomson down the path that leads unambiguously from the Mother to the Father, from matriarchy to patriarchy. Among them, R. F. Willetts, who worked mainly on ancient Crete, was interested in the "necessary" transition from a matrilinear to a patrilinear system. He described Crete in the Minoan period as a primitive agrarian matriarchy dominated by the Great Mother.[54] Though an adept of matriarchy, Willetts scarcely alluded to Bachofen; in his bibliography he cited the 1861 edition of *Das Mutterrecht* rather than the exemplary 1948 edition put together by Karl Meuli and his collaborators. Other proponents of the theory of matriarchy have taken a similar cavalier attitude toward the founder. Kaarle Hirvonen explains "Homeric courtesy" toward heroines and women in general by assuming, without mentioning Bachofen, that Homer was unable to root out all survivals of a supposed "Aegean matriarchy" despite his total adherence to the patriarchy of his time.[55] Similar remarks apply to a study by C. G. Thomas, who takes it for granted that Minoan society was "matriarchal" and dominated by the Mother Goddess.[56]

Bachofen's true champion, however, was the Greek philologist Panagis Lekatsas, who devoted his life to making Bachofen's theory known as accurately as possible in modern Greece. As late as 1970 he wrote that the existence of a "matriarchal stage of humanity," first discovered by that "man of genius," Bachofen, had been proven "beyond all doubt."[57] In short, Bachofen's work has given rise to a sort of Bachofenian vulgate, whose influence periodically resurfaces in ancient history. The same "proofs" of the existence of the matriarchy, bearing on the same subjects, are continually recycled. Properly interpreted, virtually any scholarly work can be mined for such proof, whether it be in archaeology, mythology, history, or literature.

Proofs and Refutations

Archaeology. Archaeology appears to support the theory of a ubiquitous Minoan Mother Goddess, allegedly the symbol of a pre-Hellenic matriarchal society. Examined closely, however, the evidence turns out to be flimsy: all representations of females, whether in frescoes, on seals, or on precious stones, are identified with the goddess; and mainly Neolithic figurines discovered on Crete are similarly supposed to represent the Great Mother. Yet serious objections have long been raised concerning the interpretation of these images. They may not all represent the same goddess; some may not be of goddesses at all, but of mortal women. The existence of a polytheistic system in the Minoan period cannot be ruled out.[58] Furthermore, proper interpretation of the female statuettes depends on comparison with a smaller number of male idols and a large number of figurines of indeterminate sex.[59] Minoan religion is, in Nilsson's words, "a great book of images without a text."[60] To deduce the existence of a matriarchal society from such images in the absence of related myths, to write history on the basis of iconographic sources alone, is a risky business that can lead only to the most dubious conclusions.

Mythology. Mythological evidence has been used in a similar way to explain the origin of the name "Athens" in terms of a "historic" conflict between a matriarchal and a patriarchal regime. In the time of Cecrops, the mythical first king of Athens, a dispute is supposed to have erupted between Athena and Poseidon over the name and ownership of the territory. After consulting the oracle at Delphi, the king convoked an assembly consisting of "citizens of both sexes," because "in this place it was then the custom for women to participate in public elections." The men voted for Poseidon, the women for Athena, and "because there was one more vote on the women's side," Athena won. This provoked the wrath of Poseidon and drove the men to seek vengeance: henceforth the women "would lose the right to vote, none of their children would bear their name, and they would not be called Athenians."[61]

For proponents of matriarchy there is not the shadow of a doubt about how this tale should be interpreted. Since, Thomson claims, the myth "so clearly [reflects] the unity of human, economic, political, social, and reproductive relations," it is nothing less than an illustration of the victory of a nascent patriarchal society over a declining matriarchal one.[62] As satisfying as this interpretation may seem to those who would see myth as a form of historical chronicle, it fails to do justice to the complexity of mythical discourse. Taken in its entirety, the story of Cecrops' life raises a number of questions that this account of a patriarchal phase succeeding a matriarchal phase cannot answer. In some versions of the myth, for example, Cecrops is described as a civilizing hero, the inventor of monogamous marriage.[63] This portrayal conflicts with Bachofen's account, according to which that invention is credited to the matriarchal Demeter. Another problem has to do with the dual nature of Athena, who is a female deity, to be sure, but also a motherless daughter descended solely from her father, Zeus. And what exactly does the myth say about filiation? Did society shift, as Bachofenians maintain, from "promiscuity" and matrilinear filiation to patrilinear filiation? Or was the change that occurred during Cecrops' reign from bilateral filiation (which took account of both the mother's and the father's name) to unilateral filiation in which only paternal ancestry counted? Cecrops, who taught that all creatures have both a father and a mother, might well have been the founder of bilateral filiation, which would account for his surname *diphyes* (dual nature).[64] Finally, how did the Athenians interpret this myth of origin? In the end the story it tells is one of women's defeat in the political and social realms. The myth is a reminder of the privileges that women enjoyed, not before the time of Cecrops, as Thomson claims, but during his reign, which "brought men from savagery to milder ways."[65]

History. If myth can be substituted for history, then surely a historian can be taken at his word. Proponents of the matriarchy theory therefore turn to Herodotus (I, 173): "In their manners [the Lycians] resemble in some ways the Cretans, in others the Carians, but in one of their customs, that of taking the mother's name instead of the father's, they are unique. Ask a Lycian who he is, and he will tell you his own name and his mother's, then his grandmother's and great-grandmother's, and so on."

To demolish all the Bachofen-like arguments about matrilinear filiation among the Lycians that have been repeated endlessly since the publication of *Das Mutterrecht,* it was enough for Simon Pembroke to look carefully at Lycian inscriptions.[66] But it has also been useful to reconsider the work of Herodotus, to ponder the relation of the ethnographer to the historian, and to reflect on the way in which *The Histories* represent the relation of barbarians to Greeks. Herodotus, it will come as no surprise, described the sexual and marital customs of the barbarians in terms of Greek categories: his *logos* was Greek.[67]

Tragedy. Ancient tragedy, particularly the work of Aeschylus, has also been plumbed for evidence of matriarchy. Bachofen's followers have interpreted the *Oresteia* in terms of a historical conflict between a declining matriarchy and a rising patriarchy. As they see it, Aeschylus' trilogy is a realistic account of the bitter struggle between powerful gynecocratic figures, represented by Clytemnestra and the Erinyes, and the new dynasties of the paternal regime, embodied in Orestes and Apollo. In this epic battle Electra and Athena abandon the female and come over to the male side, symbolizing woman's voluntary submission to the paternal order in recognition of its superior justice.[68]

The tenuousness, not to say the falsity, of this "historical" reading of Attic tragedy has been demonstrated time and again by studies that, far from denying the importance of male-female conflict in the *Oresteia,* have shown how rich the work is from the standpoint of current research interests. Scholars have shed a great deal of light on the way in which Aeschylean tragedy explores the social, biological, and religious implications of male-female relations.[69]

The Creation of a Myth

For some years historians and anthropologists have been embarked on a critical reexamination of Bachofen and his theories. Scholars have explored the theoretical preconceptions, ideological biases, and methodological procedures that helped shape the theory of maternal law.[70] This work has brought into sharper focus the Basel scholar's faults as well as his not inconsiderable contributions to ancient studies. Bachofen's emphasis on the importance of myth was not the least of the constructive aspects of his work. In myth he saw and accurately described the Greeks' representation of woman's demand for and exercise of power: dark Gaia, proud of her prophetic powers; the man-killers Clytemnestra, the Danaides, the Lemnians; the Amazons, bellicose enemies of Greek heroes and attackers of Athens. He saw, in short, the obsession of the good Greek citizen with all that was thought to be primitive, chaotic, obscure, undisciplined, and dangerous in the "female element."

Some Greek myths placed this fearsome female element at the beginning of time and endowed it with venerable primordial power. To relegate woman's power to the remote past, to assign it a place in "prehistory," to associate it with barbarian, "gynecocratic" regimes characterized by the absence of law and morality—to do these things was no doubt to write women out of the picture, to exclude them from Greek history, indeed from all history.[71] Bachofen and his followers clearly saw this legendary "reality." Their error was to take the Greeks at their word, to mistake myth for history. In so doing, they unwittingly created a myth of their own, itself a worthy object of study: the myth of the matriarchy.[72]

11

Women and Ancient History Today

Pauline Schmitt Pantel

WHAT ARE THE MAJOR AREAS of current research on women in antiquity? There is considerable ferment in this field, and the excitement transcends not only international borders but disciplinary boundaries as well. Historians and anthropologists have engaged in much fruitful exchange of ideas. In part this exchange reflects the interest of a new generation of historians and is not confined to women's studies per se. But it is also true that female investigators are particularly likely to venture across disciplinary boundaries to read whatever is written about women in their period of interest.[1]

From the History of Women to the History of "Gender"

Once upon a time there was no women's history, only a sort of portrait gallery of famous women—Penelope to Cleopatra—that went by the name "women in history." Amazons, warrior women, and matriarchs figured in an anguished quest for the prehistoric origins of civilization. In a well-known scholarly debate Michael Rostovtzeff among others linked the confinement of women in the home to the rise of Athenian democracy, while A. W. Gomme portrayed Athenian women as no less free than the gentle ladies of his own day. Scholars like Victor Ehrenberg who chose the middle ground insisted that ancient women were indeed confined, but for their own protection, and that within the home they reigned as undisputed mistresses.[2]

This controversy belongs to another era, although some are pleased to behave as though it were still a live issue. A new age began when it became possible to study the history of women, a subject previously neglected or dismissed as impossible. The explosion of feminism in the 1970s played an important part in this enterprise, as did progress in anthropology and the history of *mentalités* (as Georges Duby and Michelle Perrot point out in their introduction to this volume). A vast effort of documentation was begun, as texts were reread in order to lay the groundwork for a history of women that would satisfy scholarly standards of rigor as well as meet the expectations of militant feminists. The aim, Sarah Pomeroy points out, was to learn more about the feelings of women, about their sexuality, and about their private lives.[3] And, I would add, it was to give women a place in history as well as a history of their own.

This work was important and necessary. Without it, it would have been impossible to establish a new discipline with all the necessary support apparatus—journals, colloquiums, professional organizations, and even, in the United States, special academic programs dedicated to Women's Studies. But as new questions arose, scholars moved beyond this initial stage in the creation of a new field of study. Some specialists in ancient history felt the need to move beyond women's history per se in order to study the relation between the two sexes. Studies of production, property, gifts, ritual gestures, death, and clothing made it possible to understand how sex roles were distributed in the ancient world and how space was organized to reflect that distribution. Scholars began systematic study of various forms of ancient discourse on sexual division: myth, history, poetry, romance, medical treatises, philosophy. Analyses of Attic tragedy and comedy in the classical era, for example, showed how the portrayal of women on the stage influenced thinking about fundamental civic problems, such as the limits of power, warfare, and the reproduction of citizens.

New Demands

Progress in the history of women and the history of representations contributed to this new line of research. Novel questions came to the fore. Methodological critiques began to appear. Objections were raised to the overuse of pairs of oppositions for describing the division between the sexes. People began to ask about the relation between forms of discourse and social practices.

More specific critiques focused on women's issues in particular. Some asked why a history of women should deal with the masculine as well as the feminine. A special issue of the journal *Helios* edited by Marilyn Skinner provocatively questioned why feminists should waste their time studying androcentric representations created by and for men.[4] Josine Blok and Peter Mason edited a collection of articles entitled *Sexual Asymmetry,* which began by asserting that the study of the thought of ancient males held little interest for scholars seeking to explore the history of women.[5] Beate Wagner-Hasel and others shared this view.[6] These critiques reflected impatience, in my view justified, with the fragmentary character of many papers, which simply treated a fashionable theme in an academic fashion without seeking to establish a broader historical perspective. The critics seemed to want work in women's history to relate to history in general and to proceed from a shared conceptual, if not theoretical, base. Recent research has responded to these challenges.

New Concepts

Three concepts have recently been proposed as a basis for further progress: sexual asymmetry, social relations between the sexes, and gender. Their content is similar, but they come out of different cultural traditions.

The notion of sexual asymmetry emphasizes differences in the power of men and women and in the value attached to each sex. In the preface to her collection Josine Blok proposes that historians focus on such sexual asymmetry and its relation to other social and cultural models.[7]

The phrase "social relations between the sexes" is intended to underscore an obvious fact: that relations between the sexes are social relations. They are social constructs, not facts of nature, and as such can be studied in the same way as other relations between social groups. Looked at in this way, "male domination" is one expression among others of inequality in social relations. Its specific nature and mechanisms can be studied for a variety of historical systems. In addition, the connection between male domination and other types of domination can be examined. In the ancient world, for example, we need to look at sex roles in relation to other social roles as defined in archaic, classical, and Hellenistic society, as well as in republican and imperial Rome.

The notion of gender may require somewhat more extensive discussion, because in recent years it has been widely used in a variety of contexts. In fact the term has become something of a catch-all, particularly in English, where scarcely an article appears in a women's studies journal without the word "gender" in its title or subtitle. Although it took a little longer for this fashion to make its influence felt in the field of ancient history, it has been flourishing for some time now, and we have been treated to countless papers on gender in ancient tragedy, Greek medicine, Homer, and what have you. The term often is used in a vague, general way simply to point out that there are women in the world as well as men. In this sense *gender* refers to the division of the world between masculine and feminine, to a sexual or sexualized categorization. It is a neutral, conventional term of description that can be used by anyone and that lends an air of seriousness to any discussion. Hence the vogue for the word, as well as its principal shortcoming. In France the notion of gender has been severely criticized and denounced as a "fig leaf" for hiding the issue of sex.

But the term gender also has a more precise meaning. Joan Scott, for example, uses it to refer to the social organization of the relation between the sexes.[8] For her it stands for: rejection of biological determinism (implicit, according to Scott, in terms such as "sex" and "sexual difference"); introduction of a relational dimension: men and women must be defined in reciprocal terms (as has been the case in much recent work); and insistence on the fundamentally social character of sex-based distinctions.

In this sense gender is an analytic category that has proved useful to scholars seeking a concept in terms of which to make sense of a wide variety of case studies. With this concept in hand we can ask general questions: How does gender relate to other types of social relation? How can the study of gender add to historical understanding? Gender clearly captures much of the content of the two concepts discussed previously: sexual asymmetry and social relations between the sexes. It is a useful term as long as one is clear about how it is being used in any particular context, much like such other general concepts as "race" and "class."

The History of Women and Ancient History

Review essays and works of bibliography are valuable tools that help historians keep track of the current state of research and keep research from becoming bogged down. Sarah Pomeroy's 1973 bibliographic review was really the starting point for contemporary work on ancient women's history; subsequent reviews of the literature have proved equally valuable.[9]

Historiographic research has also yielded useful results, as scholars have explored the past to gain deeper understanding of the kinds of historical models that are in use today. It is not enough to say that the old debate on the condition of women in the ancient world has become a thing of the past. The origins of the debate have to be explained, its place in the history of ideas must be explored, in order to prevent these issues from recurring in some new guise. One issue that has been clarified by historiographic research is how "woman" or "women" came to be a distinct field of study within ancient social history. Josine Blok has shown that this feature of the discipline can be traced back to the nineteenth-century distinction between public and private. The nineteenth century was also responsible for the view of woman as "other" that informs so many studies of the ancient world.[10] Historiographic study has also shed light on another topos of ancient history bequeathed to us by the last century: the supposed seclusion of women in the east. According to Beate Wagner-Hasel, this notion grew out of two aspects of the nineteenth-century conception of antiquity: the idea that modern democracy is the child of ancient democracy, and the idea that east and west represent two distinct cultural forms.[11]

This historiographic research has made it clear that many subjects long considered controversial are the products of ideological constructs. Once recognized for what they are, these ideological constructs must be rejected as bases for thinking about ancient practices and ideas. Historiography enables us to remain critical about many of the concepts put forward in the name of the "history of women." It keeps us thinking about the relation between our own special subject and historical research in general.

The Big Picture

Research on the history of women has added to our knowledge of ancient history in general. Consider the notion of *stasis* (civil conflict). In a series of articles Nicole Loraux has shown that stasis cut across various aspects of civic life: politics, family life, the life of women.[12] In times of acute crisis, when the existence of the city was in doubt, women intervened, usually in groups. When there was fighting in the city—civil war—women put in an appearance. Their political involvement pointed up the proximity of political division to sexual division. One of the historian's tasks is to show how the two were related.

Let us turn next to Helen King's work on the Hippocratic corpus.[13] Hippocratic texts compare female blood—menstrual blood and the blood of childbirth—to the blood of sacrificial victims: "Woman's blood flows like the blood of the victim"— hot, red, quick to coagulate. The blood of the hero who died in combat was never compared to sacrificial blood. Helen King analyzes this analogy by examining stories of sacrifices, the story of Pandora's creation, and fragment 70 of Empedocles, where the term for the membrane enveloping the fetus, *amnion*, is the same word that Homer uses for the vessel that receives the sacrificial blood. She shows how this analogy reveals Greek thinking about gender and about social organization in general. Her conclusions can be carried even further: there is a parallelism between the role of sacrificial blood in the foundation of the city and female blood in the perpetuation of the city.

Marriage, an institution that lies at the heart of the economic, social, and political life of the city, provides my third example. In this volume Claudine Leduc considers marriage as a free gift.[14] A woman was always given to her husband, and the man authorized to give the bride away always gave her in conjunction with certain forms of wealth. Leduc examines how different cities dealt with this fundamental organizing principle. She explores the relation between the matrimonial and social systems and reconsiders, in a totally new light, the well-known contrast between the liberty of Spartan women and the constraint of Athenian women. The status of the married woman and her property was very different in Athens and Sparta because the two cities defined the civic community very differently. Sparta preserved the household organization and limited citizenship to landowners. Since the bride was tied to civic land, she was mistress of her person and property. Athens did away with the household structure and refused to limit citizenship to owners of civic lands. The bride, who was given away with a cash dowry, was an eternal victim. This analysis, which links the status of woman not only to the transmission of property but also to the definition of citizenship, at last makes it possible to resolve the long-standing controversy over the contrast between the status of woman in Athens and Sparta. Marriage and the status of the married woman can be seen as part of the larger and more central problem of the definition of citizenship.

Finally, consider the division of space within the ancient city. In our own day space is divided between the private home, where woman reigns, and public space, where man is paramount. I have suggested elsewhere that research on the sexual division of space might shed light on sexual roles in general. Phyllis Culham has called for research into the use of public space by women and into women's perception of space.[15]

Lurking behind these questions is the old controversy over the seclusion of women. Beate Wagner-Hasel has demonstrated convincingly that male space and female space in ancient Greek cities were not distinct but closely intertwined.[16] The oikos, she argues, was just as masculine as it was feminine. It is wrong to think of private space in the ancient world as feminine and public space as masculine. In this volume François Lissarrague examines the evidence of vase painting and concludes, prudently, that it makes no sense to speak of a particular space reserved exclusively for women.[17] We must avoid imposing our modern categories on the ancient world.

Sarah Humphreys has examined the relation between oikos and polis with respect to death, kinship, religion, and finance. In considering the relation between the economic and the political in the ancient world, Domenico Musti touches on similar themes.[18] Anyone who thinks about the emergence of politics in the ancient city runs into the question of the definition of public and private spheres. How were they related, and in what ways did they come into conflict?[19] Thinking about the delimitation of male and female space may prove useful to historians working on politics, economics, and social practices.

In the 1970s it was legitimate to ask: Do women have a history? It made sense for historians to spend their time amassing the materials needed to answer. By the early 1980s the question had changed, and researchers in this field felt a pressing need to overcome their isolation and move from a history of women to a history of the relation between the sexes. Today, the history of gender marks a new stage in the evolution of the subject. Historians are now showing that women were at the center of important social, economic, and political processes and intellectual developments.

Gillian Clark was being a trifle ironic when she remarked of work in women's history, "we await the new season's collection with interest."[20] But to those who have stood on the sidelines and watched "with interest," we can now ask: Can ancient history be written without taking women's history into account? Not, to be sure, without taking women into account; there is consensus on this point. But we can go further still: henceforth all ancient historians must take note of the contribution offered by the feminist perspective, by the "history of women."

The Woman's Voice

TO LET WOMEN SPEAK for themselves is difficult. To be sure, the gods gave Pandora, the first woman, a voice, and from the day of her creation the ancient world resounded with female voices. Women screamed when animals were put to death in blood sacrifices; they cried as they accompanied the body of a dead household member to the cemetery; they chanted in choruses during festivals; they gossiped at home behind closed doors; according to the comic poets, they spoke in hectoring tones in imitation of citizens in the assembly; and those who called themselves Amazons made inarticulate and therefore incomprehensible sounds. But did women speak? Cries, lamentations, chants, gossip, foreign tongues—all these were within women's grasp, but did they have access to the only generally recognized language? Throughout this book we have pointed out how the nearly total absence of texts written by women complicates the task of writing a history of women in the ancient world. There are, however, a precious few texts that are reputed to contain the authentic expression of women's feeling, and among them we have chosen one written on the eve of her martyrdom by the Christian Saint Perpetua, which recounts her suffering. Monique Alexandre introduces it.

P.S.P.

Perpetua or Self-Knowledge

In 202 Septimius Severus issued an edict banning proselytism, whether Christian or Jewish, in the Roman Empire. In Africa, most likely in Carthage, "they arrested young people, catechumens: Revocatus and Felicity, his companion in slavery; Saturninus and Secundulus; with them, Vibia Perpetua, of distinguished birth and liberal education, married according to the rules for the marriage of matrons. Perpetua still had her father and mother. She had two brothers, one of whom was also a catechumen, and a son, still at the breast. She was about twenty-two years old." The catechumens were baptized at the beginning of their incarceration. "The man who had converted them, Saturus, surrendered to the authorities and joined them in prison." After questioning and a "confession of faith," they were condemned "to the animals" and transferred to a military prison to await the beginning of Games in honor of the birthday of Caesar Geta, the emperor's son. Perpetua and her companions died in the arena with the animals, probably on March 7, 203.

We know of these events from an anonymous contemporary account in Latin, which served as the basis for a later Greek version and abridged summary *(Acts)*. For believer and unbeliever alike, the narrator hails "this latest testimony to the continued operation of the Holy Spirit in our own time," and he gives a lengthy account of the martyrs' triumphant struggles. The centerpiece of his account, however, is a verbatim reproduction of the words of two of the condemned prisoners, Saturus and Perpetua. Perpetua's testimony, brilliant and detailed, is said to have been "written by her own hand, based on her impressions." After the silence of so many others, a woman's words had finally found their way into a written document. This autobiographical fragment concentrates on the essential: the ultimate confession of faith "in the resistance of the flesh." From her first conversation with her father to her appearance before Hilarianus, the public prosecutor, Perpetua defines herself by this simple statement: "I am a Christian." But the text, with the analysis of emotions it contains, tells us what obstacles had to be overcome by a young woman who was closer to her family and nursing child than to her strangely absent husband. She speaks of her anxieties as a mother and of the mixture of opposition and pain in her relations with her father. She assumes and transcends her femininity. We witness the emergence of a new family configuration, stronger than the old: the family of faith. Painful moments alternate with moments of joy intensely experienced and expressed. In prophetic nocturnal visions Perpetua glimpses another Father and takes heart. A white-haired shepherd feeds her mouthfuls of sweet cheese, and the master of the gladiators offers her a green branch bearing golden apples.

Other visions herald the struggle with the Devil, with a dragon waiting at the foot of a ladder bristling with arms, with a dark Egyptian fierce in combat. Still others foretell victory "in the name of Jesus Christ," the crushing of an adversary's head beneath a heel, and revenge against the serpent of Eden. The visions show the way through the Gate of the Living to the Tree of Life and its fruits in Paradise regained. Using the virile image of the pancratium, an athletic contest involving both wrestling and boxing in which all blows were permitted, Perpetua sees herself "made male" (facta sum masculus), paradoxically transcending the limits of feminine weakness. From that moment on a power inhabits her, bringing her powers of vision and prophecy and, at long last, sovereign freedom of speech and action in the face of jailers, magistrates, and executioners. In these terms Perpetua proclaimed the power that the Christian faith would recognize in her and her companions. In 354 the names Perpetua and Felicity figured in the Roman calendar of martyrs on the date March 7.

Perpetua's Vision

We were still with our guards [in Thuburbo]. My father tried to talk me into forsaking my vows. Out of love he stubbornly sought to shake my faith.

"Father," I asked, "do you see these things? This vase sitting on the ground, for example, or this jug?"

"I see them," he answered.

And then I asked, "Can you call this thing by anything other than its true name?"

And he said, "Certainly not."

"Well, I am the same. I cannot call myself anything other than what I am: a Christian."

Exasperated, my father hurled himself at me as if to tear out my eyes. But he did not go beyond insults and left with his devilish arguments a defeated man. I did not see him for several days, and for that I thanked the Lord, for his absence was a relief to me.

During that time we were baptized. Inspired by the Spirit, I asked only one thing of the holy water: the power to resist in my flesh.

A few days later we were moved to a prison [in Carthage]. I was frightened, because I had never been in such a dark place. A sad day! The large number of prisoners made the place stifling. The soldiers tried to extort money from us. I was also tormented by worry for my child. Finally, Tertius and Pomponius, the blessed deacons responsible for taking care of us, bribed the guards to allow us a few hours in a better part of the prison to regain our strength. All the prisoners were released from the dungeon and allowed to do as they wished. I gave suck to my starving child. I spoke to my mother about my concerns for my baby. I comforted my brother by promising to give him the child. I was consumed with sorrow at the sight of my loved ones suffering on my account. My worries caused me many days of anguish. I was permitted to keep my child with me in prison. His strength came back quickly, which alleviated my pain and anguish. The prison was suddenly like a palace; I felt more comfortable there than anywhere else.

On the eve of the day set for our combat, I had this vision: I saw the deacon Pomponius beating on the gates of the prison. I went down and opened them. He was wearing a beltless white tunic and boots with many straps. He said, "Perpetua, we are waiting, come." He took my hand and we followed a winding path across rough terrain. Finally, after an arduous journey, we arrived out of breath at the amphitheater. He led me to the middle of the arena and said, "Have no fear. I am with you and will help you." Then he disappeared.

At that point I noticed a huge crowd, seemingly spellbound. Since I knew I was condemned to be fed to the animals, I was surprised that no one threw me to the beasts. A terrifying Egyptian approached the place where I was standing. He and his assistants girded themselves for the coming battle. Several good-looking youths, my assistants and supporters, also arrived. I was undressed and became a man. My supporters began rubbing me with oil, as was customary before a fight. Meanwhile I saw the Egyptian rolling in the sand in front of me. Then a man of extraordinary height drew near, a man taller than the amphitheater. He wore a beltless purple tunic and fancy boots decorated with gold and silver. He carried a club like that of a master gladiator and a green branch with golden apples. After calling for silence, he said: "If the Egyptian wins, he will smite the woman with this sword. If she wins, she will receive this branch." He then withdrew. The adversaries approached one another and began to exchange blows. The Egyptian tried to grab my feet. I kicked at his face with my heels. All at once I was lifted up into the air, and I could land my blows without touching the ground. Finally, to hasten the end, I knitted together the fingers of both hands, grabbed the Egyptian's head, fell upon his face, and with a kick of the heel smashed his head. The crowd cheered, and my supporters gave the victory chant. I approached the master gladiator and accepted the branch. He kissed me and said, "My daughter, peace be with you." Triumphant, I headed for the Gate of the Living.

At that moment I woke up. I understood that I would be fighting not beasts but the Devil, and I knew that I would win.[1]

Notes

Writing the History of Women
GEORGES DUBY AND MICHELLE PERROT

1. Marie-Véronique Gauthier, "Les sociétés chantantes au XIXe siècle. (Chansons et sociabilité)," thesis, University of Paris I, supervised by Maurice Agulhon.

2. Michel Foucault's method of analysis can readily be applied to our case; see *Folie et déraison. Histoire de la folie à l'âge classique* (Paris: Plon, 1961), pp. 200 ff.

3. Marguerite Yourcenar, *Carnet de Notes pour Mémoires d'Hadrien* (Paris: Gallimard, 1951), I, 526.

4. Nicole Loraux, *Les expériences de Tirésias. Le féminin et l'homme grec* (Paris: Gallimard, 1989).

5. Renate Bridenthal and Claudia Koonz, *Becoming Visible. Women in European History* (Boston: Houghton Mifflin, 1977).

6. Jane Austen, *Northanger Abbey,* chapter 14.

Representations of Women
PAULINE SCHMITT PANTEL

1. *Plutarch's Moralia,* ed. T. E. Page et al. (London: Heinemann, 1931), pp. 475–479.

Chapter 1. What Is a Goddess?
NICOLE LORAUX

1. Although Artemis states the rule in personal terms ("I must not"), it is actually as general as the previous one. In Greece the gods were supposed to have nothing to do with death, which was by definition impure. In places David Grene's translation has been made more literal to correspond to Nicole Loraux's argument.

2. *Khaire,* farewell, has the additional sense of "be happy." Hence Hippolytus is saying to Artemis, "Be happy, you who are leaving."

3. Jean-Pierre Vernant, *Mythe et pensée chez les Grecs,* 2nd ed. (Paris: Maspero, 1971), II, 84–85.

4. See Charles Segal, "Penthée et Hippolyte sur le divan et sur la grille," in *La musique du sphinx. Poésie et structure dans la tragédie grecque* (Paris: La Découverte, 1987), pp. 166–168. Georges Devereux, *Femme et mythe,* 2nd ed. (Paris: Flammarion, 1982), p. 42, bluntly alleges that what Hippolytus feels for Artemis is "amorous lust."

5. J. von Arnim, *Stoïcorum veterum fragmenta,* II, 315 (fr. 1076: Chrysippus); 313, fr. 1070 (Servius, commentary on Virgil, *Aeneid,* IV, 638: citation); see also Cicero, *De natura deorum,* I, 34. *Effeminarunt, fictos:* Cicero, *De natura deorum,* II, 66, 70; Servius, ibid.

6. Clémence Ramnoux, *Mythologie ou la famille olympienne,* rev. ed. (Brionne: Monfort, 1982), p. 11.

7. Walter Burkert, *Greek Religion,* trans. John Raffan (Cambridge, Mass.: Harvard University Press, 1985), p. 218.

8. Hesiod, *Theogony,* 664–667.

9. Clémence Ramnoux, "Philosophie et mythologie. D'Hésiode à Proclus," in Y. Bonnefoy, ed., *Dictionnaire des mythologies,* II, 257.

10. Aristophanes, *Birds,* 830–831. The word *theos* used in the feminine deserves to be in the lesson on grammatical genders that Socrates gives to Strepsiades in the *Clouds;* see Nicole Loraux, *Les expériences de Tirésias. Le féminin et l'homme grec* (Paris: Gallimard, 1989), pp. 8–9.

11. I take the characterization of Athena from Paul Friedrich, *The Meaning of Aphrodite* (Chicago: University of Chicago Press, 1978). On page 7 Friedrich styles himself a "Freudian (or Jungian)," implying that he sees no difference between the two. In this instance he is perhaps more Jungian: it was Kerényi, following Jung, who proposed that "the Greek gods stand for ideas"; see C. G. Jung and Karoly Kerényi, *Introduction à l'essence de la mythologie* (Paris: Payot, 1974), pp. 149–150.

12. *Theogony,* 205–206, 224.

13. Vernant, *Mythe et pensée,* II, 138–139.

14. Ibid., I, 124–170.

15. Pausanias, II, 38, 2.

16. Pausanias, VIII, 22, 2.

17. Friedrich, *Meaning of Aphrodite,* pp. 82–85.

18. Burkert, *Greek Religion,* p. 161.

19. Giulia Sissa, in Giulia Sissa and Marcel Detienne, *La vie quotidienne des dieux grecs* (Paris: Hachette, 1989), p. 52.

20. See Jean-Pierre Vernant, "Mortels et immortels: le corps divin," in *L'individu, la mort, l'amour* (Paris: Gallimard, 1989), pp. 7–39.

21. In tragedy the summit represents something quite different for women, namely, the husband's stature. See Nicole Loraux, *Façons tragiques de tuer une femme* (Paris: Hachette, 1985), p. 52.

22. The *Clouds* (340–365) raises the question whether goddesses must appear in female form.

23. *Homeric Hymn to Demeter,* 275–276.

24. *Homeric Hymn to Aphrodite*, 40–44; compare *Homeric Hymn to Hera*, 2.

25. Hesiod, *Works and Days*, 61.

26. Ibid., 79.

27. At the beginning of *Hippolytus Rex* (line 86), when Hippolytus boasts of hearing *(auden)* the goddess' voice and conversing with her even if he cannot see her, I take it that Euripides' scathing irony has her uttering words better suited to a mortal.

28. *Odyssey*, X, 36; XI, 8; XII, 150; XII, 449. The expression occurs in M. N. Nagler, "Dread Goddess Endowed with Speech," *Archaeological News* 6(1977):77–85.

29. Hesiod, *Works and Days*, 61–62.

30. Jean Rudhardt, "Pandora: Hésiode, *Théogonie*, vers 885 à 955," *Museum Helveticum* 43 (1986): 231–246.

31. See the epilogue to Nicole Loraux, *Enfants d'Athéna* (Paris: Seuil, 1990).

32. See Alcman, fr. 3, 16 Calame.

33. *Homeric Hymn to Aphrodite*, 189–190.

34. Euripides, *Ion*, 506–508.

35. The only union between a god and a mortal that is not portrayed as having unfortunate consequences is Zeus's abduction of Ganymede (*Homeric Hymn to Aphrodite*, 200–217). Was homosexuality considered less dangerous in relations between gods and mortals? It was not so regarded among humans, as is shown by the fate of Laius, the "inventor" of homosexuality.

36. See Ileana Chirassi-Colombo, "L'inganno de Afrodite," in *I labirinti dell'Eros* (Florence: Libreria delle Donne, 1984), p. 114, and Stella Georgoudi, "Les jeunes et le monde animal: éléments du discours grec ancien sur la jeunesse," in *Historicité de l'enfance et de la jeunesse* (Athens, 1986), p. 228.

37. This is not a primitive (and modern) projection of incest, and the ancients had already remarked on it: see Karoly Kerényi, *The Gods of the Greeks* (London, 1977), p. 97, on the scholium to Theocritus, XV, 64 (which may allude only to a young girl's modesty in the presence of her mother), as well as Ramnoux, *Mythologie*, pp. 160, 165. On incest among gods, kings, and heroes, see Sigmund Freud, *Moses and Monotheism*, trans. Katherine Jones (New York: Random House, 1955).

38. Ramnoux, *Mythologie*, p. 52.

39. Pindar, *Eleventh Nemean Ode*, 1–2.

40. Marcel Detienne, "Puissances du mariage I. Entre Héra, Artémis et Aphrodite," in Y. Bonnefoy, ed., *Dictionnaire des mythologies*, II, 65–69.

41. *Iliad*, XIV, 213.

42. *Theogony*, 928.

43. Pierre Lévêque, "Pandora ou la terrifiante féminité," *Kernos* 1(1988):60. See also E. Simon, "Griechische Muttergottheiten," in *Matronen und verwandte Gottheiten* (Cologne, 1987), pp. 160–161, who makes it a

hypostasis of the Great Mother Goddess of Anatolia and the Aegean, like Cybele, Meter, and Rhea.

44. Burkert, *Greek Religion,* pp. 133–134.

45. On Ares and Hera, *Iliad,* V, 890–893. Recall that the "just" mother gives birth to sons who resemble their father: see Nicole Loraux, *Les mères en deuil* (Paris: Seuil, 1989), pp. 107–114. On Hera and Hephaestus, see Friedrich, *Meaning of Aphrodite,* p. 84. On Hera giving birth alone, see Jung and Kerényi, *Introduction,* p. 98, where Typhon, Hephaestus, and Ares are mentioned.

46. Jung and Kerényi, *Introduction,* p. 151.

47. Hesiod, *Homeric Hymn to Aphrodite,* 8–35; adapted from H. G. Evelyn-White, trans., Loeb Classical Library (London–Cambridge, Mass., 1982).

48. Euripides, *Hippolytus,* 1301–1302.

49. Loraux, *Les expériences de Tirésias,* pp. 263–270. Jung and Kerényi, *Introduction,* p. 151.

50. See Nicole Loraux, *Les enfants d'Athéna. Idées athéniennes sur la citoyenneté et la division des sexes* (Paris: Maspero, 1981).

51. Marcel Detienne, *L'écriture d'Orphée* (Paris: Gallimard, 1989), p. 98.

52. List of twelve gods in P. Séchan and P. Lévêque, *Les grandes divinités de la Grèce* (Paris: de Boccard, 1966), p. 26; on the organization of the *Dodekatheon,* see Sissa and Detienne, *La vie quotidienne des dieux,* pp. 181–182.

53. Burkert, *Greek Religion,* pp. 119–121.

54. Vernant, *Mythe et pensée,* II, 86.

55. Clémence Ramnoux, "Les femmes de Zeus: Hésiode, *Théogonie,* vers 885 à 955," in *Poikilia. Etudes offertes à Jean-Pierre Vernant* (Paris: l'EHESS, 1987), p. 159.

56. Madeleine Jost, *Sanctuaires et cultes d'Arcadie* (Paris, 1985), p. 308. On the question of multiple representations, see T. Hadzisteliou-Price, "Double and Multiple Representations in Greek Art and Religious Thought," *Journal of Hellenic Studies* 97 (1971): 48–69.

57. Pierre Brulé, "Arithmologie et polythéisme. En lisant Lucien Gerschel," in *Lire les polythéismes. I. Les grandes figures religieuses. Fonctionnement pratique et symbolique dans l'Antiquité* (Besançon and Paris, 1986), p. 35.

58. Ibid., p. 42; italics mine.

59. Ramnoux, "Les femmes de Zeus," pp. 157–158.

60. On this subject the reader may wish to consult various works on comparative Indo-European grammar, according to which the neuter plural was originally a collective noun with the form of a feminine singular "abstract" noun. Charles Malamoud, who first called my attention to this phenomenon, suggests that with a problem this large and this fundamental it might be wise to look beyond the Indo-European, because the question is one of general linguistics.

61. *Theogony,* 976: *theaon phulon.* "Societies of gods" could be male:

Burkert, *Greek Religion,* p. 173, gives several examples. But these male collectives appear to be more recent, and their connection with a Mother often places them in the service of a female divinity.

62. Brulé, "Arithmologie et polythéisme," p. 41.

63. On Goethe's "Mothers," see W. Granoff, *La pensée et le féminin* (Paris: Minuit, 1976), pp. 130–131.

64. Hesiod, *Works and Days,* 764; Pindar, *Eighth Olympian Ode,* 106.

65. Hesiod, *Works and Days,* 200, 102–104.

66. Burkert, *Greek Religion,* p. 125.

67. Marcel Detienne, *L'écriture d'Orphée* (Paris: Gallimard, 1989), pp. 89–90.

68. Vernant, *Mythe et pensée,* II, 87–88.

69. *Homeric Hymn to Aphrodite,* 97–98; Callimachus, *Hymn to Delos,* 82–85.

70. *Homeric Hymn to Aphrodite,* 257.

71. Jean Humbert's French translation of the hymn incorrectly translates "those women" as "the goddesses" on line 259.

72. Callimachus, *Hymn for Pallas' Bath,* 85–86.

73. *Homeric Hymn to Aphrodite,* 259. On the intermediate status of the Nymphs as the central subject of the hymn (relation of divine to human, immortal to mortal), see V. Pirenne-Delforge, "Conception et manifestations du sacré dans l'*Hymne homérique à Aphrodite,*" *Kernos* 2(1989):193.

74. *Theogony,* 159.

75. *Choephorae,* 45.

76. This is the view of A. Dieterich, *Mutter Erde* (1925; rpr. Stuttgart: Teubner, 1967), p. 54.

77. Plato, *Menexenes,* 237e–238a; for citations of the formula see Loraux, *Les enfants d'Athéna,* p. 89, n. 71; Erich Neumann, *The Great Mother. An Analysis of the Archetype,* trans. R. Manheim (London: Routledge and Kegan, 1985), p. 51; and above all J. J. Bachofen, *Myth, Religion and Mother Right,* trans. R. Manheim (Princeton: Princeton University Press, 1967), p. 132 (who cites the legal scholar Cujas, VI, 219e: *mater enim est similis solo, non solum simile matri*) and 195 (where the phrase occurs without quotes in the course of the argument).

78. Loraux, *Les enfants d'Athéna,* p. 89, n. 71.

79. J. Przyluski, *La Grande Déesse. Introduction à l'étude comparative des religions* (Paris: Payot, 1950), p. 31; Pierre Lévêque, *Les premières civilisations. I. Des despotismes orientaux à la cité greque* (Paris: PUF, 1987), p. 16.

80. Neumann, *Great Mother,* p. 51; M. Gimbutas, "The Earth Fertility Goddess of Old Europe," *Dialogues d'Histoire ancienne* 13(1987):23; and especially Bachofen, *Myth, Religion and Mother Right,* p. 80.

81. Euripides, *Phoenician Women,* 685–686.

82. Bachofen, *Myth, Religion and Mother Right,* pp. 80, 86–87; Simon, "Griechische Muttergottheiten," pp. 164–165. Another common identifica-

tion was of Pandora with the Earth. See, most recently, the subtle observations of Lévêque, "Pandora," pp. 56–57.

83. Jung and Kerényi, *Introduction*, p. 156; see also Burkert, *Greek Religion*, p. 159.

84. Burkert, *Greek Religion*, p. 175. Simon, "Griechische Muttergott-heiten," p. 164, suggests a distinction between *Ge* as Attic Earth and *Gaia* as a principle in the *Theogony* and in philosophical reflection.

85. Loraux, *Les enfants d'Athéna*, pp. 66–67, 130.

86. Pausanias, IX, 25, 3.

87. In discussing the reliefs in the Sparta Museum, admittedly of late date (first century A.D.), Juliette de la Genière, "Le culte de la Mère des Dieux dans le Péloponnèse," *Comptes rendus de l'Académie des Inscriptions et Belles Lettres*, attributes to the Great Mother what archaeological tradition attributed to Helen.

88. Pausanias, X, 12, 10.

89. Solon, fr. 36 West, lines 4–5.

90. Burkert, *Greek Religion*, p. 45.

91. For further insight we must await Philippe Borgeaud's forthcoming book on the Mother (to be published by Editions du Seuil).

92. Lévêque, *Les premières civilisations*, pp. 9–10, 14.

93. See, for example, Przyluski, *La Grande Déesse*, p. 23, n. 79, and Lévêque, *Les premières civilisations*, p. 16.

94. See Bachofen, *Myth, Religion and Mother Right*, p. 27 (the large container); Neumann, *Great Mother*, pp. 39, 42, 43 (woman=body=vessel=world), 44; Gimbutas, "The Earth Fertility Goddess"; Pierre Lévêque, *Colère, sexe, rire. Le Japon des mythes anciens* (Paris: Belles Lettres, 1988).

95. In the *Theogony* Uranos, out of hatred for his children, hides them all inside Gaia, "rather than let them climb toward the light," and "a moan came from the depths of the vast Earth, a sound of choking" (154–160). In Bachofen, as Neumann (*Great Mother*, p. 25) observes, it is the feminine that holds fast to everything that wells up from within and surrounds it and engulfs it as an eternal substance, so that all that is born from the feminine both belongs to *and* is subject to it.

96. Note what Neumann, *Great Mother*, pp. 62–63, says in criticism of Bachofen, for whom man in the matriarchy was a sower of seeds, whereas "the Great Vessel produces its own seed; it is parthogenetic."

97. On this subject see Chapter 10, "The Creation of a Myth of Matriar-chy," by Stella Georgoudi.

98. Bachofen, *Myth, Religion and Mother Right*, pp. 76–78.

99. Neumann, *Great Mother*, pp. 120–146, 147–208.

100. Lévêque, *Colère, sexe, rire*, p. 40. Lévêque gives this concept a specific Jungian root, which is no doubt correct: the Mother is terrifying because she and others close to her were the victims of sexual violence.

101. Euripides, *Heraclidae*, 771–772.

102. Pausanias, V, 3, 2.

103. Jung and Kerényi, *Introduction*, p. 151.

104. Hubert Petersmann, "Altgriechischer Mütterkult," in *Matronen und Verwandte Gottheiten* (Cologne: Rudolf Habelt, 1987), pp. 171, 173.

105. Burkert, *Greek Religion*, p. 179.

106. Neumann, *Great Mother.*

107. I am borrowing here from M. Moscovici, *Il est arrivé quelque chose. Approches de l'événement psychique* (Paris: Ramsay, 1989), pp. 76–79 (from a discussion of mothers as an issue in the debate between Freud and Jung).

108. Neumann, *Great Mother*, p. 11.

109. Ibid., p. 293.

110. Ibid., p. 11.

111. Ibid., p. 95.

112. Bachofen, *Myth, Religion and Mother Right*, p. 71.

113. Lévêque, *Colère, sexe, rire*, pp. 110–111.

114. Neumann, *Great Mother*, p. 309.

115. See Loraux, *Les mères en deuil*, pp. 78–84.

116. Alexandra Dimou points out that *theos* supplanted the feminine *thea* not only in the accusative but also in related constructions: *toin theoin*, for example, supplanted *tain theain*.

117. Petersmann, "Altgriechischer Mutterkult," pp. 173, 184; see also Jung and Kerényi, *Introduction*, p. 173.

118. See L. Kahn-Lyotard and Nicole Loraux, "Mythes de la mort," in Yves Bonnefoy, ed., *Dictionnaire des mythologies* (Paris: Flammarion, 1981), II, pp. 121–124.

119. Simon, "Griechische Muttergottheiten," p. 157.

120. Burkert, *Greek Religion*, p. 161. On the reorganization, perhaps at a late date, of the Arcadian cults around a pair of goddesses, see Jost, *Sanctuaires et cultes d'Arcadie*, pp. 297–301, and Madeleine Jost, "Les grandes déesses d'Arcadie," *Revue des études anciennes* 72(1970):141.

121. See Friedrich, *Meaning of Aphrodite*, pp. 46–47, n. 11.

122. Przyluski, *La Grande Déesse*, p. 29, n. 79; Neumann, *Great Mother*, p. 170; Friedrich, *Meaning of Aphrodite*, passim; Lévêque, "Pandora," pp. 60–61.

123. Marie Delcourt, *Légendes et cultes de héros en Grèce* (Paris: Presses Universitaires de France, 1942), pp. 88, 100; *L'oracle de Delphes* (Paris: Payot, 1955), p. 139.

124. See S. G. Kapsomenou, *Deltion* 19 (1964): 24 (col. 18): "Earth, *Meter*, Rhea, and Hera are the same . . . She was called Demeter, moreover, as well as *Ge Meter*—two names that make one." A. Henrichs, "Die Erdmutter Demeter (P. Derveni und Eurip. Bakch. 275 f.)," *Zeitschrift für Papyrologie und Epigraphik* 3(1968):111–112, compares this text to a passage in the *Bacchantes* where Cadmus and Tiresias, newly converted to Dionysus, give the same etymology and notes that the Demeter/*Ge Meter* etymology thus antedates stoicism, to which it is often attributed.

125. Petersmann, "Altgriechischer Mütterkult," p. 172.

126. Przyluski, *La Grande Déesse*, p. 29, n. 79; Lévêque, *Colère, sexe, rire*, pp. 37, 66.

127. Moscovici, *Il est arrivé quelque chose*, pp. 317–318, n. 107 (on Ferenczi finding "God the Mother behind God the Father").

128. Burkert, *Greek Religion*, p. 46.

129. Ibid., pp. 11–12, 14.

130. "Mother goddesses probably originated when the matriarchy entered its decline, in compensation for the decreased importance of the mother" (Sigmund Freud, *Moses and Monotheism*).

131. Moscovici, *Il est arrivé quelque chose*, p. 88; on Freud's suspicion of the Great Goddess, pp. 345–346.

132. Nicole Loraux, *Les expériences de Tirésias. Le féminin et l'homme grec* (Paris: Gallimard, 1989), pp. 219–231.

133. Madeleine Biardeau, *L'hindouisme. Anthropologie d'une civilisation* (Paris: Flammarion, 1981), p. 136.

134. Ibid., pp. 55, 150.

135. Ibid.

136. Although there were important differences between Greek cities, I cannot explore them here.

137. I am relying mainly on Clémence Ramnoux, *Mythologie ou la famille olympienne* (1959; rpr. Brionne: Gérard Monfort, 1982), a work that is not cited as often as it should be, probably because its lack of footnotes makes it appear "unscholarly."

138. *Iliad*, XIV, 260, 261.

139. Clémence Ramnoux, *La Nuit et les enfants de la Nuit dans la tradition grecque* (Paris: Flammarion, 1959), p. 23.

140. This birth by pure division is to be distinguished from growth within the earth.

141. Ramnoux, *La Nuit,* p. 64.

142. Ibid., p. 25.

143. Ibid., p. 52.

144. Aeschylus, *Agamemnon,* 170–173.

145. Ramnoux, *Mythologie,* pp. 27–29.

146. Ibid., p. 165.

147. *Phradmosuneisin* (*Theogony,* 884); on *Gaia*, Zeus, and the *phrazein*, see A. Iriarte, *Las redes del enigma. Voces femininas en el pensaimento griego* (Madrid: Taurus, 1990), pp. 38–39.

148. Aeschylus, *Choephorae,* 148.

149. Ramnoux, *Mythologie,* p. 50.

150. Detienne, "Puissances du mariage," and *L'écriture d'Orphée,* p. 40.

151. Detienne, *L'écriture d'Orphée,* p. 33; Ramnoux, "Les femmes de Zeus," pp. 160 (and 156).

152. Ramnoux, *Mythologie,* p. 50.

153. Ibid., p. 56.

154. Walter Otto, *Les dieux de la Grèce. La figure du devin au miroir de l'esprit grec,* trans. C.-N. Grimbert and A. Morgant (Paris: Payot, 1981), pp. 50, 41.

155. Ibid., p. 177.

156. Ibid., pp. 72, 283.

157. Aeschylus, *Eumenides,* 428.

158. Otto, *Les dieux de la Grèce,* p. 158 (with an etymology endlessly repeated by proponents of the Great Goddess: Poseidon is said to be the husband *(posis)* of Do, Dos, Deo, that is, Demeter, allegedly another name for the Earth). See Petersmann, "Altgriechischer Mütterkult," pp. 175–177, and the reservations of Burkert, *Greek Religion,* p. 136.

Constructing Gender
P.S.P.

1. Other aspects are dealt with in Danielle Gourevitch, *Le triangle hippocratique dans le monde gréco-romain* (Rome: BEFAR, 1983), and *Le mal d'être femme* (Paris: Les Belles Lettres, 1984); Aline Rousselle, "Observation féminine et idéologie masculine: le corps de la femme d'après les médecins grecs," *Annales. Economies, Sociétés, Civilisations* 1980, pp. 1089–1115, and *Porneia* (Paris: Presses Universitaires de France, 1983).

Chapter 2. The Sexual Philosophies of Plato and Aristotle
GIULIA SISSA

1. Philo of Alexandria, *De onificio mundi,* 165. I am grateful to Francis Schmidt for calling my attention to passages in Philo concerning the sexual connotation of the psychological and cognitive functions. I examine these issues in "Il segno oracolare. Una parola divine e femminile," in *Il mondo classico. Percorsi possibili* (Ravenna, 1985), pp. 244–252.

2. See Henri Iréné Marrou, *Histoire de l'éducation dans l'antiquité* (Paris: Seuil, 1950), p. 50.

3. Plato, *Republic,* II, 377: Socrates considered the possibility of recasting the myths that mothers and nurses taught to children because "most of those that are told today should be thrown out."

4. Plato, *Symposium,* 209a–c. Quotations from Plato are taken from *The Collected Dialogues,* ed. E. Hamilton and N. Cairns (New York: Pantheon, 1963).

5. Ibid., 212a.

6. Ibid., 206d.

7. Ibid., 206d–e.

8. There is surely displacement, as Nicole Loraux suggests in *Les expériences de Tirésias* (Paris: Gallimard, 1989), p. 21. There is probably also appropriation by the philosopher of the feminine power to give birth, as Page DuBois points out in *Sowing the Body: Psychoanalysis and Ancient Representation of Women* (Chicago: 1988), pp. 169–183.

9. Plato, *Republic,* VI, 490a–b.

10. Plato, *Phaedrus,* 251.

11. Plato, *Theaetetus,* 160e.

12. On maieutics see Miles Burnyeat, "Socratic Midwifery, Platonic In-

spiration," *Bulletin of the Institute for Classical Studies* 24(1977):7–16. While working on a book on the subject, I have published preliminary findings in "La loi dans les âmes," *Le Temps de la réflexion* 6(1985):49–72, esp. 68–72.

13. Philo of Alexandria, *De opificio mundi,* 76.

14. Ibid., 152.

15. Albert Jacquard, *Moi et les autres* (Paris, 1983), p. 26.

16. C. Bocquet, "Espèce biologique," *Encyclopaedia Universalis* 6, pp. 545–548, esp. 545. The definition of species is borrowed from Ernst Mayr.

17. A definition of species in terms of a morphological criterion would run into difficulties with sexual dimorphism, which in some cases is so marked that individuals of different sexes appear to belong to different types.

18. See the works of Pierre Pellegrin, especially "Aristotle: A Zoology without Species," in A. Gotthelf, ed., *Aristotle on Nature and Living Things (Essays in Honor of David M. Balme)* (Pittsburgh, Pa.–Bristol, 1985), pp. 95–115.

19. Plato, *Statesman,* 262c–263a.

20. Plato, *Republic,* V, 450d.

21. Ibid., 452b–c.

22. Ibid., 453e–455e.

23. Ibid., 455c–d.

24. Ibid., 455d. See Monique Canto, "Le livre V de la *République:* les femmes et les platoniciens," *Revue Philosophique* 3(1989):378–384.

25. The social groups responsible for biological reproduction go unrecognized. Kinship terms are applied to recognized age groups. The guardians constitute a single lineage for classificatory purposes.

26. See Pellegrin, "Aristotle," p. 95.

27. Aristotle, *Metaphysics,* IV, 28, 1024a, 29–30.

28. Plato, *Symposium,* 192a.

29. Plato, *Timaeus,* 42b; 90e.

30. Hesiod, *Theogony,* 589 ff.

31. See Nicole Loraux, "La race des femmes et quelques unes de ses tribus," *Arethusa* 11(1978):43–89.

32. See the comprehensive overview put together by P. Judet de la Combe, D. Rolet, and A. Lernould for the *Hesiod* colloquium organized by the Centre de Recherche Philologique of Lille in October 1989. The authors rightly insist on woman as the advent of want for man.

33. The magnitude of the discontinuity caused by the appearance of woman has been stressed by Piero Pucci, "Il mito di Pandora in Esiodo," in Bruno Gentili and Gino Paioni, eds., *Il mito greco. Atti del convegno internazionale. Urbino 7–12 maggio 1973* (Rome, 1977), pp. 207–229.

34. Jean Rudhart insists on this point, even denying that Pandora was the first woman: "Pandora: Hésiode et les femmes," *Museum Helveticum* 43(1986):231–246.

35. Aristotle, *Metaphysics,* 1024a 29–30.

36. Ibid., X, 1058a: "It may be asked why woman is not a different species from man, female and male being contraries and their specific difference, a contrariety."

37. Aristotle, *On the Generation of Animals* (GA), 716b 32.

38. Ibid., 716a 23–27.

39. On defects of the female, see Giulia Sissa, "Il corpo della donna," in Sissa, Silvia Campese, and Paola Manuli, *Madre Materia* (Turin, 1983).

40. Aristotle, *On the History of Animals* (HA), 638b 7–24.

41. Aristotle, *On the Parts of Animals* (PA), 653a 27–b3.

42. Aristotle GA, 728a 17–25.

43. Ibid., 775a 16–22.

44. Ibid., 775a 14–16.

45. Ibid., 728a 17–25.

46. This distinction between quantitative difference and analogy seems to me the real fruit of the critique of dichotomy, because analogy makes it possible to establish a system of correspondence between groups (PA, 645b ff.). As Pellegrin shows, Aristotle classifies not animals but parts of animals. It is analogy that enables him to envision a classification based on parts and their functions (distinctive features) taken together rather than as successive dichotomies.

47. Aristotle, GA, 738a–b.

48. Ibid., 716a 5.

49. As Françoise Héritier-Augé would say. Héritier-Augé has been interpreting Aristotle's ideas in the light of African biological theories.

50. Sissa, "Il corpo della donna."

51. Aristotle, GA, 740b 18–25.

52. Hippocrates, *On Generation*, IV, 1 ff.

53. Pseudo-Demosthenes, *Contra Macartatos*, 51.

54. Aristotle, GA, 767b 16–24.

55. Ibid., 767b 29–30.

56. Ibid., 768a 1–9.

Women and the Law

P.S.P.

1. Women's place in the legal codes of Hellenistic times is discussed in Claude Vatin, *Recherches sur le mariage et la condition de la femme mariée à l'époque hellénistique* (Paris: de Boccard, 1970). Joseph Mélèze Modrzejewski, "La structure juridique du mariage grec," *Scritti in onore di Orsolina Montevecchi* (Bologna, 1981), pp. 231–268. Sarah Pomeroy, *Women in Hellenistic Egypt* (New York: Schocken, 1984).

Chapter 3. The Division of the Sexes in Roman Law
YAN THOMAS

Roman legal sources are cited in the following abbreviated forms:

CJ. *Code of Justinian,* preceded by the name of the emperor to whom the law is attributed and followed by the date of the law (e.g., Septimius Severus and Caracalla, CJ 3, 28, 3, a.197).

CT. *Code of Theodosius* (preceded and followed by the same indications as for the *Code of Justinian*).

D. *Digest.* Where necessary, references to the *Digest* are preceded by mention of the author of the text and the title of the work, followed by the number of the book from which the compilers took it (e.g., Ulpian, *Commentary on Sabinus,* 1.1, D.1, 5, 10).

FV. *Fragments of the Vatican.*

Gaius. *Institutes of Gaius.*

I. *Institutes of Justinian*

SP. *Sententiae of Paul.*

Ulp. *Regulae of Ulpian.*

1. P. Legendre, *L'inestimable objet de la transmission. Etude sur le principe généalogique en Occident* (Paris, 1985), pp. 41 ff.

2. Ulpian, *Commentary on Sabinus,* 1.3, D.28, 2, 6, 2.

3. Paul, D.22, 5, 15, 1.

4. Ulpian, *Commentary on Sabinus,* 1.1, D.1, 5, 10.

5. The theory of physical irregularities derives from that of "voluntary corporeal vices" (i.e., mutilations), which are treated in the *Decretum of Gratian,* part 1, distinction 55 in conjunction with other "permanent" impediments, both psychic and legal. See Bartolomeo Ugolinus, *Tractatus de irregularitatibus* (Venice, 1601), and *Code of Canon Law,* canons 1040 ff.

6. Pliny, *Natural History,* 7, 34; Galen, *Definitiones medicae,* 478, in Kühn, *Medicorum graecorum operae quae extant,* XIX (Leipzig, 1830), p. 453.

7. Titus Livy, 27, 37, 5 in 207 B.C. and 31, 12, 8 in 200; numerous examples between 142 and 95 in Julius Obsequens (chaps. 81, 86, 92, 94, 96, 106, 107, 110).

8. These sexual definitions were combined with metaphors of weaving (see John Scheid, *Annuaire de l'Ecole Pratique des Hautes Etudes,* 5th sec., 1985–86, pp. 443 ff.) and the yoke (Servius, *Commentaries on the Aeneid,* IV, 16; Isidore, *Etymologies* 9, 7, 9, 19).

9. Cicero, *On Duties* I, 17, 54; Columella, *On Agriculture* XII, preface, 1; Ulpian, D.1, 1, 1, 3; I.1, 2, pr; Modestinus D.23, 2, 1.

10. Matronal majesty: Afranius, *comica,* fragment 326 of the 3rd ed. of Ribbeck, Titus Livy 32, 2, 8; Donatus, *Commentaries on the Aeneid* IX, 185.

11. J. Gaudemet, "Le statut de la femme dans l'Empire romain," in *La femme,* anthology of the Société Jean Bodin XI (Brussels, 1959), pp. 191–

222; S. Pomeroy, *Goddesses, Whores, Wives and Slaves: Women in Classical Antiquity* (New York, 1975); G. Fau, *L'émancipation féminine dans la Rome antique* (Paris, 1978); J. A. Crook, "Feminine Inadequacy and the *Senatus-consultum velleianum,*" in Beryl Rawson, ed., *The Family in Ancient Rome* (Ithaca, N.Y., 1986), pp. 83–91.

12. P. Gide, *Etude sur la condition privée de la femme* (Paris, 1867).

13. Pierre Vidal Naquet, *Le chasseur noir. Formes de pensée et formes de société dans le monde grec* (Paris, 1981), p. 26.

14. Nicole Loraux, *Les Enfants d'Athéna. Idées athéniennes sur la citoyenneté et la division des sexes,* 2nd ed. (Paris, 1984). On the incorporation of the feminine into the Greek concept of virility, see Nicole Loraux, *Les expériences de Tirésias. Le féminin et l'homme grec* (Paris, 1989). The introduction (pp. 7–26) is a methodological manifesto of great importance concerning the validity of the notion of sexuality for isolating and analyzing men's thoughts about their sexual natures (and not only for the Greeks).

15. Fau, *L'émancipation féminine.*

16. Ulpian, *Commentary on the Edict,* 1.46, D.50, 16, 195pr. See also D.50, 16, 56, 1, and Pomponius, *Commentary on Quintus Mucius,* D.50, 16, 122. The survey of semantics entitled "On the Meaning of Words" by the compilers of the *Digest* (5, 16) opens with a brief fragment from Ulpian: "The expression 'if someone' includes both men and women." Medieval judicial thinking began with this text: see the *Great Gloss* of Accursus, ad loc.: "The masculine sex includes the feminine sex within it, because it outstrips it in dignity." Humanist interpretation also started here; see the important exegesis of Johannes Goddaeus in his *Commentary* on D.50, 16 (Herborn, 1608), on which one can read E. Koch, "Vom Versuch, die Frage, ob die Weiber Menschen sein, oder nicht, aus den Digesten zu beantworten," *Rechtshistorisches Journal* (Frankfurt, 1982), 1, 171–179.

17. Acquisition of the *patria potestas* on the death of the ancestor possessing this power: D.50, 16, 195, 2.

18. Yan Thomas, "Le ventre: Corps maternel, droit paternel," *Le genre humain* 14(1986):211–236.

19. Gaius 3, 4.

20. Gaius 3, 2; *Berlin Fragments,* 2 (in P. F. Girard, *Textes de droit romain,* 7th ed. [Paris, 1967], p. 409).

21. Gaius 3, 26; Pomponius, *Commentary on Sabinus,* 1.4, D.38, 6, 5pr; 1.3, 1, 9.

22. R. P. Saller, "*Patria potestas* and the Stereotype of the Roman Family," *Continuity and Change* (Chicago: University of Chicago Press, 1986), I, 7–22. On p. 19 it is stated that, since the rules were no longer applied, there was no need under the Empire to change the old rules of *patria potestas.*

23. The "exercise" of paternal power has been the subject of extraordinarily fruitless debate concerning the frequency with which the "right of life and death" was actually applied. On the pointlessness of subjecting institutional analysis to the steamroller of sociological interpretation, see P. Legendre, *Le désir politique de Dieu* (Paris, 1988), pp. 63–103.

24. Yan Thomas, "*Vitae necisque potestas*. Le père, la cité, la mort," *Du Châtiment dans la cité* (Rome: Ecole Française de Rome, 1984), pp. 499–548; "Remarques sur la juridiction domestique à Rome," in J. Andreau, ed., *Stratégies familiales dans le monde antique* (Rome: Ecole Française de Rome, 1990).

25. Undifferentiated kinship groups coexisted with the agnatic family in the earliest recorded times. See P. Moreau, "La terminologie latine et indo-européenne de la parenté et le système de parenté et d'alliance à Rome: questions de méthode," *Revue des Etudes Latines*, 1979, pp. 41–53.

26. Twelve Tables, 5, 4; Gaius 3, 1–8; D.38, 16, "On Proper and Legit-imate Heirs."

27. Twelve Tables, 5, 4; Gaius 3, 9–17; Ulp. 11, 4.

28. Gaius 3, 14; 1.3, 2, 5; SP 4, 8, 20; Ulp. 26, 6.

29. "Natural" filiation as qualification of a legitimate filiation after ex-tinction of the *patria potestas: Tabula Hebana* (*Année épigraphique* 1949, no. 164) 1.2; cf. *Tabula Sairensis* (*Zeitschrift für Papyrologie und Epigraphik* no. 55, 1984), Frag. 1, 1.20, which should be punctuated: *Patris eius natu-ralis, fratris . . .* and not, as the editor, J. Gonzalez, has done in *Patris eius, naturalis fratris*); D.1, 7, 1; 28, 2, 23; 50, 16, 195, 2, etc.

30. Gaius 2, 161 (cf. 1, 104; 3, 43; 3, 51); D.38, 16, 3; Diocletian and Maximian, CJ 8, 47, 5, a.291; 1.1, 11, 9.

31. Gaius 1, 104.

32. Gaius 2, 161.

33. Gaius 3, 24 (cf. 3, 3); 1.1, 3, 3pr.

34. Consanguine kin were supposed to have been under the same *potestas* and to have escaped from it at the same time, or to have been born after their father's death or capture (for then the paternal power was either fictively continued until birth or suspended and retroactively reestablished when the father regained his citizenship). Ulpian, *Commentary on Sabinus*, 1.12, D.38, 16, 1, 10.

35. D.38, 16, 8; cf. 38, 8, 1, 8; 38, 16, 6.

36. D.50, 16, 195, 2.

37. *Rhetoric to Herennius*, 1, 3, 23; Quintilian, *Oratorical Institutions* 7, 8, 6; 8, 6, 35.

38. Murder of a *parens*, father or mother: Festus, p. 174, Lindsay edition; Plautus, *Epidicus*, v. 449; Priscianus, *Grammatical Institutions*, 5, 56. On the punishment for matricide, see *Rhetoric to Herennius*, 1, 3, 23; Tacitus, *Annals*, 13, 21, 2; 14, 8, 5.

39. D.25, 3, 5: "Let us examine whether children are required to give food only to their father, grandfather, great-grandfather, and other paternal ancestors, or whether they must also give food to their mother and other maternal ancestors. The judge must exert his authority in all such cases on behalf of those suffering from indigence or disease. And since the obligation stems from equity and from the affection felt by those joined by blood *(caritate sanguinis)*, the judge must examine the justice of each person's requests."

40. D.2, 4, 4, 1–2; "The praetor declared: 'No one shall pursue his *parens* in court without my permission.' Here *parens* should be interpreted as referring to both sexes."

41. D.27.10, 4; 37, 15, 1.

42. Evidence: *lex iulia* of Augustus, D.22, 5, 4; municipal law of the colony Genetiva Julia (Caesarean period), chap. 95 (in *Fontes iuris Romani Anteiustiniani* I, p. 187). The same formulation of undifferentiated kinship is also found in a law of Caius Gracchus between 123 and 121 B.C. (FIRA I, p. 90, l. 20).

43. Suetonius, *Life of Galba*, 2, shows that ancestors on both sides figured in the atriums of noble households (and therefore in public funerals). Galba traced his maternal background back to Pasiphae, wife of Minos. The *stemmata* of kinship that jurists used included both parents. The design of the *stemma*, with its lines (*lineae*, D.38, 10, 9) and branches (*ramusculi*, Isidore, *Etymologies*, 9, 6, 29), is reminiscent of the "lines" that link painted images (Pliny, *Natural History*, 35, 2), which Cicero called "curved lines of the *stemmata*" (*De beneficiis*, 3, 28, 2). In the painted *stemmata* in noble households, we must therefore assume that women and maternal kin were present, as we know they were in the legal diagrams that were probably derived from the paintings.

44. Imperial diplomas studied by E. Volterra, *"Tollere liberos,"* in *Festschrift F. Schulz* (Weimar, 1951), I, 388–398; "Ancora sul tema di tollere liberos," in *Iura* 3, 1951, pp. 206–217.

45. P. Moreau, "Structures de parenté et d'alliance à Larinum d'après le Pro Cluentio," *Les "bourgeoisies" municipales italiennes aux IIe et Ie siècles avant J.C.* (Naples, 1983), pp. 99–123, esp. 121 ff.; "Patrimoines et successions à Larinum (Ier s. av. J.C.)," *Revue historique de droit français et étranger*, 1986, pp. 169–189. S. Dixon, "Family Finances: Terentia and Tullia," in Rawson, ed., *Family in Ancient Rome*, pp. 93–119.

46. Practice attested in Cicero, *De finibus*, 2, 55 and 58, and *Pro Cluentio*, 7, 21.

47. On Terentia's dowry, see Plutarch, *Life of Cicero*, 8, 2; on Tullia's dowry, see Cicero, *Letters to Atticus*, 11, 23, 3 and 11, 25, 3. On the size of dowries in the republican senatorial aristocracy, see I. Shatzman, *Senatorial Wealth and Roman Politics* (Brussels, 1985), pp. 413 ff.

48. S. Dixon, *The Roman Mother* (London–Sydney, 1988); J. A. Crook, "Women in Roman Succession," in Rawson, *Family in Ancient Rome*, pp. 58–82.

49. See the chapter entitled "On the Successoral Order Observed in Orders to Take Possession of Property," in D.38, 15.

50. D.38, 8, 1, 9; 38, 8, 2; 38, 8, 4; 38, 8, 8.

51. See note 21.

52. D.38, 16, 13.

53. On the instantaneity of male successions, see Paul, *Commentary to Sabinus*, 1.2, D.28, 2, 11; Gaius 2, 157; D.38, 16, 14. On the discontinuity in female successions, see Gaius 2, 161; Ulpian, *Commentary to Sabinus*, 1.6,

D.29, 2, 6, 3. On "jacent heritage," see P. Voci, *Diritto ereditario romano*, 2nd ed. (Milan, 1967), I, 516–576.

54. For example, Dinaea's will to Larinum (Moreau, *Patrimoines et successions*, p. 184) in favor of her sons and grandsons; or that of Cesennia (Cicero, *Pro Caecina*, 17) in favor of her husband. Murdia bequeathed her sons equal shares, with an equal portion for her daughter and a monetary bequest in addition to her dowry to her husband (FIRA III, no. 70, p. 219, first century A.D.). Ummidia Quadrata, survived only by grandchildren, bequeathed her grandson two-thirds of her estate and her granddaughter one-third (Pliny the Younger, *Letters*, VII, 24, 2), while the wife of Aquilius Regulus instituted her son on condition that he would have been emancipated by his father (Pliny, *Letters*, IV, 2,2. See D. Dalla, *Praemium emancipationis* (Milan, 1983).

55. Marcellus, *Digest* 1.3, D.5, 2, 5; cf. Papinian D.5, 2, 16.

56. Will invalidated by Augustus: Valerius Maximus 7, 7, 4; Curianus eliminated from maternal testament: Pliny, *Letters*, 5, 1.

57. Cicero, *Pro Cluentio*, 14, 45; cf. *Pro Caecina*, 17: young Fulcinius had bequeathed his father's entire fortune to his mother.

58. CJ 3, 28, 28.

59. D.5, 2, 5; 5, 2, 16; 5, 2, 18; CJ 3, 28, 1 (a.193); 3, 28, 3 (a.197). On the invalidity of wills of children attacked by their mothers, see Quintilian, *Oratorical Institutions* 9, 2, 34; CJ 3, 28, 17 (a.287): 3, 28, 28 (a.321).

60. Septimius Severus and Caracalla, CJ 3, 28, 3, a.197; cf. SP 4, 5, 2; D.5, 2, 6pr.; 38, 8, 1, 9.

61. *Praeterire:* Valerius Maximus 7, 7, 4; D.5, 2, 5; D.5, 2, 18; SP 4, 5, 2; *Berlin Fragments* 8 and 8a (Girard, *Textes*, p. 410). This concerns sons emancipated by their fathers and unmentioned in their wills. CJ 3, 28, 17 (mother *praeterita*). *Neglegere:* CJ 2, 28, 3. This absence of forms was *de jure,* but nothing prevented a mother from being explicitly disinherited. Thus Quintilian, *Oratorical Institutions,* 9, 2, 34, or, for a mother, her son (Pliny, *Letters*, 5, 1, 1: *exheredato filio.* Disinheritance had no specifically juridical function at the time. It was merely a superfluous expression of anger.

62. Gaius 2, 123 ff. Numerous examples in D.28, 2.

63. T. Masiello, *La donna tutrice. Modelli culturali a prassi giuridica fra gli Antonini e i Severi* (Naples, 1979), pp. 67 ff.

64. Nevertheless, such a relation is the basis of B. D. Shaw, "Latin Funerary Epigraphy and Family Life in the Later Roman Empire," *Historia* 33(1984):455–497.

65. Ulpian, *Commentary on Sabinus,* L.13 D.38, 17, 2; SP 4, 10; I.3, 3.

66. Ulp. 26, 7.

67. *Hereditas legitima:* D.38, 7, 1, 4; D.38, 17, 1, 2, 3; SP 4, 10, 1 and 4.

68. D.38, 7, 2, 4–5; 38, 8, 1, 9 (which, despite what is sometimes argued, does not mean that children were then considered to be their mother's "closest agnates").

69. D.37, 17, 1, 10.

70. Addition of heredity: D.38, 17, 1, 4; 10; 11; SP 4, 10, 4.

71. Ulpian, *Commentary on the Edict*, L.46 D.38, 8, 1, 9 (cf. D.38, 17, 1, 5).

72. Ibid., 1.14 D.5, 2, 6pr.

73. On the notion of *heres legitimus*, see Gaius 3, 32 and D.38, 7, 2, 4 (where second-century senatus-consults complement the Law of the Twelve Tables).

74. See note 67.

75. SP 4, 10, 1; compare Ulpian D.38, 17, 1, 2.

76. Julian, cited by Ulpian D.38, 17, 2, 1; SP 4, 9, 1. Pregnant freed slave: D.38, 17, 2, 3.

77. D.38, 17, 1, 2.

78. Freeborn or freed mother: D.38, 17, 1pr; delay of emancipation: D.38, 17, 1, 3.

79. CJ 6, 57, 5; the remainder of the text allows for successoral equality between children of a woman living in regular concubinage and those born to the same woman in legitimate marriage.

80. Gaius 1, 77; 1, 99; V.F. 168; 194.

81. SP 4, 10, 2.

82. D.38, 17, 1, 4; 8.

83. D.38, 17, 2, 2; in this passage Ulpian quotes a constitution of Caracalla of similar import.

84. Gaius 1, 145; Paul, *Commentary on the lex iulia et Papia*, 1.2 D.50, 16, 137. R. Astolfi, *La "lex iulia et Papia"* (Padua, 1970).

85. Gaius 1, 29; Ulp. 3, 3.

86. The 1855 Boecking edition does not correct the Vatican manuscript, but since the 1878 Krüger edition and the 1926 Schulz edition all editors have corrected the original text. Nevertheless, the reading *vulgo quaesit te re nexa* is certain.

87. D.1, 5, 15.

88. Gaius, *Commentary on the Provincial Edict*, 1.16, D.38, 8, 2; Ulpian, *Regulae* 1.6 D.38, 8, 4.

89. The jurists' distinction between "legal" (i.e., adoptive) father and "natural" father (presumed to be the biological father in a legitimate marriage) does not exist for the mother, who is never called *naturalis* either in legal texts or in inscriptions (in CIL 6, 25711, *parens naturalis* refers to the father). *Filius naturalis*, which sometimes refers to a bastard in relation to his progenitor, is never used in relation to the mother (see D.20, 1, 8 and 31, 88, 12 and CT 4, 6, *De naturalibius filiis et matribus eorum*, where none of eight compiled laws covering the period 336–428 concerns relations between mother and child, only relations between the progenitor and the child or its mother.

90. Gaius 1, 89; *Epitome Gai*, 1, 4, 9 (in Girard, *Textes*, p. 244); Ulp. 5, 10.

91. Gaius 1, 56; 76; 156; Ulp. 5, 8; Celsus, *Digest*, 1.29 D.1, 5, 19; Ulpian, *Commentary on Sabinus*, 1.26 D.1, 7, 15pr. The formula "*patrem*

sequuntur liberi" comes from republican law: Cicero, *Topics,* 4, 20; Livy 4, 4, 11.

92. Gaius 1, 64; Ulp. 4, 2, 2; 57; D.1, 5, 23; 2, 4, 5; CJ 5, 18, 3. In Livy the mother of Romulus and Remus refers to Mars as the father of an "illegitimate line"—*incertae stirpis patrem:* 1, 4, 2); Aeneas, on the other hand, was born of a legitimate marriage: *certe natum* (1, 3, 3).

93. Gaius 1, 89; Ulp. 5, 10; *Epitome Gai,* 1, 4, 9.

94. D.3, 2, 11, 2; 38, 16, 3, 11–2. F. Lanfranchi, *Richerche sulle azioni di stato nella filiazione in diritto romano* (Bologna, 1964), II, 71 ff.

95. J. J. Bachofen, *Das Mutterrecht* (Stuttgart, 1861), pp. 328 ff.

96. Aulus Gellius, *Attic Nights,* 5, 19, 9.

97. Boethius, *Commentary on the Topics of Cicero,* 3, 14, which includes an allusion to Ulpian's *Institutes* (cf. D.1, 6, 4).

98. Servius, *Commentary on the Georgics of Virgil,* 1, 31.

99. Wife of a *paterfamilias:* Festus, p. 112 Lindsay; Aulus Gellius, *Attic Nights,* 18, 6, 9; Servius Auctus, *Commentary on the Aeneid,* 12, 476. Boethius, *Commentary.* Wife: references to the Digest in M. Kaser, *Das römische Privatrect* (Munich, 1971), I, 59, n. 11. W. Woldkiewicz, "Attorno al significato della nozione di *materfamilias,*" *Studi in onore di Cesare Sanfilippo,* vol. 3 (Milan, 1983), pp. 733–756.

100. Emile Benveniste, *Le vocabulaire des institutions indo-européennes* I (Paris, 1969), p. 243.

101. Aulus Gellius, *Attic Nights,* 18, 6, 5 ff.; Servius Auctus, *Commentary on the Aeneid,* II, 476; Nonius Marcellus, p. 709 Lindsay.

102. Aulus Gellius, *Attic Nights,* 18, 6, 5; Servius, *Aeneid,* 11, 476; Isidore, *Etymologies* 9, 5, 8.

103. On the dignity of matronal status and its protection, see Suetonius, *Life of Augustus,* 43; Seneca the Rhetor, *Controversies,* 2, 7; D.43, 30, 3, 6; 47, 10, 15, 15; 50, 16, 46, I; *Mosaicarum et romanarum legum collatio,* 2, 5, 4, to which must now be added an inscription from Larinum (Tiberius period), on which see V. Giuffrè, "Un senato-consulto ritrovato: il '*sc. de matronarum lenoncinio coercendo,*'" *Atti dell accademia di scienze morali e politiche* (Naples) 91(1980):7–40. On the vestimentary signs of matronal status, see L. Sensi, "*Ornatus* e *status* sociale delle donne romane," in *Annali Fac. Lettere e Filosofia* (University of Perugia) 18(1980):55–90. Matronal dignity was also granted to certain concubines: to women who were concubines of their patrons (Marcellus, D.27, 2, 41pr), which in case of infidelity made it possible to apply the punishments for adultery, normally reserved for married women (Ulpian D.48, 5, 14; see J. Plassard, *Le concubinat romain sous le haut-empire* [Paris, 1921], p. 67). Hence it was impossible for a freeborn concubine whose status was public knowledge to be considered a matron. Only a freed slave who was the concubine of her patron could be regarded as possessing a dignity that was a corollary of her sexual subjection. In a different sense, see Aline Rousselle, "Concubinat et adultère," *Opus* 3(1984):75–84.

104. References in D. Dalla, *L'incapacità sessuale in diritto romano* (Milan, 1978), pp. 235 ff.

105. S. Tafaro, *Pubes e viripotens nella esperienza giuridica romana* (Bari, 1988), pp. 139 ff. on *viripotens*.

106. I.1, 22pr. The two passages from Servius cited in a note by Tafaro, *Pubes*, p. 137, do not prove the existence of a practice of physically examining young girls. See Aline Rousselle, *Porneia* (Paris, 1983), pp. 47 ff., where it appears that, according to Soranus, prepubescent Roman girls were deflowered prior to their first menses.

107. Respectively: D.23, 2, 6; 7 (Dala, p. 243); CJ 5, 5, 8.

108. D.28, 2, 4–6; 9pr.

109. Child born free: Gaius 1, 88–89; Ulp. 5, 10; D.1, 5, 5, 2; PS 2, 24, 1; born slave of a mother who became a slave during pregnancy: *Epitome Gai,* 1, 4, 9.

110. D.1, 5, 18.

111. SP 2, 24, 2; I.1, 4pr.; Marcian, *Institutes,* 1.1, D.1, 5, 5, 2: very likely an interpolated passage.

112. SP 2, 22, 3; I.1, 4pr.; D.1, 5, 5, 3, interpolated (E. Alberterio, *Studi di diritto romano* [Milan, 1933], I, 29 ff.).

113. Tryphoninus D.1, 5, 15; Ulpian D.1, 5, 16.

114. D.38, 16, 13.

115. D.38, 17, 1, 8.

116. D.38, 17, 1, 6.

117. From which the problem of "matriarchy" and "patriarchy," to which the immense contribution of J. J. Bachofen to the study of Roman law has unfortunately been reduced. (Bachofen is strangely absent from the purview of Romanists. Kaser's textbook does not mention him at all.) On "matriarchy" in historiography, see E. Cantarella, preface to J. J. Bachofen, *Il potere femminile. Storia e teoria,* trans. A. Maffi (Milan, 1977), pp. 7–40.

118. Maternal *Origo:* 50, 1, 1, 2 (granted by imperial privilege: according to the jurists refuted by Celsus, for the *vulgo quaesiti* only and, according to Celsus, for children whose parents were born in different cities; in certain exceptional cases a man adopted the city of his mother, if she came from a place such as Delphi, Ilion, or the Pontus). In any case, the *vulgo quaesiti* had no *origo* other than their mother's city: Celsus, loc. cit., and Neratius, D.50, 1, 9.

119. *Origo,* the city from which the father derived his own *origo:* D.50, 1, 6, 1; Philip (between 244 and 249), CJ 10, 38, 3. Compare Livy 24, 6, 2; Brambach, *Corpus des inscriptions de Rhénanie,* 1444.

120. Neratius, *Membranae* 1.3 D.50, 1, 9.

121. See S. Solazzi, "*Infirmitas aetatis e infirmitas sexus,*" in *Scritti di diritto romano* (Naples, 1960), III, 357–377; and J. Beaucamp, "Le vocabulaire de la faiblesse féminine dans les textes juridiques romains du IIe au VIe siècle," *Revue historique de droit français et étranger* 54(1976):485–508; S. Dixon, "Infirmitas sexus: Womanly Weakness in Roman Law,"

Tijdschrift voor Rechtsgeschiedenis 52(1984):343–371. On the ignorance of law, see P. Van Warmelo, *"Ignorantia iuris," Tijdschrift . . .* 22(1954):1–32.

122. Livy 34, 2–4, and Zonaras 9, 17. See L. Peppe, *Posizione giuridica e ruolo sociale della donna romana in età republicana* (Milan, 1984), pp. 43 ff.

123. See, respectively, Livy 34, 2, 1; Cicero, *Pro Murena,* 27; Tacitus, *Annals,* 3, 33, 2; Quintilian, *Declamation,* 368; Gaius 1, 190; Columella XII, Praef. 6.

124. J. Beaucamp, "La situation juridique de la femme à l'époque pro-tobyzantine," diss., Paris, 1987, I, 49 ff.; see also Crook, "Feminine Inadequacy."

125. Gaius 1, 103; I.1, 11, 10; Ulp. 8, 8a. E. Albertario, "La donna adottante," in *Studi di diritto romano* (Milan, 1953), VI, 221–234; E. Nardi, "Poteva la donna, nell'impero romano, adottare un figlio?" in *Studi A. Biscardi* (Milan, 1982), I, 197–210.

126. For unmarried men, see Paul, D.1, 7, 30 and Ulp. 8, 6. On the absence of kinship created by adoption, see D.1, 7, 23.

127. Absence of the wife of the adoptee in the act of adoption before the magistrate: Gaius I, 134; fiction of a filiation stemming from a marriage with a *materfamilias* in adrogation before the *comitiae curiates:* Aulus Gellius, *Attic Nights,* 5, 19, 9. Adoptions with or without the fiction of a marriage in the classical era: Proculus, *Letters,* 1.8, D.1, 7, 44.

128. On "nature" and age gap, see Javolenas, D.1, 7, 16; Modestinus, D.1, 7, 40, 1; I.1, 11, 4: "adoption imitates nature, and it would be a monstrous feat if the son were older than the mother."

129. Cicero, *Letters to Atticus,* 7, 8, 3: Dolabella could not agree to take the name of Livia, the condition set in Livia's will. See J. J. Bachofen, *Ausgewählte Lehren des römischen Civilrechts* (Bonn, 1848), pp. 230–234.

130. Diocletian, CJ 8, 48, 5, a291. On this text see Beaucamp, *La situation juridique,* pp. 41 ff.

131. Neratius D.26, 1, 1: *Munus masculorum;* Gaius D.26, 1, 16pr: *virile officium;* CJ 5, 35, 1.a.224; *munus virile.* Masiello, *La donna tutrice,* pp. 7 ff.

132. Quintus Mucius Scaevola (around 100 B.C.), D.50, 17, 73, 1.

133. D.26, 1, 1pr.

134. The best account is still O. Karlowa, *Römische Rechtsgeschichte* II, 1, *Privatrecht* (Leipzig, 1901), pp. 278 ff.

135. Livy 39, 11: Aebutius lived with his mother and stepfather even though he was an adult. Driven from his mother's home, he took refuge with his father's second wife. Cicero, *Pro Cluentio,* 9, 27: Oppianicus kept the young son he had by Novia but left Papia his elder son, whom she raised far from Larinum, at Teanum in Apulia. Tacitus, *Annals,* 6, 49: Sextus Papirius, raised by his divorced mother, killed himself because of his disastrous upbringing. Epigraphic documentation (epitaphs to a remarried mother and a stepfather) can be found in Humbert, *Le remariage à Rome,* pp. 296 ff.

136. D.43, 30, 1, 3; 3, 5, variously interpreted by Humbert, *Le remariage*

à *Rome*, pp. 296 ff. (according to which the condition of nonremarriage of the mother was interpolated); R. Bonini, "Criteri per l'affidamento della prole dei divorziati in diritto romano," *Archivio giuridico* 181(1971):25–30; and M. Massarotto, "In merito ai decreti di Antonino pio sull'affidamento della prole alla madre," *Bolletino dell'istituto di Diritto Romano* 80(1977):354–365. See Alexander Severus CJ 5, 48, 1, a.223, and Diocletian CJ 5, 24, 1, a.294: "The judge shall decide, after divorce, if the children should live with and receive their upbringing from their father or their mother."

137. D.33, 1, 7.

138. *Consolation to Maria*, 24, 1.

139. B. Küebler, "Uber das *ius Liberorum* der Frauen und die Vormund-schaft der Mutter, ein Betrag zur Geschichte der Rezeption des römischen Rechts in Aegypten," *Zeitschrift der Savigny Stiftung, Romanistische Abteilung* 31(1910):176–195; Humbert, *Le remariage à Rome*; Masiello, *La donna tutrice*, pp. 43 ff.; Beaucamp, *La situation juridique*, pp. 316 ff. On the papyrological evidence, see also R. Taubenschlag, "Die *materna potestas* im gräko-ägyptischen Recht," 1929, *Opera minora* (Warsaw, 1959), II, 323–337, and P. Frezza, "La donna tutrice e la donna addministratrice di negozi tutelari nel diritto romano classico e nei papiri greco-egizi," *Studi Economico-giuridici dell'università di Cagliari* 12(1933–34):3–37.

140. Scaevola D.32, 41, 14; Ulpian D.38, 17, 2, 46. Some texts indicate that the child was disinherited in favor of the mother, who would then restore the child's fortune when it reached puberty: D.36, 1, 76, 1; 28, 2, 18; 38, 2, 12, 2.

141. Neratius, *Rules*, 1.3, D.26, 1, 18, possibly interpolated (but for its authenticity, see Masiello, *La donna tutrice*, pp. 11 ff.). For rejection of such a request, see D.26, 2, 26pr; CJ 5, 31, 1, a.224.

142. For Egyptian practices, see works of B. Kuebler, R. Taubenschlag, and P. Frezza cited in note 138. For rejection of provincial practices in Roman law, see Papinian D.26, 2, 26pr.; Gordian, CJ 5, 37, 12, a.241.

143. CT 3, 17, 4, with exegesis by G. Crifo, "Sul problema della donna tutrice," *Bolletino dell'istituto di diritto romano* 67(1964):87–166, esp. 88 ff.

144. P. Zannini, *Studi sulla tutela mulierum* (Turin, 1976), vol. I.

145. Gaius 1, 190.

146. Reform of Augustus: see note 84 above. Reform of Claudius: Gaius 1, 157 and 171.

147. On the decline of the *manus*: Humbert, *Le remariage à Rome*, pp. 183 ff.; A. Watson, *The Law of Persons in the Later Roman Republic* (Cambridge, 1976), p. 25; a subtler view is in Moreau, "Patrimoines et successions à Larinum," pp. 178–179. On the disappearance of unions of this type under Tiberius, see Tacitus, *Annals*, 4, 16.

148. "Remancipation" was an operation that nullified a prior "mancipation," as defined by the jurist Aelius Gallus toward the end of the first century A.D. in Festus p. 342 Lindsay: "The remancipated woman is one who was mancipated by a man with whom she had concluded a union under the regime of the *manus*." Compare Gaius 1, 137: "Women *in manu* cease to be

so by a single mancipation and become legally autonomous," and 1, 137a: "A daughter cannot in any way force her father to remancipate her, even if she is an adoptive daughter; a wife, on the other hand, who has been repudiated [by] (or has repudiated) [her husband], can force her husband [to remancipate her], as if she had never been married to her."

149. Only stillborn children were considered "unborn": D.50, 16, 19; on "monsters," see 50, 16, 135, and 1, 5, 14.

150. Gaius 1, 112, and 115a; compare Cicero, Topics, 4, 18. Interpretations of this legal ritual diverge. Watson, Law of Persons, p. 153, sees it as residual evidence that women had to have been married in manu in order to make wills. Zannini, Studi sulla tutela mulierum, pp. 154 ff., holds that the woman left her "family of origin"; Peppe, Posizione giuridica e ruolo sociale della donna romana in età republicana, pp. 53 ff., considers the case of nubile girls as well as that of widows.

151. On the absence of guardians: Gaius 1, 185; 195 ff. (the patroness could not serve as guardian for a freed slave woman); Epitome Gai, 1, 7, 2. On the law Atilia concerning dative guardianships: Ulpian 11, 18. Imperial practices: F. Grelle, "Datio tutoris e organizzazioni cittadine nel Basso impero," Labeo 6(1950):216 ff., and J. Modrezejewski, "A propos de la tutelle dative des femmes dans l'Egypte romaine," in Akten des XIII internationalen Papyrologenkongresses (Munich, 1974), pp. 263–292.

152. Gaius 1, 195. Petitio tutoris in practice: Papyrus of Oxyrhynchos IV 720, L. Mitteis, Chrestomatie der Papyruskunde 324 (a.247); also P. Oxy. XII 1466 (a.245) and P. Michigan III 165 (a.236).

153. Gaius 1, 190–191.

154. Ulpian 11, 27. I am following the excellent exegesis by Zannini, Studi sulla tutela mulierum, pp. 98 ff., in opposition to the traditional doctrine, which sees this text as proof that women were excluded from all acts of civil law. In reality, and taking account of other texts in which we find women admitted to civile negotium gerere, "si se obligent si civile negotium gerant" means "to contract an obligation according to the formalist modes of civil law." See Cicero, Pro Caecina, 25, 72, on the nonvalidity of a solemn promise made without the guardian's auctoritas.

155. Zannini, Studi sulla tutela mulierum, chap. 2.

156. Mitteis, Chrestomatie, 328 (a.168): FIRA III, no. 26, pp. 69 ff., and P. Oxy. XII 1467, FIRA III no. 27, pp. 171 ff. (a.263).

157. S. Treggiari, "Jobs in the Household of Livia," Papers of the British School at Rome 43(1975):48–77; "Jobs for Women," American Journal of Ancient History 1 (May 1976):76–104. See also Ramsay MacMullen, "Women in Public in the Roman Empire," Historia 29(1980):208–218.

158. Corpus des Inscriptions Latines, 15, 3729; 3845–47; 3960–61: female boat owners. Notizie degli Scavi di Ostia, 1953, p. 166, no. 27, and p. 174, no. 39: companies in Ostia. Women were nevertheless excluded from banking and exchange operations, these being masculine responsibilities according to Callistratus, D.2, 13, 12, no doubt because banking and exchange required acting on behalf of others. On the management of affairs that were

not necessarily commercial, see, however, D.3, 5, 3, 1. On all these feminine occupations, see N. Kampen, *Image and Status. Roman Working Women in Ostia* (Berlin, 1981).

159. L. Huchthausen, "Herkunft und ökonomische Stellung weiblicher Adressaten von Reskripten des Codex iustinianus (2 und 3 Jh. u. Z.)," *Klio* 56(1974):199–228.

160. D.3, 3, 54; D.50, 17, 2pr.

161. CJ 2, 12, 4, a.207.

162. Incapacity to bring popular action: D.47, 23, 4, and 6. Prohibition against making accusations except to avenge the death of a relative: Pomponius, D.48, 2, 1; Papinian D.48, 2, 2pr; Macer D.48, 2, 11.

163. Ulpian D.3, 1, 1, 5, which takes up the scandalous example of "Carfania," already treated in Valerius Maximus 8, 3, 2 (Caia Arfania).

164. Intercession (guaranteeing a debt) was a *civile officium* for the jurists: Paul, *Commentaries on the Edict,* 1.33 D.17, 1, 1. Hence there is no reason to view the senatus-consult Velleian outside this interpretive framework (and this structure of prohibited mediation), as does Crook, "Feminine Inadequacy."

165. Testifying in court: Paul D.22, 5, 4; 22, 5, 18. A key text is D.22, 5, 3, 5, which shows that testimony by women was envisioned in the *lex iula de vi.*

166. The ban on testifying in court in the archaic period can be deduced from the privilege granted to the Vestals: Plutarch, *Life of Publicola,* 8, 9; Tacitus, *Annals,* 2, 34; Aulus Gellius 7, 7, 2. See also John Scheid's chapter in this volume (Chapter 8, "The Religious Roles of Roman Women"). On testimony as the basis for an absolute right in the archaic period, see A. Magdelain, "Quirinus et le droit," *Mélanges de l'Ecole Française de Rome* 96(1984):222 (on Livy 3, 47, 1: *civitas in foro*); and, by the same author, *Ius. Imperium. Auctoritas* (Rome, 1990), preface (a new and convincing exegesis of Valerius Probus' *Litterae singulares* 4, 7: "Since I see you [the witness] present in court, I ask you if you will vouch [for my right]."

Chapter 4. *Figures of Women*
FRANÇOIS LISSARRAGUE

1. See P. Schmitt Pantel and F. Thelamon, "Image et histoire: illustration ou document," in F. Lissarrague and F. Thelamon, eds., *Image et céramique grecque* (Rouen, 1983), pp. 9–20.

2. On the history of this discovery, see F. Lissarrague and A. Shnapp, "Imagerie des Grecs ou Grèce des imagiers," *Le Temps de la Réflexion* 2(1981):275–297.

3. London 1971.11–1.1; Beazley, *Para* 19(16bis). Published by D. J. R. Williams, *Greek Vases in the J. Paul Getty Museum* 1(1983):9–34.

4. Florence 4209; Beazley *ABV* 76(1). For a comparison of the two vases, see T. Carpenter, *Dionysian Imagery in Archaic Greek Art* (Oxford, 1986), pp. 1–12.

5. London 1920.12–21.1; Beazley *ARV2* 1277(23). Cf. I. Jenkins, "Is There Life after Marriage?" *BICS* 30(1983):137– 145. On this type of vase, see S. R. Roberts, *The Attic Pyxis* (Chicago, 1978).

6. Paris, Louvre L 55; Beazley *ARV2* 924(33).

7. Salerno, unnumbered.

8. East Berlin F 2372; A. Furtwängler, *La collection Sabouroff* (Berlin, 1883), pl. 58.

9. Copenhagen 9165; Beazley *ARV2* 514(2). On this type of vase, see F. Harl-Schaller, "Zur Entstehung und Bedeutung des attischen Lebes gamikos," *JOAI Beiblatt* 50(1972–75):151–170.

10. Copenhagen 13113; *CVA* 8, pl. 345.

11. Athens National Museum, 1629; Beazley *ARV2* 1250(34).

12. For this interpretation, see B. Schweitzer, *Mythische Hochzeiten* (Heidelberg, 1961), and A. Shapiro in E. La Rocca, ed., *L'esperimento della perfezione* (Milan, 1988), pp. 334–344.

13. London E697; Beazley *ARV2* 1324(45). Cf. L. Brun, *The Meidias Painter* (Oxford, 1987). For a political interpretation, see D. Metzler, "Eunomia und Aphrodite," *Hephaistos* 2(1980):73–88.

14. Paris, Cabinet des Médailles, 508; Beazley, *ARV2* 1610. See Robert F. Sutton, "The Interaction Between Men and Women Portrayed on Attic Red-Figure Pottery," Ph.D. diss., University of North Carolina, pp. 208, 255.

15. See G. Ahlberg, *Prothesis and Ekphora in Greek Geometric Art* (Göteborg, 1971).

16. Paris, Louvre CA 453; Beazley *ARV2* 184(22). On the function of the bath, see R. Ginouvès, *Balaneutike, recherches sur le bain dans l'antiquité grecque* (Paris, 1962).

17. Paris, Louvre MNB 905; Haspels, *ABL* 229(58). See J. Boardman, "Painted Funerary Plaques and Some Remarks on Prothesis," *BSA* 50(1955):51–66.

18. Berlin F 1813; Beazley, *ABV* 146(22); see H. Mommsen, "Der Graphinax des Exekias," in H. Brijder, ed., *Ancient Greek and Related Pottery* (Amsterdam, 1984), pp. 329–333.

19. Athens, 1935; Beazley *ARV2* 1227(1). See J. Beazley, *Attic White Lekythoi* (London, 1938).

20. Tarquinia RC 1646; *CVA* 2(26), pl. 32(1181)2. On this entire series, see F. Lissarrague, *L'Autre guerrier* (Paris–Rome, 1990), chap. 4.

21. Munich 1553; *CVA* 8(37), pl. 370(1788)2. Cf. Lissarrague, *L'Autre guerrier*, chap. 2.

22. See Odette Touchefeu, *LIMC* IV, s.v. Hector, nos. 17, 20.

23. Rome, Villa Giulia; Beazley, *ABV* 693(8bis).

24. Baltimore 48.262; Beazley, *ARV2* 591(25).

25. Berlin F 2535; Beazley, *ARV2* 825(11).

26. Palermo V 676; Beazley, *ARV2* 641(83).

27. Munich 2336; Beazley, *ARV2* 989(35).

28. Ferrara, inv. 1684, T 308 VT; Beazley, *ARV2* 1664.

29. Athens, Vlasto Collection; Beazley, *ARV2* 847(200).

30. Berlin, F 2444; Walter Riezler, *Weissgrundige attische Lekythen* (Munich, 1914), no. 15.

31. See Nicole Loraux, "Le lit, la guerre," *L'Homme* 21(1981):37–67.

32. See Gérard van Hoorn, *Choes and Anthesteria* (Leyden, 1951).

33. See Semeli Pingiatogiou, *Eileithyia* (Würzburg, 1981).

34. Berlin, F 2395; *LIMC*, s.v. Amphiaraos, no. 27.

35. Boston 65.908. On women's choruses, see Claude Calame, *Les choeurs de jeunes filles en Grèce archaïque* (Rome, 1977), I, 52 ff.

36. Paris, Louvre CA 2567; Beazley, *ARV2* 698(37).

37. Karlsruhe B 39; *CVA* 1(7), pl. 27. See Nicole Weill, "Adoniazousai ou les femmes sur le toit," *BCH* 90(1966):664–698.

38. See Chapter 7.

39. Berlin, F 2290; Beazley, *ARV2* 462(48). For more, see Jean-Louis Durand and Françoise Frontisi-Ducroux, "Idoles, figures, images," *RA* 1982, pp. 81–108, and Françoise Frontisi-Ducroux, *Le dieu masqué* (Paris–Rome, forthcoming).

40. Rome, Villa Giulia 983; Beazley, *ARV2* 621(33).

41. Munich 8934. See Martin Robertson in *Studies in Honour of A. D. Trendall* (Sydney, 1979), p. 130.

42. London E 773; Beazley, *ARV2* 805(89).

43. London E 772; Beazley, *ARV2* 806(90).

44. Paris, Louvre CA 2587; Beazley, *ARV2* 506(29).

45. Würzburg L 304; Beazley, *ABV* 676(2). On this theme, see L. Hannestad, "Slaves and the Fountain House Theme," *Ancient Greek and Related Pottery* (Amsterdam, 1984), pp. 252–255, and Y. Manfrini, "Les nymphai à la fontaine" (forthcoming).

46. See Claude Bérard, "Erotisme et violence à la fontaine," *Etudes de lettres* 1983(4):20–27.

47. Brussels, A 11; Beazley, *ARV2* 266(86). Jean-Louis Durand and François Lissarrague, "Un lieu d'image? L'espace du louterion," *Hephaistos* 2(1980):89–106.

48. Paris, Louvre S 3916; Beazley, *ARV2* 432(60).

49. Bologna 261; Beazley, *ARV2* 1089(28).

50. Paris, Louvre G 557; Beazley, *ARV2* 1131(158).

51. Würzburg L 521; Beazley, *ARV2* 1046(7). See A. Frederick Beck, *Album of Greek Education* (Sydney, 1975).

52. Lecce, 572; Beazley, *ARV2* 564(21).

53. Milan, Torno Collection, C 278; Beazley, *ARV2* 571(73). See also Marjorie S. Venit, "The Caputi Hydria and Working Women in Classical Athens," *CV* 81(4)1988:265–272.

54. Paris, BN 652; Beazley, *ARV2* 377(103).

55. New York 31.11.10; Beazley, *ABV* 154(57).

56. New York 56.11.1; Beazley, *Para* 66. See also Dietrich Bothmer, *The Amasis Painter and His World* (New York, 1985), pp. 182–187.

57. Berlin F 2289; Beazley, *ARV2* 435(95). On working with wool, see Eva Keuls, "Attic Vase Painting and the Home Textile Industry," in Warren

G. Moon, ed., *Ancient Greek Art and Iconography* (Madison, Wisc., 1983), pp. 209–230.

58. See Kenneth Dover, *Greek Homosexuality* (London, 1978); Gundel Koch-Harnack, *Knabenliebe und Tiergeschenke* (Berlin, 1983); Alain Schnapp, "Eros en chasse," *La cité des images* (Paris–Lausanne, 1984), pp. 67–83.

59. Rome, commerce; see Gundel Koch-Harnack, *Erotische Symbole* (Berlin, 1989), p. 82, fig. 66.

60. The term comes from Eva Keuls, *The Reign of the Phallus* (New York, 1985), p. 262. See Alain Schnapp, "Comment déclarer sa flamme ou les archéologues au spectacle," *Le genre humain* 14(1986):147–159.

61. Berlin 2279; Beazley, *ARV2* 115(2).

62. Paris BN 439; Beazley, *ARV2* 209(168). Iconographic data in Sophia Kaempf-Dimitriadou, *Die Liebe der Götter in der attischen Kunst des 5 Jhs.v.Chr.* (Bern, 1979). See also Froma Zeitlin, "Configurations of Rape in Greek Myth," in S. Tomaselli and R. Porter, eds., *Rape* (Oxford, 1986), pp. 122–151, and Christiane Sourvinou-Inwood, "A Series of Erotic Pursuits: Images and Meaning," *JHS* 107(1987):131–153.

63. See Hans Herter, *Reallexikon für Antike und Christentum,* vol. 3 (Stuttgart, 1957), s.v. Dirne, col. 1149–1213.

64. London E 68; Beazley, *ARV2* 371(24). On the imagery of the *symposion,* see François Lissarrague, *Un flot d'images; une esthétique du banquet grec* (Paris, 1987).

65. Brussels R 351; Beazley, *ARV2* 31(7). Iconographic data in Jean Marcadé, *Eros kalos* (Geneva, 1962); John Boardman and Eugenio La Rocca, *Eros in Greece* (New York, 1975). For a survey of the topic, see Otto Brendel, "The Scope and Temperament of Erotic Art in the Greco-Roman World," in T. Bowie and C. V. Christenson, eds., *Studies in Erotic Art* (New York, 1970).

66. Madrid 11267; Beazley, *ARV2* 58(53).

67. Rome, Villa Giulia 57912; Beazley, *ARV2* 72(24).

68. Paris, Louvre G 285; Beazley, *ARV2* 380(170). See also Françoise Frontisi-Ducroux and François Lissarrague, "De l'ambiguité à l'ambivalence," *AION Arch St.* V 1983, pp. 11–32.

69. On maenads and wine, see Marie-Christiane Villanueva-Puig, "Les ménades, la vigne et le vin," *REA* 1988, pp. 35–64, and Françoise Frontisi-Ducroux, "Qu'est-ce qui fait courir les ménades?" in Salvatore d'Onofrio, ed., *Il fermento divino* (Palermo, forthcoming).

70. Munich 2645; Beazley, *ARV2* 371(15).

71. Rouen 538.3; Beazley, *ARV2* 188(68). On the relation between satyrs and maenads, see Sheila Mac Nally, "The Maenad in Early Greek Art," *Arethusa* 11(1978):101–135.

72. Syracuse 24554; Beazley, *ARV2* 649(42).

73. Paris, Louvre G 416; Beazley, *ARV2* 484(17).

74. Athens 2184; Haspels *ABL* 228(53); Beazley *ABV* 481(a). Iconographic data in Dietrich von Bothmer, *Amazons in Greek Art* (Oxford, 1957).

75. Paris, Louvre G 197; Beazley, *ARV2* 238(1).
76. Athens 15002; Beazley, *ARV2* 98(2).

Marriage Strategies

P.S.P.

1. Another approach to the subject would have been to review the various social roles of women systematically. We rejected this approach, which would have meant dividing up the narrative according to occupation: weaving, cooking, buying and selling, serving, farming, healing. François Lissarrague's chapter, "Figures of Women," has already touched on these activities, and several books have treated these aspects of ancient life more fully than we could hope to do here. (See, for example, Ivanna Savalli, *La donna nella società della Grecia antica* [Bologna: Patron, 1983], and David Schaps, *Economic Rights of Women in Ancient Greece* [Edinburgh: Edinburgh University Press, 1979].) Some may be surprised that there is no chapter on recent archaeological discoveries, which have done so much to enrich our understanding of the ancient world. But medieval historians took the lead in using archaeological data to advance their knowledge of material life, and ancient historians have only recently begun to catch up. Soon it will be possible to attempt a synthesis of recent discoveries that shed new light on how the ancients lived, what objects they kept in their homes, and what they had buried with them when they died. The interior of a tomb near Paestum, for example, was divided into two parts. From items found inside it was possible to infer that one chamber was used for the burial of a male, the other for a female. The woman had been buried with a hydria, phiale, and *lebes gamikos* (wedding vase), whereas the man had been buried with a krater, skyphos, kylix, and lance. (See Angelo Bottini and Emmanuelle Greco, "Tomba a camera dal territorio pestano: alcune considerazioni sulla posizione della donna," *Dialoghi di Archeologia* 8[2]1974–1975:231–274.)

2. Jean-Pierre Vernant, *Mythe et société en Grèce ancienne* (Paris: Maspero, 1974), p. 38.

3. Luc de Heusch, *Pourquoi l'épouser et autres essais* (Paris: Gallimard, 1971).

Chapter 5. Marriage in Ancient Greece

CLAUDINE LEDUC

N.B. All dates are B.C.

1. Hesiod, *Theogony*, 570–612; *Works and Days*, 60–105.

2. Nicole Loraux, *Les enfants d'Athéna* (Paris: Maspero, 1981), pp. 75–91.

3. For Pandora's arrival, see Geneviève Hoffmann, "Pandora, la jarre et l'espoir," *Etudes rurales* (January–June 1985):119–132.

4. Jack Goody and S. J. Tambiah, *Bridewealth and Dowry* (Cambridge: Cambridge University Press, 1973), p. 17.

5. Louis Gernet, "Le mariage en Grèce," lecture at the Institut de Droit Romain of the Université de Paris, April 1953.

6. Jean-Pierre Vernant, *Mythe et société en Grèce ancienne* (Paris: Maspero, 1974), pp. 70–71.

7. Joseph Modrzejewski, "La structure juridique du mariage grec," *Scritti in onore di Orsolina Montevecchi* (Bologna, 1981), pp. 261–263, 268.

8. Claude Mossé, "De l'inversion de la dot antique?" *Familles et biens en Grèce et à Chypre* (Paris: L'Harmattan, 1985), pp. 187–193.

9. Emile Benveniste, *Le vocabulaire des institutions indo-européennes* (Paris: Editions de Minuit, 1969), pp. 66–70.

10. Evelyne Scheid-Tissinier, "Etude sur le vocabulaire et les pratiques du don et de l'échange chez Homère," Ph.D. thesis, University of Paris IV, 1988.

11. Robin Fox, *Kinship and Marriage, An Anthropological Perspective* (Harmondsworth, 1967).

12. Claude Lévi-Strauss, "Histoire et ethnologie," *Annales E.S.C.* 38(November–December 1983):1217–1231.

13. In a series of articles (beginning in 1973) on the status of Greek women from the time of Homer to the fourth century, Marilyn Arthur came to a similar conclusion, although her conceptual framework, summarized by Pauline Schmitt Pantel in *Une histoire des femmes est-elle possible?* (Marseille: Rivages, 1984), pp. 116–118, is quite different.

14. Claude Lévi-Strauss, *La pensée sauvage* (Paris: Plon, 1962), p. 32, note.

15. Moses I. Finley, *The World of Ulysses* (New York, 1977).

16. Maurice Godelier, *L'idéel et le matériel* (Paris: Fayard, 1984), pp. 197 ff.

17. Claude Mossé, *La femme dans la Grèce antique* (Paris: Albin Michel, 1983), pp. 17–18.

18. Claude Lévi-Strauss, "Nobles sauvages," *Mélanges offerts à C. Morazé* (Toulouse: Privat, 1983), pp. 41–54, esp. 47.

19. Raymond Descat, "L'acte et l'effort: Une idéologie du travail en Grèce ancienne," *Annales Littéraires de l'Université de Besançon* 73 (1986):266–267.

20. Homer, *Iliad,* XV, 497, and *Odyssey,* XIV, 64.

21. Gilbert Durand, *L'imagination symbolique* (Paris: Presses Universitaires de France, 1964), p. 13.

22. This discussion of the Homeric household summarizes a long chapter of my still unfinished dissertation.

23. Homer, *Odyssey,* V, 59–61.

24. Aristotle, *Metaphysics* D26.

25. These rituals of the hearth persisted well after the classical period.

26. Homer, *Iliad,* XVII, 250 ("public wine"); *Iliad,* I, 23 (the king as "devourer" of the territorial community); *Odyssey,* XIX, 197 (on wine, flour, and cattle provided by the territorial community), and XIII, 14 (taxes on the territorial community).

27. Lévi-Strauss, "Nobles sauvages," p. 53.

28. Georges Augustins, "Esquisse d'une comparaison des systèmes de perpétuation des groupes domestiques dans les sociétés paysannes européennes," *Archives européennes do sociologie* 23(1982):39–69, esp. 40–41.

29. Homer, *Iliad,* XXII, 51.

30. Lévi-Strauss, "Nobles sauvages," p. 53.

31. "Patrivirilocal residence" means that the couple took up residence in the husband's father's household.

32. A hypogamic marriage is a marriage in which the wife's social position is inferior to that of her husband.

33. Homer, *Odyssey,* VII, 54 ff.

34. Ibid., XVIII, 276 ff.

35. Ibid., XVI, 391.

36. Ibid., XXIV, 294.

37. Anna Lucia Di Lello-Finuoli, "Donne e Matrimonia nella Grecia Arcaica (Hes. *Op.* 405–406)," *Studi Micenei ed Egeo-Anatolici,* XXV (Rome: Editioni dell'Ateneo, 1984), pp. 275–302.

38. In Homeric societies women did not tend cows, goats, or sheep, but geese were kept by Helen (*Odyssey,* XV, 161, 174) and Penelope (*Odyssey,* XV, 535 ff., esp. 543).

39. Luc de Heusch, *Le sacrifice dans les religions africaines* (Paris: Gallimard, 1986).

40. Hesiod, *Works and Days,* 406.

41. Christiane Klapisch-Zuber, "Le complexe de Griselda: Dot et dons de mariage au Quattrocento," *Mélanges de l'Ecole Française de Rome* 94(1)1982:7–43, esp. 13–19.

42. See Fox, *Kinship,* pp. 130–145, on the role of complementary filiation in a patrilinear system.

43. Homer, *Iliad,* IX, 460.

44. Homer, *Odyssey,* XV, 273.

45. A "parentela" is a group defined as stemming from "ego." According to Fox, *Kinship,* its existence depends on an ad hoc grouping that intends to achieve some specific goal.

46. Homer, *Odyssey,* I, 429 ff.

47. Ibid., XIV, 199 ff.

48. Benveniste, *Le vocabulaire,* pp. 212–215.

49. "Son-in-law" means the husband of any daughter given away in daughter-in-law marriage. Similarly, "father-in-law" means the father of any such daughter. "Nephew" is any consanguine male who left the household.

50. Marie Madeleine Mactoux, "Penelope," *Annales Littéraires de l'Université de Besançon* 16 (1975).

51. Homer, *Odyssey,* II, 196 ff.

52. Ibid., *Odyssey,* XX, 341–342.

53. Ibid., *Odyssey,* XXIII, 183 ff.

54. Homer, *Iliad,* IX, 53 ff. (The myth of Meleagrus: the hero accidentally kills his mother's brothers, and his mother wishes openly for his death.)

55. Pierre Brulé, "La fille d'Athènes. La religion des filles à Athènes à l'époque classique. Mythes, cultes et société," *Annales Littéraires de l'Université de Besançon* (1987), pp. 203 ff.

56. Homer, *Iliad*, VI, 192, and *Odyssey*, VII, 313.

57. Homer, *Odyssey*, VII, 312.

58. Homer, *Iliad*, VI, 155 ff.

59. Ibid., IX, 146 and 288.

60. Ibid., IX, 147 ff. and 289 ff.

61. Benveniste, *Le vocabulaire*, II, pp. 50–55.

62. Homer, *Iliad*, VI, 249. Priam "kept" a dozen sons-in-law in his palace.

63. Hesiod, *Works and Days*, 406.

64. Homer, *Iliad*, XXIV, 769.

65. Homer, *Odyssey*, VII, 54 ff.

66. Aristotle, *Politics*, I, 3, 1253b.

67. Brulé, "La fille d'Athènes," pp. 360–379.

68. Claude Lévi-Strauss, *Le regard éloigné* (Paris: Plon, 1983), pp. 127–140.

69. For my earlier reflections on the Athenian matrimonial system in the city-state period (sixth to fourth century B.C.), see "La dot, la valeur des femmes," *Travaux de l'Université de Toulouse-Le Mirail* 21(1982):7–29; and on diverging devolution in Athens and Gortyn, see my contribution to G. Ravis-Giordani, ed., *Femmes et patrimoine dans les sociétés rurales de l'Europe méditerranéenne* (Marseilles: Centre National de Recherche Scientifique, 1987), pp. 211–226.

70. Pauline Schmitt Pantel, "La cité au banquet," diss., University of Lyons II, 1987, I, 130.

71. For published editions of the code, see R. Dareste, B. Haussoulier, and T. Reinach, *Recueil des inscriptions juridiques grecques* (Paris, 1891–1904), I, 352 ff.; M. Guarducci, *Inscriptiones Creticae*, vol. 4, *Tituli Gortynii* (Rome, 1950); and Ronald F. Willetts, *The Law Code of Gortyn* (Berlin, 1967).

72. Dareste, *Recueil*, V, 30.

73. Alberto Maffi, "Ecriture et pratique juridique dans la Grèce classique," in Marcel Detienne, ed., *Les savoirs de l'écriture en Grèce ancienne*, Cahiers de Philologie, University of Lille III, vol. 14, pp. 188–210.

74. Dareste, *Recueil*, X, 49.

75. Ibid., V, 25.

76. Ibid., III, 16.

77. Ibid., V, 26.

78. On acknowledgment of paternity see Jean Rudhardt, "La reconnaissance de la paternité, sa nature et sa portée dans société athénienne," *Museum Helveticum* (January 1962):39–64.

79. Dareste, *Recueil*, IV, 21.

80. Ibid., VIII, 41.

81. Ibid., IV, 22.

82. Schmitt Pantel, "La cité au banquet," pp. 67–92.
83. Dareste, *Recueil*, X, 55.
84. Ibid., V, 25.
85. Ibid., V, 26, 27, 28.
86. Ibid., V, 29, 30.
87. Ibid., X, 52.
88. Ibid., X, 43–55.
89. Evanghelos Karabelias, "Recherches sur la condition juridique et sociale de la fille unique dans le monde grec ancien," typescript, Institut de Droit Romain de l'Université de Paris, pp. 7–73.
90. Claude Lévi-Strauss, *Les structures élémentaires de la parenté* (Paris: Presses Universitaires de France, 1949), pp. 57–61; in English: *The Elementary Structures of Kinship,* trans. and ed. Rodney Needham (Boston: Beacon, 1969).
91. Dareste, *Recueil,* III, 14.
92. Ibid., III, 17.
93. Ibid., III, 16.
94. Ibid., V, 31.
95. Willetts, *The Law Code of Gortyn,* pp. 23–27.
96. Diagram of the marriage of the *patrouchus* to her paternal uncle:

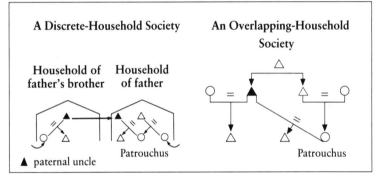

97. Pierre Lévêque, "Les communautés dans la Grèce ancienne," *Peuples Méditerranéens-Mediterranean Peoples* 14(January–March 1981):3–13.
98. The bibliography is enormous, and the oldest books are not the least interesting. Here I cite only those works to which I refer implicitly in the discussion: G. Barilleau, "De la constitution de dot dans l'ancienne Grèce," *Revue historique de droit français et étranger,* 1883, pp. 10–185; L. Beauchet, *Histoire du droit privé de la République athénienne* (Paris, 1897), vol. 1; Hans Julius Wolff, "Marriage Law and Family Organization in Ancient Athens," *Traditio* 2(1944):43–95; Anne Joseph, "La condition de l'Athénienne aux Vème et IVème s. d'après les orateurs attiques," thesis, University of Liège, 1947–48; Gernet, 1954, Hans Julius Wolff, "Proix," in *Pauly Wissowa Real Enzyklopädie,* XXIII, 1, 1957, cols. 133–170; A. R. W. Harrisson, *The Laws of Athens,* vol. 1 (Oxford, 1968); W. K. Lacey, *The Family in Classical Greece* (London, 1968); Vernant, *Mythe et société;* E. J. Bicker-

man, "La structure juridique du mariage grec," *Bolletino dell'Istituto di Diritto romano*, 1975, pp. 1–28; Sarah C. Humphreys, *Anthropology and the Greeks. Part III: Structure, Context, and Communication* (London, 1978); David M. Schaps, *Economic Rights of Women in Ancient Greece* (Edinburgh, 1979); Modrzejewski, "La structure juridique du mariage grec"; Mossé, *La femme dans la Grèce antique.*

99. Demosthenes, XLVI, 19.

100. Lévi-Strauss, *Le regard éloigné*, p. 71: (1) "The origins of the family lie in marriage." (2) "It includes the husband, the wife, and the children born of their union, thus forming a nucleus around which other relatives may gather." (3) "Members of the family are united by (a) legal bonds; (b) rights and obligations of an economic, religious, or other nature; and (c) a well-defined set of sexual rights and taboos and a variable, diversified set of feelings."

101. On the composition of Athenian fortunes in the fourth century, see Claude Mossé, *La fin de la démocratie athénienne* (Paris: Presses Universitaires de France, 1962), pp. 162 ff.

102. Emile Boisacq, *Dictionnaire étymologique de la langue grecque* (Paris–Heidelberg, 1938), p. 211.

103. Menander, *Perikeiromene*, 1012–1015; *Samia*, 897–900; *Dyskolos*, 842–845.

104. Isaeus, X, 10.

105. Demosthenes, XVII, 4–5.

106. Aeschinus, I, 171.

107. Modrzejewski, "La structure juridique du mariage grec," p. 267.

108. Lysias, XIX, 9, 11, 32. When the property of a condemned man was confiscated, his wife's dowry was included. Lysias, XLII, 27. In drawing lists of citizens obliged to perform liturgical services, income from the dowry was added to ordinary income.

109. E. Greis, "Le concubinat à Athènes pendant la période classique (chez Démosthène)," *VDI* 103(1968):28–52.

110. Isaeus, III, 39.

111. Demosthenes, LIX, 122.

112. Aristotle, *Constitution of Athens*, XXVI, 4, and XLII, 1.

113. Demosthenes, LIX, 16, 52, 112.

114. Demosthenes, LVII, 32 ff. The plaintiff had been stricken from the register of the *deme* and was trying to prove that he had been born a citizen by showing that his mother had married a citizen and therefore must have been a citizen herself.

115. Isaeus, III.

116. Isaeus, VI.

117. Ibid. Euktemon, having left his wife for another woman, tried unsuccessfully to pass the son of his seductress off as the offspring of a legitimate marriage (27). He then tried to have him admitted to his phratry by giving him a piece of land (23). The text does not specify on what grounds this land was transferred, but it cannot have been on the grounds that the son was a

legitimate child (30). We may therefore assume that Euktemon had in some way recognized the bastard as his own. Since land belonged exclusively to citizens, the gift of land was a way of making a bastard a citizen, though not a family member.

118. Demosthenes, XL, 4.

119. Aeschylus, *Eumenides, 738.*

120. Euripides, *Medea, 230* ff.

121. Brulé, *La fille d'Athènes,* pp. 370 ff. (with bibliography), discusses the selective exposure of female children.

122. Maurice Godelier, *Rationalité et irrationalité en économie* (Paris: Maspero, 1966). My research on dowries is greatly indebted to the work of Agnès Fine on dowries in southwestern Occitania. See Agnès Fine and Claudine Leduc, "Le dot de la mariee," *Actes du colloque national "Femmes, Féminisme et Recherche,"* Toulouse, 17–19 December 1982, pp. 168–175; and Agnès Fine, "Le prix de l'exclusion. Dot et héritage dans le Sud-Ouest occitan," *Bulletin du MAUSS* 10(1984):68–88.

123. Mossé, *La fin de la démocratie athénienne,* pp. 147 ff.

124. Claudine Leduc, "En marge de l'*Athenaion Politeia* attribuée à Xénophon," *Quaderni di storia* 13(January–June 1981):281–334.

125. Lucy Mair, *Le mariage* (Paris, 1974), p. 74.

126. Pierre Bourdieu, "Les stratégies matrimoniales dans le système des stratégies de reproduction," *Annales E.S.C.* (1972):1105–1127.

127. Demosthenes, XL, 25.

128. Isaeus, XI, 40.

129. Isaeus, VII, 11.

130. Wesley E. Thompson, "The Marriage of First Cousins in Athenian Society," *Phoenix* 21(1967):273–282; Sarah C. Humphreys, "Marriage with Kin in Classical Athens," typescript of paper read at the Collège de France, 1989.

131. Demosthenes, XLIII, 54.

132. E. Karabelias, "L'épiclérat attique," typescript, Paris, Institut de Droit Romain, p. 92bis.

133. Plutarch, *Life of Solon, XX, 4.*

134. Demosthenes, LVII, 41.

135. Isaeus, III, 64, and X, 19.

136. Hagnias' abundant legacy (Isaeus, IX, and Demosthenes, XLIII) gave rise to prolonged and bitter legal battles. Demosthenes' client, who had given his son in posthumous adoption to the house of Hagnias, used the term *oikos,* which was far less common among Attic orators than *oikia,* and touched several times on the problem of the house without an heir.

137. Isaeus, XI, 49.

138. Eva Cantarella, *Tacita Muta: La Donna nella Città Antica* (Rome: Riuniti, 1985).

139. Demosthenes, XLVI, 19, and XLIII, 54.

140. Plutarch, *Life of Solon, XX, 6.*

141. Pierre Chantraine, "Deux notes sur le vocabulaire juridique dans

les papyrus grecs," *Mémoires Maspero*, II, 219–224. This hypothesis is repeated in the articles on *proix* and *pherne* in the *Dictionnaire étymologique de la langue grecque*.

142. Mossé, *La fin de la démocratie athénienne*.

143. Euripides, for example, does not use the term *proix* but mentions *pherne* ten times.

144. Xenophon, *Cyropedia*, VII, 5, 19.

145. Aristotle, *Constitution of Athens*, II–XIII.

146. The bibliography is enormous. The most complete commentaries on Aristotle's work are C. Hignett, *A History of the Athenian Constitution to the End of the Fifth Century* (Oxford, 1952), pp. 32–123, and P. J. Rhodes, *A Commentary of the Aristotelian Athenaion Politeia* (Oxford, 1981), pp. 35 ff. The brief article by F. Cassola in *PP* (1964):26–34 is very convenient and still up to date.

147. Pierre Lévêque and Pierre Vidal-Naquet, "Clisthène l'Athénien," *Annales de l'Université de Besançon*, vol. 65.

148. Aristotle, *Constitution of Athens*, V, 2.

149. *Inscriptiones Graecae*, 12, 115. R. S. Stroud, *The Axones and Kyrbeis of Drakon and Solon* (Berkeley–Los Angeles–London, 1979).

150. Augustins, "Esquisse," p. 57.

151. Jean-Michel Servet, *Nomismata: Etat et origines de la monnaie* (Lyons: Presses Universitaires de Lyon, 1984), pp. 72–74.

152. J. K. Davies, "Athenian Citizenship: The Descent Group and the Alternatives," *The Classical Journal* 73(December–January 1977/8):106–121.

153. Aristotle, *Metaphysics* A,I,993 a30–b7.

Chapter 6. Body Politics in Ancient Rome

ALINE ROUSSELLE

1. Jean-Pierre Vernant, "Le mythe hésiodique des races. Essai d'analyse structurale," *Mythe et pensée chez les Grecs* (Paris: Maspero, 1965), I, 13–41. See also Nicole Loraux, *Les enfants d'Athéna. Idées athéniennes sur la citoyenneté et la division des sexes* (Paris: Maspero, 1981), p. 78.

2. Lucian, *Histoire véritable*, 22.

3. Benjamin Kilborne, *Interprétations de rêves au Maroc* (Grenoble: La Pensée Sauvage, 1978), pp. 4–5.

4. Keith Hopkins, "On the Probable Age Structure of the Roman Population," *Population Studies* 20(1966):245–264.

5. Edward Shorter, *A History of Women's Bodies* (New York: Basic Books, 1982); Jacques Gélis, *L'arbre et le fruit. La naissance dans l'Occident moderne, XVIè–XIXè siècles* (Paris: Fayard, 1984); Mireille Laget, *Naissances. L'accouchement avant l'âge de la clinique* (Paris: Seuil, 1982).

6. Raffaele Pettazzoni, "Carmenta," *Essays on the History of Religions* (Leiden: Brill, 1967), a 1941–42 article.

7. Augustine, *City of God*, 4, 21.

8. André Adnès and Pierre Canivet, "Guérisons miraculeuses et exorcisme dans l'*Histoire Philothée* de Théodoret de Cyr," *Revue de l'Histoire des Religions* 171(1967):53–82, 149–179; on childbirth, 157–159; Pierre-André Sigal, "La grossesse, l'accouchement et l'attitude envers l'enfant mort-né à la fin du moyen âge d'après les récits de miracles, *Santé, Médecine et assistance au Moyen Age, Actes du 110è Congrès National des Sociétés savantes,* Montpellier, 1985 (Paris: Editions du Comité des Travaux Historiques et Scientifiques, 1987), I, 23–41.

9. Ann Ellis Hanson, "The Eight Months' Child and the Etiquette of Birth: *Obsit omen!*," *Bulletin of the History of Medicine* 61(1987):589–602.

10. Seneca, *De matrimonio, Opera* suppl., ed. F. Haase (Leipzig: Teubner, 1902), p. 28.

11. Aline Rousselle, *Porneia. De la maîtrise du corps à la privation sensorielle* (Paris: PUF, 1983), p. 71; Soranus, *Gynecology,* I, 34, II, 42, ed. P. Burguière, D. Gourévitch, and Y. Malinas, vol. I (Paris: CUF, Belles Lettres, 1989).

12. Cicero, *Correspondence to Atticus,* XII, 18, ed. and trans. J. Beaujeu (Paris: CUF, Belles Lettres, 1983), VIII, 23, 39–40 (Letter DXCII).

13. Aline Rousselle, "Observation féminine et idéologie masculine: Le Corps de la femme d'après les médecins grecs," *Annales ESC* (1980):1089–1115.

14. Aline Rousselle, "Abstinence et Continence dans les monastères de Gaule méridionale à la fin de l'Antiquité et au début du Moyen-Age. Etude d'un régime alimentaire et de sa fonction," *Hommages à André Dupont, Fédération Historique du Languedoc méditerranéen et du Roussillon* (Montpellier, 1974), pp. 239–254; Emmanuel Le Roy Ladurie, "L'aménorrhée de famine (XVIIè–XVIIIè siècle)," *Annales ESC* (1969); rpr. in *Le Territoire de l'Historien* (Paris, 1973), pp. 331–348.

15. For the Orient, see Adnès and Canivet, "Guérisons miraculeuses"; on sterility, p. 160. For the Occident, see Gregory of Tours, *Virtutes Martini,* 4, 11.

16. Seneca, *Consolation to Marcia,* 12–16.

17. Mario Tabanelli, *Gli ex-voto poliviscerali etruschi e romani* (Florence, 1962), fig. 3.

18. Simone Deyts, *Les bois sculptés des Sources de la Seine,* XLIIth Supplement to *Gallia* (Paris, 1983), p. 89, and pls. XX, CXXVa.

19. Hanson, "Eight Months' Child"; Campbell Bonner, *Studies in Magical Amulets, Chiefly Greco-Egyptian* (Ann Arbor: University of Michigan Press, 1950), pp. 84–85, 275–277, esp. nos. 140, 147; Alphon A. Barb, "Diva Matrix," *Journal of Warburg and Courtault Institutes* 16(1953):214, and n. 23.

20. Edwin M. Yamauchi, "A Mandaeic Magic Bowl from the Yale Babylonian Collection," *Berytus* 17(1967–68):49–63, and pls. XIV–XVII.

21. Sigal, "La grossesse," pp. 31–33.

22. Ulpian, *Regulae,* XV, 1.

23. Benys Gorce, ed. and trans., *Life of Saint Melanie*, 1, 5, 6, 61 (Paris: Collection Sources Chrétiennes, 1962; cited hereafter as SC), 90, pp. 131–137, 249.

24. Pierre Fabre, *Paulin de Nole et l'amitié chrétienne* (Paris, 1947).

25. Danielle Gourévitch, *Le mal d'être femme. La femme et la médecine dans la Rome antique* (Paris: Belles Lettres, 1984), pp. 233–259; Keith R. Bradley, "Wet Nursing at Rome: A Study in Social Relations," in Beryl Rawson, ed., *The Family in Ancient Rome: New Perspectives* (Ithaca, N.Y.: Cornell University Press, 1986), pp. 201–229.

26. Emir Maurice Chehab, "Terres cuites de Kharayeb," *Bulletin du Musée de Beyrouth* 10(1951–52):31, and pl. XII.

27. Sharon Kelly Heyob, *The Cult of Isis among Women in the Greco-Roman World*, Etudes Préliminaires aux Religions Orientales 51 (Leiden: Brill, 1975).

28. Ramsay MacMullen, *Paganism in the Roman Empire* (New Haven, Conn.: Yale University Press, 1981), p. 115.

29. Seneca, *De superstitione,* quoted by Augustine, *City of God,* 6, 10.

30. J. Roger, *Paléontologie générale* (Paris, 1974), p. 1; Lucienne Rousselle, "La Paléodémécologie: Une ouverture nouvelle vers la compréhension des phénomènes d'interaction entre les organismes fossiles et leurs environnements," *Bulletin de l'Institut Géologique du bassin d'Aquitaine* 21(1977):3–11.

31. Emmanuel Le Roy Ladurie, "L'Histoire immobile," *Annales ESC* (1974):673–691.

32. Claude Vatin, *Recherches sur le mariage et la condition de la femme mariée à l'époque hellénistique* (Paris: Boccard, 1970), pp. 145–163.

33. Emiel Eyben, "Antiquity's View of Puberty," *Latomus* 31(1972): 678–697.

34. Galen, quoted from Oribasius, *Collection médicale,* 6, 15, ed. and trans. E. Bussemaker and Ch. Daremberg (Paris, 1851), I, 481.

35. Rufus, quoted from Oribasius, *incerti,* 2, Daremberg, III, 82–83.

36. Ibid., III, 83.

37. Soranus, *Gynecology,* I, 22–23.

38. Jean-Yves Nau, "La puberté programmée," *Le Monde,* Feb. 24, 1988, pp. 21, 23.

39. Soranus, *Gynecology,* I, 25.

40. Keith Hopkins, "The Age of Roman Girls at Marriage," *Population Studies* 18(1965):309–327; Brent Shaw, "The Age of Roman Girls at Marriage: Some Reconsiderations," *Journal of Roman Studies* 77(1987):30–46.

41. Keith Hopkins, "Brother-Sister Marriage in Roman Egypt," *Comparative Studies in Society and History* 22(1980):303–354.

42. Soranus, *Gynecology,* I, 17; Rousselle, *Porneia,* p. 41.

43. Rousselle, "Observation féminine," pp. 1089–1115.

44. Gordon J. Wenham, "Betulah: A Girl of Marriageable Age," *Vetus Testamentum* 22(1972):326–348.

45. *Digest,* 48, 5, 14.

46. Louis M. Epstein, *Sex Laws and Customs in Judaism* (New York, 1948), pp. 206–207.

47. Giulia Sissa, *Greek Virgins,* trans. Arthur Goldhammer (Cambridge, Mass.: Harvard University Press, 1990).

48. Carston Niebuhr, *Description de l'Arabie,* based on observations by Forskal and Niebuhr (Copenhagen, 1773), pp. 31–35.

49. Psellus, text and trans. in Jean-René Vieillefond, *Les "Cestes" de Julius Africanus. Etude sur l'ensemble des fragments avec édition, traduction et commentaires* (Florence–Paris, 1970).

50. S. Itzchaky, M. Yitzhaki, and S. Kottek, "Fertility in Jewish Tradition," *Proceedings of the Second International Symposium on Medicine in the Bible and the Talmud, Koroth* 9(1985):131.

51. Françoise Dunand, "Images du féminin dans le roman grec," *Mélanges Pierre Lévêque* (Paris–Besançon, 1989), pp. 173–182.

52. John Chrysostom, *On Single Marriage,* ed. and trans. Bernard Grillet (Paris: Cerf, SC 138, 1968), p. 191.

53. Jerzy Kolendo, "L'esclavage et la vie sexuelle des hommes libres à Rome," *Index. Quaderni camerti di Studi romanistici. International Survey of Roman Law* 10(1981):288–297.

54. Evelyne Patlagean, "L'entrée dans l'âge adulte à Byzance aux XIIIè–XIVè siècles," *Historicité de l'enfance et de la jeunesse* (Athens, 1988), pp. 263–270.

55. Emmanuel Le Roy Ladurie, "Biographie de la femme sous l'Ancien Régime," in Denis Hollier, ed., *Panorama des Sciences Humaines* (Paris, 1973), pp. 626–628.

56. Tacitus, *Germany,* 19.

57. Tacitus, *Histories,* 5, 5.

58. Strabo, 17, 2, 5; Aristotle, quoted from Oribasius, 22, 5, Daremberg, III, 62.

59. Flavius Josephus, *Contra Apion,* 199–201.

60. Beryl Rawson, "Children in the Roman Family," in Rawson, ed., *Family in Ancient Rome,* pp. 170–200.

61. Jean Hubeaux, "Enfants à louer ou à vendre. Augustine et l'autorité parentale," *Les lettres d'Augustine découvertes par Divjak. Colloque des 20–21 sept. 1982,"* Etudes Augustiniennes (1983), pp. 189–204.

62. *Codex Theodosianus,* 11, 17, 1–2; cited hereafter as *CTh.*

63. Olivia Robinson, "Women and the Criminal Law," *Raccolta di Scritti in memoria di Raffaele Moschella* (Perugia: Università degli Studi di Perugia, 1989), p. 539.

64. Yan Thomas, "Le 'ventre.' Corps maternel, droit paternel," *Le Genre humain* 14(1986); "La valeur," pp. 211–236.

65. Rufus of Ephesus, end of first century A.D., quoted from Oribasius, 6, 38, Daremberg, I, 541.

66. Jacques André, *L'alimentation et la cuisine à Rome* (Paris: Klincksieck, 1961), p. 140, and n. 32; Columella, 7, 9, 5; Pliny, 8, 209.

67. Aline Rousselle, "L'Eunuque et la poule: La logique de la reproduc-

tion," *Mi-Dit. Cahiers méridionaux de Psychanalyse* 2–3 (June 1984):57–65; Galen, *De spermate*, II, Kühn (1822), IV, 569.

68. Keith Hopkins, "Contraception in the Roman Empire," *Comparative Studies in Society and History* 8(1965):124–151.

69. Diocles and Rufus, quoted from Oribasius, 7, 26, Daremberg, II, 136–139, 143.

70. E. Nardi, *Procurato aborto nel mondo antico* (Milan, 1971); Marie-Thérèse Fontanille, *Avortement et contraception dans la Médecine gréco-romain* (Paris, 1977); A. Keller, "Die Abortiva in der römischen Kaiserziet," *Quellen und Studien zur Geschichte des Pharmazie*, ed. R. Schmitz 46(1988):309 ff.

71. Aristotle, quoted from Oribasius, 22, 5, Daremberg, III, 62; Plutarch, *Lycurgus*, 3.

72. Rousselle, *Porneia*, p. 51; Danielle Gourévitch, *Le mal d'être femme*, p. 209.

73. Thomas, "Le 'ventre,'" pp. 211–236, esp. 234, n. 88.

74. Jean Gagé, *Matronalia. Essai sur les dévotions et les organisations cultuelles des femmes dans l'ancienne Rome*, Collection Latomus 60 (Brussels, 1963), p. 95.

75. Dario Sabbatucci, "Magia ingiusta e nefasta," *Studi di storia in memoria di Raffaela Garosi* (Rome, 1976), pp. 233–252.

76. Robinson, "Women and the Criminal Law," p. 539.

77. Thomas, "Le 'ventre,'" p. 224.

78. Robinson, "Women and the Criminal Law," p. 539; *Digest*, 48, 8, 8 (Ulpian); 48, 19, 38, 5 (Paul); app., 39 (Tryphoninus).

79. *Digest*, 48, 5, 14, 7–8 (Ulpian).

80. Iza Biezunska-Malowist,"Les enfants-esclaves à la lumière des papyrus," *Hommages à M. Renard* (Brussels: Latomus, 1969), II, 91–96; "Les esclaves nés dans la maison du maître et le travail des esclaves en Egypte romaine," *Studi Classici* (1961), III, 147–162.

81. P. R. C. Weaver, "Gaius I, 84 and the S. C. Claudianum," *Classical Review* (1964):137–139; Tertullian, *Ad uxorem*, II, 8, 1, ed. and trans. Charles Munier (Paris: Cerf, SC 273, 1980), p. 145.

82. Aulus-Gellius, *Nuits Attiques*, IV, 2, 6–10, p. 194.

83. Sermon 44, 2–3, ed. M.-J. Delage (Paris: Cerf, SC 243, 1978), II, 331. See also Sermon 19.

84. Clement of Alexandria, *The Pedagogue*, III, 33, 2–3.

85. *Querolus*, ed. and trans. L. Havet, III, 1, frag. 56, 6–13, Bibliothèque des Hautes Etudes 41 (Paris, 1880), p. 275.

86. J.-T. Milik, *Recherches d'épigraphie proche-orientale. Dédicaces faites par des dieux (Palmyra, Hatra, Tyr) et des thiases sémitiques à l'époque romaine*, Institut Français d'Archéologie de Beyrouth, Bibliothèque archéologique et historique 92 (Paris: Geuthner, 1972), pp. 63–64.

87. Claude Vatin, *Recherches sur le mariage et la condition de la femme mariée à l'époque hellénistique* (Paris: Boccard, 1970), p. 128.

88. *Digest*, 23, 2, 44 (Paul); Leo Ferrero Raditsa, "Augustus' Legislation

Concerning Marriage, Procreation, Love Affairs and Adultery," *Aufstieg und Niedergang der römischen Welt* II, *Principat* 2(1980):278–339.

89. Chariton, *Chairéas et Callirhoé*, I, 12, ed. and trans. Georges Molinié (Paris: CUF, 1979), p. 57.

90. Horace, *Satires*, I, 2, ll. 80–108.

91. Horace, *Satires*, I, 2, l. 131, and *Satires*, II, 7, ll. 46–71.

92. *Satires*, I, 1, l. 93.

93. Paul-Louis Gatier, "Aspects de la vie religieuse des femmes dans l'Orient paléochrétien: Ascétisme et monachisme," *La femme dans le monde méditerranéen*, Travaux de la Maison de l'Orient 10 (Lyons, 1985), pp. 165–183, esp. 171, n. 38.

94. Alfredo Mordechai Rabello, "Divorce of Jews in the Roman Empire," *The Jewish Law Annual* (1981) IV, 79–102, and p. 82, n. 12; Plaute, *Mercator* 817 ff.; Valerius Maximus, 6, 3, 10–12; on the Jews, Michna, Ketubot, 7, 6.

95. Pliny the Younger, *Letters*, IV, 19, ed. and trans. Anne-Marie Guillemin (Paris: CUF, Belles Lettres, 1962), II, 19.

96. Robert E. A. Palmer, "Roman Shrines of Female Chastity from the Last Struggle to the Papacy of Innocent I," *Rivista Storica dell'Antichità* 4(1974):113–159.

97. *Digest*, 47, 10, 15, 15; Marcel Morabito, *Les réalités de l'esclavage d'après le Digeste*, Annales Littéraires de l'Université de Besançon 254, Centre de recherches d'Histoire ancienne 39 (Paris: Belles Lettres, 1981), p. 190.

98. Ethel and L. Edelstein, *Asclepius: A Collection and Interpretation of the Testimonies* (Baltimore, 1945), I, nos. 31, 34, 39, 42, 426.

99. Ammiaus Marcellinus, XVI, 10, 18.

100. M. Durry, ed. and trans., *Eloge funèbre d'une matrone romaine* (Paris: CUF, 1950), p. 22.

101. Rousselle, *Porneia*, pp. 58–59; Voir Oribasius, *Collection Médicale, incert.* 6; Soranus, *Gynecology*, I, 46, 56; Galen even recommends extending this period of abstinence while breast-feeding, quoted from Oribasius, *incert.* 14, III (1858), p. 130.

102. Keith Hopkins, *Death and Renewal: Sociological Studies in Roman History*, 2 vols. (Cambridge: Cambridge University Press, 1983), pp. 31–200; François Jacques, "Le renouvellement du Sénat romain," *Annales ESC* 6(1987):1287–1303.

103. Evelyne Patlagean, "Sur la limitation de la fécondité dans la haute époque byzantine," *Annales ESC* 6(1969):1353–1369.

104. Joseph Mélèze-Modrzejewski, "Les Juifs et la droit hellénistique," *IURA* 12(1961):175; Rabello, "Divorce of Jews."

105. *Genération des animaux*, IV, 6, 775a.

106. For the modern era, see Laget, *Naissances*, pp. 236, 246–247.

107. John Chrysostom, "To a Young Widow," trans. Bernard Grillet (Paris: Cerf, SC 138, 1968), 2, 139–142, p. 125; John Chrysostom, *Sur le mariage unique*, 2, p. 169, ll. 80–81.

108. Horace, *Satires*, I, 2, ll. 24–63; Jerzy Kolendo, "L'esclavage et la

vie sexuelle des hommes libres à Rome," *Index. Quaderni camerti di Studi romanistici. International Survey of Roman Law* 10(1981):288–297.

109. Henry Chadwick, "The Relativity of Moral Codes: Rome and Persia in Late Antiquity," in William R. Schoedel and R. L. Wilcken, eds., *Early Christian Literature and the Classical Intellectual Tradition in Honor of R. M. Grant,* Collection Théologie Historique 53 (Paris: Beauchesne, 1979), pp. 135–153.

110. Aline Rousselle, "Personal Status and Sexual Practice in the Roman Empire," *Zone 5, Fragments for a History of the Human Body,* pt. III (1989), pp. 300–333.

111. Epictetus, *Conversations,* 1, 18, 21–23, and 4, 1, 15; Philo of Alexandria, *Quod omnis Probus,* 38, ed. and trans. Madeleine Petit, *Oeuvres* 28 (Paris: Cerf, 1974), p. 167.

112. Twelve Years, *Digest,* 25, 7, 1, 4; fidelity, *Digest,* 48, 5, 14 (13), 8; Aline Rousselle, "Concubinage and Adultery," *Opus* 3(1984):75–84.

113. P. R. C. Weaver, "The Status of Children in Mixed Marriages," in Rawson, *Family in Ancient Rome,* pp. 145–169.

114. D. M. MacDowell, "Bastards as Athenian Citizens," *Classical Quarterly* 26(1976):88–91.

115. Aristophanes, *The Wasps,* 480.

116. Catherine Simon, "Mères au bereau," *Le Monde,* Nov. 21, 1989.

117. Valerius Maximus, 6, 7, 1.

118. Suetonius, *Augustus,* 71.

119. Tertullian, *Ad uxorem,* ed. and trans. Charles Munier, I, 6, 4 (Paris: Cerf, SC 273, 1980), p. 113.

120. Tertullian, *De culte feminarum,* ed. and trans. Marie Turcan (Paris: Cerf, SC 273, 1971), II, 2, 1, p. 95.

121. Hippolytus of Rome, *La tradition apostolique,* ed. and trans. Bernard Botte (Paris: Cerf, SC 11, 1968), p. 75.

122. Iro Kajanto, "On Divorce among the Common People of Rome," *Mélanges M. Surray, Revue des Etudes Latines* 47(1969):99–113.

123. S. Itzchaky, M. Yitzhaki, and S. Kottek, "Fertility in Jewish Tradition," p. 132; Epstein, *Sex Laws and Customs in Judaism,* p. 140.

124. Seneca, *Consolation to Helvia,* 16, 3.

125. Horace, *Odes,* 1, 2, 19.

126. Virgil, *Aeneid,* IV, 266.

127. Pliny, *Natural History,* 7, 60.

128. Seneca, *On Clemency,* 3, 8, trans. François Préchac, 3rd ed. (Paris: CUF, 1967), p. 28.

129. Pliny, *Natural History,* 5, 57.

130. Dio Cassius, 58, 22.

131. Marcus Aurelius, *Meditations,* I, 29.

132. Juvenal, *Satire,* 6, ll. 306–313; cf. Palmer, "Roman Shrines," p. 143.

133. *Femmes pythagoriciennes. Fragments et lettres de Théano, Périctione, Phintys, Mélissa et Mya,* trans. with notes by Mario Meunier (Paris, 1980).

134. *Conseils à mari et femme,* 140 B.

135. Georges Fabre, *Libertus, Recherches sur les rapports patron-affranchi à la fin de la République romaine* (Paris: Boccard, 1981), pp. 192–193.

136. Arnaldo Momigliano, "La Libertà di parola nel mondo antico," *Sesto Contributo alla Storia degli Studi classici* (Rome, 1980), pp. 403–436, and Arnaldo Momigliano, "Epicureans in Revolt," *Journal of Roman Studies* 31(1941):151–157.

137. Tacitus, *Annals,* I, 72–73.

138. Suetonius, *Tiberius,* 28.

139. Tacitus, *Annals,* 6, 15, 3.

140. Frederick H. Cramer, "Bookburning and Censorship in Ancient Rome," *Journal of the History of Ideas* 6(1945):157–196.

141. Yolande Grisé, *Le suicide dans la Rome antique* (Paris: Belles Lettres, 1982).

142. Pliny the Younger, *Letters,* 3, 16.

143. Livy, 1, 58.

144. Livy, II, 13; Pliny the Elder, *Natural History,* 34, 13.

145. Seneca, *Consolation to Marcia,* 16, 2.

146. Plato, *Symposium,* 179b–d.

147. Marc Philonenko, ed. and trans., *Joseph and Aseneth* (Leiden: Brill, 1968).

148. Plutarch, *On Love,* 25, 770D–771C.

149. Plutarch, *Life of Marius,* 19, 9.

150. Radu Vulpe, "Prigioneri romani suppliziati da donne dacie sul rilievo della colonna traiana," *Rivista storica dell'Antichità* 1(1973):109–125.

151. Dio Cassius, *Roman History,* 78, 14.

152. A. Dupont-Sommer, intro. and trans., *Le Quatrième Livre des Maccabées,* Bibliothèque des Hautes Etudes 274 (1939).

153. Charles Saumagne, "Thraséa et Perpétue."

154. Anonymous Latin, *Treatise on Physiognomy,* text established, trans. and commented on by Jacques André (Paris: Collection des Universités de France, 1981).

155. Galen, *De spermate,* 1, Kühn, IV, p. 569.

156. Télès and Musonius, *Prédictions,* trans. André-Jean Festugière (Paris: Vrin, 1978). See C. E. Lutz, *Musonius Rufus, the Roman Socrates,* Yale Classical Studies 10 (New Haven, Conn., 1947), pp. 3–147.

157. Antoine Guillaumont, *Aux origines du monachisme chrétien,* Spiritualité orientale 30 (1947), p. 15, and nn. 9–10.

158. *Collatio,* 6, 4.

159. *Justinian Code,* 1, 9, 7.

160. Chadwick, "Relativity of Moral Codes," p. 145.

161. *CTh,* 3, 12, 1, de 342, Constance; Jean Gaudemet, *"Justum matrimonium,"* *Société et mariage* (Strasbourg: Cerdic, 1980), p. 83.

162. Gaudemet, *"Justum matrimonium,"* p. 84.

163. *CTh,* 9, 1, de 326, Clémence Dupont, "Le constitutions de Constantin et le droit privé au début du IVè siècle," thesis, Lille, 1937, p. 26.

164. *CTh,* 4, 6, 3, de 336, Constantine; Theodosius and Valentinian, Gaudemet, *"Justum matrimonium,"* pp. 85–86.

165. Sermon 19, 4, SC 175, I, 489.

166. Hippolytus of Rome, *Apostolic Tradition,* ed. Bernard Botte, 16 (1968), pp. 71–72.

167. Rousselle, *Porneia,* p. 133.

168. C. St. Tomulescu, "Justinien et le concubinat," *Studi in Honore di Gaetano Scherillo* (Milan, 1972), I, 299–326; C. Van De Wiel, "La légitimation par mariage subséquent de Constantin à Justinien. Sa réception sporadique dans le droit byzantin," *Revue Internationale des Droits de l'Antiquité* 25(1978):307–350; Clémence Dupont, *Les constitutions,* sec. VIII.

169. *CTh,* 9, 15, 1 (318); see J. H. W. G. Liebeschuetz, *Continuity and Change in Roman Religion* (Oxford: Clarendon, 1979), pp. 294–295.

170. *Justinian Code,* 9, 16, 7=*CTh,* 9, 14, 1 (374).

171. *CTh,* 11, 36, 1 (314 or 315); 9, 9, 29; 38, 1 (322).

172. Dupont, *Les constitutions,* pp. 110–112.

173. Hopkins, "Contraception," p. 139, contains references to the Church Fathers.

174. Jean-Louis Flandrin, *Un temps pour embrasser. Aux origines de la morale occidentale* (Paris: Seuil, 1983), p. 130.

175. Clément of Alexandria, *The Pedagogue,* III, 4.

176. Theodoret of Cyrrhus, V, 55–57; I, 244–245.

177. Isidore Lévy, *La légende de Pythagore de Grèce en Palestine* (Paris, 1927), pp. 81–82.

178. *Les Apocryphes du Nouveau Testament,* trans. J. B. Bauer (Paris: Cerf, 1973).

Chapter 7. Pandora's Daughters and Rituals in Grecian Cities
LOUISE BRUIT ZAIDMAN

1. François de Polignac, *La naissance de la cité grecque* (Paris, 1984), p. 79.

2. Hesiod, *Theogony,* 590–591; see Nicole Loraux, "Sur la race des femmes," in *Les enfants d'Athéna* (Paris, 1984).

3. Marcel Detienne, *Dionysos mis à mort* (Paris, 1977), pp. 177–179.

4. Susan Guettel Cole, "The Social Function of Rituals of Maturation: The Koureion and the Arkteia," *Zeitschrift für Papyrologie und Epigraphik* 55(1984):233–244.

5. Pierre Brulé, *La fille d'Athènes* (Paris, 1987).

6. On male initiations, see Henri Jeanmaire, *Couroi et Courètes* (Paris, 1939). For a discussion of female initiation, compare Angelo Brelich, *Paides e Parthenoi* (Rome, 1969), pp. 229 ff., with Claude Calame, *Les choeurs de jeunes filles en Grèce archaïque* (Rome, 1977), esp. pp. 67–69.

7. Christiane Sourvinou-Inwood, *Studies in Girls' Transitions* (Athens, 1988), pp. 136–148.

8. Calame, *Les choeurs,* I, 263 ff. See also Brûlé, *La fille,* pp. 83 ff.

9. Brulé, *La fille,* p. 116.

10. See the various publications on this subject by L. Kahil, in particular "L'Artemis de Brauron, rites et mystères," *AK* 20(1977):86–98, and "Le 'cratérisque' d'Artémis et le Brauronion de l'Acropole," *Hesperia* 50(3)1983: 253–263.

11. Sourvinou-Inwood, *Girls' Transitions,* pp. 15–66.

12. Brelich, *Paides,* I, 280 ff.

13. For a detailed analysis of this ritual, see Jean-Louis Durand, *Sacrifice et labour en Grèce ancienne* (Paris–Rome, 1986).

14. See, for example, Sophia Kaempf-Dimitriadou, *Die liebe der Götter in der Attischen Kunst des 5. Jahrhunderts von Christ* (Berne, 1979), esp. p. 36 for Boreas and Oreithyia, and plates 27–31.

15. Calame, *Les choeurs,* pp. 367 ff.

16. Sourvinou-Inwood, *Girls' Transitions,* pp. 39–66.

17. See Pierre Vidal-Naquet, *Le chasseur noir,* pp. 151–174, 191–207.

18. Polignac, *La naissance de la cité grecque,* p. 78.

19. Detienne, "Violentes 'Eugenies'" in *La cuisine du sacrifice en pays grec,* pp. 183–214.

20. Loraux, "Le nom athénien," p. 127.

21. Jean-Pierre Vernant and Pierre Vidal-Naquet, *Mythe et tragédie en Grèce ancienne* (Paris, 1986), II, 260–264.

22. Marcel Detienne, *Dionysos à ciel ouvert* (Paris, 1986), p. 42.

23. Ibid., pp. 79–89, and note 202.

24. René Ginouvès, *Balaneutikè: recherches sur le bain dans l'antiquité grecque* (Paris, 1962), pp. 268–276.

25. Cole, "The Social Function," and Pauline Schmitt Pantel, "Athena Apatouria et la ceinture: les aspects féminins des Apatouries à Athènes," *Annales E.S.C.* 6(1977):1059–73.

26. Brulé, *La fille,* pp. 361 ff.

27. Ibid., p. 260.

28. Jean-Pierre Vernant, *Mythe et pensée chez les Grecs* (Paris, 1965), pp. 131–137.

29. See Robert Parker, *Miasma. Pollution and Purification in Early Greek Religion* (Oxford, 1983).

30. Euripides, *Iphigenia in Tauris,* ll. 381–383.

31. "Le pur et l'impur" in *Mythe et société en Grèce ancienne* (Paris, 1974), pp. 121–140.

32. Marcel Detienne, *Les jardins d'Adonis* (Paris, 1972), pp. 187–226.

33. Giulia Sissa, *Le corps virginal* (Paris, 1987), pp. 27–65.

34. Hesiod, *Theogony,* trans. Dorothea Wender, ll. 570–593.

Chapter 8. The Religious Roles of Roman Women
JOHN SCHEID

1. John Scheid, *Romulus et ses frères. Le collège des frères arvales, modèle du culte public dans la Rome des Empereurs* (Rome: Ecole Française, 1989).

2. Cato the Censor in Festus, p. 466 Lindsay.

3. Cato, *Treatise on Agriculture,* 143.

4. Paulus Diaconus, *Abridgment of Festus,* p. 72 Lindsay.

5. Olivier de Cazanove, "*Exesto:* L'incapacité sacrificielle des femmes à Rome (A propos de Plutarque. Quaest. Rom. 85)," *Phoenix* 41(1987):159–174.

6. Ibid., pp. 165 ff.

7. Scheid, *Romulus,* pp. 320 ff.

8. Paulus Diaconus, *Abridgment,* p. 124. Cazanove, "Exesto," pp. 166 ff.

9. Plutarch, *Life of Romulus,* 15.4 ff., 19.9.

10. Cazanove, "*Exesto,*" pp. 164 ff.

11. Ibid., p. 159.

12. Plutarch, *Roman Questions,* 85.

13. Mary Beard, "The Sexual Status of Vestal Virgins," *JRS* 70(198):12–27, esp. 14.

14. Aulus Gellius, *Attic Nights,* 1, 12, 14; Beard, "The Sexual Status," pp. 15 ff.

15. Luigi Sensi, "Ornatus e status sociale delle donne romane," *Annali della Facoltà di Lettere e Filosofia di Perugia,* Sez. Studi Classici 18, n.s. IV (1980–81): 55–102.

16. Augusto Fraschetti, "La sepoltura delle Vestali e la città," *Du châtiment dans la cité. Supplices corporels et peines de mort dans le monde antique,* Collection de l'Ecole Française de Rome, vol. 9 (Rome: Ecole Française, 1984), pp. 97–128.

17. Servius augmented, *Commentary on the Eclogues,* 8.82, according to Cazanove.

18. Scheid, *Romulus,* pp. 320 ff.

19. Cazanove, "*Exesto,*" p. 170, n. 57.

20. Paulus Diaconus, *Abridgment,* p. 473.

21. Georges Dumézil, *Religion romaine archaïque,* 2nd ed. (Paris: Payot, 1974), p. 376.

22. Ovid, *Fasti,* 4, 637–640.

23. Tertullian, *Spectacles,* 5.

24. Dumézil, *Religion,* pp. 168 ff., concerning Varro, *On the Latin Language,* 6.21.

25. Prudentius, *Contra Symmachus* 2.1107 ff. *(in flammam iugulant pecudes).*

26. Beard, "The Sexual Status," pp. 17 ff.

27. Ibid.; John Scheid, "Le flamine de Jupiter, les Vestales et le général triomphant," *Le Temps de la réflexion* (Paris: Gallimard, 1986), pp. 213–230.

28. Nicole Boels, "Le statut religieux de la Flaminica Dialis," *REL* 51(1973):77–100.

29. Macrobius, *Saturnalia,* 1.16.30.

30. Ibid., 1, 15, 18.

31. Paulus Diaconus, *Abridgment,* p. 473.

32. Cato, *Treatise on Agriculture*, 143.

33. Paulus Diaconus, *Abridgment*, p. 419.

34. See, e.g., Jacqueline Champeaux, *Fortuna. Le culte de la Fortune à Rome et dans le monde romain. I*, Collection de l'Ecole Française de Rome, vol. 64 (Rome: Ecole Française, 1982), pp. 290 ff.

35. Pierre Drossart, "Nonae Captrotinae. La fausse capture des Aurores," *RHR* 185(1974):129–139.

36. Ovid, *Fasti*, 3.233.

37. Dumézil, *Religion*, pp. 63 ff., 343 ff.

38. Champeaux, *Fortuna*, pp. 311 ff.

39. Dumézil, *Religion*, p. 72.

40. Ibid., pp. 341 ff.

41. For sources, see Champeaux, *Fortuna*, pp. 378 ff.

42. Ibid., pp. 379 ff.

43. Ovid, *Fasti*, 4.135–156.

44. Ibid., 4.153 ff.

45. Ibid., 4.149.

46. Filippo Coarelli, *Il Foro Boario. Dalle origini alla fine della Repubblica* (Rome: Quasar, 1988), pp. 299 ff.

47. Champeaux, *Fortuna*, pp. 391 ff.

48. Ibid., pp. 348 ff.

49. Ibid., pp. 335–373.

50. Livy 2.39 ff.; Dionysius of Halicarnassus 8.22–62; Plutarch, *Life of Coriolanus*, 37.4 ff.; Valerius Maximus, 5.2.1. See also Dario Sabbatucci, "L'extra-romanità di Fortuna," *Religione e Civiltà* 3(1982):511–527, esp. 519.

51. See Champeaux, *Fortuna*, pp. 335–373.

52. Ibid.

53. Valerius Maximus, 1.8.4.

54. Plutarch, *Roman Questions*, 57.

55. Ibid., 56.

56. Dumézil, *Religion*, p. 355.

57. Plutarch, *Life of Cicero*, 19; *Life of Caesar*, 9.

58. Macrobius, *Saturnalia* 1.12.27.

59. Ovid, *Fasti*, 5.148–158.

60. Propertius 4.9.21–36; 51–61.

61. Giulia Piccaluga, "Bona Dea. Due contributi all'interpretazione del suo culto," *SMSR* 35(1964):195–237, see 221.

62. For the affair of Clodius, see Philippe Moreau, *Clodiana religio. Un procès politique en 61 avant J.C.* (Paris: Les Belles Lettres, 1982).

63. Propertius 4.9.51; Juvenal, *Satires*, 2.84 ff.

64. Propertius 4.9.28; Plutarch, *Life of Cicero*, 20.1; *Life of Caesar*, 10.

65. Juvenal, *Satires*, 2.86 ff.; Macrobius, *Saturnalia*, 1.12.23 ff.

66. Plutarch, *Life of Caesar*, 9.9; Juvenal, *Satires*, 6.314.

67. Henri Le Bonniec, *Le culte de Cérès à Rome. Des origines à la fin de*

la République, Etudes et commentaires, vol. 27 (Paris: Klincksiek, 1958), p. 430.

68. Plutarch, *Roman Questions,* 20.

69. *Pro populo:* Cicero, *Laws,* 2.9.21.

70. Juvenal, *Satires,* 9.115–117.

71. Macrobius, *Saturnalia,* 1.12.25.

72. Palladius 11.19; Piccaluga, "Bona Dea," p. 217.

73. Servius, *Aeneid,* 8.314; Macrobius, *Saturnalia,* 1.12.27.

74. Macrobius, *Saturnalia,* 1.12.27.

75. Michel Gras, "Vin et société à Rome et dans le Latium à l'époque archaïque," *Modes de contacts et processus de transformation dans les sociétés anciennes,* Collection de l'Ecole Française de Rome, vol. 67 (Rome: Ecole Française, 1983), pp. 1067–1075, esp. 1072.

76. Beard, "The Sexual Status," pp. 24 ff.

77. Livy 27.37.

78. Giovanni Battista Pighi, *De ludis saecularibus populi Romani Quiritium,* second edition (Amsterdam: Hakkert, 1965), pp. 155 ff.: IV, 1.4, ll. 9–30; Va, l. 52; Va, ll. 83–90.

79. Harold Mattingly, *Coins of the Roman Empire in the British Museum,* III (London, 1966), no. 424.

80. Ovid, *Fasti,* 6.475.

81. *Matrones honestissimas:* Cicero, *For Milo,* 10.27.

82. Champeaux, *Fortuna,* p. 244.

83. Cazanove, "Exesto," p. 168.

84. Plutarch, *Life of Numa,* 12.3.

85. Aulus Gellius, *Attic Nights,* 4.3.

86. Juvenal, *Satires,* 6.

87. Cicero, *On the Nature of the Gods,* 1.20.55; 2.28.70; etc.

88. Anne-Marie Tupet, *La magie dans la poésie latine. Des origines à la fin du règne d'Auguste,* Collection d'études anciennes (Paris: Les Belles Lettres, 1976).

89. Jean-Marie Pailler, *Bacchanalia. La répression de 186 avant J.-C. à Rome et en Italie; vestiges, images, tradition,* Bibliothèque des Ecoles françaises d'Athènes et de Rome, vol. 270 (Rome: Ecole Française, 1988), p. 251.

90. For all problems and interpretations, see ibid.

91. Ibid., p. 582.

92. Livy 34.1 ff.

93. Pailler, *Bacchanalia,* p. 582.

94. Livy 34.1 ff.

95. Pailler, *Bacchanalia,* pp. 592 ff. for sources.

96. Livy 8.18.1 ff.

97. Ibid., 40, 43 ff.

98. Livy, *Abridgment,* 98.

99. Quintillian, *The Art of Oratory,* 5.11.39; Plutarch, *Life of Cato the Elder,* 9.11.

100. Robert Schilling, *La religion romaine de Vénus depuis les origines jusqu'au temps d'Auguste,* 2nd. ed. (Paris: Boccard, 1982).

101. Macrobius, *Saturnalia,* 1.12.26.

102. Ibid.

103. Horace, *Odes,* 3.30.8.

104. Rutilius Namatianus, *My Return,* 2.52.

105. Festus, p. 79.

106. Aulus Gellius, *Attic Nights,* 10.15.14.

107. Servius, *Aeneid,* 4.29.

108. See Nicole Boels, "Le statut religieux de la Flaminica Dialis," *REL* 51(19)3:77–100.

109. Plutarch, *Roman Questions,* 50.

110. Boels, "Le statut religieux"; Scheid, "Le flamine de Jupiter," p. 215.

111. Scheid, *Romulus,* pp. 214 ff.

112. Cato, *Treatise on Agriculture,* 143.1.

113. *Rem divinam facere:* ibid., 5.3.

114. See Chapter 3, "The Division of Sexes in Roman Law," by Yan Thomas.

115. Ibid.

116. Compare Dionysius of Halicarnassus 2.25.5 on the domestic status of wives: "So long as a woman showed herself to be virtuous and obedient to her husband in all ways, she was mistress of the household by the same right as he was master."

Chapter 9. Early Christian Women

MONIQUE ALEXANDRE

1. I, 1–2, *Sources chrétiennes* 173, Marie Turcan (Paris, 1971) (Carthage, c. 202). *Sources chrétiennes* is cited hereafter as SC.

2. Sermon 5, "Praise of the Holy Virgin and Mother of God Mary," *Patrologiae Grecae* 65, 720B, fifth century. Cited hereafter as PG.

3. Galatians 3:28.

4. 1 Timothy 2:11–15. For the silence of the congregation, compare 1 Corinthians 14:34, possibly an interpolation. For feminine submission, see Colossians 3:18; Ephesians 5:22; Titus 2:3; 1 Peter 3:1–5; all to be understood in the general context of "domestic codes."

5. Matthew 27:56, 61; 28:1–10; Mark 15:40, 47; 16:1, 9–10; Luke 8:2; 24:10; John 19:25; 20:1, 11–18.

6. Luke 10:38–42; John 11–12.

7. John 4:1–42.

8. Acts 16:13–15, 26, 40.

9. Acts 13:2–3, 18, 26; 1 Corinthians 16, 19; Romans 16:3–5; 2 Timothy 4:19.

10. Romans 16:1.

11. *Actes de Paul,* trans. L. Vouaux (Paris, 1913).

12. Eusebius, *Ecclesiastical History,* V, 1, 17–19, 37, 41–42, 53–56 (SC

41, G. Bardy, Paris, 1955). Cf. Marie-Louise Guillaumin, "Une jeune fille qui s'appelait Blandine. Aux origines d'une tradition hagiographique," in J. Fontaine and Charles Kannengiesser, eds., *Epektasis: Mélanges patristiques offerts au Cardinal Daniélou* (Paris, 1972), pp. 93–98.

13. *Passio Perpetuae et Felicitatis*, in Herbert Musurillo, *The Acts of Christian Martyrs* (Oxford, 1972), pp. 106–131.

14. Pio Franchi de' Cavalieri, *Scritti agiografici* I, "Studi e Testi," 221 (Vatican City, 1962), pp. 293–381.

15. Cyprian of Carthage, *The Conduct of Virgins* 3(243).

16. SC 296, Pierre Maraval, 1982.

17. Epistle 22. Compare Epistle 107 to Iaeta, in *Correspondence,* 8 vols. ed. J. Labourt (Paris: CUF, 1949–1963).

18. Epistle 130.

19. *Sentences des Pères du Désert* (alphabetical collection), trans. Lucie Regnault (Solesmes, 1981). Theodora: 309–315; Sacra: 885–891; Syncleticus: 892–909.

20. *Oeuvres monastiques* I. *Oeuvres pour les moniales* (SC 345, Adalbert de Vogüé, Joël Courreau) (Paris, 1983).

21. Palladius, *Lausiac History,* 46 (*La Storia Lausiaca,* ed. G. J. M. Bartelink, Mondadori, 1974).

22. Jerome, Epistle 127 (411).

23. Epistle 103 (404).

24. Gregory Nazianzen, PG 37, 1542–1550.

25. *Life of Melania* (SC 90, D. Gorce, Paris, 1962).

26. Pierre Petitmengin et al., *Pélagie la pénitente. Métamorphoses d'une légende.* Vol. 1. *Les textes et leur histoire* (Paris, 1981); Vol. 2. *La survie dans les littératures européennes* (Paris, 1984), and Evelyne Patlagean, "L'histoire de la femme déguisée en moine et l'évolution de la sainteté à Byzance," *Studi medievali* 17(1976):597–623.

27. See, for example, pseudo-Sophronius, *Life of Mary the Egyptian,* PG 87, 3697–2736.

28. *Journal d'Egérie* (SC 296, Pierre Maraval, Paris, 1982).

29. PG 35, 757–760 (Caesarius' funeral oration); 991–1000A (his father's funeral oration); PG 37, 969 s., 1029 s. (poems about himself and his life); Epitaphes, *Anthologie Palatine* VIII, 34074, ed. Pierre Waltz (Paris: CUF, 1944).

30. PG 35, 789–817.

31. Basil of Caesarea, *Epistles,* 204, 6; 210, 1; 223, 3 (*Letters,* ed. Yves Courtonne, 3 vols. [Paris: CUF, 1957–1966]), for Macrina the Elder; Gregory of Nyssa, *Life of Macrina* 2, for Emmelia.

32. *Confessions,* I, 11; III, 11–12; V, 8–9; VI, 1–2, 13; VIII, 12; IX, 8–13; X.

33. *Gregorii Nysseni opera* IX, ed. Andreas Spira (Leiden, 1967), pp. 461–490; see also Kenneth Holum, *Theodosian Empresses: Women and Imperial Dominion in Late Antiquity* (Berkeley, 1982).

34. Jerome, Epistle 46.

35. See *Oeuvres monastiques I,* pp. 441 ff.

36. *Life of Anthony,* 3, 1, ed. G. J. M. Bartelink (Milan: Mondadori, 1974).

37. Palladius, *Lausiac History,* 33, for example. *Vie grecque de Pacôme,* 32, trans. A. J. Festugière (Paris, 1965); *Vie bohaïrique,* chap. 27, trans. A. Veilleux, "Spiritualité orientale," no. 38, Bellefontaine, 1984.

38. Augustine, *Epistle,* 211; L. Verheijen, *La Règle de Saint Augustin* (Paris, 1967), I, 105 ff.

39. SC 70, 108, 159, Henri-Irénée Marrou, Marguerite Harl, Claude Mondésert (Paris, 1960–1970).

40. (Frankfurt: Christoph Stücklin, 1974); P. A. Gramaglia, *De virginibus velandis. La condizione femminile nelle prime communite cristiane,* 3 vols. (Rome, 1985).

41. Trans. Denys Gorce (Namur, 1958).

42. PG I, 350–452.

43. SC 95, H. Musurillo, V. H. Debidour (Paris, 1963).

44. See Michel Aubineau, "Les écrits de Saint Athanase sur la virginité," *Revue d'ascétique et de mystique* (1955):140–173.

45. PG 30, 669–810.

46. SC 119, Michel Aubineau (Paris, 1966).

47. SC 125, H. Musurillo, B. Grillet (Paris, 1966); cf. *Sur les cohabitations suspectes,* ed. J. Dumortier (Paris: CUF, 1955).

48. Saint Ambrose, *Ecrits sur la virginité,* trans. Marie-Gabriel Tissot (Solesmes, 1981).

49. *Bibliothèque augustinienne,* 3, trans. J. Saint Martin (Paris, 1949).

50. PL 16, 367–384.

51. *A son épouse* (SC 273, Charles Munier, Paris, 1980); *Le Mariage unique* (SC 343, Paul Mattei, 1988); *Exhortation à la chasteté* (SC 319, J. C. Fredouille, Paris, 1985).

52. *A une jeune veuve. Sur le mariage unique* (SC 138, B. Grillet, Paris, 1968).

53. *Bibliothèque augustinienne,* 3; cf. translation cited in note 48.

54. *Bibliothèque augustinienne,* 2, trans. Gustave Combés (Paris, 1948).

55. FG 51, 217–241.

56. See, e.g., Kari Borresen, "L'usage patristique des métaphores féminines dans le discours sur Dieu," *Revue théologique de Louvain* 13(1982):205–220.

57. See Jeanne-Marie Demarolle, "Les femmes chrétiennes vues par Porphyre," *Jahrbuch für Antike und Christentum* 13(1970):42–47.

58. SC 320, 3–9, 336, Marcel Metzger (Paris, 1985–1987).

59. See, e.g., Basile of Caesarea, *Epistles,* 188, 199, 217.

60. The texts collected in Ross S. Kraemer, *Maenads, Martyrs, Matrons, Monastics* (Philadelphia, 1988), also rely on this type of documentation. For the use of epigraphic evidence, see, e.g., Charles Piétri, "Le mariage chrétien à Rome, IVe–Ve siècles," *Histoire vécue du peuple chrétien* (Toulouse, 1979), I, 105–130.

61. *A Diognète*, 6, 1 (SC 33, Henri-Irénée Marrous, Paris, 1951).

62. Jerome, *Epistles*, 22, 16.

63. See *Les Martyrs de Lyon* (177), Colloque de Lyon, 1977 (Paris, 1978): Garth Thomas, "La condition sociale de l'Eglise de Lyon en 177," pp. 93–106.

64. *Life of Macrina*, 7; *Life of Olympias*, 6.

65. Augustine, *Epistles*, 211, 5–6; *Rule of Caesarius*, 21, 42.

66. Siricius, *Epistles*, 7, 3.

67. Michel Foucault, *Histoire de la sexualité* (Paris, 1976–1984): vol. 2: *L'usage des plaisirs;* vol. 3: *Le souci de soi;* cf. Averil Cameron, "Redrawing the Map: Early Christian Territory after Foucault," *Journal of Roman Studies* 76(1986):266–271.

68. Aline Rousselle, *Porneia. De la maîtrise du corps à la privation sensorielle, IIe–IVe siècles de l'ère chrétienne* (Paris, 1983).

69. Paul Veyne, "La famille et l'amour sous le Haut Empire romain," *Annales E.S.C.* 33(1978):35–63.

70. Peter Brown, *The Body and Society. Men, Women and Sexual Renunciation in Early Christianity* (New York, 1988).

71. John Paul II, *Mulieris dignitatem* (1988).

72. Simone de Beauvoir, *Le deuxième sexe* (Paris, 1949), I, 153.

73. Karl Borresen, *Subordination et Equivalence. Nature et rôle de la femme d'après Augustin et Thomas d'Aquin* (Oslo–Paris, 1968).

74. Compare two collections of articles: Rosemary Ruetner, *Religion and Sexism: Images of Women in the Jewish and Christian Traditions* (New York, 1974), and, with Eleanor McLoughlin, *Women of Spirit: Female Leadership in the Jewish and Christian Traditions* (New York, 1974).

75. Elizabeth Schlüsser-Fiorenza, *In Memory of Her* (New York, 1983).

76. Elizabeth Clark, *Jerome, Chrysostom and Friends* (Lewiston, N.Y., 1979); *Women in the Early Church* (Wilmington, Del., 1983), a collection of texts; *Studies in Women and Religion*, 7 (New York–Toronto, 1981).

77. Proverbs 31:10.

78. Compare, e.g., *Talmud Babylone, Guittin* 90a: "The immoral man allows his wife to come and go in the streets with her hair and shoulders bared and to wash with men. The Torah recommends divorcing such a wife."

79. *Pirke Avot*, I, 5 (Josi ben Johanan, ca. 150 B.C.).

80. Philo, *Special Laws*, III, 169–175.

81. Deuteronomy 24:1.

82. Compare the treatise on *Ketoubot* in the *Talmud,* and, e.g., Colette Sirat et al., *Le Papyrus Inv. 5853 de l'Université de Cologne; un contrat de mariage écrit en caractères hébraïques: Antinopolis 417,* Papyrologica Colonensia, Kölner Papyri, 1987.

83. *Antiquités juives*, IV, 219.

84. Leviticus 12, 15.

85. Compare *Talmud B, Kiddushin* 34–36a.

86. *Berakot* 7, 18 (Rabbi Mayer, second century A.D.).

87. Compare J. B. Segal, "The Jewish Attitude towards Woman," *Journal of Jewish Studies* 30(1979):121–137.

88. *Contra Apion*, II, 102–104.

89. Exodus 38:8.

90. *Contemplative Life*, 33–34.

91. Bernadette Brooten, *Women Leaders in the Ancient Synagogue*, Brown Judaic Studies 36 (Chico, Calif.: Scholars Press, 1982).

92. *Talmud B, Sotah* 22 b.

93. *Talmud B, Pessahim* 62 b; cf. David Goodblatt, "The Beruriah Traditions," *Journal of Jewish Studies* 26(1975):68–85, reprinted in William S. Green, ed., *Persons and Institutions in Rabbinic Judaism*, Brown Judaic Studies 3 Mont. (Chico, Calif.: Scholars Press, 1977).

94. *Talmud B, Berakot* 16 b.

95. *Talmud B, Meguilla* 14 a: Sarah (cf. Genesis 21:12), Minam (Exodus 15:20), Deborah (Judges 4:4), Hannah (1 Samuel 2:1), Abigail (1 Samuel 25:29), Huldah (2 Kings 22:14).

96. 2 Maccabees 7 and 4.Maccabees.

97. Contra Apion II, 202. Is the biblical text Genesis 3:16? Compare Philo of Alexandria, *Hypothetica, 7.3.* But the word here is "to be a slave."

98. Matthew 1:1–17.

99. Matthew 1:3; cf. Genesis 38:1, 5; Joshua 2:1, 5; Ruth 1:6; 2 Samuel 11, 12. On the significance of the four mothers, see, e.g., André Paul, *L'Evangile de l'enfance selon St. Matthieu* (Paris, 1968), pp. 29–35.

100. Matthew 1–2; Luke 1–2.

101. Matthew 1:23, cf. 1:25: "And knew her not till she had brought forth her firstborn son: and he called his name Jesus."

102. See E. Ammann, *Le Protévangile de Jacques et ses remaniements latins*, text and [French] translation (Paris, 1910); E. Strycker, "La forme la plus ancienne du Protévangile de Jacques," *Subsidia Hagiographica* 33 (Brussels, 1961); H. R. Smid, *Protevangelium Jacobi. A Commentary* (Assen, 1965).

103. See, for example, Ambrose, *De virginitate*, II, 6–15: Mary, model of virgins.

104. On the arch of Saint Mary Major in Rome, Mary is portrayed spinning purple and scarlet for the temple at the time of the Annunciation.

105. Matthew 12:46–50; cf. Mark 3:31–35; Luke 8:19 and 11:27–28.

106. John 2:1–12.

107. John 19:25–27.

108. Acts 1:14.

109. Galatians 4:4.

110. Luke 10:38–42.

111. John 11.

112. John 4:27.

113. John 4:9.

114. Matthew 15:21–28; cf. Mark 7, 24–30.

115. Matthew 21:31.

116. Luke 7:36–49; cf. Matthew 26:6–13 and Mark 14:3–9, which attribute the gesture to a woman. John 12:1–8 attributes it to Mary, sister of Martha.

117. John 8:1, 11.

118. John 4:17–18.

119. Matthew 9:20–22.

120. Luke 7:11–15.

121. 1 Kings 17:17–24.

122. Luke 21:1–3; Mark 12:41–44.

123. Luke 8:1–3 (*diakoneo* = to assist).

124. Matthew 27:56; Mark 15:40–41.

125. Matthew 27:55–56; Mark 15:40–41.

126. John 19:25–27.

127. Matthew 27:61; Mark 15:47; Luke 24:55–56.

128. Mark 16:1; Luke 23:56, 24:1.

129. Matthew 28, Mark 16, Luke 24, John 20; cf. Martin Hengel, "Maria Magdalena und die Frauen als Zeugen," in P. Schmid, ed., *Abraham unser Vater* (Leyden, 1963), pp. 243–256.

130. Acts 1:14.

131. Acts 5:14; 8:3; 9:2.

132. Acts 9:36–42.

133. Acts 12:12–16.

134. See, e.g., Juvenal, *Satire*, 6, 511–541.

135. Cf. 1 Corinthians 16:9 in Ephesus for Priscilla and Aquila; Romans 16:5 in Rome for the same individuals; Colossians 4:15 in Laodicea for Nympha.

136. Acts 16:13–15.

137. Acts 17:4.

138. Acts 17:12.

139. Acts 17:34.

140. Acts 18:2–3.

141. Acts 18:24–26.

142. Romans 16:3–5.

143. Romans 16:1 and 2; Romans 16:6 and 12.

144. Romans 16:13.

145. Romans 16:15.

146. Romans 16:7.

147. Romans 16:15 if the feminine form of the latter name is preserved.

148. Philemon 2.

149. 1 Corinthians 9:5.

150. Philippians 4:2–3.

151. Cf. Exodus 22:20–23; Deuteronomy 10:18; 14:29; 16:11, 14; 24:17–22; 26:12–13; Psalms 68:6; Isaiah 1:17; Job 29:12–13; Mark 12:42; Luke 7:12 and 18:3.

152. 1 Kings 17:7–24.

153. Luke 2:36 ff.

154. Acts 6:1; 9:36–39; Mark 1:27.

155. 1 Corinthians 7:8–9; 39–40.

156. 1 Timothy 5:11–15.

157. 1 Timothy 5:9–10.

158. Titus 2:3–5.

159. Cf. 1 Corinthians 7, 8:25–35.

160. R. Gryson, *Le ministère des femmes dans l'Eglise ancienne* (Gembloux, 1972), pp. 30–31.

161. 1 Timothy 3:11.

162. Joel 2:28, cited in Acts 2:17.

163. Acts 21:9.

164. 1 Corinthians 11:2–16. Compare, e.g., M. D. Hooker, "Authority on Her Head: An Examination of 1 Corinthians 11:10," *New Testament Studies* 10(1963–64):410–416; Annie Jaubert, "Le voile des femmes: 1 Cor. 11:2–16," *New Testament Studies* 18(1972):419–430; A. Feuillet, "Le signe de puissance sur la tête de la femme," *Nouvelle Revue Théologique* 95(1973):945–954; William Walker, "1 Corinthians 11:2–16 and Paul's Views Regarding Women," *Journal of Biblical Literature* 94(1975):94–110.

165. Apocrypha 2:20–24.

166. *Dialogue with Tryphonus*, 88.

167. *Passion of Perpetua and Felicity*, 4–10. The story, whose Montanist aspects are emphasized by some scholars, begins with a passage from Joel.

168. PG 51, 191.

169. Marguerita Guarducci, *Epigrafia Graeca*, 4 vols. (Rome, 1967–78), IV, 445.

170. Compare, e.g., G. Fitzer, "Das Weib scheige in der Gemeinde," *Uber den unpaulinischen Character der Mulier-taceat Verse in I Korintheir 14* (Munich, 1963), with Robert Allison, "Let Women Be Silent in the Churches: 1 Corinthians 14:33b–36: What Did Paul Really Say and What Did It Mean?" *Journal for the Study of the New Testament* 32(1988):27–60.

171. Ephesians 133:4 citing 2 Thessalonians 2:7; cf. Ephesians 75:3 on Basilite Gnostics denounced in Spain and 84:6 on Origenists.

172. See, e.g., *Gospel of Thomas*, Logion 61, in James H. Robinson, ed., *The Nag Hammadi Library* (Leiden, 1977), p. 124.

173. Gospel of Mary 9:20; op. cit., p. 472.

174. See Elaine Pagels, *The Gnostic Gospels* (New York, 1979), and Karen L. King, ed., *Images of the Feminine in Gnosticism* (Philadelphia, 1988).

175. See, e.g., Irenaeus, *Adversus Haereses*, I, 1 (Ptolemy, disciple of Valentinus); I, 11 (Valentinus).

176. Apocrypha of John 2:9–14: "I am he who [stays with you] always. I am the Father, I am the Mother, I am the Son." *The Nag Hammadi Library*, p. 99.

177. Compare Irenaeus, *Adversus Haereses*, I, 2, 2–3; I, 5, 1–3.

178. Madeline Scopello, "Jewish and Greek Heroines in the Nag Ham-

madi Library," in King, ed., *Images of the Feminine in Gnosticism,* pp. 70–95.

179. See Gospel of Thomas, Logion 22.

180. See also Gospel of Thomas, Logion 114.

181. See Pagels, *The Gnostic Gospels,* pp. 99–101. Like the other images, this one was well known outside of Gnostic circles. Compare Wayne A. Meeks, "Some Uses of a Symbol in Earliest Christianity," *History of Religion* 13(1974):165–208.

182. Justin, I *Apol.* 26, 3; Irenaeus, *Adversus Haereses,* I, 16, 2–3; Hippolytus, *Ref.* 6, 19, 2–3; Epiphanius, *Panarion,* 21, 3, 1–3.

183. Jerome, *Epistles,* 133, 4.

184. Epiphanius, *Panarion,* 42, 4.

185. Irenaeus, *Adversus Haereses,* I, 25, 6; Origen, *Contra Celsus,* 5, 61; Epiphanius, *Panarion,* 37, 6.

186. Tertullian, *Prescription for Heresies,* 6, 6; 30, 5–6.

187. Irenaeus, *Adversus Haereses,* I, 13, 3.

188. Ibid.

189. Ibid., 41:1–4.

190. Tertullian, *Baptism,* 1, 2 (note the play on words *pisciculi/piscis*).

191. Ibid., 17, 4, with citation of 1 Corinthians 14:35 and denunciation of *Acts of Paul and Thecla.*

192. Compare *Exhortation to Chastity,* 10, 5.

193. *De virg. velandis,* 9, 1.

194. Epiphanius, *Panarion,* 49, 1.

195. Eusebius, *Ecclesiastical History,* V, 16, 17, citation of an anonymous anti-Montanist.

196. Ibid., V, 18, 3, citation of Appolonius.

197. Firmilian of Caesarea, Cyprian, *Epistles,* 75, 10, 5.

198. Epiphanius, *Panarion,* 49: 1(1)–9(4).

199. Origen, Fragments on 1 Corinthians, in C. Jenkins, *Journal of Theological Studies* 10(1909):41–42.

200. *On the Trinity,* 3, 41, 3.

201. Epiphanius, *Panarion.*

202. Gryson's work (see n. 160) has been challenged by Aimé-Georges Martimort, *Les Diaconesses. Essai historique* (Rome, 1982). To follow the ensuing debate, see A.-G. Martimort, "A propos du ministère des femmes," *Bulletin de littérature ecclésiastique* 74(1979):102–108; R. Gryson, "L'ordination des diaconesses d'après les *Constitutions Apostoliques,*" *Mélanges de Sciences Religieuses des Facultés Catholiques de Lille,* 1974. Feminist calls for women to be allowed to become deacons inspire Marie-Josèphe Aubert's *Des femmes diacres* (Paris, 1987).

203. Polycarp, *Phillipian Epistles,* 6, 1.

204. Justin, I *Apol.,* 67, 6.

205. Eusebius, *Ecclesiastical History,* VI, 43, 11.

206. Philemon 4, 3.

207. *Smyrn.,* 13, 1.

208. Tertullian, *Virg. vel.*, 9, 2, 3, attacking the scandalous admission of an unveiled twenty-year-old virgin among the *viduae*.

209. *Apostolic Constitutions*, II, 57, 12; VIII, 13, 14. Compare Antonia Quacquarelli, *Il triplice frutto della vita cristiana: 100, 60, and 30, Matteo XIII, 8 nelle diverse interpretazioni,* 2nd ed. (Bari, 1989).

210. *Exhortation to Chastity*, 13, 4.

211. Hippolytus of Rome, *La tradition apostolique d'après les anciennes versions*, SC 11bis, Bernard Botte, 2nd ed. (Paris, 1968), chap. 10.

212. But Theodore of Mopsuesta moderates the requirement: the woman has only to remain faithful, even in successive marriages (*PG* 66, 944 AB: in 1 Timothy 5:9). Whether to accept or reject a second marriage was a matter of fierce controversy.

213. Epistle 199 (To Amphilochus on the canons), 24.

214. *Didascalia*, III, 5, 3–6, ed. Funk, pp. 188–190 (fifty years); *Apostolic Constitutions*, III, 1, 1–2 (cf. SC 329, Marcel Metzger, Paris, 1986).

215. *Didascalia*, III, 5, 3–6; 6, 1–2; 8, 1–3.

216. *Apostolic Constitutions*, III, 7, 7.

217. *Didascalia*, III, 8, 1–5.

218. Ibid., 6–7.

219. Ibid., 9, 1–3.

220. *Apostolic Constitutions*, III, 9, 1–4.

221. *Didascalia*, III, 6, 1–2; cf. *Apostolic Constitutions*, III, 6, 1 and 2, which seems to leave latitude to certain better educated women.

222. Hermas, *Pastor*, 8, 2–3 (SC 53, Robert Joly, Paris, 1958).

223. Pliny, *Letters*, X, 96, 8–9.

224. See Phoebe, *diakonos*, in Romans 16:1.

225. *Didascalia*, II, 26, 6, trans. R. Gryson; cf. Ignatius, *To the Magnesians*, 6, 1: the bishop is in the image of the Father, the deacon is in the image of Christ, and the priests are in the image of the apostles. In Syria the deaconess, said to be in the image of the Holy Spirit, was added to the list. Was this because the gender of the word "spirit" is feminine in the Semitic languages?

226. *Didascalia*, II, 28, 6; 44, 2–4; 57, 6–7.

227. *Didascalia*, III, 12, 1–13, 1.

228. *Apostolic Constitutions*, VI, 17, 4. In Egypt widows rather than deaconesses performed these kinds of duties (see Gryson, *Le ministère des femmes*, pp. 81 ff.

229. Ibid., II, 16, 1–4.

230. Ibid., III, 14, 1.

231. Ibid., II, 26, 6.

232. Ibid., II, 58, 4–6.

233. Ibid., VIII, 28, 6.

234. Ibid., VIII, 13, 14 (precedence).

235. Ibid., VIII, 20, 1–2 (prayer parallel to that of the ordination of deacons).

236. Ibid., VIII, 31, 2.

237. Ibid., VIII, 13, 14.

238. *Epistles, 199, Canon,* 44. Justinian, *Novella,* 6, 6 provided for capital punishment, as for unfaithful vestals; *Novella,* 123 provided for confinement in a monastery in case of seduction.

239. *Life of Olympias,* 5.

240. *Notice,* 37 (ed. I. Sbordone, Rome, 1936, pp. 118 ff.), citing Ecclesiasticus 9:8.

241. Chapter 18.

242. *Didascalia,* II, 57; *Apostolic Constitutions,* II, 57.

243. John Moschus, *Pratum Spirituale,* chap. 3 (SC 12, ed. Rouet de Journel).

244. D. Feissel, "Recueil des inscriptions chrétiennes de Macédoine du IIIe au VIe siècle," *Bulletin de correspondance hellénique,* suppl. VIII, no. 241 (Paris, 1983), fourth and fifth centuries.

245. Ibid., no. 20, fifth and sixth centuries.

246. Ibid., no. 256, fifth and sixth centuries.

247. Ibid., no. 274, fourth century.

248. *Life of Olympias,* 7.

249. Palladius, *Dialogue sur la vie de Jean Chrysostome,* X, 50–52 (SC 341–342, Anne-Marie Malingrey, Paris, 1988).

250. Pentadia, *PG* 52, *Letters,* 94, 104, 185; Amprucla, *Letters,* 96, 103, 141.

251. *Letters to Olympias* 6(13), SC 13bis, p. 130; cf. Palladius, *Lausiac History,* 41.

252. *Novella,* 3, 1, 1.

253. Gregory of Nyssa, *Life of Macrina,* 29.

254. Texts quoted in Martimort, *Les diaconesses,* pp. 138–142.

255. Ibid., p. 183.

256. *Apostolic Constitutions,* III, 6, 1–2; cf. *Didascalia,* III, 6, 1–2.

257. Ibid., III, 9, 1–4; cf. *Didascalia,* III, 9, 2.

258. See Gryson, *Le ministère des femmes,* p. 94.

259. I, 41, 1.

260. I, 42.

261. *Ecclesiastical Canons of the Apostles,* chap. 21.

262. Ibid., chap. 24.

263. Epiphanius, *Panarion,* 79: 3(6)–4(1).

264. II, 2.

265. Ambrosiaster, *Questions Concerning the Old and New Testaments,* 45, 2–3.

266. *Chronicle,* 2, 50, 8.

267. *Canon,* 25.

268. *Letter,* 14, 13, and 21.

269. See Pierre de Labriolle, *Les sources de l'histoire du montanisme* (Paris, 1913), pp. 226–230.

270. Venantius Fortunatus, *Life of Saint Radegund,* 12, 26–28.

271. Adolf von Harnack, "Porphyrius gegen die Christen. 15 Bücher.

Zeugnisse, Fragmente und Referate," *Abh. der königl. Preuss. Akad. der Wiss.* 1916, *Philos.-Hist. Kl.* 1, n. 97 (Jerome, *Com. in Esaïam* 3, 2).

272. *On the Priesthood*, III, 9.

273. Palladius, *Dialogue on the Life of John Chrysostom*, IV, 22 ff., VIII, 76–85.

274. See, e.g., *Letters to Olympias* IX (XIV), 4e–5b.

275. *Epistles,* 127, 10.

276. Palladius, *Lausiac History,* 54, 3.

277. Ibid., 46, 3–4.

278. Ibid., 46, 6.

279. *Life of Melania,* 54.

280. Cyril of Scythopolis, *Life of Saint Euthymia,* 30.

281. See K. G. Holum, *Theodosian Empresses: Women and Imperial Dominion in Late Antiquity* (Berkeley, Calif., 1982), chaps. 3, 5, 6.

282. *Epistles,* 127, 7.

283. See Evelyne Patlagean, *Pauvreté économique et pauvreté sociale à Byzance, 4e–7e siècle* (Paris–The Hague, 1977), pp. 181–203.

284. Feissel, "Recueil," nos. 276, 275 (fourth century).

285. Jerome, Epistles 77, 6, 10.

286. Fragment no. 58 Harnack (Macarius Magnus III, 5).

287. Palladius, *Lausiac History,* 10, 2–4.

288. Ibid., 46, 5–6.

289. *Life of Olympias,* 4–5. In 390 Theodosius nullified wills in which widows and deaconesses left their property to clerics (Theodosian Code, XVI, 2, 27–28). This provision of the code was abrogated by Marcian in 455.

290. *Life of Olympias,* 14, 12–13.

291. Ibid., 5, 17–33.

292. Ibid., 7, 3–6.

293. Ibid., 6, 2.

294. Ibid., 14–15. Cf. Palladius, *Dialogue on the Life of John Chrysostom,* 17, 200 ff.

295. *Life of Olympias,* 8, 14–16; Palladius, *Dialogue on the Life of John Chrysostom,* 17, 185–186.

296. See Gilbert Dagron, *Naissance d'une capitale, Constantinople* (Paris, 1974), pp. 501–506.

297. *Life of Melania,* 9–19.

298. Ibid., 20–22.

299. Ibid., 41.

300. Ibid., 49.

301. Ibid.

302. Ibid., 57–59.

303. See Elizabeth Clark, "Claims on the Bones of Saint Stephen," *Ascetic Piety and Women's Faith. Essays on Late Ancient Christianity* (Lewiston–Queenston: Edwin Mellen Press, 1986).

304. Mark the Deacon, *Life of Porphyry of Gaza,* 43, 53, 75–78, 83–84, 92.

305. Holum, *Theodosian Empresses,* pp. 189, 219.

306. Ibid., pp. 103, 137, 142, 144.

307. 2 Timothy 1:5; cf. Acts 16:1.

308. Origen, *Contra Celsus,* III, 55 (SC 136, M. Borret, Paris, 1968).

309. *Epistles,* 204, 6; cf. 210, 1.

310. Gregory Nazianzen, *Funeral Oration for Basil,* V, 1.

311. *Life of Macrina,* 3.

312. André Chastagnol, "Le sénateur Volusien et la conversion d'une famille de l'aristocratie romaine sous le Bas-Empire," *Revue des Etudes anciennes* 58(1956):241–253; *L'Italie et l'Afrique au Bas-Empire, Scripta varia* (Lille, 1987), pp. 235–248.

313. Letter to Saint Jerome, *Epistles,* 107, 1.

314. *Epistles,* 135, 136.

315. *Life of Melania,* 50–56. According to Gerontius, Volusian risked dying as a catechumen, which is evidence for a first degree of Christianization.

316. *PG* 35, 812C–813A.

317. *Confessions,* IX, 9, 19; cf. IX, 9, 22.

318. *Confessions,* III, 12, 21.

319. *Letters* 2, 4 (Bibliothèque augustinienne, 46 B, 1987, pp. 64–67).

320. Palladius, *Lausiac History,* 38.

321. Ibid., 54, 4.

Chapter 10. Creating a Myth of Matriarchy
STELLA GEORGOUDI

1. Johann Jakob Bachofen, *Das Mutterrecht. Eine Untersuchung über die Gynaikokratie der Alten Welt nach ihrer religiösen und rechtlichen Natur,* in Bachofen, *Gesammelte Werke,* ed. Karl Meuli (Basel, 1948), 2, 293 ff. Cited hereafter as JB.

2. JB, 2, 34–35.

3. JB, 2, 31.

4. "Le droit de la mère dans l'Antiquité," preface to the French translation of Bachofen's *Das Mutterrecht,* translated and published by the Groupe Français d'Etudes Féministes (Paris, 1903), p. 26.

5. Ibid., p. 22.

6. Uwe Wesel, *Der Mythos vom Matriarchat: Uber Bachofens Mutterrecht und die Stellung von Frauen in frühen Gesellschaften* (Frankfurt, 1980), p. 33.

7. See H. R. Hays, *From Ape to Angel. An Informal History of Social Anthropology* (New York: Capricorn, 1958), pp. 32 ff.

8. Karl Meuli, "Nachwort," in Bachofen, *Gesammelte Werke,* 3, 1097.

9. Walter Benjamin, "Johann Jakob Bachofen," in *Johann Jakob Bachofen (1815–1887): Eine Begleitpublikation zur Ausstellung im Historischen Museum Basel* (Basel, 1987), p. 22.

10. JB, 2, 15–16.

11. Meuli, "Nachwort," pp. 1107–1108.

12. See Plutarch, *Isis and Osiris*, 56, *Moralia*, 373 E.

13. JB, 2, 40–41.

14. JB, 2, 36 ff.

15. JB, 2, 238.

16. JB, 2, 375 ff.

17. JB, 3, 747.

18. JB, 2, 41, 385 ff.

19. JB, 2, 385.

20. JB, 2, 386–387.

21. JB, 2, 36.

22. JB, 2, 88, 387–388.

23. Ibid.

24. JB, 2, 121.

25. JB, 2, 37.

26. JB, 2, 48 ff.

27. JB, 2, 100.

28. JB, 2, 104 ff.

29. JB, 2, 50; cf. Meuli, "Nachwort," p. 1108.

30. JB, 2, 53 ff.

31. JB, 2, 44 ff.

32. JB, 2, 47.

33. JB, 2, 61–64.

34. J. J. Bachofen, "Briefe," *Gesammelte Werke*, X, 512–515, letter no. 309, dated June 7, 1881, ed. Fritz Husner (Basel, 1967).

35. Hans-Jürgen Heinrichs, ed., *Materialen zu Bachofens "Das Mutterrecht"* (Frankfurt, 1975), pp. 408–443. Compare Erich Neumann, *The Great Mother. An Analysis of the Archetype*, Bollingen Series XLVII, 2nd ed. (Princeton: Princeton University Press, 1963).

36. Friedrich Engels, *The Origins of the Family, Private Property, and the State* (New York: International, 1945).

37. Brigitta Hause-Schaüblin, "Mutterrecht und Frauenbewegung," in *Johann Jakob Bachofen (1815–1887)*, pp. 137–150; cf. Evelyn Reed, *Woman's Evolution. From Matriarchal Clan to Patriarchal Family* (New York–Toronto: Pathfinder, 1975).

38. Hans-Jürgen Heinrichs in *Johann Jakob Bachofen (1815–1887)*, p. 107; Claudio Cesa, "Bachofen e la filosofia della storia," in *Seminario su J. J. Bachofen*, in *Annali della Scuola Normale Superiore di Pisa* 18(2)1988:621–642.

39. JB, 3, 655 ff.

40. JB, 2, 263; compare Strabo, VII, 7, 2, 321–322.

41. Arthur Bernard Cook, *Zeus. A Study of Ancient Religion* (Cambridge: Cambridge University Press, 1940), 3, 89, n. 1.

42. Martin P. Nilsson, *Geschichte der griechischen Religion*, 2nd ed. (Munich: C. H. Beck, 1955), I, 456, n. 6. H. J. Rose, "Prehistoric Greece and Mother-Right," *Folk-Lore* 37(1926):213–244.

43. Walter Burkert, *Griechische Religion der archaischen und klassischen Epoche* (Stuttgart: Kohlhammer, 1977), p. 46 and n. 22. English translation

by John Raffan, *Greek Religion* (Cambridge, Mass.: Harvard University Press, 1985).

44. W. K. Lacey, *The Family in Classical Greece,* 2nd ed. (Auckland, N.Z.: University of Auckland Press, 1980), p. 11.

45. Rose, "Prehistoric Greece and Mother-Right," p. 213.

46. W. K. C. Guthrie, *The Greeks and Their Gods* (London: Methuen, 1950); Jane Harrison, *Prolegomena to the Study of Greek Religion,* 3rd ed. (Cambridge: Cambridge University Press, 1922; rpr. New York: Meridian, 1955).

47. See Moses I. Finley, *The Ancient Greeks: An Introduction to Their Life and Thought* (New York, 1963).

48. Harrison, *Prolegomena,* pp. 260 ff.

49. Jane Harrison, *Themis. A Study of the Social Origins of Greek Religion,* 2nd ed. (Cambridge: Cambridge University Press, 1927; rpr. New York: Meridian, 1962), pp. 492 ff.

50. Harrison, *Prolegomena,* pp. 260 ff.

51. Carl Kerenyi, *Zeus and Hera. Archetypal Image of Father, Husband and Wife.* Bollingen Series LXV (Princeton: Princeton University Press, 1975).

52. George Thomson, *The Prehistoric Aegean,* 3rd ed. (London, 1961), p. 7.

53. Ibid., p. 199.

54. R. F. Willetts, *Cretan Cults and Festivals* (London: Routledge & Kegan Paul, 1962).

55. Kaarle Hirvonen, *Matriarchal Survivals and Certain Trends in Homer's Female Characters* (Helsinki, 1968).

56. C. G. Thomas, "Matriarchy in Early Greece: The Bronze and Dark Ages," *Arethusa* 6(1973):173–195.

57. Panagis Lekatsas, *The Matriarchy and Its Conflict with the Patriarchy in Greece* (Athens: Keimena, 1970), in Greek.

58. Burkert, *Griechische Religion,* pp. 76–82.

59. Peter J. Ucko, "Anthropomorphic Figurines of Predynastic Egypt and Neolithic Crete with Comparative Material from Prehistorical Near East and Mainland Greece," Royal Anthropological Institute Occasional Paper no. 24 (London, 1968).

60. Martin P. Nilsson, *A History of Greek Religion,* 2nd ed. (Oxford: Clarendon, 1949), p. 10.

61. Augustine, *City of God,* XVIII, 9.

62. Thomson, *The Prehistoric Aegean,* p. 267.

63. See scholia to Aristophanes, *Plutos,* 773; Klearchos ap. Athenaeus, XIII, 555 cd.

64. See scholia to Aristophanes, *Plutos,* 773.

65. Ibid.

66. Simon Pembroke, "Last of the Matriarchs: A Study in the Inscriptions of Lycia," *Journal of the Economic and Social History of the Orient* 8(1965):217–247.

67. See Michèle Rosellini and Suzanne Saïd, "Usages de femmes et autres

nomoi chez les 'sauvages' d'Hérodote: Essai de lecture structurale," *Annali della Scuola Normale Superiore di Pisa* 8(1978):949–1005; François Hartog, *Le miroir d'Hérodote. Essai sur la représentation de l'autre* (Paris: Gallimard, 1980).

68. George Thomson, *Aeschylus and Athens. A Study in the Social Origins of Drama,* 4th ed. (London, 1973); Lekatsas, *The Matriarchy.*

69. Froma I. Zeitlin, "The Dynamics of Misogyny: Myth and Mythmaking in the Oresteia," *Arethusa* 11(1978):149–184.

70. See Heinrichs, *Materialen;* Wesel, *Der Mythos;* Hartmut Zinser, *Der Mythos des Mutterrechts* (Frankfurt, 1981); *Seminario su J. J. Bachofen,* etc.

71. See Nicole Loraux, "Et l'on déboutera les mères," in *Les expériences de Tirésias* (Paris: Gallimard, 1989), pp. 219–231.

72. Joan Bamberger, "The Myth of Matriarchy: Why Men Rule in Primitive Society," in Michelle Zimbalist Rosaldo and Louis Lamphere, eds., *Woman Culture and Society* (Stanford: Stanford University Press, 1974), pp. 263–280.

Chapter 11. Women and Ancient History Today

PAULINE SCHMITT PANTEL

1. See my earlier assessment of the state of research, "La différence des sexes, histoire, anthropologie et cité grecque," in Michelle Perrot, ed., *Une histoire des femmes est-elle possible?* (Marseilles: Rivages, 1984), pp. 98–119.

2. Michael Rostovtzeff, *A History of the Ancient World I: The Orient and Greece* (London, 1930); A. W. Gomme, *Essays in Greek History and Literature* (Oxford, 1937), pp. 89–115. Victor Ehrenberg, *Aspects of the Ancient World* (New York, 1946), pp. 65–66.

3. Sarah B. Pomeroy, *Goddesses, Wives, Whores and Slaves: Women in Classical Antiquity* (New York, 1975).

4. Marilyn Skinner, ed., "Rescuing Creusa: New Methodological Approaches to Women in Antiquity," special issue of *Helios,* 1987.

5. Josine Blok and Peter Mason, eds., *Sexual Asymmetry: Studies in Ancient Society* (Amsterdam, 1987).

6. Beate Wagner-Hasel, "Das Private wird politisch: Die Perspektive 'Geschlecht' in der Altertumswissenschaft," in Ursula A. J. Becher and Jörn Rüsen, eds., *Weiblichkeit in geschichtlicher Perspektive* (Frankfurt, 1988), pp. 11–50.

7. Josine Blok, "Sexual Asymmetry: A Historiographical Essay," in Blok and Mason, eds., *Sexual Asymmetry.*

8. Joan Scott, "Gender: A Useful Category of Historical Analysis," *American Historical Review* 91(1986).

9. For example, Sarah B. Pomeroy, "Selected Bibliography on Women in Antiquity," *Arethusa* 8(1973):127–155, expanded in John Perradoto and John P. Sullivan, eds., *Women in the Ancient World: The Arethusa Papers* (Albany, N.Y., 1984); Elain Fantham, "Women in Antiquity: A Selective (and

Subjective) Survey, 1979–1984," *E.M.C.* 30(1986):1–24; Phyllis Culham, "Ten Years After Pomeroy: Studies of the Image and Reality of Women in Antiquity," *Helios* (1987):9–30.

10. Blok, "Sexual Asymmetry," pp. 1–57.

11. Beate Wagner-Hasel, "Frauenleben in orienalischer Abgeschlossenheit? Zur Geschichte und Nutzanwendung eines Topos," in *Der Altsprachliche Unterricht* 2(1989):18–29.

12. Nicole Loraux, "La cité, l'historien, les femmes," *Pallas* (1985):7–39; "Notes sur un impossible sujet de l'histoire," in "Le Genre de l'Histoire," *Les Cahiers du GRIF* 37–38(1988):113–124.

13. Helen King, "Sacrificial Blood: The Role of *amnion* in Ancient Gynecology," in Skinner, ed., "Rescuing Creusa," pp. 117–126.

14. See Chapter 5, "Marriage in Ancient Greece," by Claudine Leduc.

15. Culham, "Ten Years After."

16. Wagner-Hasel, "Das Private wird politisch."

17. See Chapter 4, "Figures of Women," by François Lissarrague.

18. Sarah Humphreys, *Family, Women and Death. Comparative Studies* (London, 1984). Domenico Musti, "Pubblico e privato nella democrazia periclea," *Quaderni Urbinati* n.s. 20(1985):7–18.

19. Bibliography in Pauline Schmitt Pantel, *La cité au banquet: Histoire des banquets publics dans les cités grecques* (Rome: Ecole Française de Rome, 1991).

20. Gillian Clark, "We Await the New Season's Collection with Interest," *The Classical Review* 1(1989):103–105.

The Woman's Voice

1. This translation, by Arthur Goldhammer, is based on Paul Monceaux's French translation of the Latin text of "The Passion of Saints Perpetua and Felicity," 3–10.

Bibliography

Adnès, André, and Pierre Canivet. "Guérisons miraculeuses et exorcisme dans l'*Histoire Philothée* de Théodoret de Cyr," *Revue de l'Histoire des Religions* 171 (1967): 53–82, 149–179.

Ahrem, Maximilian. *Das Weib in der antiken Kunst.* Jena, 1914.

Arrigoni, Giampiera. "Amore sotto il manto e iniziazione nuziale," *QUCC* (1983): 7–56.

———, ed. *Le donne in Grecia.* Bari and Rome: Laterza, 1985.

——— "Tra le donne dell'Antichità: Considerazioni e ricognizioni," in Renato Uglione, ed., *La donna nel mondo antico.* Turin, 1987, pp. 39–71.

Arthur, Marilyn B. "Early Greece: The Origins of the Western Attitude Towards Women," *Arethusa* 6 (1973): 7–58.

——— "Liberated Women: The Classical Era," in R. Bridenthal and C. Koontz, eds., *Becoming Visible: Women in European History.* Boston: Houghton Mifflin, 1977, pp. 60–89.

——— "Review Essay-Classics," *Signs* 2 (1976): 383–403.

——— "Sexuality and the Body in Ancient Greece," *Mètis* (1990).

——— "Women and the Family in Ancient Greece," *The Yale Review* (Summer 1982): 532–547.

Bachofen, Johann Jakob. *Das Mutterrecht: Eine Untersuchung über die Gynaikokratie der alten Welt nach ihrer religiösen und rechtlichen Natur,* in Karl Meuli, ed., *Gesammelte Werke,* vols. II, III. Basel, 1948.

——— *Myth, Religion and Mother Right: Selected Writings of J. J. Bachofen,* trans. R. Manheim. Princeton: Princeton University Press, 1967.

——— *Du règne de la mère au patriarcat.* Lausanne: Editions de l'Aire, 1980.

Bamberger, Joan. "The Myth of Matriarchy: Why Men Rule in Primitive Society," in Michelle Zimbalist Rosaldo and Louise Lamphere, eds., *Woman, Culture and Society.* Stanford: Stanford University Press, 1974, pp. 263–280.

Barb, Alphon A. "Diva Matrix," *Journal of Warburg and Courtault Institutes* 16 (1953): 193–238.

Bazant, Jan. *Les citoyens sur les vases athéniens.* Prague, 1985.

Beard, Mary. "The Sexual Status of Vestal Virgins," *JRS* 70 (1980): 12–27.

Beaucamp, Joelle. *La situation juridique de la femme à l'époque protobyzantine.* Paris: Université de Paris, 1987.

————— "Le vocabulaire de la faiblesse féminine dans les textes juridique romains du IIIe au VIe siècle," *Revue historique de droit français et étranger* 54 (1976): 485–508.

Becher, Ursula A. J., and Jörn Rüsen, eds. *Weiblichkeit in geschichtlicher Perspektive.* Frankfurt am Main: Suhrkampf, 1988.

Benveniste, Emile. *Le vocabulaire des institutions indo européennes.* Paris: Minuit, 1969.

Bérard, Claude. "L'impossible femme athlète," *Aion ArchSt* 8 (1986): 195–202.

————— "L'ordre des femmes," *La Cité des images.* Lausanne and Paris, 1984, pp. 85–103.

Biardeau, Madeleine. "Devi: La Déesse en Inde," in Y. Bonnefoy, ed., *Dictionnaire des mythologies* I. Paris: Flammarion, 1981, pp. 295–298.

————— *L'hindouisme. Anthropologie d'une civilisation.* Paris: Flammarion, 1981.

Bickerman, E. J. "La structure juridique du mariage grec," *Bulletino dell'Instituto di Diritto romano* (1975): 1–28.

Blok, Josine, and Peter Mason, eds. *Sexual Asymmetry: Studies in Ancient Society.* Amsterdam: Gieben, 1987.

Bluestone, Nathalie Harris. *Women and the Ideal Society.* Oxford: Oxford University Press, 1987.

Boardman, John, and Donna C. Kurtz. *Greek Burial Customs.* London, 1971.

Bocquet, C. "Espèce biologique," *Encyclopedia Universalis,* vol. 6.

Boels, Nicole. "Le statut religieux de la Flaminica Dialis," *Revue des études latines* 51 (1953): 77–100.

Borresen, Kari-Elisabeth. *Subordination et equivalence. Nature et rôle de la femme d'après Augustin et Thomas d'Aquin.* Oslo and Paris, 1968.

Bourriot. *Recherches sur la nature du génos.* Paris: Ampion, 1976.

des Bouvrie, Synnove. *Women in Greek Tragedy: An Anthropological Approach.* Oslo: Norwegian University Press, 1990.

Bradley, Keith R. "Wet Nursing at Rome: A Study in Social Relations," in Beryl Rawson, ed., *The Family in Ancient Rome: New Perspectives.* Ithaca, N.Y.: Cornell University Press, 1986, pp. 201–229.

Brelich, Angelo. *Paides e Parthenoi.* Rome: Ateneo, 1969.

Brooten, Bernadette. *Women Leaders in the Ancient Synagogue, Brown Judaic Studies* 36. Chico, Calif.: Scholars Press, 1982.

Brown, Peter. *The Body and Society: Men, Women and Sexual Renunciation in Early Christianity.* New York: Columbia University Press, 1988.

————— *The Cult of the Saints.* Chicago: Peter Smith, 1981.

Brulé, Pierre. "Arithmologie et polythéisme. En lisant Lucien Gerschel," *Lire les polythéismes* 1. *Les grandes figures religieuses. Fonctionnement pratique et symbolique dans l'Antiquité.* Paris: Besançon and Paris, 1986, pp. 35–47.

————— *La fille d'Athènes. La religion des filles à Athènes à l'époque classique. Mythes, cultes et société. Annales littéraires de l'Université de Besançon* 363. Paris, 1987.

Burguiere, André, Christiane Klapisch-Zuber, Martine Segalen, and Françoise Zonabend, eds. *Histoire de la Famille*, vol. 1, *Mondes lointains, Mondes anciens*. Paris: Armand Colin, 1986.

Burkert, Walter. *Greek Religion*, trans. J. Raffan. Cambridge, Mass.: Harvard University Press, 1985.

———— *Griechische Religion der archaischen und klassischen Epoche*. Stuttgart, 1977.

Burnyeat, Miles. "Socratic Midwifery, Platonic Inspiration," *Bulletin of the Institute for Classical Studies* 24 (1977): 7–16.

Burrus, W. *Chastity as Autonomy: Women in the Stories of Apocryphal Acts*. Studies in Women and Religion 23. New York: Edwin Mellen, 1987.

Byl, Simon. *Recherches sue les grandes traités biologiques d'Aristote: Sources écrites et préjugés*. Brussels, 1980.

Calame, Claude. *Les choeurs de jeunes filles en Grèce archaïque*. Rome: Ateneo, 1977.

Cameron, Averil, and Amélie, Kuhrt, eds. *Images of Women in Antiquity*. London: Croom Helm, 1983.

———— "Women in Ancient Culture and Society," *Der Altsprachliche Unterricht* 2 (1989): 6–17.

Campese, Silvia, Paola Manuli, and Giulia Sissa. *Madre Materia. Sociologia e biologia della donna greca*. Turin: Boringhieri, 1983.

Cantalamessa, Raniero. *Etica Sessuale e Matrimonio nel Cristianismo delle Origine*. Milan, 1976.

Cantarella, Eva. *L'ambiguo malanno. Condizione ed immagine della donna nell'antichità greca e romana*. Rome: Riuniti, 1981.

———— Introduction to J. J. Bachofen, *Il potere feminile. Storia e teoria*, trans. A. Maffi. Milan, 1977.

Canto, Monique. "The Politics of Women's Bodies: Reflections on Plato," *Poetics Today* 6 (1985).

Cassimatis, Hélène. "Imagerie et femme," *La femme dans le monde méditerranéen*, I, *Antiquité*. Travaux de la Maison de l'Orient 10. Lyons: Maison de l'Orient Méditerranéen, 1985, pp. 19–28.

de Cavalieri, Pio Franchi. *Scritti agiografici I*. Studi e Testi 221. Vatican City, 1961, pp. 41–155.

de Cazanove, Olivier. *Exesto. L'incapacité sacrificielle des femmes à Rome, Phoenix* 41 (1987): 159–174.

Champeaux, Jacqueline. *Fortuna. Le culte de la Fortune à Rome et dans le monde romain* I. Collection de l'Ecole Française de Rome 64. Rome: Ecole Française, 1982.

Clark, Elizabeth A. *Asceticism, Piety and Women's Faith: Essays on Late Ancient Christianity*. Studies in Women in Religion 20. Lewiston and Queenston: Edwin Mellen, 1986.

———— *Women in the Early Church*. Wilmington: Michael Glazier, 1983.

Coarelli, Filippo. *Il Foro Boario. Dalle origini alla fine della Repubblica*. Rome: Quasar, 1988.

Colombo, I. Chirassi. "Paides e Gynaikes: Note per una tassonomia del comportamento rituale nella cultura attica," *Quaderni Urbinati Nuova Serie* 1 (1979): 25–58.

Crook, J. A. "Feminine Inadequacy and the Senatus-Consultum Velleianum," in B. Rawson, *The Family in Ancient Rome,* pp. 83–92.

Culham, Phyllis. "Ten Years After Pomeroy: Studies of the Image and Reality of Women in Antiquity," *Helios* (1987): 9–30.

Dalla, D. *L'Incapacita sessuale in diritto romano.* Milan, 1978.

Davies, Stevan L. *The Revolt of the Widows: The Social World of the Apocryphal Acts.* Carbondale: Southern Illinois University Press, 1980.

De Heusch, Luc. *Pourquoi l'épouser? et autres essais.* Paris: Gallimard, 1971.

Detienne, Marcel. *Dionysos à ciel ouvert.* Paris: Hachette, 1986.

—— *L'écriture d'Orphée.* Paris: Gallimard, 1989.

—— *Les jardins d'Adonis.* Paris: Gallimard, 1972.

—— "Puissances du mariage I. Entre Héra, Artémis et Aphrodite," in Y. Bonnefoy, ed., *Dictionnaires des mythologies* II. Paris: Flammarion, 1981, pp. 65–69.

—— "Violentes Eugénies. En pleines Thesmophories des femmes couvertes de sang," in Marcel Detienne and Jean-Pierre Vernant, eds., *La cuisine du sacrifice en pays grec.* Paris: Gallimard, 1979.

Dixon, Suzanne. "Family Finances: 'Terentia and Tullia,'" in B. Rawson, *The Family in Ancient Rome,* pp. 93–120.

—— *Praemium emancipationis.* Milan, 1983.

—— *The Roman Mother.* London and Sidney: Croom Helm, 1988.

Dörmann, Johannes. "War J. J. Bachofen Evolutionist?," *Anthropos* 60 (1965): 1–48.

Dowden, Ken. *Death and the Maiden: Girls' Initiation Rites in Greek Mythology.* London: Routledge, 1989.

Drossart, Pierre. "'Nonae Caprotinae.' La fausse capture des Aurores," *RHR* 185 (1974): 129–139.

du Bois, Page. *Sowing the Body: Psychoanalysis and Ancient Representations of Women.* Chicago: University of Chicago Press, 1988.

Dumézil, Georges. *Religion romaine archaïque,* 2nd ed. Paris: Payot, 1974.

Dunand, Françoise. "Images du féminin dans le roman grec," *Mélanges Pierre Lévêque.* Paris: Besançon, 1989, pp. 173–182.

Duval, Yvette. *Loca Sanctorum Africae. Le culte des martyrs en Afrique du IVème au VIème siècles,* 2 vols. Collection Ecole Française de Rome. Rome, 1982.

Epstein, Louis M. *Sex Laws and Customs in Judaism.* New York, 1948.

Evans-Pritchard, E. E. *The Position of Women in Primitive Societies and Other Essays in Social Anthropology.* London: Faber and Faber, 1965.

Eyben, Emiel. "Antiquity's View of Puberty," *Latomus* 31 (1972): 678–697.

Eynard, Laure. *La Bible au féminin. De l'ancienne tradition à un christiànisme hellénisé.* Paris, 1990.

Fayer, Carla. "L'ornatus della sposa romana," *Studi Romani* 34 (1986): 1–24.

La Femme dans le Monde Méditerranéen I, Antiquité. Travaux de la Maison de l'Orient 10. Lyons: Maison de l'Orient Méditerranéen, 1985.

Finley, Moses I. *The World of Odysseus* (New York: Viking, 1965).

Flandrin, Jean-Louis. *Un temps pour embrasser. Aux origines de la morale sexuelle occidentale.* Paris: Seuil, 1983.

Foley, Helen P., ed. *Reflections of Women in Antiquity.* New York: Gordon and Breach, 1981.

Fontanille, Marie-Thérèse. *Avortement et contraception dans la médecine gréco-romaine.* Paris: Laboratoires Seale, 1977.

Foxhall, Lin. "Household, Gender and Property in Classical Athens," *The Classical Quarterly* 39 (1989): 22–44.

Fraschetti, Augusto. "La sepoltura delle Vestali e la città," *Du châtiment dans la cité. Supplices corporels et peines de mort dans le monde antique.* Collection de l'Ecole Française de Rome 79. Rome: Ecole Française, 1984, pp. 97–128.

Fridh, Ake. *Le problème de la Passion des saintes Perpétue et Félicité.* Stockholm, 1968.

Friedländer, L. *Darstellungen aus der Sittengeschichte Roms,* vol. 1. Leipzig, 1919.

Frontisi-Ducroux, Françoise. "Images du ménadisme féminin: Les vases des Lénéennes," *L'association dionysiaque dans les sociétés anciennes.* Rome: Ecole Française de Rome, 1986.

Gardner, J. F. *Women in Roman Law and Society.* London: Croom Helm, 1986.

Gaudemet, Jean. *Le mariage en Occident. Les moeurs et le droit.* Paris, 1985.

Giannarolli, Elena. *La tipologia femminile nella biografia e nell'autobiografia cristiana del IV secolo.* Studi Storici 127. Rome, 1980.

Gide, P. *Etude sur la condition privée de la femme.* Paris, 1867.

Ginouves, René. *Balaneutiké: Recherches sur le bain dans l'Antiquité grecque.* Paris: Ecole Française d'Athenes, 1962.

Godelier, Maurice. *La production des Grands Hommes.* Paris: Fayard, 1982.

Gonzalez, E. Garrido, ed. *La mujer en el mondo antique.* Madrid, 1986.

Goodwater, Leanna. *Women in Antiquity: An Annotated Bibliography.* Metuchen, N.J.: Scarecrow Press, 1975.

Gossman, Lionel. *Orpheus Philologus: Bachofen Versus Mommsen on the Study in Antiquity.* Transactions of the American Philosophical Society LXXV. Philadelphia, 1983.

Götte, Erika. *Frauengemachtbilder.* Munich, 1957.

Gould, John. "Law, Custom and Myth: Aspects of the Position of Women in Classical Athens," *JHS* 100 (1980): 38–59.

Gourevitch, Danielle. *Le Mal d'être femme. La femme et la médecine dans la Rome antique.* Paris: Belles Lettres, 1984.

Gras, Michel. "Vin et société à Rome et dans le Latium à l'époque archaïque," *Modes de contacts et processus de transformation dans les sociétés anciennes.* Collection de l'Ecole Française de Rome, vol. 67. Rome: Ecole Française, 1983, pp. 1067–1075.

G.R.I.E.F. *La dot, la valeur des femmes*. Travaux de l'Université de Toulouse-Le Mirail XXI. 1982.

Gryson, Roger. *Le ministère des femmes dans l'Eglise ancienne*. Gembloux, 1970.

Guettel-Cole, Susan. "The Social Function of Maturation: The *koureion* and the *arkteia*," *ZPE* 55 (1984): 233–244.

Hallet, Judith P. *Fathers and Daughters in Roman Society: Women and the Elite Family*. Princeton: Princeton University Press.

—— "Women as Same and Other in Classical Roman Elite," *Helios* 16 (1989): 59–78.

Halperin, David M., John J. Winkler, and Froma I. Zeitlin, eds. *Before Sexuality: The Construction of Erotic Experience in the Ancient Greek World*. Princeton: Princeton University Press, 1990.

Harrison, A. R. W. *The Law of Athens: The Family and Property*. Oxford: Oxford University Press, 1968.

Havelock, Christine M. "Mourners on Greek Vases: Remarks on the Social History of Women," in Stephan Hyatt, ed., *The Greek Vase*. New York, 1979.

Heinrichs, Hans-Jürgen, ed. *Materialen zu Bachofens "Das Mutterrecht."* Frankfurt am Main, 1975.

Héritier-Augé, Françoise. "La cuisse de Jupiter. Réflexions sur les nouveaux modes de procréation," *L'Homme* 94 (1985): 5–22.

—— "L'individu. Le biologique et le social," *Le Débat* 36 (1985): 27–32.

Herter, Hans. "Dirne," *Reallexikon für Antike und Christentum* 3 (1957): 1154–1213.

Hirvonen, Kaarle. *Matriarchal Survivals and Certain Trends in Homer's Female Characters*. Helsinki, 1968.

Hoffmann, Geneviève. *La jeune fille, les pouvoirs et la mort dans la société athénienne du Vème siècle*. Paris: Université de Paris, 1987.

L'Homme XIX (1979). Issue on the categories of sex in social anthropology.

Hopkins, Keith. "The Age of Roman Girls at Marriage," *Population Studies* 18 (1965): 309–327.

—— "Brother-Sister Marriage in Roman Egypt," *Comparative Studies in Society and History* 22 (1980): 303–354.

—— "Contraception in the Roman Empire," *Comparative Studies in Society and History* 8 (1965): 124–151.

—— *Death and Renewal: Sociological Studies in Roman History*, 2 vols. Cambridge: Cambridge University Press, 1983.

—— "On the Probable Age Structure of the Roman Population," *Population Studies* 20 (1966): 245–264.

Huchthausen, L. "Herkunft und ökonomische Stellung weiblicher Adressaten von Reskripten des Codex iustinianus," *Klio* 56 (1974): 199–228.

Humbert, M. *Le remariage à Rome. Etude d'histoire juridique et sociale*. Milan, 1972.

Humphreys, Sarah. *The Family, Women and Death: Comparative Studies*. London: Routledge and Kegan Paul, 1983.

Iriarte, Ana. *Las redes del enigma, Voces feminas en el pensamiento griego.* Madrid, 1990.

Jeanmaire, Henri. *Couroi et Courètes.* Paris, 1939.

—— *Dionysos.* Paris, 1951.

Jost, Madeleine. *Sanctuaires et cultes d'Arcadie, Etudes Peloponnésiennes IX.* Paris: Vrin, 1985.

Jung, C. J., and Ch. Kerényi. *Introduction à l'essence de la mythologie.* Paris: Payot, 1974.

Just, Roger. *Women in Athenian Law and Life.* London: Routledge, 1989.

Kaempf-Dimitriadou, Sophia. *Die Liebe der Götter in der attischen Kunst des 5 Jahrhunderts v. Chr.* Bern, 1979.

Kahil, Lily. "L'Artémis de Brauron. Rites et mystères," *Antike Kunst* 20 (1977): 86–98.

—— "Le cratérisque d'Artémis et le Brauronion de l'Acropole," *Hesperia* 50, pp. 253–263.

—— "La déesse Artémis: Mythologie et l'iconographie," *Greece and Italy in the Classical World.* Acts of the XII International Congress of Classical Archaeology. London, 1979, pp. 73–87.

Kammerer-Grothaus, Helke. *Frauenleben-Frauenalltag im antiken Griechenland.* Berlin: Staatliche Museen Preussischer Kulturbesitz, 1984.

Kampen, Natalie. *Image and Status: Roman Working Women in Ostia.* Berlin, 1971.

Karabelias, Evanghelos. *L'épiclérat attique.* Paris: Institut de droit romain, 1974.

Kauffmann-Samaras, Aliki. "Mères et enfants sur les lébétès nuptiaux à figures rouges attiques du Vème siècle," *Third Symposium on Ancient Greek and Related Pottery.* Copenhagen, 1988, pp. 286–299.

Keuls, Eva. *The Reign of the Phallus: Sexual Politics in Ancient Athens.* New York: Harper and Row, 1986.

King, Helen. "Sacrificial Blood: The Role of the *amnion* in Ancient Gynecology," *Helios* (1987): 117–126.

King, Karen, ed. *Images of the Feminine in Gnosticism.* Philadelphia: Augsburg Fortress, 1988.

Klingenberg, G. "Die Frau im römischen Abgaben und Fiskalrecht," *Revue internationale des droits de l'Antiquité* 30 (1983): 141–150.

Kraemer, Ross S. *Maenads, Martyrs, Matrons, Monastics: A Sourcebook on Women's Religion in the Greco-Roman World.* Philadelphia: Augsburg Fortress, 1988.

Lacey, W. K. *The Family in Classical Greece.* Ithaca, N.Y.: Cornell University Press, 1968.

Laporte, Jean. *The Role of Women in Early Christianity.* Studies in Women and Religion 7. New York and Toronto: Edwin Mellen, 1981.

Le Bonniec, Henri. *Le culte de Cérès à Rome. Des origines à la fin de la République.* Etudes et commentaires 27. Paris: Klincksiek, 1958.

Leduc, Claudine. "Observations sur la 'diverging devolution' dans deux cités grecques: Athènes et Gortyne," *Femmes et patrimoine dans les sociétés rurales de l'Europe méditerranéene.* Marseilles, 1987, pp. 211–226.

Lefkowitz, Mary R. *Heroines and Hysterics.* London, 1981.

———— *Women in Greek Myth.* London: Duckworth, 1986.

———— and M. B. Fant. *Women's Life in Greece and Rome.* London and Baltimore: Johns Hopkins University Press, 1982.

Legendre, P. *L'inestimable objet de la transmission. Etude sur le principe généalogique en Occident.* Paris, 1985.

di Lello-Finuoli, Anna Lucia. "Donne e matrimonio nella Grecia arcaica," *Studi Micenei ed Egeo-Anatolici* XXV (1984): 275–302.

Lennox, J. G. "Aristotle on Genera, Species and the More and Less," *Journal of the History of Biology* 13 (1980): 321–346.

Lerner, Gerda. *The Creation of Patriarchy.* New York and Oxford: Oxford University Press, 1986.

Lévêque, Pierre. *Colère, sexe, rire. Le Japon des mythes anciens.* Paris: Belles Lettres, 1988.

———— "Pandora ou la terrifiante féminité," *Kernos* 1 (1988): 49–62.

———— *Les premières civilisations* I, *Des despotismes orientaux à la cité grecque.* Paris: PUF, 1987.

Levy, Edmond, ed. *La femme dans les sociétés antiques.* Actes des colloques de Strasbourg (May 1980 and June 1981). Strasbourg: Université des Sciences Humaines de Strasbourg, 1983.

Lissarrague, François, and Alain Schnapp. "Imagerie des Grecs ou Grèce des imagiers?" *Le Temps de la Réflexion* II (1981).

Loraux, Nicole. "La cité, l'historien, les femmes," *Pallas* (1985): 7–39.

———— *Les enfants d'Athéna.* Paris: Maspero, 1981.

———— *Les expériences de Tirésias. Le féminin et l'homme grec.* Paris: Gallimard, 1989.

———— *Façons tragiques de tuer une femme.* Paris: Hachette, 1985.

———— *Les mères en deuil.* Paris: Seuil, 1990.

———— "Notes sur un impossible sujet de l'histoire," *Le Genre de l'Histoire. Les Cahiers du GRIF* (1988).

MacCormack, C., and M. Strathern, eds. *Nature, Culture and Gender.* Cambridge: Cambridge University Press, 1980.

MacMullen, Ramsay. *Paganism in the Roman Empire.* New Haven, Conn., and London: Yale University Press, 1981.

———— "Women in Public in the Roman Empire," *Historia* 29 (1980): 208–218.

Mactoux, Marie Madeleine. *Pénélope.* Annales littéraires de l'Université de Besançon. Paris, 1975.

Magli, Ida, ed. *Matriarcato e potere delle donne.* Milan, 1978.

Marrou, Henri Irénée. *Histoire de l'Education dans l'Antiquité.* Paris: Seuil, 1950.

Martha, Jules. *Les sacerdoces athéniens.* Paris, 1882.

Martimort, Aimé-Georges. *Les Diaconesses. Essai historique.* Rome, 1982.

Masiello, T. *La donna tutrice. Modelli culturali e prassi giuridica fra gli antonini e i severi.* Naples, 1979.

Mattingly, Harold. *Coins of the Roman Empire in the British Museum* III. London, 1966.

Mayer, Gunther. *Die jüdische Frau in der hellenistich römischen Antike.* Stuttgart, Berlin, and Cologne, 1987.

Metz, René. *La consécration des vierges dans l'Eglise romaine: Etude d'histoire et de liturgie.* Paris, 1954.

Metzger, Henri. *Les représentations dans la céramique attique du IVème siècle.* Paris, 1951.

Meyer, P. M. *Der römische Konkubinat.* Leipzig, 1865, rpr. 1966.

Miralles, C., ed. *La dona en l'antiguitat.* Barcelona, 1987.

Modrzejewski, Joseph. "La structure juridique du mariage grec," *Scritti in onore di Orsolina Montevecchi.* Bologna, 1981, pp. 231–268.

Monceaux, Paul. *Histoire littéraire de l'Afrique chrétienne,* I, 70–96.

Moreau, Philippe. *Clodiana religio. Un procès politique en 61 avant J.C.* Paris: Belles Lettres, 1982.

———— "Patrimoines et successions à Larinum au Ier siècle avant J.C.," *Revue historique de droit français et étranger* (1986): 169–189.

———— "Structures de parenté et d'alliance à Larinum d'après le *pro Cluentio,*" *Les "bourgeoisies" municipales italiennes aux IIe et Ier siècles avant J.C.* Naples, 1983, pp. 99–123.

Morgan, Lewis H. *Ancient Society,* intro. Leslie A. White. Cambridge, Mass.: Harvard University Press, 1964.

Morsin, J. *Aristotle on Generation of Animals: A Philosophical Study.* Washington, D.C.: University Press of America, 1982.

Mossé, Claude. *La femme dans la Grèce antique.* Paris: Albin Michel, 1983.

Munier, Charles. *Mariage et virginité dans l'Eglise ancienne (Ier–IIIème siècles),* Traditio Christiana VI. Bern, 1987.

Murdock, George Peter. Social Structure. New York: Macmillan, 1949.

Musurillo, Herbert. *The Acts of the Christian Martyrs.* Oxford: Oxford University Press, 1972, pp. 108–118.

Nardi, Enzo. *Procurato aborto nel mondo antico.* Milan: Giuffrè, 1971.

Nau, Jean-Yves. "La puberté programmée," *Le Monde,* February 1988, pp. 21, 23.

Needham, Rodney, ed. *Rethinking Kinship and Marriage.* London: Tavistock, 1971.

Neumann, Erich. *The Great Mother: An Analysis of the Archetype,* trans. R. Manheim. London: Routledge and Kegan, 1985.

Neumer-Pfau, Wiltrud. *Studien zur Ikonographie und Gesellschaftlichen Funktion hellenisticher Aphrodite Statuen.* Bonn: Rudolph Halbelt, 1982.

Opitz, Claudia, ed. *Weiblichkeit oder Feminismus?* Drumlin, 1983.

Otto, Walter. *Les dieux de la Grèce,* trans. C. N. Grimbert and A. Morgant. Paris: Payot, 1981.

———— *Die Götter Griechenlands.* Frankfurt am Main, 1929.

Pagels, Elaine. *The Gnostic Gospels.* New York: Random House, 1979.

Pailler, Jean-Marie. *Bacchanalia. La répression de 186 avant J.C. à Rome et en Italie: Vestiges, Images, Tradition.* Bibliothèque des Ecoles françaises d'Athènes et de Rome 270. Rome: Ecole Française, 1988.

Pallas: Revue d'Etudes antiques, vol. XXXI (1985): *La femme dans l'Antiquité Grecque.*

Parke, H. W. *Festivals of the Athenians.* London: Thames and Hudson, 1977.

Parker, Robert. *Miasma: Pollution and Purification in Early Greek Religion.* Oxford: Oxford University Press, 1983.

Patlagean, Evelyne. "L'entrée dans l'âge adulte à Byzance aux XIIIè–XIVè siècles," *Historicité de l'enfance et de la jeunesse.* Athens, 1988, pp. 263–270.

——— *Structure sociale, famille, chrétienté à Byzance IVème–XIème siècles.* London, 1981.

——— "Sur la limitation de la fécondité dans la haute époque byzantine," *Annales ESC* 6 (1969): 1353–1369.

Pellegrin, Pierre. "Aristotle: A Zoology without Species," in A. Grotthelf, ed., *Aristotle on Nature and Living Things.* Pittsburgh and Bristol: Mathesis, 1985, pp. 95–115.

Pembroke, Simon. "Last of the Matriarchs: A Study in the Inscriptions of Lycia," *Journal of the Economic and Social History of the Orient* 8 (1965): 217–247.

——— "Locres et Tarente: Le rôle des femmes dans la formation de deux colonies grecques," *Annales ESC* 25 (1970): 1240–1270.

——— "Women in Charge: The Function of Alternatives in Early Greek Tradition and the Ancient Idea of Matriarchy," *Journal of the Warburg and Courtauld Institutes* 30 (1967): 1–35.

Peppe, L. *Posizione giuridica e ruolo sociale della donna in età republicana.* Milan, 1984.

Peradotto, John, and J. P. Sullivan, eds. *Women in the Ancient World: The Arethusa Papers.* Albany: State University of New York Press, 1984.

Petersmann, Hubert. "Altgriechischer Mütterkult," *Matronen und Verwandte gottheiten.* Cologne: Rudolf Habelt, 1987, pp. 172–199.

Piccaluga, Giulia. "Bona Dea. Due contributi all'interpretazione del suo culto," *SMSR* 35 (1964): 195–237.

Pietri, Charles. "Le mariage chrétien à Rome IVème–Vème siècles," in Jean Delumeau, ed., *Histoire vécue du peuple chrétien,* vol. 1. Toulouse, 1979, pp. 105–130.

Pighi, Giovanni Battista. *De ludis saecularibus populi Romani Quiritium.* Amsterdam: Hakkert, 1965.

Plassard, J. *Le concubinat romain sous le Haut-Empire.* Toulouse and Paris, 1921.

de Polignac, François. *La naissance de la cité grecque.* Paris: Découverte, 1984.

Pomeroy, Sarah B. *Goddesses, Whores, Wives and Slaves: Women in Classical Antiquity.* New York: Schocken, 1975.

——— *Women in Hellenistic Egypt.* New York: Schocken, 1984.

————, with Ross S. Kraemer and Natalie Kampen. "Selected Bibliography on Women in Classical Antiquity," in J. Peradotto and J. P. Sullivan, *Women in the Ancient World.*

Raditsa, Leo Ferrero. "Augustus' Legislation Concerning Marriage, Procreation, Love Affairs and Adultery," *Aufsteig und Niedergang der römischen Welt* II, *Principat* II (1980): 278–339.

Ramnoux, Clémence. "Les femmes de Zeus: Hésiode, Théogonie, vers 885 à 955," *Poikilia. Etudes offertes à Jean Pierre Vernant.* Paris: l'EHESS, 1987, pp. 155–164.

———— *Mythologie ou la famille olympienne.* Brionne: Gérard Monfort, 1982.

———— *La Nuit et les enfants de la Nuit dans la tradition grecque.* Paris: Flammarion, 1959.

———— "Philosophie et mythologie. D'Hésiode à Proclus," in Y. Bonnefoy, ed., *Dictionnaire des mythologies* II. Paris: Flammarion, 1981, pp. 256–268.

Rawson, Beryl. "Children in the Roman Family," in B. Rawson, *The Family in Ancient Rome,* pp. 170–200.

————, ed. *The Family in Ancient Rome: New Perspectives.* Ithaca, N.Y., and London: Cornell University Press, 1986.

Reiter, Rayna R., ed. *Toward an Anthropology of Women.* New York and London: London Review Press, 1975.

Ritzer, K. *Formen, Riten und religiöses Brauchtum der Eheschliessung in den christlichen Kirchen des ersten Jahrtausends,* 2nd ed. Munich, 1981.

Rosaldo, Michelle Zimbalist, and Louise Lamphere. *Women, Culture and Society.* Stanford: Stanford University Press, 1974.

Rousselle, Aline. "Observation féminine et idéologie masculine: Le corps de la femme d'après les médecins grecs," *Annales ESC* (1980): 1089–1115.

———— "Personal Status and Sexual Practice in the Roman Empire," *Fragments for a History of the Human Body,* pt. III, 1989, pp. 300–333.

———— *Porneia. De la maîtrise du corps à la privation sensorielle.* Paris: PUF, 1983.

Roux, Georges. *Delphes, son oracle et ses dieux.* Paris: Belles Lettres, 1976.

Rudhardt, Jean. "Pandora: Hésiode et les femmes," *Museum Helveticum* 43 (1986): 231–246.

Ruether, Rosemary, ed. *Religion and Sexism: Images of Women in the Jewish and Christian Traditions.* New York, 1974.

———— and Eleanor McLaughlin, eds. *Women of Spirit: Female Leadership in the Jewish and Christian Traditions.* New York, 1979.

Sabbatucci, Dario. "L'extra-romanità di Fortuna," *Religione e Civilita* 3 (1982): 511–527.

Savalli, Ivanna. *La donna nella società della Grecia antica.* Bologna: Patron, 1983.

Saxer, Victor. *Saints anciens d'Afrique du Nord.* Vatican City, 1979, pp. 42–49.

Scafuro, Adele, ed. *Studies on Roman Women. Helios* 16 (1989).

553

Schaps, David. *Economic Rights of Women in Ancient Greece.* Edinburgh: Edinburgh University Press, 1979.

Scheid, Evelyne. "Il matrimonio omerico," *Dialoghi di Archeologia* (1979): 60–73.

Scheid, John. "Le flamine de Jupiter. Les Vestales et le général triomphant," *Le Temps de la réflexion.* Paris: Gallimard, 1986, pp. 213–230.

――― *Romulus et ses frères. Le collège des frères arvales, modèle du culte public dans la Rome des Empereurs.* Rome: Ecole Française, 1989.

Scheid-Tissinier, Evelyne. *Etude sur le vocabulaire et les pratiques du don et de l'échange chez Homère.* Paris: Université de Paris, 1988.

Schelp, J. *Das Kanoun. Der griechische Opferkorb.* Würzburg, 1975.

Schilling, Robert. *La religion romaine de Vénus depuis les origines jusqu'au temps d'Auguste,* 2nd ed. Paris: Boccard, 1982.

Schmitt, Pauline. "Athéna Apatouria et la ceinture: Les aspects féminins des Apatouries à Athènes," *Annales ESC* 32 (1977): 1059–1073.

Schmitt Pantel, Pauline. "La différence des sexes, histoire, anthropologie et cité grecque," *Une histoire des femmes est-elle possible?* Marseille: Ed. Rivages, 1984, pp. 98–119.

Schneider, David M., and Kathleen Gough. *Matrilineal Kinship.* Berkeley, Los Angeles, and London: University of California Press, 1961.

Schuller, Wolfgang. *Frauen in der griechischen Geschichte.* Konstanz, 1985.

――― *Frauen in der römischen Geschichte.* Konstanz, 1987.

Schüssler-Fiorenza, Elizabeth. *In Memory of Her: A Feminist Theological Reconstruction of Christian Origins.* New York: Crossroad, 1983.

Scott, Joan. "Gender: A Useful Category of Historical Analysis," *American Historical Review* 91 (1986).

Sensi, Luigi. "Ornatus e status sociale delle donne romane," *Annali della Facoltà di Lettere e Filosofia di Perugia.* Studi Classici 18 (1980–81): 55–102.

Shaw, Brent. "The Age of Roman Girls at Marriage: Some Reconsiderations," *Journal of Roman Studies* 77 (1987): 30–46.

Sissa, Giulia. *Le corps virginal. La virginité féminine en Grèce ancienne.* Paris: Vrin, 1987.

――― "La famille dans la cité grecque" (Vème–IVème siècle avant J.C.), *Histoire de la Famille,* vol. 1. Paris: Armand Colin, 1986, pp. 163–194.

――― "La loi dans les âmes," *Le Temps de la Réflexion* 6 (1985): 49–72.

Skinner, Marilyn, ed. *Rescuing Creusa: New Methodological Approaches to Women in Antiquity. Helios* 13 (1987).

Solazzi, S. "Infirmitas aetatis e infirmitas sexus," *Scritti di diritto romano.* Naples, 1960, III, 357–377.

Sourvinou Inwood, Christiane. *Studies in Girls' Transitions: Aspects of the Arkteia and Age Representation in Attic Iconography.* Athens, 1988.

Swerdlow, Amy. "The Greek Citizen Woman in Attic Vase Painting: New Views and New Questions," *Women's Studies* 5 (1978): 267–284.

Tafaro, S. *Pubes e viripotens nella esperienza giuridica romana.* Bari, 1988.

Thomas, Yan. "Le 'ventre.' Corps maternel, droit paternel," *Le Genre Humain* 14 (1986): 211–236.

Thomson, George. *Aeschylus and Athens: A Study in the Social Origins of Drama*. London, 1973.

———— *Studies in Ancient Greek Society*, vol. 1, *The Prehistoric Aegean*. London, 1961.

Thraede, Karl. "Frau," *Reallexikon für Antike und Christentum* VIII, pp. 197–269.

Toepffer, Johannes. *Attische Genealogie*. Berlin: Weidmannsche, 1889.

Treggiari, S. "Jobs for Women," *American Journal of Ancient History* 1 (1976): 76–104.

Tupet, Anne-Marie. *La magie dans la poèsie latine. Des origines à la fin du règne d'Auguste*. Paris: Belles Lettres, 1976.

Uglione, Renato, ed. *La Donna nel Mondo Antico*. Turin, 1987.

Van Beek, Cornelius. *Passio Sanctarum Perpetuae et Felicitatis*. Nimègue, 1936.

Vatin, Claude. *Recherches sur le mariage et sur la condition de la femme mariée à l'époque hellénistique*. Paris: Boccard, 1970.

Verdier, Yvonne. *Façons de dire, façons de faire: La laveuse, la couturière, la cuisinière*. Paris: Gallimard, 1979.

Vérilhac, Anne Marie, and Claude Vial, with L. Darmezin. *La Femme dans L'Antiquité classique: Bibliographie*. Travaux de la Maison de l'Orient 19. Lyons: Maison de l'Orient Méditerranéen, 1990.

Vernant, Jean-Pierre. "Hestia-Hermes," *Mythe et pensée chez les Grecs*. Paris: Maspero, 1965, pp. 97–143.

———— "Le Dionysos masqué des 'Bacchantes' d'Euripide," in J.-P. Vernant and P. Vidal-Naquet, eds., *Myth et tragèdie Deux*. Paris: Découverte, 1986.

———— *Mythe et pensée chez les Grecs*.

———— "Le mariage," and "Le pur et l'impur," *Mythe et Société en Grèce ancienne*. Paris: Maspero, 1974.

Veyne, Paul. "La famille et l'amour sous le Haut-Empire romain," *Annales ESC* 33 (1978): 35–63.

Vidal-Naquet, Pierre. *Le chasseur noir*. Paris: Maspero and Paris: Découverte, 1981.

Wagner, Beate. *Zwischen Mythos und Realität: Die Frau in der frühgriechischen Gesellschaft*. Frankfurt am Main: Haag and Herchen, 1982.

Wagner-Hasel, Beate. "Frauenleben in orientalischer Abgeschlossenheit? Zur Geschichte und Nutzanwendung eines Topos," *Der Altsprachliche Unterricht* (February 1989): 18–29.

———— "Das Private wird politisch. Die Perspektive 'Geschlecht' in der Altertumswissenschaft," in Ursula A. J. Becher, and Jörn Rüsen, eds., *Weiblichleit in geschichtlicher Perspektive*. Frankfurt, 1988, pp. 11–50.

Walter, Hans. *Die Gestalt der Frau. Bildwerke von 30000–20 V.Chr.* Stuttgart, 1985.

Weaver, P. R. C. "The Status of Children in Mixed Marriages," in B. Rawson, *The Family in Ancient Rome,* pp. 145–169.

Webster, Paula. "Matriarchy: A Vision of Power," in R. Reiter, *Toward an Anthropology of Women,* pp. 141–156.

Weiner, Annette B. *Women of Value, Men of Renown: New Perspectives in Trobriand Exchange,* Texas Press Sourcebook in Anthropology 11. Austin and London: University of Texas Press, 1976.

Wenham, Gordon J. "Betulah: A Girl of Marriageable Age," *Vetus Testamentum* XXII (1972): 326–348.

Wesel, Uwe. *Der Mythos vom Matriarchat: Über Bachofens Mutterrecht und die Stellung der Frauen in frühen Gesellschaften.* Frankfurt am Main, 1980.

Williams, Dyfri. "Women on Athenian Vases: Problems of Interpretation," A. Cameron and A. Kuhrt, *Images of Women in Antiquity,* pp. 92–105.

Zannini, P. *Studi sulla tutela mulierum* I. Turin, 1976.

Zevi, Elena. "Scene di gineceo e scene di idillio nei vasi greci delle seconda metà del secolo quinto," *Mem. Linc.* 6 (1937): 291–350.

Zinser, Hartmut. *Der Mythos des Mutterrechts: Verhandlung von drei aktuellen Theorien des Geschlechterkampfes.* Frankfurt am Main, 1981.

Zinserling, Verena. *Die Frau in Hellas und Rom.* Leipzig and Stuttgart, 1972.

——— "Zum Problem von Alltagsdarstellungen auf attischen Vasen," in Max Kunze, ed., *Beiträge zum antiken Realismus.* Berlin, 1977, pp. 39–56.

Contributors

MONIQUE ALEXANDER Born in 1932 in Marseilles. Professor at the University of Paris IV–Sorbonne. Her research is concentrated on Hellenistic Judaism and Greek patristics. She is the editor of Philo of Alexandria's *Le commerce avec les connaissances préparatoires* (Paris: Editions Le Cerf, 1967) and the author of *Le commencement du livre Genèse 1–5. La version grecque de la Septante et sa réception* (Paris: Editions Beauchesne, 1988).

LOUISE BRUIT ZAIDMAN Born in 1938 in Paris. Lecturer at University of Paris VII. Her field is Greek religious anthropology, and she is presently working on priestesses. In addition to various articles, she has published, in collaboration with Pauline Schmitt Pantel, *La religion grecque* (Paris: Armand Colin, 1989).

STELLA GEORGOUDI Born in 1937 in Athens. Lecturer at the Ecole Pratique des Hautes Etudes (Religious Sciences Division). Her areas of research include Greek institutions and religion and historiography. Her most recent book is *Des chevaux et des boeufs dans le monde grec. Réalités et représentations animalières à partir des livres XVI et XVII des Géoponiques* (Paris–Athens, 1990).

CLAUDINE LEDUC Born in 1936 in La Grand'Combe (Gard). Lecturer at the University of Toulouse-Le Mirail. Her areas of research include religion, kinship, and politics in Hellenic societies. She is the author of *La Constitution d'Athènes attribuée à Xenophon* (Paris, 1976) and of several studies of Greek women.

FRANÇOIS LISSARRAGUE Born in 1947 in Paris. Research assistant at the Centre National de Recherche Scientifique (Louis Gernet Center). A specialist in the anthropological aspects of Greek imagery, he contributed to the volume *La cité des images* (Paris–Lausanne, 1984) and is the author of *Un flot d'images* (Paris: Adam Biro, 1987) and *L'Autre guerrier* (Paris: La Découverte-Ecole Française de Rome, 1990).

NICOLE LORAUX Born in 1943 in Paris. Professor at the Ecole des Hautes Etudes en Sciences Sociales. Her work is concerned with Greek ideas of division—the division of the sexes, division in the city, civil war. Among other works, she has published *Les enfants d'Athéna* (Paris: Maspero, 1981), *Les expériences de Tirésias. Le féminin et l'homme grec* (Paris: Gallimard, 1990), and *Les mères en deuil* (Paris: Le Seuil, 1990).

ALINE ROUSSELLE Born in 1939 in Rabat (Morocco). Lecturer at the University of Perpignan. Her research is focused on cultural aspects of the conversion of the Romans to Christianity, including ideas of authority, attitudes toward the body, and iconography. She is the author of *Porneia. De la maîtrise du corps à la privation sensorielle, II–IV siècle* (Paris: Presses Universitaires de France, 1983) and *Croire et guérir. La foi en Gaule dans l'Antiquité tardive* (Paris: Fayard, 1990).

JOHN SCHEID Born in 1946 in Luxembourg. Professor at the Ecole Pratique des Hautes Etudes (Religious Sciences Division). His areas of research include Roman religion and institutions. Among other works he has published *Religion et piété à Rome* (Paris: La Découverte, 1985) and *Romulus et ses frères. Le collège arvale, modèle du culte public dans la Rome des empereurs* (Rome: Ecole Française de Rome, 1990).

PAULINE SCHMITT PANTEL Born in 1947 in Vialas (Lozère). Professor at the University of Amiens. Her research is concerned with the history of Greek collective practices and, in particular, mores. She contributed to Michelle Perrot, ed., *Une histoire des femmes est-elle possible?* (Marseilles, 1984), and has published *La cité au banquet. Histoire des repas publics dans les cités grecques* (Rome: Ecole Française de Rome, 1991).

GIULIA SISSA Born in 1954 in Mantua. Research Assistant at the Centre National de Recherche Scientifique (Laboratory of Social Anthropology, Paris). Her areas of research include kinship, the anthropology of the body, and the history of sexuality in the ancient world. Her publications include *Madre Materia* (Turin, 1983), with S. Campese and P. Manuli; *Le corps virginal* (Paris: Vrin, 1987); and *La vie quotidienne des dieux grecs* (Paris: Hachette, 1989), with Marcel Detienne.

YAN THOMAS Born in 1945 in Lyons. Professor of Law and professor at the Ecole des Hautes Etudes en Sciences Sociales. His work concerns the law of kinship, the history of legal procedure, and the legal constructs of the Roman state. His publications include "A Rome, pères citoyens et cité des pères," in *Histoire de la famille,* vol. 1 (Paris: Armand Colin, 1986), and "Le 'ventre.' Corps maternel, droit paternel," *Le Genre humain* 14 (1986).

Illustration Credits

1. FN, 1971.II–1.1. British Museum, London.
2. FR, pl. 1. Archaeological Museum, Florence.
3. FR, British Museum, London.
4. FR, L 55. Réunion des Musées nationaux, Paris.
5. From Pfuhl, fig. 580.
6. Provincial Museum, Salerno.
7. Lissarrague.
8. FR, A 9165. Lennart Larsen.
9. FR, 13.113. Lennart Larsen.
10. FR, 1629. National Archaeological Museum, Athens.
11. FR, E 697. Lissarrague.
12. FR, 508. Bibliothèque nationale, Paris.
13. FR, CA 453. Réunion des Musées nationaux, Paris.
14. Chuzeville.
15. FN, F 1813. Lissarrague.
16. From Riezler, pl. 23.
17. FN, RC 1646, Soprintendenza Archeologica per l'Etruria meridionale, Rome.
18. FN, 1553. Kruger-Mösner.
19. FN, 693. Soprintendenza Archeologica per l'Etruria meridionale, Rome.
20. FR, inv. 48.262. Walters Art Gallery, Baltimore.
21. FR, F 2535. Jutta Tietz-Glagow.
22. FR, V 676. Gabinetto.
23. FR, 2336. R. Bauer.
24. FR, T 308. Lissarrague.
25. From Beazley AWL, pl. 2.
26. From Riezler, pl. 15.
27. From AZ 1885, pl. 15.
28. Inv. 65.908. Museum of Fine Arts, Boston.
29. FR, CA 2567. Réunion des Musées nationaux, Paris.
30. FR, B 39. Badisches Landesmuseum, Karlsruhe.
31. After kraters from the sanctuary of Artemis at Brauron.
32. FR, 2290. Ingrid Geske-Heiden.
33. FR, Soprintendenza Archeologica per l'Etruria meridionale.
34. FR, B KM 2565, inv. 8934. Kruger-Mösner.
35. FR, E 773. Furtwängler Reichhold, pl. 57.
36. FR, E 772. Furtwängler Reichhold, pl. 57.
37. FR, CA 2587. Réunion des Musées nationaux, Paris.
38. FN, L 304. Martin von Wagner Museum.
39. FR, A 11. A.C.L., Brussels.
40. From Chuzeville photo.
41. FR, 261. Archivo Fotografico.
42. FR, G 557. Réunion des Musées nationaux, Paris.
43. Fr, L 521. Martin von Wagner Museum.
44. FR, 572. "Sigismondo Castromediano" provincial museum.
45. From *Annali*, 1876, d–e.
46. FR, 652, fragment. Bibliothèque nationale, Paris.
47. FN, 31.11.10. Metropolitan Museum of Art, New York.
48. FR, 2289. Jutta Tietz-Glagow.
49. FR, 57.780–57.781. Deutschen Archäologischen Institut, Rome.

50. FR, F 2279. Lissarrague.
51. FR, 439. Bibliothèque nationale, Paris.
52. FR, E 68. Trustees of the British Museum, London.
53. FR, R 351. A.C.L., Brussels.
54. FR, 11267. Archaeological Museum, Madrid.
55. FR, 57912. Soprintendenza Archeologica per l'Etruria meridionale, Rome.
56. FR, G 285. Réunion des Musées nationaux, Paris.

57. FR, 2645. Kruger-Mösner.
58. FR, 538.3. Ellebé.
59. Archivo della Soprintendenza ai Beni Culturali e Ambientali.
60. FR, G 416. Réunion des Musées nationaux, Paris.
61. FN, 2184. National Archaeological Museum, Athens.
62. FR, G 197. Réunion des Musées nationaux, Paris.
63. From Mon. Piot 26, pl. 3.

560

Index

Crete, 233, 261, 348, 447, 459, 460, 461. *See also* Gortyn
Crook, J. A., 100
Culham, Phyllis, 470
Cults. *See* Festivals
Cyprian: "On the Conduct of Virgins," 412
Cypris, 365, 371

Dala, D., 120
Dance, 184–224 passim, 346, 359, 360, 392, 395, 396
Darwin, Charles: *Origin of Species*, 451
Deaconesses, 423, 431–435, 437
Dea Dia, sacrifice to, 378, 403
Death, 368–369. *See also* Childbirth: death in
de Beauvoir, Simone, 415
Delcourt, Marie, 35
Delia (festival), 347–348
Delphic oracle, 345, 375, 460
Demeter, 20, 35, 301, 358, 359, 360, 373; and agriculture, 371, 452; festivals of, 340, 349, 350, 351, 352; gynecocracy of, 452–454; images of, 139, 145, 188; and Kore, 33–34, 351; and marriage ceremonies, 363, 364, 452; as matriarch, 459, 461; priestesses of, 372, 373. *See also Homeric Hymn to Demeter*; Thesmophoria
Democracy, 239, 291, 293, 465, 468
Demosthenes, 272, 275, 276, 278, 280, 358; *Against Neara*, 358
Dendrites, 296–297
Descat, R., 240
Desert Fathers, 411
Desert Mothers, 412
Detienne, Marcel, 22, 41, 339, 357, 358
Devi, 37–38. *See also* Great Goddess
Devolution, diverging, 236, 262, 263, 268, 278, 280
Didascalia Apostolorum, 430, 431–432, 434
Diocletian, 128–129, 298, 331
Diodorus of Sicily, 3, 375
Dionysus, 339, 340, 355–360, 362, 454; images of, 152, 189–194, 219–224
Diotima, 47, 49
Disinheritance, 105–106, 131. *See also* Inheritance
Divorce, 133, 134, 268, 315, 316, 396; and children, 130, 317; and dowries, 99, 120, 275, 416–417; and Jewish

women, 416–417; of priests, 401, 402; remarriage after, 281, 334
Dixon, S., 99, 100
Domitian, Emperor, 103, 317, 396, 402
Dowries, 130, 132, 134, 135, 142, 236; in Athenian matrimonial system, 273–281, 286, 290, 291, 470; in cash, 238, 239; and divorce, 99, 120, 275, 416–417; and inheritance, 262–263, 267; loss of, for unfaithful wives, 314
Dracon, 288
Duby, Georges, 4, 465
Dumézil, Georges, 20, 383, 386–387
Durand, G., 240
Durry, Marcel, 303

Earth Mothers, 28–29. *See also* Great Goddess; Mother Earth
Ecclesiastic Canons of the Apostles, 436
Ecology, 302–307
Edict of Milan, 413
Education, 46–47, 51, 78, 323, 334, 348
Egypt, 35, 131, 300, 304, 327, 350, 409, 414; children in, 307; custom of levirate in, 120; and Great Goddess, 33; images in, 139; marriage in, 312; and myth of matriarchy, 449–450; slavery in, 311; status of women in, 3, 194
Ehrenberg, Victor, 465
Eileithyia, 26, 182, 366
Electra, 368, 462
Eleusinian Mysteries, 339, 372
Eliezar, Rabbi, 418
Elijah, 300
Empedocles, 469
Endogamy, 266, 269, 270, 292. *See also* Kinship
Engels, Friedrich, 455, 458, 459
Epictetus, 319, 328
Epicureans, 326
Epiphanius of Salamis: *Panarion*, 437
Equality, 90, 295; in priesthood, 373; successoral, 91, 106; and wills, 103
Erichthonius, 341–342, 346
Erinyes, 25, 28, 462
Eros, 301, 364; images of, 153–162 passim; 183–218 passim
Eudocia, Empress, 439, 442
Eudoxia, Empress, 438, 442
Euripides, 1, 24, 25, 28, 350; *The Bacchae*, 192, 356–357, 359; *Electra*,

Property, 233, 239, 252, 257, 259, 262;
and daughters, 262, 281, 451; and
dowries, 99–100; management of,
130–131, 135, 136; sale of, 134, 135;
and status of women, 250, 470; and
succession, 110, 262; and wealth,
273; and wills, 102. *See also* Devolu-
tion, diverging; Wealth; Wills
Prophetesses, 374–376, 416, 418, 424–
425, 427, 428, 429
Prostitution, 135, 315, 319, 332, 427
Puberty, 303, 306, 343
Public speaking: prohibitions on, 425–
426
Pudicitia, 315, 323, 390, 396. *See also*
Chastity
Pulcheria, 442
Punic War, 398, 399
Pythagoras, 25, 53, 316, 323, 324, 328
Pythia of Delphia, 374–375

Ramnoux, Clémence, 22, 38, 39, 41
Rape, 224, 313, 326, 334, 367
Religion, 5, 377–408, 417–419; and
cults, 337; and matriarchy, 456; vs.
matronal magic, 400. *See also* Christianity, early
Remus, 322
Reproduction, 4, 80, 233, 295, 330; celebrations of, 401; class, 333–334; and
law, 83, 86; legitimate, 236, 245, 256,
265; male system of, 296–297; regulation of, 302, 324; and species difference, 54, 58, 61–62, 64–65, 67; and
status, 311–313, 340. *See also* Legitimacy
Rhea, 20, 35, 39, 40, 41
Rituals, 4, 5, 7, 233; of death, 368–369;
Dionysiac, 189–194; funerary, 163–
170, 180; postpartum, 367–368; purification, 367–370; sacrificial, 379–
380; of women, 183–194, 401, 405–
408; of young girls, 343–349. *See also*
Blood sacrifices
Roman Rites, 395
Rome: age of marriage in, 302–303;
compared with Greece, 4, 7; heroines
of, 326; life expectancy in, 318; number of widows in, 429–430; paternal
principle of, 454–455; religious role
of women in, 377–408; status of
women in, 414. *See also* Christianity,
early; Law; Religion

Romulus, 322, 380, 386
Rose, H. J., 457, 458
Rostovtzeff, Michael, 464–465
Rousselle, Aline, 7, 120, 295, 296–336,
415
Rudhardt, Jean, 21
Ruetner, Rosemary, 416

Sabine women, rape of, 379, 381, 388,
406, 408
Sacred Wars, 359
Sacrifices: exclusion of women from,
379–381, 404, 405; and Vestals, 382–
384, 396; by women, 385, 386–387,
388, 389, 390, 392, 395, 396, 406,
407. *See also* Blood sacrifices; Vestals
Saints, female, 5, 473–477
Salian virgins, 385
Saller, R. P., 93
Sappho, 2, 4, 206, 346
Satyrs, 222–224
Scheid, John, 7, 377–408
Schlüsser-Fiorenza, Elizabeth, 416
Schmitt Pantel, Pauline, 1–8, 256, 464–
471
Scipio Africanus, 321
Scott, Joan, 467
Secular Games, 393, 395, 396, 404
Sejanus, 325
Selenites, 296
Semonides of Amorgos, 62, 65, 72
Senatus-consult Orphitian (Roman de-
cree), 106, 109, 110, 111, 112, 124
Senatus-consult Tertullian (Roman de-
cree), 106, 112–113
Senatus-consult Velleien (Roman decree),
137
Seneca, 130, 299, 300, 301, 302, 321,
322, 326
Septimius Severus, 104, 136, 394, 396,
474
Servius, 117, 382
Servius Sulpicius, 120, 129, 437
Sexes, social relations between, 466–
468, 471
Sexual asymmetry, 466, 468
Sexual Asymmetry (Blok and Mason),
466
Sexual intercourse, 306, 308, 316, 318,
319, 320, 334, 360, 452
Sexuality, 24, 227, 233, 328, 346, 405,
465
Sibyls, 374, 378, 401